Routledge Handbook of Applied Sport Psychology

The *Routledge Handbook of Applied Sport Psychology* is a definitive guide to the theory and practice of applied sport psychology. It goes further than any other book in surveying the full variety of issues that practising sport psychologists will confront in their working lives. It introduces the most important tools and skills that psychologists will need to be truly helpful to their clients, and it also adopts a holistic definition of the role of the sport psychologist, explaining how effective counseling, assessment, and therapeutic models can add important extra dimensions to professional practice. The book is divided into seven thematic sections, addressing:

- counseling;
- assessment;
- theoretical and therapeutic models;
- issues for the individual athlete, from injury and overtraining to depression;
- issues for teams, from conflict resolution to travel;
- working with special populations;
- mental skills, such as imagery, goal setting, and concentration.

Moving beyond the traditional tracks of clinical psychology and performance enhancement, the authors in this book argue convincingly that psychologists would benefit from attempting to understand athletes' social and familial contexts, their health, happiness, and interpersonal dynamics in the broadest sense, if they are to serve their clients' best interests. With contributions from many of the world's leading sport psychologists, and with clear descriptions of best practice in each chapter, the *Routledge Handbook of Applied Sport Psychology* is essential reading for all serious students and practitioners of sport psychology, counseling, applied sport science, health psychology, and related fields.

Stephanie J. Hanrahan is an Associate Professor and the Director of the sport psychology programs at the University of Queensland, Australia. She has authored/edited books on coaching, games, and cultural sport psychology, has been the editor of the *Journal of Applied Sport Psychology*, and is a registered psychologist.

Mark B. Andersen, a registered psychologist in Australia and the USA, is a Professor in the School of Sport and Exercise Science and also teaches in the School of Social Science and Psychology at Victoria University (VU) in Melbourne, Australia. He is also a member of the Institute of Sport, Exercise and Active Living at VU. He is the editor/author of four other books on applied psychology in sport and rehabilitation.

Routledge Handbook of Applied Sport Psychology

A comprehensive guide for students and practitioners

Edited by
Stephanie J. Hanrahan and
Mark B. Andersen

LONDON AND NEW YORK

First published 2010
by Routledge
2 Park Square, Milton Park, Abingdon, Oxon, OX14 4RN

Simultaneously published in the USA and Canada
by Routledge
270 Madison Avenue, New York, NY 10016

Routledge is an imprint of the Taylor & Francis Group, an informa business

Typeset in Goudy by Glyph International Ltd.
Printed and bound in Great Britain by CPI Antony Rowe, Chippenham, Wiltshire

British Library Cataloguing-in-Publication Data
A catalog record for this book is available from the British Library

Library of Congress Cataloging in Publication Data
Routledge handbook of applied sport psychology : a comprehensive guide for students and practitioners / edited by Stephanie Hanrahan and Mark Andersen.
    p. cm.
1. Sports–Psychological aspects–Handbooks, manuals, etc. 2. Applied psychology–Handbooks, manuals, etc. I. Hanrahan, Stephanie J., 1961- II. Andersen, Mark B., 1951-
GV706.4.R68 2011
796.07–dc22   2010017600

ISBN 13: 978-0-415-48463-3 (hbk)
ISBN 13: 978-0-203-85104-3 (ebk)

Contents

Contributors

Mark B. Andersen, PhD, Victoria University, Australia
Ruth Anderson, MPsych Sport & Ex, Australian Institute of Sport, Australia
Glenn S. Brassington, PhD, Sonoma State University / Stanford University, USA
Britton W. Brewer, PhD, Springfield College, USA
Kevin L. Burke, PhD, Illinois State University, USA
Melissa A. Chase, PhD, Miami University, Ohio, USA
Rebecca A. Clark, PhD, private practice, New York City, USA
Emily Claspell, EdD, private practice, Kamuela, Hawaii, USA
Damien Clement, PhD, West Virginia University, USA
Kathryn A. Conley, MA, Virginia Commonwealth University, USA
Steven J. Danish, PhD, Virginia Commonwealth University, USA
Lars Dzikus, PhD, University of Tennessee, USA
Edward Etzel, EdD, West Virginia University, USA
Leslee A. Fisher, PhD, University of Tennessee, USA
Thaddeus France, EdD, Springfield College, USA
Frank L. Gardner, PhD, Kean University, USA
Petah M. Gibbs, PhD, University of Ballarat, Australia
Chris Goode, BA, Sonoma State University, USA
Pippa Grange, DPsych, Australian Football League Players' Association, Australia
Melanie Gregg, PhD, University of Winnipeg, Canada
Jeff Greenberg, PhD, University of Arizona, USA
Christy Greenleaf, PhD, University of North Texas, USA
Daniel F. Gucciardi, PhD, University of Queensland, Australia
Stephanie J. Hanrahan, PhD, University of Queensland, Australia
Kate F. Hays, PhD, The Performing Edge, Private Practice, Toronto, Canada
Ken Hodge, PhD, University of Otago, New Zealand
Kerrie Kauer, PhD, California State University, Long Beach, USA
Michael Kellmann, PhD, Ruhr-University of Bochum, Germany
Vikki Krane, PhD, Bowling Green State University, USA

Elsa Kristiansen, PhD candidate, Norwegian School of Sport Science, Norway
David Lavallee, PhD, Aberystwyth University, Wales
Trisha Leahy, PhD, Hong Kong Sports Institute, Hong Kong
Ronnie Lidor, PhD, Zinman College, Wingate Institute, Israel
Ellen T. Luepker, MSW, LICSW, University of Minnesota, USA
Lynda Mainwaring, PhD, University of Toronto, Canada
Clifford J. Mallett, PhD, University of Queensland, Australia
Daryl B. Marchant, PhD, Victoria University, Australia
Jeffrey J. Martin, PhD, Wayne State University, USA
Jason Mazanov, PhD, University of New South Wales, Australia
Nikola Medic, PhD, Edith Cowan University, Australia
Lisa Mitzel, MFA, Youth and Parent Programs, Community Relations at Kepler's Books &
   Magazines, Menlo Park, CA, USA
Samantha Monda, PhD candidate, West Virginia University, USA
Zella E. Moore, PsyD, Manhattan College, USA
Aidan Moran, PhD, University College, Dublin, Ireland
Tony Morris, PhD, Victoria University, Australia
Annemarie I. Murphy, PhD, Gold Medal Consultants, Monroe, CT, USA
Shane M. Murphy, PhD, Western Connecticut State University, USA
Jonah Oliver, PhD candidate, University of Queensland, Australia
Sunghee Park, PhD candidate, Aberystwyth University, Wales
Gloria Park-Perin, PhD, Temple University, USA
Cassandra D. Pasquariello, EdM, Virginia Commonwealth University, USA
Jessica C. Peacock, PhD candidate, West Virginia University, USA
Albert J. Petitpas, PhD, Springfield College, USA
Trent A. Petrie, PhD, University of North Texas, USA
Glyn C. Roberts, PhD, Norwegian School of Sport Sciences, Norway
Michael L. Sachs, PhD, Temple University, USA
Vanessa Shannon, PhD, West Virginia University, USA
Julia Shiang, PhD, Stanford University, USA
Jeff Simons, PhD, California State University East Bay, USA
Harriet D. Speed, PhD, Victoria University, Australia
Traci A. Statler, PhD, California State University, Fullerton, USA
Peter C. Terry, PhD, University of Southern Queensland, Australia
David Tod, PhD, Aberystwyth University, Wales
Judy L. Van Raalte, PhD, Springfield College, USA
Robin S. Vealey, PhD, Miami University, Ohio, USA
Dan Vernau, Miami University, Ohio, USA
Jennifer E. Vose, PhD candidate, Springfield College, USA
Barbara Walker, PhD, Center for Human Performance, Cincinnati, USA
Jack C. Watson II, PhD, West Virginia University, USA
Robert Weinberg, PhD, Miami University, Ohio, USA
Dave Weise, PhD candidate, University of Arizona, USA
Michael Zito, PhD, Montclair State University, USA
Sam J. Zizzi, EdD, West Virginia University, USA

Preface

"What? *Another* handbook for sport psychology? There are already about four handbooks out there." That was what a colleague said to one of us early in the development of this book. It's a good question, and part of the answer lies in the professional and personal experiences of both of us who have been training and supervising applied sport psychology students and practitioners for the past 15 to 20 years. Another part of the answer as to "why another handbook on sport psychology?" stems from the experiences of our students as they have explored the landscapes of employment and service after leaving our universities.

To begin answering the question, we would like to go back to a story told in the Coleman Griffith Keynote Address at the Association for Applied Sport Psychology (AASP) 2005 annual conference in Vancouver, Canada. Rainer Martens opened that conference with a talk titled "Does Sport Psychology Matter?" In his speech Martens described the growth of two sport service delivery fields, athletic trainers and strength and conditioning practitioners, over the past 30 to 35 years. These two fields' histories have followed similar paths. For example, Martens related, around 30 to 35 years ago a small group of about 300 athletic trainers came together, formed a professional organization for support in practice and research, and today there are about 30,000 athletic trainers in that association working in service and academic settings. In the previous sentence one could replace "athletic training" with "strength and conditioning," and the story would be essentially the same.

The historical tale for sport and exercise psychology starts out similarly (a group of about 300 people coming together some decades ago), but the ending is quite different. Today there are about 1200 members of AASP, and that membership number is about the same for, or considerably more than, other sport psychology professional organizations (e.g., Division 47 of the American Psychological Association, European Federation of Sport Psychology, the Sport and Exercise Psychology Division of the British Association of Sport and Exercise Sciences, International Society of Sport Psychology). There is also considerable overlap in membership among these organizations, and although it cannot be determined precisely, the world-wide figure for sport and exercise psychologists in professional associations probably does not exceed 3000. AASP is also one of the few certifying bodies for practitioners in the world, and currently there are approximately only 200+ certified consultants. The difference between the numbers of sport and exercise psychology practitioners and academics and the professionals in each of the fields of athletic training and strength and conditioning is about a factor of 10.

Martens answered the question he posed in the title of his keynote address in the affirmative, "Yes, sport and exercise psychology does matter." Many of us in the audience, however, heard a less optimistic message. The perennial complaint from students at most of the sport and exercise psychology conferences is: "There aren't enough jobs," and the number of employed practitioners in the field seems to support that complaint. But the numbers we have reported here are most assuredly deceptive. If we only consider jobs that are supposedly the bread-and-butter of sport psychology practitioners (i.e., performance enhancement through cognitive-behavioral interventions such as imagery, relaxation, concentration, goal-setting, and self talk), then the students are probably correct. If, however, we consider all the psychologists, psychiatrists, counselors, psychotherapists, hypnotherapists, and social workers who, as some part of their professional lives, work with athletes, coaches, and exercisers (especially in sport-mad countries such as Australia and the USA), then the number of clients involved, and the number of practitioners working, could well be equal to or exceed the total number of people involved in the athletic training and strength and conditioning professions.

For students who want to be performance enhancers, we believe they are correct; there aren't enough jobs if one's focus is on the narrow band of specific behaviors around the execution of physical skills. Taking this approach to sport and exercise psychology service delivery is like a house painter who is more than happy to paint your home, but only if you want it done in one specific shade of blue. The book you are holding is not blue; it covers a great deal of the visible spectrum of athletes' and coaches' lives. It also delves into the usually unexamined infrared and ultraviolet realms of hidden fears, desires, abuse, trauma, and shattered dreams.

Why another sport and exercise psychology handbook? Because we wanted to present the full spectrum of the issues psychologists, counselors, and consultants encounter when they focus on working with people, and not just when they dip their brushes into blue paint. There is a reason as to why we relegated the performance enhancement section of this book to the last chapters. It's not because we think such interventions are unimportant; we think they can be of tremendous value. Those cognitive-behavioral techniques have been covered many times in other books, but we still needed to include them here. What's a rainbow without some blue in it? But we wanted to present the rest of the spectrum first: the full range of what may be encountered when we look at whole people rather than specific behaviors such as sport skills and mental training. Even when we focus on performance, we have to see how sport behavior fits, or doesn't fit, in the lives of those we serve. An 800-meter run does not take place in a vacuum. All the relaxation exercises in the world will probably have little effect on competition anxiety if those fears are tied to some dire imagined and real consequences of failure such as parental psychological abuse, the withdrawal of love, and feelings of worthlessness and emptiness.

As educators, researchers, and practitioners, we have tried to help make applied sport psychology, in a word, more "psychological." We have tried to move the focus from a set of behaviors (i.e., performance) to a broader lens of the entire person, the social and familial contexts, the intrapsychic and interpersonal struggles and successes, and the health and happiness of those we serve.

As the title suggests, this book is intended to be a handbook of applied sport psychology that can guide advanced students as well as be a useful source of information for practitioners and academics who are training future sport psychologists. The central idea of the book is to combine the knowledge from counseling, assessment, therapeutic models, and mental skills as they apply to the practice of applied sport psychology. We want to present a picture of service that is more complex and multi-faceted than most other applied sport psychology texts have done in the past.

The book contains seven sections. The first focuses on counseling, from establishing to terminating therapeutic relationships and many things in between. Having a toolbox or a bag of tricks that can help people improve their performances or their lives will be of little use to clients if practitioners cannot develop rapport, establish mutual respect, and communicate effectively. The second section contains information about assessment, a necessary step often overlooked in many sport psychology textbooks. How can practitioners determine what interventions may be useful if they don't first establish what is actually going on with the client? Many of the questionnaires developed within the field of sport psychology have been created for research purposes. Although they may demonstrate validity and reliability when comparing groups or establishing trends, they may not be appropriate for obtaining information on which to base a case formulation of a single individual. In this section the authors explore objective and projective tests as well as observations and intake interviews.

The third section of the book includes descriptions of nine different theoretical or therapeutic models on which interventions can be based. The old adage of "if the only tool you have is a hammer, you tend to see everything as a nail" unfortunately parallels the work of some practitioners who only consider their clients from a single viewpoint. Sometimes the situation calls for a tool other than a hammer. This section looks at a variety of different frameworks as they can apply to sport. The fourth section delves into how to help athletes (and coaches) cope with specific individual issues. There are guidelines for dealing with issues specific to sport (e.g., injury rehabilitation, career termination, overtraining) as well as non-sport-specific issues often ignored in the applied sport psychology literature (e.g., eating disorders, depression, anxiety). The fifth section provides similar views on team-related issues (e.g., conflict resolution, travel, death of a teammate).

Considerations when working with specific populations are the spotlight of the sixth section. Too often sport psychology knowledge has been presented in ways that suggest that once students learn particular techniques, they can apply them to most if not all athletes, with few variations. What makes for appropriate content and structure of sessions will differ if the athletes are children or older adults, novices or professionals. In addition, individual factors such as sexual orientation, disabilities, nationality, and ethnicity can affect attitudes, beliefs, and behaviors of both clients and practitioners. The final section focuses on mental skills, the tools in the toolbox that practitioners often teach to athletes to help them enhance the quality and consistency of their performances.

The contributors to this book have a range of backgrounds, experiences, and viewpoints, but what they all provide is concise expertise based on a combination of research and professional experience. The chapters should provide guidance to graduate students undertaking their first placements as well as seasoned professionals exploring new frameworks or dealing with specific issues.

Section I

Counseling

1

Therapeutic relationships in applied sport psychology

Mark B. Andersen and Harriet D. Speed

We begin this book with the topic of relationships because we believe that in applied sport psychology there is no aspect of service that is more important or central to the quality and outcomes of the collaborative work than how the two parties involved get along with each other. The issue of establishing therapeutic relationships or working alliances, between psychologists and their clients forms the underlying connective thread throughout most of the chapters in this book. The editors did not think they were being redundant in having authors repeat the relationship importance litany over and over again. Rather, they were being emphatic.

One could argue that relationships in sport are the foundations upon which performance, satisfaction (or dissatisfaction) with participation, and happiness are built. If we consider the most obvious working relationship in sport, the coach–athlete dyad, then it becomes immediately apparent how the quality of that relationship underpins performance, happiness, effort, and a whole host of positive or negative results and outcomes. We know what happens when coaches are loving, caring, respectful, and genuinely concerned with the health and welfare of athletes in their charge (athletes usually thrive). We also know what happens when coach–athlete relationships are chaotic, manipulative, exploitative, and inconsistent (athletes fall into anxiety, acting out, depression, and victimization). Relationships fuel outcomes in both positive and negative ways.

We (the authors) are both psychotherapists, and we firmly believe that most of the issues in psychotherapy, and even sport psychology performance enhancement work with athletes, are almost always about love. For example, in working with athletes who only want to learn some mental skills for performance enhancement, we may teach those skills, and then the athletes go on their way. But why did the athletes want to learn mental skills to improve performance? We don't know, but the underlying reasons probably have something to do with love. For example, "I really want to perform better so I can feel good about myself (self-esteem, self-love)," or "I want to get better so my parents will love me because when I perform poorly they withdraw love (seeking the parental contingent love reinforcement)," or "I love my coach, and I want to give her a gift that proves my love and dedication (good performance as an expression of love and devotion)." Freud supposedly said, "All giving is asking, and all asking is an asking for love." (Freud, n.d.). Whether or not he actually said or wrote that epigram, we don't really care because it sums up, for us, what therapeutic relationships are all about.

When athletes tell their stories (gift-giving) to sport psychologists, what are they asking? It may take some time to figure out their questions, but what they are probably asking are questions such as, "Can you really hear my story?," "Do you understand my story?," "Will you lovingly hold and care for my story?," or even, "Now that you have heard my story, am I still worthy of love?"

When a sport psychologist gives an athlete the gifts of mental skills training, of unconditional positive regard, of loving care, of genuineness, of an agenda that has only the health and happiness of the athlete as the goals, then what is the sport psychologist asking? Depending on the quality of the character of the sport psychologist, the questions may be, "Will you admire my expertise (narcissistic love)?," "Will we connect as human beings with mutual care and respect (by another name, 'love')?," "Will I be able to help you achieve what you so desire (mentor or parental love)?," "Will you come back in a few months' time and tell me that my gifts and I were helpful (giving as an asking for love)?" As Freud mentioned often, healing is achieved through love (see McGuire, 1974).

Therapeutic relationships in counseling and clinical psychology

The importance of the therapeutic relationship in counseling and clinical psychology has long been recognized, first in clinical practice and theory and, more recently, in a wealth of psychotherapy outcome research (e.g., Sexton & Whiston, 1994). Various theorists conceptualize the effective component of the therapeutic relationship in different ways. For example, psychodynamic theorists focus on transference as the vehicle for therapeutic change, whereas client-centered theorists suggest that it is the relationship conditions offered by the therapist (e.g., empathy, unconditional positive regard, congruence) that provide the environment for change. Regardless of one's theoretical orientation, positive therapeutic relationships, or working alliances, are consistently associated with positive outcomes (Horvath, 2000). As long as the relationship is strong, caring, and mutually respectful, the likelihood of positive outcome is increased.

Psychodynamically, the therapeutic relationship is a fundamental and necessary component of successful therapy because it provides the therapist and client with a mechanism – transference – to build a collaborative working alliance and explore and resolve the enduring influences of the client's past relationships, both positive and negative. Transference refers to the client's attachment to the therapist based on unconscious redirection or projection onto the therapist of qualities and emotional responses that stem from past relationships (real or fantasized) of the client. For example, children who had loving, caring, nonintrusive, supportive parents are likely to transfer those positive responses and parental histories onto the therapist, resulting in a positive working alliance. On the other hand, children who experience physical or sexual abuse or neglect may, as compensation, develop rich fantasies about the "good mother" or "good father" they wish they had and positively transfer those wishful fantasies onto the therapist. One sees this phenomenon frequently in sport. For example, a boy physically abused by his father meets a loving caring coach and falls in love. The coach becomes the good dad that he fantasized about and wished he had. Freud believed that the client's positive attachment to the therapist is essential for fostering a collaborative alliance or "pact" because it instills in the client a sense of security and the personal strength and confidence necessary to deal with unconscious obstacles and painful memories that impede the growth and healthy functioning of the client.

Similar to a psychodynamic formulation of therapeutic relationships, existential psychotherapists such as Yalom (1980) consider the therapeutic relationship to be fundamental to positive therapeutic outcome because it provides the client a "dress rehearsal" for new ways of relating to significant others, as well as the experience of a genuine relationship with someone whose caring is indestructible. Andersen (in press), in a similar vein, suggested that the psychologist, through the therapeutic relationship, provides the client with a model for healthy living. He stated:

> Ideally, in time, the psychologist becomes (we hope) a model for the athlete of self- and other-acceptance, a model for rational thought, and a model for how to be in the world. The psychologist has the ability to "hold" (not control) the athlete's anger, anxiety, and sadness and not become overwhelmed by them, even though the athlete may feel overwhelmed and discombobulated at times. ... Athletes often take the qualities of the psychologist and make internal representations of how the psychologist acts, thinks, feels, and behaves. These internal representations act as guides for the athlete to change or alter his or her thinking, emotional reactions, and behaviors. When athletes say to their sport psychologists, "I was at the tournament and getting nervous, and then I heard your voice in my head ... " we know that the internalization of the psychologist is on its merry and helpful way.

These processes also have support in the neuroscience literature. For example, Schore (1996) suggests that

> experiences in the therapeutic relationship are encoded as implicit memory, often effecting change with the synaptic connections of that memory system with regard to bonding and attachment. Attention to this relationship with some clients will help transform negative implicit memories of relationships by creating a new encoding of a positive experience of attachment.
>
> (p. 63)

The therapeutic relationship may create or recreate the ability for clients to bond or develop attachments in future relationships.

Fostering the therapeutic relationship

In thinking about nurturing therapeutic relationships, we always come back to Rogers (1946), who emphasized that if a practitioner "can create a relationship permeated by warmth, understanding, safety from any type of attack, no matter how trivial, and basic acceptance of the person as he is, then the client will drop his natural defensiveness and use the situation" (p. 419). Rogers believed that all people have the internal resources required for personal growth but need a warm and nonthreatening environment to enable and nurture that growth. In the therapeutic relationship he turned to interpersonal qualities of the therapist, namely empathy (experiencing the client's emotional state as if it were one's own), unconditional positive regard (being accepting and nonjudgmental of the client no matter what the presenting behaviors), and congruence (being nondefensive, genuine, and open) as providing the necessary conditions for releasing the client's inner healing processes.

The relationship conditions offered by the therapist are, in themselves, the foundation for change.

More recently, Hick and Bien (2008) suggested that one way to foster the relationship is for the therapist to be mindfully present (moment-to-moment, nonjudgmental awareness). We believe this stance to be similar to what Rogers was suggesting and has its roots in Freud's "evenly suspended attention" as the means to be physically and emotionally available to clients (Freud, 1912/1958; see also Chapters 20 and 21 for further discussions of mindfulness in applied sport psychology practice).

The sport psychologist's agenda

Some practitioners define the scope of sport psychology practice as primarily performance enhancement and divide athlete concerns into the false dichotomy of performance issues versus personal ones. As Andersen (2006) stated:

> Performance is only one part of the performer, and success or failure on the playing field is intimately tied to feelings of self-worth (and a host of other "self" issues such as self-concept, identity, self-esteem, and self-efficacy), family dynamics, ontogenetic histories, relationships between coaches and athletes and, ultimately, happiness and misery. It is quite surprising that sport psychologists still make the distinction between *performance* and *personal* issues. This distinction has been present and argued loudly in sport psychology circles for a considerable time. It is about time it was seen for the false dichotomy it is. Performance is a deeply personal issue, and counseling athletes on performance touches areas of their lives that go to the core of their being. Improving performance may be the manifest goal of sport psychology work, but the health, welfare and happiness of athletes are the foundations of why sport psychologists do what they do.
>
> (pp. 689–690)

In a recent debate (Brady & Maynard, 2010), a prominent sport psychologist argued that "at an elite level the role of a sport psychologist is entirely about performance enhancement." (p. 59). The agenda of focusing solely on performance enhancement apparently will not die. We do not understand this unholistic and fragmented stance. When athletes come to sport psychologists, they bring with them their entire worlds. As we mentioned at the beginning of this chapter, if the athlete's agenda is learning mental skills then, of course, we follow that athlete's lead and address his/her performance concerns, but it is the athlete who determines the focus of the work, not the sport psychologist. It is our experience that many athletes start out wanting to learn mental skills, but as trust and the therapeutic relationship develop, other "personal issues" begin to emerge.

Therapeutic relationships in applied sport psychology

Studies of sport psychologist–athlete relationships do not have a long history. One of the earliest investigations that touched on this issue was an evaluation of sport psychology services delivered to Canadian Olympic athletes (Orlick & Partington, 1987). The researchers found that athletes described the best consultants as having good listening skills, being able to develop rapport, and caring about what was happening with the athletes – all qualities for building therapeutic relationships. More than a decade later, the first journal article dedicated completely to the sport psychologist–athlete relationship appeared (Petitpas, Giges, & Danish, 1999). The authors were trying to pull mainstream counseling psychology therapeutic relationship paradigms into sport psychology training and practice. They stated, "it may be time for a paradigm shift in sport psychology training models from an emphasis on skill-based instruction to greater awareness of self and the processes involved in the sport psychologist–athlete interaction." (p. 347).

Since Petitpas *et al.* (1999), there have been numerous book chapters (often case studies) and journal articles that focus in whole, or in part, on the qualities of the relationships formed between sport psychologists and the clients in their care. Andersen (2000), in a case example, discussed relationship building from the first intake session, along with the client's transference and his own countertransference, and how these dynamic processes can be found in the early stages of counseling. Price and Andersen (2000) showed the development of a profound therapeutic relationship that occurred over a five-year period with an American football player who moved from university sport to the professional ranks. Andersen (2007) also showed, in two case examples, how the relationships between a sport medicine physical therapist and a swimmer, and a sport psychologist and a track athlete, led to positive and negative outcomes, respectively. Recently, Andersen (2009) described a case of a ballet dancer with performance concerns who benefited from classic psychological skills training (PST). The heart of the case study, however, was the therapeutic relationship and the dancer's positive transference to the therapist. As a final example, Andersen and Speed (in press), in several case examples, described how the story telling and metaphors generated by both sport psychologists and their clients act as building blocks and signposts of the developing working alliances.

We are not so sure there has been the paradigm shift for which Petitpas *et al.* (1999) had hoped. It seems more like a "paradigm nudge." But the therapeutic relationship ball is rolling in the applied sport psychology literature.

Training sport psychologists: therapeutic relationships in supervision

There are several supervision models that can be used in applied sport psychology (see Van Raalte & Andersen, 2000). No matter what the model, we would hope that in the training and supervision of sport psychologists there is a parallel process with the therapeutic relationship in the supervisee–client dyad that is being mirrored in, or running in parallel with, the supervisor–supervisee collaboration. The therapeutic alliance in supervision may actually be more difficult to establish than the one in practitioner–client relationships because of a different kind of power imbalance. In supervision, the supervisor has an evaluative role that may be perceived as threatening (Andersen & Williams-Rice, 1996). As Batten and Santanello (2009) suggested:

> Trainees are likely to encounter difficult emotional experiences, such as shame related to making mistakes and anxiety related to concerns about providing effective therapy, routinely during the course of both supervision and clinical work. In an attempt to minimize the distress associated with these experiences, supervisees may avoid discussion about their shortcomings in supervision.
>
> (p. 149)

If supervisors model unconditional positive regard, care, appreciation of their own frailties and the frailties of others, love, and genuineness, then the supervisory environment may become relatively threat-free for initially anxious supervisees. If there is positive transference and countertransference between a supervisor and a supervisee, a therapeutic alliance is likely to form, and the supervisee may begin to internalize the supervisor as a model of what it is to be a competent psychologist and a loving and caring human being. As in therapy, so too in supervision, it is the therapeutic relationship that fuels change.

Problems in professional relationships

Sport psychologists working relatively long-term with individual athletes and teams may experience schisms, ruptures, or breakdowns in those relationships. Such ruptures may occur for a variety of reasons. For example, a psychologist may be working with a team as a whole and with individual players one-on-one. At first, things are going well, and everyone is happy, but as time goes by a schism between the coach and the sport psychologist begins to manifest. This schism may result from the insecurities of the coach who sees the athletes spending a lot of time with the sport psychologist. The athletes may be coming to the sport psychologist because they are uncomfortable talking to the coach. When I (Mark) was working for a university team, several of the athletes I saw individually had difficulties with the coach who was inconsistent, constantly irritated at the athletes, and a bit of a bully. My office was a safe haven from the often unpleasant training environment. One day the coach called me into his office, sat me down, and blurted out, "Why is it that all the athletes I have trouble with are the ones who are seeing you?" The schism I had been feeling between the coach and me had now widened into a canyon with what amounted to an accusation of a conspiracy, between the athletes and me, against him. At first I felt like I had been professionally suckerpunched, and then I started to become defensive and angry because I also felt bullied. I took a deep breath, told my bruised ego it could have some "poor me" time later, but not now, and I began to speak. I said something like,

> Coach, I value my working relationship with you and the team so highly, and I would never want something to happen that damaged our work together. You know I see several of the women on the team one-on-one, and we talk about a lot of things. Sometimes we talk about coach–athlete interactions and communications and how they may go smoothly and how there may be some concerns. I always discuss with them that communication is a two-way street, and that if there are any problems then it is usually both parties who are contributing to the problem. When these sorts of issues come up, I always encourage them to talk to you so that you too can figure out a way to best help the athlete move forward. I think my title as "team psychologist" makes me the "go to" guy when athletes are struggling with something, so if you are having difficulties with some athletes, then those athletes are probably having difficulties too, and I am kind of the natural outlet for them. But I can also see it from your point of view, and it doesn't look good. Please believe me, I am not trying to undermine your role as coach; I am trying to help the athletes understand the difficulties and tensions and figure ways to resolve them. As I said, I encourage them to talk to you about what they and I have talked about in private.

Even as I read it now, it still sounds defensive. I was trying to mollify the coach, keep my anger and hurt in check, and lay some groundwork for possible future communication. I wasn't truly successful at any of those tasks, but I didn't get fired. This event also started to sow seeds of doubt. Was it possible that I had, in some way, colluded with the athletes in their struggles with the coach? Had I turned my working alliances with the athletes into misalliances?

When the working alliance becomes a misalliance

The therapeutic relationship can devolve into a misalliance for a number of reasons. One way is for the psychologist to become an ally in an athlete's struggles against a powerful other (e.g., coach, parent, administrator). This misalliance is fueled by the two parties having a common enemy. In psychodynamic terms, it is like siblings bonding together against an abusive parent. It is almost always unhelpful and usually damaging for the client, and the psychologist is feeding the dissatisfaction.

Another type of misalliance is dependency-fostering. I have seen some sport psychologists "over-serve" athletes, go to every home and away event, and become so ubiquitous in athletes' lives that their athletes feel lost without them. This sort of dependency-fostering is manipulative and exploitative and probably fills the narcissistic needs of the psychologist at the cost of the athlete's autonomy and dignity. A cousin to dependency-fostering is the psychologist using the athlete to bask in reflected glory. We and our students call these (un) professionals (rather colorfully) "jock-sniffers." The reflected glory seekers probably have the same neediness and narcissism as those sport psychologists who foster dependency.

Probably the most egregious form of a misalliance is when a sexual/romantic liaison develops between the sport psychologist and the client. We know from past literature that such boundary violations are nearly always damaging to the client and to the psychologist. It is a profound betrayal of trust that may leave vulnerable individuals feeling exploited, depressed, and even suicidal (see Stevens & Andersen, 2007).

All of us are flawed in some ways, and working with high-profile athletes can be glamorous and seductive. We need to be vigilant so that we can recognize when the therapeutic alliance is threatened by external or internal factors that pull us away from being helpful and into misalliances that may damage and collapse our professional relationships.

Conclusions

Over 75 years ago, Rosenzweig (1936) used a competition described in Lewis Carroll's classic *Alice's Adventures in Wonderland* as a parable for the outcomes of therapy. He called this tale the "The Dodo Bird Verdict." The competition was running around a lake. Several of the characters in the book had become wet, and the objective of the race was to keep running around the lake until everyone was dry. Neither the distance the characters ran nor how long they took mattered; "dry" was the goal. Once everyone dried out, they looked to the dodo to determine the winner. He pondered the issue for a while and announced, "Everybody has won and all must have prizes." What Rosenzweig was suggesting is that, in general, it is not so important what specific interventions one uses, or what psychotherapy models one adheres to, but rather, it is the common factors of most therapies, such as having a warm, caring, respectful, and nurturing relationship with another human being, that brings about positive change. So, we might say (with caution) that most approaches to applied sport psychology service delivery are roughly equivalent, and that "all must have prizes." But the rough equivalence of treatments is not the issue so much as is the process of building the therapeutic relationship and the interpersonal skills of the psychologist. See Box 1.1 for a summary of the key points from this chapter.

Box 1.1

Summary of key points about therapeutic relationships

- Therapeutic relationships lie at the heart of applied sport psychology service delivery, training, and supervision.
- Therapeutic relationships have been studied intensely in mainstream clinical and counseling psychology, but only relatively recently in applied sport psychology.
- Psychodynamic formulations of the therapeutic relationship view the client's transferential connections to the therapist as the primary agent for positive outcomes.
- The Rogerian qualities of unconditional positive regard, empathy, genuineness, and being nonjudgmental form the foundation upon which a therapeutic alliance can be built.
- In supervisory relationships, therapeutic alliances, similar to what happens in therapy, may occur and help fuel supervisees' growth and change.
- Contratherapeutic misalliances may occur because of psychologists' needs, and even psychopathology, taking precedence over client concerns and desires.

References

Andersen, M. B. (Ed.). (2000). *Doing sport psychology*. Champaign, IL: Human Kinetics.

Andersen, M. B. (2006). It's all about performance ... and something else. In J. Dosil (Ed.), *The Sport Psychologist's Handbook: A guide for sport-specific performance enhancement*. Chichester, England: Wiley, pp. 687–698.

Andersen, M. B. (2007). Collaborative relationships in injury rehabilitation: two case examples. In D. Pargman (Ed.), *Psychological Bases of Sport Injuries* (3rd ed.). Morgantown, WV: Fitness Information Technology, pp. 219–234.

Andersen, M. B. (2009). The "canon" of psychological skills training for enhancing performance. In K. F. Hays (Ed.), *Performance Psychology in Action: A casebook for working with athletes, performing artists, business leaders, and professionals in high-risk occupations*. Washington, DC: American Psychological Association, pp. 11–34.

Andersen, M. B. (in press). Who's mental, who's tough, and who's both? Mutton constructs dressed up as lamb. In D. F. Gucciardi & S. Gordon (Eds.), *Mental toughness in sport: Developments in theory and research*. London: Routledge.

Andersen, M. B., & Speed, H. D. (in press).The practitioner and client as storytellers: Metaphors and folktales in applied sport psychology practice. In D. Gilbourne & M. B. Andersen (Eds.), *Critical essays in applied sport psychology*. Champaign, IL: Human Kinetics.

Andersen, M. B., & Williams-Rice, B. T. (1996). Supervision in the education and training of sport psychology service providers. *The Sport Psychologist*, 10, 278–290.

Batten, S. V., & Santanello, A. P. (2009). A contextual behavioral approach to the role of emotion in psychotherapy supervision. *Training and Education in Professional Psychology*, 3, 148–156.

Brady, A., & Maynard, I. (2010). At an elite level the role of a sport psychologist is entirely about performance enhancement. *Sport & Exercise Psychology Review, 6*, 59–66.

Freud, S. (1958). Recommendations to physicians practicing psychoanalysis. In J. Strachey (Trans. & Ed.), *The standard edition of the complete works of Sigmund Freud, Vol. 12, pp. 111–120)*. London: Hogarth Press. (Original work published in 1912)

Freud, S. (n.d.). *Sigmund Freud Art Quotes*. Online. Retrieved from http://quote.robertgenn.com/auth_search.php?authid=1242

Hick, S. F., & Bien, T. (2008). *Mindfulness and the therapeutic relationship*. New York: Guilford Press.

Horvath, A. O. (2000). The therapeutic relationship: From transference to alliance. *Psychotherapy in Practice, 56*, 163–173.

McGuire, W. (Ed.). (1974). *The Freud/Jung letters: A correspondence between Sigmund Freud and C. G. Jung*. (R. Manheim & R. F. C. Hull, Trans.). Princeton, NJ: Princeton University Press.

Orlick, T., & Partington, J. (1987). The sport psychology consultant: Analysis of critical components as viewed by Canadian Olympic athletes. *The Sport Psychologist, 1*, 4–17.

Petitpas, A. J., Giges, B., & Danish, S. J. (1999). The sport-psychologist–athlete relationship: Implications for training. *The Sport Psychologist, 13*, 344–357.

Price, F., & Andersen, M. B. (2000). Into the maelstrom: A five-year relationship from college ball to the NFL. In M. B. Andersen (Ed.), *Doing sport psychology, pp. 193–206*. Champaign, IL: Human Kinetics.

Rogers, C. R. (1946). Significant aspects of client-centered therapy. *American Psychologist, 1*, 415–422.

Rosenzweig, S. (1936). Some implicit common factors in diverse methods of psychotherapy. *American Journal of Orthopsychiatry, 6*, 412–415.

Schore, A. N. (1996). The experience-dependent maturation of a regulatory system in the orbital prefrontal cortex and the origin of developmental psychopathology. *Development and Psychopathology, 8*, 59–87.

Sexton, T. L., & Whiston, S. C. (1994). The status of the counseling relationship: An empirical review, theoretical implications, and research directions. *The Counseling Psychologist, 22*, 6–78.

Stevens, L., & Andersen, M. B. (2007). Transference and countertransference in sport psychology service delivery: Part I. A review of erotic attraction. *Journal of Applied Sport Psychology, 19*, 253–269.

Van Raalte, J. L., & Andersen, M. B. (2000). Supervision I: From models to doing. In M. B. Andersen (Ed.), *Doing sport psychology, pp. 153–165*. Champaign, IL: Human Kinetics.

Yalom, I. D. (1980). *Existential psychotherapy*. New York: Basic Books.

2

Attending and listening

Shane M. Murphy and Annemarie I. Murphy

The foundation of most training programs for mental health practitioners is the process of becoming a good listener. All approaches to counseling emphasize the critical importance of listening and attending to the client. These skills are not easy to develop. Many graduate counseling training programs devote two years or more to the development of basic counseling skills. Yet listening and attending skills are infrequently discussed in sport psychology. Research in our field almost never focuses directly on the basic skill of listening, although advanced skills such as goal-setting and imagery-training have been studied extensively. Despite the limited attention in the literature on becoming a good listener, experts in sport psychology attest to the high degree of importance they attach to this process. As Orlick (1989) stated:

> First I start with the athletes' needs ... I really listen to athletes. I listen intently. I focus totally on what they are saying and really draw from their experiences. I encourage them to reflect upon and continue to discover what works best for them in different circumstances.
>
> (p. 362)

The core of this chapter is the presentation and discussion of the microskills approach to counseling, originally developed at Colorado State University in the late 1960s (Ivey, Normington, Miller, Morrill, & Haase, 1968). As elaborated over the years, especially by Allen Ivey (Ivey, Ivey, & Zalaquett, 2010), the microskills model identifies a hierarchy of skills, beginning with basic building blocks such as ethics, competence and wellness, and culminating in the ability to integrate skills from theories of psychology into a personal counseling style. In this chapter, we focus on the basic skills of attending the nonverbal and body language attributes that signal a readiness to listen, and listening, which can be further broken down into such basic skills as questioning, paraphrasing, and reflecting. This approach has been influential in the training of counselors, psychologists, social workers, psychiatrists, and others in the helping professions (Egan, 2007a). These microskills are critical to effective sport psychology consulting.

Terms such as counseling and therapy will be used throughout this chapter with particular meanings. *Counseling* is the work of helping people cope with everyday problems and opportunities. It is a fundamental part of most applied work in psychology, including applied sport psychology. Because it usually occurs within the context of a helper (the sport psychologist) and a client (the athlete), it depends on a process of interaction between two people. *Interviewing* is the basic process of information gathering and information sharing between people. Conversations between the practitioner and client in counseling are part of a helping *dialogue*. Egan (2007a) suggested that an effective dialogue comprises turn-taking, connecting, mutual influencing, and co-creating outcomes. *Therapy*, or *psychotherapy*, is an intense process focused on helping clients deal with persistent and distressing life problems, such as anxiety or eating disorders. Throughout this chapter, the terms *counselor*, *sport psychology consultant*, and *sport psychologist* will be used interchangeably to refer to the person conducting applied sport psychology work, and *client* will refer to the athlete in a counseling relationship.

The building blocks of helpful listening

Your skill as a counselor depends upon how comfortable you can make your clients feel in your relationship with them, so that they feel safe discussing the issues that concern them. Even if athletes come to you to ask for help, they may be reluctant to talk about emotional and upsetting issues. Any problems with sport performance can be distressing for clients because self-confidence and self-image may be directly derived from past performances. What are the building blocks of helpful listening? How does the initial counseling interview begin?

Initiation of counseling

There are generally two types of initiations of counseling: nontraditional or traditional. In a traditional model, an athlete approaches a counselor directly to talk about some important issues that have been of concern. The sport psychologist has usually prepared for the interview, and may have some knowledge of the presenting issues. Although typical of many professional counseling situations, this mode of interaction may be less frequent in sport psychology services than in other counseling or consulting practices. Common in sport psychology practice is a nontraditional model, in which athletes may seem to have nonprofessional or casual relationships with sport psychology consultants, but at some point begin to talk about their private concerns or challenges. It is sometimes possible to steer a nontraditional beginning toward an effective counseling relationship, but to do so requires tact and empathy from the counselor. In either model of initiation, it is important to have a quiet and relatively private setting to discuss the athlete's concerns.

Attending behavior

The initial moments of the first interview are spent listening to the athlete about their concerns. Remember, these problems developed over time; resist the tendency of many novice counselors to try to solve the issue immediately. The first part of the session should be about developing rapport and connection with the client. As Carl Rogers first emphasized, a critical quality of a genuine relationship is immersing oneself in the immediacy of the moment, which means paying full attention to the client (Rogers, 1961). Attending behavior has the critical aspects of: eye contact, positive vocal qualities and questions, verbal tracking, and attentive body language (Ivey *et al.*, 2010). In predominant Western cultures, body language that suggests full attention includes facing the client squarely, leaning slightly forward, expressing appropriate emotions via facial expressions, and using encouraging gestures. Attending involves focusing on the athlete and what they may be saying or feeling, and not getting caught up in problem solving. It is a time to listen and attend to verbal and nonverbal behavior.

Attending behavior should also convey respect for the client and an appreciation of any differences between counselor and client. Sport psychologists should listen carefully to all their clients have to say, and make no assumptions about them. All listeners bring their own listening filters to the helping relationship, and these filters are influenced by one's gender, ethnicity, religion, culture, and so on. Being aware of one's own filters is essential for successful listening, but so is learning that athletes are not defined by labels but must be respected for their individuality.

Questions

Having athletes tell their stories is important for developing interventions and building positive relationships. In the early stages of interviews, a few well-placed and focused questions will show that consultants are listening and understanding the importance of the stories the athletes are telling. Avoid getting sidetracked with unimportant elements; counselors can ask some of these questions later on in the interviews. Consultants should look at the athletes, not at their computers or notepads. Although taking some notes is important (for professional reasons of best practice, as well as for aiding memory; see Chapter 6), remember that the first few minutes tend to be important in developing a connection through nonverbal behavior.

Four microskills that are central to the initial interviews are paraphrasing, reflection of feelings, reflection of meaning, and summarizing. These verbal skills show athletes that counselors are listening to their stories and are concerned about their well-being. They are the foundation of effective listening.

Paraphrasing

Paraphrasing is restating the essential content of what the athlete has said, using other words. The paraphrase needs to preserve the meaning of the story but indicate that the consultant has been able to identify the main sources of concern. When paraphrasing the information, make sure to exhibit encouraging nonverbal communication such as positive facial expressions and looks of concern. Nothing is more off-putting to a client than when a consultant's nonverbal expressions do not match verbal expressions. You may have noticed this issue while viewing the television news, such as a commentator talking about a serious accident while smiling.

Reflecting feelings

The second basic listening skill is the reflection of the athlete's feelings. A reflection of feeling occurs when, while paraphrasing a statement, the sport psychologist includes an explicit identification of the athlete's feelings (Egan, 2007b). Observe clients' verbal and nonverbal communications and, while listening to their words, try to feel what they are feeling. Reflection can be a questioning way to "check out" what they are really feeling. Use an empathic tone with positive facial expression. It is not helpful to say things such as, "Don't be upset,"

"You should not worry about that," or "It will be OK." Such comments can appear to your clients that you are making light of their experiences. If you make an inaccurate reflection, say something such as, "It seems I have not quite grasped what is going on for you," and then ask clients to explain more about how they feel so that you can better understand them.

Reflecting meaning

The third basic listening skill is reflection of meaning. Reflection of meaning occurs when sport psychology consultants paraphrase the stories their clients may be trying to tell them. Consultants fill in the blanks of the stories, while asking the athletes to elaborate and clarify. Reflection of meaning should be tentative. If consultants are wrong, this mistake gives athletes the opportunity to "set the record straight," which will assist them in understanding their own experiences. This approach also helps athletes see that the sport psychologist is following the story and the experience.

Summarizing

The fourth basic skill of a good listener, summarizing, helps with both attending and the next stage, which is setting goals and developing an intervention. These topics are covered in later chapters (e.g., Chapter 51). In summarizing, sport psychologists paraphrase both the information and the emotional content the clients shared, restating them as accurately as possible. Summarizing takes longer than simple paraphrasing and moves the counseling forward toward action. It usually happens toward the end of an interview. Summarizing helps to provide clarity, especially with complex issues (Ivey *et al.*, 2010).

An advantage of many sport psychology approaches to counseling is that they build upon the strengths of athletes, drawing out the athletes' personal strengths and resources and reflecting them back, helping to create an atmosphere of optimism and providing focus and direction to the interview. The next section summarizes how various theoretical orientations can guide the listening process.

Theory-guided listening: focusing attention

As much as any applied area of psychology, sport psychology is strongly identified with the set of specific interventions its practitioners commonly use. These various interventions, usually identified as a group under the rubric "psychological skills training," or PST (Vealey, 1988), have been described as the "canon" of sport psychology (Andersen, 2009) and include approaches such as goal-setting, relaxation training, concentration training, imagery work, self-talk, and emotional control. Yet the application of these interventions does not occur in a vacuum, and the basic work between sport psychologist and athlete happens within a counseling relationship. The counselor/therapist (sport psychologist) listens to and talks to the client (athlete) and together they establish the goals for their work together. Even if PST is used, its introduction and implementation will be strongly influenced by the approach of the sport psychologist to this counseling relationship.

Theoretical approaches to counseling and behavior change are foundational in sport psychology consulting and good consultants are guided by their theoretical frameworks at every step of the process. One of the markers of a suboptimal sport psychology consulting relationship is the lack of a theoretical orientation to guide the interactions. Researchers who asked athletes to describe the characteristics of effective and ineffective sport psychology consultants found that the atheoretical application of PST programs, what they described as a "canned" approach to consulting, was one of the main markers of consultants who were perceived as ineffective (Gould, Tammen, Murphy, & May, 1991; Orlick & Partington, 1987). A theoretical orientation provides direction for the consultant by highlighting certain issues, concepts, and situations that deserve attention. The consultant will be listening for these key concepts and will attend to them when they occur. The theoretical orientation of the consultant also provides an explanation for what is happening in the relationship with the athlete. It predicts that certain interventions will be effective in certain situations and helps guide the consultant in choosing strategies.

In Section III of this book, a variety of theoretical models within sport psychology are discussed, including cognitive-behavioral, humanistic, psychodynamic, and family systems approaches. Here, we will briefly highlight how three such theoretical approaches influence the work of attending and listening within the sport psychologist–athlete counseling relationship. It is not feasible to discuss the many theoretical approaches, so we have focused on those that appear to be the ones that sport psychologists commonly employ. For each, we highlight some of the critical issues, concepts, and situations to which the consultant will be attending.

Behavioral theory

In one sense, the behavioral theories of B. F. Skinner (1971) could be said to underlie all attempts to influence the dialogue between counselor and client. We have emphasized that the counseling relationship is one of shared work, a collaboration between sport psychologist and athlete, but because the relationship begins with the athlete seeking help and the sport psychologist as the expert providing assistance, whatever the sport psychologist chooses to attend will have a great influence on the direction of subsequent discourse. Behaviorists consider the mere act of attention to be a powerful reinforcer, something that is readily apparent in social situations. For example, consider the following hypothetical conversation between a sport psychologist and an athlete:

> Athlete: I'm still upset about the last match I suppose, and I'm not looking forward to the tournament this weekend. I haven't been sleeping well this week; I keep thinking about how the last match ended. I think I wanted coach to get upset and yell at me; maybe I need that. I'm worried this is going to be a pattern, a habit or something. My parents have noticed, they're bugging me to talk to you about it.

> Sport Psychologist: I'm hearing that you're still upset about last week and you're worried about this weekend. Tell me about what happened with your coach.

Even the briefest consulting situations give rise to a host of information, and one of the main responsibilities of the sport psychologist is to help focus the dialogue in a manner that moves the process forward. In this interaction, the sport psychologist uses the microskill of paraphrasing to establish empathy, and this tactic reinforces the athlete for disclosing feelings. By attending to the coaching relationship, the sport psychologist subtly reinforces the discussion of this issue. Several other issues such as the athlete's negative self-talk, the inability to let go of a defeat, and the relationship with parents are also worthy of attention. The act of attending directs the discussion toward some topics at the expense of others.

A skilled counselor will keep track of the issues raised and may wish to come back to them at a later point in the interview.

In a related fashion, issues or concerns raised by the athlete that the sport psychology consultant chooses to ignore are likely to be mentioned less, due to lack of reinforcement. The process of not reinforcing a behavior with the goal of eliminating it or greatly decreasing its frequency is known as extinction. The practice of extinguishing an athlete's verbal focus on an issue is usually used with respect to thoughts and feelings such as anxiety and depression that may interfere with performance.

The behavioral framework is a natural fit for a sport psychologist due to the strong focus on behavior change in both approaches. Behavioral theory suggests that sport psychology consultants pay special attention to the environmental and social factors that shape and maintain athlete behaviors (contingencies of reinforcement), especially those that athletes wish to change.

Cognitive theory

As formulated by theorists such as Beck (1976) and Ellis (1973), cognitive theories propose that behavior change occurs when cognitions change, reversing the half-century trend of minimizing the importance of cognitions, initiated by the behavioral movement of Watson (1913) and Skinner (1971). Sport psychology consultants using a cognitive therapy approach listen carefully to the thoughts and emotions expressed by the athletes-clients, paying special attention to cognitions that seem to trigger strong feelings and seeking to identify irrational thoughts that lead to ineffective learning, maladaptive emotions, and poor performance.

One of the challenges for the counselor in identifying negative thinking is that some cognitions are believed to be automatic (Beck, 1976); that is, they occur frequently, have strong emotional connotations (e.g., "I can't beat this guy," "my coach is disappointed in me"), but the client is initially unaware of the thoughts because they are routine. Not only must the sport psychologist use expert listening skills, but athletes must also learn to recognize, or listen to, their own self-talk, with the goal of identifying ineffective cognitions and changing them.

Many psychologists and sport psychologists today identify themselves as cognitive-behavioral therapists (Mahoney & Meyers, 1989), merging the cognitive and behavioral approaches into a system that emphasizes client behavior change via both reinforcement strategies and the facilitation of changes in thoughts and feelings. This model is a good fit for sport psychology consultants because it places a strong responsibility on the client–athlete to make behavioral changes and to be accountable for practicing new behaviors and implementing agreed-upon goals. The counseling relationship becomes an alliance between sport psychologist and athlete to identify goals and initiate desired changes. In this approach, listening and attending skills are crucial for the successful creation of a working partnership.

The transtheoretical stages of change model

Prochaska and colleagues developed the transtheoretical model of change in an attempt to clearly explain the change process as it occurs within most therapeutic relationships, irrespective of theoretical orientation (Prochaska, Norcross, & DiClemente, 1994). Identification of the stages of change themselves was an important contribution to the helping literature, but the critical insight provided by the transtheoretical model is that clients' behaviors and willingness to change will reflect the stages they are in – pre-contemplation,

contemplation, preparation, action, or maintenance. This model is relevant for applied sport psychology, because athlete clients are often spread widely across the stages of change spectrum. Some are ready to begin behavioral change (i.e., they are in the preparation stage), but many have only vaguely thought about applying a mental skills approach to their sport, perhaps through conversations with a teammate or because a sport psychologist has been assigned to their team, program, or school. The challenge for sport psychology consultants is to help the athletes move forward in the change process. Two critical listening tasks face sport psychologists in the early stages of helping relationships. First, consultants must identify the stage of change occupied by the athletes. Straightforward questions about how serious athletes are about changing specific behaviors and what their change plans are will usually enable determinations to be made. Second, to assist athletes in moving toward desired changes, listening to their rationales for change is essential. Helping athletes identify pros and cons of change is the most effective way of helping them move toward the next stage.

Skill development for sport psychologists in attending and listening

Listening and attending are skills to be learned and practiced. Becoming an effective listener is a lifelong process. Here are some general suggestions to develop the skills outlined in this chapter:

1. Become aware of your own verbal and nonverbal communication style. It is important to have accurate awareness of your own tendencies. To gain such awareness, you can obtain feedback from colleagues and other professionals. With modern technologies, it is possible to record a sample session from your own practice (with the client's permission) and subsequently review what you said and how you said it, examining both verbal and nonverbal interactions. Analyze your own listening and attending microskills. Another way to engage in critical self-reflection is to practise interviewing with a colleague or a friend and ask for specific feedback. A great resource is found in Ivey et al. (2010). Their format, analyzing a counseling interview in a systematic and objective fashion, may help you to develop these important skills.
2. Obtain continuing education training not only at sport psychology seminars but through a variety of professional development activities and workshops that may introduce you to different orientations and approaches. Choose seminars that will challenge your counseling attitudes and add to your repertoire of skills.
3. Find a mentor, supervisor, or other individual who can be relatively objective about your work. When starting your journey as a counselor, it is important to obtain consistent feedback on your skills. But even the most experienced counselors benefit from the opportunities to discuss situations that are complex and challenging. Sport psychology consulting is rarely as simple and straightforward as it might seem from the reading of an introductory sport psychology textbook.

Conclusion

Sport psychology has a strong research tradition of examining a variety of psychological strategies that are commonly employed to change performance (Hays, 2009). The psychological skills training approach of sport psychologists must rest on a firm foundation of excellent communication skills, of which listening and attending are the most basic (Ivey *et al.*, 2010). This chapter described the microskills approach to developing good communication skills and suggested ways to strengthen and improve these skills in sport psychology consulting. Good communication skills are a necessary foundation for effective counseling, but these skills are just the first step in becoming an effective sport psychology consultant. "Communication skills are essential for building the helping partnership and for helping clients move through the stages and steps of the helping model. But they are the essential tools for making the model work and not the model itself" (Egan, 2007b, p. 45). See Box 2.1 for a summary of the key points made in this chapter.

Box 2.1

Summary of key points about attending and listening

- Expert sport psychologists place a high priority on excellent listening as an essential foundation for effective applied sport psychology consultations.
- Sport psychology consulting often involves a nontraditional counseling approach, with athletes often having an informal relationship with a sport psychology consultant that can suddenly develop into a serious counseling relationship.
- The *microskills* approach suggests that specific behaviors form the foundation of effective communication in all counseling relationships.
- Attending behavior includes the critical aspects of: eye contact, positive vocal qualities, questions, verbal tracking, and attentive body language.
- Listening skills include: paraphrasing, reflection of feelings, reflection of meaning, and summarizing.
- Consultants using a *behavioral* model will be listening for stories that reveal the contingencies of reinforcement and punishment in the athlete's life.
- Consultants using a *cognitive therapy* approach will listen to the thoughts and emotions expressed by athletes, seeking to identify irrational thoughts that lead to poor performance.
- Consultants guided by the *transtheoretical model* will listen to identify the stages of change occupied by athletes, and will help athletes identify the pros and cons of change.
- Analyze your own listening and attending microskills, using recordings of actual client sessions if possible, or conducting practice interviews with colleagues.
- Obtain continuing education training at sport psychology seminars and at applied workshops offered by therapists, counselors, and other experts.
- Develop a mentee or supervised relationship with a skilled sport psychologist who can provide you with feedback and guide your development as an expert listener.

References

Andersen, M. B. (2009). The "canon" of psychological skills training for enhancing performance. In K. F. Hays (Ed.), *Performance psychology in action: Casebook for working with athletes, performing artists, business leaders, and professionals in high-risk occupations* (pp. 11–34). Washington, DC: American Psychological Association.

Beck, A. (1976). *Cognitive therapy and the emotional disorders.* New York: International Universities Press.

Egan, G. (2007a). *The skilled helper: A problem-management and opportunity-development approach to helping* (8th ed.). Belmont, CA: Thomson.

Egan, G. (2007b). *Skilled helping around the world* (booklet accompanying *The skilled helper* (8th ed.)). Belmont, CA: Thomson.

Ellis, A. (1973). *Humanistic psychotherapy: The rational-emotive approach.* New York: McGraw-Hill.

Gould, D., Tammen, V., Murphy, S., & May, J. (1991). An evaluation of U. S. Olympic sport psychology consultant effectiveness. *The Sport Psychologist, 5,* 111–127.

Hays, K. F. (Ed.). (2009). *Performance psychology in action: Casebook for working with athletes, performing artists, business leaders, and professionals in high-risk occupations.* Washington, DC: American Psychological Association.

Ivey, A., Normington, C., Miller, C., Morril, W., & Haase, R. (1968). Microcounseling and attending behavior: An approach to pre-practicum counselor training. *Journal of Counseling Psychology, 15,* Part II, 1–12.

Ivey, A., Ivey, M. B., & Zalaquett, C. P. (2010). *Intentional interviewing and counseling: Facilitating client development in a multicultural society* (7th ed.). Belmont, CA: Brooks/Cole.

Mahoney, M., & Meyers, A. (1989). Anxiety and athletic performance: Traditional and cognitive-behavioral perspectives. In D. Hackfort (Ed.), *Anxiety in sports: An international perspective* (pp. 77–94). Washington, DC: Hemisphere.

Orlick, T. (1989). Reflections on sportpsych consulting with individual and team sport athletes at Summer and Winter Olympic Games. *The Sport Psychologist, 3,* 358–365.

Orlick, T., & Partington, J. (1987). The sport psychology consultant: Analysis of critical components as viewed by Canadian Olympic athletes. *The Sport Psychologist, 1,* 4–17.

Prochaska, J. O., Norcross, J. C., & DiClemente, C. C. (1994). *Changing for good.* New York: HarperCollins.

Rogers, C. (1961). *On becoming a person.* Boston: Houghton Mifflin.

Skinner, B. F. (1971). *Beyond freedom and dignity.* New York: Vintage.

Vealey, R. S. (1988). Future directions in psychological skills training. *The Sport Psychologist, 2,* 318–336.

Watson, J. B. (1913). Psychology as the behaviorist views it. *Psychological Review, 20,* 158–177.

3

Training and professional development in applied sport psychology

David Tod

In the last 40 years, the demand for applied sport psychology has increased as coaches, athletes, and exercise participants have sought help with performance and other issues, and as practitioners have marketed their services. Concurrent with the increased demand, researchers have conducted investigations to examine whether applied sport psychology can help athletes and exercisers with their issues. The lion's share of researchers' attention has been towards evaluating practitioners' typical interventions (e.g., goal setting, self-talk). A much smaller number of studies have focused on effective practitioners' characteristics. There are even fewer investigations examining optimal ways to train practitioners.

Some professionals believe training to become an applied sport psychologist involves more than learning the typical interventions used in the profession, because psychological service delivery is intimately tethered to practitioners and their client relationships (Tod & Andersen, 2005), a feature recognized in other applied psychology disciplines (Sexton & Whiston, 1994). Findings from research on applied sport psychologist training and development have strong parallels with results from mainstream psychology investigations (Tod, Andersen, & Marchant, 2009), providing evidence that parent literature can help guide educators' and supervisors' attempts to mentor trainees. One purpose of this chapter is to explain typical trends in applied sport psychologist development and training. Another purpose is to suggest ways that educators, supervisors, trainees, and practitioners may benefit from practitioner maturation knowledge. Given the parallels between the sport and mainstream psychologist development literature, this knowledge may also help practitioners from other disciplines wishing to reconfigure their skills to work with exercise participants and athletes (e.g., counselors, psychologists).

Trends in applied sport psychologist development

When trainees first begin working with clients, they typically adopt problem-solving perspectives, in which they attempt to provide solutions to athletes' issues (Tod *et al.*, 2009). Associated with a problem-solving approach, trainees also behave in rigid ways and try to adapt clients' issues to fit the interventions they (trainees) have at their disposal. For example, trainees may apply goal setting in ways they have been taught by respected mentors without much consideration for clients' specific needs. Trainees' service delivery practices often result from their desire to justify their involvement with clients (Andersen, 2000a). With experience, practitioners may start collaborating more with clients, acting as facilitators rather than problem solvers, and adapt interventions to suit athletes' specific needs (Rønnestad & Skovholt, 2003). For example, rather than tell an athlete she should write her goals on paper, a practitioner may help the individual create a pictorial montage because the client believes that approach will be more helpful for her motivation to train regularly.

Trainees may have difficulty adapting interventions to clients' needs because they can be distracted during service delivery by their own cognitive activity (Tod et al., 2009). In addition to listening to athletes' stories, beginning practitioners are normally trying to coach themselves through sessions, and attempting to recall advice from supervisors, educators, and their readings. One trainee in the Tod et al. study (not reported in the published article), for example, described that he didn't just have the voice of Homer Simpson in his head, referring to his own self-dialogue, but it felt like he had to contend with the voices of the entire Simpson family (e.g., Marge, Lisa, Bart, Grampa, Santa's Little Helper, Snowball II). As practitioners develop a sense of competence, the level of internal Simpson family domestic chaos reduces and trainees report that they are better able to listen to clients.

Beginning consultants' high levels of cognitive activity may reflect their anxieties and self-doubts about their service delivery competence (Tod et al., 2009). Although excited about helping people, neophyte practitioners are acutely aware they have limited knowledge and skills. They may also be fearful that they will be stripped naked professionally in front of clients and supervisors and be exposed as frauds. With client experience, anxiety intensity is likely to be reduced as practitioners come to realize they can help athletes. Also, they might reinterpret their anxieties as a sign that they care about helping clients and want to improve their service delivery. Mature practitioners, however, are not immune from service delivery anxiety, and may experience self-doubts when working in novel situations and with client groups with whom they have not previously interacted (Rønnestad & Skovholt, 2003).

The change from directive advice-giving and problem-solving approaches to more collaborative and facilitative perspectives is usually associated with an increased recognition of the role of relationships in service delivery, a decreased sense of self as a change agent, and greater appreciation for the ways individuals' needs and personalities influence service delivery (Tod et al., 2009). Trainees often develop their interpersonal skills and attempt to realign the balance of service delivery power to allow clients more control over relationships (Rønnestad & Skovholt, 2003). Trainees may also reflect on ways they can draw on their issues and needs to inform their client-interactions or ensure their "stuff" does not hinder service delivery. For example, a neophyte consultant may draw on his experiences of locker room homophobia to help understand gay male athletes' difficulties functioning in threatening and inimical environments.

The recognition of the role of the self in service delivery reflects the individuation process in which practitioners develop service delivery styles that mirror their personalities and the theoretical orientations resonating with their worldviews (Rønnestad & Skovholt, 2003). For example, individuals who like to adopt a philosophical and rational approach to problems and believe that the cognitive model readily explains much human functioning may base their service delivery on cognitive therapy principles (Beck, 1995). Individuation often involves experimentation, and over time practitioners may try on for size the mantles of various schools of thought as they search for the one(s) that fits comfortably.

Given that initially trainees have limited internal cognitive and behavioral maps to guide service delivery, it is understandable they will seek information from external sources (Tod et al., 2009). The principle of specificity from exercise physiology might help make sense of the types of information trainees' value. The specificity principle suggests that athletes benefit more from modes of training closely resembling their sports than those methods placing different demands on their bodies. Trainee applied sport psychologists value most sources of information providing models or knowledge about how to work with clients (Tod, Marchant, & Andersen, 2007). One such source includes taking part in or observing actual or simulated (e.g., role plays) service delivery. A second source involves discussing service delivery with a supervisor or other colleagues. Although trainees (and practitioners) do find theory and research useful sources of knowledge, the professional literature dealing with the service delivery processes is typically deemed more helpful than the latest research on interventions (Tod et al., 2009). Examples include books and articles dealing with how to interact with clients or use interventions, and those that include examples of service delivery in action (e.g., Andersen, 2000b). With increasing amounts of client interaction, neophyte practitioners' reliance on external knowledge sources decreases, and they are able to draw on their accumulated experiences.

Optimizing professional growth

Applied sport psychologists begin their careers sticking closely to recipes of action dictated to them by their mentors. As individuals accumulate service delivery experience, they are able to explore different ways of operating and develop consulting styles reflecting their personalities and theoretical orientations. One challenge for educators, supervisors, and practitioners is to find ways to facilitate professional development, such as helping trainees manage and learn from their anxieties. Some professional development issues, however, probably receive insufficient attention from professionals in the discipline. For example, a substantial proportion of qualified sport psychology practitioners do not seem to have regular or frequent supervision (Winstone & Gervis, 2006). Also, the supervised work experience hours students undertake in many places may be considered minimal compared with those from other applied psychology disciplines (see Williams & Scherzer, 2003).

Supervised experience

Given that research indicates client interactions and supervision are the most potent influences on professional development (Rønnestad & Skovholt, 2003), it is understandable many educators argue that formal supervised experience is one pillar of effective training programs. Through supervised experience trainees have opportunities to explore their craft and develop their skills, in a safe (one would hope) environment under the guidance of a caring supervisor. Through supervised experience, beginning practitioners can learn to cope with the messiness of real-world service delivery and deal with the ethical, interpersonal, logistical, and other issues that crop up when operating in helping professions (e.g., Andersen, 1994). Supervision can also help practitioners from other fields of psychology receive assistance from an experienced applied sport psychologist when they expand their work to athletes.

Just as some writers believe the working alliance is one (if not the central) cornerstone of psychotherapy and applied sport psychology (Tod & Andersen, 2005), some researchers have suggested that the supervisory working alliance is a (or the) foundation of effective supervision (Ladany & Inman, 2008). In addition to providing one of the most cogent descriptions of supervisory working alliances, Bordin's (1983) approach may also guide supervisors and supervisees as they embark on what can be, at times, a turbulent, yet rewarding, relationship. For Bordin, supervisory working alliances refer to relationships in which participants collaborate to achieve the desired objectives of supervision and consist of: (a) mutually agreed goals, (b) shared understandings of the tasks each party will undertake, and (c) interpersonal bonds between partners.

Bordin (1983) included eight broad goals in his model that may help supervisors and supervisees identify specific aims relevant to their particular needs and situations. Bordin's goals included helping supervisees to: (a) master specific skills, (b) enlarge their understanding of clients' concerns, (c) increase their awareness of service delivery process issues, (d) expand their self-knowledge about how they influence client interactions and outcomes, (e) deal with personal obstacles hindering development, and (f) deepen their appreciation of theory. Two additional goals Bordin mentioned were using supervision as a stimulus for research, and the maintenance of service delivery standards.

The achievement of supervision goals, according to Bordin (1983), is influenced greatly by the negotiated tasks and the interpersonal bonds among the parties. Examples of tasks he proposed as being typically associated with supervisees include preparing and presenting service delivery reports for discussion. Examples of tasks within the supervisor's realm include providing feedback, suggesting alternative conceptualizations, and directing supervisees' attention to relevant phenomena such as their feelings during service delivery. One characteristic of effective supervisors is their ability to tailor tasks to suit supervisees' developmental needs and to negotiate specific goals. The strength of the interpersonal bond is in the degree to which the parties involved care for, like, respect, and trust each other. One particular issue influencing interpersonal bonds specifically, and supervisory alliances generally, is the evaluative component of supervision. Supervisors are gatekeepers tasked with the responsibility of protecting the public and profession. Given the intimate role that practitioners' personal factors play in service delivery, for both qualified and trainee professionals, supervisors' feedback may be approached (and received) with trepidation. The development of a strong interpersonal bond will help buttress potentially sensitive feedback.

Supervision relationships provide a structure within which parties can deal with issues and problems that arise in service delivery. Supervision can quickly become a messy interpersonal minefield because trainees and supervisors bring their strengths, frailties, desires, and needs, of which they may or may not be aware, to the relationship. Reading suitable literature may be a useful way to help people prepare for supervision, and be able to recognize and deal with problems and issues. For example, Andersen (1994) briefly addressed ethical issues in supervision and provided case examples that readers can discuss with colleagues.

Supervision contracts are another vehicle by which the potential messiness of supervision can be addressed (Rønnestad & Skovholt, 1993). The degree of formality and structure of contracts has probably varied across supervisors in applied sport psychology. The trend, however, toward accountability in higher education and the workplace may lead to contractual processes becoming more explicit and documented. In the absence of accountability and legal pressures, a number of additional benefits may be accrued when individuals consider their rights and obligations in supervision. Issues that may hinder supervision can be acknowledged before they arise and possible solutions discussed. A contract may provide a basis for decision making and a way to resolve conflicts if either party feels aggrieved.

According to Rønnestad and Skovholt (1993) there are four areas to consider when establishing supervision contracts: (a) students' developmental needs; (b) supervisors' competencies;

(c) goals, methods, and focus; and (d) the opportunities provided by the work setting. In many situations, such as when supervisees work in the same organizations as supervisors, addressing each of the areas may be relatively straightforward. There are indications, however, that some applied sport psychology supervisors may not have much service delivery experience, may not have training in how to foster students' development, and may not work in the same organization as supervisees (Tod *et al.*, 2007). In less than ideal situations, contracts may be needed to clarify people's rights and obligations because opportunities for conflict and unhappiness may be greater than when supervisors are active practitioners, have training and experience in mentoring others, and operate in the same workplaces as supervisees.

Consideration of students' developmental needs will inform goal setting (Rønnestad & Skovholt, 1993). There are various theories through which to view and address supervisees' developmental needs, and supervisors may change their approaches as supervision progresses. Van Raalte and Andersen (2000), for example, suggested beginning trainees may find behavioral models helpful because the focus is on skill development and supervisors give direct advice. Phenomenological and psychodynamic approaches may be suitable for advanced students. Based on these models, supervisors create environments conducive to supervisee growth and encourage trainees to examine how their needs and histories influence service delivery relationships and outcomes (Van Raalte & Andersen , 2000). A brief discussion about the models supervisors adopt may help trainees understand why their mentors act and react in particular ways during supervision. More broadly, student practitioners will likely benefit from experiencing multiple supervisors (although not for the same client at the same time). Receiving supervision from a range of practitioners will expose trainees to different perspectives and modes of service delivery. Supervision from a variety of people may help trainees develop flexibility in their client interactions.

Given that some sport psychology supervisors may have limited service delivery experience, have little supervision training, and work away from the locations where trainees are gaining experience, reflecting on their competencies may help them identify ways to ensure goals are achieved. In some cases, it may be prudent for individuals to turn down requests for supervision. In other instances, after beginning supervision relationships, supervisors may realize they are not able to help trainees with issues that have arisen in service delivery. The ethical response is to refer trainees to other supervisors.

Educators and practitioners who seek supervision training may find that the quality of their supervisory working alliances improves, and their trainees are better prepared for their careers. Metasupervision is one way that individuals may develop their abilities to mentor others, and refers to when individuals receive supervision for their supervision of others. Metasupervision was a feature of Barney, Andersen, and Riggs' (1996) supervision training model in which beginning students were supervised by advanced trainees, who in turn were overseen by faculty. It is doubtful, however, that metasupervision procedures are included in many training programs.

Although Rønnestad and Skovholt (1993) acknowledged the value trainees may find in clear supervision goals, they recommended the need to consider goal specificity and permanence. Specificity refers to the balance between making goals general enough to be meaningful and specific enough to be measurable. Permanence refers to striking a balance between rigid adherence to outdated targets and changing goals too frequently. There is a great deal of theory and literature on goal setting (see Chapter 51) to help guide supervisors in setting supervision goals. As with many interventions, with experience supervisors will learn how to tailor and negotiate supervision goals to meet trainees' needs.

Supervision methods may be conceptualized at different levels, and Rønnestad and Skovholt (1993) specifically discussed the need to be explicit about procedures (e.g., written reports), interventions, (e.g., modeling), and more pervasive issues (e.g., the use of the supervisory relationship as the vehicle of change). Another level not mentioned by Rønnestad and Skovholt, but which may assist supervision if established at the contractual stage, includes practical and organizational components, such as payment, supervisor availability, legal constraints, grievance procedures, and referral processes (see Andersen, Van Raalte, & Harris, 2000, for an example of how some of these issues can be negotiated).

Another area, focus, refers to the objects, people, and events of primary attention in supervision (Rønnestad & Skovholt, 1993). The main areas of focus in supervision include clients, trainees, and therapeutic relationships. The areas of focus in supervision may vary according to factors such as supervisors' theoretical orientations and trainees' developmental needs. Detailing the areas of focus may help avoid misunderstanding and frustration. For example, a misunderstanding may arise if supervisors focus on the supervisory working alliance, as a parallel process for the therapeutic alliance, when trainees expect the primary attention to be given to their mastery of specific interventions.

One of Bordin's (1983) supervision goals was helping trainees overcome personal obstacles to learning, and this goal may blur the boundaries between supervision and personal counseling. Supervision is the suitable place where trainees can examine how personal issues influence service delivery processes and outcomes, such as how their past experiences with drugs may cause them to react if athletes admit to steroid use. The roots and treatment of trainees' personal issues, however, are best addressed in personal therapy and not supervision. More broadly, authors have advocated the value of applied sport psychologists undertaking personal counseling (Petitpas, Giges, & Danish, 1999).

Undertaking counseling for personal issues

Research provides evidence that practitioners derive personal and service delivery benefits from receiving counseling (Tod et al., 2009). One benefit, for example, is an increase in self-awareness, in addition to resolving personal issues. Increased awareness allows practitioners to be cognizant of their reactions and behaviors, and explore how they might influence service delivery. The opportunity to sit in the client's chair helps practitioners gain insights into how athletes might experience service delivery. Undertaking personal psychotherapy may also help trainees develop confidence and manage their anxieties because observing a practitioner in action may help them to develop a cognitive map of service delivery.

Reflective practice

Reflective practice is one central pillar to optimal professional growth (Rønnestad & Skovholt, 2003), because the cognitive processing of experience may stimulate changes in the ways practitioners understand their craft and behave. Although self-reflection can help practitioners develop new service delivery insights and practices, they can find it uncomfortable because they may need to admit to limitations and mistakes. Also, practitioners' blind spots and finite worldviews may limit the benefits gained from reflective practice. Self-reflection can be improved with guidance and support (Johns, 1994). Individuals can obtain guidance by following a reflective framework. Johns' model, for example, consists of a series of questions that help practitioners describe, reflect on, and learn from their experiences. Further guidance can be sought from the writings of other sport psychology professionals who have discussed reflective practice. For example, Anderson, Knowles, and Gilbourne (2004) discussed techniques and methods to enhance self-reflection, such as journaling. Also, practitioners might find value in comparing their own service delivery experiences with the published accounts of others (e.g., Cropley, Miles, Hanton, & Niven, 2007).

Reflective practice need not be a solitary experience, and additional guidance and support can be obtained by including others in the process (Anderson *et al.*, 2004). For example, practitioners can establish ongoing relationships with peers in which they discuss service delivery experiences together. Shared reflection underpins effective supervision. Supervisors may also draw on the reflective practice literature to consider their own supervisory practices and help trainees engage in self-investigation. Also, applied sport psychologists can learn a great deal about the human condition and service delivery from reflecting on a range of experiences, not only athlete interactions (Tod *et al.*, 2007). For example, practitioners who reflect on traumatic events they have experienced (e.g., divorce) may find that their levels of tolerance, empathy, and acceptance for difficult clients increase (Rønnestad & Skovholt, 2003).

Developing strong professional networks

Sport and mainstream psychologists report that interactions with colleagues contribute to professional development (Tod *et al.*, 2007). Learning how colleagues operate and exposing one's practice to peer review may lead to improved service delivery or reassure individuals they are already acting ethically, safely, and effectively. Professional networks might include clinical and counseling psychologists, psychiatrists, social workers, pastoral care providers, sport and exercise scientists, coaches, marriage and family therapists, horse whisperers, career guidance and substance abuse counselors, sport administrators, sports medicine specialists, and physical therapists. Interacting with a wide range of professionals may provide practitioners with alternative perspectives on service delivery and greater insights into the various issues with which athletes grapple. Having a wide range of contacts also helps ensure practitioners will be able to find suitable professionals for referral and supervision purposes. Psychologists and counselors have also reported that supervising others leads to professional growth because it stimulates self-reflection on one's knowledge and skills (Rønnestad & Skovholt, 2003). Through helping trainees, for example, experienced practitioners might uncover blind spots about how they influence athlete interactions. Networking might be achieved by attending and presenting at professional organizations' conferences and meetings. Establishing informal but regular contact with groups of peers, or individuals, are other ways to network. Collegial interaction is not limited to face-to-face meetings, and practitioners can make use of various other communication modes including email, discussion boards, and blogs.

Conclusion

The conditioning of many athletes is based on systematic training plans and regular feedback and instruction from coaches and other experts to help individuals achieve their targeted goals. Perhaps sport training provides a metaphor for effective applied sport psychologist training: competence results from the use of specific goals, expert feedback, and guided practice. The content presented in the current chapter may help trainees and practitioners strive toward specific goals and seek the feedback and guided practice that will allow them to develop their service delivery skills to better meet their clients' needs. See Box 3.1 for a summary of practical suggestions.

Box 3.1

Practical suggestions for sport psychologists' training and development

- Develop patience regarding professional development, realizing it takes many years to master the service delivery process.
- Accept that anxiety is a typical experience when first engaging in service delivery and when working in novel situations.
- Avoid being negatively self-critical, but accept your level of self-development.
- Remember nearly everybody experiences similar emotions and developmental themes.
- Engage in self-reflection and find ways to make it an interpersonal experience.
- Draw on reflective practice models to facilitate the process.
- Keep good case notes to aid in self-reflection and supervision.
- Receive regular supervision from a range of individuals (but not for the same client at the same time).
- Establish a clear and explicit contract at the start of supervision.
- Develop conflict resolution and management skills to help deal with difficult situations in service delivery and supervision.
- Engage in supervision training, and when suitable be open to supervising others.
- Read professional literature to stay up-to-date about what works in service delivery.
- Engage in self-analysis through personal therapy.
- Develop relationships with professionals from a range of disciplines.
- Join and become involved in professional organizations.

References

Andersen, M. B. (1994). Ethical considerations in the supervision of applied sport psychology graduate students. *Journal of Applied Sport Psychology*, 6, 152–167.

Andersen, M. B. (2000a). Beginnings: Intakes and the initiation of relationships. In M. B. Andersen (Ed.), *Doing sport psychology* (pp. 3–16). Champaign, IL: Human Kinetics.

Andersen, M. B. (Ed.). (2000b). *Doing sport psychology*. Champaign, IL: Human Kinetics.

Andersen, M. B., Van Raalte, J. L., & Harris, G. (2000). Supervision II: A case study. In M. B. Andersen (Ed.), *Doing sport psychology* (pp. 167–179). Champaign, IL: Human Kinetics.

Anderson, A. G., Knowles, Z., & Gilbourne, D. (2004). Reflective practice for sport psychologists: Concepts, models, practical implications, and thoughts on dissemination. *The Sport Psychologist*, 18, 188–203.

Barney, S. T., Andersen, M. B., & Riggs, C. A. (1996). Supervision in sport psychology: Some recommendations for practicum training. *Journal of Applied Sport Psychology*, 8, 200–217.

Beck, J. S. (1995). *Cognitive therapy: Basics and beyond*. New York: Guildford Press.

Bordin, E. S. (1983). A working alliance based model of supervision. *The Counseling Psychologist*, 11, 35–42.

Cropley, B., Miles, A., Hanton, S., & Niven, A. (2007). Improving the delivery of applied sport psychology support through reflective practice. *The Sport Psychologist*, 21, 475–494.

Johns, C. (1994). Guided reflection. In A. M. Palmer, S. Burns, & C. Bulman (Eds.), *Reflective practice in nursing* (pp. 110–130). Oxford, England: Blackwell.

Ladany, N., & Inman, A. G. (2008). Developments in counseling skills training and supervision. In S. D. Brown & R. W. Lent (Eds.), *Handbook of counseling psychology* (4th ed., pp. 338–354). Hoboken, NJ: Wiley.

Petitpas, A. J., Giges, B., & Danish, S. J. (1999). The sport psychologist-athlete relationship: Implications for training. *The Sport Psychologist, 13*, 344–357.

Rønnestad, M. H., & Skovholt, T. M. (1993). Supervision of beginning and advanced graduate students of counseling and psychotherapy. *Journal of Counseling & Development, 71*, 396–405.

Rønnestad, M. H., & Skovholt, T. M. (2003). The journey of the counselor and therapist: Research findings and perspectives on professional development. *Journal of Career Development, 30*, 5–44.

Sexton, T. L., & Whiston, S. C. (1994). The status of the counseling relationship: An empirical review, theoretical implications, and research directions. *The Counseling Psychologist, 22*, 6–78.

Tod, D., & Andersen, M. B. (2005). Success in sport psych: Effective sport psychologists. In S. Murphy (Ed.), *The sport psych handbook* (pp. 305–314). Champaign, IL: Human Kinetics.

Tod, D., Andersen, M. B., & Marchant, D. B. (2009). A longitudinal examination of neophyte applied sport psychologists' professional development. *Journal of Applied Sport Psychology, 21* (Suppl. 1), S1–S16.

Tod, D., Marchant, D., & Andersen, M. B. (2007). Learning experiences contributing to service-delivery competence. *The Sport Psychologist, 21*, 317–334.

Van Raalte, J. L., & Andersen, M. B. (2000). Supervision I: From models to doing. In M. B. Andersen (Ed.), *Doing sport psychology* (pp. 153–165). Champaign, IL: Human Kinetics.

Williams, J. M., & Scherzer, C. B. (2003). Tracking the training and careers of graduates of advanced degree programs in sport psychology, 1994 to 1999. *Journal of Applied Sport Psychology, 15*, 335–353.

Winstone, W., & Gervis, M. (2006). Countertransference and the self-aware sport psychologist: Attitudes and patterns of professional practice. *The Sport Psychologist, 20*, 495–511.

4

Challenging and confronting clients with compassion

Sam J. Zizzi and Jessica C. Peacock

From the first three chapters of this book, the importance of building a strong relationship with each client should be evident. Many things can be accomplished with clients once this foundation is built, such as taking the risk of challenging or confronting them on critical issues. Regardless of experience level or theoretical orientation, facilitating strong working alliances with clients and helping them navigate behavior change are two common threads we need to manage in most therapeutic situations. Therapists commonly serve as "agents of change" – so let's explore how we can become highly skilled facilitators of clients' behavior change processes by looking at our own self-awareness.

Looking inward: the therapist's perspective

Understanding the purpose of challenging and confronting clients in therapy

One of the first steps to facilitating the process of confrontation within therapy for sport psychology practitioners is to understand why we would even want to challenge our clients. Aren't they responsible for change? Depending on the level of direction typically provided to clients in therapy (and the therapeutic models used), we may be more or less comfortable with the idea of confronting client issues directly.

The primary purpose of challenging or confronting clients' key issues is because one believes it will help them reach their therapeutic goals. The desired outcome, at least from the therapist's perspective, is to keep the issue in the present moment so that it cannot be ignored (Hanna, 2002). Research has suggested that keeping clients focused in the present (i.e., how the client's problem is being experienced right now) is a more effective method of facilitating working alliances compared to focusing on past experiences (Kivlighan & Schmitz, 1992). The process of confrontation, however, may lead to considerable distress on the part of clients because it is usually more comfortable to ignore (or deny) difficult or recurring issues. Consciously or subconsciously, clients may have developed a variety of skills or strategies to keep these issues out of their present awareness due to the distress that may be caused by bringing them to the surface.

So how should we view our roles in this process? The term *confrontation* may lead to images of the therapist in an adversarial role battling with the client and arguing for change. Most research on behavior change in therapy, however, suggests quite the opposite. Based on qualitative and quantitative studies of successful behavior change experiences, clients most often describe their therapists as warm and supportive (Hanna & Ritchie, 1995). Highly compassionate practitioners define compassion as being fully present with clients and helping clients take action to change (Vivino, Thompson, Hill, & Lanady, 2009). Pushing or pulling clients to help them alleviate suffering or grow as people may be a compassionate act when handled effectively, and may be needed for some clients to initiate change (Vivino *et al.*, 2009).

Some clients may not be ready or motivated to change, and this lack of readiness may be the first target for confrontation in therapy. One model that can be helpful in analyzing a client's readiness to change is the transtheoretical model (TTM; Prochaska, Norcross, & DiClemente, 1994). The five stages of the model include: (1) precontemplation (not even considering change); (2) contemplation (thinking about changing, but not ready to act); (3) preparation (making specific plans to initiate change in the next month); (4) action (the first six months of engaging in a new behavior; and (5) maintenance (more than six months of behavior change). The stages within this model, and the corresponding processes of change, can be used as guidelines to plan confrontations to help move clients from the precontemplation or contemplation stages into the preparation stage. Consciousness raising is one process that is helpful for moving clients toward contemplation. For example, if one wanted to confront an individual in precontemplation about changing a behavior, incorporating education about the benefits or consequences of change might assist the client in moving into contemplation:

> Dr. Psi: Lee, we've been working together for quite some time now, and I don't think I've ever seen you take a day off. I know you want to make it to the championships this year, but I'm worried that your training might be putting your health at risk. Have you noticed any negative effects over the last few weeks?

> Lee: Well, not really. I mean, I am pretty tired, but I make do.

> Dr. Psi: Making do doesn't sound like the best way to be going through life. What might be some benefits of taking a day off and getting more rest?

Other processes of change can be used throughout the various stages of the TTM. Stage-matched processes of change can be incorporated at any point in the behavior change process, so we encourage practitioners to explore this work further (Prochaska *et al.*, 1994). Many theorists and practitioners espouse the basic concept of "meeting clients where they are," and using the TTM is only one frame of reference for helping clients achieve their therapeutic goals.

One of the key purposes of looking inward is to remind ourselves why we are sitting in our offices, in locker rooms, or on the practice fields (e.g., to help our clients), and that there may come a moment when we will need to confront or challenge our clients to help them achieve their goals. Cormier and Cormier (1979) recommended that prior to implementing any helping strategy, therapists weigh their own characteristics and preferences as well as the client's, along with any salient environmental factors. One way to begin this process is to explore how our personalities may interact with clients and the circumstances in which they are living.

31

How might our personalities affect our approaches to confrontation?

In our roles as counselors or therapists, we serve as facilitators of attitude and behavior change for our clients. Two important factors that will greatly affect *how* we facilitate change are our personalities and therapeutic styles (e.g., models of therapy we use).

Are we aware of our own dominant personality traits and how they interact with traits in others, in particular our clients? For example, a psychologist might be a highly conscientious, goal-oriented type of professional who gets frustrated with disorganized, unmotivated clients. Another could be an amenable helper who is uncomfortable with conflict and distress. Any dominant personality characteristics we possess, we bring with us into nearly every situation, including our roles as therapists. Typically, these dominant traits include functional strengths and Achilles heel-like weaknesses that we will want to be aware of in our roles as sport psychology professionals (not to mention our personal relationships!). Self-awareness of these characteristics is part of being an effective therapist, and will certainly help us understand how we may cognitively and emotionally react to the process of challenging our clients.

One useful exercise we recommend for supervision sessions is for students to discuss their personality characteristics with their supervisors, using a 1–10 scale for each bi-polar characteristic. If students have completed a personality test, then of course they can use the results as the basis for discussion, but for simplicity's sake, let's just use the five-factor personality model as our guide (McCrae & Costa, 2008). The characteristics within this model include: (a) open to experience–closed, (b) conscientious–disorderly, (c) extraverted–introverted, (d) agreeable–disagreeable, and (e) neurotic–calm. These five global traits don't really do justice to the complexities of our personalities, but they may help us think about core characteristics in ourselves and our clients. The factors in this model can have a strong influence on how we approach and react to specific types of clients or clinical situations.

The purpose of this discussion with a supervisor (or colleague) would be to identify one or two dominant characteristics and then brainstorm on types of clients or specific scenarios that match, and do not match, well with the therapist's personality. The point of the discussion is not to change dominant traits but to increase awareness of how these traits influence client interactions, the development of the therapeutic alliance, and the propensity for conflict. We believe, as Corey (1991) has articulated, that "you are your best technique" (p. 437), so it follows that we should spend considerable time studying this critical technique (ourselves) and understanding our own personalities, interpersonal skills, and therapeutic styles. Supervision is a logical place to facilitate this process because it helps sometimes to get an external view, and keep ourselves accountable and honest.

How might therapeutic style affect approaches to confrontation?

Some approaches to counseling, such as some cognitive-behavioral models, include direct confrontation as a key component of effective counseling. Rational–emotive behavior therapy, for example, includes confrontation as a critical therapist skill along with genuineness, empathy, and concreteness (Whalen, DiGiuseppe, & Dryden, 1992). This didactic approach to therapy emphasizes directly challenging clients' dysfunctional thoughts. Training in one of the cognitive-behavioral models of therapy may result in the inclination to build effective confrontation into some sessions.

Nearly all major models of therapy outline different techniques for managing conflict within clients (Corey, 1991). Some approaches focus on exploring repressed conflicts (psychodynamic), making choices and understanding purposeful behavior (e.g., Adlerian, existential, transactional analysis, reality therapy), or revisiting denied or repressed emotional experiences (e.g., Gestalt, person-centered therapy). Regardless of the approach or technique adopted, sport psychology professionals will need to build rapport and find positive ways to challenge and confront clients if they hope to be effective practitioners.

Ultimately, after building self-awareness of our own therapeutic foundations, which are in turn built from personal tendencies and professional training, we might ask these two questions before making a plan for confrontation:

1. How do I rate the quality of my client–therapist relationship?
2. Have I earned the right to confront this client?

By reflecting on these two questions, or discussing them in supervision, we will be able to understand if we are ready to build a specific plan for confrontation or if we need to re-invest time in our next client session to build a stronger foundation (working alliance) so we can take advantage of a challenge/confrontation later on in therapy. Now that we have discussed self-awareness by looking inward, let's change our focus and begin to evaluate client-specific variables to come up with a plan for approaching some challenging situations.

Looking outward: the client's perspective

Much of the literature on challenging therapy situations or confrontation focuses on specific client populations including those in prison, or clients with drug or alcohol problems. (Miller & Rollnick, 2002). In many cases, clients are "nonvolunteers," and the context of therapy requires a strategy to help these clients achieve major outcomes in key life domains (e.g., work, relationships, jail time). Although some athletes struggle with similar concerns, many sport psychology clients don't fit this profile because we have the luxury of working with fairly motivated individuals. There can be circumstances, however, when athletes are mandated by coaches or administrators to see a sport psychology professional (e.g., alcohol or drug violation, team suspension).

Applied sport psychology provides a different therapeutic context for understanding behavior change and confrontation because the "need" to change may not be as critical compared to other client populations. For example, if people with addictions do not find new ways to approach their disorders in a fairly quick manner, they may experience significant, meaningful, and negative consequences across many life domains (loss of work, restricted freedom, diminished social support, death). The need to change is often easy to illustrate, although not always embraced by clients in these difficult circumstances.

In contrast to the extreme examples above, a tennis player may seek sport psychology services to reduce his performance anxiety so he can serve better and play more freely in performance situations. If he doesn't manage to change his approach in the next few weeks, it is unlikely that he will experience significant consequences outside of sport. The good news is that because many sport psychology clients voluntarily seek help, they have implicitly recognized the need for change, and they may possess stronger coping skills and support than many mental health clients. The bad news is that because the client is functioning fairly well in sport and other areas of his life, he may be ambivalent towards putting significant effort into achieving a perceived small change. To help evaluate a client's perspective

33

on change, there are several useful questions to guide the process based on the motivational interviewing work of Miller and Rollnick (2002).

Evaluating the client's perspective on, and capability for, change

Motivational interviewing (MI) is an approach to counseling centered on preparing people for change by helping them resolve ambivalence and low motivation (Miller & Rollnick, 2002). The interviewing nature of this client-centered approach poses clients as the experts navigating their own paths to change, with therapists holding an indirect, nonconfrontational stance. There is plenty of MI-related literature on working with difficult clients, but it is unclear how applicable this work is to sport psychology interventions, particularly for those who are oriented toward performance. Unless sessions are mandated by a coach for some violation of team rules, sport psychology practitioners may not encounter many difficult clients or those at earlier stages of readiness to change (i.e., precontemplation). There are many circumstances, however, where we may encounter athletes who are ambivalent or unmotivated toward change, so the key principles of MI can still apply to sport psychology work. Here are a few examples:

- A basketball player complains about her coach's and teammates' behaviors toward her but doesn't follow through on strategies to manage her emotional reactions (i.e., she likes to complain and doesn't accept responsibility for her role in the interpersonal conflicts).
- A cricket bowler continues to show up for psychological skills training sessions but does not complete homework assignments week after week (i.e., he doesn't appear to want to put in extra effort to develop self-talk and imagery skills to improve performance).
- A coach refers a track athlete because of a bad attitude problem. She shows up for sessions, talks a good talk about making attitude and behavior changes related to improved work ethic at practice, but discreet observation during recent practices and competitions reveals negative attitudes and behaviors (i.e., discrepancy between session and external behavior).

MI theorists suggest that ambivalence can be expressed in two key sentiments, "I want to, but I don't know how" or "I want to, but I'm afraid of failing again" (Miller & Rollnick, 2002, p. 12). Successful athletes are often tuned into a training–performance cycle that includes investing significant amounts of effort to achieve a stated goal (e.g., improved personal performance, individual or team outcomes). They may evaluate sport psychology interventions skeptically, and could be unsure if mental training will be worth the effort for a potential change in one of these outcomes. To help explore the potential for change in each client and how to challenge the client to pursue a different path, the "ready, willing, and able" model is useful as a guide (Miller & Rollnick, 2002).

Question 1: Is your client ready to change?

One factor to consider is whether the client feels that the potential behavior change is important enough at this specific moment in time to invest the necessary effort. If the client is ready for change, then think clearly about whether she has the motivation and skills to navigate the path ahead.

Question 2: Is the client willing to change?

Typically, athletes don't lack willpower or motivation to achieve their goals, but in some cases their understanding of how to go about correcting long-term problems or repeated failures may be limited and lead to low motivation. Attempting to change, therefore, may disrupt a comfortable state of persistent unsatisfactoriness. One of the key issues involves understanding if clients are willing to experience additional failures along the way for the potential of increasing the consistency or level of performance in the future.

Question 3: Is the client able to change?

Elite athletes are often creatures of habit. They manage their food intake, sleep, hydration, training, and recovery often with military precision so they can achieve predictable and consistent levels of performance. Taking on the challenge of changing most, or part, of this routine may result in significant distress and frustration. So, does the client have the coping skills to overcome the negative mood commonly experienced during change? If not, time may be needed to help them build up critical coping skills to manage the stress response likely to be experienced.

The game plan for confrontation

Timing

We should allow plenty of time within a session for confrontation, because we may need to attend to clients' feelings before they leave our presence. For example, some clients may bring up a sensitive issue towards the end of a session to present material that is "therapy-worthy" without actually having to discuss it. Although it is important to confront clients who repeat this pattern, it is rarely a good idea to broach the topic with only a few minutes left in a session. Instead, consider approaching the client at the start of the next meeting so that there is ample time to discuss both the issue at hand and the client's motivation for avoiding "doing the work."

Direct or indirect?

When formulating game plans, consultants should consider whether a direct or indirect approach is best for confrontation. The approach that one decides to take will ultimately depend on a combination of factors, including personal therapeutic style, the client, and the specific scenario. It is important to have a clear sense of the clients' worlds and to be able to anticipate how they will react to particular challenges. It might be helpful to think of planning for confrontation as an imagined chess match, thinking several steps ahead before acting. If I say "x," how might the client respond? If the client reacts with "y," what would I do next? Thinking about the "what ifs" might help determine which approach will work best for the client in that situation; as well, this thinking ahead can allay anxiety and ready the therapist for the various reactions the client might exhibit. It is useful to imagine both positive and negative outcomes to be optimally prepared.

If one is not comfortable openly challenging a client, or if the client exhibits characteristics such as anxiousness or defensiveness, an indirect approach may work best. Indirect approaches that are often effective include the use of humor, identifying discrepancies in behavior, and other techniques found in motivational interviewing (Miller & Rollnick, 2002). The following is an example of a confrontation using an indirect approach with a client:

> Amy was referred to Dr. Psi by her swimming coach because her competitive times have continually increased throughout the season, and she seems totally unmotivated. Amy has been to see Dr. Psi twice already, and has expressed a desire to "do whatever it takes" to get back to her previous levels of performance. Nevertheless, Amy has agreed during both previous sessions to complete a practice journal for homework, but arrives for the third session without having completed the log.
>
> Dr. Psi: So Amy, do you have the journal that we agreed you would complete for this week?
>
> Amy: No Doc, I'm sorry I don't have it.
>
> Dr. Psi: Well, I was never a big fan of homework assignments either, so I can appreciate where you're coming from (stated in a humorous tone). However, you've said a number of times to me already that you want to do everything that you can to get back to your previous performance, so I can't figure out why else you would agree to keep the journal and then not follow through on it (identifying discrepancies).
>
> Amy: I know Doc, and I really do want to improve, I do!
>
> Dr. Psi: Okay, so what gives? Help me understand why you haven't completed something that could help us get you back to those faster swimming times (clarify motivation).

In this scenario, the counselor challenged the client about discrepancies between her words and her actions, but did so indirectly by refocusing attention on the counselor's empathy for the client and her situation. The end goal to confront Amy about her not completing a homework assignment was attained, but was done so without provoking defensiveness or placing blame on the client.

At times, a direct approach to challenging a client may be more helpful than an indirect one. Being direct with a client does not mean being combative or attacking. Instead, it is helpful to think of direct confrontation as an invitation to clients to examine their own behaviors, thoughts, and attitudes, with the intention of cooperation toward behavior change. In addition, confrontation does not necessarily have to emphasize negatives, but can instead be reframed in such a way as to challenge clients to stop blocking their strengths and to live to their potential. When the working alliance is strong, or the client has the perceived skills to handle open confrontation, then a directive stance may be useful. An assessment of the level and severity of the issue that needs confrontation may also help dictate whether a direct or indirect approach is warranted. When the consequences of an issue are high, such as if a client is abusing substances or self-harming, then a direct approach may be warranted. Strategies that are often helpful in direct confrontation include the use of visual aids, asking for evidence, and various Gestalt techniques (Hanna, 2002). The following is an example of a direct approach to confrontation:

> Troy has been seeing Dr. Chi for several weeks regarding his anger management and mood issues. Troy reports experiencing conflicts with his girlfriend, his teammates, his coach, and several friends that are causing him stress. Troy, however, refuses to take

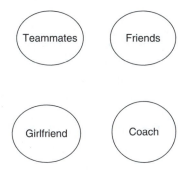

Figure 4.1 Areas of conflict for Troy.

any responsibility for his own actions or role in the problems that he is having, instead placing all blame on external factors.

Troy: None of them ever call or text me back. I'm always the one who has to make plans or get in touch. If I don't do it, I won't hear from them. It's so unfair.

Dr. Chi: Well Troy, can you think of any reasons why your friends might not call or text you? (Trying to hint at several recent arguments Troy has started with the same friends.)

Troy: No. Because they aren't really my friends. My teammates are the same way. I'm always the one doing all the work, and they just act like they do as much as me. Then when I try to help them or tell them how to do something, they get all mad! That's why when I get home I'm in a bad mood. Then instead of making me feel better, my girl will pick a fight!

Dr. Chi: Troy, I want to stop you right there. I want you to take a look at something for me, ok? (goes to a whiteboard). Over the last couple of weeks I've listened to you talk about how much drama and conflict you have to put up with, and how it's coming from all different fronts. (draws "what if" Figure 4.1) But what I'm not hearing from you is your role in all this. Look at all those parts of your life. There's conflict in each area (draws harsh lines in each bubble to represent conflict; Figure 4.2). Now tell me, the conflict experienced by your teammates, your friends, your girlfriend. What do they all have in common in this scenario?

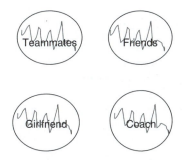

Figure 4.2 What do these conflicts have in common?

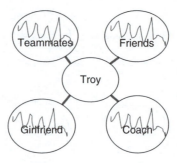

Figure 4.3 These conflicts have Troy in common.

Troy: Me.

Dr. Chi: That's right, you're the thing that all those pieces have in common (draws Figure 4.3). You and conflict. Don't you think it's time you own up to your responsibility in the drama? I know you want to mend these relationships, and I think we can make them better. But you have to be willing to look a little more at yourself and less at the people around you. It might be hard, but you're a strong guy, and I know you have what it takes to improve yourself. What are your thoughts Troy?

In this scenario, the counselor confronted Troy directly about his external blame and used diagrams to help illustrate that it was time for Troy to take responsibility for his own actions. Although the counselor was direct in his challenge to Troy, he was respectful, encouraging, and, above all, compassionate. By pushing or placing demands on clients you are showing them that you care, and that you believe that they can change. What's important to remember though, is that ultimately the decision to make that change lies with the clients.

Conclusions

Ultimately, as sport psychology practitioners our job is to work ourselves out of a job. One of the ways to ensure this outcome occurs is to help clients confront persistent barriers to achieving their therapeutic goals. If we have confronted our clients effectively and helped plan a successful course of change, the clients will have gained the autonomy, competence, and motivation necessary to maintain these changes on their own, and we will no longer be needed.

Box 4.1

Practical take-home messages about challenging and confronting clients

- Effective confrontation is a compassionate act meant to help clients grow – when done well, it is not bullying or attacking a client and may actually improve the therapeutic alliance.

- Take time to understand how your core personality characteristics affect your approach to confronting clients.
- Ask yourself, "Have I established a foundation of trust and rapport, from which I can build?"
- Think carefully about each specific client and the potential consequences of confrontation. Planning will help you prepare for possible negative and positive client reactions.
- List some of the steps the clients will need to take, and help them identify support that will assist them in moving through the processes of change.

That's a good result. See Box 4.1 for a summary of the take-home messages from this chapter.

References

Corey, G. (1991). *Theory and practice of counseling and psychotherapy* (4th ed.). Pacific Grove, CA: Brooks-Cole.

Cormier, W., & Cormier, S. (1979). *Interviewing strategies for helpers: A guide to assessment, treatment, and evaluation.* Monterey, CA: Brooks/Cole.

Hanna, F. J. (2002). *Therapy with difficult clients: Using the precursors model to awaken change.* Washington, DC: American Psychological Association

Hanna, F. J., & Ritchie, M. H. (1995). Seeking the active ingredients of psychotherapeutic change: Within and outside of the context of therapy. *Professional Psychology: Research and Practice, 26,* 176–183.

Kivlighan, D. M., & Schmitz, P. J. (1992). Counselor technical activity in cases with improving working alliances and continuing-poor working alliances. *Journal of Counseling Psychology, 39,* 32–38.

McCrae, R., & Costa, P. (2008). Empirical and theoretical status of the five-factor model of personality traits. In G. Boyle, G. Matthews, & D. Saklofske (Eds.). *The SAGE handbook of personality theory and assessment, Vol 1: Personality theories and models,* pp. 273–294. Thousand Oaks, CA: Sage.

Miller, W. R., & Rollnick, S. (2002). *Motivational interviewing: Preparing people for change.* New York: Guilford Press.

Prochaska, J. O., Norcross, J. C., & DiClemente, C. C. (1994). *Changing for good.* New York: Quill.

Vivino, B. L., Thompson, B. J., Hill, C. E., & Ladany, N. (2009). Compassion in psychotherapy: The perspective of therapists nominated as compassionate. *Psychotherapy Research, 19,* 157–171.

Whalen, S. R., DiGiuseppe, R., & Dryden, W. (1992). *A practitioner's guide to rational-emotive therapy.* New York: Oxford University Press.

5

Working with reluctant and resistant clients

Julia Shiang and Lisa Mitzel

Why would an athlete be resistant to treatment? Some quick answers might be: pressure from a coach, fear of being perceived as mentally weak, worry that one's shameful secrets will be revealed, or doubts about psychology really helping. To begin to address these reasons and others, we will first consider what characterizes resistance. Resistance is a psychological state that comprises the forces in the client that oppose getting help from others, or prevents a client from confronting deep personal issues during treatment (Beutler, Moleiro, & Talebi, 2002). One must consider the many forces within an athlete – what are they, and how do they contribute to resistance to (and in) therapy?

This chapter is divided into two parts: components of sports participation that shape athletes' perceptions, and ways of reducing resistance to participation in therapy. Additionally, we weave in a third element: a sport psychology case example. This personal example provides an intimate lens into a young athlete's life. It illustrates how the internal and external pressures in competitive and familial environments can influence an athlete's perceptions and, subsequently, create resistance toward and during treatment.

We will shift back and forth from personal experiences in the case study to various teaching points. We hope to demonstrate how sport psychologists can prepare themselves to work with athletic clients who are resistant to initiating treatment and with athletes who manifest resistance once therapy is in progress.

A sport psychology case study of resistance

Cathy has been passionate about gymnastics since age nine when she saw the Olympic Games on TV. Since then she trained and competed, won trophies, spent 20+ hours a week at the gym, and grew to love her "gymnastics family." Her father thinks she is good enough to get an athletic scholarship to a university. But Cathy is now 15, and things are changing. Physically, Cathy's maturing. She grew several inches in the last year and gained weight; her body resembles more a woman's than a girl's, which can be a disadvantage in gymnastics. Her practice sessions have been inconsistent for over the past month, and younger girls on the team have started to outshine her in the gym. Cathy's coaches are frustrated – competition is around the corner, and she's not ready. Her head coach confronts her at practice one day. "What's the problem? We have a meet in three weeks. It looks like you don't even want to compete." Cathy replies, "Nothing's wrong. I'm just off." "Well," he says, "Get back on," and lifts his eyebrow.

Components of sports participation that shape athletes' perceptions

To better understand resistance in athletic clients and the underlying forces in athletes' lives, we discuss the following components of sports participation:

- physical play, sports culture, and the learning process;
- intrinsic desires and expressions through physical movement;
- athletes' tenacity;
- "weaknesses" and the consequences of hiding them;
- athletic identity: The self connected to sport, winning, and the sports family.

Physical play, sports culture, and the learning process

Physical movement in exercise, recreation, and sport is a defining feature: A gymnast flips; a boy kicks a ball; a woman runs a marathon. Movement is concrete; it is also a primary factor in one's exposure to the culture of sport and what athletes do. In the case study, Cathy watched gymnastics on TV and was immediately fascinated. The desire to emulate top athletes and participate is prevalent across many sports. For example, at a swimming pool, a child might see kids and adults playing and become interested. That same child will then get in the water, imitate the stroke of a parent, and may ultimately decide to join a swim team. The initial exposure to physical play can lead to participation in the organized structure of sports.

As athletes begin to compete, they become familiar with sports culture. They find games are measured in a concrete frame of rules, scores, and results. Basketball, tennis, soccer – playing sports can be intense: fans come to watch; pressures build; athletes are pushed to do their best. Coaches say, "Let's get down to business," and "Give me 100 percent," and athletes respond. In practices they run, push, and sweat; their bodies develop, get stronger and faster; and skills improve.

In the athlete's learning process, a foundation of beliefs develops through sports culture and ongoing training regimens. A primary example is that physical preparation is of the utmost importance – at times, urgent. Athletes experience continual pressure to physically train and perform, and they may develop assumptions, such as, *I can't ever miss practice*, and *I'm not tough if I can't endure a little injury*. Keith Henschen (personal communication, February 16, 2009) stated, "When athletes struggle, many don't admit they have any problems, and if they do, the answer to any and all of their problems is physical." They think, *work harder* (physically), because that's what they've learned for years. Many athletes will likely have no personal history (or proof) that practising mental skills, or psychological treatment, can help their performances. With little to no prior education of *how* psychology can help, along with the stigmatizing power of the word *psychology*, athletes often resist seeing a sport psychologist; it is unfamiliar territory, and historically they've resolved problems through their physical efforts.

Cathy's progress

Three days later, Cathy is at practice with five of her teammates. They are doing routines on the uneven parallel bars, and Cathy is struggling. With each trick and swing around the bar, she feels heavy, slow, and strains to complete each movement. Her coach barks, "Come on Cathy, your knees are bent. The whole routine is sloppy."

On the other set of bars nearby, a younger teammate nails her routine. A couple of girls say, "Nice job!" and her coach high-fives her. Later, after practice, Cathy breaks down in tears. Her assistant coach says, "Cathy, I can tell you're having a tough time, but we'll work it out." He then speaks with her mother and suggests taking Cathy to a medical doctor to rule out the possibility of an infection, anemia, or any other serious condition. "If nothing is physically wrong," he adds, "then you might consider a sport psychologist." Cathy's mom relays the message to Cathy, who reluctantly agrees to see a physician.

Intrinsic desires and expressions through physical movement

As exercisers and athletes increase their aptitudes in the physical realm, preparation and performance often become habitual and produce a sense of gratification. Individuals create rhythms and rituals. They feel at home with their surroundings. In gymnastics, it may be the feel of vinyl mats under bare feet, or the smell of chalk dust in the air. Athletes are at home and don't have to think – they are in a comfortable state and easily execute learned movements and skills.

One can understand that an athlete's happiness often comes from movement. Athletes become absorbed into the sport's environment; their skills and passions soar as they run, shoot, jump, or spin. In short, athletes highly desire ongoing physical challenges and expression. Some athletes do various types of training six or seven days a week! To take time away from sport can lead to discomfort and cause a disconnection from their bodies and from training. Sport psychology and going for treatment, a sedentary and reflective practice, is often the last thing they want to do or make time to do.

Cathy's progress

Cathy sees her medical doctor several days later. A few test results come back and the doctor finds no physical issues to address. She can see that Cathy is unhappy. The doctor says, "You seem very healthy. No injuries keeping you out of the gym." Cathy sighs. She explains the problems she's having in practice. "What do your coaches say?" asks the doctor. "My assistant coach mentioned seeing a sport psychologist." She looks down. Her doctor speaks up, "Do you know of any psychologists who work with athletes?" Cathy says 'no'. "If you're open to the idea," says the doctor, "you never know, it could really help." Cathy doesn't buy in. Seeing a psychologist sounds extreme, and her problems are not *that* bad. She is determined to fix the problem on her own. The doctor encourages Cathy to think about it.

Athletes' tenacity

As athletes become astute, develop body competence, and realize what they are capable of, clear aspirations and a determined mindset take root. When faced with mental distractions such as doubt or fear, individuals often find ways to cope, rise to the challenge, and take control. In the case study, Cathy had learned this attitude and expectation, this (often false) aura of confidence. For years she had dealt with the pressure to perform, and many times over she had been successful. So in the moment of question, with frustrated coaches, with teammates outperforming her, and with not being prepared for competition, Cathy faced the challenge head-on. Her determined mindset – an athlete's tenacity – caused her to resist outside assistance (in this case, a sport psychologist) and pushed herself to keep trying on her own.

One might call this attitude "an inner arrogance that makes you believe that you can achieve anything you set your mind to" (Jones, Hanton, & Connaughton, 2007, p. 249). In competition or difficult workouts, this attitude and irrational self-belief trigger an internal drive to prevail over any and all failures to achieve success. The notion that strong and capable athletes *should* be able to conquer their problems becomes fixed in an athlete's mind and takes over logical thinking. The disadvantage for athletes with great tenacity is that they close themselves off to other problem-solving ideas; they especially tend to resist methods of psychological training or treatment because they believe they have (or should have) the intelligence and inner strength to overcome obstacles on their own.

Cathy's progress

Two weeks pass. Cathy competes. She not only performs poorly, but her confidence is now fading. Her father says, "You'll never get a scholarship with that kind of performance." Cathy feels pressured. In the gym, her assistant coach takes her aside, "Cathy, talk to me." She can't help it – she begins to cry. "I don't know what's wrong with me," she says, "why I'm falling, why I can't concentrate." He asks her, "Do you want to try talking with a sport psychologist? It couldn't hurt." Cathy feels conflicted. She still thinks she should be tough and overcome the problems. If she saw a psychologist it would mean she has serious problems, and she hates that she might appear weak.

Weaknesses and the consequences of hiding them

Thompson (1995) reported hearing a soccer coach repeatedly yell at his players, "Never let up!" during games; over and over, the coach shouted it. Thompson said that all athletes at some point must let up, or they run themselves into the ground. But what many athletes fear is that if they do let up, their coaches and teammates will judge them to be weak players who won't perform well at crucial moments.

In the world of sport, courage and grit count. Athletes unite as they work together and make sacrifices together. Coaches select top players as starters in games, or part of special travel teams when athletes demonstrate toughness, talent, and a sharp focus in pressure situations. If a player keeps repeating mistakes in practice, the team members come to perceive the player as a weak link. In attempts to hide problems, athletes will not easily admit something is wrong. To protect their status and reputation on the team, athletes will also try to ignore problems (e.g., pains, minor injuries). At most they will say, "It's not a big deal," given the need to appear tough and to prove the problem is temporary. In that way, athletes commonly resist seeing doctors, and especially sport psychologists, because of the stigma of being perceived as mentally weak.

43

Cathy's progress

Another day at practice and her problems persist. Cathy tells her coach and her mother that nothing's helping her in the gym. If they know a sport psychologist, she will try one session. "But," she says, "I don't want anyone to know." As Cathy rides in the car toward home, she is scared. She feels anxious about seeing a psychologist – it's so extreme. But she also imagines her career coming to an end, all her gymnastics friends gone. No more competitions. She has always been an athlete. If she doesn't get this problem fixed, what will she do?

Athletic identity: self-connected to sport, winning, and the sports family

Groff and Kleiber (2001) defined athletic identity as one's view of self in relation to physical activity and involvement in sport. The more time people engage in physical activity, the more likely they are to identify with being athletes. Coaches and teammates validate individuals by spending many hours together. Often local businesses support them with team sponsorships, merchandise discounts, and articles in newspapers. When their team wins, they begin to perceive that they are special compared to other people. What becomes evident is through their athletic prowess they represent strength, uniqueness, and a position of high value in society.

On the other side of this special identity, Groff and Kleiber (2001) suggested that negative consequences could emerge. Individuals seriously committing themselves to the role of athlete could easily engage in overtraining or develop emotional vulnerability (see Chapter 30). In regard to poor performances or career-ending injuries, athletes can experience self-blame, self-criticism, or even depression (Brewer, 1993). They tend to associate their athletic identities with their personal identities. So if athletes struggle, or they decide to quit, devastation may set in. In some cases, athletes hold so tightly to their passion of performing that they are willing to try anything and will eventually seek out psychological help. Others, to avoid further emotional pain or jeopardize their identities, resist asking for assistance or confronting their issues.

Reducing resistance to participation in therapy

We have discussed the ways athletes' training habits and sport environments contribute to specific mindsets that make resistance a common part of entering and staying in therapy. Finding ways to address these normal oppositions is a challenge, but with collaboration between the athlete and therapist, it is possible to find a means to change pre-established perceptions, doubts, and understandable fears.

We should also mention that, at times, there are practical reasons why an athlete might not enter or might drop out of therapy – these include: limited financial resources, complex and time-consuming work/school schedules, significant relationships that are unsupportive or even hostile to psychological treatment, or geographical distances that make transportation and time an issue. These matters are quite challenging and depend largely on the individual or family to find feasible options if treatment is desirable.

When athletes finally take the step toward treatment, therapists can be pro-active in reducing resistance during therapy. At the outset, athletes may often lack an understanding of the therapeutic process and expect to be "cured" in a short period of time. Meanwhile, therapists can briefly share their sports knowledge/history and perhaps anecdotes about

RELUCTANT AND RESISTANT CLIENTS

former (unnamed) clients. This casual talk can help therapists gain some credibility as professionals linked to sports, and allow the athletes a level of comfort as they connect through the sports world.

Cathy's progress

Cathy arrives at the sport psychologist's office. "What brings you here today?" she asks. Cathy responds, "Well, to be honest, I really didn't want to come. I'm going through some stuff in the gym, but I don't see how you can help me." The therapist leaves the door open and says, "I don't know if I'll be of any help either, but why don't we sit down and have a chat about what's going on." Cathy begins to share a little about her training regimen and what's been going on lately, but she is still not convinced the psychologist will be helpful. She also admits that her father has high expectations. But she resists giving any details because she is embarrassed to reveal anything that might indicate she has problems.

As the psychologist sees Cathy suppress emotions, the therapist talks about her work with other athletes and describes how common it is for them to resist therapy. She assures Cathy that whether there are pressures to achieve success, or there are interpersonal relationships that get in the way, all people have parts of themselves that are difficult or painful. At the end of the session, Cathy denies she has a serious problem and says, "I don't think I need to come back for another appointment." The therapist says, "I can see the situation is difficult ... maybe the pressure from your family is part of what's going on. I think if we work together, we can make it better. Can I call in two weeks and check in with you?" Cathy nods, "Okay," and leaves.

As athletes step into treatment and show resistance, sport psychologists can use a number of techniques and interventions including: (a) build and maintain a therapeutic alliance, (b) work on focused short-term and long-term goals, (c) collaborate on negotiating the use of interventions, and (d) discuss with the client the therapist's own limitations. Each of these issues can be raised separately, but as experienced therapists know, these ingredients interact with each other and contribute to the overall success or failure of the therapy.

Developing the therapeutic alliance

The potential of the therapist to help athletes work through resistance and achieve their goals depends primarily on the quality of the relationship. The therapeutic alliance, defined as the quality and strength of the collaborative relationship, is based on trust, respect, mutual understanding, and common goals (Safran & Muran, 2000). This process is mutually collaborative and develops over time with potential for both personal growth and improvement in athletic performance. If the therapy is meaningful and voluntary, and learning takes place, athletes will usually commit to the process of therapy. In addition, the more the therapist knows about the habits of athletes and the specific mechanics of the sport, the better the therapist and athlete can work together, address resistance, and achieve their goals.

Collaborating and negotiating successful interventions

At each stage of therapy athletes can exhibit resistance in a number of ways: Skipping a session, frequently coming in late, avoiding difficult issues, and "forgetting" to practise skills that are taught in the sessions. Nevertheless, if a strong therapeutic alliance based on collaboration can be established, then athletes can play key roles in creating interventions that help attain agreed-upon goals.

Accomplishing small tangible tasks at the outset of therapy is self-reinforcing and confidence-boosting for clients. For example, agreeing on "homework" to do between sessions can reinforce new skill sets. But, if athletes repeatedly come in without completing the homework, then the therapists can take the lead to explore and express curiosity about what is making therapy difficult (see Chapter 4). To re-engage the athletes, the therapists can express empathy, respect, and warmth to alleviate doubt and minimize potential threats. Interventions may need to be revised, and in some situations it is useful to encourage an athlete to stop therapy because little progress is being made. The suggestion to end therapy, in the long run, may actually motivate athletes to re-engage in the change process or resume therapy sometime in the future when they are ready.

Goals: short-term vs. long-term

Athletes often enter therapy with concerns about their struggles with performance, but they also face trouble with confidence, communication issues, and coach– or parent–athlete relationships. To address these issues, measurable goals are necessary. Goals can range from short-term improvement in performance to long-term work with deep-seated, often suppressed problems.

Cathy's progress

When the therapist called Cathy two weeks later, Cathy said she'd been thinking about how her relationships might be affecting her performance. Cathy told the therapist that when her father came to practice one day, she began to shake and had trouble performing. When they got in the car he started yelling at her, and for the first time she felt scared that she might never regain her previous poise as a gymnast. Cathy said she's embarrassed about her problems, but she realizes she needs to talk to someone about what's happening. The therapist offers an appointment for the next day.

Cathy comes in, but she is reluctant to blame her father for the incident. She sighs, "I should have worked harder." The therapist steps back to take a broader view, "How have your parents supported you over time?" Cathy describes the differences between her mom and dad. As she talks, it becomes apparent that her father's approach is more authoritarian and that he has extremely high expectations for Cathy's future.

Over the next several sessions, the therapist empathizes with Cathy: "It seems you are under an enormous amount of pressure to please your father." Cathy agrees. They work together to clarify Cathy's own personal goals in gymnastics and explore how they may or may not be different from her parents' hopes for her. Through this process, Cathy and the therapist come up with a number of coping strategies to help her handle the pressures. Gradually, as Cathy tries new skills, reviews them with the therapist, and learns from trial and error in interactions with her parents, her gymnastics performance begins to improve.

If a therapist discovers that an athlete has a serious emotional/psychological issue – for example, self-induced abuse, an eating disorder, or dysfunctional/damaging relationships – then long-term therapy may be suitable, potentially with a specialist consultant. At this point, it may be necessary to refer the client to another psychologist who is an expert in that area of treatment (see Chapter 22).

Therapist obstacles in helping the athlete

As therapists work with athletes, they may experience a number of difficult reactions within themselves. In therapy, this influence is called countertransference (Gelso & Hayes, 2002). The interactional patterns that occur in the presence of a sports star can create an environment of conflicting pressures. For example, a therapist may unconsciously wish for gratification – to be part of the spotlight or to be chosen into an athlete's inner circle.

When treatment is taking place during the competitive season, the athlete, who is the "expert" in the sport, may tend to focus mainly on the goal of winning. Therefore, it can be easy for the therapist also to become highly invested in outcome goals. The emphasis may be on better times, bigger jumps, and as a result, issues of underlying conflict may not be addressed. Being seduced into this frame of mind can lead to feeling that therapy is a failure when the athlete does not win. Thus, the therapist, in a sense, has colluded with the athlete in increasing resistance to treatment. By focusing on measurements of sports success, the therapist can be derailed from taking the long-range view of the overall purpose of therapy (the athlete's happiness and well-being). Being aware of blind spots, seeking supervision, and maintaining an open stance to learning will help sport psychologists increase their competence.

Sport psychologists need to be prepared to address ruptures and misunderstandings in treatment that they may have caused. Because intense and personal relationships are susceptible to ruptures, even small misunderstandings in therapy can cause a client to disengage and resist further treatment. The critical issue is to navigate in the here-and-now reactions of the client, for both parties to take responsibility for their contributions to the misunderstanding, and to work toward restoring trust. Once the relationship is repaired and trust re-established, the work of therapy can continue.

Conclusion

Because of the many underlying forces within their lives, athletes are often resistant to treatment. Sport psychologists routinely encounter various forms of resistance when an athletic–client engages in therapy. Preparing for and overcoming resistance involves various approaches, including: establishing a therapeutic alliance, defining clear goals, negotiating interventions, directly confronting resistant behaviors (e.g., missing sessions, not doing homework), and addressing the therapist's countertransference reactions. Being aware of and addressing resistance is an ongoing process. Collaboration between therapist and client throughout treatment will help athletes to reach their goals. See Box 5.1 for a summary of practical points from this chapter.

Box 5.1

Practical points on working with reluctant and resistant clients

- Through training regimens, developed beliefs, and sports culture, the many forces within athletes contribute to specific attitudes, which may cause them to resist seeking help.

- Deep-seated mindsets, related to the pressures and expectations in sports, influence athletes to typically "tough it out" in training, hide perceived weaknesses, or avoid identity threats rather than talk about their problems with a psychologist.
- The potential of the therapist to help athletes work through resistance and achieve their goals depends primarily on the quality of the relationship – empowering clients, trust, and confidentiality can minimize potential threats, doubts, and fears.
- The use of short-term goals and simple mental tools can reduce clients' negative perspectives of treatment and further engage them in the therapeutic process.
- Directly addressing athletes about resistance during treatment may result in athletes re-engaging with the process or indicating that they are not currently ready to continue.
- Therapists need to be aware of conflicting pressures, influences, and their own patterns of behavior (while treating athletic-clients) that can affect their abilities to provide quality treatment.

References

Beutler, L. E., Moleiro, C. M., & Talebi, H. (2002). Resistance. In J. C. Norcross (Ed.), *Psychotherapy relationships that work: Therapist contributions and responsiveness to patients* (pp. 129–144). New York: Oxford University Press.

Brewer, B. W. (1993). Self-identity and specific vulnerability to depressed mood. *Journal of Personality*, 6, 87–100.

Gelso, C., & Hayes, J. (2002). The management of countertransference. In J. C. Norcross (Ed.), *Psychotherapy relationships that work: Therapist contributions and responsiveness to patients*, pp. 267–284. New York: Oxford University Press.

Groff, D. G., & Kleiber, D. (2001). Exploring the identity formation of youth involved in an adapted sports program. *Therapeutic Recreation Journal*, 35, 318–332.

Jones, G., Hanton, S., & Connaughton, D. (2007). A framework of mental toughness in the world's best performers. *The Sport Psychologist*, 21, 243–264.

Safran, J., & Muran, J. C. (2000). *Negotiating the therapeutic alliance: A relational treatment guide*. New York: Guilford Press.

Thompson, J. (1995). *Positive coaching: Building character and self-esteem through sports*. Palo Alto, CA: Warde Publishers.

6

Records

Purposes, characteristics, and contents for protecting our clients and ourselves

Ellen T. Luepker

Today's sport psychologists focus on establishing rapport with their clients (e.g., athletes, coaches, whole teams), and may not document their work as much as would be required of licensed clinical psychologists. They work long hours, have limited time for paper work, balance competing demands for increased accountability against their clients' needs for privacy, and, in difficult economic times, may experience job uncertainty and decreased income for their services. Where is the time to document each professional encounter? Why not just rely on memory or scribbled notes? Are records really necessary anyway? If so, what should go in them?

As we struggle to make our way, it helps to realize we are not alone. Many psychologists express uncertainty about what constitutes good record keeping practices. (Luepker, 2003; Scaife & Pomerantz, 1999) They have not received training or support in how to manage these essential professional tasks, much less how to use records as therapeutic tools. Further, even though professional organizations highlight the importance of maintaining high standards to protect client welfare and professional ethics codes and regulatory boards specifically require records (e.g., American Psychological Association [APA], 2007; Australian Psychological Society [APS], 2004, 2007; British Psychological Society [BPS], 2008), none adequately define nor describe the characteristics of competent record keeping. Only recently have academic programs begun recognizing the urgent need to include knowledge about record keeping in psychological counseling curricula. Although some psychologists are lucky enough to learn about documentation during their clinical or counseling practice and internships, most are left to muddle through. To help fill this gap, in this Chapter I share tips on key issues in record keeping including: purposes, what to include, how to say it, how to keep it simple, and how to plan for records in the event of interruptions or closure of practice.

Purposes

Even when our clients request that we keep no records, if we are to be ethical, we do not have a choice (APA, 2007; APS, 2004; BPS, 2008). Reasons systematic clinical records are essential include, but are not limited to, the following:

■ to facilitate communication between psychologist and clients;

- to form the basis of sound assessment and appropriate treatment plans;
- to provide continuity of care;
- to facilitate supervision;
- to satisfy requirements of regulatory boards and ethical codes of conduct (e.g., APA, APS, BPS);
- to satisfy contractual obligations with third-party payers;
- to facilitate writing reports (e.g., formal assessments, legal documents);
- to protect clients, practitioners, supervisors, and employers.

General characteristics

The majority of records I have reviewed when providing consultations to attorneys in malpractice cases, and to anxious practitioners regarding complaints against them, were, unfortunately, nonexistent, sparse, illegible, or incoherent. Sadly, this state of affairs meant that reputations and careers of competent practitioners and their supervisors (and their employers) were needlessly at risk due to inadequate documentation of their professional services.

In one case, a grief-stricken mother sued her son's psychologist, alleging that sub-standard counseling care caused his suicide. Unfortunately, the practitioner's progress notes did not show what her professional interventions were and what transpired in each session. Although her writing was legible, it was limited to scattered words, apparently jotted down during sessions. No quotation marks or pronouns helped to clarify who said or did what (e.g., "he stated ... ," "I asked him ... ").

Fortunately, however, the record included copies of the psychologist's letters to other professionals, which revealed the competent care she provided. Her letters clearly summarized the young man's problems, his difficulties functioning, his lack of progress, and the need for further professional evaluation and collateral services. Her correspondence showed her compassionate, conscientious, and professional efforts to help this young man, whose personal daily journals depicted his chronic despair and wish to die. Although it was a tragedy the young man killed himself, and even though the counseling professional's records of sessions did not convey her quality work, the letters provided sufficient documentation to indicate that the treatment she provided met the standard of care in her community.

In addition to being practitioners' best protection against specious claims, competent records also help to protect the professional relationships, the building blocks for success. Whether clients choose to exercise their rights to access their records or whether psychologists choose to share their records as part of the therapeutic process (e.g., sharing their documentation with clients when crafting evaluations and plans with their clients, monitoring progress, terminating treatment), records can become a dynamic therapeutic aid (Luepker, 2003).

When records convey professional work in humane, legible, and plain language, they can become invaluable therapeutic tools to help clients see themselves within the context of their life experiences, the work they have done in therapy, their progress or lack thereof, and our genuine concerns for their well-being. When records contain inaccurate or pejorative language, records can hurt clients. For example, a professional woman confided she felt devastated when she read in her own record that her counseling practitioner described her as "ugly." Had the professional used more neutral, less value-laden language, this woman could have been spared unnecessary emotional pain.

For practitioners to protect themselves and their clients, and to be able to use records to enhance the professional relationship and work with their clients, here are some essential characteristics of adequate records:

- legible (to self and others);
- germane (only information relevant to assessment/diagnosis, intervention/treatment, progress or lack thereof, and outcomes);
- reliable (e.g., cite specific source of information, document all risk situations and preventive action taken, take care in deciding when and how to document sensitive information, avoid conjectures and prejudicial comments);
- logical (intervention/treatment plans follow logically from assessment/diagnosis; progress notes show interventions geared to problems);
- chronological (organized by date);
- concise (ongoing progress notes can often be limited to 4–5 sentences).

General contents

Our goal is simple: to make what we do and why we do it clear to ourselves, to our clients, and to any other party who may have a legitimate need to see the records. It helps to ask ourselves questions such as the following: Is it clear from reading the record *who* the client is (e.g., athlete, coach, team)? How did we arrive at the intervention plan? Have we discussed options? Were we careful (e.g., informed clients whom they may call in case of emergency during our absences)? Did we record specific action we took to protect an identifiable victim of potential violence, or suicide, or other harm? Did we provide the rationale for our intervention and what progress the client made or didn't make? Did we explain why and how the client ended the work with us? If we were to die or become unexpectedly incapacitated tomorrow, could another practitioner look at the record and be able to find enough information about the client and our work to pick up where we left off? The framework for holding this necessary information includes the following:

- Standard Face Sheet (if individual – name and date of birth, address, home and work numbers, including emergency contacts, legal guardianship information, if appropriate; if team – name and type of team, and so forth);
- client's name on each page;
- date, psychologist's signature, and degree on each entry;
- billing record with matching dates, type of sessions (e.g., individual or team, length of sessions);
- evaluation, assessment, treatment plan (progress notes);
- appropriate, signed consent forms (including policies for confidentiality and exceptions);
- preventive action taken, including referrals related to life-threatening risks and/or client's inability to conduct daily activities of living;
- documentation of appropriate coordination and continuity of care between providers serving the client;
- record of other "nonroutine" disclosures (date/time of disclosure, purpose, information provided and to whom [name, organization, telephone, or fax response of receiving party]);

■ documentation of informed consent discussions;
■ closing summary (termination planned or unplanned).

Assessment or evaluation

Summarizing the assessment of a client need not be difficult. Styles of record keeping can vary. Although check lists are valuable in helping us to systematically gather essential information that we might forget in an interview, the narrative form is far easier to understand. Reserving an hour immediately after an initial assessment to write while the material is still fresh in our memories saves trouble later. Using an outline that includes the following makes an assessment summary relatively simple to compose:

■ brief statement that describes client (e.g., gender, age, educational status, socio-economic status, marital status, children, with whom living, type of employment or course of study, reasons for referral, source of referral, diversity / multicultural factors);
■ presenting problems;
■ history of problems (include onset of problems, specific description of context of onset, who has done what to whom, what / how client has tried to solve problems, what's worked, what hasn't worked);
■ significant bio-psychosocial and cultural history (family, work, school, relationships, religiosity, social activities);
■ significant history of medical problems;
■ interview observations, including description of client's appearance and mental status (e.g., affect, speech, mood, thought content, judgment, insight, memory, impulse control, attention/concentration);
■ assessment consistent with data; document any dual or multiple diagnoses, assessments ruled out;
■ documentation of any referrals made or any received (for what purpose and to/ from whom).

Treatment plan

Treatment plans come alive as therapeutic tools when practitioners discuss them with clients. The plan sets the stage, like a road map for the journey ahead. Mutual discussion of the individualized or team plan assures clients' informed consent and collaboration. The plan includes the following:

■ statement of problems, goals, treatment procedures, estimated duration of time needed to achieve goals;
■ informed consent to assessment and treatment plan.

Ongoing progress notes

Progress notes also can be used as therapeutic tools with clients. They document what occurs during the treatment, especially whether clients are achieving the goals they identified in their plans. Progress notes are part of the official record. Notes that are only of use to the practitioner who wrote them and not required for the official record are stored securely and shredded periodically to prevent confusion.

Progress notes can be brief, often only a paragraph. But they should show the focus of the session. Taking a few minutes immediately after every session to document is expedient, saves time and angst later, and ensures notes are legible, coherent, and contemporaneous. Here are essentials to include in progress notes:

- documentation from session to session regarding client's concerns/issues/problems, response or lack of response to mutually agreed upon treatment;
- modifications of original treatment plan;
- discussion of any calculated risks taken by practitioner (e.g., rationale for controversial decisions, such as accepting a client's invitation to a social event that could run the risk of crossing professional boundaries);
- follow-up notes on action/inaction related to earlier recommendations;
- reports to and from other professionals related to client's counseling;
- correspondence related to work with client;
- documentation of client receiving or being denied health insurance payment for psychological services; any efforts the psychologist made to obtain or to appeal denial of insurance payment;
- telephone contacts from and to client;
- date of any modifications of records for accuracy;
- documentation of consultations with other professionals related to assessment and intervention (e.g., peer supervision on the case);
- documentation of informed consent to changes in mutually agreed-upon plan of action.

Progress notes when working with groups, families, or teams

In addition to maintaining a record to document progress of a group, family, or team, practitioners ensure privacy and confidentiality of individuals by simultaneously keeping separate records for individuals. Maintaining separate documentation in individual files requires a few extra minutes, but is the only way to guarantee adequate documentation and to protect each individual's privacy and confidentiality. The following examples illustrate the different types of progress notes a sport psychologist created following her consultation to a team during which an individual team player shared problems that could possibly indicate a clinical depression. Note that none of the individual players' names are cited in the team progress note.

Example of a team progress note

The focus of my session today with the women's soccer team was on interpersonal tensions team players began feeling following the resignation of their former head coach two weeks ago, which the new coach and players felt were impeding team members' abilities to focus and freely cooperate in the game. I helped them to clarify their concerns, which included anxiety over having differences of opinion regarding their previous coach; divided loyalty between old and new coach; fear of retaliation from previous coach; and should they be successful this season under the leadership of the new coach. We identified various strategies that could help the players let go of their worries in order to focus on their play. We agreed to meet again next week to continue monitoring the team's progress in handling the recent crisis.

Example of an individual progress note

Nancy, a sophomore player on the women's soccer team, stated during my consultation to the team today that she was feeling overwhelmed by the team's interpersonal tensions over the previous coach and his recent resignation. She felt grateful to the previous coach for her support during her first season last year. After the coach's unexpected departure this fall, she felt anxious, began having difficulty sleeping and making more errors during games. She felt team players were wanting her to take sides, either "for or against" the previous coach. She felt anxious about forming a working relationship with the new coach. As I helped team members to clarify their respective feelings, Nancy said it dawned on her that the current situation felt reminiscent to how she'd felt following her parents' conflicted divorce when she was four years old. I helped her to clarify in what ways the recent situation and previous conflicts she experienced during childhood were similar and different. I shared techniques to anchor one's self in the present in order to relinquish feelings of responsibility and regain freedom to focus on play. I inquired but did not see indications of clinical depression in Nancy. My impression is that ongoing counseling to the team will be sufficient to help with her anxiety. However, I offered her and all team players individual appointments as needed in addition to my ongoing help to the team.

Client Name _____

Date of Birth _____

Date of Initial
Evaluation _____

Assessment
DSM, IV, or ICD Code

Reasons (specific assessment criteria)

Problems	Goals	Treatment Procedures	Estimated Time For Tx	Progress

Date:

Therapist Signature: Client Signature:

Figure 6.1 Treatment (Tx) plan.

For a sample treatment plan form that can be used as a therapeutic tool with clients, see Figure 6.1 (sections labeled "assessment" may be called "diagnosis").

Termination or closing summary

Endings in counseling work are as important as beginnings (see Chapter 8). A closing summary that reviews the problems, treatment, progress or lack of progress, and how the work with the client ended, is indispensable. If clients return a month, or a year later, a closing summary helps us recall them and the earlier work together. It facilitates focus on the next phase of problems. When clients transfer to another therapist, a closing summary helps ensure continuity of care. When we receive requests for records from a third party, a closing summary makes it possible to encapsulate the minimum necessary information to achieve the goal of the request.

The closing summary can also be used as a therapeutic tool to benefit clients and to support the professional relationship. Few people have a chance to say what a professional counseling relationship has meant to them and to say goodbye. A chance to review the work together, including problems for which clients sought help, what clients and therapists did together, what clients experienced in therapy, and what they found helpful/not helpful aids in facilitating closure. Closure with one's practitioners makes it easier in the future to seek help as needed. The following is how the psychologist can create a closing summary:

- document date and nature of ending (e.g., by mutual agreement, precipitously and unexpected);
- summarize brief descriptive information about client (e.g., athlete or team, reason/source of referral, original presenting problems, assessment and treatment, length of treatment, progress, outcome and status at closure).

For a sample of a closing summary form that can be used as a therapeutic tool with clients, see Figure 6.2.

Inappropriate contents

Some of the most common aspects of psychological work do not belong in the official record. These aspects include, for example, practitioners' personal reactions in response to clients and complex feelings such as confusion, fragmentation, anger, or sexual attraction. Although understanding one's own personal responses to individual clients is crucial for clarifying assessment or for preventing or ameliorating re-enactment of clients' previous problematic relationships with significant persons in their lives – documenting such feelings in records may burden clients when they choose to read them. Practitioners can limit discussion of their own troubling personal feelings to their own external consultation or supervision. They can document they did so in a way that reflects they conscientiously sought help (e.g., "I obtained consultation to clarify my role within the professional relationship and the best intervention approach"). They can document in the record what they learned from supervision or consultation (e.g., "supervision clarified assessment and working relationship issues, including the need to set firmer limits with the client in our work together").

Client Name _____	Assessment: _____	Reasons (specific
Date of Birth _____	At Initial Evaluation _____	assessment criteria)
Dates of Services _____ To _____	At Termination _____	
Frequency of Sessions _____		

Problems and Goals	Description of Services	Progress	Outcome and Status at Termination

Date:

Therapist Signature:

Figure 6.2 Closing summary.

Here are items to omit from records:

- personal reactions (in psychodynamic terms, these are countertransference feelings and thoughts);
- information not used to establish assessments or to conduct interventions;
- names of anyone who has not consented to receive services (e.g., clients' friends);
- details about clients' privileged communications with their attorneys;
- personal notes (notes understandable to, and meant only for, the practitioner, which are not part of the official clinical record, should be shredded periodically).

Considerations in how long to keep records

All psychology ethics codes address clients' needs for continuity of care through maintenance of records and recommend that psychologists know their local legal responsibilities in determining how long to retain records (APA, 2007; APS, 2004; BPS, 2008). Some ethical guidelines specify how long to retain records (APS, 2007; APA 2007). See, for example, the Australian Psychological Society's guidelines on record keeping that refer to

APS Code of Ethics, Section B2: "Members must make and keep adequate records for a minimum of seven years unless legal requirements specify otherwise. In the case of records collected while the client was a child, records should be retained at least until the individual attains the age of 25 years."

How long to retain records beyond minimum requirements for retention can be difficult to answer. It can be helpful for various reasons to retain records indefinitely. Realistic considerations, however, such as storage space limitations, often preclude this luxury. For example, an athlete who received counseling from a sport psychologist 16 years ago due to troubles running related to a traumatic head injury, returned to the psychologist requesting help for anxiety learning to ski. His anxiety was re-surfacing at a new developmental stage in his life. Even though the psychologist retained the record well past her regulatory board's record retention requirement, she now regretted shredding it for practical reasons during a recent office move. Although she recalled this former client and the focus of his previous therapy, not having his record made it more difficult to piece together some of the historical context. She worked collaboratively with the client in the initial interviews to refresh her memory and to clarify the client's current needs.

Here are issues to consider when determining how long to keep records:

- Know your own setting's regulations regarding length of retention of records for minors and adults.
- Consider clients' needs for continuity of care.
- Consider statute of limitations in personal injury legal cases (for self-protection).
- In general, keeping adult records at least seven years post termination and minor children's records seven years after age of majority is prudent practice.
- Have a consistent records destruction policy; never alter or destroy records with intent to avoid judicial proceedings.

Planning for interruptions or closures of practice

All mental health professions' ethics codes include requirements for continuity of care in the event of interruptions or closures of practice (APA, 2007; APS, 2004; BPS, 2008). Nevertheless, many retired practitioners and the colleagues and spouses of deceased practitioners are unaware of their responsibilities to maintain and to manage records following their retirements or deaths (Luepker, 2003).

For professionals working within institutions, meeting ethical and legal requirements and protecting clients from adverse effects of abandonment can be easier when colleagues can assume care of clients and other administrative tasks in the event of practitioners' illnesses, deaths, or other interruptions or closures of their practices. Solo practitioners, however, must proactively designate external colleagues who can agree to assume responsibility for their clients and to manage and maintain client records for the required length of time. Practitioners can help their clients by creating the following procedures:

- Communicate with clients about who will assume care as needed when the practitioner is unavailable.
- Ensure that another trusted practitioner has the means to gain access to client files, including names, addresses, phone numbers, and contact persons in case of emergency.

- When a practice closes permanently, notify current clients and help them make other arrangements for professional services as needed.
- Ask clients at termination regarding their wishes in the future to be notified should the practice close.
- When a practice closes permanently, make arrangements for secure storage and management of records for the duration of time required by law or professional ethics.
- Define the role and tasks of a designated colleague, which include but are not limited to the following: assume clinical work, attend to financial and clerical matters, monitor client billing and ensure up-to-date payments of bills, communicate with professional organizations and regulatory boards, negotiate contracts (or secure an attorney to do so), cancel subscriptions, work with the practitioner's attorney to dissolve the professional estate (in the event of the practitioner's death), respond to legitimate requests for access to clients' records.
- Provide a designated colleague with a professional directive regarding role and tasks and specific directions necessary to accomplish each task (e.g., how to change voice mail greeting, location of keys, list of subscriptions).

Conclusions

In closing, having knowledge about record keeping – its purposes, what to include, how to write records, how to plan for records in the event of interruptions or closure of practice – puts us in a strong position to protect ourselves and our clients. Using strategies such as outlines for our narratives and documenting evaluations and progress notes immediately after each session can help us to prevent problems later. But even when fortified with facts about competent record keeping, we can expect to sometimes fall short of our intentions. We can comfort ourselves by realizing that no practitioner writes perfect records. Good faith effort is what we can expect of ourselves. See Box 6.1 for practical take-home messages from this chapter.

Box 6.1

Practical take-home messages regarding record keeping

- All mental health organizations have codes of ethics that highlight the importance of protecting client welfare, including the need to appropriately document professional services.
- Few mental health organizations and regulatory bodies define and describe the characteristics involved in competent record keeping.
- Recently, increasing pressures for accountability challenge practitioners to obtain knowledge and specific methods in record keeping to protect themselves and their clients.
- Records form the basis of sound assessment and appropriate treatment plans.
- Records can become positive therapeutic tools, promoting communication about problems and strengths, enhancing mutual collaboration and trust in the working relationship between client and practitioner.

- Records are supervisory tools that facilitate a supervisor's capacity to reflect on and support the learner's work.
- Records satisfy contractual obligations and facilitate writing reports about clients.
- Records provide for continuity of care, allowing new practitioners to pick up where former practitioners ended.

References

American Psychological Association (2007). Record keeping guidelines. *American Psychologist, 62,* 993–1004.

Australian Psychological Society (2004). *Guidelines on record keeping.* Melbourne, VIC, Australia: Australian Psychological Society. Available from: http://www.psychology4change.com/forms/APS_record_keeping_guidelines.pdf

Australian Psychological Society (2007). *Code of Ethics.* Melbourne, VIC, Australia: Australian Psychological Society. Retrieved from: http://www.psychology.org.au/about/ethics/#s1

British Psychological Society (2008). Access to records and record keeping. In *Generic professional practice guidelines* (2nd ed., section 4, pp. 12–15). London: British Psychological Society. Retrieved from: http://www.bps.org.uk/publications/prof-pract/prof-pract_home.cfm

Luepker, E. T. (2003). *Record keeping in psychotherapy & counseling: Protecting confidentiality & the professional relationship.* New York: Routledge.

Scaife, J. M., & Pomerantz, M. (1999). A survey of the record-keeping practices of clinical psychologists. *Clinical Psychology and Psychotherapy, 6,* 210–226.

7

Ethical practice in sport psychology

Challenges in the real world

Jonah Oliver

In general, those who choose to pursue careers in the helping professions are motivated to act morally and ethically (of course, this ideal is sometimes not the case). But a desire to do good is not sufficient to ensure good practice. The majority of practitioners who have acted unethically have not done so through explicit malicious intent, but rather through passivity, inattention, ignorance, or limited competence to deal with the challenges of applied practice.

Key ethical principles

Challenges faced by sport psychologists cut across a number of ethical principles. In particular these challenges tend to pertain to the areas of confidentiality, boundaries, and competence.

Confidentiality

Respect for clients' confidentiality is among the oldest and honored ethical standards in the practice of psychology. Confidentiality is a necessary precondition for the development of an effective client–therapist alliance, without which safe, trusting, and effective therapeutic relationships cannot be formed (Andersen, 2005; Brown & Cogan, 2006; Moore, 2003). Most practitioners and trainee sport psychologists have a reasonable grasp of what confidentiality is, why it is fundamental to the practice of psychology, and when they are required to breach it. Nevertheless, translating these guidelines into applied practice is complicated. There are a multitude of environmental and social demands placed on sport psychologists that are qualitatively different from those usually experienced by our clinical, counseling, and school psychologist counterparts for whom the codes of ethics were originally written.

Sport psychologists often consult with their clients in untraditional ways with respect to time, place, confidentiality, and boundaries. It is not unusual for sessions to take place on pool decks, in gyms, on team buses, or in hotel foyers. These settings are often public, and even if the space in which the session takes place is private, it is frequently known to other people that the athlete is speaking with the psychologist. The process by which athletes are commonly referred to psychologists also raises issues of confidentiality. Coaches, administrators, player-managers, parents, and teachers are among those who refer athletes to psychologists. They have vested interests in the welfare of their athletes, and in many cases are paying for the psychologist's services. In some instances, sports clubs and government-based sport institutes not only fund psychological services, but also make athletes sign legal waivers enabling the sharing of information between medical, support, and coaching staff. Considering these challenges, practitioners need to understand how to navigate the treacherous waters of maintaining confidentiality while keeping third parties satisfied (and in many cases keeping their jobs).

Boundaries

When the original codes of ethics were written for countries such as the United States, the United Kingdom, and Australia, only typical workplace environments were considered, such as consulting rooms, hospital settings, or boardrooms. Sport psychologists, however, frequently deliver therapy in nontraditional settings (Andersen, 1996). Sport psychologists may travel for extended periods with either large teams or single athletes. Often they are in places such as locker rooms where athletes in various stages of undress are bleeding, vomiting, being injected, crying, fighting, hugging, drinking alcohol, singing, joking, or screaming in physical and emotional pain. Similarly, the countless hours of nontraditional interactions often spent with athletes traveling on planes, eating in hotel rooms, or "hanging out" as Andersen et al. (2001) put it, all contribute to the formation of blurred boundaries between the athlete and the sport psychologist. Typically, some level of blurring is unavoidable through spending extended periods of time together. When sharing hotel rooms and long-haul international flights, it is natural that some degree of disclosure will occur between the psychologist and the clients. Self-disclosure is not a problem per se in therapeutic settings, and when used judiciously can enhance therapeutic effectiveness. Therefore, it is not so much about preventing disclosure from occurring, but rather ensuring that it is relevant to the task at hand and not just unfiltered sharing of stories common between travel companions or friends (Knapp & Slattery, 2004).

Because of the heightened potential for the blurring of boundaries, sport psychologists would benefit from some self-monitoring skills and should strive to be astute in identifying, defining, and managing boundaries to prevent the ethical dilemmas that arise from dual-relationships and boundary violations. Managing these boundaries can be challenging because team psychologists work in environments where they are among professionals who may not be ethically and legally required to maintain these boundaries. For example, coaches and dieticians do not have the same level of ethico–legal obligations relating to professional boundaries. Athletes may expect that relationships with psychologists will mirror those developed with other professionals, with "work" occurring within the context of some form of personal relationship. Practically, sport psychologists initially devote much time to developing relationships with the team or the individual athlete before actively intervening. Caution is required to ensure that this form of relationship looks and feels different from other relationships that may be formed within the team (e.g., teammates, coaches, strength and conditioning specialists).

Competence

The ethical requirement to deliver services only within the confines of one's competence is another area that may occasionally be violated by psychologists across different specialties.

Those practising as sport psychologists may be particularly vulnerable to the pressures to make this ethical breach due to the complex nature of the work settings and the relationships they form with clients. Psychologists may be pushed to work with clients who have presenting problems that are beyond the psychologists' training because of the interaction of pressure from the client and the sporting organization to handle all things psychological. It is not uncommon for sport psychologists to come across clients who seek assistance with a raft of presenting problems that are of a clinical psychological nature. Athletes, like the general population, experience psychopathologies such as depression, anxiety, eating disorders, and substance abuse. In traditional clinical psychology practice, clients are screened and given clinical interviews at the commencement of therapy to ensure that the presenting problem matches the competence of the treating therapist. In sport psychology settings, often there is already a working relationship with the client before clinical issues are raised. Pressure to treat clients for presenting problems outside sport psychologists' competence can arise as a result of athletes' resistance to seeing and developing relationships with other psychologists. Athletes may have good rapport with sport psychologists and may not like the stigma of seeing clinical psychologists, or feel that traditional therapists may not understand them in the way the sport psychologists do. Resistance to seeking help from other psychologists may even take the form of athletes choosing not to seek any help rather than undertake treatment from different psychologists. The result of clients' resistance is that they may implicitly and/or explicitly place pressure on the sport psychologists to continue to treat them.

From the perspective of those running sporting organizations, sports psychologists have been employed and receive payment explicitly for assessing and delivering treatment for psychological difficulties to athletes. Often, sports psychologists are considered "one-stop shops" for all difficulties relating to the athletes' intra- and interpersonal functioning, and their role is to "fix" these difficulties in order to restore or improve performance. It may be difficult for personnel in management to understand that there are parameters defining sports psychologists' work and that some presenting difficulties fall outside their professional training and require referral. Here is where it is the job and the professional duty of sport psychologists to explain explicitly to coaches and other sport personnel (e.g., managers, finance officers) exactly what sorts of treatment fall into the psychologist's service delivery and what sorts of psychological care (e.g., treatment for depression) are outside of the psychologist's competencies and that referrals to other mental health professionals will likely need to be made. Not making one's professional competencies and limits clear from the outset to all interested parties is a professional gaffe. Much of the pressure from athletes and sport personnel to treat beyond one's competencies could be obviated by holding "competency conversations" with members of the sport organization. Some sporting organizations may be especially reluctant because referral constitutes an additional financial burden when liaising with a professional who is outside the organizational structure. These external pressures sometimes interact with sports psychologists' own issues around feeling or being seen as incompetent. For a few psychologists, their professional sense of competence is threatened if they are not directly managing and dealing with the problems with which they are presented.

Pressures from both internal and external sources may influence the sports psychologists' decisions regarding referral. Clearly, referral to appropriate external providers is required whenever presenting issues fall outside one's training and expertise. Sport psychologists seeking to expand professional competencies and to treat conditions outside the traditional sport psychology repertoire can undertake further training. Like all professional development, training must be done through suitable and board accredited avenues such as courses, workshops, and supervision (Hays, 2006).

Case vignettes and discussion

Case vignettes outlining real-world experiences from my practice and from colleagues working in the field are presented below, along with some guidance about their management. These cases highlight a number of challenges to the ethical principles outlined above.

Scenario 1

You are employed as a psychologist to work with athletes at a government-based academy of sport (e.g., U.S. Olympic Training Center, Australian/English/New Zealand Institute of Sport). A coach refers an athlete to you, because she is concerned that the etiology of his recent underperformance is psychological. The coach wants to know if her assessment was correct and whether her star player will be able to overcome his problem.

Ethical challenges and management

One setting where applied sport psychologists are employed to work with athletes is in government-based sporting institutions. These institutions are often the training grounds for many of the world's top athletes. A defining characteristic of these institutions is the comprehensive approach they take to sport sciences. Athletes frequently have access to the services of sports physicians, dieticians, physiologists, biomechanists, and sport psychologists. Athletes receive scholarships that enable them to access these services, but most institutes require that scholarship holders sign legal waivers agreeing to the sharing of information between staff (coaches, other service providers, management) within the institute.

The open sharing of a client's information may not seem contentious for the majority of service providers working with the athletes. For example, a biomechanist telling the head coach that a particular athlete drops her head too early prior to serving in tennis would not be damaging to the athlete's psychological welfare. When the disclosure of client information is extended to a psychologist, it may be a different matter. As an employee of the institution, one may be contractually obliged to share information gathered from scholarship holders (e.g., drug use), but this divulging of information may come into conflict with one's professional code of conduct and ethical principles.

The major ethical consideration in this instance pertains to confidentiality. The key is in understanding from the outset who your client is. Clearly defining the client is best practice and will determine *who* has access to *what* information. In these settings there are generally two possible options. Option one would involve transparency with the athletes about your obligations to report information if requested by the institution. Being transparent and reporting client information would satisfy the organization's requirements and ensure that you are not in breach of a workplace contract. The consequences of this approach for your therapeutic effectiveness, however, may be substantial. This contractual requirement strips therapists of one of their most powerful tools – confidentiality. The effect on the therapeutic relationship of having no confidentiality could dramatically limit the scope of the work that might be done. The second option is negotiating with the institution a separate workplace agreement that enables you to protect your clients' information from third parties.

This process is not simple and may require the involvement of legal support. In my work I have always chosen to pursue the second option, because I feel that in our profession we should not compromise client confidentiality. A consequence may be that the institution does not wish to retain your services if you take this stance. I suggest that being ethically and morally compromised and having your therapeutic effectiveness diminished to maintain a contract with an institution is not worth the cost to your professional integrity. Thankfully, sport institutes are beginning to realize the consequences of making athletes sign these waivers and are being more open to allowing psychologists to work around this requirement (e.g., I have personally negotiated workplace contracts that allow me to protect my clients' confidence in state sport institutes in Australia as well as professional clubs in Australia).

Scenario 2

You are employed as the sport psychologist for a professional sporting team. The head coach refers an athlete, who is underperforming, to you. Your assessment of the athlete leads you to the conclusion that he is psychologically unfit to compete at his peak, and his participation in competition could have a negative influence on the overall team's performance. The coach asks you whether he should select him for the big match this weekend.

Ethical challenges and management

The scenario above raises the ethical dilemma of confidentiality and boundaries – who is your client, and do you get involved in player selection? When employed by a professional sporting organization, you are by definition entering a contract with multiple organizational demands and relationships. The CEO is paying for your services, the head coach wants you to help the team as a whole to perform better, and your ethical obligation to your individual athletes is to help them function optimally with respect to both their personal well-being and sporting prowess. Sometimes these competing goals place the sport psychologist in precarious situations. Looking at the scenario above, if you were to inform the coach that the player is not psychologically fit to perform at his peak, then you would be fulfilling your role in helping the team perform optimally, thus keeping the CEO, coach, and probably the other teammates happy. The welfare of the individual athlete, however, might be compromised. The mental health of many athletes is tightly linked to their sporting identities and senses of competence. In the scenario above, if you were to provide information that led to the athlete being dropped from the team, your actions may directly lead to the further deterioration of the individual's mental health (of course the reverse is also true – if he plays poorly he may also experience deterioration in mental health). You can, and probably should, have a candid conversation with the athlete about the situation and the potential consequences mentioned above. Ultimately, it is the athlete's decision as to whether he puts himself up for selection to play.

This scenario is common in professional sport settings. It often occurs due to sport psychologists not clearly defining the boundaries in which they operate with the team and coaching staff. The duress that may be placed upon sport psychologists by coaches is understandable because coaches daily interact with other medical staff (e.g., team doctors or physiotherapists) about whether players are fit to play. The onus of responsibility lies with psychologists to prevent this situation from occurring in the first place through clear establishment of boundaries with regard to player selection. Of course, clearly defining boundaries with a head coach does not prevent the coach from still attempting to engage you on such matters throughout the duration of a season. Coaches are not psychologists and typically do not have the working understanding of ethical codes of practice. Therefore, if you are placed in this situation it will be important to remind the coaching staff of the boundaries you set up at the beginning of the contract and the purpose and value of maintaining these boundaries. Alternatively, if your professional role includes informing decisions regarding team selection then this information needs to be clearly communicated to all parties, and athletes need to know that the information they share will not be held in confidence.

Personally, I strongly discourage my colleagues and students from engaging in team selection. There are several potential detrimental consequences associated with psychologists being involved in selection, including the potential for athletes to limit or conceal certain information, to view the therapist as an ally to the coaching staff, and to undermine aspects of the therapeutic relationship such as trust, empathy, and understanding.

Scenario 3

An athlete asks you to travel with him to a major competition overseas for two weeks.

Ethical challenges and management

Traveling with athletes is often viewed as glamorous and rewarding. Although it is personally exciting and often reflective of the practitioner's competence to be asked to travel with athletes and provide support as they enter major competitions, several factors must be considered prior to embarking on this journey. First, the usefulness of traveling with the athlete must be weighed. It is easy for the excitement and lure of traveling to get in the way of the basic needs of the client. You must be sure of your purpose and the benefit to your client before agreeing to travel with him. He may be anxious about upcoming competitions and ask you to come to help control these emotions. In the short term if an athlete is in treatment for performance anxiety and that anxiety is not yet under control, then you going along on the trip as a psychological coach may be useful. In the long term, however, it is possible that you could be fostering dependency in your client and an external locus of control, thus doing more harm than good. It is worth considering if the travel is for the benefit of the athlete, or if it is servicing your own desire to be needed. Additionally, it costs money for an athlete to take a sport psychologist to a competition, therefore, the financial "cost–benefit" must be taken into account as well. On the flip side, traveling to a competition with an athlete is often the best way you for you to see your client performing *in situ*.

When traveling with clients, some ethical considerations need to be made in relation to boundaries, unwarranted disclosure, and confidentiality. You are spending extended periods of time together in trains, planes, and automobiles; sharing meals; and staying in the same hotel (but, one would hope, not the same room), meaning that keeping traditional boundaries is not possible. There will be some natural spilling of information between the two parties, which is expected in such an environment, however it is important that there are some parameters guiding the nature, content, and level of disclosure by the therapist. In essence therapists' disclosures should be limited to information that is in the service of the client's needs.

Confidentiality is often inadvertently breached when traveling with athletes. The daily occurrence of being introduced to new people is the most common place where confidentiality is breached. How do you introduce yourself to new people when asked what you are doing with your client at the tournament? "Hi, I'm his sport psychologist ... " Saying this could be easy to do, and may not seem like a big deal when working in an environment where people are familiar with the role of a sport psychologist. Nevertheless, revealing your role with your client is a blatant breach of your client's confidentiality. To prevent it you must set up clear guidelines for yourself that the athlete dictates. Sometimes you may be required to fabricate a story about who you are and your role to people. The second main breach of confidentiality is when the sport psychologist uses the opportunity to recruit new clients while at a competition. Seeking out new clients can easily happen, because competitions are environments where athletes, coaches, managers, and parents congregate. It would be easy to have conversations with parents or coaches and mention your qualifications and provide them with your business card (being careful not to mention anything about the athlete with whom you are working). The problem arises when those parents or coaches then see you consulting your client at the event. Through inference it can be assumed that they now know who your client is. Again, I recommend that all of these potential scenarios be discussed openly with your clients prior to traveling and a clear understanding of what will and will not be said or done by yourself with respect to protecting their confidentiality.

Scenario 4

A concerned coach refers a 14-year-old talented tennis player to you. During the course of your intake assessments you learn that she is the possible victim of physical abuse by her mother.

Ethical challenges and management

Working with minors is fraught with ethical challenges. Who has access to the minor's information and when are practitioners required to report incidents of suspected abuse? The answers to these questions are not simple, and they vary according to where one is registered/licensed/chartered. There are clear differences between countries, and even between states within the same country with regard to psychologists' obligations to report suspected abuse. Some countries mandate that psychologists must report all suspected cases of physical abuse to minors, whereas others have no such requirement. The ethical and legal ramifications for failing to notify abuse of a minor are significant (as is breaching a client's confidence when you have no ethical or legal basis to do so). The example above is provided to highlight that before acting on suspected abuse, familiarity with your relevant ethical and legal obligations is a necessity.

Concluding thoughts

I hope this chapter provoked some thought about ethical practice in sport psychology. The one central theme I did want to convey was the potential for sport psychologists to inadvertently act in questionable ways. As outlined above, these breaches typically arise through the interaction of practitioners' passivity, ignorance, limited competence, the environments, and clients with whom we work. I encourage readers to access and study their registration (licensing, chartering, certifying) boards' ethical principles and codes of conduct for further information on the specific guidelines for practitioners in the field (see American Psychological Association [APA], 1992, for a standard reference point, but note that each country has its own code that applies to the practitioners within that locale). See Box 7.1 for some practical take-home messages from this chapter.

Box 7.1

Take-home messages regarding ethics in sport psychology

- The majority of practitioners who act unethically do so through passivity, inattention, ignorance, or limited competence to deal with the challenges of applied practice, not through malicious intent.
- Sport psychologists often consult their clients in less traditional ways with respect to time, place, confidentiality, and boundaries. A consequence of the nature of sport psychology service delivery is that sport psychologists are at times vulnerable to pressures to breach ethical guidelines.
- Understanding what confidentiality is, why it is fundamental to the practice of psychology, and when to breach it, is not sufficient to successfully navigate applied practice. Most breaches of confidentiality can be prevented by having transparent discussions with clients about how the therapist can manage the competing demands of third-parties (e.g., government sporting academies, IOC, parents, coaches).
- Sport psychologists deliver therapy in nontraditional settings, frequently spending extended periods of time traveling with clients. Typically, some level of boundary blurring is unavoidable in these settings. Because of the heightened potential for the blurring of boundaries, sport psychologists benefit from some self-monitoring skills and should strive to be astute in identifying, defining, and managing boundaries to prevent the ethical dilemmas that arise from dual-relationships and boundary violations.
- Working with clients who have presenting problems that are beyond the psychologists' training can occur due to the interaction of pressure from the client and the organization, as well as the therapist's own desires to be helpful or to be seen as competent. Sport psychologists must clearly define the scope of their competence to their clients and avoid practising outside of it.

References

American Psychological Association (1992). *Ethical principles of psychologists and code of conduct.* Washington, DC: American Psychological Association. Retrieved from: http://www.apa.org/ethics/code2002.html.

Andersen, M. B. (1996). Working with college students-athletes. In J. L. Van Raalte & B. W. Brewer (Eds.), *Exploring sport and exercise psychology,* pp. 317–334. Washington, DC: American Psychological Association.

Andersen, M. B. (2005). "Yeah, I work with Beckham": Issues of confidentiality, privacy and privilege in sport psychology service delivery. *Sport & Exercise Psychology Review, 1*(2), 5–13.

Andersen, M. B., Van Raalte, J. L., & Brewer, B. W. (2001). Sport psychology service delivery: Staying ethical while keeping loose. *Professional Psychology: Research and Practice, 32,* 12–18.

Brown, J. L., & Cogan, K. D. (2006). Ethical clinical practice in sport psychology: When two worlds collide. *Ethics & Behavior, 16,* 15–23.

Gardner, F. (2001). Applied sport psychology in professional teams: The team psychologist. *Professional Psychology: Research and Practice, 32,* 34–39.

Haberl, P., & Peterson, K. (2006). Olympic-size ethical dilemmas: Issues and challenges for sport psychology consultants on the road and at the Olympic Games. *Ethics & Behavior, 16*, 25–40.

Hays, K. F. (2006). Being fit: The ethics of practice diversification in performance psychology. *Professional Psychology: Research and Practice, 37*, 223–232.

Knapp, S., & Slattery, J. M. (2004). Professional boundaries in nontraditional settings. *Professional Psychology: Research and Practice, 35*, 553–558.

Moore, Z. (2003). Ethical dilemmas in sport psychology: Discussion and recommendations for practice. *Professional Psychology: Research and Practice, 34*, 601–610.

8

Endings

More than saying goodbye

Lynda Mainwaring

Professional relationships and therapeutic treatments often, but not always, begin together. Each has its own life cycle, and the conclusion or cessation of treatment does not indicate the conclusion or cessation of the professional relationship. Therapists need to be mindful of the professional, legal, and ethical obligations that survive the delivery of services. Planning for the ending of therapeutic relationships is a fundamental, but often neglected, step in the therapeutic process (Kramer, 1990). Endings can be frightening for the client or the therapist and involve more than saying goodbye.

Ending treatment: treatment starts with the end in mind

Eagerness to develop mastery in a particular domain of functioning motivates clients to pursue therapy. The treatment begins with a presenting goal, which guides the process toward the end of treatment. In broad terms, the process of therapy involves three phases, each with its own structure and function: the intake or introduction phase (understanding the presenting issue and settling on the treatment plan), the middle phase (working through the treatment plan), and the end or termination phase (ensuring that the client is prepared for the conclusion of treatment and return to autonomous functioning). The initial treatment plan sets the stage for the course of therapy including its nature, treatment goals, timeframe, and expected end date. Incorporating end-phase goals into the overall treatment plan from the outset facilitates the ultimate closure of the therapeutic, but not the professional, relationship.

Treatment and termination goals

Treatment goals provide the vectors that guide the course of therapy. To be most effective, it is usually best that they be established early in consultation with the athlete (Bassett & Petrie, 1999). Specific goals give the treatment plan focus and instill a sense of confidence in the client that positive results are achievable. Not establishing specific goals from the beginning is an error that is likely to propagate throughout the course of treatment, resulting in a disappointing outcome (Kramer, 1990). Like treatment goals, discharge and end-phase goals should be clear, obtainable, and modifiable (see Chapter 51).

Scheduling an end-date helps to identify the conclusion of treatment as a "real" event (Firestein, 2001). It inspires, influences, and pervades the treatment plan. As a real event, the ending of treatment carries the seeds for unintended, though not unforeseeable, consequences. The end of treatment may elicit affective reactions such as grief, sorrow, dependency, and insecurity, carrying the risk of treatment relapse (Firestein). The therapist should be aware of such reactions and address them, well before the last session.

In the case of short-term treatment, a circumscribed number of sessions designated for learning a particular skill or realizing a goal is clearly identified. Time-limited therapy firmly establishes the end at the beginning and side-steps the process of identifying when it would be suitable to end treatment. Even so, the therapist needs to remain sensitive to the emergence of end-of-treatment issues.

For some clients engaged in long-term therapy, setting termination goals may create anticipation for new beginnings or resumed high-level performance. For others, the prospect of ending therapy may evoke myriad negative emotions that trigger feelings of abandonment, sadness, and loss. Such feelings are normal, and avoiding these feelings with long-drawn-out endings may prove problematic and signal termination difficulties for both the client and therapist. When discussing end-phase goals, it is a good idea to observe and record clients' responses, especially those that indicate potential distress, or are associated with setbacks or transference reactions (See Chapters 1, 6, & 17). A gradual approach to ending is usually preferable in respect of the intimate working alliance and bond created during long-term therapy. Discussing post-termination expectations allows the therapist to assess and prepare for client reactions to the end of therapy. It also allows for adjustments to goals and treatment protocols, acknowledgment of the client's current state of functioning, and ideally, a comfortable transition to the end of the therapeutic alliance.

Therapist tasks for the end-phase of treatment include confirming the desired outcome (identified or modified from the intake phase), summarizing the progress made, identifying the number of scheduled visits prior to the last treatment session, explaining the nature of follow-up visits (if any), establishing maintenance exercises or routines identifying specific time-targeted goals for ending treatment including the date and nature of the last session, and preparing the client for the end of a professional, yet intimate, relationship. These tasks can be developed over a number of sessions depending on the length of treatment.

Ending a session

Just as the overall process of therapy has a structure, which includes an end-phase, so too does each session. Ending a session can be awkward if it is not given prior thought. Session length is determined and communicated during intake, but the actual work of preparing a client for the end of a session occurs during each and every session.

Telegraphing the ending in advance allows both client and therapist opportunities to acknowledge outstanding issues. Therapist and client preferences will shape the structure of the sessions. Some therapists will anticipate the ending of a flowing format by stating that "time is almost up" and some will structure sessions more rigidly with designated amounts of time for client expression; therapist formulation and communication of plans, concerns, and direction; and finally, session wrap-up statements.

Session endings that are abrupt and not anticipated can leave clients feeling unsettled. Worse, if therapists are not aware of session end times, an end of session emotional event could leave insufficient time to diffuse or manage the emotional reaction before the client leaves. This problem can be avoided for the most part with the appropriate management of session endings.

How do you know when the end of treatment is near?

For explicitly established time-limited performance enhancement training, and short-term solution-oriented therapy, the completion of treatment is clearly indicated by the treatment plan and a specified number of sessions. Time-limited treatment establishes the ending at the beginning and precludes the problem (and possible therapeutic value) of deciding when it would be best to end treatment.

In therapies addressing psychological issues that go beyond enhancing performance, or for extended treatment, there is hardly ever a perfect recipe for ending. Murdin (2000) stated that endings are never complete, or perfect, and suggested that therapists are not always good at recognizing the right time for a client to end therapy.

The therapist's training and experience informs decisions about the overall course and nature of treatment. Psychological training in graduate schools does not always include instruction on ending treatment, and this educational lacuna is especially true for sport and performance psychology. All of us at sometime ask the obvious and important question, how does one know when clients are near the end, or completion, of treatment? The answer is not straightforward; the issues involved may not be obvious, but they are not insignificant.

Therapists usually have their own indicators of readiness to end treatment whether explicit or implicit. Practitioners construct different therapeutic tasks depending on their theoretical models and the interplay between their professional training, their experiences, and client responses to treatment and treatment endings. Often, therapists' objectives for treatment are quite different from their clients' expectations. If clients believe that the therapist's objectives for termination are unreasonable, or not in line with their own, they probably will not agree or comply with the plan. Both the therapist and the client need to work toward mutually agreed upon treatment ending objectives and goals. It is important to understand the client's perspective on treatment and what the end of treatment means so that a manageable schedule for ending therapy favorably is set in motion. Endings in therapy are as different as individual clients and therapists: no two endings are the same.

The overall therapeutic enterprise involves a basic uncertainty, and the client's symptoms themselves may prevent the client from identifying what can be achieved realistically (Murdin, 2000). This uncertainty can be difficult because a client may request help with a particular issue, and the therapist may identify another issue that needs to be addressed to accomplish certain therapeutic goals aligned with the client's interests.

Criteria for ending treatment

The experienced practitioner considers a variety of factors in determining when treatment is complete; they vary with the client, the therapist, and the therapy. For both the therapist and the client to proceed with a clear picture of how the treatment progresses and ends, objective, clear, realistic, and mutually agreed upon criteria for termination should be established at the beginning of treatment (Kramer, 1990). It can be difficult to establish and adhere to strict termination criteria because of the varied issues and uncertainties that constitute the therapeutic process. Even though it seems as though these criteria can be readily established, they may not be identified easily, and the vicissitudes of treatment may prove set criteria to be more of a hindrance than a help. Nevertheless, there are general guidelines for making decisions about when treatment should end.

During the course of treatment, experienced practitioners gauge readiness to end treatment by reference to one or more of five general criteria: the attainment of treatment goals, symptom resolution, global improvement in functioning (therapists' judgments that the clients have improved in all or most psychological, physical, social, and behavioral domains), improved intra-psychic functioning (e.g., recognized enhancement in self-esteem, reduced internal conflict), or observable improvements in specific behaviors (e.g., improvement in eating patterns, a reduction in negative self-talk). Objective assessments of improvement in psychological parameters are not always used by practitioners.

Empirically identified client decisions about terminating treatment focus primarily on global improvement (i.e., feeling better) gauged by specific external or internal factors (Kramer, 1990) and a type of cost–benefit analysis whereby the client questions whether the additional gains from continued treatment justify the additional financial and emotional investment. Within the end-phase itself, "the single most important guideline for negotiating a successful termination is to unambiguously acknowledge the reality of the ending" (Teyber, 2000, p. 297).

Ending the therapeutic relationship

Given that the therapeutic relationship is established for a limited purpose, it follows that once the purpose is achieved (or abandoned), therapy ought to end. The treatment may end, but what about the relationship?

The professional engagement initiates a process involving two individuals – the therapist and the client. The intended consequence is effecting some change in the client through the instrumentality of the therapeutic process. Not only should the client be ready for personal change, the therapist must be ready to accommodate a change in the quality of the relationship (Murdin, 2000). Practitioners bear the burden of managing therapeutic relationships with a view to achieving good outcomes and salubrious endings. That task is far from easy.

Natural and consensual endings

A consensual ending to treatment emerges when the therapist and client agree that the work is complete. Both the client and therapist feel satisfied about the outcome. In consensual endings, the therapist acknowledges the appropriateness of the ending of therapy, reviews treatment achievements, sets a definite end date, and obtains the client's consent. To ensure that the consent is informed, the therapist may ask probing questions to assess the client's understanding about the ending of treatment. Short-term termination phases of about two weeks may be fitting in cases where there is consensus about ending (Teyber, 2000). Even with a consensual ending, the client may experience conflicting emotions in anticipation of ending what may have become an important relationship.

The therapist ought to affirm the client's mixed feelings, if any, about not just ending therapy, but their relationship as well. The therapist, apart from acknowledging the client's achievements and readiness for independent and autonomous functioning, should acknowledge the significance of their relationship to the client's achievement, and the sense of loss that may be experienced with the formal ending of their relationship. This type of ending is the most satisfying one for both client and therapist, and there is usually a sense of accomplishment.

Truncated endings

Client-initiated endings

Unilateral client-initiated endings may not be aligned with the therapeutic targets identified in the treatment plan. The therapeutic work is incomplete, and therefore, the ending is premature. Clients may decide to end therapy for any number of reasons – some well founded and some not. Therapists may find it difficult to navigate issues surrounding client withdrawal. Assuming the client withdrawal comes as a surprise, the therapist needs to evaluate his or her own countertransference reactions to the client's decision. Outside of extenuating circumstances that rationally explain the client's decision to withdraw, issues of control often lie at the heart of the matter and formal negotiations of the end of treatment are not made. Suitable referrals can be made if clients announce their withdrawal, but when clients withdraw abruptly, a follow-up phone call or letter offering referral options is warranted.

Therapist-initiated endings

Endings initiated by the therapist may arise in a variety of instances represented in the following four broad categories: (a) the therapist concludes that therapeutic objectives have been reached earlier than expected, (b) the student-therapist has graduated or finished her term, (c) the therapist has become unavailable owing to some change in life circumstances, or (d) a referral to another professional is needed to address certain therapeutic issues beyond the therapist's competence or tolerance. In all but the first instance, external circumstances lead to the truncated ending. Substantial therapeutic gains may have occurred when the decision to end was made, but the treatment may have begun to only scratch the surface of the presenting problem. Regardless, adequate provision for continuity of care/ referral is indicated (see Chapter 22). If not handled sensitively, this truncated ending may adversely influence future relationship endings for the client, induce negative transference reactions, or dissuade the client from trusting a therapist again.

It is crucial that the therapist and client work through the complex issues arising from any externally imposed ending. Clients need time to work through their feelings of anger, frustration, abandonment, disappointment, betrayal, or loss associated with interrupted therapy and relationship endings. Sufficient advance notice of the termination date is necessary so that client concerns, frustrations, defenses, and transference reactions can be addressed adequately. Success in moving through a truncated ending depends on the "therapists' ability to remain non-defensive and tolerate clients' protests – rather than feel guilty, become defensive, and make ineffective attempts to talk clients out of their feelings" (Teyber, 2000, p. 300).

It is the therapist's responsibility to work through the issues with the client. Negative transference or countertransference reactions are more likely to occur in truncated endings, especially when they are therapist-initiated (Kirk-Sanchez & Roach, 2001; Kramer, 1990). The potential differences in opinion between therapist and client about what constitutes readiness to end treatment necessitate an open discussion about expectations and the realities related to continuing or concluding treatment. It may not be easy for therapists to take the time to work through these issues when their own life stressors are overwhelming and, perhaps, the reason for the unilateral termination. In the case of student therapists, the limits on their availability and level of responsibility should be identified for the client at the outset of therapy and emphasized again during end-phase discussions.

Death

Death presents many challenges for the surviving client or therapist. If a client dies unexpectedly, the therapist must work through feelings of grief (e.g., sadness, guilt, anger, despair). At the same time, professional responsibilities associated with the termination of the alliance must be completed. For example, the notification of death needs to be documented in the client's file, which is then retained for the requisite time specified by the regulatory body. If the therapist dies unexpectedly, ideally the therapist had adequate advanced arrangements in place to cover that eventuality to provide for the management of client referrals and files. If not, those duties will fall to the accreditation boards of the appropriate jurisdictions (e.g., state or national boards). The client is faced with either the transition to another therapist or an abrupt ending to the treatment altogether. The loss of the therapist presents the client with real difficulties such as grief, treatment disruption and interference of progress, possible relapse, and the inconvenience of seeking and acquiring a new therapist.

Third-party-initiated endings

With third-party payer involvement (e.g., sport governing body, insurer, employer), the potential for interrupted or curtailed service because of funding issues is heightened. National sport organizations, for example, typically have a set fee schedule or limited term for funding treatment. Therapists must be clear about their professional obligations, and ensure that clients understand the nature of such engagements and the limits of confidentiality and the scope and extent of treatment. Should treatment need to be extended beyond the approved number of sessions, and to avoid an interruption of service, the practitioner needs to contact the third party to request continued treatment well before the treatment time has elapsed. In the event of a delay or withdrawal of funding, clients need to be informed, and a course of action determined. Continued or alternative funding may be requested, treatment may be terminated, or it may be continued under different payment options. Keeping the client apprised of these issues and options is important.

Managing sensitive issues and vulnerable clients

Clients who engage in performance enhancement counseling, like all therapy clients, may bring psychological experiences or characteristics to treatment that put them at risk for tumultuous terminations. For athletes with affective (e.g., depression) or adjustment difficulties, eating disorders and associated issues, or for those facing the prospect of career-ending injuries, there may be risks of affective reactions or suicidal ideation associated with termination. Astute practitioners will recognize the importance of addressing these issues by validating client feelings and orchestrating the termination to be as smooth as possible. The gravity and nature of any potential distress requires the practitioner to address it sufficiently to avoid or buffer termination disequilibrium.

Suicidal ideation may emerge during the end-phase of therapy when clients realize that their main support will no longer be available. Individuals who fear abandonment and rejection, or who have attachment difficulties or few social supports, may be particularly vulnerable. Clients with certain personality profiles, or those who have experienced physical or emotional abuse, also may be prone to suicidal ideation. These reactions are expressions of intense helpless feelings (albeit, they may be manipulative behaviors for clients with certain personality disorders), and in the worst scenario they may be signs that a suicide attempt is imminent (for details about the management of suicidal clients see Kramer, 1978, Chapter 12).

In general, individuals with personality disorders, or those with histories of early, intense, repeated, or prolonged psychic and physical trauma can be challenging to treat. Special attention to ending treatment with such individuals is warranted. When the security of the therapeutic relationship is in question for these clients, transference reactions may arise, such as feelings of abandonment or rejection. The reality of termination may exacerbate symptoms, undo some of the positive changes that have occurred throughout treatment, or create new concerns for the client.

For clients with histories of trauma, the anniversary of the traumatic event (and also the weeks prior to that date) is usually a vulnerable time. Termination dates, if at all possible, should not coincide with that time period. Similarly, the prospect of termination for clients with post-traumatic stress syndrome may trigger a resurgence of stress symptoms such as insomnia, nightmares, cognitive dysfunction, anxiety, or depression. This reactivation of symptoms often occurs if the client anticipates resuming activity related to, or in the vicinity of, the traumatic event.

The seasoned practitioner will recognize the link between the prospect of termination and affective distress, validate the client's feelings, provide support, and may help the client to resolve some of the issues. Overly dependent or superstitious clients may react to the imminent ending of therapy by becoming obviously dependent or attached to the therapist or the ritual of therapy. In such cases, clear end dates and a gradual progression emphasizing successful autonomous functioning are the best path.

Professional obligations related to ending therapeutic relationships

Confidentiality considerations

There is more to fulfilling the duty to maintain client confidentiality than biting one's tongue. The practitioner's duty to maintain client confidentiality is addressed elsewhere (see Chapter 7) and only information pertinent to ending relationships and treatment is outlined here. Apart from purely ethical considerations that are aspirations, there are normative standards imposed by the rules of professional conduct. The failure to adhere to those rules exposes the practitioner to professional discipline that may lead to reprimand or all the way to revocation of license (deregistering, revoking charter). The duty to maintain confidentiality is enduring and survives the end of treatment and even the death of the client.

One major consideration is document and records management (see Chapter 6). Attention to the duty of confidentiality weighs heavily at each step in the document and record life cycle if the inadvertent disclosure of client information is to be avoided. The practitioner may disclose client information with the client's signed (and informed) consent. Consensual disclosure may be requested long after treatment ends, and the minimum period of document and record retention has expired. The practitioner should keep in mind that even though the rules of professional conduct permit the destruction of client documents and records after a time, the rules are not reason, in and of themselves, for their destruction. The practitioner may well do a disservice to clients by destroying their documents and records at the first opportunity.

Requests for information frequently are made on behalf of clients well beyond the minimum document retention period. A letter request may be made by the client's lawyer in the context of a personal injury claim where the defendant alleges that the client's mental distress had its origin in an earlier time and not from the recent road accident. Alternatively, it may be from the authority charged with preparing a presentence report where the client's mental history has been called into question. Even though treatment has ended, responsibility for the professional relationship endures.

Legal considerations

The failure of the professional to exercise the requisite degree of skill, care, judgment, and diligence measured by professional standards, which results in compensable harm to the client, exposes the professional to civil liability for malpractice. The abrupt or inept termination of professional services may amount to malpractice if it results in significant mental distress for the client.

Fiduciary obligations

The practitioner–client relationship is recognized as imposing fiduciary obligations on the practitioner. Expressed simply, the fiduciary bears a duty of loyalty to the client that requires it to act in the best interests of the client. The fiduciary either significantly influences the client's decision through the advice given to the client, or exercises the power of decision for the client. Because the client is reliant on the fiduciary, the law imposes on the fiduciary the duty to act in the client's best interests. So, for example, the practitioner may be obliged, in the best interests of the client, to make a referral to another professional, even if that is to the practitioner's financial disadvantage. To do otherwise is to put the interests of the practitioner ahead of those of the client.

Because the practitioner, in a fiduciary capacity, represents an influential force, professional boundaries must be recognized and maintained. As long as the therapist, or former therapist, is in a position to exercise an improper influence over the client, the client remains at risk of exploitation. Client vulnerability does not stop with the end of treatment.

When a friend is not a friend: maintaining professional boundaries post-termination

Following termination, therapists need to maintain their ethical standards especially as they relate to avoiding dual or multiple relationships with clients. Kagel and Giebelhausen (1994) suggested that a dual relationship is one where a boundary violation has, or may occur. When a therapist, or former therapist, engages the client in a different type of relationship, or assumes an additional role, so that the two are now business associates, friends, or romantic partners, professional boundaries have been crossed.

Travel, competition, social events, and the nature of team interaction may make it difficult to draw strict professional boundaries for sport psychology practitioners. The nature of some performance enhancement therapies does not usually involve intense emotional issues and attachments arising from in-depth therapeutic processing. That scenario, in itself, could lure the client (and sometimes the therapist) into thinking that after performance-enhancement treatment has terminated, they are not only practitioner and client, but friends, too.

In a different context, Rangell (1980) identified two possible errors that psychoanalysts can make when happening upon clients post-termination: (a) they may maintain an analytic attitude at unsuitable times and places, or (b) they may conduct themselves with premature and excessive displays of intimacy. Both may precipitate anxiety or difficulty for the client. In a sporting context, athletes may not want to acknowledge publicly that they have seen a therapist, so it is a good idea to be cautious with post-termination contacts and let the client take the first steps in the initial greeting.

Ethical codes vary with respect to the length of time that is required to elapse between the termination of a therapeutic relationship and the beginning of an intimate relationship between therapist/former therapist and client. Many major professional associations stipulate that sexual contact more than two years after termination of a therapeutic relationship is *per se* ethical. Others maintain that a sexual relationship before or after termination is never ethical. Much more remains to be said on the need to maintain professional boundaries following the termination of the therapeutic relationship, but that topic goes well beyond the scope of this chapter.

Conclusions

In this chapter issues related to ending treatment and therapeutic relationships have been outlined. Endings involve processes that can be complex, complete or incomplete, cause for celebration, or cause for concern. Successful endings to treatment can be rewarding for both the client and the therapist. Mismanaged endings can be disastrous.

Even though treatment and the therapeutic relationship end, the professional relationship never ends. By addressing the practical, ethical, and legal implications accompanying the conclusion of the therapeutic alliance, the therapist advances the interests of the client and attends to professional responsibilities. In doing so, case closure may not always lead to a happy ending, but the ending will be a well-managed one. See Box 8.1 for take-home messages from this chapter.

Box 8.1

Take-home messages about client–practitioner relationship endings

- Ending treatment is not the same as ending the therapeutic relationship.
- The professional relationship extends beyond the end of treatment.
- Client confidentiality does not end with treatment.
- Start the ending of treatment from the intake.
- During treatment, identify potential difficulties with ending the relationship.
- Endings evoke feelings and transference reactions for clients and therapists.
- Prepare guidelines and goals for end-phases of treatment.
- Clearly set an end-date.
- Maintain professional boundaries post-termination.
- Ending professional relationships is not always simple or easy.
- Endings entail much more than saying goodbye.

References

Bassett, S. F., & Petrie K. J. (1999). The effect of treatment goals on patient compliance with physiotherapy exercise programs. *Physiotherapy, 85,* 130–137.

Firestein, S. K. (2001). Termination in psychoanalysis and psychotherapy (Rev. ed.). New York: International Universities Press.

Kagel, J. D., & Giebelhausen, P. N. (1994). Dual relationships and professional boundaries. *Social Work, 39,* 213–218.

Kirk-Sanchez, N. J., & Roach, K. E. (2001). Relationship between duration of therapy services in a comprehensive rehabilitation program and mobility at discharge in patients with orthopedic problems. *Physical Therapy, 81,* 888–895.

Kramer, E. (1978). *A beginning manual for psychotherapists* (2nd ed.) New York: Grune & Stratton.

Kramer, S. A. (1990). *Positive endings in psychotherapy.* Oxford, England: Jossey-Bass.

Murdin, L. (2000). *How much is enough? Endings in psychotherapy and counseling.* London: Routledge.

Rangell, L. (1980). Some notes on the post-analytic phase. *International Journal of Psychoanalytic Psychotherapy, 8,* 165–170.

Teyber, E. (2000). *Interpersonal process in psychotherapy: A relational approach.* (4th ed.). London: Wadsworth.

Section II

Assessment

9

The applied sport psychology intake

Jeff Simons

Listening is a rare happening among human beings. You cannot listen to the word another is speaking if you are preoccupied with your appearance or with impressing the other, or are trying to decide what you are going to say when the other stops talking, or are debating about whether what is being said is true or relevant or agreeable. Such matters have their place, but only after listening to the word as the word is being uttered. Listening is a primitive act of love in which a person gives himself to another's word, making himself accessible and vulnerable to that word.

William Stringfellow

Well before diving into psychological work with athletes, one would do well to heed the beautiful words of Stringfellow, listening with the accessibility and vulnerability that invite relationship and foster insight. From the start, it is important to take the time to listen as the words reveal the athlete's stories. In this chapter, I will focus on the applied sport psychology intake, relatively free from assessments. A great many protocols for clinical or counseling intake include an assessment schedule. For example, Taylor and Schneider (1992) have offered a method for athlete intakes that includes a well-considered and comprehensive assessment. Nevertheless, as Andersen (2000) pointed out, even though such a protocol is a valuable resource for practitioners, it is often too formal and clinical for the far more loose initiations of service common to applied sport psychology situations. Furthermore, jumping into assessment during the initial intake will often implicitly constrict the process to the tools favored by the clinician before adequate time has been spent determining whether or not psychological counseling is even warranted (Van Audenhove & Vertommen, 2000). Based on extensive investigations into the subject, Van Audenhove and Vertommen stated that they "became more and more convinced of the importance of the intake phase preceding the start of psychotherapy" (p. 296), even to the point of recommending several sessions prior to formally proceeding in clinical settings. So here, I will examine the value and practical issues surrounding intakes in applied sport psychology that are light on assessment.

Essentially, most or all of the important aspects of an intake are the same, or closely related, across any area of psychological work (Lukas, 1993; Perry, 2002). The practitioner wants to create a welcoming space for the client that is comfortable, safe, open, and is

81

accompanied by a sense of optimism for positive change. The intake, one hopes, begins to establish the foundation of a relationship between client and practitioner that will determine much of the opportunity to do significant work. It is a time to set basic boundary conditions (e.g., confidentiality) and modulate expectations (e.g., no magic wand). And the intake allows the psychologist (and often the client) to develop understanding around the objective and subjective realities of the client's position and situation. None of these processes and procedures is unique to applied sport psychology.

If, however, an athlete is referred specifically to a sport psychologist, it is usually *because* the client is a performer, and service expectations are often centered on areas of athlete training and performance support. These expectations cannot be understated. Even if the athlete is referred because of a recognizable issue of psychological adjustment or disorder, we need to be mindful that most expectations of a "sport" psychologist are, ultimately, to help the athlete perform better. Certainly, this may not be the case if the referral is to a clinical/counseling psychologist or psychiatrist without the "sport" title or inference. But because we are assuming a referral to a sport psychology practitioner here, the intake may differ from other clinical examples due to the nature of expectations for performance results.

One of the persistent issues underlying referrals of athletes is that the sport psychologist is often just one possible solution to "something that is not right." The situation is not much better when the sport psychologist is viewed potentially as "the next secret to a higher level of performance." It may be that the athlete is not performing well and no one knows what to do, or the athlete might be hoping for some new (magical) techniques, capabilities, or skills to improve and gain an edge. It may be a last-gasp effort (e.g., day before competition) or just a trial of something different. But the *necessity* of sport psychology is often not implicit in the search (unlike the surgery needed to repair a detached ACL). If there is a clear psychological issue (e.g., eating disorder, suicidal thoughts, relationship difficulties) the connection is much clearer. But often the mostly vague notion that behavior or performance could possibly be improved with the help of a psychologist leads to less-than-half-hearted attempts at securing support. Sport psychology is most often seen as a "potential" fix – something to try – and only a few athletes and coaches seem to fully embrace a psychological approach to athlete issues. It is like a wet bar of soap – hold too loosely and it slips away; grasp too tightly and it squirts off. Establishing an attraction and connection for the athlete is part of the professional's art.

Thus, the intake becomes incredibly important. It is up to the sport psychologist to hold the soap firmly but with sensitivity. The practitioner needs to be clear and positive and to convey the value of the service. One cannot afford to be too abstract, theoretical, or vague. The psychologist will, conversely, not want to come on too strong, or make the process of psychological work seem like a life-sentence of commitment. A gentle hand and an open perspective are needed to cultivate a relationship that might lead to continuing and significant work.

To be effective, the psychologist needs to determine a philosophy and a set of objectives for the intake. Essential elements of the philosophy are the centrality of care for the benefit of the athlete and the importance of developing a positive relationship between athlete and psychologist. Without a reasonably positive connection, little is likely to be accomplished no matter the technical expertise of the practitioner. Several objectives also seem universal for the intake: clearing a psycho-social space in which to explore issues, cultivating the athlete–practitioner relationship, tapping diverse perspectives of the athlete and the situation, creating engagement by the athlete to a process of change, and setting the course for effective reflection and action. None of these objectives needs be pursued in depth, much less completed. But the "first impression" created by the intake will significantly influence further work.

Setting

Some professionals may meet athletes in a traditional psychotherapeutic office setting, but classically this situation is often not the case in applied sport psychology. Commonly, first meetings are held in and around performance venues, training spaces, dorms, airports, hotels, or cafés (see Andersen, 2000). While in full-time practice, my time was largely spent at training venues, competitive events, on the road with athlete groups, and in and around sport institutions with no dedicated office space. Such circumstances mean far less control over the environment. Not only does one have to deal with the standard disruptors such as phones and PDAs (personal digital assistants; see Perry, 2002), but there seems to be an ever-changing variety of distractions and potential interruptions in these settings.

I would not say that an office is necessarily a better space. Athletes are comfortable in their familiar locales, and privacy is a relative thing. I distinctly recall a first meeting with a well-known professional athlete at my office located in a city university building. He was having some (well-publicized) performance issues and had taken the major leap to seek professional help. By the time I arrived to greet him in the waiting area, he had been inundated by a small hoard of fans wanting autographs and asking why he was there. I still remember vividly the "deer-in-the-headlights" look on this otherwise impressive sport star, and I don't think we ever really got into a reasonable and relaxed intake on that day in my office. We would have been far better off meeting at his team venue or a more secluded place.

Whatever the setting, one needs to create the essentials of a comfortable conversation space. Beware of letting the physical dynamics happen haphazardly. Physical and social discomforts will often be difficult to overcome once the conversation begins. Consider lines of sight for background distractions, lighting (including glare outdoors), and seating comfort. Make sure that orientation and spacing between you and the athlete are conducive to relaxed and dynamic conversation. In sum, purposefully apply your professional and personal judgment in setting up the meeting dynamics to optimize the chances of a quality discussion.

Getting started

Initial words and nonverbal communications create first impressions that set the psychological climate for relationship building. As with all therapeutic situations, the practitioner needs to create a relaxed but professional tone and a receptive, engaging atmosphere. When the two have never met before, it is important that the athlete senses the nature of the relationship that will be shared with the sport psychologist, as this is likely to be unique in their relationships around sport. In other situations, it is common that the sport psychologist and athlete may have some level of existing relationship (e.g., team interactions, travel), and the "first impressions" now are a reorienting towards a practitioner–client relationship. Either way, deliberately set the psychosocial tone that you wish to carry into a working situation at the outset.

To a reasonable extent, try to meet the culture of the sport and athlete. One needs to be wary of coming off as a fake "insider," (e.g., overuse of the sport jargon), but athletes tend to appreciate the psychologist who understands the language, culture, and experiences of sportspeople. Position yourself as part of the working aspects of sport and as a resource for athletes and coaches, and watch that your interests are not interpreted as fan attraction, particularly when working with high-profile athletes. The last thing a client needs is another enthusiast hoping to get intimate with an athlete. It is up to practitioners to be clear as to their purpose and to remember for whom the relationship is designed.

Set the boundaries of confidentiality early. Sport is particularly public, and there are many people who feel they have rights to personal information about athletes. Many athletes are accustomed to a type of "sport confidentiality," where everyone offers non-disclosure, but it is regularly violated. In addition, there tends to be a whole network of "unseen people in the room" (see Henschen, 1998) who have dual relationships with the athlete. To set the intake on the right course, be specific and clear about the nature of the psychologist–athlete relationship and establish clear expectations of confidentiality.

Interview

Unlike many mental health settings, sport psychology clients rarely have accompanying files or records. Not often will one be able to read through professional notes. Performance records, however, are often readily available, and it is advisable, when possible, to do a little advance research on the athlete's situation. It is common that a coach or administrator may have already provided some perspectives on the athlete's issues, or that the athlete has offered some performance information when making the appointment. Despite what information you have or what you think you know, a primary objective of the intake is to elicit the client's understanding of what is happening. Accomplishing this task is where professional listening skills become essential. You want to hear the client's version and perspective (Lukas, 1993).

The practitioner's task is to convey to clients that they will be *listened* to, and that the psychologist is working at *understanding* (Lukas, 1993). Throughout the session, active listening entails stimulating the dialogue and discussion, but also much waiting – being quiet long enough to hear emergent stories, images, emotions, and thoughts as they arise from the client (see Chapter 2). As Andersen (2000) stated in reference to intakes, "the bottom line is helping athletes tell their stories" (p. 4).

Intake is best viewed as a process of relationship-building and uncovering the "objective" facts. Unless there is a mutual agreement that the intake is an in-depth assessment, it is usually pushing it to do deep exploration and analysis. Stimulate discussion with questions, but don't make the client take a quiz (Andersen, 2000). Especially in a first meeting, you want to ask questions that they can readily answer. Over-probing or intense analysis of causal factors is usually too much for a first session. For example, Lukas (1993) advised, "ask who, what, when, where, and how. Don't ask why" (p. 8). The client may not know the answer to "why" questions (and experience embarrassment or confusion), or maybe the answer is the source of conflict (forced into an emotional place), or it may lead to too much emotional exchange for a first discussion (leading to the client feeling vulnerable and then withdrawing), any of which could stifle relationship building.

Reflect, summarize, and follow lines of thought, while being careful of leading towards your own conclusions or biases, or of putting words or emotions into the client's mouth. In particular, stay clear of your own personal "Maslow's hammer"[1] and be wary of "over-psychologizing" – pushing the client toward underlying issues. Important issues and suitable interventions will arise in due time, given insight and trust. The dance at intake is to engage the client in ways that allow a broad and safe discussion that reveals important perceptions and experiences, and engenders a sense of understanding.

Contrary to the conventional wisdom in psychological practice, the presenting problem in applied sport psychology may well be *the* problem, especially when it relates to underdeveloped mental skills for the high-performance demands of elite sport. For example, an age-group athlete requested my help in the case of a severe batting slump. After requesting a few details of his situation, I asked him what he was focusing on while at bat. He produced a list of outcomes on his mind such as scoring, winning, being successful, moving up to higher levels of play, and so forth. I replied that none of those things was likely to help him make contact with the ball, and that he might try focusing on batting one ball at a time (a brilliant idea that I thought up myself, of course). His response was, "OK that makes sense." And he simply did it, immediately ending the slump and continuing on to his best season ever. I'm glad I didn't begin the long exploration into why the expectations of his parents and an outcome-mad society were leading to his sense of failure about himself. The point here is that the presenting problem is often directly related to a real and highly desired outcome.

Nevertheless, even if the concern seems easily remedied, the practitioner should keep a healthy sense of skepticism about the facts and connections the client and others present (Lukas, 1993). One must remain open to other possible elements and follow professional curiosity about the situation. Certainly, this approach is the same in most of the helping professions. I have encountered many athletes seeking psychological assistance to raise performance when their primary issue was limited physical capabilities or inadequate training. Members of teams are notorious for only seeing their side of the equation. Ask "where's the proof" of the clients' perceptions, conclusions, and causal connections. Be aware that presenting issues may be distractions from the real underlying or otherwise obscured ones, and appreciate the possibilities of both embellished and attenuated stories.

Although an intake, as described here, is not targeted at assessment, psychologists still need to monitor and record (mentally or in notes during or after the session) their perceptions of their clients – personalities, styles, verbal and nonverbal communication, emotions, moods, and general presentation. We need to note the objective situation and apparent constraining/supporting factors, record a professional reading of affective flows and underlying themes or issues that appear to be in play, and keep track of questions that arise that are not necessary to address in this first meeting (see Chapter 6). All of these tasks aid in determining the possible needs of the client and the feasibility of providing professional help.

Covering the bases

During the intake, practitioners are faced with the challenge of eliciting stories relevant to potential service needs. Returning to the central assumption that expectations of applied sport psychology are that ultimately the *athlete's* needs will be addressed, the interview should cover a range of training and performance issues prior to determination of intervention, if any. In particular, matters beyond the psychology of the person are centrally important. What demands are placed on the athlete by the sport? What are the cultural norms (sport, family, community)? How do the athlete's objective skills work into the equation? How do all of these factors pose problems, and how can one identify potential solutions to the needs of the athlete?

Jim Loehr, in Simons and Andersen (1995), made the cogent point that psychologists' training tends to skew the investigation to mental problems. Many experienced practitioners would agree that focusing too early or solely on deep psychological issues puts many athletes off ("oh no, the *Psychologist*"). Further, as Loehr stated:

> The mind–body dichotomy, looking at things from a mental or psychological perspective is a very limiting way to view the athlete ... I'm much more effective in my work today, and I think it's largely because I tend to see things much more integrated, as kind of a mental, physical, and emotional whole.
>
> (in Simons & Andersen, p. 455)

The applied sport psychologist is well-advised to maintain a broad view, from intake to intervention.

A framework that aids the practitioner in eliciting stories from different perspectives is most helpful. It is important that the structure be as unbiased as possible, because if the intake is primarily client driven, theory driven, or technique driven, the perspectives arising are invariably myopic (Marquis, 2008). One simple framework borrowed from dynamical systems concepts of motor control and performance allows the practitioner to consider the interacting perspectives of person x task x environment (Newell, 1991). Applying this approach, stories would be elicited from perspectives of the athlete's perceptions, feelings, and psychological processing (person), the general and specific training and performance demands in relation to the athlete's skills (task), and sport, institutional, physical, and psycho-social settings in which the athlete lives (environment). Whatever the presenting problem is claimed to be, the issues are embedded within these interacting factors. Moving between person, task, and environment allows checks of congruence between stories, strengths and weaknesses within the whole situation, and varied potential avenues for interventions.

Another framework that I have increasingly favored is based on Wilber's (2000a) integral model. One of the fundamental tenants of the integral model is that there are four basic perspectives of being, which can be illustrated as quadrants of a 2 x 2 matrix (see Figure 9.1). Wilber's insight is that all things exist in terms of external and internal features, both as a singular entity and as part of a collective. With regard to humans, the internal singular contains the individual's experience and psycho-spiritual development that constitute "I" (first person perspective). The internal collective contains the norms, expectations, and values of the culture(s) within which the individual operates, constituting "We" (first person plural). The external singular is the empirical world of facts, events, and other observable or recordable things, and can be identified as "It" (third person singular). The external collective, labeled by Wilber as "Its," encompasses identifiable systems, including natural/physical systems, societies, institutions, infrastructure, and methodological approaches of knowledge, training, and so forth (third person plural). Because integral theory eschews reductionism in all forms, it is recognized that "being" is an irreducible confluence of interactions among these perspectives. Yet there is significant value in the consideration of the quadrants as an intellectual tool for fuller understanding, particularly when looking from outside of the subject.

The depth and extent of integral theory is substantial, and the interested reader can readily access a multitude of resources on and around it. In particular, psychologists might begin the challenge with Wilber's (2000b) volume on *Integral Psychology* and the thorough guide to integral assessment by Marquis (2008). For the present discussion, however, just the simple outline of the four quadrants provides a valuable framework from which to explore what may be happening with a new athlete client. It is a meta-theoretical model, and

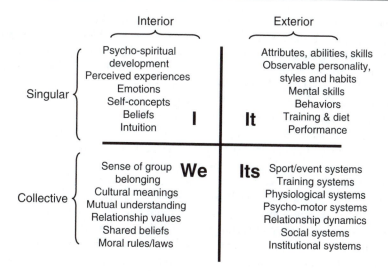

Figure 9.1 The four quadrants of being, based on Wilber's (2000a) integral model, with examples of elements that might be explored by the sport psychologist within each.

therefore brings no bias to evaluations or interventions. Further, it is ultimately practical in evoking stories covering the bases of influence in the athlete's life situation (see examples in Figure 9.1). Pursuing stories of "I" not only gives the practitioner windows into the athlete's experience, but also psychological processing, and stories of "We" provide reflections of shared values and expectations. Stories of "It" speak to physical and mental skills, objective performance, and situational demands, and stories of "Its" inform the practitioner of at least some of the institutional, programmatic, environmental, and social demands. Just a few explorations of each quadrant will fill an intake with substantial sharing and a high likelihood of openings to a positive athlete–psychologist relationship.

Moving forward

Throughout the intake the practitioner wants to normalize the nature of psychological work. Particularly with reference to practical applications, we want athletes to understand that psychology is not outside, or different, or an add-on to who they are and what they do and how they perform, but rather it is inextricably linked to all of their experiences. The intake is an opportunity to help dissolve the artificial separateness of the Western mind–body dichotomy (dualism). Without invoking theory or jargon, it is possible to highlight the natural influences of the four quadrants of experience. Living, training, and performing are not just external things nor just internal subjective interpretations, but both simultaneously. There are distinct individual aspects and shared/connected aspects. The work of psychology is inherent in all that sportspeople do – it is already and forever part of their game. The question then to clients is whether they would rather let this arena just progress by chance or by purposeful development. The psychologist may be viewed as a facilitator, providing guidance or coaching within this essential domain.

The intake should typically conclude with goals. Perry (2002) suggested, asking what the client thinks would be important. What changes would make the work worth the time?

If treatment were successful, what would be different? What would the client like to see happen? What does the client want to work on? Answers to such questions indicate what is meaningful, and therefore motivating, to the athlete. In addition, the practitioner can easily expand or add to the ideas expressed by the athlete according to professional insight. Goals may be related to some directed assessment or exploration, or they may include some practical applications. In my experience, athletes are particularly eager for action-oriented goals. They want more than instructions for reflection or the promise of another conversation later. Consider specifically directed inquiry or exploration, and whenever possible provide a particular step to take. The action goal can be a perspective, a thinking process, a communication process, or a behavior. Just get them engaged in the work.

Make sure to finish with a next step to a working relationship that is planned and scheduled. Even if it is simply, "I will stop by/call next Tuesday to check in on how you are doing." Remember, athletes seeking help from sport psychologists are notoriously slippery. Particularly in situations where casual contact is common (sport teams, athletic departments, institutes of sport), it is easy to be vague or assume a good chance will arise in the near future. The commitment needs to be more than "see you around" or "catch you at practice sometime." These vague plans too often never materialize, and the relationship started during intake becomes one of unease and avoidance. Clearly, the athlete has the right to opt out in most cases, and should be granted such a decision graciously. But if the relationship is to continue and develop, the onus is on the psychologist to keep the momentum and organization. Create the supportive expectation, set the meeting, and follow through. That engagement in itself will demonstrate that the psychologist–athlete relationship is qualitatively different than so many others in the athlete's life, and an opportunity for meaningful work.

A final thought

In accordance with Stringfellow's observations, the intake interview is a loving and caring encounter centered on listening and truly hearing the athlete's story. Being heard and understood is often the beginning of therapeutic change. See Box 9.1 for a summary of the key points of this chapter.

Box 9.1

Key points about applied sport psychology intakes

- The intake is first and foremost about building an athlete–practitioner relationship to support potential psychological work.
- A primary objective is to listen with an open and unbiased ear as possible to create an accepting environment and to develop understanding of the athlete and the situation.
- No matter what the apparent reason for an athlete referral, keep in mind from the outset that nearly everyone involved will expect that a *sport* psychologist will assist with sport performance.

- One of the challenges for sport psychologists is to be conscious of traditional guides for the intake environment while often working in the nontraditional settings of sport venues, cafés, hotel lobbies, and so forth.
- The psychologist needs to meet the culture of the athlete as well as possible, but also be cautious about resembling the fan or any of many others around sport who have dual relationships with the athlete.
- It is helpful to have a framework for eliciting athlete stories that encompasses the multitude of perspectives that interact to create the whole situation for the athlete.
- Make sure to end the intake with clear plans for future contact and action-oriented goals for next steps.

Note

1 " ... it is tempting, if the only tool you have is a hammer, to treat everything as if it were a nail" (Maslow, 1966/2002).

References

Andersen, M. B. (2000). Beginnings: Intakes and the initiation of relationships. In M. B. Andersen (Ed.), *Doing sport psychology* (pp. 3–16). Champaign, IL: Human Kinetics.

Henschen, K. P. (1998). The issue behind the issue. In M. A. Thompson, R. A. Vernacchia, & W. E. Moore (Eds.), *Case studies in applied sport psychology: An educational approach* (pp. 27–34). Dubuque, IA: Kendall/Hunt.

Lukas, S. (1993). *Where to start and what to ask: An assessment handbook.* New York: Norton.

Maslow, A. H. (2002). *The psychology of science: A reconnaissance.* Richmond, CA: Maurice Bassett Publishing (Original work published 1966).

Marquis, A. (2008). *The integral intake: A guide to comprehensive ideographic assessment in integral psychology.* New York: Routledge.

Newell, K. M. (1991). Motor skill acquisition. *Annual Review of Psychology, 42,* 213–237.

Perry, C. W. (2002). *Basic counseling techniques: A beginning therapist's toolkit.* New York: 1st Books Library.

Simons, J. P. & Andersen, M. B. (1995). The development of consulting practice in applied sport psychology: Some personal perspectives. *The Sport Psychologist, 9,* 449–468.

Taylor, J. & Schneider, B. A. (1992). The sport-clinical intake protocol: A comprehensive interviewing instrument for applied sport psychology. *Professional Psychology: Research and Practice, 23,* 318–325.

Van Audenhove, C., & Vertommen, H. (2000). A negotiation approach to intake and treatment choice. *Journal of Psychotherapy Integration, 10,* 287–299.

Wilber, K. (2000a). *A theory of everything: An integral vision for business, politics, science, and spirituality.* Boston: Shambhala.

Wilber, K. (2000b). *Integral psychology: Consciousness, spirit, psychology, therapy.* Boston: Shambhala.

10

Individual and group observations

Purposes and processes

Jack C. Watson II and Vanessa Shannon

You can discover more about a person in an hour of play than in a year of conversation.
Plato, *The Republic*

Assuming this statement of Plato's is at least partly true, one might also believe that by watching how athletes behave during practice and competition, psychologists may be able to gain valuable information from these observations in addition to talking with the athletes in counseling sessions. Although traditional discussion and assessment strategies can be excellent ways to learn about clients, observations can also be useful components of the information-gathering process. This chapter will focus on the role of observation in consultation and provide the reader with an overview of the techniques and strategies that can be used to make informative observations.

What is observational assessment?

Why are observations important for sport psychologists, and in what ways can they help consultations? Observational assessment is an out-of-session opportunity for practitioners to monitor clients in their sport environments where they may be less guarded and act more naturally. These observations may provide practitioners with information beyond what they can glean from clients during one-on-one sessions. This information can be used to facilitate relationship building, inform consulting, and track effectiveness.

Face time: building rapport and trust

Effective sport psychology consulting relationships are often built on a foundation of trust and rapport (Ravizza, 1988). Early interactions between consultants and clients provide professionals with opportunities to make connections with athletes and develop rapport and trust by communicating understanding and commitment. Conducting practice and game observations can also be excellent ways to develop rapport with individual clients or teams. By putting in "face time" at team events and demonstrating commitment, consultants may be able to engage athletes in the consulting process by reducing resistance to sport psychology and facilitating the development of trust.

Observational assessment may afford consultants an opportunity to peak the curiosity of team members and foster interest in how the psychologist might function within the team. In settings with existing relationships, observations may provide opportunities for bonding between professionals and athletes/teams. In situations where consultants have been hired without team knowledge, observations may provide the first face-time exposure with the team. Often a sport psychologist, new to a team, may be introduced by the coach saying, "We have a new member of the team, she's a sport psychologist, and she'll be observing the team. I want you all to get to know her better." When the psychologist is regularly seen at practices and games, athletes begin to interact with him/her and rapport and trust (may) develop naturally. These early interactions can pay dividends later in consulting relationships.

Holistic understanding: how observations can inform consulting

Successful consultations often start with the development of rapport between athletes and consultants. Nevertheless, it is important not to overlook the value of developing a thorough assessment of the athletes and the social environments influencing their behaviors. Assessment facilitates successful consultations because it informs psychologists about the clients' backgrounds and underlying issues that may affect their sport behaviors and their lives. These issues may be related to factors that clients are unwilling to discuss, or may even be outside of the clients' awareness. In either case, proper assessment of clients can facilitate the efficacy of the consultation process.

Assessing athletes and their successes and failures related to sport and other aspects of their lives can be accomplished using two forms of assessment information: pre-assessment and corroborating assessment. Pre-assessment information is collected prior to consulting and provides the benefit of allowing the consultants to develop tentative understandings of individuals and teams. Corroborating assessment occurs after consulting relationships have begun and allows the psychologists to triangulate information gathered from athletes or teams during treatment sessions.

One may ask, beyond watching athletes and how they perform and interact with teammates and coaches, what other value can come from observing clients in their natural environments? To answer this question, one must consider that all individuals have their own perceived realities. Every person views life and situations differently (Berger & Luckmann, 1966). For example, when police officers interview witnesses of a crime, they likely get different accounts. These accounts differ based upon the physical perspective of the witnesses as well as the factors to which the witnesses paid attention, which were affected by personal biases and experiences. Similarly, athletes view themselves through biased lenses. Clients may believe they are being "objective" in one-on-one sessions, but their accounts are likely biased by their past experiences and self-perceptions. Even though it is the clients' perceptions of reality that matter, the clients' perceptions may not be completely accurate. Consultants will benefit from determining whether or not their clients view situations with particular biases. When bias is observed, it should be used as a caveat for future observations and interpretations and may be a beneficial topic of discussion.

Sport psychology consultants would benefit from having a thorough understanding of the ways in which athletes act and react during both minimally and highly competitive situations. Although many of the mental and psychological barriers athletes encounter may be related to previous experiences in their lives, it is helpful to consider the current social factors that could affect athletes' mental states or performances. Observational assessment is another way to gain perspective on the social factors affecting life and performance. Athletes and their concerns do not develop in a vacuum. Observational assessment, along with questioning, can facilitate the understanding of the social environments in which athletes live and compete. Factors that may be observed and assessed include the athletic subculture, athletic and team identities, social networks, and leadership styles (Brustad & Ritter-Taylor, 1997).

Tracking learning

Although observations can be a central component of an initial assessment, it should not take the place of a traditional intake interview. If done effectively, observational assessments can supplement information gathered during traditional intakes (Gardner & Moore, 2005). Observations can be used as a feedback loop that provides information about client change throughout the consultation. Consultants can observe client behaviors, such as the use of anger-reducing strategies and routine implementation, to help quantify behavior change. Such knowledge can inform the consultation process. In addition, observations may be informative later in the consultation process by helping professionals learn how clients use the skills taught during individual sessions. Observational assessment should be seen as something that takes place throughout the consultation process.

When and where to observe?

Initial observations are often started from a distance, which can help provide a perspective of the entire field, gym, or practice venue by allowing consultants to observe the entire team. From this distance, consultants may be less likely to focus their attention on specific individuals and skills; instead, their attention is focused on the overall process. Observations of teams at a distance may help professionals develop an idea of normal interactions, cliques, coaches' interactions with each other, and coach–player communication.

After observing the general processes of the team (i.e., 1–2 observations), and learning more specifics about presenting problems, consultants might observe practice from a closer vantage point. Such observations allow psychologists to hear specific interactions between players, coaches, and support staff, and to observe specific personal responses to success and failure through comments, facial expressions, and other reactions. These observations become purposeful, and with more knowledge about the team, consultants will start observing players and teams with specific ideas in mind. The goal of these observations should no longer be to soak in information to better understand the client, but should progress to using this information to assess and confirm (or reject) previous speculations and perceptions.

In time, observations may progress to where consultants are observing from the playing field (or pool deck, or golf links). Observations at such close proximity serve two needs. First, personal observations can be made about team and individual reactions to situations. Second, information can be made quickly available to athletes, and with permission could even lead to immediate interventions. Nevertheless, during these observations, psychologists should not spend a significant amount of time talking with or standing beside the coaches. It is important to balance consulting time between coaches and athletes (Jowett, Paull, Pensgaard, Hoegmo, & Riise, 2005); if players view consultants as extensions of the coaching staff, the relationship between them may change.

Coaches may, at times, ask consultants to help with practice. Consultants should use their best judgment with regard to helping, because they do not want to be seen as coaches. Roles that would be perceived by players to help the team and are not likely to be seen as coaching roles can have positive consequences and help to decrease distance between players and consultants. For example, while working with a volleyball team, one of the authors would frequently help collect balls during practice. Collecting balls was done in situations when team members were in a rush to gather balls. Such a small action was viewed positively by the players.

Practice settings

A great deal can be learned about athletes, their presenting problems, environmental factors that may trigger negative responses, and possible treatment approaches through observations made in settings where the consequences of mistakes are less meaningful than in competitive situations. Practice settings are great places to observe how athletes interact with coaches and teammates, respond to or engage in leadership, and deal with successes and failures.

With practice often being less stressful than games, athletes and coaches are more likely to behave in their usual manner. Observations of typical behaviors during warm-ups, drills, and competitive simulations allow consultants to form a picture of the team's athletic subculture (e.g., values and beliefs, roles and status that affect communication and support). Such observations allow consultants to identify cliques and subtleties in leadership. Many presenting problems and treatment plans have social components to them, and practitioners should consider identifying these social interactions as possible components in future treatments.

Competitive settings

Even though practice observations are important, we also encourage consultants to observe competitions to gather information not available during practices. Competition observations may provide insight into how athletes behave, react, and interact in outcome-oriented environments with respect to sportspersonship, pride, shame, and self-worth. Competition also allows for observations of the influence of external factors that are not relevant during practice settings (e.g., responses to perceived errant calls, fan interactions). Finally, competition observations help consultants examine how teams respond to pressure, winning, and losing.

Other settings

Beyond practices and competitions, athletes often interact with each other in settings such as the locker room, weight room, training room, cafeteria, and during travel. Observing interactions in these settings can help practitioners garner a great deal of information. These observations can provide evidence about the athletic subculture of the team, athletes' personal identities, social networks of influence, motivation, communication patterns, cohesion, and social support.

Observations in weight rooms and training rooms (where athletes receive treatments) may focus on social issues, but one should also be open to gather information about motivation, athletic subculture, athletic identity, and self-perceptions. In these settings, psychologists should pay close attention to how hard athletes work, how much they need to be pushed to perform, the motivation they provide to others, how they interact with support personnel, how strongly they identify with the role of athlete, and how they carry themselves in terms of confidence. Although several of these issues may be observed via overt behaviors, observations related to athletic identity can be made by listening to athletes and how, and how often, they discuss their sports, the importance of sport to them, and by observing their reactions to injury and the influence that it has upon other aspects of their lives.

Although the weight and training rooms are areas where athletes may be encouraged to push their limits using both intrinsic and extrinsic motivational strategies; locker rooms, cafeterias, buses, and planes provide athletes with informal social opportunities. In these settings, consultants should look for illustrations of the athletic subculture and social networks. Observations in these areas could focus on communication between teammates, seating arrangements, eating and exercise habits, evidence of social support, and friendships. This information can provide the consultant with an understanding of how the team members affect each other and how they fit, or don't fit, together. Such observations can also provide evidence of social support opportunities for athletes who may be struggling with athletic, personal, or social problems. Observations made in the locker room can at times resemble observations made in less structured (e.g., cafeteria) and more structured (e.g., practice) environments. In some instances, these observations may provide evidence about social networks and support systems, and in other instances may result in learning a great deal about leadership styles and motivation.

Inconsistencies in observations

An important component of observational assessment is identifying potential discrepancies between practice and competition behaviors. For individual athletes, discrepancies between practice and competition behaviors may provide evidence about attitudes or sources of motivation. Other individual behaviors to compare between practice and competition include arousal, anxiety, focus and concentration, confidence, and differences in social interactions.

It is equally important to identify possible changes in coach behaviors and team interactions from practice to competition settings. Coaches' behaviors can have major effects on athletes, and if these behaviors change between practice and competition, athletes may be confused by the inconsistencies. Inconsistent coaching can leave athletes not knowing what to expect, and can result in anger and a loss of trust. Differences in team interactions between practice and competition may also be useful information for psychologists. How teams behave and how the members interact with one another are indicative of the team climate. If that climate were to change between practice and competition settings, it may signify a disruption in the team unit.

It is also important to be aware of any discrepancies between what athletes are saying during one-on-one sessions and their behaviors during observations. Individuals live in their perceived realities, and what they think they are doing and what they are actually doing may be different. For example, if an athlete suggests in session that he is confident about his performance under pressure and then is observed by the psychologist to be cracking under pressure (e.g., errors, negative body language), there may be a disconnect between the athlete's perceptions and reality. This disconnect could be something that the psychologist and athlete discuss in session to figure out what may be happening for the athlete. To be consistent with observations across communication type and settings, practitioners should consider using a behavior tracking from (see Figure 10.1 for a sample form).

Athlete/Team: _____   Date: _____

Practice/Competition against _____   Location:_____

	Warm-Up	Practice/Competition	Post-Practice/Competition
Nonverbal Communication			
Interactions with Teammates			
Interactions with Coaches			
Energy Level			
Reactions to Successes and Failures			
Overall Assessment Comments			

Figure 10.1 Individual observation tracking form.

What to observe?

Observational assessment can provide practitioners with an opportunity to examine verbal and nonverbal communication among players and coaches. This information can be useful in understanding team dynamics. The majority of communication is nonverbal (Mehrabian, 1981), and as Plato's quote at the beginning of this chapter implies, athletes' body language can be equally as telling as their words. Nonverbal cues paint a picture of both interpersonal and intrapersonal communication. High fives and positive verbal communications may suggest high cohesion among team members, whereas limited verbal communication and no physical touching may imply team tension. Similarly, athletes who always have their heads up and shoulders back regardless of the score or previous outcome exude confidence, and athletes who slouch and whose eyes are pointed at the floor may lack confidence or be feeling dejected.

Other forms of nonverbal communication for practitioners to be aware of include facial expressions, stride length, visual gaze, breathing, ritualistic behaviors, and speech patterns (Weinberg & Gould, 2007). For example, athletes may be showing signs of fear or stress if they take short and indecisive strides, have a lost or apprehensive expression on their faces, seem to be having trouble focusing on the task, breathe faster and shallower than expected, use short or fast speech patterns, or perform ritualistic behaviors. On the other hand, athletes may be perceived as confident and comfortable if they display multiple behaviors opposite to those identified above.

Individual observations

Pre-performance observations

Observing the way an athlete prepares for competition can be informative. Many athletes use pre-performance routines to regulate arousal and mentally prepare for competition. Athletes with systematic and consistent routines may be more aware of the importance of arousal regulation and mental preparation. If athletes use their pre-performance routines inconsistently, they may not see the usefulness of the routine, be distracted, or be unable to focus on the routine. In addition, by observing athletes' pre-performance routines, practitioners may be able to better understand the issues the athletes may have related to performance anxiety, focus, and concentration. The activities in which athletes engage prior to performance may illustrate how they feel about the impending competitions. For example, overconfident athletes may not feel the need to prepare as much as athletes who have a suitable level of confidence or are underconfident.

Anxiety and arousal

If athletes experience anxiety, or are unable to attain optimal levels of arousal, it may negatively affect their performance. In such instances it is important for consultants to use observations to identify behaviors that may indicate anxiety or issues with arousal regulation. Examples may include athletes swaying back and forth or constantly drying their sweaty palms. Similarly, athletes with difficulty attaining optimal levels of arousal may appear lethargic at intense moments or over-aroused when it might be more effective to be less intense.

Composure and emotional control

The best scenarios in which to gauge athletes' composure and emotional control are during successes, failures, and situations in which they have minimal control. Athletes' responses to successes and failures say a great deal about their composure and emotional control; athletes with composure and control maintain a similar gracious attitude in success and failure. If athletes are boastful after a win or good play, or unsportsmanlike after a loss or mistake, they may need to work on their composure and emotional control.

Confidence and concentration

Oftentimes, athletes who lack confidence have heightened levels of performance anxiety, experience frequent lapses in concentration, talk a bigger game than they play, and struggle with indecisiveness (Weinberg & Gould, 2007). Many of these behaviors and cognitive changes can be observed (or inferred) during competition. Performance anxiety may manifest itself through observable behaviors (discussed in the previous section). Lapses in concentration and indecisiveness are both apparent when athletes experience a number of unforced errors during competition. An athlete with diminished confidence may struggle to focus and may appear to be physically disengaged (e.g., wandering eyes). In addition, if athletes are indecisive, they may appear tight or tentative.

Low confidence is only one of the many reasons athletes have difficulty maintaining focus and concentration. External and internal distractions, such as the opponent(s), the previous point, the score, and negative self-talk can lead to lapses in concentration. Observable examples of distracters may take the form of "trash talking" or athletes verbally criticizing themselves.

Motivation, dedication, and commitment

Although psychological attributes are less tangible than physical attributes, practitioners can still use observation to assess behaviors that may illustrate an athlete's motivation, dedication, and commitment. If athletes demonstrate responsible behavior, adhere to team norms, and try hard to succeed, they are demonstrating high levels of motivation, dedication, and commitment. Athletes who loaf around or are disengaged when not in the competition, may have limited motivation and dedication and may not be truly committed to their team or individual performance.

Group observations

When psychologists are hired to work with entire teams, their observations should be somewhat different than those discussed for individual athletes. When working with teams, consultants should focus on both coach-related and team-related factors.

Coaching behaviors

When consulting with teams, we encourage practitioners to use their observation time to focus on team-related issues that may affect performance. Because the team is bigger than the sum of the individual parts, it is important for observations to extend beyond the individual athletes themselves. Such observations should also focus on gathering information about coaches, and how the coaches influence the team through their interactions with the athletes, their leadership styles, and the emotional and motivational climates they promote.

Coach–athlete issues

The relationships between athletes and their coaches can strongly affect performance and other aspects of athletes' lives (Jowett & Poczwardowski, 2007). Through observational assessment, psychologists can examine verbal and nonverbal interactions between coaches and athletes to gain information about the way coaches interact with athletes. Consistency, or lack thereof, can heavily influence the coach–athlete relationship. If coaches demonstrate inconsistencies in their interactions across time or athletes, these inconsistencies may affect team dynamics and subsequent performance. Specific coaching behaviors to observe include modeling, reinforcement, and feedback style. By observing these behaviors, practitioners will be able to better determine whether or not coaches interact consistently and/or effectively with athletes.

Leadership

Team settings provide opportunities for learning and developing leadership skills. The leadership tendencies of coaches and athletes affect behavior and performance and are important to assess during games and practices. Information about the leadership tendencies of players and coaches can be garnered from warm-ups, encouragement given during drills and games, and feedback or instruction provided to players. Other leadership observations might include assessments of leadership practices on the team (e.g., autocratic vs. democratic) and responses to differing leadership styles.

Questions that consultants may want to ask when observing coach leadership styles include: how does the coach teach? How does the coach communicate with athletes following successes or failures? How does the coach react to player feedback/comments? In addition, psychologists should pay particularly close attention to how athletes or teams react to their coaches in these situations.

While observing athlete leaders, consultants may want to focus on questions such as: How does the athlete leader motive his/her teammates? Are there "unofficial" leaders, beyond the captain, who emerge during practice or competition? What leadership strategies appear to be working best? Do different team members respond to leadership styles differently? All of this information can be used to help the athlete leader become more aware of the team landscape and to provide guidance for improvement of leadership strategies in the future.

Climate

Some coaches create climates where athletes are free to learn and make mistakes as long as they work toward improved performance, but other coaches create climates that are rigid and threatening, where athletes are shamed and reprimanded for mistakes. The setting influences player autonomy and satisfaction, but can also influence other factors such as self-confidence, role expectations, cohesiveness, stress, and anxiety (Ames, 1992). Observations of team climate can help consultants understand player thoughts and behaviors. For instance, observing coach–player interactions following different situations (e.g., success and failure in practice or competitive situations, individual mistakes, personal crises) and more so, player reactions (e.g., hanging head, tentative movements, frustration) to these interactions can provide the psychologist with information about the perceived climate and the influence of the climate on individuals and the team.

Team processes

By observing teams across settings, consultants can learn how athletes communicate. Communication strategies should be observed in as many situations as possible, but may be particularly informative when teams are under pressure. Stressful and evaluative situations that demonstrate communication patterns include successes and failures, position challenges, and team scrimmages. These situations give information about communication patterns, but also team processes such as leadership characteristics, team support structures, and team roles.

Observations of team processes such as leadership, status, social support, and roles are important for practitioners to understand. Not only does knowledge of these factors affect how practitioners understand the information obtained from clients in session, but also provides information that can inform interventions. When consultants know the roles, support systems, and/or leadership styles on the team, they are better able to judge the potential efficacy of team interventions. Further, if effective social support is not present, or players do not understand their roles or status, consultants may want to develop initial interventions that target improvements of these factors.

Conclusion

In conclusion, psychologists need to be aware of the roles that observations can play in the consultation process. Not only do observations play an important role in the development of rapport between client and psychologist, they also provide information to consultants that can be used to better understand and corroborate information learned in one-on-one sessions, provide information that can help develop and maintain effective interventions, and assess the effectiveness of interventions. Given the importance of observations, we recommend that psychologists consider conducting both practice and competition observations as early and often as possible. These observations should focus on the social and situational factors influencing athlete and team attitudes and behaviors. These social factors include social networks of influence, the athletic subculture, leadership styles, and communication patterns.

Observational assessments provide information that helps with evaluation. Although observational assessments may not provide specific information about why athletes experience stress, anger, fear, or limited focus or self-confidence, they can provide insight into the athletes' experiences. If conducted well, these observations can benefit the consultation process. Although we have provided an outline for conducting effective observations, psychologists will need to develop their own methods of practice/competition and individual/group observations. In addition, they will need to develop strategies for using the information that they gain from these observations. See Box 10.1 for the main take-home messages from this chapter.

Box 10.1

Take-home messages about observing clients

- A significant amount of information can be learned from observations that may not be possible to obtain in traditional consultation sessions.
- Observations can help build rapport and inform the consultation process with information about clients' experiences, ideas for effective interventions, and assessment of client change.
- Consultants should attempt to gather pertinent information from clients (individual athletes, whole teams, coaches) using observations of both practice and competition situations.
- Observations should start from a distance. With time and rapport development, they can periodically move to closer proximities.

References

Ames, C. (1992). Achievement goals, motivational climate, and motivational processes. In G. C. Roberts (Ed.), *Motivation in sport and exercise* (pp. 161–176). Champaign, IL: Human Kinetics.

Berger, P. L., & Luckmann, T. (1966). *The social construction of reality: A treatise in the sociology of knowledge.* Garden City, NY: Anchor Books.

Brustad, R., & Ritter-Taylor, M. (1997). Applying social psychological perspectives to the sport psychology consulting process. *The Sport Psychologist, 11,* 107–119.

Gardner, F., & Moore, Z. (2005). *Clinical sport psychology.* Champaign, IL: Human Kinetics.

Jowett, S., Paull, G., Pensgaard, A.M., Hoegmo, P. M., & Riise, H. (2005). Coach–athlete relationship. In J. Taylor & G. Wilson (Eds.), *Applying sport psychology: Four perspectives* (pp. 153–170). Champaign, IL: Human Kinetics.

Jowett, S., & Poczwardowski, A. (2007). Understanding the coach–athlete relationship. In S. Jowett & D. Lavallee (Eds.), *Social psychology in sport* (pp. 3–14). Champaign, IL: Human Kinetics

Mehrabian, A. (1981). *Silent messages: Implicit communication of emotions and attitudes* (2nd ed.). Belmont, CA: Wadsworth.

Ravizza, K. (1988). Gaining entry with athlete personnel for season-long consulting. *The Sport Psychologist, 2,* 243–254.

Weinberg. R. S., & Gould, D. (2007). *Foundations of sport and exercise psychology* (4th ed.). Champaign, IL: Human Kinetics.

11

Psychological assessment

Projective techniques

Petah M. Gibbs

The development of early projective techniques was strongly influenced by the psychoanalytic movement. According to Rabin (1986), clinical psychologists, pre-1930, had few assessment tools (e.g., the Stanford-Binet, and some personality inventories of limited range). Essentially, the clinicians of this era mainly used quantitative indices, IQ tests, percentiles on introversion or dominance scales, and similar pieces of nomothetic information. Rabin suggested the introduction of projective techniques gave clinicians the opportunity to communicate something meaningful to professional colleagues about the personality structure, dynamics, and diagnoses of clients. Results from projective techniques also contributed to the planning of therapeutic processes. According to Rabin, the clinical tradition provided a setting for the development of projective techniques, and today projective techniques remain favored instruments of many clinical psychologists, and common methods of assessing personality.

As early as 1907, a simple projective test consisting of a series of pictures was available for personality assessment of children. Since the early 1900s, the use of psychodynamically driven personality tests have waxed and waned. For example, in the 1920s and 1930s there were groundbreaking developments such as the Rorschach Ink Blot Test (Rorschach, 1921) and the Thematic Apperception Test (TAT; Morgan & Murray, 1935). These classic early personality tests, which have stood the test of time and are still widely used, have spawned a huge number of derivative tests. A gradual shift took place when the development and popularity of self-report tests led to a reappraisal of, and in some instances skepticism towards, older projective methods. During the 1950s, many psychologists were strident in asserting that projective techniques did not meet established psychometric criteria of reliability and validity.

The popularity of sport psychology as a specific discipline has largely coincided with an era dominated by objective (self-report) testing (1960s to present). Like mainstream psychologists, some sport psychologists use various tests and techniques to assess personality. The many instruments that have been developed to assess personality in sport are essentially objective/self-report. With the increasing maturation of the field of sport psychology, there appears to be a greater appreciation for diversity of training models, research methodologies, and other approaches beyond the dominant cognitive-behavioral paradigm. For example, psychodynamic interpretations and formulations have begun to appear more frequently in the sport psychology literature (Andersen, 2005; Strean & Strean, 1998).

Historical traces and theoretical foundations

Freud introduced the term *projection* as early as 1894. He stated that projection is a process of ascribing one's own drives, feelings, and sentiments to other people or the outside world as a defensive tactic that allows one to remain unaware of these undesirable phenomena in oneself. Murray (1938) first introduced the term *projection test* in a ground breaking study titled *Explorations in Personality*. The term is the generic label for a collection of varied psychological assessment tools. This collection includes inkblot methods (e.g., Rorschach), storytelling methods (e.g., TAT), drawing techniques (e.g., human figure drawing, house–tree–person), and verbal stimuli techniques (e.g., sentence completion, word association). Murray described these methods as, "an attempt to discover the covert (inhibited) and unconscious (partially repressed) tendencies of normal persons ... simply different methods of stimulating imaginative processes and facilitating their expression in words or in action" (p. 248).

One of the most accepted and widely used projective tests to investigate the dynamics of personality is the TAT (Morgan & Murray, 1935), which involves a psychodynamic process of interpretation. Using the TAT in a therapeutic setting enables clinicians to gain insights into how the dynamics of personality are manifested in interpersonal relations, and how clients describe and interpret their environments. The TAT consists of 30 cards (and one blank card) with the majority of images depicting people in a variety of life situations. Clients are asked to interpret the scene by identifying the central (main) character, telling what is taking place, describing the thoughts and feelings of the characters, recounting events leading to the scene, and telling what the outcome will be. Clients reveal their personal apperception of the images through the medium of *projection*. They project onto the images their own hopes, dreams, fears, frustrations, relationships, and so forth.

Interpreting projective tests

Clinicians working with the TAT differ in how they use the tool as source material for finding characteristics of their clients they believe are significant. For example, a clinician may use the TAT solely to determine diagnostic characterizations of behavior, or to locate important emotional relationships in a person's world. According to Rotter (1946), interpretations from the TAT should be considered only as hypotheses or leads for further investigation, and "the value, significance, nature, and validity of the tests are dependent upon the interpreter, his experience, and his approach to the field of personality" (p. 206).

Interpretation can include identifying the "degree" of projection (how much projection is going on) and complementing responses with case notes of interactions with clients. Adcock (1965) suggested that practitioners should appreciate the difficulty of interpreting the degree of projection involved in a client's storytelling. Adcock warned against practitioners relying on mere counting of needs and conflicts and being too concerned with group averages. The interaction between the clinician and client is also a central component of the interpretation process and understanding the degree of projection.

The problem with most projective tests is always the same; they allow the interpreter to project as much as the client. Interpretation of respondents' stories requires clinicians to be highly aware of their own needs and projections. Similarly, transference and countertransference also play important roles in the interpretation of clients' stories. Eron (1959) suggested there is a tendency to distort in storytelling due to the effects of transference. For example, clients may make conscious (or unconscious) efforts to please practitioners and present themselves as specific kinds of persons. There may also be a tendency for practitioners to misinterpret the meaning of stories due to a lack of awareness, or analysis, of their own countertransference. If clients have some behaviors or personality features that remind practitioners (unconsciously) of others in the past who have disappointed them, then there may be a tendency to interpret the stories in a more negative light than if clients remind professionals of positive past experiences with significant others.

Validity and reliability

Projective tests have been a matter of concern to psychometricians because they generally do not conform to the usual methods of establishing reliability and validity. Critics have pointed to validity problems (or limitations) of projective tests especially when interpretation is not based on quantified scores or normative data, and have dismissed their usefulness as personality assessment techniques. According to Jensen (1959), "if the TAT is short on actual validity, it certainly is not lacking in what might be called *subjective validity* (akin to *faith validity*)" (p. 312). Jensen suggested some psychologists have greater capacities than others for experiencing subjective validity. This capacity seems to be associated with training and experience in psychoanalysis, psychotherapy, and projective techniques in general. Jensen also asserted that one reason for the survival of the TAT in clinical practice is this subjective validity. "While research has shown the TAT to have low reliability and negligible validity, many clinical psychologists continue to use it, apparently with some satisfaction" (Jensen, 1959, p. 313). Applying the rules of quantitative test validation to projective tests, however, is actually a misapplication. Trying to fit the TAT into a quantitative psychometric mode is akin to applying quantitative positivist paradigms to qualitative research such as ethnography and life histories. It's an unfair comparison, and it misses the point that projective tests are clinical instruments designed to help us understand people.

Projective assessment in sport

There is a prevailing trend in sport psychology to focus on observable and self-reported traits of athletes. According to Apitzsch (1995), trait theory and social learning theory have received the most attention in sport personality research, whereas, little attention has been given to psychodynamic theory. An advocate of psychodynamic therapy for athletes, Cratty (1989), suggested that the interpretation of athletes' dreams is useful in conjunction with projective tools to "assess such concepts as achievement needs in sports, aggressive reactions to frustrating sports situations, and perhaps anxiety in sporting contexts. Projective tools have existed for decades, but they were not designed with the specifics of sport in mind" (p. 37). The interpretation of projective tests, according to Cratty, may differ depending on the tester and test environment. Individuals may also fluctuate in their responses to visual stimuli depending on external factors during administration. These differences and fluctuations, however, are useful because they may provide a great deal of information for the clinician. As Cratty stated, "Projective tests give breadth and depth to clinical psychology. Fortunately, they are not dead" (p. 36). Although Cratty appears pleased that projective tests have not died, these tests have been in a serious slumber.

Although projective testing is rarely mentioned in the sport psychology literature, a few researchers have attempted to develop projective tests specifically for athletes (Bouet, 1970; Missoum & Laforestrie, 1985). Bouet, and Missoum and Laforestrie, are among the few sport researchers to show concerted interest in the development of projective tests for sport and the application of projective tests to an athlete population. Bouet developed a sport-specific version of the TAT, the Projective Sport Test (PST). In a similar study, Missoum and Laforestrie developed the Projective Test for Sportspersons (PTS) as a part of a psychological assessment battery adapted for athletes. The PST was also designed to aid in the selection and training of sports personnel. The Bouet study and Missoum and Laforestrie's test development provided evidence that in sport psychology there was at least "latent" interest in projective methods. Their efforts, however, were incomplete and neither drove research in the area to a point of applied use for practitioners, or to any significant academic journal publication. Bouet's PST is referenced in the *Directory of Psychological Tests in Sport and Exercise Sciences* (Ostrow, 1998) and stands as the only psychodynamically themed test of the 314 tests listed. Bouet's test and administration material, however, are not available.

There have been few serious attempts over the last 20 years to develop a projective test for use in a sport context. Although there are some prevailing opinions on the usefulness of a sport-specific projective test, a few sport psychology researchers have found projective tests to be, at least, useful means of gathering information. For example, Benzi and Michelini (1987) administered a series of projective tests with the aim of describing the psychological profiles of artistic roller skaters. Johnson, Hutton, and Johnson (1954) also attempted to describe and measure the personality traits of "champion" athletes using projective tests. Although these two examples demonstrate some applications of projective tests in sport, further examples of researchers using projective tests in sport settings are extremely rare. Often the criticism of using projective tests focuses on the belief that information is based on dated research and literature. In particular, the criticism that arises from sport researchers and clinicians is often sourced from information found outside of the sport literature. Projective tests are readily available as sources of complementary information but not as an all-encompassing answer to personality dynamics. Clinicians may expect too much from this one source rather than taking a projective test as part of a battery of personality assessment tools (a holistic view of assessment).

There remain differing opinions regarding the use of projective techniques in sport psychology service delivery (e.g., Cox, 2007; Cratty, 1989). These differences appear to revolve around two primary points: (a) the value of the instruments as tools in collecting information about athletes that is not easily obtained with self-report techniques, and (b) the psychometric adequacy of the instruments. In specific reference to point (b), opponents focus on psychometric inadequacies of projective techniques, and proponents focus on the potential usefulness of such instruments. Proponents also point out that projective techniques allow considerable freedom for clients to generate responses that provide information about their psychological constitutions.

Projective tests are attractive as clinical tools, but they are often difficult to score and interpret. Projective tests were, however, not originally designed or intended for quantitative studies.

Cratty (1989) suggested that they provide insightful information for psychologists and researchers, but are not suited for statistical inferences for athletic populations; rather, "they are tools for clinical psychologists and psychiatrists who are both intuitive and expert." (p. 36). Essentially, the use of projective tests gives practitioners a means to gain insight into a patient's innermost feelings and current conflicts and needs. Cox (2007) maintained a more traditional psychometric approach to sport psychology assessment. According to Cox, projective techniques are "unstructured," allowing people to be open and honest in their responses. He suggested that projective methods are not often used by sport psychologists, but that is not to say they should not be used. In reference to the TAT in particular, Cox suggested, "its validity and reliability are highly dependent upon the skill and training of the individual administering and interpreting the results" (p. 26). In the field of projective testing, problems of validation are particularly salient. Anzieu and Chabert (1960) maintained that projective tests, "do not explore a single variable, but describe an individual in terms of a dynamic system where the variables themselves are in inter-correlation" (p. 217). Projective tests do, however, provide an alternative to nomothetic approaches to assessment.

Although there has been widespread resistance to projective tests in sport psychology (and to some extent the psychological community as a whole) since the 1950s, the premise that projective tests use has limited application is questionable. According to Lazarus (1989), all assessment and treatment of human problems should be holistic, or totalistic, as exemplified by multimodal therapy. Multimodal therapy involves an assessment of the individual using the integration of different but interrelated modalities, or psychological parameters (e.g., behavior, physiology, cognition, interpersonal relationships, sensation, imagery, affect). In other words, the use of multiple assessment tools and divergent theoretical approaches when assessing an individual can only enhance the understanding of the individual's needs, motives, and drives.

In describing personality, psychologists have relied heavily on developing, administering, and interpreting personality tests and techniques. It is difficult to measure personality directly, but projective tests provide an opportunity for people to describe their feelings and thoughts about a range of stimuli. For example, someone might be shown a photo of an exhausted runner crossing a finishing line at the end of a track race and be asked to write about what is happening. A high-achieving, confident person might emphasize how the runner made an effort to achieve a goal, whereas a low-achiever might project feelings of disappointment at losing the race in a close finish. An athlete can answer any pencil and paper tests, or interview questions (objective/self-report methods) with verbal and conscious decisions. There may be, however, unconscious motives and conflicts that cannot be measured on self-report inventories. A well-trained and intuitive clinician may pick up the conflict through discussion, but projective methods can be effective techniques to assist the athlete in (unconsciously) sharing such information.

The Athlete Apperception Technique (AAT)

The construction of the Athlete Apperception Technique (AAT; Gibbs, Marchant, & Andersen, 2005) followed the developmental model of the TAT. An important element in the construction of any projective test is the creation of a unique and suitable image set that goes beyond a pictorial view of traditional family/associate relationships. The AAT represents a new technique that practitioners can use to dynamically produce an idiographic understanding of athletes' and coaches' characteristics, motivations, anxieties, and dreams.

The two specific aims of the development of the AAT were to: (a) create a sport image set using past expert-driven guidelines as a blueprint, and (b) investigate potential interpretive methods. The first aim was completed by following a process that included collating a large set of sport images, trialing images with a large and diverse sample of athletes, using experts to judge the appropriateness of images, engaging a professional artist to recreate images, and carrying out additional testing to achieve a small and workable image set. Following the progressive reduction of a large number of sport images, this work has culminated in three general image sets: (a) an adult image set (AAT), (b) a supplementary set (AAT-S), and (c) a children's set (AAT-C). The AAT includes 10 images that evoke a range of sport-related themes and latent stimulus properties such as relationships with other athletes and coaches, anxiety and arousal issues, concentration, leadership, team cohesion, preparation and routines, flow and optimal performance, confidence, motivation, attributional styles, and self-talk. The AAT-S (5 images) provides an option for sport psychologists to choose supplementary images that evoke specific themes such as apprehension over body contact, vulnerability, arousal-aggression, faith, boasting or gloating, and conflict. Between the AAT and the AAT-S, many themes can be evoked, and I believe future research will

Figure 11.1 Image 6 from the AAT.

demonstrate the depth and breadth of themes and stories that these images can produce. The AAT-C images (appropriate for children–adolescents) evoke stories reflecting sport development and barriers to sport involvement themes. Considerable data have been collected for each image set, but to date, exclusively with adults (Gibbs, 2006). Additional research on the AAT-C images with children is needed.

AAT image interpretation example

The following section is an example of a typical story response to an AAT image (Image 6; see Figure 11.1) followed by two forms of analysis: a sport psychology interpretation and a dynamic interpretation. It is important to note that the case example used here is somewhat limited because I had no life history or background information for the respondent (other than gender, age, and sport participation) and such limited knowledge, and lack of dialogue, greatly restricts attempts to interpret this respondent's stories. The interpretations of just one image (of 10 images administered) is presented here for illustrative purposes only.

The participant, Jenny, 19-year-old female basketball player, responded with this story for Image 6:

> This is a group of kids, and a couple of them look to be either brother or sister or very close friends. They look like they are about to play soccer. At the moment it looks like they are having trouble picking the teams. This is because they all don't agree it is fair. The boy with his leg on the ball is the oldest, and he has the responsibility of picking the next player, but he can't decide because the two players left don't look that good. One of the players to choose from is his sister, and he wants to pick her because he doesn't want her to be the last picked, but the problem is that she is shit at soccer. He knows he is the best player and wants to have the best team, but he has to be fair because the others look up to him. I think they won't end up playing as they won't be able to agree on teams. They will just have a kick around and go home for tea.

Sport psychology analysis and interpretation

Jenny described the boy with his foot on the ball as the oldest player who is feeling pressure from others to make a decision on team selection. The primary sport psychology theme for Image 6 is group cohesion, with secondary themes being leadership and team dynamics, confidence, inclusion–exclusion, and rejection. Jenny's story appears to be focused on these sport themes. Jenny indicated that the central character was feeling in a position of responsibility for making a decision that would satisfy all the other children. There was also some conflict for Jenny with the boy's responsibility of picking the next player and feeling that although the girl (the central character's sister) is not good at soccer, there is some pressure to choose her. Questions may be raised and discussed with Jenny regarding issues such as shouldering the responsibility for others' happiness, and why she interprets the central character's decision as important for his and others' enjoyment. Also interesting to examine with Jenny would be the conflict of wanting to "have the best team," "being fair," and pressure to choose his (her) sister even though "she is shit at soccer." Jenny's response integrated feelings of inclusion–exclusion, rejection, and a strong relationship with a sibling.

Dynamic interpretation

Jenny's story, at first read, seems to be about the older, dominant boy, but Jenny probably identifies with the sister who is "shit at soccer." Given themes evident in Jenny's responses to the other images, she likely identifies with the incompetent young girl who makes mistakes, who is a loser, but who wants to be chosen and have a go. The older competent boy may represent an actual older sibling, or if Jenny does not have an older sibling, then he may represent a fantasized older brother whom she wanted to have around and admire (like some of her other female friends probably had growing up). I did not have a family history on Jenny, so these thoughts are quite speculative. This story may be about wanting to be "chosen," and that desire holds all sorts of possibilities (to be loved, to be valued). Those needs to be chosen and to be valued are thwarted because she is not any good at what she wishes to be chosen for. Jenny may feel that worthiness, attention, and love are contingent on playing well, and she knows she does not have the skills that equate to that worthiness. The older, admired (he is the "best" player) brother is a positive authority figure, but he is caught up in the values of sport (he wants the best team) and cannot make a decision between brotherly protection (he does not want her to be the last one chosen) and being the best. I think the central theme of this story is that there is no solution for Jenny. She may see no way out of her desire for love and her perceived lack of the qualities (sport skills) that she believes will bring her to that special status of being "chosen" and loved. Jenny may be stuck with no way out. It all comes to naught, and then we just go home (for tea, in this story).

The above is a brief example of how someone with a psychodynamic orientation might begin to analyze Jenny's responses. For many in sport psychology, this territory would be rather foreign, and some might even say that this approach is really just spinning Freudian fairy tales. I would disagree and suggest that this approach may be helpful if an athlete, such as Jenny, wants to do some deeper exploration of her life, rather than learn some relaxation for her competition anxiety.

Thoughtful analysis and interpretation of AAT responses may provide an in-depth and idiographic understanding of athletes' characteristics, motivations, and anxieties, as well as assisting in the assessment of personality features. At the very least, discussion of AAT responses can be a useful way of initiating dialogue, engaging the client, and possibly unmasking issues that might otherwise lay dormant (latent personal issues, of which athletes may not be consciously aware, or which they may be reluctant to voice openly). Further, the use of the AAT may help sport psychologists identify and assess personality features relevant to performance and the health and wellbeing of athletes. The AAT should not be used as a stand-alone instrument, but rather in conjunction with other sources of information (e.g., questionnaires, intake interviews, ongoing service delivery encounters).

The AAT may also become a useful tool in educational settings, and academics in sport psychology programs may find it to be an instructive and challenging tool in the education of applied sport psychology students. The AAT may also assist educators in providing some balance, in regard to the dominance of paper and pencil self-report measures, when discussing personality assessment administration, analysis, and interpretation.

Conclusions

In athlete–sport psychologist encounters, the aim is not to judge athletes' personalities, but to explore and embrace their lives. When used judiciously, projective techniques may be of

---

Box 11.1

Take-home messages about projective testing

- Psychodynamic interpretations and formulations have begun to appear in the sport psychology literature.
- In sport psychology there appears to be an appreciation for diversity of research methodologies and other approaches beyond the dominant cognitive-behavioral paradigm.
- In the past 30 years, only a few researchers have attempted to develop projective tests specifically for athletes (e.g., the AAT).
- Projective tests are readily available as sources of complementary information but not as an all-encompassing answer of personality dynamics.
- Projective techniques are best suited as one part of a battery of personality assessment tools (a holistic view of assessment).
- Projective tests provide an alternative to nomothetic approaches to assessment.
- Projective methods can be effective as techniques to assist the athlete in (unconsciously) sharing sensitive personal information.
- The AAT may assist educators in providing some balance, in regard to the dominance of paper and pencil objective measures, when discussing personality assessment administration, analysis, and interpretation.

---

assistance in revealing athletes' worlds. The AAT, for example, is not a technique designed to predict success in sport, identify leadership skills, measure anxiety, or assign a range of values to explain personality. The AAT follows the developmental and theoretical guidelines of the TAT, and to that extent, is designed to assist sport psychologists in understanding their athletes' motives, attributions, wishes, dreams, conflicts, and desires, and in some ways may help practitioners better serve the people in their care. See Box 11.1 for the main take-home messages from this chapter.

References

Adcock, C. J. (1965). Thematic Apperception Test. In O. Buros (Ed.), *The sixth mental measurement yearbook* (pp. 533–535). Highland Park, NJ: Gryphon Press.

Andersen, M. B. (Ed.). (2005). *Sport psychology in practice.* Champaign, IL: Human Kinetics.

Anzieu, D., & Chabert, C. (1960). *Les méthodes projectives.* Paris: P.U.F.

Apitzsch, E. (1995). Psychodynamic theory of personality and sport performance. In S. J. H. Biddle (Ed.), *European perspectives on exercise and sport psychology* (pp. 111–127). Champaign, IL: Human Kinetics.

Benzi, M., & Michelini, L. (1987). Psychological aspects of a group of national team artistic roller skaters. *Medicina Dello Sport, 40,* 419–422.

Bouet, M. A. (1970). A projective test for sport participants. In G. S. Kenyon (Ed.), *Contemporary psychology of sport* (pp. 747–752). Chicago: Athletic Institute.

Cox, R. H. (2007). *Sport psychology: Concepts and applications* (6th ed.). New York: WCB/McGraw-Hill.

Cratty, B. J. (1989). *Psychology in contemporary sport* (3rd ed.). Englewood Cliffs, NJ: Prentice-Hall.

Eron, L. D. (1959). Thematic Apperception Test. In O. Buros (Ed.), *The fifth mental measurements yearbook* (pp. 306–310). Highland Park, NJ: Gryphon Press.

Gibbs, P. M. (2006). Development of the Athlete Apperception Technique (AAT). *Unpublished doctoral dissertation*, Victoria University, Melbourne, Australia.

Gibbs, P. M., Marchant, D., & Andersen, M. B. (2005). Development of the Athlete Apperception Technique (AAT). In T. Morris *et al.* (Eds.), *ISSP 11th World Congress of Sport Psychology: Promoting health and performance for life* (3 pages), CD-ROM. Sydney, NSW, Australia: International Society of Sport Psychology.

Jensen, A. R. (1959). Thematic Apperception Test. In O. Buros (Ed.), *The fifth mental measurements yearbook* (pp. 310–313). Highland Park, NJ: Gryphon Press.

Johnson, W. R., Hutton, D. C., & Johnson, G. B. (1954). Personality traits of some champion athletes as measured by two projective tests: Rorschach and H-T-P. *Research Quarterly, 25,* 484–485.

Lazarus, A. A. (1989). *The practice of multimodal therapy.* Baltimore: Johns Hopkins University Press.

Missoum, G., & Laforestrie, R. (1985). L'image de soi du sportif. *Bulletin de Psychologie, 38,* 909–917.

Morgan, C. D., & Murray, H. A. (1935). A method for investigating fantasies: The Thematic Apperception Test. *Archives of Neurology and Psychiatry, 34,* 289–306.

Murray, H. A. (1938). *Explorations in personality: A clinical and experimental study of fifty men of college age.* New York: Oxford University Press.

Ostrow, A. C. (1998). *Directory of psychological tests in the sport and exercise sciences* (2nd ed.). Morgantown, VA: Fitness Information Technology.

Rabin, A. I. (1986). Concerning projective techniques. In A. I. Rabin (Ed.), *Projective techniques for adolescents and children* (pp. 3–11). New York: Springer.

Rorschach, H. (1921). *Psychodiagnostik.* Bern, Switzerland: Bircher.

Rotter, J. B. (1946). Thematic apperception tests: Suggestions for administration and interpretation. *Journal of Personality, 15,* 70–92.

Strean, W. B., & Strean, H. S. (1998). Applying psychodynamic concepts to sport psychology practice. *The Sport Psychologist, 12,* 208–222.

12

Psychological assessment

Objective/self-report measures

Daryl B. Marchant

Test use in sport psychology practice can certainly be controversial. The widely discussed credulous versus skeptical debate (Morgan, 1980) regarding the efficacy of psychological test use in sport psychology had a significant effect on the field. Sport psychologists who were professionally active in the 1970s will recall the earnest and somewhat divisive discussions. Perhaps as a result of these discussions sport psychologists gravitated toward becoming either staunch advocates (i.e., credulous) or staunch adversaries (i.e., skeptical) of testing. For example, the credulous side believe that personality data derived from questionnaires are extremely useful in predicting success, whereas the skeptical side believe questionnaire data have little relevance and usefulness (cf. Morgan, 1980). Now, some 35 years after the fervor of the credulous–skeptical debate, we can reflect that both sides were using data derived from somewhat dubious methods based on current standards and arguments. Also, in reviewing the relevant literature from the period, there were many inflammatory comments and statements proposed from both the skeptical and the credulous.

Later, when *The Sport Psychologist* published two special issues on consultants working with professional and Olympic athletes (Roberts, 1989; Roberts & Halliwell, 1990), forthright opinions were again expressed that echoed the earlier debates. In more recent times, the development and psychometric evaluation of standardized tests in sport psychology has remained highly visible in the published literature, but the debate over the use of testing has waned. Nevertheless, readers who have entered the field since the early 1990s might be unaware of the credulous–skeptical debate. Sport psychologists who were active participants in the debate may still harbor attitudes about testing, informed largely from a sport psychology landscape that bears only some resemblance to that of the present time. I have no intention, however, of reviving debate about the relative merits of testing here, but rather to engender an applied practitioner perspective of test use and relevant considerations. Nevertheless, the credulous–skeptical debate provides an historical backdrop to current use and non-use of psychometric instruments in applied sport psychology service delivery.

Perhaps as a result of the fervor of earlier debate, the subsequent decades of psychological testing discussions have, in my view, retained an austere quality largely conducted within the walls of academia. Sport psychologists nowadays are sometimes asked to provide testing for talent identification and athlete profiling purposes. Some sport psychologists can be adamant about not using tests, or alternatively, professionally irresponsible in using tests without due diligence. There is certainly a delicate balance to be sought when using tests in applied contexts. I encourage practitioners who choose to adopt psychological testing as part of their services to reflect on the issues presented here. Graduate students and early-career applied sport psychologists should at least find some "grist for the mill" in answering practical questions that have largely been ignored in the published literature in terms of informing professional practice.

Testing times: reflections on test development and use in sport psychology

After years of research in sport psychology, the number of sport-specific tests available is now rather daunting (see Ostrow, 2002). Although the quantity of tests has grown substantially over the years, the quality of tests is varied. Even though the following list is deliberately cynical, experienced test users might recognize these types of instruments:

- *The pre-statistical revolution test* – Developed in an era when statistical methods were less sophisticated and the spotlight of examination less bright. These tests that were generally developed in good faith and based on accepted test construction practices have sometimes been found, after reexamination, to be fundamentally flawed.
- *The unsuccessful prototype test* – Developed specifically for doctoral studies and usually accompanied by the following lamentation, "If only I had known how difficult it would be to develop a test".
- *The model of propriety test* – Developed using modern standards in statistical analysis (e.g., confirmatory factor analysis). Yet the robust statistical indicators of such tests belie the questionable repetition of items that ensures excellent internal consistency at the expense of a decent representation of the construct, and in turn, diminishes the practical usefulness or external validity of the test.
- *The search for the Holy Grail test* – Developed to identify or unlock the psyche of sporting greatness. Fortunately, the lure to develop such tests generally hooks those from outside or on the fringes of sport psychology, and clearly reflects a degree of naïveté.
- *The open to deception test* – Developed for a specific purpose but with little thought given to social desirability issues and self-deception (where the respondents actually believe their positive self-reports) and impression management (where the respondent consciously obscures the truth). Currently, many test respondents are relatively savvy and test-item transparency is becoming a highly relevant issue depending on the type and purpose of the test.
- *The top-down theoretically derived test* – Developed with careful consideration of research findings but with little relevance, sensitivity, and hence, practical usefulness in consulting situations.

Admittedly, there are many well-constructed tests in sport psychology. Excuse the analogy, but at times it seems that test construction is akin to an uncleared minefield where treading carefully might simply not be enough. Many sport psychologists have experienced the scorched earth of developing tests that probably seemed like good ideas at the time: I certainly have! The point is that psychological testing is a serious business, and to extend the minefield metaphor, the soldiers might appreciate a little forewarning about the dangers that lie ahead. Clearly, sport psychology as a field needs to provide our "soldiers" (i.e., applied sport psychologists) with the most advanced and sophisticated weaponry. OK, enough of that metaphor!

Collectively, do we feel that the psychological tests available for use by sport psychologists represent best practice tools? The question needs to be asked because the expectations from elite sport organizations that contract sport psychologists are often quite lofty in terms of what they believe practitioners can deliver. Common questions sound something like, "what tests do you have that will enable us to identify the most promising athletes in advance or those with good character and attitude?" In this context of high expectations and athletes becoming better educated about mental skills and psychology generally, the instruments we use need to be of the highest quality. Historically, sport-psychology-specific tests have been developed in university settings, primarily for research purposes. Although a number of tests have been constructed that are adaptable to both research and applied settings, there is certainly scope for further development of tests that reflect the specific needs of applied sport psychology practitioners. The challenge is to develop tests that are market driven and remain reliable while being ecologically valid. Andersen, McCullagh, and Wilson (2007) have mounted a case for a stronger focus on calibrating tests against real-world behaviors. Arbitrary measurement of psychological constructs is relatively common in sport psychology and can be misleading (e.g., does a score of 4 on an anxiety test item imply an athlete is twice as anxious as an athlete scoring 2 on the same item?). Furthermore, and along the lines of Andersen *et al.*'s concerns, what do scores on psychological inventories tell us about real-world performance or behavior? Andersen *et al.* argued that when sport psychology tests are calibrated against real world behaviors, the metric or evidence is more trustworthy and hence legitimizes the testing enterprise. In reality, few psychometrics in sport psychology research and practice are calibrated against the real-world variables of interest (e.g., performance).

Understanding fundamentals: a psychometric mindset

Included in the training for most psychologists is a course or two on assessment/psychological testing. These courses are invaluable in providing foundations about the broader parent discipline of psychological assessment, and specifically, test development, administration, and reporting. Before moving to developing a "psychometric mindset," it would be remiss not to recall that quantitative psychological tests represent just one class of technique in psychological assessment. Well-rounded assessments involve multiple sources of information such as interviewing and observation in addition to psychological testing. Some psychologists (e.g., Lines, Schwartzman, Tkachuk, Leslie-Toogood, & Martin, 1999) advocate the use of sport-specific behavioral assessments such as a type of checklist that reflects the specific technical language of the sport (e.g., on backstroke: "Head still," "Hips high").

Although there are thousands of psychological tests and hundreds of sport psychology tests available, many of them are unsuitable for applied settings. The limitations of tests are many and varied, but can generally be traced back to limitations in reliability or validity. Familiarity with the foundations of psychometrics assists sport psychologists in making informed choices about which tests to use, for what populations, and in what contexts. Because tests do not get published if they are not reliable, test developers often pay close attention to assessing and demonstrating reliability. Beyond basic inter-item and test-retest reliability, various forms of validity testing such as factor analyses (or principle components

113

analysis) are minimum requirements. From a psychometric viewpoint, the current gold standard in terms of construct validity is confirmatory factor analyses. Although construct validity is well catered for with factor analytic techniques, test developers are sometimes not as diligent about the many other aspects of validity that require attention.

Few tests are initially published with systematic attention and coverage of: content validity, face validity, convergent/discriminant validity, criterion/predictive validity, and particularly internal/external validity. Yet from a practitioner's perspective, validity questions are central. For example, does the test measure a characteristic that will carry over or transfer to the sports context? It may be years before all the relevant psychometric properties of a test have been examined. Tests that stay in vogue are characterized by some of the following features: resilience to peer-reviewed scrutiny; clearly defined uses and limitations; adequate administration, standardized scoring, and accepted reporting procedures; and, to a lesser extent, attractive presentation. Irrespective of whether a research or applied sport psychology career path is pursued, it is worth periodically scanning the latest psychometric studies regularly published in the sport psychology journals. Questions worth considering include: has the test been peer reviewed and published in a reputable journal? Beyond publication, how widely is the test used by other sport psychologists in research and/or applied work? Have other sport psychologists, apart from the test developers, published research pertaining to the psychometric qualities of the test? In what specific context could this test be useful in consulting?

Watch your step: suggestions for responsible and effective test use

Understanding the fundamentals of psychometric testing provides a reasonable starting point for the responsible use of tests in applied contexts. At this point, however, we are merely rounding first base. Before requesting that clients, who are generally coaches and athletes, take up their valuable time completing a psychological test, a number of issues require forward thinking. For efficiency, these issues are presented here as a series of questions akin to a checklist.

- First and foremost, for what particular purpose is the test designed?
- Is the test only available to registered psychologists, or is it in the public domain?
- Is there a cost associated with using the test, and what are the copyright limitations?
- Is there available normative data for target populations?
- What sport psychology colleagues (e.g., supervisor, professional mentor) have used the test and can provide you with professional guidance if necessary?
- What are the limitations of the test? Even the so-called gold-standard tests have limitations with which users need to be familiar.
- Have you completed the test yourself?
- Are you familiar with the nuances of the test and the administrative procedures?
- How should the test be introduced to the client?
- What type of reporting or feedback are you going to provide to the client?

Choosing tests: start with the end in mind

I expect that most readers are familiar with the rationale that for researchers the objective is to find the best fit between the research problem and the method chosen to investigate the research question (i.e., elegant design). Similarly, in applied sport psychology contexts, tests/inventories/questionnaires are adopted with an expectation of better understanding a person, group, or presenting issue. By commencing with a clear view of what will be achieved by using a psychological test, we are at least envisaging the complete process from start to finish. Intentionality is the key. A broad overview of potential reasons for testing is a useful starting point. Possibly the most recognized reasons for using tests in applied settings is to measure susceptibilities, characteristics, tendencies, abilities, traits, states, and styles in relation to performance, training, mental skills, and topics frequently associated with applied sport psychology.

The term "diagnostic test" is broadly relevant to all tests but also carries clinical connotations. Making a clinical diagnosis of psychopathology may not necessarily form a substantial part of service delivery, or be part of how some sport psychologists conceptualize their work. Nevertheless, there are numerous studies that have demonstrated that significant psychopathology is present within athletic populations (see Brewer & Petrie, 2002). Irrespective of whether an applied sport psychologist has completed substantial clinical training, there is a professional responsibility to at least be familiar with prevalent clinical issues (e.g., personality disorders, eating disorders, substance abuse, anxiety disorders) and make referrals to suitably trained colleagues (e.g., clinically trained sport psychologist, clinical psychologist) if needed. We have moved well beyond the era of the educational sport psychologists who absent themselves from professional responsibilities regarding clinical recognition or awareness based on a limited clinical training. For identifying maladaptive behaviors and mental disorder symptomatology, a range of psychological tests are available that can be of assistance. For example, the Beck Depression Inventory (BDI-11; Beck, Steer, & Brown, 1996), a 21-item scale, guides respondents through an assessment of depressive symptoms over the past two weeks; the Eating Attitudes Test (EAT; Garner & Garfinkel, 1979), a 26-item scale, is a useful screening tool for clients who present with possible pathogenic eating; the Revised NEO Personality Inventory (NEO-PI-R; Costa & McCrae, 1992), despite primarily being designed to measure the big five personality traits, has a useful feature whereby the professional report generated with the NEO-PI-R software also includes a clinical diagnostic section that quantifies the likelihood of personality disorders (i.e., an Axis II diagnosis from the *Diagnostic and Statistical Manual of Mental Disorders-IV-TR* [American Psychiatric Association, 2000]). Where clients are shown to have an elevated pre-disposition to a particular personality disorder, the clinician could choose to carry out a follow-up assessment using a scale such as the Personality Disorder Interview-IV (PDI-IV; Widiger, Mangine, Corbitt, Ellis, & Thomas, 1995), which represents an in-depth clinical guide to assessing 10 personality disorders. Applied sport psychologists, depending on their level of clinical training and competence, will normally need to make judicious decisions about whether to refer or treat clients who present with clinical issues.

A great place to start: tests for developing insight

Postgraduate students often ask questions about psychometrics and express an interest in gaining proficiency in administering, scoring, and interpreting psychological tests. Apart from designated university psychometrics courses that students are generally required to complete as part of their training, how do students gain experience in psychometrics? Given the (often healthy) skepticism still prevailing in the field of sport psychology regarding test use, there is certainly value in working with tests to establish your own view of whether psychological tests are potentially useful (or not useful) in your professional practice or research. Using selected tests and forming your own opinions is similar to reading the original primary work of Freud before forming opinions, as opposed to relying on secondary sources. A brief sketch of how to start will probably include, at the least, the following steps: (a) seeking supervision from an experienced psychologist; (b) reading the relevant current literature; (c) networking and talking to colleagues; (d) researching what tests are sometimes used with what populations and with what results; (e) establishing a clear purpose for administering a test while bearing in mind that tests are simply one assessment tool; (f) familiarizing yourself with local guidelines for ethical test use; (g) working with the client (e.g., consultation) or participant (research) to educate them on test use and establishing the reasons for testing, likely pros and cons, and responding to client questions; (g) administering, scoring, and interpreting the test; (h) possibly writing/producing a client report and debriefing the client; and finally, and importantly, (i) establishing a "where to from here?" That is, how will the test results inform ongoing work or benefit the client? See also Beckmann and Kellmann (2003) for a number of additional suggestions and perspectives on procedures for test use and feedback to clients.

A test use example: The NEO-PI-R

One of the few tests that I have regularly used with clients is the longer version of the NEO-PI-R (Costa & McCrae, 1992), which includes scales that measure susceptibility to anxiety, depression, and angry hostility within the neuroticism (emotional stability) factor. The NEO-PI-R is widely cited in the psychological literature. It has sound psychometric properties and is based on the modern 5-factor personality standard. The NEO-PI-R is not sport-specific and primarily serves three purposes within the sport psychology consultation context. First, it can be used to assist in establishing a relatively quick assessment into 30 personality characteristics and may facilitate initial intakes and help me come up to speed with the type of person with whom I am working. Second, its use may enhance insight by providing information that clients expand on in counseling sessions, and it may serve as a self-narrative primer. Third, although the NEO-PI-R is not sport-specific, it does provide a window into potential areas for future exploration and interventions and almost endless lines of behavioral inquiry that might later be observed, discussed, or connected to athletes' sport and exercise involvement.

Another advantage of having an athlete complete a 5-factor personality measure such as the NEO-PI-R is the potential to better identify strengths and weaknesses in mental skills. For example, with some experience, combination scores on particular factors provide valuable clues that can then be followed up in further investigation in one-on-one work. A *high anxiety–high self-consciousness* combination might indicate a possible susceptibility to choking. A *high angry hostility–low deliberation–high impulsiveness* combination might indicate impulse control issues. *High fantasy* scores might indicate acuity for imagery. A *high order–high achievement striving–high self-discipline* combination might indicate perfectionist tendencies. The repeated use of a personality instrument, combined with working directly with athletes for an extended period, provides opportunities to test hunches about the potentially endless connections between personality profiles and observations of everyday behavior. In my consulting work with professional Australian Football League (AFL) players, I have found the NEO-PI-R to be exceptionally useful in the early stages of a consulting contract with AFL squads, which comprise close to 60 athletes and approximately five full-time coaches. Apart from enabling the consultant to identify potential clinical issues, a NEO-PI-R profile will likely represent a useful personality overview of individuals with whom consultants will potentially be working over an extended period. Moreover, debriefs with clients, including access to their NEO-PI-R report, largely confirm in their verbal feedback that they find their personality profiles to be accurate. Occasionally, clients are almost astounded at how accurate they feel the reports are, and this feedback provides an opportunity to demystify the process by emphasizing that they are essentially "describing themselves through a questionnaire." I must stress, however, that much of the above is contextual and based on personal experience, albeit over a 15-year period.

Debriefing with the client, if carried out sensitively, can improve the athlete's self-awareness and insight. Goleman (1998) stated, "Self-awareness serves as an inner barometer, gauging whether what we are doing (or are about to do) is, indeed, worthwhile" (pp. 57–58). Giges (2004) encapsulated the interplay between self-awareness, sporting performance, and behavior:

> Self-awareness involves knowledge of one's own behavior, thoughts, feelings, needs, and wants ... A major advantage of such knowledge is an increased ability to be in charge of oneself, enabling individuals to be less distracted by their own feelings, wants, and values and better able to respond to others effectively. Self-awareness can also lead to improvement in sport performance. Without it, feelings can surface in unexpected or undesired ways. Consider coaches who ... to avoid feeling guilty about selecting poor strategy blame their athletes for not trying hard enough. Awareness of guilt might be difficult, however, for coaches who are unable to make an internal attribution and accept responsibility for their mistakes.
>
> (p. 432)

Cautionary tales: indentations, potholes, and craters

Mistakes in the use of psychological testing can have relatively dire consequences. There isn't the space here to provide an exhaustive list of potential pitfalls, but I will introduce a range of considerations that might be described as indentations (e.g., misinterpretation of an item) to craters (e.g., aggrieved clients angrily confronting a psychologist about their "negative profiles"). Potential pitfalls in using psychological tests generally fall into six broad categories: (a) choice of the test; (b) psychometric properties of tests; (c) administration and scoring errors; (d) interpretation errors; (e) reporting errors; and (f) safe-guarding profiles, scores, results, and associated reports. Choice errors can be avoided by being thorough in: assessing the psychometrics properties, determining the theoretical basis or construct validity of a test (not necessarily taking test developers' promotional material or test retailers' claims at face value), trialing tests with limited samples, investigating (where possible) tests within a domain that represents current best practice, subscribing to catalogs from reputable test providers, avoiding tests that are primarily geared for research purposes, and using other forms of assessment if you are uncomfortable with the quality of tests in a particular domain. Errors relating to psychometrics have been touched on earlier. To reiterate, however, although reliability is critical, applied sport psychologists are equally interested in various forms of validity. Administration and scoring errors are annoying because they can often be traced back to human error. Interpretation errors can result from a lack of in-depth knowledge about the test, under-interpretation/over-interpretation, limited sensitivity to sport context variables, poor debriefing skills, and misinterpretations from the client. In applied

117

settings, test use is unlikely to be a straight two-way exchange. Applied sport psychology environments are generally complex in delineating ownership of tests materials and best-practice procedures.

Understandably many sport psychologists are concerned about the ethical ramifications, the lack of predictive power of many tests, and the practical considerations in relation to athlete recruitment. Professional sporting organizations, will, however, argue their right to use psychological assessment tools to assist in minimizing risks, especially in terms of potential absorption of resources and the financial ramifications of poor selection decisions. Although familiarity with professionally drafted guidelines and procedures for test use is helpful, the specifics vary depending on the governing structure, local history of psychological accreditation, training requirements, psychological registration, and governing bodies. Furthermore, sport psychologists will inevitably be faced with challenging practical dilemmas and vexing questions that guidelines may not necessarily directly address.

Conclusions

In writing this chapter, I am acutely aware that we are touching on issues that warrant a more detailed and comprehensive discussion. Even with the sheer number of tests available, there is a notable absence of references to specific tests used in real-world consulting apart from a few examples showing how tests might be used for a particular purpose. The absence of real-world references is a reflection of the scarcity of dedicated contributions geared specifically to test use in applied settings. Perhaps this limited available literature on specific issues confronting applied sport psychologists who are contemplating using tests harks back to the history of tests in sport psychology being controversial. Irrespective of the issues raised here, psychological tests are merely tools that have the capacity to add both depth and breadth to assessment practices when used judiciously. Sport psychology remains a niche field and psychological testing a small sub-discipline. At present, the published sport psychology literature, in my view, is skewed toward psychological tests from an academic or researcher perspective. You may have heard the phrase "the psychologist is the instrument." Thus, "the instruments might be more instrumental if better instruments were at their disposal." See Box 12.1 for the main take-home messages from this chapter.

Box 12.1

Take-home messages about psychometric testing

- ▪ Attitudes to psychological testing in sport psychology have historically been informed by the credulous–skeptical debate.
- ▪ The quality of psychological tests developed in sport psychology varies considerably. Practitioners who intend to use tests are duty bound to choose psychometrically robust tests.
- ▪ The many challenges of using psychological tests and inventories responsibly should not be underestimated. Psychologists will often cite anecdotes or case examples of where test use has gone awry.

- Sport psychologists will often be particularly interested in evidence of external validity and predictive validity when choosing tests in applied practice.
- Well designed psychological tests can provide extremely useful information about clients' personalities, abilities, tendencies, and traits. Being clear about the purpose of using a test(s) in the early stages of a consultation is important for both the psychologist and the client.
- When using tests, careful attention to administration and scoring procedures, safe keeping of data, and report writing can circumvent potential problems.
- It is unlikely that psychologists will desist from continuing to employ tests and inventories. The challenge for the field of sport psychology is to develop high quality tests. That is, psychometrically sound tests that are *tested* for their own internal qualities.

References

American Psychiatric Association (2000). *Diagnostic and statistical manual of mental disorders* (4th ed., text Rev.). Washington, DC: American Psychiatric Association.

Andersen, M. B., McCullagh, P., & Wilson, G. J. (2007). But what do the numbers really tell us? Arbitrary metrics and effect size reporting in sport psychology research. *Journal of Sport & Exercise Psychology, 29*, 664–672.

Beck, A. T., Steer, R. A., & Brown, G. K. (1996). *Beck Depression Inventory–II*. San Antonio, TX: Psychological Corporation.

Beckmann, J., & Kellmann, M. (2003). Procedures and principles of sport psychological assessment. *The Sport Psychologist, 17*, 338–350.

Brewer, B., & Petrie, T. (2002). Psychopathology in sport and exercise. In J. L. Van Raalte & B. W. Brewer (Eds.), *Exploring sport and exercise psychology* (2nd ed., pp. 307–324) Washington, DC: American Psychological Association.

Costa, P. T., & McCrae, R. R. (1992). *Revised NEO Personality Inventory (NEO-PI-R) and NEO five-factor inventory (NEO-FFI): Professional manual*. Odessa, FL: Psychological Assessment Resources.

Garner, D. M., & Garfinkel, P. E. (1979). The Eating Attitudes Test: An index of the symptoms of anorexia nervosa. *Psychological Medicine, 9*, 273–279.

Giges, B. (2004). Helping coaches meet their own needs: Challenges for the sport psychology consultant. *The Sport Psychologist, 18*, 430–444.

Goleman, D. (1998). *Working with emotional intelligence*. London: Bloomsbury.

Lines, J. B., Schwartzman, L., Tkachuk, G. A., Leslie-Toogood, S. A., & Martin, G. A. (1999). Behavioral assessment in sport psychology consulting: Applications to swimming and basketball. *Journal of Sport Behavior, 22*, 558–569.

Morgan, W. P. (1980). Sport personology: The credulous–skeptical argument in perspective. In W. F. Straub (Ed.), *Sport psychology: An analysis of athlete behavior* (2nd ed., pp. 218–227). Ithaca, NY: Movement.

Ostrow, A. C. (Ed.). (2002). *Directory of psychological tests in the sport and exercise sciences* (2nd ed.). Morgantown, WV: Fitness Information Technology.

Roberts, G. C. (Ed.). (1989). Delivering sport psychology services to the 1988 Olympic athletes [Special Issue]. *The Sport Psychologist, 3*(4).

Roberts, G. C., & Halliwell, W. (Eds.). (1990). Working with professional athletes [Special Issue]. *The Sport Psychologist, 4*(4).

Widiger, T. A., Mangine, S., Corbitt, E. M., Ellis, C. G., & Thomas, G. V. (1995). *Personality Disorder Interview–IV: A semistructured interview for the assessment of personality disorders. Professional manual*. Odessa, FL: Psychological Assessment Resources.

Section III

Theoretical and therapeutic models

13

The humanistic/person-centered theoretical model

Barbara Walker

A humanistic model is one that emphasizes the personal worth and dignity of all people. Happiness and a person's quest for happiness are important themes. A pivotal notion among humanistic psychologists is that human beings continue to develop throughout their entire lives (Jacobsen, 2007).

The humanistic psychologist, Carl Rogers, formulated a model and a psychotherapy that centers on happiness and the self. He saw the goal of the human being as becoming a "fully functioning person" (Rogers, 1961). The fully functioning person is engaged in a process of change, and is not characterized by having achieved a certain stable, lasting condition. The primary therapeutic goal is for the client to become less defensive and more receptive to the experiences of inner and outer life. A secondary goal is for the client to achieve an increased ability to live in the here and now. A basic tenet is that what one does in the future grows out of the experience of what one does in the present. A third goal is that one develops an increased confidence in one's self, so that one can increasingly base decisions and actions on what immediately feels right (Jacobsen, 2007).

In the 1940s and 1950s, Rogers developed person-centered therapy (PCT), which is also known as client-centered therapy or Rogerian psychotherapy. The basic elements of PCT, for the therapist, involve showing genuineness, authenticity, empathy, and unconditional positive regard toward clients. By taking this stance, the therapist creates a supportive, nonjudgmental environment in which the practitioner encourages clients to reach their full potential (Bruno, 1977). Roger's humanistic theory and model for psychotherapy focus on the client as the agent for self-change. A foundation of the person-centered approach is the self-authority and self-determination of the client. It is the client who directs and orchestrates the process and progress of therapy.

Rogers is sometimes called a self-theorist. He believed that the self is constantly evolving and that people have free will and the ability to make choices that are growth-enhancing. He also believed in the concept, similar to other humanistic theorists, of self-actualization. Self-actualization is based on the assumption that there is an internal, biological force to develop one's capacities and talents to the fullest. The individual's central motivation is to learn and grow. Growth occurs when individuals confront problems, struggle to master them, and through that struggle develop new aspects of their skills, capacities, and views

123

about life. Life, therefore, is an endless process of creatively moving forward, even if only in small ways (Robbins, 2007).

Rogers looked at the self in terms of the "ideal self" versus the "real self." The ideal self is the person one would like to be; the real or actual self is who one currently perceives oneself to be. When one is self-actualized, there is congruence (i.e., harmony or agreement) between the real and the ideal selves. One has become the self one wants to be. There is congruence for an athlete who is working hard every day, following prescribed physical training, sleeping well, eating well, following a sound mental routine, and feeling that the place the athlete is in right now is where the person needs and wants to be. Rogers also described a second kind of congruence. This congruence is between the actual self and experience. The experiences in one's life should fit with the type of person one thinks one is. An example of this type of congruence would be, "If I work hard, I will obtain good results. If I think I am important and valuable as a person, good things will happen to me within my life experience." Individuals feel incongruence as negative and detrimental experiences, and consider it something to avoid. When someone is experiencing incongruence, it means there is a break-down in one's unitary sense of self. Incongruence may lead to anxiety, whether the incongruence is between ideal and real selves or between actual self and experience. For example, if athletes are naturally mild-mannered or passive, but need to be aggressive to participate in their sports, there may be incongruity. Many athletes may quit their sports during times of incongruence. Rogers believed we defend ourselves against incongruence or even the perceptions of incongruence; we are always trying to seek ways to become congruent.

When athletes are experiencing congruence, they trust themselves and their training. They are motivated and have a desire to compete, and believe that they can continue to grow and improve. With incongruence, they may experience low confidence, early stages of burnout, loss of motivation, lack of improvement, an inability to be able to perform well at competitions, and either performance anxiety or choking. Athletes would be sensing differences between their current selves and experiences and of needing to move closer toward their ideal selves. The key idea is that consciously or subconsciously, athletes know they are not performing to their ideal or optimal performance states.

One example of experiencing incongruence is Ivan, a professional boxer. He had a history of physical abuse and violence in his childhood by his father. As a result of this abusive childhood, Ivan felt that he had so much rage and anger within him, that "competing in this sport was quite easy" for him. Ivan stated that it felt natural to unleash this anger onto his opponents during competition, which served him well in his sport. After competing for a number of years, he fell in love, got married, and started a family. He was cognizant of his more positive emotions, and his ability to feel love and care for others. With these new-found feelings, he had difficulty competing at the same intensity as he had in the past, but was still interested in boxing, not only because he still enjoyed it, but because it was his livelihood. He began consulting with me to help him get back in the ring, and he wanted to find a way "to tap back into his anger," which he believed was the reason for his past success. His love for his family literally felt incompatible with competing, and he felt incongruent within himself. He recognized that he did not want to go back to carrying around anger most of the time, but he didn't know how to move forward. Over a period of time, after establishing a genuine trusting rapport and good relationship with each other, we were able to develop a type of pre-competitive routine that allowed him to create a level of intensity similar to the energy he had when he was angry, but without the negative emotions, to compete again successfully at a high level. Seeing himself in a healthier place had now allowed him to establish authentic congruence.

124

Another example of incongruence is a young professional golfer, named Ryan. Ryan was performing well in his sport and climbing his way up the ranks. One afternoon while competing in a high-level tournament, he found himself doing so well that his name was on the leader board. His first thought, as he told me later, was "I'm not as good as these guys." It is not hard to guess what happened next. The incongruence he was experiencing created anxiety. Rather than believing in himself and his capabilities and feeling he deserved to compete at the top level of this tournament, his confidence diminished, along with his level of play. Never recovering from his incongruent thinking, he continued to feel anxiety and tension throughout the remainder of the round. His scores went up dramatically, and he performed poorly throughout the rest of the tournament, reinforcing to him that he truly was not as good as his competitors.

Core theoretical concepts

Within person-centered therapy, for change to occur in a therapeutic relationship, Rogers (1959) believed that six necessary and sufficient conditions are needed.

Therapist–client psychological contact

A relationship between the client and the therapist must exist, and either person's perceptions of the other are important. One central consideration is the understanding that many athletes have not experienced working with a therapist and may have preconceived notions that need to be demystified. Establishing rapport with an athlete is early core business. A therapist does not have to have experience playing the sport of the athlete(s) or that of actually being an athlete, but demonstrating an interest in, and understanding of, the sport is foundational to the extension of trust from the individual to the therapist that creates the groundwork for the therapeutic relationship.

In addition to establishing rapport, the therapist tries to meet individual athletes where they present, from their own experiences. A major goal is to treat all athletes as individuals and to recognize that they bring their own life experiences, their varying skills in communicating with others, and their abilities to identify and verbalize their own thoughts and feelings.

Client incongruence or vulnerability

Incongruence often exists between clients' experiences and awareness. Furthermore, clients are vulnerable to anxiety, which motivates them to stay in the relationship with the therapist. Administering pencil and paper assessments to athletes to help both parties understand where gaps may be in experiences and awareness may be useful especially with taciturn clients. It is my experience that the majority of athletes who consult sport psychologists recognize that their problems are that they are not getting the results they once had, that they have lost their confidence, or that they have been told by others that their problems are "mental." Giving them assessments related to sport performance and then asking specific questions that relate to their subjective experiences helps them evaluate their strengths and weaknesses and see areas for improvement. Rather than thinking they are head cases, they now know what specific situations make them tense or when they have lost their confidence. We then work on the skills necessary to increase their performances. This process allows each athlete to be in control of their own performances by working on specific objectives, similar to them working on their physical skills.

Therapist congruence or genuineness

Therapists using a humanistic model are congruent within therapeutic relationships. Therapists are deeply themselves. They are not acting, and can draw from personal experiences (self-disclosure) to facilitate the relationships. Demonstrating genuineness is a starting point for change to occur. If therapists are unclear about, or are simply unfamiliar with, the jargon and sport-specific experiences athletes are discussing, they need to ask questions to gain clarity. I have had athletes draw examples of plays or provide websites that would be helpful for me to better understand their sports. In my experience, athletes have appreciated my interest in understanding their sports, especially when they know the objective is to help their performances.

Therapist Unconditional Positive Regard (UPR)

Person-centered therapists accept clients unconditionally, without judgment. This acceptance facilitates increased self-regard in clients, because they can begin to become aware of experiences in which their views of self-worth were distorted by the influences of others. Depending on the level of competition (e.g., junior, sub-elite, elite) and the strength of perceived social support, athletes rarely have opportunities to discuss personal, and sometimes painful, issues openly. Discussing how they feel about themselves or their roles in their sports is often perceived by athletes as too risky, especially if their thoughts are unpleasant. These thoughts may clash with the perceptions others may have of them, including fans, coaches, teammates, spouses, parents, and agents. Due to self-induced or perceived external pressures, athletes may feel they will let down or disappoint coaches, teammates, or parents if they express their thoughts or feelings. Furthermore, there is a perceived fear of current or future contracts being put at risk should sponsors become aware of their sport-related anxieties. Therapists' abilities to be nonjudgmental, allowing conversations to happen without negative consequences, can prove extremely helpful for athletes to sort out feelings and career/life paths in a psychologically safe place.

One example demonstrating UPR is a middle-aged, married, competitive recreational athlete named John who came to see me for performance enhancement for golf. I gained his trust after a number of sessions, and he began to share that he was gay and stated that he had never discussed his sexuality with anyone before. He felt he could not live in his current situation any longer, but did not know what step to take to move forward. Over the next few months, because of the establishment of a comfortable, safe, nonjudgmental place to explore his feelings, John was able to discuss his issues with his wife and family and made arrangements for separation. Because John sensed nonjudgment and unconditional positive regard from me, he felt sufficiently comfortable and safe within the relationship to share an incongruent and uncomfortable part of his life. A therapist with UPR sends the message to clients that all that is shared will be cared for, in a respectful, nonjudgmental manner. The UPR stance helps open many closet doors.

Therapist empathic understanding

Therapists experience empathic understanding of clients' internal frames of reference. Accurate empathy on the part of therapists helps clients believe in the therapists' unconditional love for them. Acknowledging understanding of the client through body language such as eye contact, leaning forward, and nodding one's head, or through sincere phrases such as "I can understand why you are feeling this way," or "I can see why … " are excellent ways to demonstrate empathy.

Client perceptions

Clients perceive, to lesser or greater degrees, therapists' UPR and empathic understanding. Therapists will see that athletes are perceiving the therapists' understanding by watching the clients' body language as well as the depth and flow of their conversations. Athletes will appear to become more relaxed, make better eye contact, move closer to the therapist, and demonstrate more open body language. The athletes may direct the consultations, revealing and discussing information openly rather than the therapists asking many questions.

Another example of providing UPR is Sam, a professional motocross athlete, struggling over his fear of injury while competing. Referred to me by his spouse, he had never seen a psychologist before. He presented cautiously and was initially guarded. For Sam, it was important to not jump into traditional sport psychology interventions immediately, but to build rapport and demonstrate patience and understanding. He was assured of confidentiality, and rapport was established quickly. His eagerness to share knowledge of his sport with me provided an avenue for trust, allowing the opportunity to move into the therapeutic process. He had been in the sport for many years. As he was getting older and had children, he had developed a fear of getting injured, resulting in being unfocused and worried prior to and between his events. Although he had never been seriously injured, he knew several friends who had. Even though he had a history of being able to produce the intensity and focus needed to perform well in his sport, he now approached his races tentatively. His friends were also his competitors, so he did not feel comfortable discussing his thoughts and feelings with them, assuming it would give them an edge, as well as make himself appear weak. He also felt in jeopardy of losing his sponsorship. Discussions involved his preconceived beliefs about age (being too old to continue to perform at a national level), that he had thus far "pressed his luck," and it being just a matter of time before he would be seriously injured. We established his overall goals, as well as pre-competition routines that included focus and intensity issues. Demonstrating patience, empathy, and understanding allowed Sam's confidence to increase dramatically, and he now feels much more in charge of his ability to compete.

As individuals are accepted and valued, they tend to develop caring attitudes toward themselves. As individuals are empathically heard, it becomes possible for them to listen more accurately to the flow of inner experiences. As people grow to understand themselves, the self becomes more congruent with their experiences. The individuals thus become more real, more genuine to themselves and to others. These tendencies, the reciprocal of the therapist's attitudes, enable the clients to be effective self-growth enhancers. There is greater freedom to be the true, whole individuals they desire to be (Rogers, 1980).

Additional applications of the model to athletes: more case examples

Rosa was an athlete who was deemed gifted in tennis at an early age. Her sister had special talents in gymnastics. Rosa's family decided Rosa could benefit from being enrolled in an elite year-round program out of state to increase her skills in tennis. Similarly, her sister and mother also moved to another state to allow her sister to fulfill her dreams in gymnastics. During Rosa's few years at the academy, the owner of the program told her that she had the capability to become a world-class tennis player. This information spurred her on, and she worked hard to achieve this dream. Her focus was to become a professional player. About six months after she began her training at the academy, Rosa was not playing well and felt she was not being given the attention she had received previously. During this same period of time, she overheard the owner telling a newer player that she also had the capability of becoming a world-class tennis player. Rosa began to develop a sense of mistrust toward the owner, wondering whether he told this story to all his athletes. Her self-esteem began to plummet, along with her play. Showing significant signs of burnout and depression, she verbalized to her parents the desire to quit her sport. Her parents were deeply concerned about her well-being and decided to move her from the academy to the city where her mother and sister lived. A psychiatrist, who thought that Rosa was depressed and anxious, referred the family to me. Rosa presented with a quiet, dejected, flat affect, and exhibited low self-esteem with significant symptoms of burnout from tennis. Knowing she had talent in the sport, the family was not ready to stop considering the possibility of her playing in the future.

With the time and space needed to work through the perceived betrayal she experienced at the academy, Rosa created a new life plan, accepted that she may not play professionally, and was able to balance her time with friends, family, academics, and tennis. She had the luxury of time and family support to help her find a comfortable path. She currently has a full sport scholarship at a highly ranked university.

The therapeutic conditions in this case were met. Rosa and I established a therapeutic relationship early on that continued solidly throughout the consultation. Rosa demonstrated incongruence/vulnerability initially, but through genuineness and UPR, she trusted me and the process, allowing her to work through her issues. In this case, family support was critical, and worked in her favor.

Most parents of adolescents in my practice are concerned that they may place undue pressure on their children to succeed or continue in their sports. I am asked to explore within sessions whether there is a feeling of pressure coming from one or both parents. If indicated, we discuss this issue collectively to alleviate any misperceptions. In some cases parents are unaware of this pressure. Their vision is myopic, and they lose site of the bigger picture as it applies to their children as whole people. When a situation like this one occurs, it is difficult to meet the therapeutic needs of the client, regardless of the client's recognition of feelings of discomfort or incongruence. For example, a client named Annie was a high school athlete and played for an elite soccer club. The club had the reputation of producing Division I (i.e., highest level of U.S. university competition) collegiate scholarship athletes. Annie's father brought her in because he felt that she was not aggressive enough on the field. He believed that for her to stay on the team, and to eventually obtain a full scholarship, it would be essential for her to be more aggressive. While her father was in the session, she was quiet, but agreeable to us working together on the presenting issues. Over a period of sessions without her father present, she expressed experiencing a great deal of stress, and said she no longer wanted to play with her particular club or at that level of soccer. She was not ready to discuss this problem openly with her parents because, from her perspective, she knew quitting was not an option: her father was determined that her sport was "*their* path to college." Her mother came into one of the sessions, and when Annie explained how she felt; it was clear that communicating this information caused tension for her mother. Annie's mother stated that they could not discuss this issue with her father.

Sometimes parents build their expectations too high and seem to lose perspective. They invest time, money, energy, and sometimes subconsciously their own self-worth into their children's futures. They seem to forget the big picture and the importance of their children and their happiness. What may have started as positive support turns into pressure. In this particular case, because the father did not see results quickly enough with his goal of increasing his daughter's aggression on the field, he refused to continue with additional sessions, so I could no longer help this athlete. Perhaps at some point in her life, this athlete will be able to become whole. It is not always possible to apply the model when there are outside agendas. In this case, it was not possible to apply the model because the father, as well as the mother (because of her own inability to be congruent within the relationship to the father) were not allowing their daughter to communicate what she now desired. Within the therapeutic setting, establishing congruence was outside of our control. Because Annie was not being heard by her parents, in the future she may feign an injury, truly get injured, or sabotage herself in some other way. What will probably result is resentment in the relationship between Annie and her parents until they can communicate about Annie's life more freely and lovingly.

Benefits of using the model

There are many advantages to using this model. It is a humanistic, whole-person model that allows athletes to consider how they feel and where they are in the here and now in order to make decisions that will influence many aspects of their experiences for the remainder of their lives. Having the opportunity to process where they are with another human being without judgment and with unconditional positive regard is often a rare experience, especially for athletes. For adolescents, there often is pressure from coaches, and especially parents, who directly or indirectly verbalize how much time, energy, and money has been contributed to their sports, along with expectations of full university scholarships. For professional athletes, there are also perceived and real pressures. Some professional athletes have no one with whom to talk because they perceive that most people involved in their lives have a vested interest in them. Applying this model also allows athletes to be not only introspective, but also able to gain perspective. Participating in sport is one aspect of life; it does not make up the whole.

Disadvantages of using the model

The disadvantages of using this model depend on the context in which the athletes are being seen. Although there are times athletes may be struggling about wanting to be involved in their sports or just wanting to improve mental performances, as they aspire or begin to climb the ranks as elite athletes, they automatically begin to create imbalances in their lives. There are times when sacrifices will be made and seeing what may be missing from their lives (e.g., social opportunities, perceived normal activities) may feel daunting or overwhelming, and perhaps impossible. Another disadvantage of the model, especially if used exclusively, is not having a set agenda with the number of sessions or the content of the sessions. Athletes are used to having a plan placed in front of them and being coached through issues. When using this model, clients are the true drivers of the agenda, not the therapist. This model may be too slow and loose for result-oriented athletes. Additionally, using this model in isolation may not be economically feasible for many, because there is no set number of sessions. Exploring one's life will take time, and can be troublesome if an athlete is already in the midst of a busy and demanding competitive season. There is also a risk, especially if athletes are in season, that they may temporarily perform worse due to being emotionally distracted from examining various incongruencies in their lives.

Conclusions

Athletes are used to being coached. Even though giving athletes space to discuss what is occurring in their environments is helpful, they are also looking for direction and effective techniques from the therapist. Using a combination of modalities seems to be beneficial. For example, using in-between session homework employed in a cognitive-behavioral approach creates a familiar structure and gives a measurable means of improvement for the athlete, aiding in the ability to create relatively rapid change (see Chapter 14 on cognitive-behavioral models). See Box 13.1 for key points from this chapter.

Box 13.1

Key points from the humanistic/person-centered model

- Unconditional positive regard, empathy, congruence, and understanding from the therapist are essential for an athlete to self-explore.
- Athletes have free will and the ability to make choices that are growth enhancing.
- The importance of self-awareness is stressed; athletes who are self-aware make better choices.
- Athletes are capable of acting in responsible and caring ways in interpersonal relationships.
- Human beings have an innate drive toward growth that enables them to benefit from counseling.
- As athletes grow to understand and value themselves, their selves become more congruent with their experiences.

References

Bruno, F. J. (1977). *Human adjustment and personal growth: Seven pathways*. New York: Wiley.

Jacobsen, B. (2007). *Invitation to existential psychology*. Chichester, England: Wiley.

Robbins, B. D. (2007). *Carl Rogers*. Retrieved from http://www.mythosandlogos.com/Rogers.html

Rogers, C. (1959). A theory of therapy, personality, and interpersonal relationships as developed in the client-centered framework. In S. Koch (Ed.), *Psychology: A study of a science. Vol. 3: Formulations of the person and the social context* (pp. 185–256). New York: McGraw-Hill.

Rogers, C. (1961). *On becoming a person: A therapist's view of psychotherapy*. London: Constable.

Rogers, C. (1980). *A way of being*. New York: Houghton Mifflin.

14

Cognitive-behavioral therapies

Emily Claspell

Cognitive-behavioral therapy (CBT) is a collection of therapies sharing philosophical assumptions and similar techniques. Two therapies that I describe in this chapter are cognitive therapy (CT; A. Beck, 1991; J. S. Beck, 1995), and rational–emotive behavior therapy (REBT; Ellis, 1994; Walen, DiGiuseppe, & Dryden, 1992; Weinrach *et al.*, 1995). Although students of CBT may view the theoretical contributions of CT and REBT researchers and therapists form only a contemporary vantage point, it may surprise them to learn that the development of CBT was influenced by schools of thought that occurred thousands of years ago. In particular, Albert Ellis was a student of Greek stoicism. During the golden age of Greek philosophy, Zeno of Citium proposed that man is a logical creature, and therefore could understand the physical world around him. His ideas emphasized that the root causes of problems for humanity were found within the emotions of man (Zeno's understandably sexist language), and that to truly understand the world, man must distance himself from his emotions.

The other philosophical roots of CBT can be found within the schools of British empiricism, behaviorism, functionalism, and pragmatism. Some names that may be familiar to the students of philosophy, or history and systems of psychology are: John Locke and David Hume within the school of British empiricism in the seventeenth and eighteenth centuries, Emile Durkheim whose writings are referenced as the basis for functionalism theory, and Burrhus Frederic Skinner who revolutionized psychology by developing his school of radical behaviorism.

Why is it important to acknowledge the historical roots of CBT or any other psychology therapy? Mark Andersen (personal communication, January 6, 2009) puts the answer to this question beautifully in his description of CBT and psychological skills training (PST):

> Let me try an extended analogy. Say we have an azalea bush. It has lovely flowers, leaves, branches, a main trunk, and a root system. Taking psychological skills training (PST) as a model is like focusing only on the flowers (representing the applied sport psychology techniques of imagery, relaxation, goal setting, positive self-talk, and so forth). Those flowers are part of a much more complex system that goes by the name of cognitive-behavioral therapy. Many PST practitioners may only know the flowers

of the azalea bush, and not be familiar with the dendritic and leafy aspects of the whole therapy. That azalea bush of cognitive-behavioral therapy also has deep and branching theoretical and philosophical roots going back to empiricism, pragmatism, functionalism, and early behaviorism. But do students and practitioners study the whole "plant"? Some may know something about the leaves and branches, but probably even fewer get to the roots.

And, if therapy or PST is provided without a clear understanding of the "roots," how effective and ethical is the practitioner who applies powerful tools without any clear understanding of why these interventions are chosen and how they facilitate change? To support standards of best practice and encourage the integration of theory and application, it is important for those who use CBT approaches with athletes to be aware of the deep basin of knowledge from which these therapies have been developed.

Basic assumptions of cognitive-behavioral therapies

Keeping these ideas in mind, what are the basic assumptions that cognitive therapy (CT) and rational-emotive behavior therapy (REBT) have in common and how are they different? According to CBT, problems in living are (primarily) a product of faulty thinking. Terms such as mistaken assumptions, irrational thoughts and beliefs, self-defeating attitudes, and thinking errors are used to describe the sources of why people develop unhealthy ways of feeling and behaving. Thoughts by themselves are not the focus of CBT. Instead, the inter-relationships between thoughts and emotions and thoughts and behaviors are tightly woven. To understand the nature of emotions and behaviors, it is important to uncover and reveal the source from which they emerge. Both CT and REBT practitioners subscribe to the idea that a systematic assessment of one's belief system, combined with an organized plan to work with that belief system, will promote positive change.

Goals of therapy

There are differences in the end goals of therapy for CT and REBT, although these differences may appear subtle to many. Ellis (1994) believed that true change occurs when people are able to modify their core-belief structures. This modification requires an overall shift in a person's philosophy and incorporates a different view of the world and the person's place within it. This transformation is a product of educating individuals on the powerful effects of faulty thinking. The significant point here is to ensure that people can truly be free of the erroneous "musts," "shoulds," and "oughts" of daily living. By disputing these harmful thoughts, attitudes, and beliefs, individuals can begin to reframe their theoretical and philosophical views of themselves and the world in which they live. By the end of therapy, a new philosophy of living is adopted that is much healthier than the client's previous world view.

Like Ellis, Aaron Beck (1991) understood the importance of addressing core-beliefs to promote positive change. Instead of an emphasis upon philosophical transformation, however, Beck believed that CT could help move people from their problems to their goals by a variety of means. He encouraged therapists to tap into a wide array of psychological techniques to help their clients. This flexibility and practical orientation in a therapeutic environment creates positive changes in a person's belief system. In both CT and REBT, the objective is to understand how beliefs can maintain problems, and by developing new ways of thinking and trying out different strategies, problems in living can be resolved. Through the techniques found in both CT and REBT, the hope is for clients and athletes to develop the skills that will allow them to carry on using these tools and other strategies themselves.

The role of the therapist

In CBT, the role of the therapist is important to the success of the therapy. The therapist serves as a guide, a coach, an advocate, and someone who questions, disputes, and identifies the irrational thoughts that are harming the person. There is the expectation that clients will fulfill their part of the work in and outside of meetings with the therapist. These efforts include completing homework assignments and participating in life experiments. The therapist is directive, verbal, and active. It is important for therapists to have good rapport with clients with whom they are working and strive for a collaborative relationship. The relationship, however, is not critical nor is it the focus for CBT practitioners.

Time orientation

The temporal focus of CBT is the present. Past experiences can be addressed, but only if they have bearing on understanding and changing how a person is thinking and behaving now. The focus stays on current problems and ways that thoughts can perpetuate these problems in the here and now.

Therapeutic practice and skills training

To link these ideas to the practice setting, it is helpful to understand that the success of CBT stems from the openness and the motivation of people who are willing and able to learn about the theoretical assumptions of these therapies, and consistently practise the techniques that go with them. Cognitive-behavioral therapy is a short-term therapy, lasting anywhere from a few hours to a few months. As clients learn about their faulty thinking patterns and work toward changing them, positive consequences to these changes can occur quickly.

Applying REBT

As described earlier, how one ascribes meaning to events can have direct consequences to feelings and behaviors. To illustrate how important this assumption is to REBT, it is helpful to learn the therapy's ABCs. Here are some definitions of terms.

A is the *activating event*. This event can be something that is external (it has already happened or is about to happen) or internal (an image or a memory, for example). The activating event is often referred to as a trigger.

B is the *belief*, which includes one's thoughts, attitudes, and what meaning an individual has ascribed to the external and internal life events. In problem formation, these beliefs are "irrational."

C comprises the emotional and behavioral *consequences* that stem from the belief.

A common misconception is that these consequences stem directly from the activating event. In the REBT model, however, it is the *belief* that one has about the activating event that creates the consequences that follow the event.

Most individuals assume that it is the activating event (A) that causes the emotional or behavioral consequences (C), and our language is filled with many examples where we perceive our experiences to be a result of something happening to us.

An example is an elite basketball player saying, "I am angry (C) because I missed that key shot" (A). In other words, **A** caused **C**. If we break this statement down into the ABCs – **A** being a missed shot, **C** being angry – it is difficult to see how **B** (beliefs) factor into this experience, at least from the athlete's point of view. Nevertheless, the **B** in this scenario may be about not being good enough: "I should have made it, what's wrong with me?" It's the meaning and how the athlete interprets that missed shot that results in feelings of anger, and any corresponding behaviors.

Because of the importance of beliefs, it is critical for the rational–emotive behavior therapist to identify thinking errors and help the client or athlete become skilled at recognizing the B to C connection. Once this connecting task is accomplished, changing the irrational beliefs becomes an active exercise of disputing, questioning, and challenging the beliefs that are leading to distress in feelings and discomfort in behavior. The other parts of learning the ABCs are D and E.

D is *disputing* the irrational beliefs: Arguing against the beliefs and proposing alternate ways of thinking about **A**, and

E makes up the new *effects* or consequences from changing the irrational beliefs.

How does one go about disputing irrational beliefs that appear to be strong and seem to be ingrained in a person's view about self? In REBT, the disputing of beliefs can be aggressive. The purpose is to take away catastrophic thinking regarding a person's belief about self. It's moving away from the "awfulizing" to acceptance of oneself and the situation (Ellis, 2001). Extreme beliefs that are rigid are signified by words such as "should," "must," "need," "ought," and "have to." Some of the guiding questions or strategies that can help dispute irrational beliefs are:

1. Are you being realistic? Could there be alternative explanations for what is happening?
2. Lead with your head and not with your heart. Emotions are strong, but are not always the best barometer of reality.
3. What is your evidence to support your thinking? Make sure that your evidence is concrete and reliable.
4. Avoid labeling and overgeneralizing. Your thoughts can make labels true. So, if it's "unfair" out there, you may act defensively and be suspicious of others.
5. Acknowledge that life can be complex and always changing.
6. It's normal to have bad days, but it doesn't mean it is the end of the world.

The practitioner of REBT, through a Socratic style of dialogue (i.e., the practitioner does not give information directly but instead asks a series of questions, with the result that the client comes to the desired knowledge by answering the questions), helps someone with irrational beliefs identify and then dispute these cognitions aggressively, pursuing a philosophical shift that (one hopes) will maintain the gains for healthier and more adaptive living. Putting in the time and effort to practise REBT is important to keep problems from surfacing. This task is rarely easy. Irrational beliefs are overlearned through years of experience and reinforcement, and that is why it is important for practitioners to give homework to athletes and find ways that the principles of this philosophy can be tested and reinforced. Athletes can continue to make progress using REBT by reviewing goals, keeping track of the ABCs, and continuing to evaluate and change irrational beliefs to realistic and growth-enhancing ones.

Applying CT

How then are the CBT strategies and techniques different for cognitive therapy, when there are similar assumptions about beliefs being forerunners to emotions and behaviors? Cognitive therapy practitioners acknowledge that core beliefs (or schemas) are developed through early childhood experiences and reinforced through learning. These schemas do not necessarily cause, but can be linked to, specific problems in mental health such as depression, panic disorder, and addictions, to name just a few (J. S. Beck, 1995). For CT to help people live healthier lives, it is important to identify what the cognitive distortions (or thinking distortions) are, and then help modify them through cognitive and experiential strategies. The problems and strategies below are only brief examples of the array of interventions used in CT. The cognitive distortions that have been most identified in the research associated with CT are:

1. *All or nothing thinking*: Extreme thinking results in black-and-white categories. If your performance falls short of perfect, you see yourself as a total failure.
   Strategies:
   - Work on being realistic.
   - Reframe mistakes as lessons for improvement.
   - Remind yourself that you can still succeed in your goals, even with some set-backs.
   - Acknowledge that life is not perfect and move on.
2. *Overgeneralization*: From a single negative event, you conclude that this event proves a never-ending pattern of problems for yourself.
   Strategies:
   - Avoid using words such as "always" or "never."
   - Remind yourself that your experiences are not unique. For example, you are not the first person who has been cut from a starting position, and even top performers have "off" days.
   - Collect more information about the event before making a judgment about yourself or others.
3. *Mental filter*: You pick out information that confirms the beliefs that you hold. By dwelling on only this kind of information, you can easily keep your opinions from ever changing.
   Strategies:
   - Play devil's advocate and look for evidence that contradicts your beliefs.
   - Remind yourself that just because you don't believe the evidence, doesn't mean that it isn't there.
   - Use a visual image to help stay open to new information and experiences: Opening petals on a flower, a pupil dilating, or several streams flowing into a deep pool.
4. *Disqualifying the positive*: You reject positive experiences by believing that they "don't count." In this way you can keep a negative belief about yourself that is (at least partially) contradicted by your experiences.

135

Strategies:

- Practise accepting positive feedback about yourself and others. If this task is difficult, develop your skills by taking an assertiveness class that focuses on giving and accepting compliments freely.
- If you begin to transform a positive experience to something that is negative, use the technique of "thought-stopping." By telling yourself to stop, or wearing a rubber band around your wrist and snapping it while you say "Stop!" you can prevent yourself from escalating into this kind of processing.
- Begin to turn negative experiences into positive or neutral ones through reframing the experience.

5. *Jumping to conclusions*: You make a negative interpretation, though there are no definite facts that convincingly support your conclusion.
   a. Mind reading: You assume that others are reacting negatively to you or have negative intentions or motives toward you.
   b. The fortune teller error: You predict that things will turn out negatively, and you feel that the outcome of your prediction is an already-established fact.

Strategies:

- Generate some alternative explanations for what you are experiencing or observing.
- Acknowledge that your beliefs may be wrong, and collect evidence to support your beliefs before thinking that they are facts.
- Avoid creating a self-fulfilling prophecy about your beliefs by taking actions that would provide opportunities for you to determine what is true or not: Experiment, and test out your predictions. Although this tactic does require openness to risk, focus your thoughts on the rewards and benefits of your actions rather than on your fears and anxieties.

6. *Catastrophizing*: From one small event, you create all kinds of disastrous thoughts and scenarios.

Strategies:

- What is your evidence to support your catastrophic assumption? Look for any reasons that would contradict your beliefs.
- Consider alternative explanations for why things in your life are occurring.
- Even in the worst case scenarios, others are not as interested in your experiences as you are. Keep the bigger picture in mind, instead of focusing on extreme ideas and emotions.

7. *Emotional reasoning*: You assume that your feelings are reality. So, if you have strong emotions, then you believe they prove how things really are: "I feel it, therefore it must be true." If you believe that your feelings are valid criteria of reality, then you will be reluctant to search out alternative information.

Strategies:

- Remember to tell yourself that feelings are not facts.
- Identify the thoughts that are linked to the feelings that you have, and ask yourself if you would be feeling differently if you were thinking differently. Ask yourself, when I am feeling better, what am I thinking?
- If your emotions are distressing, give yourself time to calm down and reevaluate your perceptions about your situation.
- Recognize when you begin to rely too much on your "gut" instead of your head.

8. *"Should" statements*: You motivate yourself with extreme and rigid beliefs such as "shoulds," "musts," and "oughts." These inflexible demands that you place upon yourself, and those around you, keep you from adapting to reality and create consequences such as guilt, anger, frustration, and resentment.
   Strategies:
   - Change language by replacing "ought to" with "like to," or "should have" with "want to."
   - Acknowledge that no matter how much you value certain behaviors, not everyone shares that same value. Avoid disappointment by not expecting others to live up to your standards.
   - Practise flexibility by not insisting that you or others have to act a certain way.
   - Recognize when you place demands upon yourself and observe what the consequences are for you and how these demands may influence others.

9. *Labeling*: This problem goes beyond general descriptors for self and others. This thinking distortion takes something that is complex and categorizes it into a single definition.
   Labels have a powerful influence on your belief system and result in problems that often are associated with you believing, and then feeling, that you and/or others are inferior. Some common labels are words such as worthless, loser, unfair, incompetent, and slacker.
   Strategies:
   - Work toward accepting yourself and others. Understand that people are complex and should not be easily judged.
   - Reinforce the idea that labels are overgeneralizations and they can impair your view of reality.
   - Labels are powerful and can lead to a self-fulfilling prophecy of poor performance.
   - Avoid labeling, and instead, use other language to describe what you are observing about yourself or others. For example, instead of saying, "I'm useless," say, "I'm having a hard time focusing now, but I'll see how I do after I take a break."

10. *Personalization*: You take responsibility for the cause of some negative external event, and believe that this event is related to you personally. If everything is somehow associated with you, then you are easily able to take the blame or feel emotionally upset for those experiences that do not go well.
    Strategies:
    - Acknowledge that what happens to others is outside of your control.
    - Just because something goes wrong doesn't mean that the event is directly related to you.
    - Look for alternative explanations for what is happening without bringing yourself into the scenario.

Additional cognitive-behavioral strategies

Cognitive therapists and REBT practitioners strive to educate their clients about the importance of identifying thoughts that interfere with healthy living, and to work on changing those cognitions. Record keeping is an important tool to help the practitioner and client in this educational process and is a means for monitoring progress as change occurs. Keeping a log of the ABCs, including the various ways of disputing the irrational or distorted belief system and consequences of such thinking, is usually a first step to understanding and identifying problematic cognitive patterns.

Another strategy is adopting the role of a behavioral scientist. Both REBT and CT promote experimenting and testing ideas in real life, rather than just talking about them. People have good intentions, but intentions are not reliable predictors of change. To encourage action, the therapist and client collaborate on setting up, conducting, and recording experiments.

There are several factors to consider in developing a reality-based experiment as part of CBT. First, it is helpful to be clear about what the definition of the problem is. State the problem in the person's own language that identifies the distorted thinking or negative meaning ascribed to the situation. For example, an athlete may state, "my problem is that my teammates don't respect my opinions, so I can't express how I truly feel." Here are some questions that the practitioners may ask themselves and their athletes, that might help clarify what the problem is: What is (are) the irrational belief(s) underlying this statement? What is the evidence for making this statement? What are the consequences that arise from this belief? How does the athlete cope with this situation, and are the strategies effective? What do you and the athlete want to know by the end of the experiment that will be useful for change?

Second, develop a hypothesis or hypotheses for the experiment. What will happen if the athlete tests out a new way of thinking and behaving? The hypothesis should be a prediction that leaves an unambiguous outcome. By testing it, the outcome will be a confirmation or disconfirmation of the belief.

In the above example, one hypothesis may be, "If I say what I honestly think, or disagree with someone on the team, my teammates will respect me less." Come up with criteria that would prove or disprove the hypothesis. In this case, how would the athlete know if the teammates are less respectful? Out of being 100% confident, what percentage does the athlete believe in the confirmation of the hypothesis? And, if the prediction comes true or not, how will the athlete respond? Review possible thinking biases that could get in the way and strategies to help avoid pitfalls that would cloud an honest appraisal of the results during the experiment. For example, instead of focusing on what people might think, focus instead on what people actually say and do.

Third, develop a way to test out the new belief or behavior in a realistic way. You want the experiment to be somewhat challenging, but also successful. Skills training would be helpful prior to executing the experiment, if this tactic would improve the opportunities for the person to successfully follow through with it. Some of these skills might be role-playing, mental rehearsal, assertiveness training, arousal control in the face of anxiety, and so forth. The plan for execution of the experiment needs to be clear about where and when it will take place, how it will be carried out, and who will be involved.

Finally, it is important to record and process the results of the experiment. Was the hypothesis confirmed or not? What are the conclusions from running the experiment? If the hypothesis was not confirmed, what does this outcome mean, and what is to be learned from this exercise? How much has the confidence rating changed in the prediction for the athlete? What other experiments can be conducted to gain further information and exploration? The life scientist approach can be useful when describing the nature of the evidence to support the realistic belief systems complementary to healthy life philosophies.

Conclusion

Cognitive-behavioral therapy has great application to both clinical as well as sport psychology settings. Because this approach is short-term and focuses upon the practical everyday problems that confront people, its role as part of an overall psychological skills training program would seem to be beneficial for athletes who are focused on short-term, leading to long-term, improvements. Those who have the propensity to grasp the concepts of the theory and who are motivated to integrate the assumptions into their life experiences will do well with this approach. Those who are inclined to seek more in-depth forms of therapy as a vehicle for change may be less open and more skeptical about the focus or strategies of this therapy. In addition, it is prudent to acknowledge that CBT may have limited application within certain multicultural contexts. As described at the beginning of this chapter, CBT is derived from an Anglo-European philosophical foundation. The practitioner needs to be sensitive to the world views of those who do not share the definitions or values found within this philosophy, including those concepts associated with problem formation and characteristics of healthy thinking. See Box 14.1 for some take-home messages from this chapter.

Box 14.1

Take-home messages about CBT for practitioners

- Teach the ABCs: Activating Event–Beliefs–Consequences.
  - Develop record sheets to track these components.
  - Have athletes begin recording their ABCs.
- Identify irrational beliefs and cognitive distortions.
  - Examine the consequences of each.
- Actively dispute the irrational beliefs.
  - Reinforce that thoughts and feelings are not facts.
  - Ask for the evidence that supports the belief.
  - Prevent language that "awfulizes" and "catastrophizes" self and others.
  - Eliminate labels and black-and-white thinking.
  - Watch for mental filtering and overgeneralizing.
  - Give feedback when distorted thinking emerges.
- Have the athlete write down new beliefs that are healthy and positive in a log.
  - Record benefits and new consequences of these healthier thoughts.
- Collaborate as life scientists.
  - Develop hypotheses that would prove or disprove beliefs.
  - Create experiments that would test these beliefs in real-life situations.
  - Record the outcomes of these experiments and learning points.
  - Reassess goals.
- Encourage your athletes.
  - You want your clients to take responsibility for implementing CBT strategies.

References

Beck, A. (1991). *Cognitive therapy and the emotional disorders.* London: Penguin Books.

Beck, J. S. (1995). *Cognitive therapy: Basics and beyond.* New York: Guilford Press.

Ellis, A. (1994). *Reason and emotion in psychotherapy: A comprehensive method of treating human distur-bances: Revised and updated.* New York: Birch Lane Press.

Ellis, A. (2001). *Overcoming destructive beliefs, feelings and behaviors: New directions for rational emotive behavior therapy.* New York: Prometheus Books.

Walen, S. R., DiGiuseppe, R., & Dryden, W. (1992). *A practitioner's guide to rational-emotive therapy* (2nd ed). New York: Oxford University Press.

Weinrach, S. G., Ellis, A., DiGiuseppe, R., Bernard, M., Dryden, W., Wolfe, J., Malkinson, R., & Backx, W. (1995). Rational emotive behavioral therapy after Ellis: Predictions for future. *Journal of Mental Health Counseling, 17,* 413–427.

15

Positive psychology

Gloria Park-Perin

Positive psychology and applied sport and exercise psychology, though different fields by name and trade, are bedfellows who have remained largely strangers to each other until recently. Most of the theories and bedrock assumptions of positive psychology will be of no surprise to sport psychology practitioners because both fields have developed with the charge of facilitating optimal functioning of human beings. In this chapter, I will discuss potential interchanges in theory between the two disciplines and make concrete suggestions for how positive psychology can inform applied sport psychology practice. What I present is not exhaustive, but it reflects my hope that collegial collaboration will produce an interdisciplinary approach and enhance the richness and complexity of both disciplines.

A brief history of positive psychology

Historically, clinical psychology as a discipline has focused on the diagnosis and treatment of psychopathology, such as anxiety disorders, depression, and schizophrenia, with the laudable goal of alleviating human suffering. This dominant paradigm of resolving issues of human frailty improved quality of life for many, but resulted in a fundamentally single-sided perspective of the human condition. In his presidential address to the American Psychological Association, Martin Seligman (1999), after decades of conducting seminal research on depression and learned helplessness, sounded a call urging social scientists to broaden empirical inquiry into what makes life worth living with the belief that human beings want to thrive, not simply survive. The plea for a study of human strength, virtue, goodness, and happiness is not without precedent, and is built on the foundations laid by the work of philosophers, religious figures, and humanistic psychologists such as Abraham Maslow, Gordon Allport, and Carl Rogers. Positive psychology represents the modern resurgence of an old theme and a collective identity coalescing different lines of theory and research from diverse scientific fields. The backbone of this identity is rigorous, empirical research into the conditions and processes that enable optimal functioning of individuals, groups, and institutions. Peterson (2006) best summarized the ancestry of positive psychology as having "a very short history but a very long past" (p. 4).

The positive psychology movement has captured the global attention of popular media, leading scientists and researchers alike, but it is not without its critics. That positive psychology is solely focused on the positive, that it suggests positive is unconditionally better or preferable over the negative, and that it implies traditional psychology is negative are common misconceptions that have been the source of much disparagement (e.g., Lazarus, 2003). Positive psychologists do not deny the existence of disease, suffering, or tragedy, nor do they aim to devalue, degrade, or mutually exclude mitigating approaches. Rather, they suggest that the other side of the human condition – goodness, strength, and all that goes right in life – deserves equally earnest exploration.

Well-being and satisfaction with life rank highly among personal desires for most individuals, but we now know that happiness is not formulaic: it is not usually the end product of realized dreams and aspirations, material gains, or life circumstances. Success can bring happiness, and according to a meta-analysis by Lyubomirsky, King, and Diener (2005), happiness is associated with, and can *precede*, success in various domains in life such as marriage, relationships, and work. Happiness is desirable because it is valuable and has practical utility; it is associated with many physical, psychological, social, and cognitive benefits through life. Happy people more frequently occupy positions of leadership, have more robust social networks and stronger interpersonal relationships, are in better health, and even live longer than their less happy counterparts.

Beyond a mere "happiology" positive psychology research serves the descriptive function of illuminating those conditions that enable the "good life," (e.g., by Aristotle's concept of eudaimonia). Eudaimonia is beyond hedonism, or subjective dimensions of experienced pleasure. Human beings desire meaningful relationships with others, strive for fulfilling careers, have ambitions toward success and achievement, and yearn to live productive and engaging lives. To capture this complexity, positive psychology is founded on three pillars. The study of positive subjective experience concerns the role of positive emotions for the past (e.g., contentment, satisfaction), the present (e.g., pleasure, happiness), and the future (e.g., hope, optimism), and optimal experiences such as flow and engagement. The study of individual strengths of character (e.g., kindness, courage, curiosity), values, and interests are contained within the pillar of positive individual traits. The study of enabling institutions examines positive psychology in the social context and the extent to which larger groups, communities, institutions (e.g., schools, families, workplaces), and relationships with others enable the "good life." Peterson's *Primer in Positive Psychology* (2006) includes an in-depth treatment of each pillar, as well as additional readings and resources. To bridge research and practice, positive psychologists have developed empirically validated interventions designed to enhance well-being.

A theory of positive interventions

A theory of positive interventions (PIs) first requires distinction between mental illness, defined as the presence of a pathological disorder, and the concept of mental health, historically defined as the absence of mental illness. Keyes and Lopez (2005) suggested that mental health, like illness, should be characterized by the presence of a certain set of symptoms and researched as a syndrome of well-being. If business-as-usual psychological interventions aim to cure mental illness, then positive interventions focus on the promotion of mental health. PIs are distinguished in their end-goals from approaches aimed at alleviating the burden of mental illness, remedying pathology, diminishing deficits, or relieving suffering.

Because shifts in positive and negative affect are often orthogonal, reductions in negative emotions, such as anger, do little in the way of increasing positive emotions, such as joy. Although treatment for depression can increase well-being, the absence of depressive symptoms is insufficient for signifying flourishing. Many positive interventions are not new and can, and often do, intersect with business-as-usual psychological therapies. Long-distinguished modalities, such as cognitive-behavioral and rational–emotive behavior therapy, have been used to enhance well-being for many years. Nevertheless, practitioners can bolster the effectiveness of strategies to ameliorate mental illness by incorporating positive psychology approaches (Duckworth, Steen, & Seligman, 2005).

Most positive psychology researchers agree that lasting change to happiness occurs from the inside out, and not through the reconstruction of external life circumstances (Sheldon & Lyubomirsky, 2006). Positive interventions are exercises, techniques, or action-based strategies intended to produce gains in positive affect, happiness, subjective well-being, meaning, engagement, optimism, and satisfaction with life by cultivating fundamental "nutrients" required for creating and ordering a good life. Psychological research consistently shows a human bias toward the negative: the bad is more powerful and often holds more weight than the good when it comes to emotions, thoughts, and events (Baumeister, Bratslavsky, Finkenauer, & Vohs, 2001). Consistent with adaptation theory, positive events are far more transitory and ineffectual than negative events. Thus, PIs are aimed at the deliberate cultivation of a positivity offset to counter the negativity bias.

Several common psychological characteristics have been identified as common denominators of highly successful athletes: emotion/arousal control, attention/focus, self-regulation, confidence, positive self-talk, and a high level of commitment (Gould, Dieffenbach, & Moffet, 2002). The following is an overview of potential ways in which positive psychology research can inform the practice of sport and exercise psychology, along with examples of empirically validated intervention strategies that may contribute to athlete well-being and success. In this chapter, the intervention strategies are organized by the target mechanism – emotional/affective, cognitive/attentional, and behavioral. Resulting transformations can extend beyond their targets: affective approaches can influence shifts in attention and cognition; behavioral approaches can alter affective states, and so on. Therefore, the categories are neither finite nor absolute, and each technique is applicable to individual, interpersonal, or group settings.

Affective approaches

The most obvious mechanisms through which positive interventions work are the emotional/affective systems. The distinction between positive emotions (e.g., joy, happiness, contentment) and negative emotions (e.g., fear, anger, grief) are derived from how they are subjectively experienced. That is, positive does not refer to a "good" emotion and negative a "bad" emotion. Negative emotions have been at the forefront of psychological inquiry because of their well-known associations with stress, coping, mood regulation, and their links to psychopathology and poor health, whereas positive emotions, which are still central to the human experience, have gone largely unexamined. Positive emotions have the capacity to broaden the scope of attention; raise awareness of the surrounding environment and increase openness to stimuli; build durable intellectual (problem solving, learning), physical (coordination, cardiovascular health), social (bonding, inter-personal relationships), and psychological (resilience, goal orientation) resources; and can serve as effective antidotes to physiological activation and cardiovascular reactivity that result from experiencing negative emotions (Fredrickson, 2009).

In sport psychology, optimal states leading to high performance include the presence of both types of emotions, as evidenced by well known models such as Hanin's (1995) individualized zones of optimal functioning, and yet most affective strategies have focused on managing psychological and physiological consequences of negative emotions. Positive emotions, such as enjoyment, have been associated with increased participation, motivation and commitment, reduced burnout, and higher quality interpersonal and team dynamics (Vallerand & Blanchard, 2000). More recently, Skinner and Brewer (2004) found that anticipatory positive emotions experienced prior to competition might be beneficial for enhancing intrinsic motivation and for framing positive appraisals of perceived challenges. Enjoyment can also facilitate opportunities for flow, or a state of deep engagement, which often accompanies moments of peak performance and can contribute greatly to quality of life (Csikszentmihalyi, 1990).

In her book, Fredrickson (2009) provided many intuitive, user-friendly suggestions for cultivating positivity, such as solidifying social connections and practising altruism and kindness. Meditative practices such as loving kindness meditation (LKM), which encourages warmth and caring toward oneself and others, produced short-term gains in the daily positive emotions among employees of a corporation. Consonant with previous studies, increased positivity promoted long-term gains in other personal resources, such as the acquisition of mindfulness skills, meaning and purpose, and social and relational benefits, which in turn decreased depressive symptoms and increased life satisfaction (Fredrickson, Cohn, Coffey, Pek, & Finkel, 2008). LKM is a low-cost intervention that can be delivered by trained facilitators or self-learned using a variety of audio and video resources (e.g., Salzberg, 2005).

Savoring, or the processes underlying individuals' capacities "to attend to, appreciate, and enhance the positive experiences in their lives" (Bryant &Veroff, 2007, p. 2), can also enable individuals to prolong the beneficial influence of experienced positive emotions. Leveraging their knowledge of psychological skills training in imagery (usually used to help athletes mentally rehearse and prepare), practitioners can encourage clients to manipulate auditory, visual, tactile, olfactory, and kinesthetic senses to retrospectively savor past successes. Video clips of peak performances, collages of particularly enjoyable team trips, or opportunities to share and celebrate accomplishments (both big and small), can aid savoring practices.

Cognitive and attentional approaches

Cognition and attention effectively regulate much of the way we construct our worlds, and our perceptions, emotions, and behaviors are often influenced directly by what we attend to and how we process, translate, and think about sensory information and external stimuli. Optimal states are achieved by involving some type of active construction or the marshaling of cognitive resources to willfully shift and control attention, a critical skill that enables human beings to have a role in experiencing and responding to life events without becoming slaves to their affective systems. Cognitions help individuals predict the future, reconcile and interpret past experiences, and regulate emotional and behavioral reactions to present events.

Dispositional optimism, or the global expectation of good things and favorable outcomes, has been linked to: (a) positive mood; (b) perseverance; (c) effective problem-solving; (d) academic, athletic, military, occupational, and political success; (e) popularity; (f) good health; and (g) a long life (Peterson & Seligman, 2004). Highly successful athletes are often optimistic, and in sport, optimism can heighten sport confidence and task-focused coping strategies in dealing with a sport-related slump (Grove & Heard, 1997). Optimism, as an attributional/explanatory style, describes the way in which individuals interpret both positive and negative events or outcomes in life. For example, a person with a pessimistic style tends to explain failures as one's own fault (internal), as unchanging (stable), and as occurring at most times across most situations (global). In contrast, a person with an optimistic style explains negative outcomes as due to environmental factors (external), as variable (unstable), and as occurring as isolated incidents in certain situations (Peterson & Seligman, 2004). Optimistic swimmers performed as well or better than their first efforts after perceived sport failure (Seligman, Nolen-Hoeksema, Thornton, & Thornton, 1990). Optimism enabled young students to perform better and experience a lower drop in success expectation and stress/anxiety compared to pessimists (Martin-Krumm, Sarrazin, Peterson, & Famose, 2003), and mediated the effects of a low perceived ability on task value in physical education classes (Martin-Krumm, Sarrazin, & Peterson, 2005). Just as certain forms of pessimism can bring benefits, excessive optimism can have its costs. For example, extreme optimism has been correlated with decreased well-being in novice exercisers who fail to meet their expectations (Jones, Harris, Waller, & Coggins, 2005).

The reinforcement of functional optimism – one that is grounded in reality and enables accurate and flexible thinking – should be the goal of an intervention rather than the simplistic encouragement to think good things. Traditional cognitive-behavioral approaches such as raising awareness of one's default thinking patterns and traps, examining how deeply held assumptions color beliefs, and reframing of events, are the best known and more effective ways to build resilience (see Chapter 57). Coaches, parents, and sport psychology practitioners can also retrain attributional style by nurturing a growth as opposed to a fixed mindset, emphasizing effort over ability, and helping athletes make accurate appraisals of what is and is not malleable or within their control. Sincere and specific effort-focused praise appeared to contribute to enhanced performance and a sense of mastery and accountability in students (Kamins & Dweck, 1999).

In addition to anticipating future events or interpreting past events, attention and cognition can be marshaled to command the present. Recording three good things that happened over the course of the day, in addition to a causal explanation for why they happened, can enrich feelings of gratitude and shift attention to illuminate and encourage positive interpretations of events. Mindfulness, a form of meditation dating back 2,500 years and rooted in the contemplative Buddhist practice called *vipassana*, can also foster moment-to-moment awareness and a passive, observational mindset with relation to thoughts, emotions, and the environment, as opposed to a reactive and change-oriented approach. Mindfulness may reduce distress, improve mood, promote inner peace, and consequently, even improve physical health. Mindfulness skills can be acquired through structured interventions, such as Kabat-Zinn's (2003) mindfulness based stress reduction (MBSR), an 8–10 week intervention, combining weekly group sessions with an all-day mindfulness retreat, somatic elements of Hatha yoga, body scans, as well as emotive constituents of loving kindness meditation.

Appreciative inquiry (AI) can shift attention from that which needs to be fixed, to what can be grown and nurtured in the pursuit of change, and be used to discover and develop the positive core of an individual, team, organization, or community. Cooperrider and Whitney (2005) defined AI as "the cooperative, coevolutionary search for the best in people, their organizations, and the world around them" (p. 8). The AI process contains four phases: (a) discovery, or the articulation of key strengths and life-giving best practices; (b) dream, or envisioning results based on collective values and sense of purpose; (c) design, or co-constructing a proposition for an organizational architecture that leverages core strengths;

and (d) destiny, or building hope, affirming the capability for, and sustaining positive momentum for change.

Behavioral approaches

The lives of athletes are complex, and intensive participation often comes at a cost to other life domains, such as academic achievement and social relationships. Helping individuals resolve goal conflict and establish equilibrium in their lives is central to performance coaching in domains other than sport. For example, executive coaches do focus on developing managerial skills needed for advancing business, but they also teach tools for constructing balance between work and family lives and leisure activities, resulting in reduced turnover, and increased productivity and performance. Similarly, sport psychology consultants can help their clients enhance behavioral self-regulation, a precursor to a broad range of positive outcomes associated with happiness and well-being.

Expressively writing about one's life goals and creating idiographic and personalized depictions of an individual's "best possible self" can be an effective tool in improving self-regulation. The following is an example of a prompt for this exercise:

> Imagine that your life has gone as well as it possibly could have. You have worked hard and achieved your goals. Think of this as your 'best possible life' or your 'happily ever after' ... write a description of the things you imagined. Be as specific as you can.
>
> (King, 2008, p. 522)

Through writing, individuals are able clarify what they value most, and reorganize and prioritize their approaches for living life in consonance with their most treasured aspirations. King (2008) found the articulation of a best possible self and daily striving for proximal goals that were related to larger life goals were highly correlated with well-being. Combined with long-established goal-setting techniques (see Chapter 51 in this book), writing exercises can provide an excellent platform for developing daily behavioral strategies.

One way to fortify self-regulation is by practising restraint over the undesired, but it can also be nurtured by harnessing strengths in the quest for the most coveted facets of life. Daily engagement in and pursuit of life activities congruent with an individual's signature strengths correlated robustly with well-being (Peterson & Seligman, 2004). Strength development supporters posit that self-actualization occurs through cultivating the best in people, rather than shoring up weaknesses. In the workplace, strength-based approaches have increased employee engagement and job satisfaction, reduced turnover, and heightened productivity (Hodges & Clifton, 2004). Strengths can also be informative in the same way as personality assessments, by raising self and other awareness of how preferences and thinking styles manifest themselves in individuals' actions and the way they relate to the world. Character strengths can also have dark sides. For example, persistence prevents athletes from giving up too quickly in the face of difficult goals and setbacks. Fisher and Wrisberg (2004), however, found that having extraordinary persistence could lead to the continuation of maladaptive behaviors that can result in injury and be detrimental to performance.

The Values in Action Survey of Character (VIA-IS) is a 240-item questionnaire that produces rankings for an individual's 24 character strengths across six broad classes of virtues: wisdom and knowledge, courage, humanity, justice, temperance, and transcendence, and can be taken online at www.viacharacter.org (Peterson & Seligman, 2004). Practitioners and coaches can help athletes devise innovative ways to deploy their strengths in their goal pursuits and in navigating adversity and challenges related to training and competition. A "strengths family tree" exercise can be used in a team setting by instructing members to take the VIA survey, and creating a visual representation of the team's aggregate signature strengths. A deepened collective understanding of how strengths play out in a group dynamic can promote awareness of the group's positive assets and foster understanding of individual styles of relating to the world, and fortify inter- and intrapersonal relationships.

A final behavioral strategy involves the deliberate structuring of a good day. This process begins with a recorded daily log of activities and scores from measures such as the Satisfaction with Life Scale (SWLS; Diener, Emmons, Larsen, & Griffin, 1985) or the Positive and Negative Affect Schedule (PANAS; Watson, Clark, & Tellegen, 1988), which can be taken online at www.authentichappiness.com. After several weeks, individuals can determine which days brought the most happiness or positive affect, learn about the potential reasons why, and use the knowledge gleaned to create more good days. Although labor-intensive, behavioral logs can be highly informative self-regulatory tools that can provide insight into what makes life most pleasurable to an individual.

Future directions

This chapter only begins to explore how positive psychology principles can be integrated or translated to applied sport psychology practice, but does not expand on the many ways that sport and exercise psychology can inform the study of human flourishing. Well-being is multi-dimensional, defined not only by psychological but also by physical health. Positive interventions can also act on physiological systems to promote well-being, and it is in this area where the decades of research on theory and practice in applied sport psychology can contribute greatly to positive psychology. Physical activity has a robust connection to cognitive and psychosocial development throughout the lifespan and can support psychological well-being by serving as an effective treatment for, and buffer to, illness. Sport can also be used as a mechanism to engage, motivate, and develop life skills and good character in youth (see Chapter 18) and has the capability to cross over racial, religious, and socioeconomic boundaries and bring people together in the pursuit and celebration of a common interest.

Positive psychology and sport psychology are two fields in their youth, still going through growing pains, and faced with similar challenges. Psychological illness remains a considerable public health concern, and with the deficiency-based and disease-focused stereotypes sustaining psychology, some may view positive psychology and sport psychology as dispensable luxuries. Practitioners in both fields continue to struggle in creating identities for themselves as valuable assets in the promotion of human flourishing. Positive psychology as an organized discipline is relatively new, but it is quickly evolving in depth and complexity. Drawing upon the deep roots of the field in the philosophy of humanism and humanistic psychology, positive psychologists continue to build on this foundation by producing a high volume of research, studying interventions and applications, creating academic programs and courses, and converging to exchange ideas at professional conferences and training institutes.

Continued research is needed to articulate whether positive psychology findings are applicable to the applied sport and exercise realm and whether specifically tailored measures and interventions need to be developed and validated for use within this domain. Future research should also illuminate how person–activity fit moderates the effect of positive interventions (e.g., Lyubomirsky, 2007) and the consequences of increased well-being and happiness on sport-related outcomes. Finally, given the natural and intuitive connection between positive psychology and sport and exercise psychology, the opportunities for fruitful cross-fertilization appear abundant. Through continuous dialogue and academic exchange, both fields are poised to benefit greatly by learning from each other's rich empirical foundations and histories. See Box 15.1 for some take-home messages from this chapter.

Box 15.1

Take-home messages about positive interventions

- Use positive interventions to augment clinical applications of sport and exercise psychology and mental skills training, and thereby enhance athlete well-being.
- Nurture positivity to offset the negativity bias and to prolong the physiological, psychological, and social benefits of positive emotions.
- Build resilience, retrain explanatory style, and command the present by nurturing cognition and attention.
- Improve self-regulation by writing about life goals, learning and using strengths in daily activities, and deliberately constructing good days.

References

Baumeister, R. F., Bratslavsky, E., Finkenauer, C., & Vohs, K. D. (2001). Bad is stronger than good. *Review of General Psychology, 5,* 323–370.

Bryant, F. B., & Veroff, J. (2007). *Savoring: A new model of positive experience.* Mahwah, NJ: Erlbaum.

Cooperrider, D. L., & Whitney, D. (2005). *Appreciative inquiry: A positive revolution in change.* San Francisco: Berrett-Koehler.

Csikszentmihalyi, M. (1990). *Flow: The psychology of optimal experience.* New York: Harper Collins.

Diener, E., Emmons, R. A., Larsen, R. J., & Griffin, S. (1985). The satisfaction with life scale. *Journal of Personality Assessment, 49,* 71–75.

Duckworth, A. L., Steen, T. A., & Seligman, M. E. P. (2005). Positive psychology in clinical practice. *Annual Review of Clinical Psychology, 1,* 629–651.

Fisher, L. A. & Wrisberg, C. A. (2004). Persistence. *Athletic Therapy Today, 9*(5), 46–47.

Fredrickson, B. L. (2009). *Positivity.* New York: Crown.

Fredrickson, B. L., Cohn, M. A., Coffey, K. A., Pek, J., & Finkel, S. M. (2008). Open hearts build lives: Positive emotions, induced through loving-kindness meditation, build consequential personal resources. *Journal of Personality and Social Psychology, 95,* 1045–1062.

Gould, D., Dieffenbach, K., & Moffett, A. (2002). Psychological characteristics and their development in Olympic champions. *Journal of Applied Sport Psychology, 14,* 172–204.

Grove, J. R., & Heard, N. P. (1997). Optimism and sport confidence as correlates of slump-related coping among athletes. *The Sport Psychologist, 11,* 400–410.

Hanin, Y. L. (1995). Individual zones of optimal functioning (IZOF) model: An idiographic approach to performance anxiety. In K. P. Henschen & W. F. Straub (Eds.), *Sport psychology: An analysis of athlete behavior* (3rd ed., pp. 103–119). Longmeadow, MA: Mouvement.

Hodges, T. D., & Clifton, D. O. (2004). Strengths-based development in practice. In P.A. Linley & S. Joseph (Eds.), *Positive psychology in practice* (pp. 256–268). Hoboken, NJ: Wiley.

Jones, F., Harris, P., Waller, H., & Coggins, A. (2005). Adherence to an exercise prescription scheme: The role of expectations, self-efficacy, stage of change and psychological well-being. *British Journal of Health Psychology, 10,* 359–378.

Kabat-Zinn, J. (2003). Mindfulness-based interventions in context: Past, present, and future. *Clinical Psychology: Science and Practice, 10*, 144–156.

Kamins, M. L., & Dweck, C. S. (1999). Person versus process praise and criticism: Implications for contingent self-worth and coping. *Developmental Psychology, 35*, 835–847.

Keyes, C., & Lopez, S. (2005). Toward a science of mental health: Positive directions in diagnosis and interventions. In C. R. Snyder & S. Lopez (Eds.), *Handbook of positive psychology* (pp. 45–59). New York: Oxford University Press.

King, L. A. (2008). *Personal goals and life dreams: Positive psychology and motivation in daily life.* New York: Guilford Press.

Lazarus, R. S. (2003). Does the positive psychology movement have legs? *Psychological Inquiry, 14*, 93–109.

Lyubomirsky, S. (2007). *The how of happiness: A new approach to getting the life you want.* New York: Penguin Books.

Lyubomirsky, S., King, L. A., & Diener, E. (2005). The benefits of frequent positive affect: Does happiness lead to success? *Psychological Bulletin, 131*, 803–855.

Martin-Krumm, C. P., Sarrazin, P. G., Peterson, C., & Famose, J. (2003). Explanatory style and resilience after sports failure. *Personality and Individual Differences, 35*, 1685–1695.

Martin-Krumm, C. P., Sarrazin, P. G., & Peterson, C. (2005). The moderating effects of explanatory style in physical education performance: A prospective study. *Personality and Individual Differences, 38*, 1645–1656.

Peterson, C. (2006). *A primer in positive psychology.* New York: Oxford University Press.

Peterson, C., & Seligman, M. E. P. (2004). *Character strengths and virtues: A handbook and classification.* New York: Oxford University Press.

Salzberg, S. (2005). *The force of kindness: Change your life with love and compassion.* Louisville, CO: Sounds True.

Seligman, M. E. P. (1999). The president's address. *American Psychologist, 54*, 559–562.

Seligman, M. E. P., Nolen-Hoeksema, S., Thornton, N., & Thornton, K. M. (1990). Explanatory style as a mechanism of disappointing athletic performance. *Psychological Science, 1*, 143–146.

Sheldon, K. M., & Lyubomirsky, S. (2006). Achieving sustainable gains in happiness: Change your actions, not your circumstances. *Journal of Happiness Studies, 7*, 55–86.

Skinner, N., & Brewer, N. (2004). Adaptive approaches to competition: Challenge appraisals and positive emotion. *Journal of Sport & Exercise Psychology, 26*, 283–305.

Vallerand, R. J., & Blanchard, C. M. (2000). The study of emotion in sport and exercise: Historical, definitional, and conceptual perspectives. In Y. L. Hanin (Ed.), *Emotions in sport.* (pp. 3–37). Champaign, IL: Human Kinetics.

Watson, D., Clark, L. A., & Tellegen, A. (1988). Development and validation of brief measures of positive and negative affect: The PANAS scales. *Journal of Personality and Social Psychology, 54*, 1063–1070.

16

What happens if you introduce existential psychology into sport psychology?

Jeff Greenberg and Dave Weise

Something good, we think. Sport psychology provides psychological help to athletes and coaches. To do so optimally, it is important to recognize that sports participants are, first and foremost, human beings with the same psychological needs as other members of the species. Existential psychology provides insights into what those psychological needs are and how they may be met. In this chapter, we will summarize these insights and illustrate their value for sport psychologists.

It is useful to begin with the realization that human beings are animals with many of the needs and attributes of other animals. Humans are equipped with many biological systems oriented toward continued survival, and some that facilitate procreation. In addition, as mammals, humans are prone toward attachment to conspecifics and care of offspring. Humans also have certain especially adaptive attributes. Perhaps most important is their intelligence.

Humans have thrived largely because of the intellectual capacities afforded by their highly developed cerebral cortex. We are aware of our existence; we use linguistic symbols to communicate and problem-solve, and we think about the past and imagine possible futures. We use past knowledge and our imaginations to respond flexibly to our environments and develop effective, often novel approaches to achieving our goals.

We can also step back and experience the awe and joy of being alive and accomplishing the amazing things we and others do. This elation is one of the main reasons we enjoy sports so much. Famous athletes such as Usain Bolt, LeBron James, and Ana Ivanovic can marvel at their accomplishments, and fans can too. We can also marvel at our own and others' more modest achievements on courts and fields around the world. And we reminisce about these things and imagine future accomplishments with relish.

These consequences of human intelligence are great, but there is another consequence not so exhilarating: an awareness of sobering facts of human existence – the certainty of death, the uncertainties of what life means and who we are, the complexities of our relations to others, and the choices we make. The term "existential" refers to these basic inescapable realities of the human condition. Accordingly, existential psychology focuses on our concerns and anxieties regarding these realities.

Existential psychology

This field builds on the insights of philosophers such as Kierkegaard, Nietzsche, Heidegger, Sartre, and Camus. Existential themes emerged in the seminal writings of William James and Sigmund Freud, but existential psychology was first developed by Otto Rank (1931/1961), and later expanded by authors such as Rollo May (1953), Victor Frankl (1959), Robert Jay Lifton (1967), Ernest Becker (1973), and Irvin Yalom (1980).

Although existential psychologists traditionally eschewed experimental psychology, since the 1980s an explosion of experimental research has investigated the nature and conse-quences of five existential concerns: death, meaning, identity, isolation, and freedom. These issues have been labeled the Big Five existential concerns, and research regarding them has led to the field of experimental existential psychology (XXP; Koole, Greenberg, & Pyszczynski, 2006). We refer readers to the *Handbook of Experimental Existential Psychology* (Greenberg, Koole, & Pyszczynski, 2004) for in-depth coverage of XXP.

Research regarding the Big Five existential concerns demonstrates that they play substan-tial roles in human behavior. From the existential perspective, people's actions serve a hierarchy of goals, and coping with these Big Five concerns constitutes the higher order, largely unconscious goals that more concrete, conscious goals ultimately serve (Pyszczynski & Greenberg, 1992; Yalom, 1980). Day to day, people focus on concrete goals that help them: (a) believe they will transcend their own deaths and that they are more than material creatures; (b) maintain the view that life is meaningful; (c) sustain a coherent sense of identity; (d) feel intimately connected to others; and (e) optimize personal freedom.

When these concrete goals are not being met, the higher order existential concerns they serve approach consciousness and arouse anxiety. This existential anxiety can fuel personal growth or maladaptive defenses that contribute to anxiety, depression, identity disorders, and alcohol and drug abuse. Existential psychotherapy (Yalom, 1980) helps individuals shift from maladaptive defenses toward more beneficial modes of addressing their existential concerns, modes that contribute to, rather than hinder, effective functioning and life satisfaction.

The existential big five and sports

Sports provide ideal examples of the culturally constructed nature of our sense of perma-nence, meaning, identity, social connection, and freedom. On the one hand, sports are highly valued; on the other, tasks such as putting a rubber ball through a hoop are arbitrar-ily assigned value and are easy to see as meaningless. This view of sports itself can be useful when it is important to help someone put sport in perspective and view it as one of many aspects of life.

For athletes and coaches, sports play significant roles in all of the Big Five existential concerns. Sports can make people feel mortal or truly immortal, imbue life with meaning or call it into question; they can solidify identities and self-worth or undermine them; they can make athletes feel all alone or an integral part of something special; they can be vehicles for asserting personal freedom or constrainers of our sense of freedom.

When things are going well, sports provide paths to feel enduringly significant, and to believe that life is meaningful. They provide a strong sense of identity and social connection and offer a good balance of autonomy and structure that provides manageable levels of freedom. The existential concerns kept at bay by these psychological resources will

151

approach consciousness primarily when events within or outside sport disrupt these ongoing functions.

Accordingly, sport psychologists should be alert to such events. When disruptions arouse one or more existential concerns, people may experience psychological difficulties with anxiety and depression, and they are likely to attempt to intensify their modes of coping in either constructive or maladaptive ways. Six major kinds of sports-related events seem most likely to arouse the Big Five existential concerns: death, injury, retirement, career change (e.g., being traded), failure, and success. Each of these six types of events could arouse any of the Big Five concerns. As we discuss each Big Five concern in turn, we will provide examples of sports events particularly likely to arouse them.

Death

The knowledge that one will inevitably die conflicts with the desire for continued life. According to terror management theory (TMT), the potential for anxiety engendered by this awareness of one's mortality is managed by embracing a culturally based conception of reality, or cultural worldview (see Greenberg, Solomon, & Arndt, 2008, for a recent review). This internalized worldview allows individuals to believe they are eternally significant members of a meaningful universe, rather than material animals fated only to obliteration upon death. Consequently, to function with minimal anxiety despite the awareness of mortality, individuals must sustain faith in a meaning-providing cultural worldview and garner self-esteem, which is provided by the belief that they are living up to the standards of value of that worldview. For athletes and coaches, sports are central aspects of their worldviews and bases of self-worth.

Experimental research consisting of over 400 studies has supported TMT. One line of research has shown that a meaningful conception of reality and a strong sense of self-worth protect people from anxiety and specifically from their fears of death. Both self-report and physiological measures of anxiety have shown these effects. The central message from this line of work is that self-esteem is the primary way people buffer anxieties in their daily lives.

A second line of research has shown that reminders of mortality lead individuals to bolster faith in their cultural worldviews and strive harder for self-worth. Two studies directly established a link between existential concern with death and sports. Taubman Ben-Ari, Florian, and Mikulincer (1999) showed that reminders of mortality led people who based their self-esteem partly on driving skills to drive more boldly in a simulated driving game and to claim to be more willing to take risks in their driving. Peters, Greenberg, Williams, and Schneider (2005) showed that for people who base self-worth partly on their physical strength, reminders of their mortality increased their displays of handgrip strength.

A third line of research has shown that these defensive responses are activated whenever death-related thoughts are on the fringes of consciousness, and they function to dissipate these thoughts and thereby avert the potential anxiety such thoughts engender. Finally, a fourth line of research has shown that when faith in the worldview or self-esteem is threatened, or when people are reminded of their corporeal nature, death-related thoughts move closer to consciousness.

Death rears its ugly head in sports in three main ways. First, physical risks of death are prevalent in a number of sports, including auto racing, boxing, and mountain climbing. This threat undoubtedly weighs on athletes and coaches involved in these sports. Second, close calls in these and other sports may be traumatic, arousing fears and intrusive memories of such events. Third, athletes and coaches may learn of the deaths of others within their sports, and this reminder can arouse death-related concerns. Even in sports such as baseball, basketball, and soccer, freak fatal accidents occur during practices and games, and these events may bring mortality to the fore. Furthermore, members of one's sport, or one's own team, may die suddenly outside the realm of their sport activities.

Athletes and coaches reminded of death in these ways often have specific methods of denying, coping with, or accepting the general risks they face, the harrowing experiences they have, and the news of the death of a fellow athlete. Some develop superstitious rituals; others may rely on religious faith or social support. Sport psychologists should be alert to these strategies and the extent to which they are constructive, harmless, or harmful.

Beyond these strategies, TMT and research suggest that faith in the meaningfulness of sports pursuits and the sense of self-worth athletes derive from them, as well as from other aspects of their lives, will play a considerable role in the effectiveness with which they cope with, and even gain motivation from, these intimations of death. In the case of the death of a current or former teammate, memorializing the individual and dedicating the season to the player or coach are common tactics for denying the finality of death by keeping memories of the fallen colleague alive (see Chapter 38 on death of a teammate).

Finally, terror management research also suggests that serious injuries and major failures can arouse thoughts of death. Serious injuries are salient reminders to athletes that they are physical beings, and hence, mortal creatures. Major failures puncture the protective bubble of symbolic self-worth that normally keeps death-related anxieties at bay. Such failures can lead to defensive lashing out at others in an attempt to deflect blame to try to restore self-esteem. It can also lead to self-medicating through anxiety-reducing alcohol and other drugs. Thus, sport psychologists may want to consider that even events superficially unrelated to death can stir death-related fears that may initiate destructive attempts to cope with this existential anxiety.

When individuals' faith in their worldviews and self-worth can be restored through concrete actions, underlying death concerns can be alleviated. Theory and research, however, suggest that when straightforward constructive paths to restoring these psychological resources are lacking, deeper probing into thoughts and emotions concerning death may be useful for guiding individuals toward new constructive paths of coping (e.g., Greenberg et al., 2004; Yalom, 1980).

Meaning

A meaningful view of life quells death-related concerns, provides purpose, and gives people clear paths to adaptive actions. Given that we will all die, that our understanding of the universe is limited, and that cultures around the world have substantially different ideas about existence, how can we sustain meaning in life? Meaning for people often comes through cultural worldviews conveyed to them over the course of socialization by parents, teachers, mass media, and religious, social, and political institutions.

Knowledge of alternative views of life's meanings and of unexpected and unjust life events, however, often challenges our beliefs about what is meaningful. Such threats can arouse feelings of personal alienation and thoughts that life is pointless, and thereby arouse anxiety and depressive ideation. People cope with threats to meaning either by compensatory efforts to strengthen elements of their worldviews or by seeking new meaning systems, as happens when people convert to a new religion or cult (see Greenberg et al., 2004).

In sports, death or serious injuries can threaten meaning. These events evoke questions such as "Why me?" and threaten one's faith that the world is just. Athletes may believe that their injuries are not fair and realize that such events can happen at any time to anybody, increasing their feelings of uncertainty about meaning in life. Framing these disturbing events as meaningful, for example, as challenges to show one's mettle, and offering hope of overcoming them, can restore a sense of meaning.

Ironically, great achievements in sports can also threaten meaning. After years of training and competing, athletes may achieve their ultimate goals. Subsequently, the athletes will probably experience a period of elation regarding the accomplishments, but then they may ask: "Now what?" On this note, Becker (1974) stated:

> It is the loneliness of the man who has found his talents, realized his identity, pushed his ambition to the fullest, and achieved something of a success in his life, a recognition of his talents. He is then often put in a position to realize that the superlative achievement of cultural heroism somehow rings hollow.
>
> (in Liechty, 2005, p. 234)

To get past this hollow feeling, practitioners can help individuals develop additional goals within the sport, such as pursuing another championship or record, or develop new goals outside the sport.

Identity

We all want to have clear identities, to know who we are. In addition to bestowing meaningful conceptions of the world, cultures provide us with roles and group affiliations that help us develop our identities and goals that support those identities. Erickson (1968) posited that adolescence is a key time for developing a clear identity. Nevertheless, throughout one's life, our beliefs about ourselves require validation from other people. When we fall short of their expectations, we may feel uncertain about aspects of our identities, which can arouse considerable anxiety. To attempt to reduce this anxiety, people often cling tightly and rigidly to their cherished beliefs about themselves. At other times, they may choose to give up an identity and seek new group affiliations, relationships, and career paths to more firmly establish a sense of who they are.

Over the lifespan, each of us has a variety of different beliefs, values, and goals: we look, feel, and act differently in different situations over time. In light of this variability, how do people maintain coherent identities? People do so primarily by viewing their lives as ongoing stories with themselves as the protagonists. McAdams (2001) suggested that we order our life experiences in logical time sequences that tell the stories of our identities, how we became who we are and where we expect to go in life. Research supports the value of having an integrated sense of self over time. Self-narrative research indicates that writing a coherent story (as opposed to making a fragmented list) about a traumatic life event has positive health benefits (e.g., Smyth, True, & Sotto, 2001). This work suggests that getting clients to write or talk extensively about such events can be beneficial because it facilitates integrating the events into their self-narratives.

For longtime athletes or coaches, identities are often tied up in their roles within their sports. When their careers end, whether due to injury, age, retirement, or being fired, their identities may become uncertain. To the extent that identity allows one to experience the world in a meaningful way and guides action, athletes may have difficulties deciding what to do with their time, or finding things to do that are as meaningful as the sporting activity.

Letting go of their primary sports identities and establishing post-sports identities that allow them to sustain their sense of value within society is often a difficult task. In the film *The Wrestler*, a professional wrestler has a chance to quit and greatly improve his social relationships outside the ring, but ultimately he can't let go of the minor heroism provided by his identity as a wrestler. In real life, sports identities may be so strong that many star athletes have difficulty staying retired (e.g., Björn Borg, Brett Favre, Martina Hingis).

Long-term plans and career-marking ceremonies can facilitate smooth transitions to post-career identities by helping individuals sustain coherent self-narratives. This transition is easiest when post-career endeavors still relate to the former sports-based identity (e.g., coaching, sports broadcasting). Furthermore, the more individuals already have well-established multiple identities outside of sports during their careers (e.g., spouse, parent, business person, philanthropist), the easier it will be to give up their center-stage sports identities when circumstances dictate this. See Chapters 26 and 30 on career termination and identity foreclosure, respectively, in this book.

Isolation

Based on our mammalian ancestry, humans have needs to attach to and feel connected with fellow humans. Nevertheless, we all have interior subjective experiences that we can never entirely share with others. We can try to communicate our inner experiences through words, facial expressions, and body language, but we can never fully know another's conscious experience, and no one can ever fully know ours. This realization can arouse feelings of loneliness and isolation that generate anxiety and depression. Research suggests that people try to cope with these feelings by seeking intimacy in their close relationships and by sustaining interpersonal affiliations and group identities that help them conceive themselves as part of a larger whole rather than as an isolated organism.

One effective way to feel less isolated is to develop a relationship with someone who seems to have similar subjective experiences of reality as oneself, a process known as I-sharing (Pinel, Long, Landau, Alexander, & Pyszczynski, 2006). Research has demonstrated that sharing subjective experiences (e.g., giggling at a quirky behavior of another) leads to more attraction than sharing objective characteristics (e.g., having the same hometown).

Another line of research indicates that we attempt to connect by including important others in our self-concepts, a process called self-expansion (Aron & Aron, 1996). In this process, as a relationship deepens, one should perceive more overlap between one's self-concept and the self-concept of a relationship partner. Consistent with this perspective, people in close relationships allocated a similar level of resources to a close other as they did to themselves (Aron & Aron).

Being cut and traded are common sports experiences that can suddenly disrupt connections to valued colleagues and groups. A severe injury that sidelines a player or coach, thereby removing the person from his or her accustomed social milieu, can have similar effects. Failure can also lead to a deep sense of isolation. In American sports, one sees this process when a football placekicker misses a last minute kick or a baseball pitcher is pulled from a game; fans turn on them, and teammates often drift away from the player.

The ensuing loss of camaraderie and connection can arouse feelings of isolation and alienation. Social support systems of family and friends outside the sport can buffer against such reactions, and establishing new social roles, personal relationships, and group affiliations

155

can help individuals recover from the blow of disrupted social connections. Although social support can lessen the sting of existential isolation, the sport psychologist may also judiciously use occasions of disrupted social connections to help clients "learn what they cannot get from others" (Yalom, 1980, p. 397).

Ironically, high-level success can contribute to feelings of isolation, hence the cliché that "it's lonely at the top." We all want to be special, but we want to maintain our connections to others as well. Superstars may feel particularly isolated because their experiences and pressures are exceptional, and they have to be guarded wherever they go. Whatever they do may become fodder for tabloids. Adulation from strangers can provide a strong sense of value, but it is strange and in some ways unsatisfying to be "loved" by people who don't really know you. Many people want to be around sports stars to bask in their reflected glory, make money, and share in the lifestyle. But with so many ulterior motives for being befriended, how can stars know if others ever genuinely care about them? How many of these people would stick around if their careers fell apart? Family and friends who were there prior to their success can help stars feel grounded, as they are people who really know and accept them, regardless of what they can gain from them. Whether they are feeling isolated because of career-ending events or because of exceptional success, being able to have people around with whom the athlete or coach can experience I-sharing and self–other overlap can help sustain the sense of intimate connection they, like all of us, need.

Freedom

Freedom is perhaps the most complex existential concern because people are ambivalent about it. On the one hand, people generally like choice, control, a sense of independence, and autonomy. Reactance theory explains how people defend against threats to their perceived freedoms (see Brehm & Brehm, 1981). Also, self-determination theory and research show how people function optimally when they have a sense of autonomy and feel that their actions are self-determined (Deci & Ryan, 2003).

On the other hand, Rank (1931/1961), Fromm (1941), and others noted that freedom offers people so many choices that they can become mired in indecision. Furthermore, freedom brings a great burden of responsibility for one's own actions, and potential guilt, shame, and regret. Consequently, people often willingly give up their freedoms to close others, groups, leaders, and social institutions (see Turner, 1991), allowing them to make their decisions, thereby reducing their potential guilt.

Athletes and coaches are usually parts of larger systems. They answer to higher authorities, such as head coaches, owners, and sports governing bodies. Sports participants can view these contextual factors as overly restrictive of their freedoms, contributing to resentment, dissatisfaction, and reactance. Sometimes the answer is to get out of the context; other times it is best to recognize the value of the larger structure and the freedoms one does have within it. Similarly, at times the larger organization may provide too much freedom and not enough structure. An individual might do well as an assistant coach but not be suited to the additional demands of being a head coach. Another individual may thrive as a head coach but not be able to handle the additional choices of simultaneously functioning as the general manager. One football quarterback could thrive calling his own plays and audibling a lot, whereas another is better off having them called by the coaches. People differ in their perceived freedoms, their desires for control, and their needs for structure (e.g., Burger & Cooper, 1979). The optimal situation is a good match between the structure provided by the organization and the needs of the individual. If there is a strong mismatch, some form of change is needed.

Fans and injuries can also restrict freedoms and arouse reactance responses. Fan expectations, adulation, and stalking, particularly for major stars, can impinge on athletes' and coaches' freedoms, both within their sport lives and their private lives as well. Some people can handle the pressures well, some not so well. There are constructive measures that can be taken to minimize these threats to freedom, but again, sometimes it's a matter of match. If a soccer player is likely to have difficulty with restrictions of freedom in his personal life, playing for Manchester United may simply not be the right choice for that individual.

Finally, injuries and age can restrict freedoms. Because of these factors, athletes may have to realize that they cannot do all the things they once could. They may have to learn to accept these restrictions and optimize their play in other ways. For example, in his later years Michael Jordan learned to rely more on his jump shot and defensive positioning, and a bit less on his leaping ability and raw speed. Rather than becoming frustrated with the physical limitations of aging, he adjusted to the point where many observers felt he became a better player later in his career (although not during his post-retirement comeback). A broad acceptance of the realities of the physical body and of aging may facilitate optimal adjustments in one's functioning within and outside sports.

Conclusion

We suggest that sport psychologists add knowledge of XXP to the theoretical basis of their therapeutic repertoires. Although athletes and coaches may sometimes be at a loss for words as to what is bothering them, the Big Five existential concerns may often be at the root of their unhappiness. XXP is a young field, so only broad recommendations for assessment and treatment can be offered at this time.

When clients experience one of the six types of events likely to arouse existential concerns, sport psychologists could administer a subset of available measures pertinent to the Big Five (Greenberg et al., 2004). These measures assess: death anxiety, the accessibility of death-related thoughts, and sense of symbolic immortality; meaningfulness of and satisfaction with life; self-clarity, self-coherence, and self-worth; self–other overlap and feelings of social disconnection; needs for control and structure; a sense of autonomy; and perceptions of being controlled.

If such assessment tools confirm a deficit in managing one or more of these existential concerns, one of two broad approaches to helping the client can be useful (cf., Yalom, 1980). Sometimes, just being aware of these deeper concerns aroused by life challenges can assist the practitioner in developing strategies to help restore salubrious paths of coping. This first approach is probably preferred when clients are not very consciously aware of their existential concerns and when specific strategies to facilitate progress toward the concrete goals that serve the higher order existential concerns are readily identifiable.

A second, more direct approach, however, is useful when clients are either: (a) self-aware and introspective, and thus conscious of the existential issues; or (b) need to make substantial changes in their concrete goals to shore up the psychological resources that quell existential concerns. For such clients, sport psychologists would find it useful to bring one or more of these concerns into awareness and help the clients confront these concerns consciously and in depth. This approach can help clients let go of concrete goals no longer feasible and move toward constructing new and more effective goal pursuits that will better serve their deepest existential needs (Pyszczynski & Greenberg, 1992; Yalom, 1980). Either way XXP is used, we believe that it can enrich the practice of sport psychology. See Box 16.1 for take-home messages from this chapter.

Box 16.1

Take-home messages about existential psychology

- Human intelligence leads to awareness of existential concerns, which can cause anxiety.
- Disruptions in concrete everyday goals (e.g., failure, retirement) arouse these largely unconscious concerns, known as the existential Big Five: death, meaning, identity, isolation, and freedom.
- Coaches' or athletes' responses to increased awareness of these existential issues can vary from maladaptive to constructive.
- A goal of the existential sport psychologist is to help guide the athlete or coach experiencing these existential concerns toward constructive means of coping.

References

Aron, E. N., & Aron, A. (1996). Love and the expansion of the self: The state of the model. *Personal Relationships, 3,* 45–58.

Becker, E. (1973). *The denial of death.* New York: Free Press.

Becker, E. (1974). The spectrum of loneliness. *Humanitas, 10,* 237–246.

Brehm, S., & Brehm, J. W. (1981). *Psychological reactance: A theory of freedom and control.* New York: Academic Press.

Burger, J. M., & Cooper, H. M. (1979). The desirability of control. *Motivation and Emotion, 3,* 381–393.

Deci, E., & Ryan, R. (2003). On assimilating the self: A self-determination theory perspective on internalization and integrity within cultures. In M. R. Leary & J. P. Tangney (Eds.), *Handbook of self and identity* (pp. 253–272). New York: Guilford Press.

Erikson, E. H. (1968). *Identity: Youth and crisis.* New York: Norton.

Frankl, V. (1959). *Man's search for meaning.* New York: Simon & Schuster.

Fromm, E. (1941). *Escape from freedom.* New York: Farrer & Rinehart.

Greenberg, J., Koole, S. L., & Pyszczynski, T. (Eds.). (2004). *Handbook of experimental existential psychology.* New York: Guilford Press.

Greenberg, J., Solomon, S., & Arndt, J. (2008). A basic but uniquely human motivation: Terror management. In J. Y. Shah & W. L. Gardner (Eds.), *Handbook of motivation science* (pp. 114–134). New York: Guilford Press.

Koole, S. L., Greenberg, J., & Pyszczynski, T. (2006). Introducing science to the psychology of the soul: Experimental existential psychology. *Current Directions in Psychological Science, 15,* 212–216.

Liechty, D. (2005). *The Ernest Becker reader.* Seattle, WA: University of Washington Press.

Lifton, R. J. (1967). *Death in life: Survivors of Hiroshima.* New York: Random House.

May, R. (1953). *Man's search for himself.* New York: Norton.

McAdams, D. P. (2001). The psychology of life stories. *Review of General Psychology, 5,* 100–122.

Peters, H. J., Greenberg, J., Williams, J. M., & Schneider, N. R. (2005). Applying terror management theory to performance: Can reminding individuals of their mortality increase strength output? *Journal of Sports & Exercise Psychology, 27,* 111–116.

Pinel, E. C., Long, A. E., Landau, M. J., Alexander, K., & Pyszczynski, T. (2006). Seeing I to I: A pathway to interpersonal connectedness. *Journal of Personality and Social Psychology, 90*, 243–257.

Pyszczynski, T., & Greenberg, J. (1992). *Hanging on and letting go: Understanding the onset, progression, and remission of depression*. New York: Springer-Verlag.

Rank, O. (1931/1961). *Psychology and the soul*. New York: Perpetua Books.

Smyth, J., True, N., & Souto, J. (2001). Effects of writing about traumatic experiences: The necessity for narrative structuring. *Journal of Social and Clinical Psychology, 20*, 161–172.

Taubman Ben-Ari, O., Florian, V., & Mikulincer, M. (1999). The impact of mortality salience on reckless driving: A test of terror management mechanisms. *Journal of Personality and Social Psychology, 76*, 35–45.

Turner, J. C. (1991). *Social influence*. Pacific Grove, CA: Brooks/Cole.

Yalom, I. D. (1980). *Existential psychotherapy*. New York: Basic Books.

17

Psychodynamic models of therapy

Mark B. Andersen

"I have done that," says my memory, "I cannot have done that," says my pride, and remains inexorable. Eventually – memory yields.

Friedrich Nietzsche (1886, 1966)

Nietzsche's epigram, written before Freud first used the term "repression," is a near-perfect poetic description of that defense mechanism. Many prototypes of Freudian concepts (e.g., id, ego, superego, the unconscious, repression, sublimation) can be found in Nietzsche's work, and he had a substantial influence on Freud and other psychodynamic theorists and practitioners (e.g., Carl Jung, Alfred Adler).

In 1874, the German physiologist, Ernst Wilhelm von Brücke, first coined the word "psychodynamics" (psychological thermodynamics). Brücke was also the supervisor of a medical student named Sigismund (later abbreviated to "Sigmund") Freud. The term "psychodynamic" is a good example of how the *Zeitgeist* (spirit of the age) exerts an influence on how theorists conceptualize psychological phenomena. For example, the *Zeitgeist* of the time of Galileo and Descartes was optics, and Descartes's model of mind and body interaction is decidedly optical. The spirit of the age at the end of the nineteenth and the beginning of the twentieth centuries was physics. Freud's model of the human psyche is physics rewritten for psychological structures and functions. Psychodynamic models (originally) were about the flow of energy (e.g., from the unconscious to consciousness), the storage or investment of energy (e.g., cathexis), and the release of energy (e.g., catharsis, abreaction). There is the energy, or "instinct force" of the libido, originally conceived as sexual, but later modified as "the energy that manifests itself in the life process and is perceived subjectively as striving and desire" (Ellenberger, 1970, p. 697). Psychodynamic psychotherapies (there are many) have survived long past the *Zeitgeist* of physics, and their visibility in clinical psychology, counseling, and clinical social work is high. In applied sport psychology, however, we haven't seen much discussion or use of psychodynamic principles until recently.

Basic psychodynamics

The history of psychodynamic therapies goes back at least to the time of Mesmer (1734–1815), but psychodynamic medicine really burst on the scene in the latter part of the 1800s with the work of Jean-Martin Charcot (see Goetz, Bonduelle, & Gelfand, 1995) and Pierre Janet (1925) in France and Josef Breuer and Sigmund Freud (Breuer & Freud, 1895/1973) in Austria. Freud gets most of the credit for the development of psychodynamic theory and practice, and so he should. Since the middle of the sixteenth century, there have been, arguably, three major revolutions in the Western world about humans and their place in the universe. The first major revolution was Copernicus's heliocentric model of the solar system (a cosmological revolution). Humans no longer sat at the center of God's creation (this may not seem so "revolutionary" to us, but back then it was a huge change). Then in 1859, Darwin published *On the Origin of Species* and kicked us out of our special place in God's creation (and being made in "His" image). We became like all the other creatures on the planet, subject to the same laws of natural selection and evolution (many people are still unhappy about the Darwinian biological revolution). Finally, Freud brought about a psychological revolution shattering our myth that even if we were animals, we were "rational" animals, and therefore, *special*. We are often irrational beings with a lot of our motivations for behavior stemming from internal conflicts, unconscious desires, and childhood histories lost to conscious access. Freud helped kick us out of our self-satisfied rational minds.

The Freudian revolution is still with us today. His language and concepts pervade our language and how we think about ourselves and others. His influence has spread deeply into art, literature, sociology, anthropology, and feminism (there is a whole movement of psychodynamic feminist theorists and psychotherapists). Concepts such as unconscious motivation, anal retentiveness, slips of the tongue (parapraxes), Oedipus complex, libido, regression, repression, denial, projection, and so forth are all part of how we talk about ourselves. Freud and his legacy (all the Neo-Freudians, the object-relations theorists, the Lacanians) are everywhere.

Core concepts

At the heart of psychodynamic theories lies the unconscious. It is the repository for early childhood memories, conflicts, unacceptable sexual and aggressive desires, and other material that cannot be consciously tolerated or endured. One of the main aims of psychodynamic psychotherapy is to attempt to reveal what is unconscious and thereby decrease the power of the internal conflicts influencing our lives in maladaptive ways. Through insights into the ways unconscious conflicts affect us, through a kind of remembering, we are able to recognize the roots of our unhappiness and maladaptive patterns of behavior and then do something different. This remembering is accomplished in a number of ways such as through dream analysis and free association.

Free association

One of the few rules in psychodynamic psychotherapy is for clients to try to report whatever is happening for them in the here and now (e.g., cognitions, emotions, desires, anxieties, somatic symptoms). When I first talk to my clients in psychodynamic psychotherapy, I say something like:

> One of the only rules to this type of therapy is that you agree to try to tell me whatever is on your mind, without censoring. That's a difficult task because we all censor our thoughts and feelings. I censor; you censor, and we have lots of practise at keeping stuff to ourselves. Even if your thoughts or feelings seem trivial or "out of left field,"

161

still try to tell me about them. They come up for a reason, and they may be connected to what we are looking for. Even if the thoughts and feelings are shameful, painful, or embarrassing, let them come out. And if you ever have something pop into your mind, and then you think, "Ooh, I don't want to tell Mark that," then that is exactly what we should talk about. Also, if you are having some reaction to me, such as you get mad at me, or you think I am being an idiot, then tell me about that too. Your reactions to me, and why they came about, may help us shed some light on your interactions with others when you have become angry with them. How does all that sound?

I also let my clients know that I will occasionally tell them how I am reacting to the stories they tell and their other free associations, because clients usually benefit from feedback on how what they do and say affects others. Examining how my clients affect me may help them understand how they are perceived by others.

Free association is also one of the ways to examine and analyze dreams. There are many ways to explore dreams, but one of the most common techniques is to have the client recall the dream and then ask, "What comes to mind when you think about X (a certain image, action, emotion, character, or place in the dream)?" The practitioner is essentially asking the client to free associate on elements of the dream. Through the connections made during free association, what the dream might be about may become clear, or at least less cryptic than when first recalled.

Early childhood experiences

When one thinks of it, we probably learn more in the first six to eight years of life than we ever learn in the next 70 years. We learn to speak; we lay the foundations for reading and writing; we learn about relationships; we learn about right and wrong; we learn about love (that it is always there, or that it is unavailable, or that it is contingent, or that it can become hate); we learn about safety and vulnerability; we learn about trust (or mistrust); we learn about pride and shame. In psychodynamic theory, these years have a vast influence on how individuals develop into adolescence and adulthood. Patterns of relationships, emotional responses to love and threat, and behavioral tendencies all get laid down in childhood. For example, a child with a physically abusive alcoholic mother will experience chaos in the areas of love and attachment. One day the sober good Mom is around, attending to and playing with the child; the next day the drunk mean Mom shows up and beats and berates the child. The following day, Mom says she is so sorry. And the pattern repeats. The child may believe it is his fault that his Mom is so angry and hurtful (children often take on the responsibility for their parents' emotional states) and do everything to make sure Mom stays happy (achieve in school, become a perfectionist). To defend himself the child may become seriously mistrustful or, as compensation, develop fantasies that his Mom is not his real Mom, and that his good, always-loving Mom will someday come back to him. These experiences, and the child's responses to manage the chaos, get the love he wants, and stay safe, all have survival value and are "adaptive" when one is a child. These patterns, however, have use-by dates, and when they manifest in adulthood, they are usually maladaptive. In this case, if the boy is heterosexual, as a man he may have difficulties trusting women he finds attractive. Or, if a woman comes along who somewhat matches his childhood fantasy of his good Mom, he may project that fantasy onto her, fall hopelessly in love, do everything he possibly can to keep her happy, and smother her to the point she runs away, which then confirms his deep mistrust of women. And the cycle goes on.

Transference and countertransference

Transference in psychodynamic psychotherapy is one of the key phenomena that helps bring about change. In transference, clients begin to transfer, or project onto the therapist, thoughts and emotional responses that are similar to how they have responded in the past to significant others (parents, grandparents, siblings) or past fantasized others (see Chapter 1). Transference occurs not only in therapy, but in life in general. Our patterns and responses to others, which we learned early in life, get applied to current relationships. The analysis of transference can help clients see and understand their adaptive and maladaptive attachments to others. As therapy progresses, we hope the transference changes as the relationship between the therapist and client deepens and becomes a model for healthy human connection. Therapy then becomes the "practice ground" where the client can try out new ways of interacting with others that then can be used in the real world in current and future relationships.

Countertransference is the same as transference, but it is the therapist transferring material from past relationships onto the client. Positive countertransference may take the form of good paternal or maternal feelings, or big brother–big sister protective responses. Some researchers in countertransference in sport consider it to be not only the projection of past or fantasized relationships, but nearly all of the feelings and thoughts the client evokes in the therapist (e.g., Winstone & Gervis, 2006). A sport psychologist may be envious of an athlete's success, or angry with the athlete for not doing psychological homework. Both negative and positive responses to clients need to be examined. When I do psychodynamic supervision, I often ask my supervisees questions such as: Do you like the athlete? Does the athlete remind you of anyone? Who do you think you are for the athlete? As the athlete told you that story, what was happening with you? Such questions may lead to insights for supervisees about their own past relationships and how those influence current interactions with clients. A substantial part of psychodynamic supervision, just as in therapy, is examining the transference and countertransference between the supervisor and the supervisee. Examining countertransference is a deep form of reflective practice and often leads to an increased self-awareness for the therapist.

Transference and countertransference reactions can move into the extremely sensitive (and sometimes dangerous) realm of the erotic. Having erotic feelings or fantasies about clients is natural. Most of us are sexual, sensuous beings, and we often work with healthy, vigorous, and attractive clients. Sport psychologists who say they have never had any erotic feelings or thoughts about clients (e.g., I wonder what he looks like naked) are either lying or they are hopelessly unself-aware and repressed (see the defense mechanism section below). It is when those thoughts and feelings get translated into some action that trouble begins. See Stevens and Andersen's (2007a, 2007b) two-part study for a thorough discussion of the erotic in applied sport psychology service delivery.

Defense mechanisms

The analysis of defense mechanisms is common in many psychotherapies, but in psychodynamic psychotherapy these mechanisms are central to the work, and analyzing them and how they function in relationships, in thoughts, in feelings, and in the clients' own self-concepts helps bring these patterns of defense to consciousness so that they can be overcome. Defense mechanisms are usually formed to protect the self (or ego) from anxiety.

Defense mechanisms operate on various levels, from unconscious to conscious. For example, repression is a process that buries memories so far into the unconscious that they are not accessible to the individual, and the person has no knowledge that repression has taken place. Likewise projection, or taking one's own unacceptable or shameful feelings and thoughts and attributing them to another person (e.g., I don't hate Dad; Dad hates me), is an unconscious process. Other defense mechanisms, such as sublimation, may be more or less conscious. An example of sublimation would be taking a taboo impulse of (consciously) wanting to punch a coach in the nose, but channeling that aggression into going for an exhausting run. Denial can also be relatively conscious when one knows at some level one has behaved in a shameful manner, but denies that the event occurred. Suppression is also a conscious process, involving actively trying to put away awareness of unpleasant thoughts or anxiety-provoking feelings. Suppression is often not successful. There are many other defense mechanisms (e.g., regression, somatization, idealization, dissociation, intellectualization), but a thorough discussion of them would take up two or three chapters in this book.

Defense mechanisms are usually automatic and over-learned, and, in a sense, one is chained to one's defensive patterns. Through free association and examining defensive transferential material, clients may get to know and understand their defensive and often maladaptive patterns, be able to recognize them as they start to pop up, and then replace them with some realistic and rational responses.

Psychodynamics in applied sport psychology

Psychodynamic-based studies in sport psychology have appeared sporadically in the literature over the last several decades. Johnson *et al.* (1954) used psychodynamic projective tests to explore the personalities of champion athletes. Berger and MacKenzie (1980) conducted an in-depth case study of a female jogger and analyzed their data psychodynamically. Strean and Strean (1998) published an article about using psychodynamic theory and practice in applied sport psychology, and Conroy and Benjamin (2001) suggested incorporating interpersonal theory (a psychodynamic model) into sport performance enhancement consultation. In a rare move, Hill (2001), in the first chapter of her book, *Frameworks for Sport Psychologists: Enhancing Sport Performance*, discussed in an even-handed manner many of the potential positive applications of psychodynamic theory in sport contexts. Andersen (2005) presented a psychodynamic case study of the supervision of a graduate student caught up in erotic transference and countertransference with his volleyball client (Strean & Strean, 2005, also added a commentary to Andersen's chapter that explored, in even further depth than Andersen had, the subterranean dynamic issues involved). And finally, Andersen (2009) presented another case study of the cognitive-behavioral treatment of a ballet dancer's performance problems and how psychodynamic principles underpinned the interventions and the success of treatment.

There are many more psychodynamic studies in the applied sport psychology literature, but they do not seem to form a coherent body of work. The good news, for those of us who are dynamically oriented, is that studies, such as the ones cited above, are appearing more frequently than they have in the past. In this book, the other dynamically oriented contribution (besides Chapter 1) is Petah Gibb's work in Chapter 11 (projective assessment).

Preparing a client for psychodynamic psychotherapy

When someone calls or emails me and asks if it is possible for me to see them in therapy, I almost always arrange for a pre-therapy meeting at no cost to the person. I usually meet them in a neutral location such as a coffee shop during a quiet time of the day. I take this tactic for a number of reasons. I only do psychodynamic psychotherapy now, and although this sort of treatment can be relatively brief (Basch, 1995), it is usually lengthy. The length of therapy equates to a substantial investment in time and money. I also want to hear at least an outline of the client's concerns. Once I understand what the client is looking for, I can then determine if I might be a good match for therapy. If I am not, then I will make a referral. After I have determined that the client would be a good candidate for psychodynamic therapy, I explain how the therapy I practise works. I usually say something like:

> The kind of therapy I do is an exploration of how you got to where you are today. We want to look at the areas in your life where things are going well, and the parts of your world where there are concerns. We'll look at your current patterns of thoughts, emotions, and behaviors, but we'll also want to explore where those thoughts and emotions came from. So we will look at how you are functioning right now, but we will also explore your past, probably going back into your childhood and teenage years too. We're like a couple of explorers trying to map out the landscape of your life. We'll look at your relationships and major events from your life and how they might be connected to what is going on for you now. As we grow to understand your life, we will then have a foundation for making changes for the better. Does this type of therapy sound like something you would want to do?

If clients say, "yes" then I usually talk about free association (as described before), and I also give them a warning. I tell them that there is a good chance that as we travel along this journey they will possibly start to feel worse than they do now. I explain that as we excavate their lives we will probably come across painful material that will be upsetting. Regarding painful material, I also explain that I need their permission when overwhelming feelings of sadness or shame or anger arise (and they will) that they grant me the right to keep my finger on the hurtful button and help them stay with the shame or sadness, and not run away from it. For example, when clients start to cry in therapy, I stay silent for awhile as their emotions flow, and then I say "tears are telling us something is important; let's stay with those tears and see if we can figure out what story they are telling us."

After warning them about getting worse and asking permission to help them stay with uncomfortable feelings, I often tell the Sufi story of the wise fool, Nasruddin, and how one day Nasruddin lost his ring in his basement, where it was dark, so he went outside to search for it because there was more light out there (for the full Islamic folktale, see Andersen & Speed, in press). I conclude the story with what Andersen and Speed (in press) wrote:

> [I think] "most of us are like Nasruddin, searching in the light for something that is missing (or not right). We stay in the light and on the surface where the search is easier (and safer, but not too fruitful). What we don't do is explore the darkness and the subterranean (Nasruddin's basement, a client's suppressed or repressed emotions, the unconscious). We may find some interesting and useful things out in the light, but often what we are looking for, like Nasruddin's ring, lies in a darkness that is uncertain and possibly scary. The process of psychotherapy often involves moving from the light to the darkness and searching there, but I will be with you in both the light and darkness as we go on this search together." Many of my clients respond with something like, "I've never heard of Nasruddin, but I like that story. I sort of feel like him. I've been looking around for a long time, but I am not finding any answers."

It is probably quite noticeable that I use the word "we" a lot. That use is intentional and designed to convey that "we" are in this adventure together. Establishing a "we" is the first major step in building a solid therapeutic relationship (see Chapter 1). Somewhere in this pre-therapy meeting, we also talk about confidentiality and fees. I usually bring the session to a close with, "OK, so when would you like to start?"

Conclusion

Psychodynamic psychotherapy is probably relatively foreign for many practising sport psychologists, given the small and disjointed literature and the dominance of the cognitive-behavioral paradigm for psychological skills training. Also, training in psychodynamic psychotherapy takes years of education and practice. But that is not to say that applied sport psychologists cannot use some of the concepts and principles of psychodynamic theory and practice, such as free association, examining relationships, exploring significant events in athletes' childhoods, and reflecting on transference and countertransference possibilities.

Here at the end of the chapter, I would like to tell a story about training fleas to jump only to a certain height. That may sound odd, but bear with me. If you take a flea, place it in a jar, and close the lid, some interesting things will happen. At first, the flea may not do much more than explore the bottom of the jar. Eventually, the flea will use its powerful flea legs and jump, usually resulting in smacking itself into the lid (ouch!). Fleas are great calculators. The one in the jar may jump another time and hit itself on the lid, but it won't be as strong of an impact as the first jump. From then on, it won't jump up high enough to reach the lid. You can remove the lid, and the flea will never jump out of the jar. In some ways, most of us are like trained fleas. We limit our behaviors or emotions or we keep making the same mistakes (not jumping high enough) because we are stuck in a pattern we learned early. We are shackled by barriers (a lid, an alcoholic parent, a horrific trauma) that no longer exist. Psychodynamic psychotherapy helps us use our current strengths to explore those barriers, see them for what they were and where they came from, and learn to walk around their non-existence. See Box 17.1 for a summary of the key points from this chapter.

Box 17.1

Summary of key points about psychodynamic psychotherapy

- Psychodynamic psychotherapy developed when the scientific *Zeitgeist* of the time was physics, and the theory behind the therapy stems from applying thermodynamics to psychological phenomena.
- One of the core concepts in psychodynamic psychotherapy is the unconscious and its influences on thoughts, emotions, and behaviors.
- Free association (and dream analysis) is one of the means by which clients start to access unconscious material.
- Early childhood experiences play a major role in establishing adaptive and maladaptive behaviors and responses in adulthood.
- Positive change in therapy often occurs through the analysis of transference.

■ Defense mechanisms serve to keep anxiety about unacceptable thoughts, feelings, and past trauma at bay.

■ The applied sport psychology literature has several examples of applying psychodynamic theories to sport and exercise, but they have been sporadic.

■ Psychodynamic psychotherapy is usually a long-term endeavor that is aimed at examining the life of a client. One needs to carefully prepare a client for such a journey.

References

Andersen, M. B. (2005). Touching taboos: Sex and the sport psychologist. In M. B. Andersen (Ed.), *Sport psychology in practice* (pp. 171–191). Champaign, IL: Human Kinetics.

Andersen, M. B. (2009). The "canon" of psychological skills training for enhancing performance. In K. F. Hays (Ed.), *Performance psychology in action: A casebook for working with athletes, performing artists, business leaders, and professionals in high-risk occupations* (pp. 11–34). Washington, DC: American Psychological Association.

Andersen, M. B., & Speed, H. D. (in press). The practitioner and client as story tellers: Metaphors and folktales in applied sport psychology practice. In D. Gilbourne & M. B. Andersen (Eds.), *Critical essays in applied sport psychology*. Champaign, IL: Human Kinetics.

Basch, F. M. (1995). *Doing brief psychotherapy*. New York: Basic Books.

Berger, B., & MacKenzie, M. M. (1980). Case study of a woman jogger: A psychodynamic analysis. *Journal of Sport Behavior, 3*, 3–16.

Breuer, J., & Freud, S. (1973). *Studies on hysteria*. In J. Stachey (Ed. & Trans.), *Standard edition of the complete psychological works of Sigmund Freud*, (Vol. 2, pp. 3–305). London: Hogarth Press. (Original work published 1895)

Conroy, D. E., & Benjamin, L. S. (2001). Psychodynamics in sport performance enhancement consultation: Application of an interpersonal theory. *The Sport Psychologist, 15*, 103–117.

Ellenberger, H. F. (1970). *The discovery of the unconscious: The history and evolution of dynamic psychiatry*. New York: Basic Books.

Goetz, C. G., Bonduelle, M., & Gelfand, T. (1995). *Charcot: Constructing neurology*. New York: Oxford University Press.

Hill, K. L. (2001). *Frameworks for sport psychologists: Enhancing sport performance*. Champaign, IL: Human Kinetics.

Janet, P. (1925). *Psychological healing: A historical and clinical study* (E. Paul & C. Paul, Trans.). London: Allen & Unwin.

Johnson, W. R., Hutton, D. C., & Johnson, G. B. (1954). Personality traits of some champion athletes as measured by two projective tests: Rorschach and H-T-P. *Research Quarterly, 25*, 484–485.

Nietzsche, F. (1886/1966). *Beyond good and evil: Prelude to a philosophy of the future* (W. Kaufmann, Trans.). New York: Vintage Books.

Stevens, L., & Andersen, M. B. (2007a). Transference and countertransference in sport psychology service delivery: Part I. A review of erotic attraction. *Journal of Applied Sport Psychology, 19*, 253–269.

Stevens, L., & Andersen, M. B. (2007b). Transference and countertransference in sport psychology service delivery: Part II. Two case studies on the erotic. *Journal of Applied Sport Psychology, 19*, 270–287.

Strean, W. B., & Strean, H. S. (1998). Applying psychodynamic concepts to sport psychology practice. *The Sport Psychologist, 12*, 208–222.

Strean, W. B., & Strean, H. S. (2005). Commentary on chapter 10. In M. B. Andersen (Ed.), *Sport psychology in practice* (pp. 193–198). Champaign, IL: Human Kinetics.

Winstone, W. & Gervis, M. (2006). Countertransference and the self-aware sport psychologist: Attitudes and patterns of professional practice. *The Sport Psychologist, 20*, 485–511.

18

Sport as a context for teaching life skills

Kathryn A. Conley, Steven J. Danish, and Cassandra D. Pasquariello

In this chapter we focus on how sport can be an environment for teaching life skills to athletes of all ages. Because we have adopted a life skills perspective, our aims may differ from other sport psychology orientations. Our objective is to promote the development of athletes both during their athletic careers and when their athletic careers are over. Life skill-oriented sport psychologists work to help athletes develop the skills necessary to perform at their best in all areas of their lives. As illustrated in Table 18.1, we at the Life Skills Center seek to have athletes learn how to have competencies in the physical, technical, mental, emotional, and social domains. Athletes who adopt a life skills perspective strive to be physically fit, aware of their strengths and weaknesses, and confident. They have the ability to focus, set goals, use positive self-talk, have fun, choose their attitudes, relax, and manage and express emotions in healthy ways. These competencies are also needed to be a happy and well-balanced individual.

The Carnegie Corporation of New York (1995), in a report from the Carnegie Council on Adolescent Development, identified a number of desired adolescent development outcomes that can be summarized as the ability to work well, play well, love well, think well, serve well, and be well (Bloom, 2000; Danish, 2000). Others who study positive development might refer to these concepts as the goals of character education, social-emotional learning, resilience, positive psychology, and/or emotional intelligence. We chose the term *life skills* because our focus is on teaching skills (Danish, Petitpas, & Hale, 1993) and because of the connection between skills and sport. By describing life skills as *skills*, we are emphasizing that the process of learning life skills parallels the learning of any skill, whether it is throwing a ball, driving a car, or baking a cake. Just as individuals are taught skills to become successful athletes, they can also be taught to become successful individuals (Danish & Forneris, 2008). Many of the skills sport psychologists use to enhance athletic performance become life skills when applied to teaching athletes to achieve personal well-being.

Life skills can enhance competence and promote personal growth throughout the life span. Life skills can be *behavioral*, communicating effectively with peers and adults; *cognitive*, making effective decisions; *interpersonal*, being assertive; or *intrapersonal*, setting goals (Danish, Petitpas, & Hale, 1995). Life skills are transferable across life domains; they are

Table 18.1 Components of a successful student-athlete (© Life Skills Associates, 2004).

1. **Physical:**
   - How fit are you? Fitness refers to your strength, cardiovascular fitness and flexibility.
   - Do you eat correctly?
   - Do you drink enough water?
   - Do you get enough rest?

2. **Technical:**
   - What areas of sport have you and your coaches identified as areas for improvement?
   - What areas of the sport have you and your coaches identified as areas of strength?

3. **Mental:**
   - How focused are you?
   - How confident are you?
   - Do you have goals for yourself and a plan to reach them?
   - Are you able to be "in the present" when you need to be rather than thinking about non-sport issues or past/future sport mistakes and successes?
   - Are you able to separate your self-talk so that it is about your performance and not about you as a person?
   - Are you able to identify key self-talk statements to focus on related to your goals?

4. **Emotional:**
   - Are you able to play/have fun when you practice and in competition?
   - Are you able to choose your attitude?
   - Are you able to balance the various aspects of your life—study, sport, family, spiritual, relationships, and social life?
   - Do you know how to relax?
   - Are you able to manage and express your emotions—be excited, hurt, calm, disappointed, excited and ready, etc. when each is appropriate?

5. **Social:**
   - Are you able to offer support to friends, even to the point of "making someone else's day?"
   - Are you able to seek support from others?
   - Are you able to give and receive feedback?

skills that are applicable and necessary for achieving success in different environments in which individuals live (Danish, Forneris, &Wallace, 2005).

The context for teaching life skills

Individuals learn best when they are in the environments they choose (Danish, Taylor, & Fazio, 2005). We often find youth participating in sport and physical activities, and thus, these activities may provide ideal environments for promoting positive development, especially for youth (Hodge & Danish, 1999). Moreover, Kleiber and Kirshnit (1991) observed that the sport environment can be a forum for learning skills associated with values such as: responsibility, conformity, persistence, risk-taking, courage, and self-control.

Despite the clear potential for sport to enhance positive development, there is little empirical evidence that participation in sport itself is sufficient for healthy development (Danish *et al.*, 1993). Positive, negative, and mixed effects of sport on youth development have been found (Shields & Bredemeier, 2001).

Strachan (2008, p. iii) asserted:

[I]f youth sport programs are delivered with an emphasis on skill development in conjunction with the growth of key assets and an appropriate contextual experience, young people have the potential to emerge as healthy, secure, and positive citizens who feel valued and invested within their homes and communities

As Hodge (1989) so aptly put it – character is not caught; it must be taught. Sport psychologists should work to ensure that the sport environment is designed to facilitate the transfer of life skills from sport to other life areas.

The role of the coach is particularly important in promoting life skills through sport (Smith & Smoll, 1996). The coach and supporting staff must work to create a positive learning environment that is both enjoyable and conducive to encouraging positive growth. The National Research Council and Institute of Medicine (2002) offered eight criteria needed to create an environment that promotes positive development. These criteria include: physical and psychological safety; clear and consistent structure and appropriate adult supervision; supportive relationships; opportunities to belong; positive social norms; support for efficacy and mattering; opportunities for skill building; and the integration of family, school, and community efforts. Although such an environment is difficult to attain and rarely achieved, it is a goal that should serve as the ideal.

Examples of sport-based programs that teach life skills

Several programs have effectively taught life skills through sport. We will describe three of them here.

Teaching responsibility through physical activity (Hellison, 2003)

Hellison developed Teaching Personal and Social Responsibility (TPSR) as a framework for teachers and coaches to teach young athletes personal and social responsibility in Chicago, and the program has been implemented elsewhere (Hellison et al., 2000). Using this framework, five levels of responsibility are emphasized: (a) respecting the rights and feelings of others, (b) understanding the role of effort in improving oneself in physical activity and life, (c) being self-directed and responsible for one's own well-being, (d) being sensitive and responsible for the well-being of others, and (e) applying what you have learned in different non-physical activity/sport settings. For a more detailed discussion of TPSR, readers are referred to Hellison et al. (2000).

Play It Smart (Petitpas, Cornelius, & Van Raalte, 2008)

Petitpas and colleagues designed the Play It Smart program to work with underserved high school student-athletes, using sport to promote the transfer of life skills from the athletic domain to the classroom and the community. Key to the program was the addition of an academic coach, trained to bridge the gap between sports and life. Academic coaches established relationships with each player through consistent interactions, facilitation of study hall, and community service activities. See Petitpas (2006) for information about the program's implementation and effectiveness.

Sports United to Promote Education and Recreation (SUPER; Danish, 2002)

SUPER, a community-based intervention that uses sport to teach life skills and encourage positive youth development, has been implemented in a variety of settings in the United

States and abroad. SUPER uses sport as a "training ground for life" in fostering youth development both in the athletic domain and in life outside of sport (Danish, Fazio, Nellen, & Owens, 2002).

The SUPER program employs an "educational pyramid" approach (Seidman & Rappaport, 1974). Life Skills Center staff at Virginia Commonwealth University first train peers (high school or college student-athletes) for ten to 20 hours to become SUPER leaders. The SUPER leaders then deliver the interventions to younger peers. Following the model that teaching is the best form of learning, Hogan (2000) found that peer leaders reported improved perceptions of their own leadership skills when teaching a life skills program.

SUPER consists of a series of 18 sport-like clinics, taught by the peer leaders. Table 18.2 provides a brief description of the SUPER workshops. Ten of the 18 modules are the core of all the Life Skills Center programs; the remaining eight modules are designed as independent workshops that add to the sport psychology orientation. The participants are involved in three sets of activities: learning the physical skills related to a specific sport; learning life skills related to sports in general; and playing the sport (Danish, Forneris, Hodge & Heke, 2004).

Table 18.2 Summary of SUPER workshops.

Workshop 1	Developing a Team – The program and the peer leaders are introduced. Participants engage in several team-building activities designed to enhance communication and understand each other's strengths and weaknesses.
Workshop 2	Dare to Dream – Participants learn about and discuss the importance of having dreams for the future. They then identify career/school and sport dreams they have for ten years in the future. The peer leaders share some of their dreams.
Workshop 3	Setting Goals (Part 1) – Participants learn the difference between dreams and goals and how to turn a dream into a goal. They identify people who support them in achieving their goals (Goal Keepers) and people who may prevent them from achieving their goals (Goal Busters).
Workshop 4	Setting Goals (Part 2) – Participants learn four characteristics of a reachable goal (positively stated, specific, important to the goal setter, and under the goal setter's control). They practise creating goals that are positively stated and important to the goal setter.
Workshop 5	Setting Goals (Part 3) – Participants practise creating goals that are specific and goals that are under their control.
Workshop 6	Making Your Goal Reachable – Participants apply the four characteristics of a reachable goal to their own goals. They set two six-week goals: one for sport and a personal goal.
Workshop 7	Making a Goal Ladder – Participants learn the importance of developing plans to reach goals (called a goal ladder) and make plans to reach the two goals they have set. Making a ladder involves placing the goal at the top of the ladder and identifying six steps to reach their goal.
Workshop 8	Identifying and Overcoming Roadblocks to Reaching Goals – Participants learn how different roadblocks (e.g., using drugs, getting into fights, lack of confidence) can prevent them from reaching their goals. They identify possible roadblocks and learn and practise a problem-solving strategy called STAR to help them overcome the roadblocks.
Workshop 9	Seeking Help From Others – Participants learn the importance of seeking social support when working on goals. They identify people in their lives, a dream team, who can provide doing and/or caring help to assist them in achieving their goals.
Workshop 10	Using Positive Self-Talk – Participants learn the importance of identifying their self-talk, how to distinguish positive from negative self-talk and how to identify key positive self-talk statements related to their goals. They then practise making positive self-talk statements.

(continued)

Table 18.2 (Cont'd).

Workshop 11	Learning to Relax – Participants learn the importance of relaxation to reduce tension and how to focus and breathe as a means to help them relax.
Workshop 12	Managing Emotions – Participants learn that managing their emotions, both in sport and life, is learning to be smart. They learn and practise a procedure, the 4 R's (Replay, Relax, Redo, Ready), to help them play smart both inside and outside sport.
Workshop 13	Developing a Healthy Lifestyle – Participants develop an understanding of the importance of being healthy in all areas of their lives. They also learn how to make changes to ensure they are living healthy lives and are asked to make a commitment to such a lifestyle.
Workshop 14	Appreciating Differences – Participants identify differences among individuals in the group and determine which ones are important and which ones are insignificant in reaching goals.
Workshop 15	Having Confidence and Courage – Participants understand the importance of believing in themselves and learn how to develop self-confidence.
Workshop 16	Learning to Focus on Your Personal Performance – Participants learn what it means to compete against oneself and understand that competing against oneself to attain personal excellence can enhance performance.
Workshop 17	Identifying and Building on Your Strengths – Participants identify personal strengths and learn how to use the skills associated with these strengths and the skills learned in the program in other areas of their lives.
Workshop 18	Goal Setting for Life – Participants learn that goal setting is a lifetime activity and they set two goals to attain over the next three months. One goal is school-related; the other relates to home or community. They assess whether the goals meet the four characteristics of a reachable goal and develop a goal ladder for each goal.

SUPER leaders also learn how to use the Sport Observation System (SOS; see Table 18.3). The SOS is used throughout the SUPER program enabling coaches, peer leaders, and teachers to provide feedback to participants on how youth participate, not just on how well they perform. Part of the feedback they receive specifically relates to helping them see how their participation in sport may transfer to other life areas (Danish *et al.*, 2002, 2004).

The program has been adapted for use in a number of countries. Three studies have been done by Greek colleagues (Goudas, Dermitzaki, Leondari, & Danish, 2006; Papacharisis, Goudas, Danish, & Theodorakis, 2005; Papacharisis, Theofanidis, & Danish, 2007). Each study assessed skill performance (either on a physical fitness test or on a sport component), knowledge of life skills, self-beliefs about their performances, and their self-assessments of their abilities to use life skills. In each study significant differences were found on each measure in

Table 18.3 The Sport Observation System.

1. How attentive are participants when given instructions or observing demonstrations?
2. What happens when participants cannot perform an activity to their expectations?
3. Do participants initiate questions when they do not understand something, or do they wait for someone else to talk first?
4. Do participants initiate conversation with others, or do they wait for someone else to talk first?
5. How do participants respond when they have a good or a bad performance?
6. How do participants respond when others have a good or a bad performance?
7. How do participants respond when someone gives them praise or criticism?
8. Do participants give up when they don't do well, or do they persist?
9. Do participants compete or cooperate with teammates?

favor of the life skills group. In New Zealand, Heke (2001) worked with New Zealand Maori to design a sport-based intervention modeled from the SUPER program. The program used Maori language and culture both in program development, implementation, and evaluation. A description of the program and the results of the intervention can be found in Danish et al. (2004). For a more detailed discussion of the conceptual framework for SUPER, readers are referred to Danish, Nellen, and Owens (1996) and Danish et al. (1993).

The importance of transferable skills

If skills are truly going to be *life skills*, they must be transferable across settings; in other words, skills must transfer from sport to other life domains. Danish and his colleagues (1993) have identified considerations for skills to transfer successfully. First, individuals must believe that they have skills and qualities that are valued in settings other than sport. If they do not, the skills will not transfer. Second, individuals must know that they possess both physical and mental skills. There is a lot more to sport than being fast and strong. For example, successful athletes need to be able to plan, set goals, make quick decisions, follow instructions, and manage their stress as a routine part of their lives during competition. Without these mental skills it is unlikely athletes can compete successfully. Until athletes understand what these mental skills are, they cannot be transferred to another domain. Third, individuals may need to test a skill in a safe setting to see how it works. By testing their skills in a safe setting, individuals can further identify their areas of strength and improvement. Finally, individuals may focus so much on their identities as athletes that they ignore their accomplishments in other areas. Such a mind-set can rob them of their confidence to try something new. Table 18.4 contains a list of transferable skills one may possess. The identified skills can be transferred to a number of domains that extend beyond sport. Recently, Fiore and Salas (2008) edited a special issue of *Military Psychology* that focused on the transferable skills that exist between expertise in sport and performance in the military. Authors in the special issue emphasized the need for practitioners to recognize that skills learned in sport can be applied in other areas where skill acquisition, attentional control, and emotional regulation are required (i.e., the military, music, art, medicine).

The ability of an individual to respond well to challenges in different contexts can be partly explained by intra-individual similarity in reactions to events. Individuals who respond effectively to one particular challenge may recognize similarities between the current challenge and challenges they have encountered in the past. At a cognitive level, they know they can deal with the event. At a behavioral level, they employ a behavioral sequence that has been successful in the past. The psychological uniqueness of the event becomes de-emphasized, and properties common to both experiences are highlighted (Danish & D'Augelli, 1980). We need to emphasize the similarity between new challenges and past experiences. We can encourage athletes and others to identify the behaviors that have been successful in similar past situations and the areas in which they might have made improvements. This process increases the potential for achieving success when taking on new challenges.

Not all skills learned in sport, however, should be transferred to other domains. Sport teaches enhanced competitiveness that can be used in a counterproductive manner in non-sport situations. Sport can teach an athlete good sportspersonship or bad sportspersonship, confidence or overconfidence, and learning limitations or ignoring limitations. The experiences one has in sport are dependent on how the sport is organized and the values that are engendered. Sport psychologists can work with coaches and others to ensure that athletes develop the competencies that will help them to function well outside of sport.

Table 18.4 List of sport-related life skills.

Please check all that apply	Important for succeeding in sport	Important for succeeding in work	Skills I have	Skills I need to develop
Making a commitment and sticking with it				
Learning to win and lose				
Working with people I don't necessarily like				
Learning patience				
Becoming disciplined				
Being fit				
Learning respect				
Learning to be creative				
Learning to take orders				
Learning self-control				
Learning communication				
Learning drive and dedication				
Learning my limitations				
Learning to compete without hatred				
Accepting responsibility for my behavior				
Learning to commit a great deal of time and effort				
Accepting feedback and criticism to learn				
Learning to take risks				
Developing a sense of accomplishment				
Learning to evaluate myself				
Learning to be flexible				
Learning to perform under pressure				

Sport has the power to enhance positive development (Petitpas *et al.*, 2008). Through sport, individuals can learn skills such as work ethic, responsibility, and persistence. It is important, however, that the sport environment is structured in a way that promotes positive development. Athletes must learn the core competencies necessary for success in sport and also learn that these same competencies, or skills, can be transferred to other life domains. In other words, we can encourage positive development by teaching life skills. Teaching life skills can enhance competence and promote personal growth throughout the life span. See Box 18.1 for the main points of this chapter.

Box 18.1

Key points about life skills and sport

- Sport is a context in which athletes can learn life skills that transfer to other life domains.
- Sport psychologists and coaches can work to promote skills that will enable athletes to function well outside of sport.
- Athletes need to identify the skills they possess and recognize that those skills transfer to other domains.

References

Bloom, M. (2000). The uses of theory in primary prevention practice: Evolving thoughts on sports and after-school activities as influences of social competence. In S. J. Danish & T. Gullotta (Eds.), *Developing competent youth and strong communities through after-school programming* (pp. 17–66). Washington, DC: CLWA Press.

Carnegie Corporation of New York (1995). Great transitions: Preparing adolescents for a new century. *Reports of the Carnegie Council on Adolescent Development.* Waldorf, MD: Carnegie Corporation of New York. Executive summary. Available from http://carnegie.org/fileadmin/Media/Publications/PDF/GREAT%20TRANSITIONS.pdf

Danish, S. J. (2000). Youth and community development: How after-school programming can make a difference. In S. J. Danish & T. Gullotta (Eds.), *Developing competent youth and strong communities through after-school programming* (pp. 275–302). Washington, DC: CWLA Press.

Danish, S. J. (2002). Teaching life skills through sport. In M. Gatz, M. Messner, & S. Ball-Rokeach (Eds.), *Paradoxes of youth and sport* (pp. 49–59). Albany, NY: State University of New York Press.

Danish, S. J., & D'Augelli, A.R. (1980). Promoting competence and enhancing development through life development intervention. In L. A. Bond & J. C. Rosen (Eds.), *Competence and coping during adulthood* (pp. 105–129). Hanover, NH: University Press of New England.

Danish, S. J., Petitpas, A. J., & Hale, B. D. (1993). Life development intervention for athletes: Life skills through sports. *The Counseling Psychologist, 21,* 352–385.

Danish, S. J., Petitpas, A. J., & Hale, B. D. (1995). Psychological interventions: A life development model. In S. M. Murphy (Ed.), *Sport psychology interventions* (pp. 19–38). Champaign, IL: Human Kinetics.

Danish, S. J., Nellen, V. C., & Owens, S. (1996). Community-based life skills programs: Using sports to teach life skills to adolescents. In J. L. Van Raalte & B. W. Brewer (Eds.), *Exploring sport and exercise psychology* (pp. 205–225). Washington, DC: American Psychological Association.

Danish, S. J., Fazio, R., Nellen, V., & Owens, S. (2002). Teaching life skills through sport: Community-based programs to enhance adolescent development. In J. L. Van Raalte & B. W. Brewer (Eds.), *Exploring sport and exercise psychology* (2nd ed., pp. 269–288). Washington, DC: American Psychological Association.

Danish, S. J., Forneris, T., Hodge, K., & Heke, I. (2004). Enhancing youth development through sport. *World Leisure, 46,* 38–49.

Danish, S. J., Forneris, T., & Wallace, I. (2005). Sport-based life skills programming in the schools. Co-published in *Journal of Applied School Psychology, 21*(2), 41–62 and in C. Maher (Ed.) *School sport psychology: Perspectives, programs and procedures,* pp. 41–61. Binghamton, NY: Haworth Press.

Danish, S. J., Taylor, T., & Fazio, R. (2005). Enhancing adolescent development though sport and leisure. In G. Adams & M. Berzonsky (Eds.), *Blackwell handbook on adolescence,* pp. 92–108. Malden, MA: Blackwell.

Danish, S. J., & Forneris, T. (2008). Promoting positive development and competency across the lifespan. In S. Brown & R. Lent (Eds.), *Handbook of counseling psychology* (4th ed, pp. 500–517). Hoboken, NJ: Wiley.

Fiore, S. M., & Salas, E. (Eds.). (2008). Cognition, competition, and coordination: Understanding expertise in sports and its relevance to learning and performance in the military. *Military Psychology. 20* (Suppl.), S1–S9.

Goudas, M., Dermitzaki, I., Leondari, A., & Danish, S. J. (2006). The effectiveness of teaching a life skills program in a physical education context. *European Journal of Psychology of Education, 21,* 429–438.

Heke, I. (2001). *The Hokowhitu Program: Designing a sporting intervention to address alcohol and substance abuse in adolescent Maori.* Unpublished manuscript, University of Otago, Dunedin, New Zealand.

Hellison, D. (2003). *Teaching responsibility through physical activity* (2nd ed.). Champaign, IL: Human Kinetics.

Hellison, D., Cutforth, N., Kallusky, J., Martinek, T., Parker, M., & Stiehl, J. (2000). *Youth development and physical activity.* Champaign, IL: Human Kinetics.

Hodge, K. P. (1989). Character-building in sport: Fact or fiction? *New Zealand Journal of Sports Medicine, 17*, 23–25.

Hodge, K. P., & Danish, S. J. (1999). Promoting life skills for adolescent males through sport. In A. Horne & M. Kiselica (Eds.), *Handbook of counseling boys and adolescent males* (pp. 55–71). Thousand Oaks, CA: Sage.

Hogan, C. (2000). *The impact of a peer led program on the peer leader's leadership-related skills.* Unpublished master's thesis, Virginia Commonwealth University, Richmond, VA.

Kleiber, D. A., & Kirshnit, C. E. (1991). Sport involvement and identity formation. In L. Diamant (Ed.), *Mind-body maturity: Psychological approaches to sports, exercise and fitness* (pp. 193–211). New York: Hemisphere.

National Research Council and Institute of Medicine (2002). In J. Eccles & J. A. Gootman (Eds.), *Community programs to promote youth development. Board on Children, Youth and Families, Division of Behavioral and Social Sciences and Education.* Washington, DC: National Academy Press.

Papacharisis, V., Goudas, M., Danish, S. J., & Theodorakis, Y. (2005). The effectiveness of teaching a life skills program in a sport context. *Journal of Applied Sport Psychology, 17*, 247–254.

Papacharisis, V., Theofanidis, G., & Danish, S. J. (2007). Education through the physical: The effectiveness of teaching life skills program in physical education. In L. Chiang (Ed.), *Motivation of exercise and physical activity* (pp. 67–77). Hauppauge, NY: Nova Science.

Petitpas, A. J. (2006). *Just the facts: Academic progress report for Play It Smart for the 2005–2006 academic year.* Unpublished manuscript, Springfield College, Springfield, MA.

Petitpas, A. J., Cornelius, A., & Van Raalte, J. L. (2008). Youth development through sport: It's all about relationships. In N. L. Holt (Ed.), *Positive youth development through sport* (pp. 61–70). New York: Routledge.

Seidman, E., & Rappaport, J. (1974). The educational pyramid: A paradigm for training, research, and manpower utilization in community psychology. *American Journal of Community Psychology, 2*, 119–130.

Shields, D. L., & Bredemeier, B. L. (2001). Moral development and behavior in sport. In R. Singer, H. Hausenblas, & C. Janelle (Eds.), *Handbook of sport psychology* (2nd ed., pp. 585–603). New York: Wiley.

Smith, R. E., & Smoll, F. L. (1996). *Way to go, coach!: A scientifically validated approach to coaching effectiveness.* Portola Valley, CA: Warde.

Strachan, L. A. T. (2008). *An ecological approach to examining positive youth development in competitive youth sport.* Unpublished doctoral thesis, Queen's University, Kingston, ON, Canada.

19

Family systems interventions in sport

Michael Zito

Some of the most powerful influences shaping an athlete's life experiences, especially in the younger years, are the primary relationships provided by the family. Although the influence of specific parental behaviors on athlete performance have been reported (Horn & Horn, 2007), there is a paucity of documented investigations examining the more complex influence of reciprocal family interaction patterns on athletic performance. The purpose of this chapter is to present a comprehensive assessment and intervention model for sport psychologists that is broader than traditional individual and/or dyadic models, by incorporating the influence of the complex reciprocal family interactions on an athlete's functioning. Family systems theory can guide us to this broader level of assessment and intervention while simultaneously embracing the influence of individual factors. An individual athlete's personality and behaviors are viewed as reciprocally interacting within a broader context. This broader context of multiple interacting factors may include an athlete's: family history, team relationships, coach–coach interactions (as they influence team functioning), social support system, communication patterns, culture, and ethnic background. It is beyond the scope of this chapter to cover all family systems theories. For a comprehensive review of family systems theory and therapies see Goldenberg and Goldenberg (2008). This chapter will address the core tenets of family systems theory, assessment, and interventions as applied to sport psychology service delivery.

In a review of the family therapy literature on common clinical concerns, the efficacy and effectiveness research indicates that family systems interventions have consistently yielded significant positive treatment effects (Shaddish, Ragsdale, Glaser, & Montgomery, 1995). Family systems athletic interventions have also been documented in the literature in the form of clinical case studies. Mintz (2003) reported on an intervention with a gymnast where a family history of violence adversely influenced the athlete's motivation and performance. Burke (2005) emphasized in a volleyball team intervention the need to consider the team dynamics in accordance with family systems thinking. Specifically, he pointed out that the interactions of coach–coach, coach–athlete, athlete–athlete, and developing subsystems (cliques) all affected individual and team performance. Hellstedt (1995) discussed the role of the "invisible player" that referenced family factors as major, yet often invisible, contributors to an athlete's performance.

Families can provide comfort and support, but may also be a source of stress. Hellstedt (1995) evaluated levels of family stress, cohesion, adaptation to change, and interaction patterns, and found that unresolved problems from a parent's family of origin had an effect on marital and parent–child interactions. These unresolved issues came from modeling and unfulfilled wishes from a parent's childhood. This pattern resulted in an avoidant conflict resolution style and parental emotional gratification from over-involvement with their children (living through a child). Often, such a history leads to excessive performance criticism from parents because the elite athlete's success becomes the emotional focus of the family. Subsequently, this criticism had a negative effect on the athlete's commitment and achievement motivation.

Major tenets of family systems theory

A major difference between interventions with family systems theory and an individual approach is that systems theory focuses on the existence of the athlete's behavior within a context of reciprocally interacting factors. The family systems model, a clinical expansion of general systems theory, places at least equal importance on the relationships between the elements of a system as with the elements themselves. An individual who comes for sport psychology counseling needs to be understood on the individual psychological level (e.g., personality traits, coping mechanisms) as well as in the context in which the problems exists. Athletes' concerns can arise in several contexts. These contexts might include team dynamics, coach–athlete communication and relationship, relationships with significant others, living arrangement (e.g., dormitory) dynamics, coach–coach relationships, school environment, and family history.

A practical example of a systems conceptualization would be an athlete who is struggling with inconsistent motivation and is feeling disconnected from her team due to the perception of a lack of acceptance from the key players on her team. Gathering contextual/systemic information would help determine whether the identified problem is real or perceived and if it is influenced by her family experiences (e.g., feeling left out as a child). Similarly, coach–athlete relationships can be affected by family history that in turn can affect motivation. For example, people who have struggled to gain approval and acceptance from parents in their younger years will often unknowingly project those same struggles onto relationships with coaches. In my experience, coaches often become symbolic parents for many athletes, and teams function like families, with the potential for developing functional and dysfunctional patterns of relationships. An athlete might complain that a coach is critical, rarely shows approval, and only comments on mistakes. As a systemic practitioner, it would be important to explore the athlete's family history to see if coach–athlete issues have a historical context for the athlete (parent–child issues often get re-enacted in coach–athlete relationships). Similarly, when working with coaches one needs to be aware that coaching styles may be influenced by their family histories as well. I find that coaching style often mirrors parenting style, and family history usually influences parenting style. An additional historical influence to consider is that coaches often coach how they were coached as athletes, which can affect the current coach–athlete interaction.

In the general systems model, systems are viewed as self-regulating and reciprocally interactive (Goldenberg & Goldenberg, 2008). A system typically self-regulates by striving for homeostasis or balance. Homeostasis refers to a systemic effort to maintain stability and resist change (Minuchin, 1974). The drive for homeostasis can occur at the individual, dyadic, family, team, or organizational level in sport. Homoeostasis can be maintained through functional and dysfunctional systems' and subsystems' (subgroups') interactions. A collegiate softball team I have worked with in which one player was frequently exhibiting emotional outbursts that disrupted team functioning and also angered the coach is an illustration of striving to maintain homeostasis. A player sought my advice about her decline in batting average. As we analyzed the problem individually and systemically, we found that this player was using much of her own mental preparation time to keep the emotional player calm, thereby maintaining team homeostasis. This dynamic occurred because the emotional player batted just before my client in the batting order. After speaking with the emotional player it became apparent that she was reacting to perceived unfair criticism from the coach and a fear of rejection from key team members if she did not perform well. Unfair criticism and fear of rejection were concerns she also had about her family experience as a child. The intervention was conducted with the original client and the emotional player and included individual mental skills focus and family history awareness as well as systemic intervention with the team and coach.

When assessing family processes, it is important to evaluate functional and dysfunctional patterns of interaction as well as roles individuals play in a family (Minuchin, 1974). Functional patterns in families include a unified parental subsystem with clear, yet flexible, boundaries where parents generally work together in discipline, managing conflicts, and daily routines. Parents often consult with each other on managing family situations and rarely work at cross-purposes. The children in the family form the sibling subsystem, and although they may try to challenge the authority of the parental subsystem, rules and expectations are generally maintained except in certain situations when modification is justified. The sibling subsystem maintains a healthy emotional connection to the parents and rarely aligns with one parent against the other. This system is an ideal arrangement, and most healthy families operate this way with varying degrees of success. If the consultant has the luxury of working with the entire family, the relative sitting position of family members in sessions often illustrates the boundaries and alliances. For example, if the parents sit next to each other, it often suggests, but doesn't guarantee, that parents are unified.

By contrast, unhealthy family boundaries are usually unclear and variable. Parents rarely work in concert and often work at cross-purposes, which reflects a poorly defined parental subsystem. With unhealthy family boundaries, maladaptive alliances often form. One parent may become protective of a child and develop an enmeshed or overly involved emotional relationship with that child. Commonly, a parent will become enmeshed with a child to protect the child from the other overbearing parent or stressful situation. Sometimes a parent and child will form an alliance against another family member to deflect or counteract that person's authority in the family. Overly rigid and inflexible boundaries can also be dysfunctional and are likely to create emotional distance in the family. These dysfunctional boundaries may take the form of inflexible rules and expectations where a child has little input to decisions, and the family resists adapting to changing circumstances. Unhealthy boundaries can also be observed in the relative sitting position of family members in a session. A parent and child regularly sitting together with the other parent across the room may reflect an enmeshed relationship and/or a maladaptive alliance. Unhealthy alliances can also occur across generations. A parent might grant greater influence about family matters to his own parent rather than to his spouse. These cross-generational alliances often reflect poor emotional separation from one's family of origin.

Another form of family dysfunction is triangulation (Bowen, 1978; Minuchin, 1974), where parental dysfunction or marital tensions are deflected from the marital unit to a child

179

within the family. A parent may displace marital tension by yelling at the child because it is too threatening to express anger directly to a spouse. This displaced marital tension leaves the child feeling "in the middle" of the parental dysfunction, which can lead to anxiety and emotional distress for the child. Triangulation is common in high-conflict divorced families.

Additional areas of family system assessment are ethnicity, gender roles, and socioeconomic status. An athlete's ethnic background can influence expectations about relationships and team functioning. The work of McGoldrick, Giordano, and Pearce (2005) contains thorough descriptions of typical ethnic family patterns, but one needs to be careful to avoid stereotyping. Asian families often have a strong theme of respect in relationships that will often influence Asian athletes' expectations of coaches and team members. Italian and Jewish families may have tendencies towards close personal family relationships that sometimes can reach the level of enmeshment. These family experiences will likely influence an athlete's expectations, and when these relationship expectations are in contrast with actual relationships, problems can ensue. Although it is beyond the scope of this chapter, a practitioner should also consider the possible role of family gender role expectations and socioeconomic issues when performing an assessment.

Application of the family systems model

I typically use a 3–5 session assessment format with the proviso that assessment and intervention are interwoven given that once a practitioner enters the system, intervention has already begun. During this assessment phase, it is often useful to begin to help the family view the identified problem in a broader context, and thereby reduce the focus on the identified client. If the client is a child or adolescent, I usually begin with a parent session so that an unadulterated discussion about the problem, and a family history can be obtained as well as an assessment of their commitment to the process. If practitioners have the luxury of access to an entire family, the next session would include all relevant family members. At the collegiate, Olympic, and professional levels there is rarely access to full families or even parents, so psychologists will have to rely on the athlete's self-reported perceptions of family history and dynamics that may or may not be accurate. Who attends the third through fifth sessions will depend on the assessment of the problem. These sessions could include the entire family, parents only, parent–child dyad or triad, or individual sessions with the athlete. When establishing an initial appointment, I listen carefully to the perceived difficulties of getting certain members in for the initial session. This reluctance may illustrate resistance and/or unhealthy alliances. For example, if a mother identifies her son as the client and comments that she will never be able to get her husband and daughter to attend, this dynamic may be an indication that there is an unhealthy alliance formed between the father and daughter or the mother and son, or both. So assessment actually starts before the initial appointment. The ideal would be to have all family members present at some point, but legitimate logistical issues may prevent access to the entire family. With an individual or partial family it would be best to obtain this information through the perceptions of the available individuals.

Obtaining a family history can be done in both parent-only and full-family sessions. Family history is explored to determine the constellation of the family, the medical and psychological conditions of family members, and then, specifically, the family's sport involvement and behaviors. The family history taking usually includes a genogram that is a pictorial schematic map of family relationships (See Figure 19.1). See McGoldrick, Gerson, and Shellenberger (1999) for a detailed procedure of coding information on a genogram.

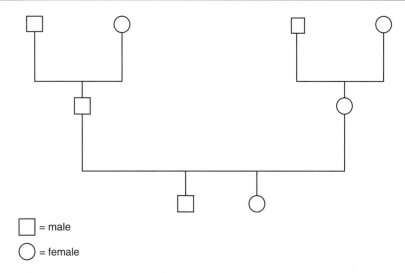

☐ = male

◯ = female

Figure 19.1 Structure of a genogram. Ages are placed inside the circles and squares. Lines could be drawn between individuals to identify certain types of relationships. For example, a jagged line (/\/\/\/\/\/\/\/\) would be drawn between members in a high-conflict relationship. I selectively use straight lines between members and place a descriptor of that relationship (e.g., enmeshed) on the line. I list personality traits next to each person in the genogram and ethnicity between the parents.

This information is analogous to a family tree where older family members are listed at the top and their offspring listed below, usually spanning two to three generations. Gender, age, and relationships are noted on the genogram. The main goal of plotting the genogram is to illuminate current and transgenerational relationship patterns that may have effects on the current presenting problem.

It is often helpful to inquire about personality traits of individuals in the current generation and one generation back to see how the interplay of personality characteristics may have influenced the family functioning. I place these personality descriptors next to the person's symbol on the genogram. The interaction of personality characteristics needs to be considered because a critical and controlling parent may not interact well with a sensitive and self-critical child, resulting in frequent conflicts that can adversely affect athletic motivation. At the completion of the genogram, I ask each parent to reflect on his or her family experience as a child and to identify the "when I'm a parent" vows each has made. Based on family experiences, parents often vow to recreate (or do the opposite of) certain experiences from their childhoods that can contribute to the current problem. For example, a parent who had an uninvolved parent as a child and who wished that his parent had urged him to achieve in sport or academics, may then vow to push his own child to stardom through over-involvement and pressure to achieve.

Application of the model to specific sport cases

The cases presented here reflect aggregate representations of family dynamics and problems. Due to confidentiality concerns, they do not reflect any one client who has been under my care.

Childhood case with direct family intervention

Cassie, an 11-year-old girl, presented with severe performance anxiety in her three sports: soccer, basketball, and softball. In soccer and basketball, she panicked when she was about to take a shot. In softball, she had high anxiety while at bat. In all cases, she feared not being successful. She came from an intact family and had an elder brother, age 14. In the first session, the mother (of Italian decent) reported that she had school anxieties as a child, and the father revealed that he had a harsh, distant, and critical father. The father (of Irish decent) described himself as strict and demanding because he wants the best for his daughter. The mother tended to protect Cassie because she had a critical father herself as a child, and she was reenacting her own mother's protectiveness. Marital tension and distance were evident in verbal and nonverbal communication.

In the first full-family session, there were five chairs for the family. The mother sat next to Cassie. There was an empty chair between the parents; then the father sat next to his son. The seating arrangement appeared to reflect the aligned relationships in the family: mother and Cassie, father and son. The observed unhealthy alliances were consistent with the reported relationships in subsequent sessions. The mother frequently complained that the father was too harsh on Cassie and that he was to blame for her performance anxiety because Cassie was sensitive. The father countered that he was just trying to help her reach her potential and that the mother was to blame because she blocked his attempts to have Cassie "tough it out." These polarized perspectives have foiled attempts to change and thereby maintain the dysfunctional homeostasis.

Two parent-only sessions were conducted to begin to create an awareness of the family dynamics and to initiate motivation to change. Despite the father's initial rejection of the idea, it became apparent that he exuded a rigid and controlling personality and was modeling his own father's relationship style. He was gradually helped to realize the connection by gently comparing his father's behavior to his own. Cassie's father vowed to help his own children be "tough" to deal with the harsh world, which was what he needed to do to deal with his own father's harsh criticism. The mother was open to the idea that she was overprotecting Cassie as a result of her own family experiences. Her vow as a parent was to not let her children experience the emotional pain and anxiety of a harsh parent as she did as a child. The parents' behaviors reflect the transgenerational process whereby past family interaction patterns (and possibly ethnic tendencies) influence the parents' current behaviors. Cassie's mother realized how her Italian heritage was a partial explanation of her enmeshment, and Cassie's father's Irish heritage may have contributed to greater tendency towards critical and distant relationships.

The parents' awareness fluctuated during treatment, and they each had a tendency to gravitate back to the blame game. Gradually, the parents realized through parent-only and family sessions that each person was operating from the assumption that there was one correct way to deal with Cassie; conveniently, it was their own way. I repeatedly helped the parents understand that both of their approaches had some merit (holding her to expectations and being sensitive to her needs) and that it would be best to blend their approaches into a method they both could accept. I had to continually refocus them to the "what was in Cassie's best interest?" approach and away from whose approach was right or wrong.

The parental and sibling subsystems were dysfunctional due to the cross alliances of mother–daughter and father–son. Ideally, the parents should be unified and working together most of the time, but they were working at cross-purposes. In the family sessions, subsystem and structural changes were made by way of the family seating arrangement. The parents were asked to sit together, separate from the children who sat next to each other, thereby reflecting healthier subsystems. As their reactions to the change were processed, it became apparent that this structural change created anxiety for all family members, but it was helpful for the family to understand healthy versus unhealthy organization. The new organization of the family was followed up in subsequent sessions to see whether day-to-day functioning reflected this new organization. As situations arose that mirrored the previous unhealthy alliances, ways to rebalance the family system and subsystems were discussed. In particular, resistance to these changes was explored and incorporated into the therapy.

Cassie appeared to be triangulated into the marital conflict because her parents deflected their negative emotion and focus onto Cassie. The increase in family stress, along with her father's chronic criticism, increased Cassie's performance pressure and negative self-talk, thereby exacerbating her performance anxiety. Cassie was also provided five individual sessions spread out over three months to promote cognitive–behavioral interventions focusing on awareness of positive and negative self-talk, reframing, and anxiety reduction techniques.

The treatment lasted for six months, and in the end, as Cassie's performance anxiety subsided, it became apparent that the parents had underlying marital problems that still needed to be worked out, and they were referred for marital therapy. Cassie made good progress, and her performance anxiety reduced significantly; over the following six months, she came in for three "booster" sessions.

Adult case with limited direct family intervention

Jackie was a 26-year-old Chinese American woman who experienced performance anxiety in the swimming portion of the triathlon. She was particularly offended by the disrespect found during the swimming portion because Jackie indicated that respect was a big part of her upbringing. In her four years of experience, she had been kicked in the head, especially when the event included men. She had developed a fear of being knocked out and drowning as a result.

Jackie was married at the age of 24 to a previously divorced 30-year-old man with two children from his previous marriage. Her husband's divorce was full of conflict and legal problems. Recently, there was a physical abuse allegation made against her husband by his ex-wife that has caused her significant stress. The child protective services investigation was still pending. Despite my encouragement, she did not want to include her husband or stepchildren in the intervention. Jackie believed she should be self-sufficient and take care of it herself and did not want to bother her husband. Her demanding self-sufficient belief system was explored in light of her family history.

As a child, she had a father who was demanding, particularly of respect, and a submissive mother who found it difficult to assert herself. Her father had a rigid approach to life and always encouraged her to have a plan that she was expected to carry out without deviation. To obtain her father's approval, she needed to be goal oriented, self-sufficient, and driven to succeed. She was successful at gaining her father's approval especially because she graduated from an Ivy League university and was currently pursuing a doctoral degree in music. Jackie was aligned with her father, and her younger brother was aligned with her mother. Her brother was not goal directed and found it difficult to obtain his father's approval. Jackie's mother played a subservient role to her father. Jackie's father was demanding and critical of his wife. Jackie's mother and brother appear to have developed an alliance because they both felt rejected by Jackie's father.

Jackie's role in her family was that of the "helper." She would often try to deflect her father's criticism of her mother and brother, and usually found herself comforting them. She often attempted to diffuse marital tension by distracting her parents. Her role in her family may be one reason she entered the "helping" profession as a music teacher.

Jackie's family history revealed a divided parental subsystem that allowed maladaptive alliances (father–daughter, mother–son) to develop. In her relationship with her husband, Jackie appeared to re-enact her mother's role model of subservience and unassertiveness. The treatment progressed using cognitive-behavioral and family-systems interventions. These interventions created an awareness of her negative self-talk regarding her swim performance. For example, Jackie defined her performance negatively if she deviated from her rigid plan of how to attack the swim, and as a result she was reluctant to make necessary adaptations to her original tactics. Through the interventions, she eventually realized how this rigidity simply replayed her father's expectations. She subsequently developed a flexible plan that included the likelihood of unknown factors, yet still defined herself as successful if she achieved it. Jackie had an unreasonably high triathlon performance goal that reflected the high achievement-oriented model in her family of origin as well as her personality. As a result of goal setting, cognitive reframing, and positive self-talk over several therapy sessions, Jackie set reasonable expectations and an achievable plan.

The family systems intervention was intertwined with the cognitive-behavioral work. Jackie needed to become aware of how her family history had affected her beliefs about herself and her marital relationship. Over several sessions, she realized how her family-of-origin experiences contributed to her limited assertiveness with adults, unreasonably high expectations, rigid goal pursuits, and her internalized need to achieve to maintain her father's approval, and perhaps now her husband's (symbolic father) approval. These factors then adversely affected her triathlon performance anxiety in the swim segment.

Jackie recognized that her over-responsibility for her husband's stress about the abuse allegations related to her triangulated role in her family of origin. The parallel experiences in her family history of feeling overly responsible for the emotions of others and a need to "fix" them created an emotional sense of being burdened. It is understandable that she would feel some stress due to the abuse allegation, but her family history led her to focus on her husband's feelings as if they were not separate from her own. Jackie reported this stress contributed to feeling overwhelmed, which lessened her ability to use anxiety-reduction techniques during the swim portion of the triathlon.

Jackie finally agreed to have her husband join her for five sessions. The focus of the sessions was to help Jackie assert herself with her husband, separate herself from his emotions, and seek the support of her husband, but not necessarily his approval via accomplishments similar to what her father expected. Jackie was asked what she did for fun. She paused for 60 seconds, and with a perplexed look on her face said, "I don't know." It became apparent that although she was achieving milestones in her life, she was not enjoying herself. Therefore, some of the couple sessions focused on developing ways to have fun individually, as a couple, and as a family.

The therapy lasted about nine months, and Jackie struggled initially with changing some of her old patterns, but eventually she did. She learned to relax and enjoy life and athletic competition. Jackie came back for five follow up sessions at monthly intervals and has significantly reduced her swim performance anxiety.

Conclusion

Contextual influence is often essential to sport performance assessment and intervention. Family interactions, roles, and history play a role in current athletic performance. A combination of family system and individual treatments can be a powerful intervention. See Box 19.1 for the main points made in this chapter about family systems interventions in sport.

Box 19.1

Main points of family systems interventions in sport

- Understand that sport performance issues occur in a context (family of origin and team) that needs to be understood and treated when appropriate.
- Family interactions and history can have profound effects on an athlete via mixed loyalties, faulty alliances, unhealthy roles, and unresolved parental issues.
- Roles athletes played in their families of origin and unresolved issues with their parent(s) can affect team and coach relationships.
- Young athletes who have divorced parents can often be caught "in the middle" of residual parental hostilities that can affect performance.
- An integrated approach that includes both family system and individual treatments can be a powerful intervention.

References

Bowen, M. (1978). *Family therapy in clinical practice*. New York: Aronson.

Burke, K. L. (2005). But the coach doesn't understand: Dealing with team communication quagmires. In M. B. Andersen (Ed.), *Sport psychology in practice* (pp. 45–58). Champaign, IL: Human Kinetics.

Goldenberg, H., & Goldenberg, I. (2008). *Family therapy: An overview* (7th ed.). Belmont, CA: Thomson Brooks/Cole.

Hellstedt, J. C. (1995). Invisible players: A family systems model. In S. M. Murphy (Ed.), *Sport psychology interventions* (pp. 117–147). Champaign, IL: Human Kinetics.

Horn, T., & Horn, J. (2007). Family influences on children's sport and physical activity participation, behavior, and psychosocial responses. In G. Tenenbaum & R. C. Elkund (Eds.), *Handbook of sport psychology* (3rd ed., pp. 685–711). Hoboken, NJ: Wiley.

McGoldrick, M., Gerson, R., & Shellenberger, S. (1999). *Genograms: Assessment and intervention*. New York: Norton.

McGoldrick, M., Giordano, J., & Pearce, J. K. (2005). *Ethnicity and family therapy* (3rd ed.). New York: Guilford Press.

Mintz, M. L. (2003). *A ghost in the gym: The invisible damage of family violence on the coach/athlete relationship*. Paper presented at the USA Gymnastics World Congress Science Symposium, Anaheim, CA, October 2003.

Minuchin, S. (1974). *Families and family therapy*. Cambridge, MA: Harvard University Press.

Shaddish, W. R., Ragsdale, K., Glaser, R. R., & Montgomery, L. M. (1995). The efficacy and effectiveness of marital and family therapy: A perspective from meta-analysis. *Journal of Marital and Family Therapy*, 21, 345–360.

20

Acceptance-based behavioral therapies and sport

Frank L. Gardner and Zella E. Moore

During the past decade, there has been a dramatic increase in the theory development, scientific research, and practice of psychological interventions often known as acceptance-based behavioral therapies (ABBT; Roemer & Orsillo, 2009). These approaches, derived from the clinical discipline within professional psychology, are often referred to as the "third wave" of behavioral psychology, and have a view of human progress, human suffering, and overall human existence that is distinctly different to previous models of therapy. The most well-known ABBT in clinical psychology is acceptance and commitment therapy (ACT; Hayes, Strosahl, & Wilson, 1999), which has demonstrated sound efficacy as an intervention for a variety of clinical issues such as depression, binge eating disorder, generalized anxiety disorder, substance abuse and dependence, and borderline personality disorder (e.g., Roemer & Orsillo, 2009). These revolutionary theoretical developments and associated interventions have not gone unnoticed in the sport-performance domain. Specifically within sport psychology, the mindfulness–acceptance–commitment (MAC) approach to performance enhancement, which Gardner and Moore (2007) developed in 2001, is an acceptance-based intervention aimed at enhancing high-level competitive performance and overall psychological well-being. In this chapter we discuss the ABBT movement and its relevance to the sport context.

Behavioral psychology through the ages

The first wave of behaviorism focused on the development of basic laws of learning, and stressed the observable relationships between stimuli, responses, and the reinforcing (and punishing) consequences following those responses (Skinner, 1953). The second wave of behaviorism was represented by the cognitive revolution within psychology (Bandura, 1969), the focus of which was to explicate and ultimately reduce, eliminate, or otherwise control maladaptive internal processes, such as cognitions and emotions, to enhance psychological wellbeing (Beck, 1976; Meichenbaum, 1977). It was during this period in the evolution of cognitive-behavioral psychology that sport psychology had its primary genesis, and the field has been strongly influenced by the theoretical models and intervention strategies that were in vogue during this time.

The foundation of behavioral psychology has always been a commitment to sound empiricism and the evolution of psychological science. Although the first two waves of the behavioral movement led to effective, albeit at times limited, interventions for a range of psychological issues (Nathan & Gorman, 2002), fascinating scientific developments began to reshape behaviorism in the late 1990s (Hayes *et al.*, 1999), giving rise to the third wave of behaviorism. Based on emerging empirical findings, the theoretical underpinnings of the acceptance-based third-wave movement take a different perspective on the link between cognitions, emotions, and behavior. Although a comprehensive review is beyond the scope of this chapter, in summary: (a) reviews of the literature indicate that little data have been accumulated over more than 30 years of research to support the position that modification of cognitions is the essential mechanism of change in cognitive-behavioral therapy (Longmore & Worrell, 2007); (b) findings within experimental psychopathology have implicated constructs such as emotion regulation, experiential avoidance, and distress intolerance as better predictors of psychopathology and more likely mediators of therapeutic change than specific cognitive changes (Roemer & Orsillo, 2009); and (c) expanding evidence suggests that ABBTs are both efficacious and work by different mechanisms than traditional cognitive-behavioral interventions (Foreman, Herbert, Moitra, Yeomans, & Geller, 2007).

Theoretical underpinning of acceptance-based behavioral therapies

The findings noted above led to the development of a new empirically derived theoretical model, which formed the basis for acceptance-based behavioral therapies. ABBTs have a fundamentally different view of the primary mechanisms by which human dysfunction occurs. This theoretical perspective posits that the *avoidance* of internal processes such as cognitions and emotions (i.e., experiential avoidance) leads to a wide array of problematic behaviors, and that the presence of experiential avoidance and lack of experiential acceptance form the basis of human suffering and dysfunction (Hayes *et al.*, 1999). Rather than seeking to change, reduce, or eliminate internal processes such as cognitions and emotions, as is typical of second-wave cognitive-behavioral interventions, the third wave acceptance-based theoretical model has spawned a number of psychological interventions (including acceptance and commitment therapy [ACT] in the clinical domain, and mindfulness–acceptance–commitment [MAC] in the sport and performance domains) that help develop mindful non-judging awareness of internal experiences, acceptance of internal states, and a willingness to experience these states *while* engaging in behaviors that are congruent with one's personal life values. These approaches explicitly suggest that the goal is not necessarily a reduction of subjective distress or an increase in attributes such as confidence, but rather, the enhancement of *behaviors* directly in the service of personal values (Hayes *et al.*, 1999).

Sport psychology and the acceptance-based movement

As the acceptance-based movement took hold in the clinical psychology domain, it generated revolutionary changes in the way scientists and clinicians conceptualized and treated psychopathological conditions. Nearly ten years ago, we (the authors) postulated that the acceptance-based behavioral movement would have direct theoretical and applied relevance to the practice of sport psychology, because research in sport psychology has long suggested the importance of maintaining a present-moment task-oriented focus of attention and full absorption in the competitive task to achieve optimal performance states. Drawing upon several clinical models, we developed an ABBT that was directly applicable to the sport-performance context, called MAC (Gardner & Moore, 2007). The development of this approach occurred as a result of the intersection between the emerging acceptance- and mindfulness-related empirical findings within clinical psychology, and the lack of consistent evidence for the efficacy of traditional psychological skills training (PST) procedures that had long dominated the North American sport psychology model. As is the case with ACT and all ABBTs, MAC practitioners do not seek to help athletes think more positively or less negatively; to feel better; or to become more confident, less stressed, or more aroused. Rather, MAC professionals help performers develop the skills necessary to engage in moment-to-moment attention (in the present), without becoming entangled in their internal experiences by judging these experiences as good or bad, right or wrong, and/or wishing or attempting to make them different. In this vein, the development of mindfulness can be seen as a core facet of ABBT. Mindfulness can be viewed as *being* with one's internal processes rather than *doing* something with those processes (as is the focus within traditional PST interventions). In this way, the development of mindfulness supports and enhances one's ability to nonjudgmentally accept internal experiences and in so doing promotes enhanced present-moment attention and awareness.

From this foundation, ABBT practitioners help clients develop the skills necessary to engage in values-driven behaviors on a day-to-day basis, regardless of internal experiences (e.g., anxiety, anger, frustration, thoughts about possible failure). Rather than engaging in behaviors aimed at reducing the form or frequency of discomfort, known as *experiential avoidance*, these approaches instead promote *experiential acceptance*, which is a willingness to approach (rather than avoid) one's life values no matter how or what one may feel or think (Gardner & Moore, 2007). For example, a primary goal of this model applied to sport would be to help athletes recognize that they can perform while experiencing a wide variety of internal states. So, an attitude of, "I want to perform well, *but* I'm feeling frustrated, and I don't feel confident," is replaced with an attitude represented by, "I want to perform well *and* I'm feeling frustrated and lacking in confidence." This conceptual shift allows for a wider range of internal states in which the person is capable of functioning effectively by maintaining a greater capacity to remain task-focused in sport, performance, and overall life contexts.

Developing mindfulness and experiential acceptance

Mindfulness has been defined as an "openhearted, moment-to-moment nonjudgmental awareness" (Kabat-Zinn, 2005, p. 24) that includes two components: (a) the self-regulation of attention so that it is maintained on immediate experience, and (b) adopting an orientation toward one's experiences in the present moment, which would best be characterized by curiosity, openness, and acceptance (Bishop *et al.*, 2004). In turn, *acceptance* reflects an active process of taking in an event or situation such that one feels emotions and bodily sensations fully (and without needing to avoid or escape) and notices the presence of associated thoughts without following, resisting, believing, or disbelieving their content. An acceptance approach helps clients alter the function of private events, rather than primarily adjusting their forms or frequencies.

The strategies used in ABBT for the promotion of acceptance include numerous exercises and dialogues, most of which convey the ultimate impossibility of eliminating or controlling normal human processes, and the idea that actions do not ultimately require an ideal state of neutral or positive emotions, cognitions, or bodily sensations. There is a direct relationship between mindfulness and acceptance, and a variety of meditative-type practices (*not* specifically aimed at relaxation) are core components of ABBT, including those used in sport and performance contexts (see Gardner & Moore, 2007, for a full discussion of sport-related mindfulness exercises and handouts). One of the hallmarks of the ABBT approach includes mindfulness (meditative) exercises (from 10–60 minutes, both in and out of practitioner–client sessions) to help develop the capacity to become both aware of one's experiences and understand the inherent transient nature of these experiences, and to direct education/discussion about the relative costs and benefits of efforts at control versus acceptance of internal experiences.

One of the core theoretical foundations of ABBT is the empirically derived idea that cognitions can take on the same meaning as the actual events that they represent (transfer of stimulus function), and that humans respond to thoughts and images as though they are real and not simply linguistic or imaginary representations of events. This phenomenon is commonly referred to as *cognitive fusion* (Hayes, Barnes-Holmes, & Roche, 2001). The strategy/process that is used to help clients recognize that thoughts are internal events that come and go (i.e., they do not have to be interpreted or changed, and do not have to guide or direct behavior) is called *cognitive defusion*. In essence, the strategy *de*-fuses the automatic connection people make between their cognitions and their behavioral responses to these cognitions. A classic defusion technique is the "milk" exercise (Hayes *et al.*, 1999) in which clients are asked to think about the word milk (including all of the associations inherent in the word). Then, clients are asked to repeat the word continuously until the word has lost its associative meaning and all that remains is its sound. This technique helps people recognize that the association between a word or phrase and its meaning can be defused, and that particular thoughts do not have to actively and automatically direct a behavioral response.

Sport psychologists unfamiliar with ABBT theory and interventions often ask how cognitive defusion differs from traditional approaches that promote relaxation, restructuring/challenging thoughts, "letting go," or refocusing. The essential difference is that in second-wave behavioral interventions, a variety of strategies are used to change the content of thoughts or reduce the frequency or intensity of affective responses to promote psychological wellbeing and attention to task. In contrast, ABBT practitioners do not seek to alter the *content* of clients' internal experiences, but instead alter the *relationships* the clients have to the internal experiences. So, whether through mindfulness training or cognitive defusion, the interventions do not alter the form, frequency, or intensity of these internal experiences to promote behavior change, but endorse the idea that one can function optimally *while having* these experiences. This state, in turn, is the essential meaning of experiential acceptance.

The ultimate purpose of developing experiential acceptance, and the mechanism by which it may promote positive outcomes, is the influence on behavior (Kollman, Brown, & Barlow, 2009). Experiential acceptance allows individuals to live through and tolerate the variety of "negative" thoughts and emotions, yet still act in a consistent and committed manner in the service of those values that mean the most to them. Through numerous experiential exercises, clients learn to view their cognitions and emotions (perceived as positive or negative) as ever-present, naturally occurring events that do not need to be controlled, reduced, or increased for optimal human functioning. ABBT practitioners place a premium on behavioral commitment and accountability for the choices that one makes, regardless of the thoughts and feelings that are present when these choices need to be made.

In the sport context, these behaviors include both on- and off-field actions that inevitably promote enhanced athletic performance, such as practise behavior and disciplined within-competition behavior.

In addition to the ABBT components presented thus far, another critical aspect is the development of commitment to values-driven behaviors. Following (or often along with) the development of experiential acceptance, clients determine the personal values that are most meaningful to their lives. Specifically, they consider how they would like their lives to be remembered, and how they would like to be remembered as individuals (such as being a good teammate, parent, or relationship partner; being known as reliable and hard working). These values can never be fully reached, but rather, require continual effort. Unlike goals, which are either achieved or not, values are always present, are never fully attained, and are available for care and direct attention. It is these personal values that ABBT practitioners help clients purposefully and consistently pursue, and clients actively aim for these values by engaging in what are known as values-driven behaviors. Behaviors congruent with these values are contrasted with behaviors that serve the purpose of fulfilling or avoiding more immediate cognitions or emotions (emotion-driven behaviors). Continuing to practise or exercise even when tired, and walking away from an on-field frustration, are examples of values-driven behaviors; feigning illness when tired, and engaging in an altercation with a resultant penalty, are examples of emotion-driven behaviors.

Both of the values-driven examples above require individuals to: be aware of their cognitions and emotions (mindful awareness), accept and tolerate these internal experiences (experiential acceptance), focus on task-relevant cues and contingencies (mindful attention), and make behavioral choices in congruence with personal values and not immediate internal states (commitment). In sport contexts, the intervention goals of enhanced mindful awareness, mindful attention, and experiential acceptance allow clients to maintain greater attention to task relevant stimuli (as opposed to internal experiences); increase understanding of, and accountability for, events (rather than avoidant behavior); and directly promote those values-driven behaviors necessary for optimal performance (e.g., practise and training intensity, self-disciplined behavior).

The goals described above are achieved through several key steps. First, systematic training and practice in mindfulness meditative exercises such as "body scans" and "mindful breathing" techniques (Gardner & Moore, 2007) allow for enhanced attention and awareness. These exercises are not intended for relaxation, but instead increase the client's capacity to be focused and aware in the present moment. Second, the use of cognitive defusion techniques reduces the power and influence of specific words, not by challenging the logic or objectivity of the words, but by learning to view thoughts as simply events that come and go, that neither need to be taken as literal truths nor responded to as if they were real-life events. Third, the use of exposure/emotion-focused techniques helps clients disrupt their emotional avoidance by confronting specific emotionally evocative situations and learn to experience, and ultimately accept and tolerate, "difficult" emotions that were previously avoided. Fourth, behavioral activation strategies help clients identify and consistently engage in specific behaviors that are congruent with personal values.

Empirical support for MAC and ABBT in sport

Since the development of the MAC approach to performance enhancement (Moore & Gardner, 2001), and its first publication (Gardner & Moore, 2004b), a number of studies have been published in support of it and associated ABBTs for the enhancement of overall wellbeing and performance.

The first phase of MAC's empirical investigation was a series of case studies demonstrating the possible utility of the approach for enhancing performance (Gardner & Moore, 2004b, 2006). Although case studies are a valuable tool in the initial development of a psychological intervention, they certainly, on their own, are not sufficient to demonstrate efficacy. Wolanin (2005) conducted an open trial of MAC within a Division I collegiate athletic department, using two intercollegiate sports. Results indicated that MAC was effective at enhancing athletic performance as judged by both self and coach performance ratings as compared to a no intervention control condition. Also, as predicted by the theory underlying MAC, ratings of attention, practice intensity, and game-related aggressiveness also increased. Of note, even though some athletes are without clinical or subclinical psychological barriers, a large number of referrals to sport psychologists are based upon non-presented subclinical psychological barriers such as worry, rumination, perfectionism, and interpersonal difficulties (Gardner & Moore, 2004a). Results from Wolanin's open clinical trial suggested that the initial 8-session MAC protocol was more effective for those athletes who manifested no subclinical psychological barriers/issues. This finding, in turn, suggested that a more flexible MAC protocol may be necessary to effectively assist the full range of athletes who come to the practitioner's attention. As a result of the study, the MAC protocol was revised from a fixed 8-session format to a flexible 7-module format, allowing the opportunity to deliver any of the modules over any number of necessary sessions (Gardner & Moore, 2007).

Following the successes of a series of case studies and the open trial, Lutkenhouse, Gardner, and Moore (as cited in Gardner & Moore, 2007) embarked upon a large ($N = 118$) randomized controlled trial (RCT) comparing MAC and a traditional psychological skills training protocol published by the United States Olympic Committee (USOC, 1999). Results indicated that a significantly greater number of athletes completing the MAC protocol demonstrated a clinically significant increase (at least 20%) in coach ratings of performance from pretest to posttest (32% of MAC participants vs. 10% of PST participants).

Additionally, a number of empirical investigations have used ABBT interventions that are closely related to MAC, both theoretically and procedurally, to enhance athletic performance. Using a sport-adapted version ACT with national level canoeists, Garcia, Villa, Cepeda, Cueto, and Montes (2004) found that the intervention resulted in statistically significant performance improvements on a canoeing training apparatus compared to a matched control of participants receiving a hypnosis intervention. In a more recent randomized controlled trial, Bernier, Theinot, Cuadron, and Fournier (2009) found that a different sport-adapted version of ACT, used with elite golfers at a national training institute, resulted in improved golf performance as defined by increases in national rank, when compared with a control group receiving a traditional PST intervention. Subjective ratings by both golfers and coaches also supported the efficacy of the ACT-based intervention as compared to the PST intervention.

Conclusion

In the last decade there has been a major shift in the theoretical and applied landscape in cognitive-behavioral psychology. The theoretical models and intervention packages once considered the gold standard in the field have been challenged by a new approach to studying and treating human behavioral issues. This new generation of behavioral psychology, often referred to as the third wave of behaviorism, focuses on the development of mindful awareness, mindful attention, acceptance of internal experiences, and commitment to act in accordance with valued life directions. These interventions, referred to as ABBT, have contributed significantly to the clinical and counseling psychology domains, garnering substantial empirical support for a variety of clinical and subclinical concerns. Within sport, the MAC approach to performance enhancement has accumulated evidence to support both its theoretical foundations and its intervention efficacy within sport-performance contexts. Evidence in basic science has supported the underlying processes of MAC and other ABBTs, and a series of outcome studies has supported the efficacy of MAC as an evidence-based intervention for the enhancement of overall psychosocial wellbeing and performance. Although it is inevitable that the process of science will continue to provide reasons to modify and enhance any intervention, ABBTs in general, and MAC in particular, have achieved an empirical level of support sufficient to be considered a first-line intervention strategy for the sport psychologist when working with athletes. See Box 20.1 for a summary of the main key points of this chapter.

Box 20.1

Summary of key points about acceptance-based behavioral therapies

- Behavioral psychology has evolved from a focus on observable relationships between stimuli, responses, and reinforcing consequences (the first wave); to a focus on reducing, controlling, or eliminating internal processes such as cognitions and emotions (the second wave); to acceptance of internal experiences and an emphasis on enhancing behaviors connected to personal values (the third wave).
- The new class of interventions based on the third wave revolution has been termed acceptance-based behavioral therapies (ABBT). These interventions help people develop mindful non-judging awareness of internal experiences, acceptance of internal states, and a willingness to experience these states *while* engaging in behaviors that are congruent with one's personal life values.
- ABBTs such as acceptance and commitment therapy (ACT) and mindfulness–acceptance–commitment (MAC) have demonstrated efficacy for the treatment of a wide variety of clinical problems and for the enhancement of performance and overall psychosocial wellbeing.
- As with clinical ABBTs, MAC professionals promote the development of: (a) mindful awareness, (b) mindful attention, and (c) an acceptance of and willingness to experience a wide range of internal experiences, in the service of (d) consistent committed behavior that is congruent with one's personal values.
- By being aware of one's cognitions and emotions (*mindful awareness*), individuals can maintain an in-the-moment focus on task-relevant cues and contingencies (*mindful attention*).
- *Experiential acceptance* is a willingness to approach (rather than avoid) one's life values no matter how or what one may feel or think.
- *Commitment* is consistent activation of behavior in the service of one's personal values.

References

Bandura, A. (1969). *Principles of behavior modification.* New York: Holt, Rinehart, & Winston.

Beck, A. T. (1976). *Cognitive therapy and the emotional disorders.* New York: International University Press.

Bernier, M., Theinot, E., Caudron, R., & Fournier, J. F. (2009). A multi-study investigation examining the relationship between mindfulness and acceptance approaches and sport performance. *Journal of Clinical Sport Psychology, 3,* 320–333.

Bishop, S. R., Lau, M., Shapiro, S., Carlson, L., Anderson, N. D., Carmody, J., Segal, Z. V., Abbey, S., Speca, M., Velting, D., & Devins, G. (2004). Mindfulness: A proposed operational definition. *Clinical Psychology: Science and Practice, 11,* 230–241.

Foreman, E. M., Herbert, J. D., Moitra, E., Yeomans, P. D., & Geller, P. E. (2007). A randomized controlled effectiveness trial of acceptance and commitment therapy and cognitive therapy for anxiety and depression. *Behavior Modification, 31,* 772–799.

Garcia, R. F., Villa, R. S., Cepeda, N. T., Cueto, E. G., & Montes, J. M. G. (2004). Efecto de la hipnosis y la terapia de aceptación y compromiso (ACT) en la mejora de la fuerza física en piragüistas. *International Journal of Clinical and Health Psychology, 4,* 481–493.

Gardner, F. L., & Moore, Z. E. (2004a). The multi-level classification system for sport psychology (MCS-SP). *The Sport Psychologist, 18,* 89–109.

Gardner, F. L., & Moore. Z. E. (2004b). A mindfulness–acceptance–commitment based approach to performance enhancement: Theoretical considerations. *Behavior Therapy, 35,* 707–723.

Gardner, F. L., & Moore, Z. E. (2006). *Clinical sport psychology.* Champaign, IL: Human Kinetics.

Gardner, F. L., & Moore, Z. E. (2007). *The psychology of enhancing human performance: The mindfulness–acceptance–commitment (MAC) approach.* New York: Springer.

Hayes, S. C., Strosahl, K. D., & Wilson, K. G. (1999). *Acceptance and commitment therapy: An experiential approach to behavior change.* New York: Guilford Press.

Hayes, S. C., Barnes-Holmes, D., & Roche, B. (2001). *Relational frame theory: A post Skinnerian account of human language and cognition.* New York: Kluwer Academic/Plenum.

Kabat-Zinn, J. (2005). *Coming to our senses: Healing ourselves and the world through mindfulness.* New York: Hyperion.

Kollman, D. M., Brown, T. A., & Barlow, D. H. (2009). The construct validity of acceptance: A multitrait-multimethod investigation. *Behavior Therapy, 40,* 205–218.

Longmore, R. J., & Worrell, M. (2007). Do we need to challenge thoughts in cognitive behavior therapy? *Clinical Psychology Review, 27,* 173–187.

Meichenbaum, D. (1977). *Cognitive behavior modification.* New York: Plenum Press.

Moore, Z., & Gardner, F. (2001, October). *Taking applied sport psychology from research to practice: Integrating empirically supported interventions into a self-regulatory model of athletic performance.* Symposium presented at the annual conference of the Association for the Advancement of Applied Sport Psychology, Orlando, FL.

Nathan, P., & Gorman, J. M. (2002). *A guide to treatments that work.* New York: Oxford University Press.

Roemer, L., & Orsillo, S. M. (2009). *Mindfulness and acceptance based behavioral therapies in practice.* New York: Guilford Press.

Skinner, B. F. (1953). *Science and human behavior.* New York: MacMillan.

United States Olympic Committee Sport Psychology Staff (1999). *Sport psychology mental training manual.* Colorado Springs: CO: USOC Sport Science and Technology Division.

Wolanin, A. T. (2005). Mindfulness–acceptance–commitment (MAC) based performance enhancement for Division I collegiate athletes: A preliminary investigation. *Dissertation Abstracts International-B, 65,* pp. 3735–3794.

21

An Eastern philosophical approach

Sam J. Zizzi and Mark B. Andersen

It is not necessary to start every chapter on Buddhist teachings with a quote.

Anonymous

Within the context of this chapter, the term "Eastern philosophy" will refer to Buddhist or Taoist principles, whereas "Western influences" will refer to European and North American approaches to psychotherapy. When adapting Eastern principles, we will cite primarily general philosophical ideals for living a happy life as opposed to specific theories focusing on working within the context of psychotherapy. The purpose of the chapter is not to resolve the major differences between Eastern and Western approaches, for there are many more comprehensive treatments on this subject. The primary objective is to outline principles from Eastern philosophies (Buddhism, Taoism, and others), and to suggest how these principles relate to therapeutic processes in applied sport psychology. The amount of literature available from the last 30 to 40 years on the topic of Buddhist principles (e.g., mindfulness) applied to psychotherapy is voluminous (e.g., Germer, Siegel, & Fulton, 2005), but there have been surprisingly few applications of these principles within the profession of applied sport psychology. Therefore, it is our goal to succinctly explore some of the ideas and the research conducted so sport psychology professionals can find their own paths in applying these principles to their work.

Common ground?

One key similarity cited between the two approaches is that Buddhism "is concerned with helping people change and with helping them overcome emotional suffering, as are the various psychotherapies" (Wray, 1986, p. 155). Eastern philosophical approaches offer insights over 2,500 years old, and provide classic lessons and principles to be applied to daily life (Reps, 1989), whereas Western psychotherapies have been developed in the context of industrialized societies founded on capitalistic principles over the last 150 years. Wray noted that because psychotherapies are recent developments, we must consider how Western cultural and social ideals helped to shape these approaches on macro and micro levels.

The primary bias within many industrialized societies is economic development, based on a variety of socialist and capitalist perspectives. In many ways, capitalism could be seen as the antithesis of Buddhism. Within a capitalistic environment, individual needs are emphasized and citizens struggle to achieve status and gain material goods (Schumacher, 1999). Aggression and risk taking are reinforced. Buddhism focuses on the interconnectedness of collective societies and the earth, simplicity in living, non-attachment to achievements and material goods, and compassion towards others (Rosenbaum, 1999).

On a micro level, the primary bias within applied psychology is an emphasis on empirical evidence and proven treatments. In the twenty-first century, the focus on the science of psychotherapy and accountability has sharpened. Shaped by economic (e.g., insurance companies, managed health care) and governmental forces, a movement has taken shape called "evidenced-based practice," although some professionals are skeptical of this structured, top-down approach to client care (Stuart & Lilienfeld, 2007). Practitioners of Eastern approaches value the evidence and experiences encountered when consciously engaged in the present moment. Western practitioners place emphasis instead on rational, linear thinking and the accumulation of knowledge via the scientific method (e.g., randomized controlled trials).

At their core, Eastern philosophies emphasize engaging in the present moment as the highest form of consciousness. Buddhist and Taoist proponents highlight the simplicity and clarity of the present moment, and they espouse the value of present experience over past events or future possibilities. Meditation and mindful awareness (i.e., simply being) might be the most common forms of psychological treatment that Buddhist-oriented practitioners prescribe (Rosenbaum, 1999). In contrast, some Western approaches to psychotherapy focus on past conflicts (Freudian/Jungian) or current emotional experiences (Gestalt), whereas others center on cognitive reactions to past and current experiences (rational–emotive behavior therapy) and how choices will affect future outcomes (Adlerian individual psychotherapy). These therapies typically have changing patterns of thoughts, emotions, or behaviors (i.e., doing versus being) as the medium of treatment.

In Watts' (1961) classic essay, *Psychotherapy East and West*, he suggested that another basic contrast between the two approaches is that clinical psychologists have been concerned with "changing the consciousness of particularly disturbed individuals . . . [whereas Taoists and Buddhist teachers have focused on] changing the consciousness of normal, socially adjusted people" (p. 16). This latter description, on the surface, would suggest that Eastern approaches would be well-suited to applied sport psychology given that many athletes do not experience serious mental illness. Watts' discussion of psychotherapy, however, must be viewed in a historical context because it largely focused on psychodynamic approaches that dominated the psychotherapy landscape in the first half of the twentieth century. In addition to these seminal approaches to psychotherapy, we need to consider the strong influence and integration of cognitive-behavioral approaches as well, given their high prevalence in the field of applied sport psychology. We'll now explore several key principles of Eastern philosophy that may be useful to consider integrating into our practices as sport psychology professionals.

Starting with an empty cup

As you consider each of the following principles, you may find yourself struggling to fit one of these "new-old" ideas into the structure of how you have been taught to be an effective sport psychology professional. It might be useful to try to "unlearn" – even for a moment – something you have been taught in your preparation as a therapist (Brandon, 1976) so that you may have the opportunity for growth as a sport psychology professional.

195

Some of the principles discussed below will appear in direct opposition to either the current cultural norms related to health care or your professional training, so it is important to start this process in the moment, or "empty your cup" as noted in the translated Zen anecdote below (Reps, 1989):

> Nan-in, a Japanese master during the Meiji era (1868–1912), received a university professor who came to inquire about Zen. Nan-in served tea. He poured his visitor's cup full, and then kept pouring. The professor watched the overflow until he no longer could restrain himself. "It is overfull. No more will go in!"
>
> "Like this cup," Nan-in said, "you are full of your own opinions and speculations. How can I show you Zen unless you first empty your cup?"
>
> (p. 5)

The meaning of unsatisfactoriness, suffering, and pain

One of the first opportunities to unlearn relates to the meaning of unsatisfactoriness, suffering, and pain, from a Buddhist perspective. Nearly all Western approaches to physical or mental health care, often through a medical model of treatment, focus on symptom or pain reduction as key therapeutic outcomes. Visits to doctors often commence with a listing of current and recurrent symptoms, and end with a prescription for treating those symptoms and/or the root cause (with pharmaceuticals or psychotherapy). The focus is typically on making people comfortable and avoiding or minimizing pain and discomfort.

Eastern approaches would instead have us help the client focus on, and accept, the pain as part of experience (Kabat-Zinn, 1990). Buddhist teachers suggest pain has meaning; there is something to be learned, and therefore, we should pay *more* attention to it, not less. In this context, our Western approach to medicine is nearly the polar opposite of what Buddhists might think of as "traditional medicine." The traditional approach to healthy living taught in Buddhist texts focuses on accepting current circumstances, and healing ourselves through moderation in eating, drinking, sleep, and other behaviors (Germer *et al.*, 2005). The most common medical intervention in modern Western society involves ingesting a manmade substance (drug) to alter body chemistry to either: (a) remove or reduce unpleasant sensations or states of mind, or (b) treat an underlying pathology. Many teaching texts of Buddhism list the "four noble truths" as the fundamental realities students should come to accept if they hope to live well. The four principles explain the central role of "suffering" in life (the first truth), the sources of suffering (the second truth), and how to stop suffering (the last two truths). The first of these noble truths of Buddhism – "life is suffering" – should be accepted as a fact of life, but not in a pessimistic sense. As Andersen and Mannion (in press) noted, there is a problem of translation of the word "suffering".

> Many Western people, when hearing the first noble truth of Buddhism, may baulk. That "life means suffering" sounds like the language of victimization. One can argue, "But life is full of joy and happiness too; this view is way too pessimistic and negative." What the first noble truth addresses is often misinterpreted … . The actual term used in Sanskrit is *dukkha*, and its translation into "suffering" has caused no end of misunderstandings. The term *dukkha* can mean a few different things, and its translation into the more accurate expressions of "pervasive unsatisfactoriness" or "disquietude" sets the first noble truth in a clearer light. That even in moments of joy there is a tinge

of unsatisfactoriness because of the transience and impermanence of the experience. Great athletic achievements, gold medals, and such, are often followed by feelings of regret, "was it really worth it?," and "I wish I could have that feeling again." The whole culture of sport could be seen as a culture of pervasive unsatisfactoriness. One is not training enough (i.e., satisfactorily); one is not achieving enough. One must do more. You're not *citius*, *altius*, and *fortius* enough.

The idea is for clients to understand that their lives will be filled at times with a certain amount of suffering and that they are not helping the situation by denying, avoiding, or over-reacting to negative life events and the dissatisfaction they cause. Fisher and Wrisberg (2005) provided an application of these concepts to career-ending injury rehabilitation. They suggested that athletic trainers (or sport physiotherapists) help their athletes develop "beginner's mind" so they can accept their present circumstances and commit to "getting on with life as it is today" (p. 44). The concept of beginner's mind is similar to the idea of emptying your cup, described above. To help athletes engage in mindful rehabilitation, it could be useful for them to quiet many of their thoughts related to why the injury happened and what they might be missing out on in the future. Emptying their minds of biases, irrelevant goals, and preconceived notions about the future will allow them to consider the new opportunities that lay ahead on their paths to recovery.

Expecting to encounter and accept adversity could certainly be taught as a critical mental skill for sport performance. Helping athletes interpret situations differently and accepting the "full catastrophe" of the worst parts of their lives (Kabat-Zinn, 1990) has the same outcome goal as more structured, situation-focused cognitive-behavioral techniques. As mentioned earlier, a critical difference when making these types of comparisons is that Buddhism is a broad philosophical approach offering guidance on most aspects of life and personal development, whereas each specific form of psychotherapy focuses more narrowly on mental health issues.

Athletes may have a different perspective on pain than general psychotherapy clients given the physicality of their work and the realistic expectation that they will encounter some amount of pain on a regular basis. Some sport sub-cultures embrace or sensationalize pain tolerance so absurdly that athletes who play injured are revered as the highest form of sport hero. Phrases such as "no pain, no gain" are all too common in sport environments. Such attitudes, however, don't necessarily encourage mindful awareness and could lead to a variety of negative consequences including injuries and overtraining. People generally try to avoid pain, but high-achieving athletes may be conditioned to think that more work and effort (and pain) are always better. In sum, Buddhism would not really differentiate painful moments from pain-free moments in terms of relative importance. We are meant to pay attention, and experience these (and other) moments so we can learn to live in the present.

The nature of behavior change

At this point, it is useful to remember that both Eastern and Western practitioners would agree that they want to reduce unsatisfactoriness, physical pain, and psychological suffering, and help clients lead fulfilling lives (e.g., perform better in life or sport). Definitions of a fulfilling life, however, might differ considerably if you asked a Western psychologist or a Japanese Zen master. Western psychologists might focus on helping their clients build self-esteem and confidence so they can become more competent in relationships, school, or work than they previously have been. They would be likely to help them set goals to lead more productive lives, based on achievements or outcomes desired by their clients. If clients are able to achieve the stated goals of therapy, then the process may be judged a success.

Notions of behavior change differ considerably in Buddhism. The attainment of *sukha* (from Sanskrit for happiness, ease, pleasure, bliss), which is a central motive for change, offers an interesting example. The Buddhist notion of *sukha* in living has been described as ending the cycle of life and death (de Silva, 1986) or cessation of *dukkha* (pervasive unsatisfactoriness). The past and future are meaningless and do not hold the weight of the present moment. In sports, an example may be a shift to ending the cycle of dwelling on future and past wins and losses. Happiness is (ideally) an acceptance of, and commitment to, the circumstances of the present moment. The process involves being present, rather than striving to do something perfectly. From this perspective, each opportunity to perform may be seen as a temporal work of art that cannot be held. Some aspects of flow are similar to *sukha*. Some Western psychotherapies, such as acceptance and commitment therapy, come close to Buddhist concepts of change.

Buddhist approaches to behavior change and self-development are conducted with an emphasis on personal restraint, and moderation in motor, verbal, and cognitive elements of life (de Silva, 1986). In a general sense, Buddhism teaches through the open interpretation of a variety of stories and examples. Specific techniques are not necessarily offered to the practitioner, but emphasis is placed instead on guiding principles to change. In a review of many of these ancient stories and examples, de Silva identified some of the following commonly used cognitive and behavioral strategies: (a) modeling, (b) reciprocal inhibition, (c) stimulus control, (d) behavioral reinforcement, (e) social skills training, (f) thought stopping, and (g) self-monitoring through mindfulness. The remarkable overlap between techniques used to facilitate behavior change in Buddhism and Western psychology suggests that sport psychology practitioners may be able to merge ideologies to experience personal and professional growth. It is also humbling to realize that many of the "new" techniques outlined by cognitive-behavioral practitioners have been practised by Buddhist and Taoist teachers for more than 2,000 years.

Buddhist practitioners would best be described as "non-directive" – they lead by standing still. Buddhist teachers do not move towards or away from clients; they might reflect the present moment (à la Carl Rogers), or they may guide clients in meditation to help them reflect on and accept their circumstances. The modeling of non-doing or sitting still (e.g., mindful meditation, *zazen*) is the primary medium to encourage change.

Mindfulness in the consulting room

The sport psychologist can take a variety of stances. He can be the expert problem solver and direct the athlete to solutions. She can be the Rogerian mirror of unconditional positive regard and genuineness. He can be the irrational thought confronter; it all depends on the therapeutic model one embraces. The Buddhist suggestion for the stance of the therapist is the same one for the person in therapy: moment-to-moment mindful attention. As Wilson and DuFrene (2008) stated:

> Present-moment contact is every bit as important for you as a therapist as it is for your clients. You need to ask of yourself the same questions you ask of your clients. To the extent that you become excessively attached to a conceptualized future for your clients ("What if I can't help them?") or a conceptualized past ("I have done them no good at all"), you'll be less available to interact with the small shifts in their behavior. In addition,

to the extent that you're worried and anxious and working hard to make these painful thoughts go away, your clients may begin to help you out by expressing less distress.

(p. 63)

Wilson and DuFrene's mindfulness of the therapist and the client (their book is titled *Mindfulness for Two*) has psychotherapy roots that go back, at least, to Freud.

Freud asked his clients to say whatever came to mind (e.g., thoughts, images, memories, emotions) with as little censoring as possible. He asked them to report their continually rolling internal world. Freud's free association can be seen as an early Western mindful exercise. Freud (1912/1958) also wrote about the stance a psychoanalyst needs to take when working with clients:

> As we shall see, it rejects the use of any special expedient (even that of taking notes). It consists simply in not directing one's notice of anything in particular, and in maintaining the same "evenly suspended attention" (as I have called it) in the face of all that one hears ... . The rule for the doctor may be expressed: "He should withhold all conscious influences from his capacity to attend," ... or to put it purely in terms of technique: "He should simply listen, and not bother about whether he is keeping anything in mind".

(pp. 111–112)

Freud's description of how a therapist should *be* (not *do*) in a state of "evenly suspended attention" sounds mindful and positively Buddhist. There have been many arguments over the decades about what Freud meant with his evenly suspended attention. Epstein (2007) probably best summed it up as:

> This attention is not just passive, receptive, empathic listening, it is a means of attending to all phenomena equally, impartially, and dispassionately with rapt interest and active close scrutiny but with a slight distance, so that one allows a thought or impulse to completely exhibit itself, noting all of the reverberations created, before acting.

(p. 118)

How is this mindfulness of the therapist helpful? This nonjudgmental state echoes with Rogers' (1957) empathy and unconditional positive regard and provides clients with a different type of interpersonal feedback than they receive from others and themselves. This evenly suspended attention is also deeply connected to Winnicott's (1971) concept of creating a safe, secure, "holding" environment. Perhaps sitting in these moments with a sport psychologist could help heal and might be the most compassionate act a therapist can do, to hold others in all their confusion and messiness, to *be* with the other. Evenly suspended attention (mindfulness) also assists in quieting our own needs to help, to find solutions, and to jump to (possibly premature) interventions.

Teaching Buddhist principles to help clients change thoughts and behaviors

One of the goals of this chapter is to help sport psychology professionals better understand the key Buddhist principles that may be applied, why they might be useful, and how they can influence work in the consulting room. Many skeptical readers may look beyond these humble goals and ask themselves, "How specifically am I supposed to teach these vague concepts to my clients to help them improve performance?" Any seasoned Zen master would not provide an answer to this question, but perhaps ask students more questions meant to lead them down their own paths of discovery. Nevertheless, given our own biases and desires to write a useful chapter, we have developed the final section of the chapter to satisfy some readers' Western urges for clarity.

Prior to implementing any of the strategies below with a particular client, we encourage readers to review some of the earlier chapters (e.g., Chapters 1, 2, 20) in this book to determine if their clients will be good matches for the strategies outlined below. Fisher and Wrisberg (2005) suggested that spiritually-minded clients may be open to adopting some of these concepts, although the timing of the consultation may be critical to success.

Strategy #1: Encourage enhanced self-awareness through meditation and mindfulness training. From our viewpoints, clients spending time "single-tasking," or just sitting, may help counteract the culturally dominant strategy of multi-tasking or disastrous dissociation. Elite athletes, who often live complicated lives with many demands on their time, may benefit from the simplicity of these moments. Time spent mindfully, on a single task, may recharge their batteries and contribute positively to recovery and mental health. This benefit alone might motivate some clients to try meditation. If clients are uncomfortable trying a sitting meditation, then perhaps guide them in a walking meditation where they focus on one step at a time and let their thoughts flow by without judgment. Clients who embrace mindfulness training may eventually develop an ability to recall this calm state of mind and body when under pressure in performance situations. Learning this coping skill could be highly useful, particularly for athletes who struggle to manage their emotional states before, during, or after competitions (see Germer, 2005).

Strategy #2: Help clients "let go" of their attachments and live and own their own "full catastrophes." One key characteristic of Westernized sport environments is the sheer volume of external rewards and punishments for success and failure. The high visibility and accessibility of modern sport make for a double-edged sword for the modern athlete – the rewards may be higher for success, yet the downfalls may be deeper and longer lasting. Attachment to either of these potential outcomes takes athletes out of the moment, and can lead them to establish tentative patterns of behavior where they are motivated to avoid failure at all costs. We can help athletes break their patterns by teaching them to embrace the idea that their careers will most likely include tremendous highs and lows, peaceful moments, and catastrophes. All of these experiences are parts of their stories, and adopting this approach might give them a happy, calm way of functioning within a challenging, distracting environment where pervasive unsatisfactoriness is guaranteed (see Kabat-Zinn, 1990).

Strategy #3: Buddhist philosophy (and all religions) is full of stories, images, and metaphors. One strategy that we have found useful in communicating Buddhist principles is to tell modern and ancient stories to capture a concept or to represent a client's situation. For example, here is a story that might help athletes with the concepts of attachment, clinging, and letting go.

> One day the Buddha was having a picnic in a lovely meadow with many monks. They noticed an unhappy farmer coming toward them. The farmer had lost his cows, and he asked the Buddha and the monks if they had seen them. They said that they had not seen any cows the whole day. The farmer, greatly distressed, said, "I'm so miserable. I have twelve cows, and now I can't find them." The Buddha said, "My friend, we have not seen any cows. You might look for them in another place." The farmer thanked

him and ran away, and the Buddha turned to his monks and said, "My dear monks, you must be the happiest people. You have no cows to lose. If you have too many cows to take care of, you will be very busy. In order to be happy, you have to learn the art of *cow releasing*." And then the Buddha laughed heartily. "Release the cows one by one. In the beginning you thought those cows were essential to your happiness, and you tried to get more and more cows. But now you realize that cows are not really conditions for your happiness; they are obstacles for your happiness. You need to release your cows."

There are thousands of Buddhist stories, metaphors, and images that can be used to communicate what may be foreign concepts to athletes and coaches. As sport psychologists, we listen to athletes' and coaches' stories all the time, but we are storytellers too. Stories have been used for millennia to entertain, to instruct, to warn, and even to enlighten. We find the telling of Buddhist stories in therapy to be a useful strategy to begin changing maladaptive thinking and behavior. See Andersen and Speed (in press) for a discussion on stories, folktales, and metaphors in applied sport psychology service delivery.

Conclusions

There are many lessons to be learned and unlearned when comparing and contrasting Western and Eastern approaches to the practice of applied sport psychology. The contradictory messages appear, at times, difficult to merge. But when put together, just as in the yin-yang symbol, the approaches form a full circle. They need each other for balance, and there are valuable lessons within each approach. See Box 21.1 for the key points of this chapter.

Box 21.1

Key points about an Eastern philosophical approach

- Learning Buddhist and other Eastern approaches is largely unlearning, so we start with emptying our cups. If we hope to be present-moment focused in a culture that makes such behavior difficult, we will probably have to unlearn some of the sociocultural lessons or specific counseling techniques that emphasize the past and the future.
- Doing less to help may help more. Techniques vary across psychotherapies, and their success often depends on rapport and timing. Techniques lead the client to where you think they should go. "Doing" less and being present more may help clients feel accepted and encourage clients to find their own paths.
- In your work with athletes, accept that you will experience *dukkha*, or pervasive unsatisfactoriness. You could always have done more, said more in a session, observed more practices or competitions, consulted with the coach more often. Learning to model acceptance of a non-perfect world in your own professional life may do wonders for the genuine rapport and empathy you model in your sessions.

■ Help clients "let go." Re-consider how you set goals with your clients, and how much time you spend helping them achieve. Outcome goals lead to judgments and relative comparisons that may undermine our efforts. If absorption in the moment is the ultimate objective, then trying to win or get better only detracts from one's focus in the now. Putting energy instead into mindful training and performing encourages athletes to focus on the quality of now instead of unknown quantities and consequences in the future.

References

Andersen, M. B., & Mannion, J. (in press). If you see the Buddha on the football field – Tackle him. In D. Gilbourne & M. B. Andersen (Eds.), *Critical essays in applied sport psychology*. Champaign, IL: Human Kinetics.

Andersen, M. B., & Speed, H. D. (in press). The practitioner and client as storytellers: Metaphors and folktales in applied sport psychology practice. In D. Gilbourne & M. B. Andersen (Eds.), *Critical essays in applied sport psychology*. Champaign, IL: Human Kinetics.

Brandon, D. (1976). *Zen in the art of the helping*. New York: Dell.

de Silva, P. (1986). Buddhism and behavior change: Implications for therapy. In G. Claxton (Ed.) *Beyond therapy: The impact of Eastern religions on psychological theory and practice* (pp. 219–231). London: Wisdom.

Epstein, M. (2007). *Psychotherapy without the self: A Buddhist perspective*. New Haven, CT: Yale University Press.

Fisher, L. A., & Wrisberg, C. A. (2005). The "Zen" of career-ending injury rehabilitation. *Athletic Therapy Today, 10*(3), 44–45.

Freud, S. (1912/1958). Recommendations to physicians practicing psychoanalysis. In J. Stachey (Ed. and Trans.), *Standard edition of the complete psychological works of Sigmund Freud*, (Vol. 12, pp. 111–120). London: Hogarth.

Germer, C. K. (2005). Teaching mindfulness in therapy. In C. K. Germer, R. D. Siegel, & P. R. Fulton (Eds.), *Mindfulness and psychotherapy* (pp. 113–129). New York: Guilford Press.

Germer, C. K., Siegel, R. D., & Fulton, P. R. (2005). *Mindfulness and psychotherapy*. New York: Guilford Press.

Kabat-Zinn, J. (1990). *Full catastrophe living: Using the wisdom of your body and mind to face stress, pain, and illness*. New York: Delacorte.

Reps, P. (1989). *Zen flesh, Zen bones: A collection of Zen and pre-Zen writings*. New York: Anchor Books / Doubleday.

Rogers, C. R. (1957). Training individuals to engage in the therapeutic process. In C. R. Strouther (Ed.), *Psychology and mental health*. Washington, DC: American Psychological Association.

Rosenbaum, R. (1999). *Zen and the heart of psychotherapy*. Philadelphia: Taylor & Francis.

Schumacher, E. F. (1999). *Small is beautiful: Economics as if people mattered*. Point Roberts, WA: Hartley & Marks.

Stuart, R., & Lilienfeld, S. (2007). The evidence missing from evidence-based practice. *American Psychologist, 62*, 615–616.

Watts, A. W. (1961). *Psychotherapy East and West*. New York: Ballantine Books.

Wilson, K. G., & Dufrene, T. (2008). *Mindfulness for two: An acceptance and commitment therapy approach to mindfulness in psychotherapy*. Oakland, CA: New Harbinger.

Winnicott, D. W. (1971). *Playing and reality*. London: Routledge.

Wray, I. (1986). Buddhism and psychotherapy: A Buddhist perspective. In G. Claxton (Ed.), *Beyond therapy: The impact of Eastern religions on psychological theory and practice* (pp. 156–172). London: Wisdom.

Section IV

Individual issues

22

Referring clients to other professionals

Judy L. Van Raalte

An athlete came to talk to the team's sport psychologist saying that she wanted to increase her confidence during games. Most of the meeting was focused on talking about confidence, but the athlete also mentioned in passing that she had "issues at home" that she might want to discuss in the future. Some time later, the coach called the sport psychologist to express concerns about the athlete. Two team members had approached the coach and told her that the athlete had sent text messages talking about suicide. When the coach spoke to the athlete directly, however, the athlete said that she was fine and denied that she was suicidal. The coach and teammates are worried.

How should the sport psychologist proceed with this case? Should she continue to work with the athlete on confidence and performance enhancement? Should she push the athlete to talk about the "issues at home?" Should she discuss the information about suicide provided by the coach? Should the athlete be referred to another practitioner? If so, how should the athlete be referred and to whom?

The answer to these questions depends on a number of factors, many of which may be explored and addressed by the sport psychologist during supervision. The focus of this chapter is referral. Therefore, attention will be primarily directed to issues pertaining to referral. Specifically, when and why referrals should be made, how to make referrals, and what happens when needed referrals are not made. Applied sport psychology work is complex, involving individual athletes, teammates, entire teams, coaches, parents, and other support service providers. Understanding the referral process can facilitate the effectiveness of applied sport psychology practice in complex situations such as the one described above and can strengthen the relationships among all those involved in sporting endeavors.

What is a referral?

In the case of applied sport psychology practice, referral typically pertains to those situations in which a client, or potential client, is directed to another professional for services. These professionals often include experts in medical, nutritional, physical, psychological, or spiritual issues (Andersen & Van Raalte, 2005).

Why referrals are made?

At a basic level, referrals are made to meet ethical obligations pertaining to the treatment of clients. Sport psychology is a diverse field consisting of practitioners with a variety of backgrounds and training, but all applied sport psychology practitioners are subject to ethical guidelines of the profession. In their review of more than 200 ethics codes, Henschen, Ripoll, Hackfort, and Mohan (1995) identified seven key ethical principles essential to the practice of applied sport psychology. Of those ethical principles, two are directly related to referral: the principle pertaining to professional competence and the principle relating to professional and scientific responsibility. In both principles sport psychologists who are asked to work beyond their training and competence should make referrals to suitable colleagues. The referral process is an effective mechanism by which sport psychologists can serve their clients' best interests and protect their welfare.

When should referrals be made?

Sport psychology consultants make referrals for a variety of reasons. For example, a sport psychology consultant may have too much business and not have the time to devote to working with a particular client. A practitioner may have the time, but simply not be interested in working with a client.

Referrals can be made when a sport psychology practitioner has limited knowledge about a particular behavioral, psychological, or spiritual concern (Andersen & Van Raalte, 2005). Referrals may also help ensure the provision of optimal services when a sport psychologist lacks experience with or does not have a full understanding of how to work with a client of a particular age, gender identity, race, ethnicity, culture, religion, sexual orientation, disability, or socioeconomic status (American Psychological Association, 2002). In these types of situations, referrals are made because another practitioner with a different set of skills and experience would be best suited to serve the client.

Why aren't referrals made when they should be?

The exact conditions that require a sport psychology consultant to refer are not completely clear (Etzel, Watson, & Zizzi, 2004). Before a referral can be made, a sport psychology consultant has to recognize that a referral is needed. Williams and Scherzer (2003) surveyed doctoral students in sport psychology and found that 44% of the students had encountered issues that were not related to sport in their applied work with athletes. Similarly, Leffingwell, Wiechman, Smith, Smoll, and Christensen (2001) found that 42% of students who sought the assistance of sport psychology consultants were dealing with personal and/or mental health issues not directly connected to sport. There appears to be recognition among sport psychology practitioners that mental health and other issues that might require referral arise during consultation.

In 2006, Gayman and Crossman surveyed sport psychology professionals, all of whom were registered with the Canadian Mental Training Registry, about how often they made referrals to mental health practitioners (Gayman & Crossman, 2006). Results indicated that the sport psychologists surveyed rarely made referrals to such professionals. Etzel *et al.* (2004) assessed sport psychologists' ethical beliefs and behaviors and found that the top two concerns identified by sport psychologists, who were asked to "list questionable ethical practices in applied sport psychology that you have recently observed" (p. 238), involved referral. Specifically, the Association for Applied Sport Psychology members surveyed expressed concerns about practitioners who did not refer clients even though the practitioners lacked sufficient training, competency, or supervision to meet client needs. Further, the members expressed concern about sport psychologists who misrepresented their credentials, skills, and training, thus confusing potential clients about their abilities and by extension the need for a referral for suitable services. Although, there appears to be recognition in the field of sport psychology that mental health and other issues arise during applied work, there seems to be little follow-through in terms of actually making needed referrals.

Why do some sport psychology practitioners not make needed referrals? There may be several reasons. Some practitioners simply do not recognize that a referral is needed. For example, sport psychology practitioners who do not recognize the signs of depression are unlikely to refer their depressed clients to mental health clinics. Ideally, sport psychology practitioners should both "know what they know" but also "know what they don't know." Continuing education can help practitioners gain knowledge of relevant issues outside of their areas of specific expertise, about intervention techniques, and about situations that require referral. The use of continuing education has been found to be nearly universally endorsed as an ethical sport psychology professional development behavior (Etzel et al., 2004). Therefore, it seems likely that many or even most sport psychology consultants are working to maintain their expertise. Reasons beyond simple lack of knowledge contribute to some practitioners' not making needed referrals.

Some practitioners may not refer clients because they are not sure how or when to make a referral. That is, they do not feel comfortable making referrals. Reis and Cornell (2008) found that counselors and teachers who had been trained to recognize and refer students with suicidal tendencies using a "Question, Persuade, and Refer" program had greater knowledge of risk factors for suicide and had made more referrals nearly six months after the training program had ended than did those participants who had not received training. Because awareness of the referral process enhances the likelihood of making effective referrals, a detailed explanation of the referral process is provided later in the chapter.

Another reason why sport psychology practitioners may not refer clients is that they have a sincere desire to help their clients. Having established strong working relationships, these practitioners may feel that referrals will interrupt the progress being made with their athlete–clients. On the one hand, sport psychology consultants who have developed rapport with their clients and are having some success in their work may ethically continue working with their athletes in areas outside of their main skill set by "stretching" to meet their clients' needs (Andersen & Van Raalte, 2005). Practitioners who take this approach should keep the best interest of their clients in mind and ensure that they are expert enough (Heilbrun, 2008) to provide appropriate services. Sport psychology practitioners who are "stretching" often benefit from extra supervision, study (e.g., reading texts on the issue), and from consultation with experts in the area of concern to strengthen the services they provide and to allow for the possibility of a future referral if needed (Andersen & Van Raalte, 2005).

On the other hand, the desire to help athletes and "stretch" can be confused with the desire to continue to work with a client for a number of less than ethical reasons such as the desire to bask in the reflected glory of a particular athlete (Haberl & Peterson, 2006) or the desire to maintain an income stream from the client. Sport psychology consultants who are self-aware and supervised are less likely to work when they are impaired

207

(Andersen, Van Raalte, & Brewer, 2000) and are more likely to identify these sorts of ethical concerns and proceed appropriately (Anderson, Knowles, & Gilbourne, 2004).

Some sport psychology consultants may not refer because they do not know, or do not have relationships with, high quality practitioners to whom they can refer clients. This problem can often be addressed by the creation of a referral network, described in more detail later in this chapter. For some practitioners, the lack of a referral network is a reflection of the limited local resources rather than the effort on the part of the practitioner to create a referral network. Although a number of challenges with the delivery of telehealth services have been identified (Miller, 2007), recent research by Mitchell *et al.* (2008) indicates that telemedicine services for the treatment of bulimia, a challenging mental health issue, were essentially as effective as a face-to-face interventions. For practitioners in areas where face-to-face referrals are not possible, the use of telemedicine may be an alternative way to provide referrals for clients (see Chapter 44).

How effective referrals are made

Effectively managing the referral process is an issue that extends beyond the field of sport psychology. Goldberg and Gater (1991) studied patients at a general medical practice in the United Kingdom and found that approximately 25% of patients entering the clinic experienced anxiety, depression, or distress. The clinic doctors recognized only about 40% of the troubled patients. Fewer than 10% of the anxious, depressed, or distressed patients were actually seen by mental health practitioners. To provide effective service for sport psychology clients, multiple steps must be taken to ensure that a network of professionals to whom clients can be referred is established, the need for a referral is identified, a referral is made, and that clients follow up by meeting with the suggested practitioner or get other support.

Referral networks

The referral process often begins before a client is even seen, with the sport psychology consultant establishing networks of professionals to confidentially discuss challenging cases and issues and to whom clients can be referred when necessary. Members of the referral network might include experts in such disciplines as career counseling, coaching, exercise science, medicine, mental health, nutrition, and religious issues/pastoral care (Andersen & Van Raalte, 2005). Issues requiring referral may include but are not limited to: anger management, biomechanical problems, career exploration, eating disorders, existential concerns, family problems, gambling, grief, injury, personality disorders (e.g., antisocial personality disorder, borderline personality disorder) and mood disorders (e.g., depression, dysthymia, cyclothymia), religious belief conflicts, retirement, strength and conditioning, sexuality issues, steroid use, study skills, substance abuse, suicidal ideation, time management, unplanned pregnancy, and weight management (Andersen & Van Raalte, 2005).

There are many benefits to identifying referral sources in advance of needing to refer a client. The first is that this process allows a sport psychologist to clearly know the quality of the services that will be provided by the referral source. Many sport psychologists cultivate their referral networks by meeting or talking on a regular basis with their referral network members. Such interactions allow them to maintain relationships that facilitate the referral process and ensure that the sport psychologist and the referral sources are "on the same team." A team-based approach to service provision is appreciated by athlete clients who find that it is an efficient and effective way to get needed services (Andersen, 1992).

A sport psychology practitioner can identify potential members of a referral network by talking with colleagues and friends about experts in various fields. Additional contacts can be found in the telephone book and by using online resources. The consultant finder services provided by the Association of Applied Sport Psychology (2010), the Australian Psychological Society (2010), and the British Association of Sport and Exercise Sciences (2010) are effective means of finding credentialed sport psychology consultants. Information about mental health practitioners in the United States is available at 4therapy.com (2010). Ethical guidelines generally require that practitioners do not receive "kickbacks" or other benefits for making referrals to particular practitioners.

Maintaining an effective referral network is a dynamic process with new referral sources being added and other resources being removed on a regular basis. New practitioners may be added who address a particular void in the referral network. Clients prefer practitioners about whom they have heard favorable comments from others and who are perceived as having high standards of confidentiality (Athanasiades, Winthrop, & Gough, 2008). Current practitioners who are unable to meet client needs may be removed. For example, referral failure may result when clients are referred to practitioners with long wait-times between the call for an appointment and the first scheduled appointment (Sherman, Barnum, Nyberg, & Buhman-Wiggs, 2008), to practitioners who do not accept a client's insurance (Beel, Gringart, & Edwards, 2008), or to practitioners whose practices are located a long distance from the client (Portone, Johns, & Hapner, 2008). It may be useful to include more than one practitioner per area of specialty in a referral network so that effective referrals can be made in case a particular practitioner is not available. Some sport psychology consultants are able to "refer in" and have a consultant come to work directly with the sport psychologist and client. This approach can be particularly useful for athletes who appreciate the convenience and/or do not want to be "abandoned" by their current sport psychology consultant (Andersen & Van Raalte, 2005).

Referral training

Sometimes people (e.g., coaches, athletes, family members, friends) believe that an athlete needs sport psychology services and want to make a referral. In these instances, it can be helpful to educate them about the referral process to enhance the likelihood that the referral will be successful (Bobele & Conran, 1988). These principles also apply to sport psychologists making referrals to other practitioners for their own clients (Andersen & Van Raalte, 2005). Van Raalte and Brewer (2005) developed the acronym REFER to help university students make effective referrals with regard to body image issues (see Table 22.1). With slight modifications, the acronym can be useful for sport psychology consultants.

R-ecognize that a referral is needed

The sport psychologist can help the referral source assess the situation and identify common situations for which referral might be appropriate. The sport psychologist might also take a proactive educational role informing coaches and athletes about the types of issues for which a referral to a sport psychology consultant or other professional might be helpful. Sport psychology consultants would be wise to consider referrals to medical professionals.

Table 22.1 Guidelines for making effective referrals.

R-ecognize that a referral is needed.
E-xplain the referral process.
F-ocus on feelings. Discuss the referral in a clear, caring, and supportive manner.
E-xit if emotions are too intense. You can return to the topic when things calm down.
R-epeat (and follow-up) as needed. It often takes more than one suggestion for a referral to be
  effective.

Robinson and James (2005) reported that over 10% of psychological symptoms are caused by medical or physical conditions such as metabolic abnormalities, infections, neoplasts (tumors), and trauma to the body.

E-xplain the referral process

Referrals work well when the people making the referrals (e.g., coaches, teammates, parents) understand the process and are confident about their abilities to effectively refer. Steps involved in making a referral might include: (a) a coach talking to the athlete about sport psychology and the sport psychologist to whom they are being referred (including why they are being referred, the type and effectiveness of the services to be provided, a discussion of confidentiality, and what is involved in meeting with a sport psychologist, all issues that are related to the success of consultation (Athanasiades *et al.*, 2008; Swift & Callahan, 2008); (b) the coach providing the athlete with the telephone number and/or email of the sport psychologist; and (c) the coach discussing an appropriate follow-up plan to ensure that the athlete meets with the sport psychologist or gets other needed assistance.

Sometimes people are unsure when the "best time" is to make a referral. There is no one best time. Athletes may need several referrals before they accept and/or find the help that they need. Making a referral sooner rather than later, therefore, may enhance the likelihood of a beneficial outcome. In general, the less time problematic behaviors have existed, the easier they are to change.

F-ocus on feelings

Emotions can run high during the referral process. Athletes may feel criticized or rejected by the referral source. Referral sources who focus on feelings when making a referral, "you seem sad" or "you seem frustrated and therefore I am suggesting that you consider meeting with our sport psychologist," allow athletes to save face, and appear more caring and supportive than those who say things like "you are a head case" (Brewer, Petitpas, & Van Raalte, 1999). Using language that emphasizes enhanced performance (e.g., "sport psychology may help you reach your full athletic potential") rather than pathology (e.g., "maybe the shrink can get your head straightened out") may also be useful in reducing stigma (Van Raalte, Brewer, Brewer, & Linder, 1992), increasing the chances that athletes are comfortable and that they follow up on the referral.

Practising or role playing the referral can enhance the likelihood that the person making the referral will communicate with the athlete in an effective manner. The person making the referral should plan to hold the conversation in a quiet, private environment in which outside distractions are minimized, if possible. It is reasonable to expect that an athlete may be hesitant to admit to a problem and may be uncomfortable with the referral process.

E-xit if emotions are too intense

When the topic of referral is raised, athletes may: (a) feel angry that they are being accused of having problems; (b) feel relieved that their problems are being brought up and can be discussed openly; (c) be in denial that problems exist; or (d) have some other reaction. The response to a referral is unpredictable. Referral sources who understand that a variety of responses are possible are better equipped to make effective referrals. Informing referral sources that it is acceptable to stop the referral process if the conversation is becoming too confrontational and resume it at a later calmer time can be helpful.

R-epeat and follow-up as needed

Referrals may be rejected the first time they are made. As with most human behaviors, repeated effort may be needed to effect change. It is acceptable to simply raise the possibility of a referral the first time the topic is discussed but to reserve the right to revisit the topic at a later date. A written contract, agreed upon and signed by the parties involved, can also promote compliance with the referral in some circumstances (Bonci et al., 2008). Discussion of why an athlete did not follow up with a referral may be useful and important for referring in the future.

Conclusion

Sport psychology consultants may make referrals for a multitude of issues related to mental, physical, and spiritual concerns when working with athletes, teams, coaches, and families. The referral process is a complex one that involves recognizing the need for a referral, knowing when to refer, and making an effective referral. Understanding the referral process and developing referral skills is likely to benefit the athlete clients whom sport psychologists serve. In this chapter we have looked at referral from two major viewpoints: the sport psychologist making the referral, and how sport psychologists can help others (athlete family members and friends, coaches, exercise science practitioners, sports medicine personnel) make referrals to the sport psychologists themselves and to other mental health professionals. See Box 22.1 for key practical points from this chapter.

Box 22.1

Key practical points about making referrals

- Making referrals meets ethical obligations.
- Making referrals meets client needs.
- Referrals should be made when sport psychology consultants lack the expertise to meet clients' needs effectively.
- Before making referrals, sport psychology consultants should:
  - learn how to make referrals;
  - r-ecognize that a referral is needed;

■ e-xplain the referral process;

■ f-ocus on feelings – discuss in clear, caring manner;

■ e-xit if emotions are too intense;

■ r-epeat (and follow-up) as needed;

■ develop referral networks;

■ obtain supervision for all applied work.

References

4therapy.com (2010). Available from http://www.4therapy.com/

American Psychological Association (2002). Ethical principles of psychologists and code of conduct. *American Psychologist, 57*, 1060–1073.

Andersen, M. B. (1992). Sport psychology and procrustean categories: An appeal for synthesis and expansion of service. *Association for the Advancement of Applied Sport Psychology Newsletter, 7*(3), 8–9.

Andersen, M. B., & Van Raalte, J. L. (2005). Over one's head: Referral processes. In M. B. Andersen (Ed.), *Sport psychology in practice* (pp. 159–169) Champaign, IL: Human Kinetics.

Andersen, M. B., Van Raalte, J. L., & Brewer, B. W. (2000). When applied sport psychology consultants and graduate students are impaired: Ethical and legal issues in training and supervision. *Journal of Applied Sport Psychology, 12*, 134–150.

Anderson, A. G., Knowles, Z., & Gilbourne, D. (2004). Reflective practice for sport psychologists: Concepts, models, practical implications, and thoughts on dissemination. *The Sport Psychologist, 18*, 188–203.

Association of Applied Sport Psychology (2010). Available from http://www.appliedsportpsych.org/

Australian Psychological Society (2010). Online. Available from http://www.psychology.org.au/

Athanasiades, C., Winthrop, A., & Gough, B. (2008). Factors affecting self-referral to counselling services in the workplace: A qualitative study. *British Journal of Guidance & Counselling, 36*, 257–276.

Beel, J. V., Gringart, E., & Edwards, M. E. (2008). Western Australian general practitioners' views on psychologists and the determinants of patient referral: An exploratory study. *Families, Systems, & Health, 26*, 250–266.

Bobele, M., & Conran, T. J. (1988). Referrals for family therapy: Pitfalls and guidelines. *Elementary School Guidance, 22*, 192–198.

Bonci, C. M., Bonci, L. J., Granger, L. R., Johnson, C. L., Malina, R. M., Milne, L. W., Ryan, R. R., & Vanderbunt, E. M. (2008). National Athletic Trainers' Association position statement: Preventing, detecting, and managing disordered eating in athletes. *Journal of Athletic Training, 43*, 80–108.

Brewer, B. W., Petitpas, A. J., & Van Raalte, J. L. (1999). Referral of injured athletes for counseling and psychotherapy. In R. Ray & D. M. Wiese-Bjornstal (Eds.). *Counseling in sports medicine* (pp. 127–141). Champaign, IL: Human Kinetics.

British Association of Sport and Exercise Sciences (2010). Available from http://www.bases.org.uk/

Etzel, E. F., Watson, J. C., II, & Zizzi, S. (2004). A web-based survey of AAASP members' ethical beliefs and behaviors in the new millennium. *Journal of Applied Sport Psychology, 16*, 236–250.

Gayman, A. M., & Crossman, J. (2006). Referral practices: Are sport psychology consultants out of their league? *Athletic Insight: The Online Journal of Sport Psychology, 8*, 1–12.

Goldberg, D., & Gater, R. (1991). Estimates of need: A document prepared for the South Manchester District Health Authority. *Psychiatric Bulletin, 15*, 593–595.

Haberl, P., & Peterson, K. (2006). Olympic-size ethical dilemmas: Issues and challenges for sport psychology consultants on the road and at the Olympic games. *Ethics & Behavior, 16*, 25–40.

Heilbrun, K. (2008). When is an 'expert' an expert? In. D. N. Bersoff (Ed.). *Ethical conflicts in psychology* (4th ed., pp. 457–458). Washington, DC: American Psychological Association.

Henschen, K., Ripoll, H., Hackfort, D., & Mohan, J. (1995). Ethical principles of the International Society of Sport Psychology (ISSP). *International Journal of Sport Psychology, 26,* 588–591.

Leffingwell, T. R., Wiechman, S. A., Smith, R. A., Smoll, F. L., & Christensen, D. S. (2001). Sport psychology training within a clinical psychology program and a department of intercollegiate athletics. *Professional Psychology: Research and Practice, 32,* 531–536.

Miller, E. A. (2007). Solving the disjuncture between research and practice: Telehealth trends in the 21st century. *Health Policy, 82,* 133–141

Mitchell, J. E., Crosby, R. D., Wonderlich, S. A., Crow, S., Lancaster, K., Simonich, H., Swan-Kremeier, L., Lysne, C., & Myers, T.C. (2008). A randomized trial comparing the efficacy of cognitive-behavioral therapy for bulimia nervosa delivered via telemedicine versus face-to-face. *Behaviour Research and Therapy, 46,* 581–592.

Portone, C., Johns, M. M., III, & Hapner, E. R. (2008). A review of patient adherence to the recommendation for voice therapy. *Journal of Voice, 22,* 192–196.

Reis, C., & Cornell, D. (2008). An evaluation of suicide gatekeeper training for school counselors and teachers. *Professional School Counseling, 11,* 386–394.

Robinson, J. D., & James, L. C. (2005). Assessing the patient's need for medical evaluation: A psychologist's guide. In L. C. James & R. A. Folen (Eds.). *The primary care consultant: The next frontier for psychologists in hospitals and clinics* (pp. 29–37). Washington, DC: American Psychological Association.

Sherman, M. L., Barnum, D. D., Nyberg, E., & Buhman-Wiggs, A. (2008). Predictors of preintake attrition in a rural community mental health center. *Psychological Services, 5,* 332–340.

Swift, J. K., & Callahan, J. L. (2008). A delay discounting measure of great expectations and the effectiveness of psychotherapy. *Professional Psychology: Research and Practice, 39,* 581–588.

Van Raalte, J. L., & Brewer, B. W. (2005). *Balancing college, food, and life* [CD-ROM]. Available from Virtual Brands, 10 Echo Hill Rd., Wilbraham, MA 01095 or http://www.vbvideo.com.

Van Raalte, J. L., Brewer, B. W., Brewer, D. D., & Linder, D. E. (1992). NCAA Division II college football players' perceptions of an athlete who consults a sport psychologist. *Journal of Sport & Exercise Psychology, 14,* 273–282.

Williams, J. M., & Scherzer, C. B. (2003). Tracking the training and careers of graduates of advanced degree programs in sport psychology, 1994 to 1999. *Journal of Applied Sport Psychology, 15,* 335–353.

23

Drug use and abuse by athletes

Jason Mazanov

The sports-drugs nexus has been around since ancient times, from enhancing the sporting prowess of athletes using anything from figs to bull's testicles (Verroken, 2005) to the alcohol-fuelled celebrations after sporting events (Dunning & Waddington, 2003). The relationship between sport and drug use is ongoing, and one of central concern to contemporary sport psychologists. The issue for sport psychologists is how best to work with and counsel athletes navigating the sport-drug relationship.

World Anti-Doping Code (WADC) responsibilities

Both athletes and sport psychologists have responsibilities under the WADC, where the use of certain prohibited drugs and methods (e.g., performance-enhancing drugs, masking agents, blood doping) are defined as being contrary to the "spirit of sport." The WADC is the framework athlete support personnel (including sport psychologists) operate under if they work in WADC-compliant sporting organizations, or work with athletes in sports bound by the WADC (e.g., Olympic sports). If sport psychologists choose to test the limits of the WADC, they could find themselves sanctioned (banned) from sport. There are eight possible sanctionable anti-doping rule violations:

- a positive drug test;
- use or attempted use by an athlete (and strict liability);
- athletes refusing, failing to provide, or evading sample collection;
- non-compliance with out-of-competition testing;
- tampering or attempted tampering with doping control;
- possession of prohibited substances or methods;
- trafficking of prohibited substances or methods;
- administration, attempted administration, assistance, encouragement, aiding, abetting, covering up, or any other type of complicity involving an attempted or actual anti-doping rule violation.

The first three make athletes culpable for drug use. The remaining five apply to all athlete support personnel, including sport psychologists. The last one is the most ambiguous; for example, it is unclear whether silence about the treatment of an athlete for anabolic-androgenic steroid (AAS) dependence contravenes the WADC. The sanctions for transgressions vary in severity by circumstance (e.g., a violation involving a minor compels a life ban for the offending athlete support person).

Under the WADC, athlete support personnel are obliged to support the objectives of anti-doping. These responsibilities include being knowledgeable and compliant with the WADC, and fostering anti-doping attitudes and behaviors in athletes. It is unclear what, if anything can be done to (or for) sport psychologists who may disagree with the WADC as a method for managing drugs in sport. For example, some sport psychologists may prefer a harm-minimization approach when counseling athletes about substance use and abuse.

Irrespective of preferred approach, all practising sport psychologists should have at least passing familiarity with the WADC, as well as the arguments and counter-arguments for anti-doping. Athletes can be easily overwhelmed by the information and rumors about doping and anti-doping. Knowledgeable sport psychologists are well placed to help athletes navigate what can be a turbulent sea of issues around doping and substance use.

The relationship between sport and drug use

There has been some debate as to the influence of sport participation on both drug use and abuse. For example, there is evidence that self-reported illicit drug use among Australian athletes is lower than that of the general population (Dunn et al., 2009), typically explained using the "deterrence hypothesis." Evidence arising from this hypothesis that participating in sport deters drug use is mixed, with some studies indicating sport has a protective effect and others that sport makes people more vulnerable to drug use and abuse (Lisha & Sussman, 2010); the latter point is particularly true for alcohol abuse. The research is inconclusive as to whether sport participation has a protective or deterrent effect on drug use. Sport may have a protective effect against some drugs (e.g., illicit ones), but may leave athletes more vulnerable to others (e.g., alcohol).

Models of athlete drug use

Investigations of athlete drug use (as a sub-population of all drug users) have been largely devoted to explaining why elite athletes use banned performance enhancing drugs (doping). The focus on doping stems from an implicit assumption that athlete licit and illicit drug use follows the same principles as use in the general population. The current discussion on athlete doping follows one of three models: the social cognitive, the life cycle, and the grounded models. The first two models stem from evidence on licit and illicit substance use outside sport and provide some conceptual background for athlete substance use. The grounded model was developed from data arising from within the sporting context, and provides the first empirically validated model of why athletes dope.

The social cognitive model

Donovan, Kapernick, Egger, and Mendoza (2002) suggested that three factors influence athlete intentions to use banned performance-enhancing drugs: appraisals (threat and benefit), individual differences in the athletes, and the influence of reference groups. Like all social-cognitive theories, this approach is explicitly rational, assuming that athletes weigh up a collection of threats (e.g., being banned, being disgraced) against presumed potential benefits (e.g., staying on the team). The threat–benefit appraisal is moderated by individual differences and reference groups (e.g., coaches, administrative structures) and the eventual formation of an intention (with attendant implications arising from the imperfect correlation between intention and behavior: see Greve, 2001). The social cognitive model provides a sound framework in which to think about why an athlete might dope. Further, with a basis in licit and illicit drug research, it is likely the model can be extrapolated to those substances as well. Therefore, sport psychologists would do well to explore the costs and benefits as athletes perceive them, the individual differences that might influence athlete drug use (e.g., self-esteem), and who might be involved in the athletes' decisions one way or the other.

The life cycle model

Petroczi and Aidman (2008) used self-regulated behavior towards achieving performance goals as an explanation for doping over an athlete's "life cycle" or career. Like the social cognitive model, the life cycle model contains personality and systemic factors that influence a cost–benefit analysis of both vulnerability and inhibiting factors that predict doping behavior. A key assumption underpinning this model is that drug use is functional. For example, use of an ergogenic substance may be functional towards injury rehabilitation. Equally, alcohol could be functional for coping with the stress of competition. This functionality is then rationally pursued in the context of committing to and executing a goal achievement strategy. The introduction of goal achievement in terms of the functionality of drug use is the main difference between the social cognitive and life cycle models.

In terms of responding to athlete drug use, the life cycle model suggests sport psychologists explore the functionality of that drug use towards achieving goals. An implication of this goal-directed functionality is that prevention of drug use might be best effected by exploring alternative ways of achieving goals (Mazanov, 2009). Interventions for treating drug use might be effectively managed by using the same psychological mechanism that got them into the drug use (i.e., goal achievement).

The grounded model

Mazanov and Huybers (in press) interviewed a range of elite athletes and support personnel to develop a grounded model that explains the observed variation in experiences and explanations of why athletes decide to dope. Four themes emerged that, in part, reflected the previous models.

The first theme was the objective of doping, usually articulated as some variation of doping "to win." Winning was characterized as a performance outcome (e.g., overcome injury, improve performance) or prize money. The second theme was the kinds of information to which athletes attend in relation to doping, such as the influence of coaches or senior athletes, or the source of information (e.g., side effect information from pharmaceutical companies). The third theme was the system in place aimed at enforcing abstinence; in the context of anti-doping, this theme was represented by the likelihood of testing positive and being prosecuted. The final theme was the consequences of being caught doping, such as being ostracized from the sporting community, irrespective of any formal bans.

In practice, this model provides some focus on what to talk about with athletes. For example, the functional objective of drug use is clearly an important part of athlete decisions.

The discussion of drug use can also explore the credibility of certain forms of information and influence. For example, it may be worthwhile discussing the role of the coach or senior athletes in the decision to use a drug, whether performance-enhancing or a beer after the game. The athlete's response to the system aimed at compelling a certain kind of behavior is also a central part of the discussion in relation to drug use, especially in the context of the WADC. Finally, the consequences of athletes' actions beyond the immediate drug use can be explored. Overarching this model is a sense that sport psychologists need to help athletes navigate the potentially difficult decision to use or abstain, rather than judge the athletes in terms of the "rightness" of their actions.

Lessons learned from the models

There has been some conjecture about whether athlete drug use is rational (Stewart & Smith, 2008), but all of the models discussed indicate that athlete drug use behavior does have a rational component (Mazanov & Huybers, in press). Although specific mechanisms may be open to debate, the models broach issues that may assist sport psychologists working with athletes either considering or using some kind of drug. It may be useful to reflect upon:

1. Why is the drug use occurring?
2. Who is involved in the drug use, and are they the right people to listen to?
3. What are the unanticipated consequences of drug use?

Answers to these questions do not fully resolve issues, but they do provide a starting point for sport psychologists counseling athletes about drug use.

Key ideas from the models

The three models include lists of variables thought to influence athlete drug use that can be broadly categorized as individual differences and social/systemic variables. What follows is a selection of variables that may inform sport psychologists working with athletes confronting drug use issues.

Individual differences

Self-esteem

Self-esteem is associated with all forms of drug use (see Byrne & Mazanov, 2001). Athletes may be vulnerable to drug use as a function of changes in self-esteem due to perceptions of the self being associated with sporting performance. When self-esteem declines athletes may turn to external coping mechanisms, one of which may be drug use. Drawing on the life cycle model, the function of drug use is coping with a decline in self esteem. Like most coping, drug use behavior can be functional if, for example, alcohol consumption ceases when self-esteem returns. Low self-esteem-driven substance use becomes problematic if the use continues or becomes critical to self-esteem. In this context the complex issues at play may benefit from clinical treatment. The role of the sport psychologist becomes preventive monitoring of both self-esteem and drug use to determine when links between the two may be potentially harmful.

217

Morality

The role of morality in substance use can be complex. There are several levels of morality in the sporting context that may cloud the judgment of both the athlete and the sport psychologist. Athletes are subject to the morality imposed upon them by the WADC: doping has been effectively defined as "immoral" in sport. This edict sometimes conflicts with societal conventions around drug use. For example, there is evidence illicit drug use has become normalized among 18–25-year-olds (Duff, 2003); athletes may judge the morality of their substance use relative to these prevailing societal norms rather than those imposed by the WADC. In addition, athletes have to contend with the morality of drug use within their sport. For example, professional cyclists may take a different view of ergogenic drug use than do "up and coming" talents (Christiansen, 2010).

This potentially conflicting context is the scene within which athletes try to make the "right" decision. For some athletes the decisions are unambiguous; for others decisions are difficult to make. Sport psychologists need to avoid confusing the issue further by imposing their moralities on athletes. Sport psychologists need to help athletes navigate the issues by providing an impartial sounding board, ready to articulate arguments and counterarguments. For example, some athletes may argue that doping is conceptually equivalent to better running shoes on the grounds that both are performance-enhancing technologies. The issue is defining what is right for the athletes and what they can live with rather than what is right according to everyone else, including the sport psychologists.

Knowledge of health consequences

The importance of physical health to sustained sporting performance suggests athletes would shun drugs on health reasons alone. Using the health consequences of drug use to promote abstinence or quitting behavior is intuitively appealing on the assumption that the potential health effects lead to a rational solution of ongoing abstinence. The three models outlined above suggest that athletes are rational in their decision-making around drug use, yet some athletes continue to use. Rationalizing drug use or abstinence is only partially influenced by knowledge of health consequences.

Results from the general population indicate users know more about the health consequences of drug use than non-users and that knowledge of health consequences appears to have little influence on whether non-users start using or users stop (Mazanov & Byrne, 2007). Applying these results to the sporting context, knowledge of health consequences is unlikely to provoke a change in behavior one way or the other, possibly because athletes prioritize other knowledge or outcomes. For example, athletes may prioritize performance outcomes above health outcomes, demonstrated by Goldman's work showing elite athletes would exchange longevity for Olympic success (Connor & Mazanov, 2009). Nevertheless, prioritizing health may vary by age. Masters level athletes may prioritize health over performance. The key message is that although knowledge of health consequences may be useful as part of counseling athletes about drug use, it is unlikely to serve as Archimedes' lever.

Social/systemic variables

Perverse incentives

The prioritization of performance over athlete welfare is common across sport (Houlihan, 2004). For example, many athletes are told about the ideal of sacrificing the self for sport, or are encouraged to play while in pain or injured. Similarly, coaches often receive rewards for medals and championships rather than for helping athletes prepare to realize their genetic potentials. Prioritization of performance means that athletes may take the teleological approach of the "ends justifies the means." That is, drug use becomes the way in which they manage performance at the expense of health. For example, in Australia a prominent rugby league player, Andrew Johns, reported self-medication of bi-polar depression with illicit drugs to preserve his prominent role in the sport. Such social/systemic issues demand social/systemic solutions, such as rewarding the path to performance as much as the end results. Sport psychologists may be unable to have input at that level, but they should be cognizant of the perverse incentives created by broader social structures, either real or perceived, that influence the context in which drug use occurs.

Culture

Although there has been no direct assessment of how the culture of a sport influences drug use vulnerability or resistance, drug use has been associated with sports that demand hyper-masculine behavior such as American football (Eitle, Turner, & Eitle, 2003). Whitehead (2005) characterized this behavior as an overemphasis on ideals of strength, stamina, pain endurance, or fearlessness in the face of danger. The pursuit of hypermasculinity can be seen in the various versions of football and rugby. For example, these sports seem to include reckless consumption of alcohol as integral to group initiation, social identity, and team cohesion. Alternatively, athletes may feel pressure to use AAS to achieve hypermasculine physiques. Of course, hypermasculinity does not explain cultures of drug use resistance or vulnerability in all sports, and is offered here as an example of the role of culture as a social/systemic force that may influence drug use by athletes.

Medicalization of society

Waddington and Smith (2009) argued that the medicalization of society has influenced drug use in sport. The medicalization of society refers to the expectation and use of medical treatment to overcome physical and social deficiencies or to enhance them in some way. Overcoming deficiencies could be the expectation of "popping a pill" in relation to illness, pain, anxiety, or fatigue. Enhancing the self is reflected in cosmetic surgery to enhance physical attractiveness, alcohol and illicit drugs to "have a good time", or blood transfusions to boost hemoglobin. For athletes medicalization leads to an expectation that barriers to sporting excellence, whether realistic or unattainable, can be resolved with medical intervention. The task for sport psychologists becomes broadly interpreting the role of medicine in sport and society. In particular, sport psychologists can point to alternative methods that achieve the same outcomes using, for example, psychological interventions.

Specific issues for drug types

Licit drugs

Alcohol perhaps represents the single greatest drug abuse threat to athletes. The culture of alcohol abuse in some sports, usually binge drinking, brings with it unambiguous dangers to athletes in terms of vulnerability to anti-social behavior and alcoholism. The vulnerability is translated into unwanted pregnancies, jail sentences, permanent injury, or death. The pressures upon athletes to abuse alcohol can also come from sponsorship. For example, athletes may feel obliged to consume a sponsor's product, whether a multi-national company or the local bar (O'Brien & Kypri, 2008). It is beyond the scope of this short review to explore the intricacies of treating athlete alcohol abuse, but having an effective response to alcohol abuse for any age range (adolescents, young adults, or mature athletes) is an essential tool for all sport psychologists.

Illicit drugs

As noted above, sport may have a protective effect against illicit drug use. Athlete sub-populations appear less likely to use illicit drugs than other sub-populations. Illicit drug use and abuse usually follow normal developmental and addictive sequelae. For example, adolescence is a period of experimentation with illicit drugs. Therefore, adolescent athletes need to receive the same intervention or treatment as other adolescents. Young adult illicit substance use is equally part of the developmental cycle, with some young adults choosing to use illicit drugs for socializing. Progression and treatment of substance use towards abuse should follow standard psychological approaches.

Ergogenic nutritional supplements

The common use of ergogenic nutritional supplements such as vitamins, minerals, proteins, herbs, creatine, and caffeine warrants their inclusion in any discussion of athlete drug use and abuse. There has been an upsurge in supplement use as a consequence of the medicalization of society, the regulation of some ergogenic substances under the WADC, and the absence of regulation in relation to nutritional supplements (Nieper, 2005). Athletes are consuming supplements at alarming rates in pursuit of legal performance enhancement. Ironically, the ergogenic effect of most of these substances is open to debate, with sports nutritionists indicating their effects are irrelevant given an appropriate, balanced diet (Rodriguez, DiMarco, & Langely, 2009). Ergogenic effects could therefore be placebo effects, with the exception of those substances proven to influence sporting performance (e.g., caffeine).

Behaviorally, athletes seem to be caught in a marketing cycle as new products are released. Athletes rush towards supplements rumored to have specific ergogenic properties. Those products that do have ergogenic effects may actually be contaminated: for example, effective protein supplements may have some level of AAS in them, which could lead to a sanction under the WADC. The best advice sport psychologists can give athletes in relation to nutritional supplements is to consult a sport nutritionist to help them better match their diets and performance goals.

Caffeine abuse has increased with the popularization of high caffeine energy drinks. Caffeine addiction and withdrawal may become serious issues for athletes given the sustained sport sponsorship and marketing of these drinks. Consequently, treatment of caffeine abuse may become as important as treating alcohol abuse.

Doping

Doping is typically constructed as an issue that exists only at the elite level. Evidence is mounting that doping is increasing in non-elite, non-athlete, and adolescent populations to the point that some commentators are suggesting it has become a public health issue (Harmer, 2010). The simple message is that doping should be an issue of concern at all levels of sport.

Huybers and Mazanov's (2010) quantitative work on the grounded model indicates that elite athletes are vulnerable to using prohibited ergogenic substances when they can be convinced of easily attained gains for little or no risk. Such gullibility represents part of the human psyche that con artists rely upon in plying their trade – it appears athletes are no different to the general population. Sport psychologists can help athletes overcome gullibility by pointing out the rapid rise and fall of prominent athletes (e.g., Marion Jones), or examining the time and effort that goes into achieving gains in other aspects of life.

Evidence is emerging that AAS use can become a substance dependence disorder, leading to signs of classic drug abuse in men akin to those seen in nicotine addiction (Kanayama, Hudson, & Pope, 2009). For example, use of AAS leads to withdrawal, self-administration by animals in controlled experiments, continued use despite adverse effects, maladaptive behavior patterns around use, and poly-drug use. The mechanisms behind AAS dependence are hypothesized to be muscle dysmorphia, biological vulnerability to the dysphoric effects of withdrawal, or overlap with other substance dependence. There is speculation that people with AAS dependence and individuals with opioid dependence may share a common diathesis (Kanayama *et al.*, 2009).

Conclusion

The role of sport psychologists in addressing issues of drug use or abuse is central to both prevention and intervention. The factors influencing use or abuse may differ by type of substance, meaning that interventions may need to reflect these differences. Sport psychologists must remain ready to counsel athletes and support personnel about the implications of drug use towards outcomes in the best interests of the athlete. See Box 23.1 for the main take-home messages from this chapter.

Box 23.1

Main take-home messages about substance use and abuse

- Sport has a protective effect against some substances, but makes athletes vulnerable to abusing others.
- Sport psychologists have a responsibility to be aware of their obligations under the World Anti-Doping Code, and to be able to discuss with athletes the issues that arise from the Code.
- A framework for guiding discussions with athletes about substance use involves reflecting on: Why is the substance use occurring? Who is involved in the substance use, and are they the right people to listen to? What are the unanticipated consequences of substance use?
- Low self-esteem-driven substance use becomes problematic if the use continues or becomes critical to self-esteem.
- Avoid making moral judgments about athlete substance use.
- Talking about health consequences is important, but unlikely to change substance use behavior.
- It may be exciting to talk about prohibited ergogenic substances, but alcohol and caffeine are the big issues for athlete substance abuse.

References

Byrne, D. G., & Mazanov, J. (2001). Self-esteem, stress and cigarette smoking in adolescents. *Stress and Health, 17*, 105–110.

Christiansen, A. V. (2010). "We are not sportsmen, we are professionals": Professionalism, doping and deviance in elite sport. *International Journal of Sport Management and Marketing, 7*, 91–103.

Connor, J., & Mazanov, J. (2009). Would you dope? A general population test of the Goldman Dilemma. *British Journal of Sports Medicine, 43*, 871–872.

Donovan, R. J., Egger, G., Kapernick, V., & Mendoza, J. (2002). A conceptual framework for achieving performance enhancing drug compliance in sport. *Sports Medicine, 32*, 269–284.

Duff, C. (2003). Drugs and youth cultures: Is Australia experiencing the 'normalization' of adolescent drug use? *Journal of Youth Studies, 6*, 433–446.

Dunn, M., Thomas, J. O., Burns, L., Swift, W., Price, J., & Mattick, R. P. (2009). *Attitudes towards, knowledge of, and prevalence of illicit substance use among elite athletes in Australia.* Sydney, NSW, Australia: National Drug and Alcohol Research Centre, University of New South Wales.

Dunning, E., & Waddington, I. (2003). Sport as a drug and drugs in sport. *International Review for the Sociology of Sport, 38*, 351–368.

Eitle, D., Turner, R. J., & Eitle, T. M. (2003). The deterrence hypothesis re-examined: Sports participation and substance use among young adults. *Journal of Drug Issues, 33*, 193–221.

Greve, W. (2001). Traps and gaps in action-explanation: Theoretical problems of a psychology of human action. *Psychological Review, 108*, 435–451.

Harmer, P. A. (2010). Anabolic-androgenic steroid use among young male and female athletes: Is the game to blame? *British Journal of Sports Medicine, 44*, 26–31.

Houlihan, B. (2004). Civil rights, doping control and the World Anti-Doping Code. *Sport in Society, 7*, 420–437.

Huybers, T., & Mazanov, J. (2010). *To take or not to take: Modelling athlete doping decisions.* Manuscript submitted for publication (copy on file with author).

Kanayama, G., Hudson, J. I., & Pope, H. G. (2009). Features of men with anabolic-androgenic steroid dependence: A comparison with nondependent AAS users with AAS nonusers. *Drug and Alcohol Dependence, 102*, 130–137.

Lisha, N. E., & Sussman, S. (2010). Relationship of high school and college sports participation with alcohol, tobacco, and illicit drug use: A review. *Addictive Behaviors, 35*, 399–407.

Mazanov, J. (2009). Debating the role of drugs in sport: A reader. *Sport in Society, 23*, 296–312.

Mazanov, J., & Byrne, D. G. (2007). Changes in adolescent smoking behaviour and knowledge of health consequence of smoking. *Australian Journal of Psychology, 59*, 176–180.

Mazanov, J., & Huybers, T. (in press, accepted 05 October 2009). An empirical model of athlete decisions to use performance enhancing drugs: Qualitative evidence. *Qualitative Research in Sport and Exercise.*

Nieper, A. (2005). Nutritional supplement practices in UK junior national track and field athletes. *British Journal of Sports Medicine, 39*, 645–649.

O'Brien, K. S., & Kypri, K. (2008). Alcohol industry sponsorship and hazardous drinking among sportspeople. *Addiction, 103*, 1961–1966.

Petroczi, A., & Aidman, E. (2008). Psychological drivers of doping: The life-cycle model of performance enhancement. *Substances Abuse Treatment, Prevention and Policy, 3*, 7. Retrieved from http://www.substanceabusepolicy.com/content/3/1/7.

Rodriguez, N. R., DiMarco, N. M., & Langely, S. (2009). Position of the American Dietetic Association, Dietitians Canada, and the American College of Sports Medicine: Nutrition and athletic performance. *Journal of the American Dietetic Association, 109*, 509–527.

Stewart, B., & Smith, A. C. T. (2008). Drug use in sport: Implications for public policy. *Journal of Sport and Social Issues, 32*, 278–298.

Verroken, M. (2005). Drug use and abuse in sport. In D. R. Mottram (Ed). *Drugs in sport* (4th ed, pp. 29–63). London: Routledge.

Waddington, I., & Smith, A. (2009). *An introduction to drugs in sport: Addicted to winning?* London: Routledge.

Whitehead, A. (2005). Man to man violence: How masculinity may work as a dynamic risk factor. *Howard Journal, 44*, 411–422.

24

Male and female athletes with eating disorders

Trent A. Petrie and Christy Greenleaf

Although clinical eating disorders (EDs) historically have been considered a woman's disorder, both male and female athletes experience body image concerns and weight and performance pressures, internalize sociocultural ideals, and engage in restrictive eating and weight control (Petrie & Greenleaf, 2007). EDs and disordered eating (DE) are serious psychological conditions that involve distortions in eating, weight-control, and body-related perceptions (American Psychiatric Association, 2000). Clinical EDs include anorexia nervosa (AN), bulimia nervosa (BN), and eating disorder not otherwise specified (EDNOS). Individuals with AN maintain very low body weight, have extreme fear of weight gain and distorted body image, experience negative self-evaluation, and are amenorrheic (for postmenarchal women). BN is identified by episodic binge eating and compensatory behaviors (e.g., vomiting), along with negative self-evaluation. Individuals with EDNOS meet some, but not all, of the criteria for AN or BN, and include disorders such as binge eating. Athletes also may experience symptoms of EDs that are problematic, which are referred to as *subclinical* disorders. Subclinical EDs are problematic because the level of psychological disturbances is similar to what is found with clinical EDs (e.g., Petrie, Greenleaf, Reel, & Carter, 2009).

The female athlete triad and muscle dysmorphia (MD) are common in athlete populations. The triad involves the co-occurrence of DE, amenorrhea, and low bone mineral density in women and can lead to health problems, such as stress fractures (American College of Sports Medicine, 2007). MD is more common among men than women and involves excessive concern and preoccupation with a perceived lack of muscularity (Olivardia, 2001). Muscle-enhancing behaviors, such as excessive weight lifting and taking anabolic steroids, and binge eating along with mood/anxiety disorders, are common.

Prevalence

The prevalence of clinical EDs among male and female athletes is slightly higher than in the general public (Petrie & Greenleaf, 2007), and rates for AN tend to be lower than those found for either BN or EDNOS (Greenleaf, Petrie, Carter, & Reel, 2009; Petrie, Greenleaf, Reel, & Carter, 2008). The prevalence of subclinical EDs is generally higher than clinical EDs.

Of the pathogenic behaviors used to control weight, athletes report using excessive exercise and fasting/dieting more frequently than self-induced vomiting or laxatives and diuretics (Greenleaf et al., 2009).

Prevalence data on the triad are sparse, though female athletes are 5 to 10 times more likely to present with two, as opposed to all three, of the components, and lean sport athletes are more likely to experience menstrual dysfunction and low bone mineral density than those in nonlean sports (e.g., Nichols, Rauh, Lawson, Ji, & Barkai, 2006). There are no large-scale, population-based studies on MD, so prevalence rates are unknown, though they are likely to be highest among men, anabolic steroid users, and body builders (e.g., Pope, Gruber, Choi, Olivardia, & Phillips, 1997).

Identification

There are psychological and behavioral signs and symptoms associated with DE and EDs (see Table 24.1; Petrie & Greenleaf, 2007), which can help practitioners identify those athletes who may be at risk for, or are experiencing, DE. Early identification reduces risk and assists athletes in obtaining treatment. Moreover, because psychological disturbances, such as low self-esteem and negative body image (Petrie et al., 2009), are associated with subclinical EDs, practitioners need to be able to recognize these as well as clinical EDs. They also should be aware of the physical and medical signs and symptoms, including amenorrhea or menstrual irregularities, constipation, dehydration, dental decay, irregular heart rhythm, gastrointestinal problems, and muscle weakness and cramps.

One identification challenge is that the psychological characteristics and behaviors associated with DE may be considered desirable for elite athletes, be viewed as "normal" within sport, and even be encouraged by coaches (Thompson & Sherman, 1999a). For example, are highly committed athletes who strive for the best demonstrating the desired "pursuit of excellence" or perfectionism associated with AN? Athletes may comply with requests to lose weight – to hopefully improve performances – by severely restricting caloric intake. They also may engage in excessive training, working out for hours outside of practice.

Table 24.1 Signs and symptoms of eating disorders and disordered eating.

Behavioral	Psychological
Avoidance of eating situations or secret eating	Anxiety/worry
Binge eating	Body image disturbance
Body/appearance checking	Depressed mood
Excessive weighing	External locus of control
Excessive exercise (in addition to normal training)	Internalized sociocultural values regarding attractiveness
Exercising despite injury or illness	Unassertiveness
Purging (e.g., vomiting)	Mood swings
Dietary restriction	Perfectionism
Sleep disturbances	Poor self-esteem
Substance abuse	Rigid thinking and beliefs
Weight loss/fluctuations	Restlessness
	Social withdrawal
	Obsessive-compulsive symptoms

Many coaches would interpret such behaviors as indications of athletes' competitiveness and coachability. For some athletes, however, these behaviors may be signs of DE. Athletes who exercise and diet to manage body- and weight-related concerns, or become anxious when they cannot achieve this, likely possess the characteristics that underlie an ED. Highly competitive athletes often push through pain and physical discomfort, which is similar to the ED symptoms of ignoring or denying physical symptoms of hunger. Practitioners should understand the similarities between the characteristics of a dedicated athlete and someone with an ED, and be attuned to their athletes' behaviors, beliefs, and attitudes. Doing so can help practitioners discern which behaviors represent a healthy performance drive and which indicate pathology.

Although most coaches have trained an athlete with an ED (Trattner-Sherman, Thompson, Dehass, & Wilfert, 2005), coaches often lack sufficient knowledge about the identification and prevention of EDs (Turk, Prentice, Chappell, & Shields, 1999). For example, 37% of U.S. college coaches indicated that amenorrhea was "normal." Further, coaches' behaviors may increase athletes' likelihood of developing EDs, such as by monitoring eating patterns, regularly weighing athletes and assessing body fat, and encouraging weight loss through food restriction and extra workouts (Heffner, Ogles, Gold, Marsden, & Johnson, 2003). Athletes may be particularly sensitive to, and influenced by, weight and body comments made by coaches (e.g., de Bruin, Oudejans, & Bakker, 2007). Even when coaches make comments they believe to be supportive, athletes may interpret them as judgmental. Practitioners can educate coaches on ED signs, symptoms, and accurate identification, while also monitoring the sport environment to reduce risk.

Psychosocial environment

Both male and female athletes (and non-athletes) are exposed to general sociocultural ideals about appearance, behaviors regarding food and exercise, body size and shape, weight, and attractiveness. For women, the ideal is thin and lean, yet curvaceous. Represented by *Sports Illustrated* swimsuit models, women are expected to attain this body through diet and exercise. For men, the ideal is defined by leanness and muscularity – wide shoulders, narrow waist, and defined muscles in the chest, arms, and abdomen – which can be achieved through muscle enhancing activities, such as weight lifting and supplements. These body ideals are often internalized and become the standard against which one's own body is evaluated. Because few people can attain these physical ideals, men and women become body dissatisfied, which can lead to the development of EDs.

Athletes also experience sport-specific body, weight, and appearance pressures, such as weight requirements, judging criteria, performance demands, revealing uniforms, and social comparisons with other athletes. Athletes in weight-related sports, such as wrestling, rowing, and judo, are at increased risk for eating pathology, particularly during their competitive seasons. These athletes may engage in pathogenic behaviors, such as intentional dehydration, caloric restriction, excessive exercise, and self-induced vomiting to cut weight. Although these behaviors may be less frequent during off-seasons, they can negatively influence psychological and physical health and should be monitored and addressed.

Judged sports, such as gymnastics and figure skating, place pressure on athletes to maintain aesthetically appealing and positively evaluated physiques. Low self-esteem and the need for approval are common ED attributes; thus it is not surprising that sports with subjective evaluations of performance and appearance might further contribute to body and weight concerns, including a strong drive for thinness (Zucker, Womble, Williamson, & Perrin, 1999).

Performance demands also can contribute to the maintenance of very low body weight and fat. Athletes and coaches may assume that there is an ideal body for each sport (or position) and that weight loss or gain will automatically enhance performance (Thompson & Sherman, 1999b). For example, a power lifter may believe that any increase in body mass is good, whereas a figure skater may think weight loss will translate into higher scores. Athletes who are too light or too heavy, however, may experience performance decrements due to inflexibility, insufficient strength, inadequate energy, or lack of confidence. Weight-loss also does not automatically translate into lower body fat; rather, athletes may lose important muscle mass. Practitioners can take a holistic approach with coaches and athletes to ensure that changes are not made to training and/or eating regimens under the mistaken assumption that weight-loss (or gain) causes improved sport performances.

Form-fitting and body-revealing attire that is part of many sports, such as swimming, may exacerbate body, appearance, and weight concerns and lead athletes to experience body objectification. Although there is a trend for women's uniforms to be more revealing than men's (e.g., two-piece swimsuits in beach volleyball), both genders may experience this pressure (e.g., in swimming and diving both men's and women's suits leave little to the imagination).

Athletes may engage in social comparisons with others on weight, body size/shape, eating patterns, and appearance and, as a result, take on their unhealthy beliefs and behaviors. For example, Engel et al. (2003) found that athletes' restrictive eating behaviors were predicted, in part, by perceptions of teammates' weight control behaviors. Further, Smith and Ogle (2006) found that "fat talk" was a common occurrence among girls on a high school athletic team. These findings suggest that healthy or unhealthy social norms about eating, body, and weight issues may develop within team environments, and that practitioners may affect the direction and influence of these norms.

Creating a body-healthy training environment

One of the most effective ways to reduce the risk and prevalence of ED and DE among athletes is creating a *body-healthy* training environment; that is, athletes' physical and psychological health is the determining factor in all decisions, recommendations, and requirements regarding training. Such an approach requires that practitioners work with coaches, sports medicine staff, sport administrators, and athletes to change the current myopic focus on performance to one that emphasizes health. Although this idea may be anathema to some, the reality is that healthy athletes – in terms of weight, physical status, physiological functioning, nutrition, and psychological well-being – will perform better than those who are compromised in any of these areas. Many athletes engage in unhealthy eating and weight control behaviors in search of the ephemeral promise of improved performance (Thompson & Sherman, 1999b).

For this approach to be successful, practitioners must align with coaches and administrators and convince them of the benefits of deemphasizing weight-change as a primary means for improving performances. At an organizational level, whether defined by an athletic department, sports club, or single team, these changes could be codified as policy that guides coaches', athletic trainers', and athletes' behaviors (see Bonci et al., 2008, for information from the National Athletic Trainers' Association that can serve as a blueprint for creating a body-healthy environment). Changes that could be made include: disconnecting weight and performance gains (deemphasizing weight loss), eliminating weigh-ins and weight requirements, changing sport subcultures that perpetuate unhealthy weight and body behaviors, educating coaches about EDs and nutrition, and integrating nutrition, strength training, and psychological skills into daily practices.

Disconnecting weight and performance

A sizable minority of coaches believe that weight loss can lead to performance gains, and thus, they engage in behaviors, such as monitoring eating patterns, tracking weight, and assessing body fat, which put an unhealthy focus on weight and body size (Heffner et al., 2003). These pressures may cause athletes to resort to pathogenic weight control measures (e.g., excessive exercising, vomiting) that can lead to additional problems, such as menstrual irregularities and/or the loss of lean body mass. Practitioners need to work with coaches to deemphasize weight change as the answer and encourage healthier avenues for improving performance, such as improving skills, eating properly, and developing psychological strategies. There is no ideal body weight or body fat percentage that translates into superior performances (Bonci et al., 2008). There is considerable variability in individual body sizes, shapes, and weights, so coaches need to look beyond the body stereotypes they hold for their sports (e.g., gymnasts are tiny, cross-country runners are tall and lean; Thompson & Sherman, 1999b) and develop individualized performance improvement plans.

Eliminating weigh-ins and weight requirements

It is our view that: (a) athletes should only be weighed for medical reasons, (b) weigh-ins should be conducted by medical personnel (e.g., athletic trainers) and *never* by coaches, (c) athletes should be informed of the weigh-ins' purpose and given the opportunity to *not* be told their weight, (d) weigh-ins should be done privately with only the athlete and medical personnel present, (e) weight should be kept private/confidential and *never* posted publicly (e.g., in the locker room), and (f) coaches and other personnel should never make comments about an athlete's weight or body shape. For example, if intensive training is being conducted in hot, humid conditions, medical personnel might weigh athletes at the beginning and end of training sessions to monitor weight loss and hydration. If such weigh-ins are consistent with the above recommendations, athletes will understand their importance in relation to keeping them healthy.

Still, there may be situations in which weight change (gain or loss) could be beneficial for the athlete's health, well-being, and potentially, performance. In such instances, decisions regarding weight change should be made by a sport management team (SMT) that comprises various professionals, such as strength and conditioning staff, medical personnel, nutritionists, exercise physiologists, and mental health practitioners. The SMT should consider all aspects of the athlete's physical condition and training before making any recommendations about weight change. If recommended because of expected health benefits, the weight change plan should be discussed with the athlete, including reasons why. Realistic short- and long-term goals should be set as well as establishing and monitoring specific daily training behaviors (Bonci et al., 2008). Athletic trainers may be in the best position to monitor progress and make weekly and monthly reports to the SMT. The focus should always be on the athlete's health, not on the weight change *per se*.

Changing the sport subculture

Cultural norms about weight, eating, body size/shape, and appearance may apply to an entire sport (e.g., wrestlers cutting weight) or exist only within a specific team (e.g., a softball team recruiting only "attractive" women). Because of coaches' power and control and the close, cohesive nature of most sport teams, such norms can be highly influential, leading athletes to adopt alternative beliefs and engage in new behaviors. When these norms are associated with pathogenic attitudes and behaviors, athletes may exercise in addition to normal workouts, not eat dinner after training, vomit after a large meal, not be satisfied with their body size and shape, and/or ingest muscle-enhancing supplements. The often not-so-subtle message of these norms is that to be considered a successful member of this team, the athletes need to conform to others' behaviors.

Some cultural norms must be changed at the organizational/departmental level, yet most practitioners work directly with coaches and teams, and their efforts should be focused in those domains. Coaches have incredible control and power, and through their messages, behaviors, and what they reward, their athletes come to understand what is expected. Such expectations may also come directly from teammates. In either case, practitioners who have close working relationships with their coaches and athletes and who understand the team's cultural norms can work to alter existing unhealthy attitudes and behaviors. For example, practitioners might help coaches become aware of how their comments affect players' confidence and how they pursue weight loss, or they might talk with the team about their expectations that everyone exercise after practices. Because such norms can be entrenched, change may take time and require strong working relationships between practitioners and coaches and athletes.

Educating coaches

Coaches may be well-informed about their sports (e.g., techniques, strategy), but may be limited in their knowledge about the effects on performance of nutrition, mental skills, physiology, and EDs (Turk *et al.*, 1999). Practitioners can provide such coaches with information directly or bring in experts in these areas. Practitioners also might coordinate with the medical staff to help educate coaches about what is normal in terms of physiological functioning (e.g., menstruation) and how training and eating behaviors may contribute to decrements in the athletes' performances. Such educational efforts can be ongoing and informal (e.g., chatting at practices), or more formal and time-limited (e.g., through scheduled presentations).

Prevention

Practitioners can work with sport teams and institutions to promote the prevention of EDs. Although creating a body-healthy environment is an important first step, practitioners also can focus on programs for at-risk athletes (i.e., those who have internalized body and weight ideals, or are body dissatisfied). Because sociocultural pressures, internalization, and body dissatisfaction are causal risk factors, programs that lessen these factors can reduce athletes' vulnerability. Recent research with athletes (e.g., Smith & Petrie, 2008) has demonstrated that targeted, time-limited programs can reduce risk factors and improve health. These programs, in as few as six 1-hour sessions, may reduce the risk of EDs without ever directly addressing their signs and symptoms.

Screening and treatment

Screening athletes for EDs can occur during two periods and be facilitated by practitioners' involvement with sports medicine staff. First, all athletes, as part of a pre-participation physical examination, can provide information regarding their eating and nutritional status, body- and weight-related attitudes, and psychological well-being and, for girls and women, their menstrual functioning (Bonci et al., 2008). This information can be obtained through paper and pencil questionnaires, though care must be taken regarding the confidentiality of their responses (e.g., not sharing them with coaches). Second, throughout the year, athletes' behaviors, attitudes, mood states, and psychological functioning can be monitored by coaches and medical staff for signs and symptoms of EDs. For example, on road trips, a coach might notice that her female soccer player is eating little at team meals and seems to have lost weight and lacks energy in practices and competitions.

When athletes are identified as having DE attitudes and behaviors or are reporting psychological distress, whether through initial screening or ongoing monitoring, the athlete should be approached and a meeting set up with a member of the SMT to gather more information. The initial approach should be made confidentially and directly with the athlete by someone who knows and has a good relationship with the athlete (e.g., assistant coach), and the focus should be on the athlete's health and well-being (as opposed to weight and/or performance). Ideally, the SMT member who conducts the interview with the athlete should be a mental health professional who has experience in the diagnosis of EDs (see Bonci et al., 2008).

Such early identification can help limit the negative effects of the suspected disorder and facilitate the athlete receiving treatment. If the athlete is subclinical, through treatment the development of more severe problems, such as the triad or a clinical ED, may be avoided. Also, sport institutes, sport organizations, and coaches have an ethical and legal responsibility to make their athletes' health and well-being a primary concern. The development of body-healthy sport environments and early identification screening programs are two ways to demonstrate that responsibility, and, from a practical perspective, reduce legal liability ("Starving for a Win," 2004). Practitioners can work within sport organizations to ensure that such environments exist and that comprehensive plans for education, identification, and treatment are developed.

We recommend other sources for readers to learn more about overall treatment effectiveness and the different modalities and theoretical perspectives that exist (e.g., Brownell & Fairburn, 1995). There are, however, a few issues to highlight regarding the treatment of athletes with EDs. First, it is likely that the licensed mental health provider, such as a psychologist, who provides the ED treatment, will not be part of the SMT nor part of the immediate sport environment. The issue of confidentiality and potential communication among interested parties (e.g., coach, SMT) must be considered and addressed at the outset of treatment. The athlete who is in treatment always should be informed about what is communicated, to whom it is communicated, and the purpose of the communication. Ideally, the athlete should be aware of such communications before they occur. Second, athletes who have subclinical or clinical EDs must decide if they are going to continue training while in treatment. It is possible for athletes to continue to train if their overall health and nutritional status and if the treatment itself are not compromised. Such a decision needs to be made collaboratively and involve the input of all the professionals who are involved in the athletes' treatment, including physicians, psychologists, and nutritionists. When athletes do train and compete while in treatment, mechanisms for effectively monitoring their health status and treatment goals need to be established and implemented. In addition, if their health and/or treatment progress is compromised, then action needs to be taken immediately to limit training. Finally, athletes are part of broader systems (e.g., teams, organizations), so they should think about how (and what) they will communicate with others about their treatment or potential absence. Such decisions should be made by the athletes in consultation with their mental health providers, but practitioners can help athletes should they decide to talk to their teammates, coaches, or family members. Also, depending on the athletes' competitive level, the media may be interested in any absence and may request information. It can be useful to view an ED as an injury and the treatment as rehabilitation. Such an approach normalizes the process and can destigmatize the disorder.

Conclusion

EDs are a reality for both male and female athletes, and practitioners are in the position to work effectively with coaches and directors of sport organizations to create sport environments that focus on the athletes' physical health and overall well-being. Practitioners also can play an important role on the SMT, which can be charged with developing ED policies for the sport organization/team, screening and identification of athletes in the system, prevention of EDs, and the management of those athletes who are in treatment. See Box 24.1 for some practical take-home messages from this chapter.

Box 24.1

Practical take-home messages regarding eating disorders

- Subclinical EDs are similar to clinical EDs in terms of associated psychological, physical, and behavioral disturbances, and thus should be considered serious health concerns.
- Behaviors that are considered "normal" within the sport environment (e.g., menstrual irregularity, training excessively) may be indicators of underlying disturbances in eating, body image, and psychological well-being.
- Pressures within the sport environment, such as weight limits, judging criteria, revealing uniforms, and social comparisons with others, may increase at-risk athletes' vulnerability. Decoupling weight loss and performance improvements, eliminating weigh-ins and weight requirements, changing sport subcultures that perpetuate unhealthy weight and body behaviors, educating coaches about EDs and nutrition, and integrating nutrition and psychological skills into daily training can help create a body-healthy sport environment.
- Practitioners can help develop screening processes to identify athletes who are at-risk for EDs. They also can implement prevention programs to reduce athletes' vulnerability.
- When treating athletes with EDs, practitioners need to consider confidentiality, whether or not to continue training, and how (and what) athletes want to communicate with others about their situations.

References

American College of Sports Medicine (2007). The female athlete triad. *Medicine and Science in Sports and Exercise, 39*, 1867–1882.

American Psychiatric Association (2000). *Diagnostic and statistical manual of mental disorders* (4th ed., text Rev.). Washington, DC: American Psychiatric Association.

Bonci, C., Bonci, L., Granger, L., Johnson, C., Malina, R., Milne, L. W., Ryan, R. R., & Vanderbunt, E. M. (2008). National Athletic Trainers' Association position statement: Preventing, detecting, and managing disordered eating in athletes. *Journal of Athletic Training, 43*, 80–108.

Brownell, K., & Fairburn, C. (Eds.) (1995). *Eating disorders and obesity: A comprehensive handbook.* New York: Guilford Press.

de Bruin, A. P., Oudejans, R. R. D., & Bakker, F. C. (2007). Dieting and body image in aesthetic sports: A comparison of Dutch female gymnasts and non-aesthetic sport participants. *Psychology of Sport and Exercise, 8*, 507–520.

Engel, S., Johnson, C., Powers, P. S., Crosby, R. D., Wonderlich, S. A., Wittrock, D. A., & Mitchell, J. E. (2003). Predictors of disordered eating in a sample of elite Division I college athletes. *Eating Behaviors, 4*, 333–343.

Greenleaf, C., Petrie, T. A., Carter, J., & Reel, J. (2009). Female college athletes: Prevalence of eating disorders and disordered eating behaviors. *Journal of American College Health, 57*, 489–495.

Heffner, J., Ogles, B., Gold, E., Marsden, K., & Johnson, M. (2003). Nutrition and eating in female college athletes: A survey of coaches. *Eating Disorders, 11*, 209–220.

Nichols J. F., Rauh M. J., Lawson M. J., Ji, M., & Barkai H-S. (2006). Prevalence of the female athlete triad syndrome among high school athletes. *Archives of Pediatric Adolescent Medicine, 160*, 127–142.

Olivardia, R. (2001). Mirror, mirror on the wall, who's the largest of them all? The features and phenomenology of muscle dysmorphia. *Harvard Review of Psychiatry, 9*, 254–259.

Petrie, T. A., & Greenleaf, C. A. (2007). Eating disorders in sport: From theory to research to intervention. In G. Tenebaum & R. C. Eklund (Ed.), *Handbook of sport psychology* (3rd ed., pp. 352–378). New York: Wiley.

Petrie, T. A., Greenleaf, C., Reel, J. J., & Carter, J. E. (2008). Prevalence of eating disorders and disordered eating behaviors among male collegiate athletes. *Psychology of Men and Masculinity, 9*, 267–277.

Petrie, T. A., Greenleaf, C., Reel, J. J., & Carter, J. E. (2009). An examination of psychosocial correlates of disordered eating among female college athletes. *Research Quarterly for Exercise and Sport, 80*, 621–632.

Pope, H. G., Gruber, A. J., Choi, P., Olivardia, R., & Phillips, K. A. (1997). Muscle dysmorphia: An underrecognized form of body dysmorphic disorder. *Psychosomatics, 38*, 548–557.

Smith, A., & Petrie, T. A. (2008). Reducing the risk of disordered eating among female athletes: A test of alternative interventions. *Journal of Applied Sport Psychology, 20*, 392–407.

Smith, P. M., & Ogle, J. P. (2006). Interactions among high school cross-country runners and coaches: Creating a cultural context for athletes' embodied experiences. *Family and Consumer Sciences Research Journal, 34*, 276–307.

Starving for a Win. (2004, April 5). *Sports Illustrated,* p. 17.

Thompson, R., & Sherman, R. (1999a). "Good athlete" traits and characteristics of anorexia nervosa: Are they similar? *Eating Disorders, 7*, 181–190.

Thompson, R., & Sherman, R. (1999b). Athletes, athletic performance, and eating disorders: Healthier alternatives. *Journal of Social Issues, 55*, 317–337.

Trattner-Sherman, R., Thompson, R. A., Dehass, D., & Wilfert, M. (2005). NCAA coaches survey: The role of the coach in identifying and managing athletes with disordered eating. *Eating Disorders, 13*, 447–466.

Turk, J., Prentice, W., Chappell, S., & Shields, E. (1999). Collegiate coaches' knowledge of eating disorders. *Journal of Athletic Training, 34*, 19–24.

Zucker, N. L., Womble, L. G., Williamson, D. A., & Perrin, L. A. (1999). Protective factors for eating disorders in female college athletes. *Eating Disorders, 7*, 207–218.

25

Adherence to sport injury rehabilitation

Britton W. Brewer

Sport injuries are a substantial public health concern across forms of physical activity and around the world (Caine, Caine, & Lindner, 1996). Athletes who sustain injuries, especially those that are severe or involve lengthy periods of time away from sport, are often prescribed a rehabilitation program as part of their medical treatment. Although adhering to rehabilitation regimens is considered central to recovery from sport injury (Taylor & Taylor, 1997), it is not uncommon for athletes to fail to complete their recommended rehabilitation activities (Brewer, 1999). Typically involving maintenance of one or more rehabilitative behaviors, adherence to sport injury rehabilitation falls squarely within the realm of applied sport psychology.

Defining adherence to sport injury rehabilitation

In the medical literature, a variety of terms (e.g., compliance, cooperation, concordance, mutuality) and operational definitions have been applied to the general concept to which client adherence refers (Bosworth, Weinberger, & Oddone, 2006). Common elements across the various definitions include the opinions or directions given by health care professionals to prevent or treat medical conditions, the role and self-care responsibilities of clients in their treatments, and the degree to which the behaviors of clients are consistent with the expert recommendations they have received (Bosworth *et al.*, 2006; Christensen, 2004). Incorporating these key elements, Christensen defined adherence as reflecting "the extent to which a person's actions or behavior coincides with advice or instruction from a health care provider intended to prevent, monitor, or ameliorate a disorder" (p. 3). In the context of sport injury rehabilitation, adherence typically involves participation in activities in clinical and home or other (nonclinical) settings. Common clinic-based activities in sport injury rehabilitation include attending appointments, experiencing therapeutic modalities (e.g., cryotherapy, electrical stimulation, massage), and completing exercises designed to enhance such parameters as agility, balance, flexibility, and strength. Away from the clinical setting, athletes undergoing injury rehabilitation may be asked to avoid potentially harmful activities, take prescribed medications, wear therapeutic devices, self-administer therapeutic modalities, and do exercises similar or identical to those featured in clinic-based regimens.

Measuring adherence to sport injury rehabilitation

Given the wide range of behaviors that can be involved in adhering to sport injury rehabilitation programs, it is not surprising that a diverse array of methods have been used to measure adherence to sport injury rehabilitation for clinical and research purposes. For any particular rehabilitation regimen, measures of adherence should, of course, correspond closely to the behavioral demands of the regimen. Accordingly, adherence measurement strategies have been developed for clinic- and nonclinic-based activities.

Clinic-based measures of sport injury rehabilitation adherence

The most commonly used measure of adherence to clinic-based sport injury rehabilitation programs is attendance at rehabilitation appointments. Objective and easily calculated by dividing the number of rehabilitation sessions that athletes attend by the number of rehabilitation sessions scheduled, attendance indices are helpful for documenting gross nonadherence to clinic-based rehabilitation in the form of failing to show up for scheduled appointments. Because there is a strong tendency for athletes to be present for their scheduled appointments and because attendance measures do not provide information on athletes' behavior during rehabilitation sessions (Brewer, 1999), additional means of assessing adherence to clinic-based sport injury rehabilitation have been developed.

The most elaborate method of assessing what athletes actually do during rehabilitation sessions is the Sports Medicine Observation Code (SMOC; Crossman & Roch, 1991), which involves observing athletes at regular time intervals during their appointments and recording their behavior in 13 categories (e.g., active rehabilitation, waiting, non-activity). Such an approach to measuring adherence to sport injury rehabilitation is labor-intensive, impractical in most rehabilitation environments, and unlikely to yield precise information about adherence unless the prescribed allocation of behaviors in each of the categories can be specified.

Another method of assessing adherence in clinical settings is to compare the number of sets of rehabilitation exercises completed with the number of sets prescribed. Although this approach is appealing in that it produces a quantifiable index of adherence, athletes undergoing rehabilitation in supervised clinical environments rarely do less than the prescribed number of sets of rehabilitation exercises, exceptions being when their medical conditions prevent them from completing exercises (in which case the exercise prescription is adjusted) or in the rare instances when they openly defy the instructions of their rehabilitation practitioners.

A fourth option for measuring adherence to clinic-based sport injury rehabilitation is to have the professionals supervising the rehabilitation of athletes rate the extent to which the individuals under their care adhere to the rehabilitation program. An example of such a measure is the Sport Injury Rehabilitation Adherence Scale (SIRAS; Brewer et al., 2000), with which practitioners evaluate clients' efforts to complete rehabilitation exercises, follow instructions and advice, and be receptive to changes in the rehabilitation program during a given clinic session. The SIRAS is a brief (i.e., three items), psychometrically sound means of assessing what athletes do relative to their rehabilitation professionals' expectations of their behavior during clinic appointments.

Nonclinic-based measures of sport injury rehabilitation adherence

Home exercise prescriptions are the central feature of many sport injury rehabilitation programs. Adherence to prescribed home exercises has been assessed in a variety of ways, ranging from single-item retrospective reports to objective methods. The most common means of measuring adherence to home exercises has been simply to ask athletes to indicate the extent to which they adhered to their home exercise prescription (Brewer, 1999). Although appealing in its convenience and simplicity, this retrospective approach is subject to forgetting and response bias (Meichenbaum & Turk, 1987). Obtaining frequent, even daily, self-reports of home exercise completion during the rehabilitation period is a way of minimizing recall inaccuracies. Objective measurement of adherence to home exercise prescriptions, which is desirable because it is not susceptible to recall and response biases and can therefore validate self-reports, can be accomplished by embedding electronic counting devices in exercise equipment (for a review of objective measures of rehabilitation adherence, see Brewer, 2004). Under the assumption that athletes who cannot correctly recall or replicate the home exercises they were asked to perform are unlikely to have done the exercises, nonadherence to prescribed home exercises can be assessed indirectly by having athletes articulate the details of (or actually demonstrate) their home exercise programs (Friedrich, Cermak, & Maderbacher, 1996; Webborn, Carbon, & Miller, 1997).

Subjective and objective means are available for assessing adherence to other nonclinic-based aspects of sport injury rehabilitation programs. For example, in the subjective realm, self-reports can be used to measure use of prescribed medications and therapeutic devices such as orthopedic braces and splints. Self-reports of medication and device use are subject to the same limitations as self-reports of home exercise completion. Objective indices of adherence to medication regimens include pill counts, pharmacy refills, reimbursement records, biochemical indicators (e.g., blood levels, drug assays), and electronic monitoring devices. As noted in a review of rehabilitation adherence measurement strategies (Brewer, 2004), adherence to prescribed use of orthotics and orthopedic braces can be measured with devices such as a hidden step-counter and a mechanical timer, respectively. Objective measurement strategies do not guarantee detection of instances in which medications have been taken or therapeutic devices have been worn or used as prescribed, but they reduce or eliminate the potential adverse effect that memory and response biases can have on subjective measurements of adherence.

Predicting and explaining adherence to sport injury rehabilitation

Researchers have adapted theoretical models of adherence that were originally developed for other health behaviors in an attempt to provide a framework for understanding associations between predictor variables and sport injury rehabilitation adherence. Among the theoretical perspectives that have been adopted are: protection motivation theory (Prentice-Dunn & Rogers, 1986), cognitive appraisal models (Lazarus & Folkman, 1984; Wiese-Bjornstal, Smith, Shaffer, & Morrey, 1998), and the theory of planned behavior (Ajzen, 1991). Because most of the theoretical approaches have been applied to sport injury rehabilitation adherence in one or, at the most, several studies, there is not an empirical basis for recommending one perspective over another. Moreover, because there are conceptual overlaps among the theories (e.g., the concept of self-efficacy figures prominently in multiple perspectives), it seems prudent to identify regularities in the research literature independent of the theoretical approach under investigation.

Factors that have consistently been associated with adherence to sport injury rehabilitation include personal characteristics, contextual/environmental characteristics, and rehabilitation-related beliefs and reactions. Personal characteristics are attributes that affect the likelihood of adhering to sport injury rehabilitation programs. Given the rigors of many injury rehabilitation regimens, it is not surprising that athletes who are self-motivated, strongly identified with the athlete role as a source of self-worth, tolerant of pain, and tough-minded are especially likely to adhere to their prescribed rehabilitation activities (Brewer, 2007).

The context in which sport injury rehabilitation occurs appears to be particularly influential in determining whether athletes adhere to rehabilitation prescriptions. Numerous characteristics (or, to be more accurate, *perceived* characteristics) of the social and physical setting of rehabilitation have been correlated with sport injury rehabilitation adherence. Athletes are more likely to adhere to their injury rehabilitation program when they report that others are supportive of their rehabilitation activities, their practitioners expect them to adhere, the clinical setting in which their rehabilitation occurs is comfortable, and the scheduling of their rehabilitation appointments is convenient (Brewer, 2007).

Beliefs and reactions associated with adherence to sport injury rehabilitation include athletes' interpretations of the severity of their injuries, perceptions of control over their recoveries, beliefs about the efficacy of their treatments, assessments of their abilities to complete their rehabilitation activities, and psychological responses to injury (Brewer, 2007). Athletes tend to adhere better to their rehabilitation when they consider their injuries severe and perceive themselves as susceptible to further health complications without rehabilitation. Athletes who report believing that they can exert control over their health in general, and their rehabilitation outcomes in particular, tend to adhere better to their injury rehabilitation programs than those who do not report such beliefs. Similarly, adherence levels are higher for athletes who deem their rehabilitation programs effective and who describe themselves as capable of completing the tasks of rehabilitation than for athletes whose perceptions of the efficacy of their rehabilitation regimens and their abilities to complete them are less favorable. Mood disturbances and fears of reinjury are psychological responses that have been associated with adherence to sport injury rehabilitation, with greater emotional distress related to lower levels of adherence.

Enhancing adherence to sport injury rehabilitation

In light of the putative importance of treatment adherence to achieving successful rehabilitation outcomes, adherence enhancement is a logical target of psychological intervention. Although a variety of interventions have been suggested to enhance adherence to sport injury rehabilitation, few experimental studies have examined the efficacy of such interventions, and a causal link with improved sport injury rehabilitation adherence has been established only for a single type of intervention – goal setting. Penpraze and Mutrie (1999) found that relative to athletes who were assigned nonspecific rehabilitation goals, athletes who were given specific rehabilitation goals exhibited greater understanding of, and adherence to, their injury rehabilitation programs. Evans and Hardy (2002) obtained complementary findings, reporting that athletes who were given a goal-setting intervention displayed better adherence to their injury rehabilitation protocols than those who received either social support or no treatment. A qualitative follow-up study revealed that the favorable effect of goal setting on adherence may have been due to increases in self-efficacy, focus on the rehabilitation program, and attributions of recovery to internal, personally controllable factors in athletes in the goal-setting group as compared with athletes in the social support and no treatment groups.

Outside the sport injury domain, empirical support has been found for several other psychological interventions as enhancers of adherence to rehabilitation regimens (Brewer, 2004). Educational approaches in which participants are provided with information and instructions about their medical conditions and rehabilitation programs have been successful in improving rehabilitation adherence. The efficacy of educational interventions in enhancing adherence can be bolstered through supervision by qualified professionals and use of instructional media that help to clarify the details of rehabilitation regimens, such as audio recordings, written/illustrated materials, and video recordings. Another beneficial approach to boosting rehabilitation adherence is reinforcement of the prescribed rehabilitation behaviors. Support also exists for multimodal interventions in which multiple procedures intended to enhance adherence are combined. Counseling/information, reinforcement, contingency contracting, modeling, self-monitoring, mental practice, and goal setting are among the procedures that have been included in successful multimodal interventions.

Although featuring correlational studies almost exclusively, the literature on predictors of adherence to sport injury rehabilitation is instructive in developing adherence enhancement interventions. Extrapolating from the synopsis of research presented in the previous section, it is possible to formulate suggestions for the foci and content of procedures designed to improve sport injury rehabilitation adherence. In clinical settings, the environment should be made as comfortable and conducive to rehabilitation activities as possible. Rehabilitation appointments should be made as convenient to athletes as is feasible so as not to pose a barrier to attendance. Rehabilitation practitioners should furnish athletes with detailed information and instructions pertaining to their rehabilitation programs, convey to athletes expectations that they will adhere to their rehabilitation regimen, provide athletes with support for their rehabilitation activities, and, where possible, assist athletes in obtaining additional support for their rehabilitation from other significant individuals (e.g., coaches, teammates, partners, family members). Practitioners should also emphasize the importance of engaging in rehabilitation activities to facilitate recovery, promote confidence in the efficacy of the rehabilitation program, build athletes' confidence in their abilities to perform the requirements of the rehabilitation regimens, and instill in athletes the belief that they are responsible for the rehabilitation outcomes that they incur. Procedures that help reduce athletes' emotional distress and fear of reinjury (e.g., counseling, cognitive restructuring, relaxation training, guided imagery) may also have beneficial effects on adherence.

An important applied consideration pertains to who implements sport injury rehabilitation adherence enhancement interventions. From a pragmatic standpoint, sport injury rehabilitation professionals (e.g., physiotherapists, athletic trainers) may be the most suitable practitioners to implement adherence enhancement interventions. By virtue of their established relationships and regular contacts with athletes undergoing rehabilitation, sport injury rehabilitation professionals are well-positioned to initiate interventions designed to enhance the rehabilitation programs that they or other sports medicine personnel (e.g., physicians) have prescribed. Although rehabilitation professionals may be concerned that adherence enhancement interventions will add tasks to their already-busy schedules and may be reluctant to administer what are essentially psychological interventions, potentially perceiving the interventions as outside their areas of expertise, they have a vested interest in the success of the rehabilitation and can easily learn the basics of adherence enhancement.

Through educational presentations (i.e., in services) and consultation, sport psychology practitioners can help rehabilitation professionals acquire adherence enhancement skills, integrate those skills into their existing methods of practice, provide athletes with treatment-related information in understandable terms, and create a rehabilitation environment conducive to adherence. For example, rehabilitation professionals can be taught that a goal-setting intervention can be incorporated into clinical practice by having the rehabilitation professionals collaborate with athletes under their care in setting short- (and possibly long-) term goals pertaining to rehabilitation processes (e.g., number of sets of home rehabilitation exercises) and outcomes (e.g., range of motion) at the time the rehabilitation prescription is given. Sport psychology practitioners can teach rehabilitation professionals how to inquire about potential barriers to goal achievement, help devise strategies to overcome those barriers, and monitor progress toward goal achievement throughout rehabilitation, revising and resetting goals as needed. Neither elaborate nor time-consuming, such interventions increase the likelihood of adherence to the rehabilitation program (Evans & Hardy, 2002; Penpraze & Mutrie, 1999) and may ultimately improve rehabilitation outcomes.

Another option – feasible in sports medicine settings where sport injury rehabilitation professionals and sport psychology practitioners work in close contact with each other – is a team approach in which athletes with injuries are seen (jointly or separately) by both types of personnel, who confer in an attempt to optimize the athletes' treatments. Procedures designed to enhance adherence to rehabilitation can be implemented by rehabilitation professionals in consultation with sport psychology practitioners or vice versa. The latter circumstance might be most likely to occur for athletes with injuries who have sought services for issues involving psychological adjustment to injury and performance enhancement. It is common for athletes to experience negative emotions such as depression, anxiety, fear, anger, and frustration following injury and during the rehabilitation period (Brewer, 2007). Emotional distress and the negative cognitions that can accompany and perpetuate it may not only be sources of concern (and targets of intervention) in their own right, but may also impair motivation and compromise adherence. Sport psychologists can help athletes gain perspective on their injuries and view their situations constructively. Athletes can be shown that the sense of identity that they may derive from sport involvement can both contribute to negative emotions and serve as a source of resilience and motivation to adhere to the rehabilitation program, presumably expediting their recovery and alleviating their distress.

A final caution about adherence enhancement is needed. Although it is widely assumed that better adherence is likely to produce better outcomes, this assumption may be unwarranted. The general medical literature is replete with interventions for which better adherence *is* associated with better outcomes (Dunbar-Jacob & Schlenk, 1996). Nevertheless, there are also examples to the contrary, where better adherence is *not* associated with better outcomes. In a compelling study of the relationship between treatment adherence and treatment outcome for multiple nonrehabilitation diagnoses and interventions, only 11 of 132 comparisons of adherent and nonadherent individuals were statistically significant (Hays et al., 1994). Despite a trend for positive associations between adherence and outcome in the rehabilitation domain, nonsignificant or negative adherence–outcome relationships have been documented in at least five studies (for a review, see Brewer, 2004). Negative associations between adherence and outcome are particularly worrisome, potentially signaling that the rehabilitation program is ineffective and should be modified. In a dramatic example of this circumstance, Shelbourne and Wilckens (1990) reported how clinical observations that people who adhered less well to a conservative rehabilitation regimen following anterior cruciate ligament reconstruction experienced *better* rehabilitation outcomes prompted a change – almost a complete reversal in rehabilitative approach – to an accelerated postoperative rehabilitation protocol. Positive adherence–outcome associations have been documented for the modified protocol (Brewer *et al.*, 2004). Because one cannot automatically assume that better adherence to rehabilitation regimens will yield better rehabilitation outcomes, practitioners should make every effort to ensure that adherence to a given rehabilitation protocol is likely to produce the desired outcomes before attempting to enhance adherence to that protocol. Doing so is consistent with the tenets of evidence-based practice.

Summary and conclusions

Injury is a common occurrence in sport. Rehabilitation programs are often prescribed for athletes who sustain injuries. Athletes frequently do not adhere fully to their prescribed rehabilitation regimens, and this limited adherence has potential implications for the rehabilitation outcomes incurred by athletes. A variety of methods can be used to assess adherence to clinic- and nonclinic-based rehabilitation activities. Numerous predictors of sport injury rehabilitation adherence have been identified and provide a preliminary basis for understanding the circumstances under which athletes are most likely to adhere to their rehabilitation programs. Several interventions to enhance rehabilitation adherence have been developed and found effective. Along with sport psychology practitioners who work in sports medicine settings, sport injury rehabilitation professionals are in a desirable position to consider the suggestions for application summarized in Box 25.1, implement methods of adherence enhancement, and, in so doing, better serve the athletes in their care.

Box 25.1

Summary of suggestions for measuring, predicting, and enhancing adherence to sport injury rehabilitation

- Adhering to sport injury rehabilitation programs typically involves completing rehabilitation activities in clinical and/or nonclinical (e.g., home) settings.
- Using attendance at rehabilitation appointments to assess adherence to clinic-based sport injury rehabilitation is objective and convenient, but does not yield information on what athletes do while they are at clinic-based sessions.
- Obtaining rehabilitation practitioner ratings of athlete adherence during rehabilitation appointments can be used to complement attendance indices in assessing adherence to clinic-based sport injury rehabilitation.
- Self-reports of adherence to nonclinic-based sport injury rehabilitation activities should be obtained as frequently as possible and should be complemented with objective measures when possible.

■ Personal characteristics of athletes who tend to adhere to their prescribed rehabilitation activities are self-motivation, strong identification with the athlete role as a source of self-worth, pain tolerance, and tough mindedness.

■ Environmental characteristics associated with high levels of clinic-based sport injury rehabilitation adherence include social support for rehabilitation, practitioner expectancies of adherence, comfortable clinical settings, and convenient scheduling of appointments.

■ Along with emotional distress, perceptions of injury severity, personal control over injury recovery, treatment efficacy, and rehabilitation self-efficacy are positively associated with sport injury rehabilitation adherence.

■ Goal setting, reinforcement, educational approaches, and multimodal interventions can be effective in enhancing rehabilitation adherence.

■ Adherence enhancement interventions are most suitable for use with rehabilitation programs for which better adherence is likely to lead to better rehabilitation outcomes.

■ Sport psychology professionals can play an educational or consultative role in helping sport injury rehabilitation practitioners learn and implement adherence enhancement interventions.

References

Ajzen, I. (1991). The theory of planned behavior. *Organizational Behavior and Human Decision Processes, 50*, 179–211.

Bosworth, H. B., Weinberger, M., & Oddone, E. Z. (2006). Introduction. In H. B. Bosworth, E. Z. Oddone, & M. Weinberger (Eds.), *Patient treatment adherence: Concepts, interventions, and measurement* (pp. 3–11). Mahwah, NJ: Erlbaum.

Brewer, B. W. (1999). Adherence to sport injury rehabilitation regimens. In S. J. Bull (Ed.), *Adherence issues in sport and exercise* (pp. 145–168). Chichester, England: Wiley.

Brewer, B. W. (2004). Psychological aspects of rehabilitation. In G. S. Kolt & M. B. Andersen (Eds.), *Psychology in the physical and manual therapies* (pp. 39–53). Edinburgh: Churchill Livingstone.

Brewer, B. W. (2007). Psychology of sport injury rehabilitation. In G. Tenenbaum & R. C. Eklund (Eds.), *Handbook of sport psychology* (3rd ed., pp. 404–424). New York: Wiley.

Brewer, B. W., Cornelius, A. E., Van Raalte, J. L., Brickner, J. C., Sklar, J. H., Corsetti, J. R., Pohlman, M. H., Ditmar, T. D. & Emery, K. (2004). Rehabilitation adherence and anterior cruciate ligament outcome. *Psychology, Health & Medicine, 9*, 163–175.

Brewer, B. W., Van Raalte, J. L., Petitpas, A. J., Sklar, J. H., Pohlman, M. H., Krushell, R. J., Ditmar, T. D., Daly, J. M., & Weinstock, J. (2000). Preliminary psychometric evaluation of a measure of adherence to clinic–based sport injury rehabilitation. *Physical Therapy in Sport, 1*, 68–74.

Caine, D. J., Caine, C. G., & Lindner, K. J. (Eds.). (1996). *Epidemiology of sports injuries*. Champaign, IL: Human Kinetics.

Christensen, A. J. (2004). *Patient adherence to medical treatment regimens*. New Haven, CT: Yale University Press.

Crossman, J., & Roch, J. (1991). An observation instrument for use in sports medicine clinics. *The Journal of the Canadian Athletic Therapists' Association*, pp. 10–13.

Dunbar-Jacob, J., & Schlenk, E. (1996). Treatment adherence and clinical outcome: Can we make a difference? In R. J. Resnick & R. H. Rozensky (Eds.), *Health psychology through the life span: Practice and research opportunities* (pp. 323–343). Washington, DC: American Psychological Association.

Evans, L., & Hardy, L. (2002). Injury rehabilitation: A goal-setting intervention study. *Research Quarterly for Exercise and Sport, 73*, 310–319.

Friedrich, M., Cermak, T., & Maderbacher, P. (1996). The effects of brochure use versus therapist teaching on patients performing therapeutic exercise and on changes in impairment status. *Physical Therapy, 76*, 1082–1088.

Hays, R. D., Kravitz, R. L., Mazel, R. M., Sherbourne, C. D., DiMatteo, M. R., Rogers, W. H., & Greenfield, S. (1994). The impact of patient adherence on health outcomes for patients with chronic disease in the Medical Outcomes Study. *Journal of Behavioral Medicine, 17*, 347–360.

Lazarus, R. S., & Folkman, S. (1984). *Stress, appraisal, and coping.* New York: Springer.

Meichenbaum, D., & Turk, D. C. (1987). *Facilitating treatment adherence.* New York: Plenum.

Penpraze, P., & Mutrie, N. (1999). Effectiveness of goal setting in an injury rehabilitation programme for increasing patient understanding and compliance [Abstract]. *British Journal of Sports Medicine, 33*, 60.

Prentice-Dunn, S., & Rogers, R. W. (1986). Protection motivation theory and preventive health: Beyond the health belief model. *Health Education Research, 1*, 153–161.

Shelbourne, K. D., & Wilckens, J. H. (1990). Current concepts in anterior cruciate ligament rehabilitation. *Orthopaedic Review, 19*, 957–964.

Taylor, J., & Taylor, S. (1997). *Psychological approaches to sports injury rehabilitation.* Gaithersburg, MD: Aspen.

Webborn, A. D. J., Carbon, R. J., & Miller, B. P. (1997). Injury rehabilitation programs: "What are we talking about?" *Journal of Sport Rehabilitation, 6*, 54–61.

Wiese-Bjornstal, D. M., Smith, A. M., Shaffer, S. M., & Morrey, M. A. (1998). An integrated model of response to sport injury: Psychological and sociological dimensions. *Journal of Applied Sport Psychology, 10*, 46–69.

26

Career termination

David Lavallee, Sunghee Park, and David Tod

One of the issues commonly encountered by sport psychology practitioners is how to help athletes cope with career termination (Lavallee & Andersen, 2000). Even though retirement from sport is one of the only certainties in the life of a competitive athlete, individuals may resist planning for career termination and sometimes experience adjustment problems when faced with the end of sport participation. Attention has increased in the literature on psychological interventions for athletes in transitions, and research has started to document the effectiveness of specific interventions to assist retiring and retired athletes. Governing bodies of sport around the world have used this research to develop career transition programs for athletes (e.g., Anderson & Morris, 2000). Many of these programs employ sport psychologists to provide pre-transition and post-transition services for athletes.

Our purpose in this chapter is to provide an overview of a range of approaches sport psychology practitioners can employ when working with athletes who intend to terminate their sports participation or who have already ended their careers. We begin by building on Danish's life development work (see chapter 18 in this book) and reviewing how life development interventions can be effective in helping athletes adjust to retirement. We then outline the beneficial role of account-making, mentoring, and traditional therapeutic approaches when working with retired athletes.

Life development interventions

In recent years researchers have focused on developing interventions to assist athletes in transition. One such approach is the life development intervention (LDI) based upon Danish and colleagues' (Danish, Petitpas, & Hale, 1995) psychoeducational-developmental model. LDI emphasizes continuous growth and development across the life span. The intervention is also based around critical life events that often disrupt daily routines and relationships, which can be sources of stress.

Danish et al. (1995) suggested an LDI can provide helpful strategies before an event (e.g., retirement), supportive strategies during an event, and counseling strategies after an event. In a sport setting, athletes experience several critical life events such as injuries, selection processes, within-career transitions, and career termination. Retirement from their sports can be seen as one of the most important life events for athletes because they have often spent long periods of time devoting themselves to their sports. When athletes have to leave their sports, they may often experience loss in many areas such as identity, public attention, everyday training, and social networks (Lally, 2007). Moreover, some athletes have to end their careers with no preparation or intention because of serious injuries or deselection. Such events often require considerable psychological adjustment due to the lack of preparation on the part of athletes.

In a recent study, Lavallee (2005) found that an LDI was effective in helping retired athletes cope with their career terminations. The intervention employed both supportive and counseling strategies. Because it is important in an LDI for the practitioner to make an initial assessment of life events (Danish et al., 1995), participants in Lavallee's study completed a personality type measurement and a career interest inventory during an intake session. Following this assessment, the intervention focused on helping the individuals identify skills they had developed in sport that could be transferred to other areas of their lives (Mayocchi & Hanrahan, 2000). The researcher used goal setting to identify new skills (e.g., interviewing skills), as well as develop future plans, and employed supportive and counseling strategies as a means of empowerment, because they helped the participants encounter their retirements constructively (Danish et al., 1995).

The third, and final, aspect of the intervention focused on the development of life skills (e.g., effective decision making) that could augment the participants' abilities to cope with their career terminations and other future events. Participants had opportunities to identify the skills as transferable, as well as new skills, to practise during intervention sessions while the researcher provided feedback, support, and follow-up to enhance personal competence (Danish et al., 1995). As part of an LDI, sport psychologists might also want to consider employing other career transition measurement tools (see Box 26.1).

Lavallee (2005) demonstrated how an LDI can help athletes broaden their social identities while also enhancing their self-confidence and self-worth. Learning new coping skills related to their current situations helped increase their abilities to cope with retirement and have positive views of the end of their sport careers. Individual counseling sessions with

---

Box 26.1

Advances in the measurement of career transitions in sport

To supplement interventions, sport psychologists might want to consider available measurement tools. There have been advances in the measurement of career transitions in sport in recent years, including the development of the following:

- *Athletes' Retirement Decision Inventory* (Fernandez, Stephan, & Fouquereau, 2006).
- *Retirement Sports Survey* (Alfermann, Stambulova, & Zemaityte, 2004).
- *British Athletes' Lifestyle Assessment Needs in Career and Education* (BALANCE) Scale (Lavallee & Wylleman, 1999; developed specifically to assess the quality of adjustment following sports career termination).
- *Athlete Retirement Questionnaire* (Sinclair & Orlick, 1993).
- *Australian Athletes Career Transition Inventory* (Hawkins & Blann, 1993).

athletes provided opportunities to evaluate how committed they were to the sport role at that point in time. If their commitment suggested identity foreclosure by showing a strong tendency to avoid their upcoming life changes, the researcher made a differentiation between psychological and situational foreclosure in subsequent parts of the intervention (see Chapter 30). Practitioners can use rapport building, effective listening, and empathic understanding during counseling sessions of the intervention to allow participants to express their emotions and reactions associated with their career terminations (Petitpas, Giges, & Danish, 1999).

Account-making

Grove, Lavallee, Gordon, and Harvey's (1998) research showed that an account-making approach is an effective framework for understanding and resolving distressful reactions to sports career termination. Harvey, Weber, & Orbuch (1990) adapted Horowitz's (1986) model of coping with loss to identify key elements in dealing with extremely distressful experiences. Compared to Horowitz's model that emphasized the role of "working through" in recovery, Harvey et al. developed the idea that individuals begin to construct stories about their traumatic experiences – why they happened, what they mean for the future. This "account" then is partially confided to close others, whose reactions may help or hinder individuals in dealing with their distressful reactions. If the close confidants react to the account with empathy (e.g., by lending an "ear," being there to listen, offering advice or encouragement, providing feedback when desired), individuals may move to confront what has happened and deal with it rationally and constructively. If the close confidants do not react with empathy, the negative effects of the distressful reactions may grow, and individuals may become discouraged in trying to engage in this confiding social interaction activity that appears to be central to positive psychological adaptation.

When athletes have distressful reactions to sport retirement, there may be several nega- tive experiences associated with their earliest recognition that their careers are over. For example, there may be a loss of material and symbolic rewards associated with their career termination. More specifically, they may have to find new ways to make a living or occupy themselves during the times that they formerly trained. Their self-identities may begin to transform toward less publicly visible and esteemed status. Their intrinsic feelings of accom- plishment and joy associated with highly competitive performances may have to be forgone, and substitute motivators may need to be found in their repertoires of skills and interests. The social environment that involves comradeship and adulation may also change as the athlete slides toward a lower profile in the minds of fans and peers.

Grove et al. (1998) found that 20% of athletes experience distressful reactions to retirement from sport. Experiences are likely to differ greatly among retired athletes who have distressful reactions to career termination. The account-making model proposes that for the best adaptation and healing to occur, individuals need to come to grips with the reality of the career termination. Retired athletes would receive substantial benefits from accepting their distressful reactions and reconstructing new identities that use their careers and experiences in constructive ways for future activities, whether for individual gain or to give back to others. Erikson (1963) termed this active concern in guiding the generations that follow *generativity* and athletes are often in a position to "give back" in terms of activities post-retirement (e.g., coaching) that still have to do with sport.

An important initial task for sport psychology practitioners is to create an atmosphere where athletes are willing to reflect openly on the current versions of their retirement stories and begin to refine them. Once a climate of meaningful involvement and trust has been established, the psychologist can offer support, validation of feelings, and assistance in reconstructing life stories. At first, practitioners might suggest constructive activities, sharing information about themselves, offering companionship, asking the athletes to teach them or others how to do something, and/or providing information about life transitions and the retirement experiences of other athletes (Grove et al., 1998). Later, both open-ended and specific questions could be asked about various phases of the athletes' careers (including the latter stages when retirement issues may have first become salient), tactfully confronting persistent denial, and encouraging self-exploration of roles, values, interests, and skills. Also during this time, as the athlete reveals more about himself/herself, the psychologist may start to feel that he/she is, in some ways, being tested by the client.

At the same time, it is important to realize that neither confiding nor account-making can be rushed. Both processes will involve periods of resistance, progress, plateau, and regression. Athletes will also differ in their abilities to understand their own experiences, express themselves, engage in personal disclosure, and construct articulate accounts. Initial attempts at confiding and account-making may best be done in writing so that athletes are better able to organize and clarify their thoughts and feelings (Pennebaker, 1990). Practitioners can use a wide variety of therapeutic writing techniques including: diaries, journals, poems, letters, stories, and autobiographies. Such activities can be approached from a number of traditional behavior-change perspectives (e.g., rational-emotive behavior therapy, as outlined later in the chapter), and various degrees of structure can also be imposed to suit athletes' preferences, abilities, and readiness to deal with specific issues. Regardless of the specific format(s) and degree of structure, it is important to encourage progressive movement toward more "complete" accounts that include explanations, memories, and emotional reactions to the athletes' prior sport involvement, transition experiences, and uncertain futures. At the same time, the establishment of new behavioral patterns (e.g., involvement in the teaching of young athletes) should be encouraged because of the potent influence of one's behavior on self-perception and identity.

These elaborated accounts and new behavioral involvements can then form the basis for private reflection, discussions with significant others, support group interactions, and/or private consultation with the sport psychologist. In the short term, feedback from these activities will enable the athletes to work through loss-related issues (e.g., denial, feelings of despair), further refine personal retirement stories, and develop plans for future behaviors. Over time, the complementary processes of account-making, confiding, refining stories, and engaging in new behavior patterns will accomplish a number of therapeutic goals. Specifically, the retirement experiences will be chronicled and their reality will be confirmed; personal memories and emotions will be formally recorded as central components of the experiences; the athletes will actively practise communication and interpersonal skills; the athletes will achieve a sense of integration, closure, and identity change; and the athletes will be prepared to embrace new and different challenges (Grove et al., 1998). Identity change can lead to generativity, and sport psychology practitioners can facilitate generativity by consciously encouraging retired athletes to discuss their refined accounts with others who are in the midst of their careers. Such an approach could be incorporated into mentoring programs as outlined in the following section.

Mentoring

Researchers have recently identified mentoring as a useful approach to assist athletes in making transitions out of sport (Lavallee, Nesti, Borkeles, Cockerill, & Edge, 2000). Kram (1992) defined mentoring as a close relationship in which a mentor counsels, supports, and guides a protégé. Research in a number of settings outside of sport has documented the benefits of such an intervention (e.g., Burke, McKeen, & McKenna, 1993), and several sport psychologists have suggested mentoring as a possible way to assist athletes in coping with career transition processes (e.g., Jackson, Mayocchi, & Dover, 1998). In addition, Perna, Zaichkowsky, and Bocknek (1996) reported the positive effects of mentoring during career transitions in sport settings. The study assessed levels of mentoring among a sample of senior-year student-athletes and found evidence that those who had mentors to guide them through the crucial stages of transition showed higher intimacy scores (which indicated a degree of comfort with emotional expression and personal relationships) when compared with athletes who received less mentoring.

In the sport career termination process, some athletes reported that they approached their coaches as mentors because they (coaches) are often former athletes who have previously experienced career transitions from participation in sport. Brooks and Sikes (1997) described desirable mentor characteristics such as being accessible, supportive, a good communicator, and a good listener, along with displaying positive and encouraging attitudes. Although coaches need to focus on their current (and potentially future) athletes, they are in a good position to offer support to retired (or soon to retire) athletes. Sport psychologists can help develop a mentoring relationship between coaches and retiring athletes. In doing so, practitioners need to consider the athletes' perceptions of coaches as mentors, the willingness of coaches to be mentors, as well as the importance of individual communication skills in mentoring. For example, when athletes show fear of an uncertain future and stressful reactions caused by career termination, mentors can reduce these negative reactions by listening, supporting, encouraging, and leading them to positive paths and building individual career development plans.

Sinclair and Orlick (1993) suggested that retiring athletes often feel alienated from their sports upon career termination, and opportunities for them to contribute to the sport system may help with their sense of isolation and disengagement. Mentoring is one method for doing so because such relationships will help current athletes plan for their post-athletic careers and assist former athletes in the adjustment process. A number of career assistance programs employ athletes to facilitate group discussions among recently retired athletes (Anderson & Morris, 2000). In addition, athletes who experience distressful reactions to retirement from sport could return to their sporting teams and discuss their retirement-related accounts with other athletes in the midst of their careers.

Traditional therapeutic approaches

Sport psychology practitioners may want to consider employing more traditional behavioral, cognitive, and emotional interventions when working with retired athletes alongside life development interventions, account-making, and mentoring. Although no research has been conducted specifically in relation to career termination, researchers have recommended emotional expression (Kennedy-Moor & Watson, 1999), cognitive therapy (Beck & Weishaar, 2000), rational–emotive behavior therapy (Ellis, 2000), and stress inoculation training (Meichenbaum & Deffenbacher, 1988) in the literature as approaches to facilitate career termination adjustment among elite athletes.

Emotional expression is based on existential psychotherapy and involves counseling that focuses on ontological experiences, one's personal values, and the present event. The approach aims to help individuals confront their existential concerns and express negative emotions based on the evidence that suppression of emotion contributes to individuals' distress (Classen, Koopman, Angell, & Spiegel, 1996). In the career transition process some athletes with strong and exclusive athletic identities at retirement may experience feelings of loss, fear of freedom, isolation, and meaninglessness (Lavallee et al., 2000). Expression of these negative emotions may reduce distress and provide opportunities for former athletes to reorder life priorities and re-establish meaning, as well as encourage them to cope with their current situations (Yalom, 1980).

Wolff and Lester (1989) have suggested that cognitive therapy is suitable to reduce retired athletes' anxiety and depression stemming from maladaptive cognitions including negative views of the self, the world, and the future that potentially occur during the career transition process. The approach aims to decrease maladaptive cognitions related to the sport career endings and build adaptive perspectives for post-sport life. Similarly, rational–emotive behavior therapy (REBT) can be an effective therapy for athletes who exhibit denial of the end of their sport careers or hold irrational views of their sport career terminations. REBT can assist athletes in shifting irrational or incongruent beliefs to rational or healthy ones, and provide them with powerful insights into their sport career terminations and current status.

Gordon and Lavallee (2004) recommended stress-inoculation training because of its utility in decreasing distress and building coping abilities through training. Practitioners can encourage retired athletes who experience their sport career terminations as problematic events to perceive them as problems to be solved and to focus on what is changeable.

Meichenbaum and Deffenbacher (1988) outlined three phases of stress inoculation training (SIT) that include educational and conceptual understanding of the treatment process, the development of coping skills, and the refining and application of the acquired coping skills. Various kinds of therapeutic methods can be applied as coping skills in SIT: cognitive restructuring, self-instructional training, problem solving, and relaxation. Practitioners can teach relaxation skills to athletes who are experiencing heightened arousal and anxiety. When athletes master a relaxation skill they can start to use it in nonanxious situations and progressively apply it in anxious circumstances as well. Cognitive restructuring aims to identify and modify negative, anxious thoughts and images. Psychologists can employ cognitive reconstructing with athletes to build positive viewpoints of their current problems. During sessions, if athletes continue to struggle with their problems, then practitioners may add other methods such as problem-solving, which refers to a direct focus on coping with the behavioral demands, and self-instructional training designed to build positive reinforcement. During the final stage of applying cognitive coping skills, practitioners should provide support and reward athletes' successful coping processes and efforts.

Conclusion

Helping athletes make successful transitions out of sport is not a simple process. Sport psychologists are sometimes approached months, and occasionally years, after athletes have ended their competitive careers for help with their transitions (Van Raalte & Andersen, 2007).

247

In some instances, it may also be the first time the athletes have sought a sport psychologist's help for any issue, transition-related or otherwise. The range of approaches reviewed in this chapter can assist sport psychology practitioners when working with athletes in transition. See Box 26.2 for some practical considerations from this chapter.

Box 26.2

Practical considerations for sport psychologists working with athletes who are dealing with career terminations

- Helping athletes cope with their career terminations is one of the most commonly encountered issues for sport psychology practitioners.
- A Life Development Intervention can help with developing: (a) coping strategies with athletes prior to retirement, (b) supportive strategies with athletes during the process of retirement, and (c) counseling strategies with athletes post-retirement.
- An account-making approach can be a useful framework for understanding and resolving distressful reactions to career termination.
- Mentoring can be useful in helping guide athletes through the career transition process.
- Emotional expression, cognitive therapy, rational-emotive behavior therapy, and stress inoculation training are recommended to facilitate career termination adjustment among athletes.

References

Alfermann, D., Stambulova, N., & Zemaityte, A. (2004). Reactions to sports career termination: A cross-cultural comparison of German, Lithuanian, and Russian athletes. *Psychology of Sport and Exercise, 5*, 61–75.

Anderson, D., & Morris, T. (2000). Athlete lifestyle programs. In D. Lavallee & P. Wylleman (Eds.), *Career transitions in sport: International perspectives* (pp. 59–81). Morgantown, WV: Fitness Information Technology.

Beck, A. T., & Weishaar, M. E. (2000). Cognitive therapy. In R. J. Corsini & D. Wedding (Eds.), *Current psychotherapies* (6th ed., pp. 241–272). Itasca, IL: F. E. Peacock.

Brooks, V., & Sikes, P. (1997). *The good mentor guide: Initial teacher education in secondary schools.* Buckingham, England: Open University Press.

Burke, R. J., McKeen, C. A., & McKenna, C. (1993). Correlates of mentoring in organizations: The mentor's perspective. *Psychological Reports, 72*, 883–896.

Classen, C., Koopman, C., Angell, K., & Spiegel, D. (1996). Coping styles associated with psychological adjustment to advanced breast cancer. *Health Psychology, 15*, 434–437.

Danish, S. J., Petitpas, A. J., & Hale, B. D. (1995). Psychological interventions: A life developmental model. In S. M. Murphy (Ed.), *Sport psychology interventions* (pp. 19–38). Champaign, IL: Human Kinetics.

Ellis, A. (2000). Rational emotive behavior therapy. In R. J. Corsini & D. Wedding (Eds.), *Current psychotherapies* (6th ed., pp. 168–204). Itasca, IL: F. E. Peacock.

Erikson. E. H. (1963). *Childhood and society.* New York: Norton.

Fernandez, A., Stephan, Y., & Fouquereau, E. (2006). Assessing reasons for sports career termination: Developing the Athletes' Retirement Decision Inventory. *Psychology of Sport and Exercise, 7,* 407–421.

Gordon, S., & Lavallee, D. (2004). Career transitions in competitive sport. In T. Morris & J. Summers (Eds.), *Sport psychology: Theory, applications and issues.* (2nd ed., pp. 584–610). Milton, QLD, Australia: Wiley.

Grove, J. R., Lavallee, D., Gordon, S., & Harvey, J. H. (1998). Account-making: A model for understanding and resolving distressful reactions to retirement from sport. *The Sport Psychologist, 12,* 52–67.

Harvey, J. H., Weber, A. L., & Orbuch, T. L. (1990). *Interpersonal accounts: A social psychological perspective.* Oxford, England: Blackwell.

Hawkins, K., & Blann, F. W. (1993). *Athlete/coach career development and transition.* Canberra, ACT, Australia: Australian Sports Commission.

Horowitz, M. J. (1986). *Stress response syndromes* (2nd ed.). Northvale, NJ: Aronson.

Jackson, S., Mayocchi, L., & Dover, J. (1998). Life after winning gold: II. Coping with change as an Olympic gold medalist. *The Sport Psychologist, 12,* 137–155.

Kennedy-Moor, E., & Watson, J. C. (1999). *Expressing emotion.* New York: Guilford Press.

Kram, K. E. (1992). *Mentoring at work.* London: Scott Foreman.

Lally, P. (2007). Identity and athletic retirement: A prospective study. *Psychology of Sport and Exercise, 8,* 85–99.

Lavallee, D. (2005). The effect of a life development intervention on sports career transition adjustment. *The Sport Psychologist, 19,* 193–202.

Lavallee, D., & Andersen, M. B. (2000). Leaving sport: Easing career transitions. In M. B. Andersen (Ed.), *Doing sport psychology* (pp. 249–261). Champaign, IL: Human Kinetics.

Lavallee, D., & Wylleman, P. (1999). Toward an instrument to assess the quality of adjustment to career transitions in sport: The British Athlete Lifestyle Assessment Needs in Career and Education (BALANCE) Scale. In V. Hosek, P. Tilinger, & L. Bilek (Eds.), *Psychology of sport and exercise: Enhancing the quality of life* (pp. 322–324). Prague, Czech Republic: Charles University.

Lavallee, D., Nesti, M., Borkeles, E., Cockerill, I., & Edge, A. (2000). Intervention strategies for athletes in transition. In D. Lavallee & P. Wylleman (Eds.), *Career transitions in sport: International perspectives* (pp. 111–130). Morgantown, WV: Fitness Information Technology.

Mayocchi, L., & Hanrahan, S. J. (2000). Transferable skills for career change. In D. Lavallee & P. Wylleman (Eds.), *Career transitions in sport: International perspectives* (pp. 95–110). Morgantown, WV: Fitness Information Technology.

Meichenbaum, D. H., & Deffenbacher, J. L. (1988). Stress inoculation training. *The Counseling Psychologist, 16,* 69–90.

Pennebaker, J. W. (1990). *Opening up.* New York: Morrow.

Perna, F. M., Zaichkowsky, L., & Bocknek, G. (1996). The association of mentoring with psychosocial development among male athletes at termination of college career. *Journal of Applied Sport Psychology, 8,* 76–88.

Petitpas, A. J., Giges, B., & Danish, S. J. (1999). The sport psychologist–athlete relationship: Implications for training. *The Sport Psychologist, 13,* 344–357.

Sinclair, D. A., & Orlick, T. (1993). Positive transitions from high-performance sport. *The Sport Psychologist, 7,* 138–150.

Van Raalte, J. L., & Andersen, M. B. (2007). When sport psychology consulting is a means to an end(ing): Roles and agendas when helping athletes leave their sports. *The Sport Psychologist, 21,* 227–242.

Wolff, R., & Lester, D. (1989). A theoretical basis for counseling the retired professional athlete. *Psychological Reports, 64,* 1043–1046.

Yalom, I. D. (1980). *Existential psychotherapy.* New York: Harper Collins.

27

Depression

Kate F. Hays

A grief without a pang, void, dark, and drear,
A stifled, drowsy, unimpassioned grief,
Which finds no natural outlet, no relief,
In a word, or sigh, or tear.
  Samuel Taylor Coleridge, *Dejection: An Ode*

Matt, a 47-year-old stock broker and runner, reluctantly sought treatment with a sport psychologist, on the recommendation of his sports medicine physician and physical therapist. During a race three months previously, he had been side-lined with a hamstring tear; recovery was both slower and more painful than he anticipated. He told the sport psychologist, "I don't know if this is going to help, but I can't think what else to do. I'm feeling empty, like a shell of myself. I'm tired all the time – I think that's because I sleep for about three hours and then spend the rest of the night going over all the things I have to do or didn't do. When I get to work, I can't focus. When I'm at home, my kids just irritate me. I know I should be enjoying my son's soccer prowess but right now I just don't care. I don't even care if I run ever again – and that was always my great passion in life."

The poem by Coleridge, and Matt's presentation, illustrate the essence of the emotional, cognitive, and behavioral manifestations of major depressive disorder (MDD) or unipolar depression. An acute depressive episode involves changes – in thoughts, feelings, and behaviors – from previous functioning. A person is diagnosed with MDD under the following conditions: for at least a two-week period, the person has had either depressed mood or loss of interest or pleasure in most activities. Additionally, during that same time the person has experienced at least four of the following: significant changes in weight or appetite; changes in sleep patterns (especially early morning awakening, without being able to return to sleep); psychomotor agitation or retardation; fatigue or loss of energy; feelings of worthlessness or unreasonable guilt; problems with concentration, indecisiveness; recurrent thoughts regarding death or suicide.

More generally classified under the rubric of mood disorders, MDD is differentiated from a number of other mood disorders: mania, at the other end of the mood spectrum; swings between mania and depression, formerly known as manic-depressive disorder but currently described as bipolar disorder; or dysthymic disorder, involving chronic or persistent depressed mood but fewer of the cognitive, affective, and vegetative symptoms mentioned above. Other manifestations of depression include seasonal affective disorder, post-partum depression, and further variants that reflect the frequency, intensity, and/or duration of episodes.

Differential diagnosis

> Grief is depression in proportion to circumstance; depression is grief out of proportion to circumstance. ... Grief is a humble angel who leaves you with strong, clear thoughts and a sense of your own depth. Depression is a demon who leaves you appalled.
>
> Andrew Solomon, *The Noonday Demon*

At different times, everyone experiences difficulties. Losses are an aspect of being alive; to be human is to suffer at least some of the time. In the quote above, though, Andrew Solomon highlighted some of the differences between "ordinary" sadness, loss, or grief as compared to depression. Depression is disproportionate to the precipitating circumstance; to the extent that depressed people feel "depth," they also feel unable to haul themselves out of those depths. Loss, bereavement, or grief involves tangible deprivation. Although loss may precipitate or co-occur with depression, ultimately, depression can be differentiated from sadness by the number, extent, and/or duration of the symptoms.

For athletes, or those who work with athletes, it is important to distinguish between depression and overtraining or burnout. Symptoms of overtraining include such mental characteristics as depressed mood, irritability, and decreased sleep. Overtraining can be differentiated from MDD in that there is both evidence of a specific precipitant (intensive training over a prolonged period of time) and a direct method of assessment: if a marked decrease in training results in a reduction of the depressive symptom cluster, most likely the issue was overtraining (see Chapter 31 in this book).

Co-morbidities and depression

Depression is not necessarily a stand-alone disorder. Anxiety disorders and substance abuse may be present along with depressive disorders (Kessler, Berglund, Demler, Jin, & Walters, 2005). Some people "self-medicate" for their depressive feelings, typically with alcohol or other substances. Because alcohol is itself a depressant, however, this attempt at a solution may further compound the problem. Also, a complex interaction exists between eating disorders and depression (see Chapter 24 in this book).

Depression can also be one characteristic or symptom of other diagnostic issues, such as traumatic brain injury or post-traumatic stress disorder (PTSD). Among chronically ill patients or those recovering from acute medical illnesses, depression may play an integral role in the course of illness and recovery (Ebmeier, Donaghey, & Steele, 2006).

Incidence, prevalence, and risk factors

> Depression has always been for me, and remains, a self-punishing language, a prolonged sensation of filthiness and worthlessness, of embarrassment at being alive;

251

a sickening deadness I enviously compare to the liveliness other people seem to enjoy.

John Bentley Mays, *In the Jaws of the Black Dogs:*
A Memoir of Depression

MDD affects approximately 16% of U.S. adults at least once in their lifetimes (Gartlehner *et al.*, 2007). Major depression is increasingly diagnosed: During 1991–92 in the USA, 3.3% of the adult population was diagnosed with MDD; in 2001–02, the percentage was 7.1%, more than double that of ten years earlier. These increases were consistent across almost all socio-demographic population sub-groups (Compton, Conway, Stinson, & Grant, 2006).

MDD affects the ways in which people feel, think, and behave. It is thus not surprising that well over 50% of MDD patients experience role impairment (Ebmeier *et al.*, 2006). The financial as well as emotional costs are enormous: major depressive disorder is the leading cause of disability among people ages 15–44 in the USA (World Health Organization, 2004).

Women are twice as likely as men to experience depression (Ebmeier *et al.*, 2006), probably due to an interaction of social, economic, biological, and emotional factors (McGrath, Keita, Strickland, & Russo, 1990). Rates of depression also vary in relation to age, cultural and ethnic differences, and various other demographic characteristics.

Depression is a high-risk factor for suicide. Although many people with major depression do not contemplate, attempt, or commit suicide, more than half of the people who commit suicide were experiencing a mood disorder. Women attempt suicide at least twice as often as men, but four times as many men as women die as a result of suicide (Weissman *et al.*, 1999).

For both men and women, the primary risk factors for an episode of depression include: certain personality traits, drug and alcohol abuse, acute and chronic stress, traumatic experiences (including childhood traumas), a family history of depression, and a previous depressive episode.

Athletes and depression

Although athletes tend in general to be healthy, they are not immune from depression. Because of its frequency and ubiquity, depression has been described as the "common cold" of mental disorders (Andersen, 2002). Elite and sub-elite athletes often experience substantial stress both within sport (e.g., performance pressures, coach–athlete conflicts) and in their everyday lives (e.g., work, school, family expectations). Managing all these demands may be taxing. Because of their sport involvement, ironically, athletes may in some ways be at risk for depression (e.g., the risk of injury, the stress of handling injury recovery and rehabilitation). Psychological adjustment to injuries and rehabilitation management can be strongly influenced by athletes' appraisals of their abilities to cope with their injuries, their attributions of the injuries' causes, and their levels of confidence in full recovery. Further, the interaction of injury and depression can have a direct effect on the process of injury rehabilitation (for a case example of treatment of an athlete with injury-related depression, see Brewer & Petitpas, 2005).

Diagnosis and treatment

Depression was a very active state really. Even if you appeared to an observer to be immobilized, your mind was in a frenzy of paralysis. You were unable to function, but were actively despising yourself for it.

Lisa Alther, *Kinflicks*

Depression is generally diagnosed by subjective account or others' reports or observations, because no laboratory tests have been developed to measure its presence. Beginning in the 1960s, a number of rating and self-rating scales were developed, designed to assess both the presence and the severity of symptoms. Among those scales most frequently used are the Hamilton Depression Rating Scale, the Beck Depression Inventory (BDI), the Symptom Checklist–90, and the Zung Self-Rating Depression Scale. Although self-rating scales are rife with a number of potential errors and inaccuracies, as general screening devices these measures operate somewhat like a thermometer: They indicate the presence and intensity of various somatic, behavioral, affective, and cognitive symptoms.

A number of types and kinds of treatment are available in the management of depression. Medication and/or psychotherapy are the most common.

Psychotropic medication

Medication designed specifically to treat depression was initially developed in the 1950s. Now described as first-generation antidepressants, tricyclic antidepressants (TCAs) are still prescribed. So-called second generation drugs include selective serotonin reuptake inhibitors (SSRIs) and serotonin and nor-epinephrine reuptake inhibitors (SNRIs). Currently, SSRIs and SNRIs are more typically prescribed for the treatment of depression; they may have fewer negative side effects and carry fewer risks than TCAs. In general, research has shown that these second-generation antidepressants have similar rates of effectiveness (Gartlehner et al., 2007).

Psychotherapy for depression

Psychoanalytic and psychodynamic treatment

Sigmund Freud developed psychoanalysis at the turn of the twentieth century: It is both a theory and a method of therapy. As currently practised, psychodynamic psychotherapy is a verbal, intensive, long-term treatment that addresses the underlying sources of a person's problems: understanding or insight is considered central to behavior change. One shorthand version of the psychodynamic understanding of depression is that it is "anger turned inward." For a case example of a depressed athlete, illustrating the use of psychodynamic therapy (in conjunction with other psychotherapy methods), see Cogan (2000).

Cognitive-behavioral therapy (CBT)

CBT came of age with the original 1979 publication of psychiatrist Aaron Beck's (and colleagues') Cognitive Therapy of Depression (see Beck, Rush, Shaw, & Emery, 1987). In contrast to earlier theories and therapies, CBT posits that depressive symptoms and behaviors are the result of dysfunctional beliefs and thoughts. By examining and challenging those negative assumptions and engaging in cognitive restructuring, positive changes in thought and behavior can result.

Mindful attention without judgment

Whereas psychodynamic treatment focuses on affect and CBT on faulty cognitions, researchers and practitioners have noted that attention to cognitions and affect, without judgment, can have profound therapeutic effects. This perspective of nonjudgmental attention is central to acceptance therapy, dialectical behavior therapy, and most recently, mindfulness treatment specifically in regard to depression. Mindfulness-based cognitive therapy (MBCT), developed as a synthesis of mindfulness-based stress reduction (MBSR) and principles and practices of cognitive therapy, is characterized as a "combination of Western cognitive science and Eastern practices" (Williams, Teasdale, Segal, & Kabat-Zinn, 2007, p. 5). MBCT has been found especially effective in the prevention of further relapse for patients with three or more episodes of depression.

Physical activity

Depression is an inter-related function of negative mood and negative thought, described as mood congruence (Thayer, 2001). When people are depressed (mood), they tend to remember and focus on the negative things that have happened to them (negative cognitions). This interaction may be directional. If low energy produces negative cognitions (rather than negative cognitions resulting in low energy), increased energy associated with physical activity can serve, at least, a moderating function with regard to negative thoughts (Thayer, 2001).

Beginning in the 1920s, researchers began studying exercise as a low-cost, effective alternative to medication or psychotherapy for the treatment of depression – and one that does not have negative side effects. A number of analyses and meta-analyses (e.g., Landers & Arent, 2001) consistently report at least moderate effect sizes for exercise in reducing depression.

Although seemingly too simple a treatment for a syndrome as serious and complex as depression, the prescription of exercise has increasingly gained legitimacy. Recent research suggests that there may even be a dose-response relationship (i.e., more exercise may result in more improvement). Dunn and colleagues (2005) conducted a randomized study of four aerobic exercise treatment groups, varying the frequency and intensity of exercise among a group of 80 adults diagnosed with mild to moderate MDD. After 12 weeks, those exercising at higher levels of intensity showed more significant recovery than those on a lower dose.

Physical activity is a particularly valuable treatment method for certain vulnerable populations. Depressed older adults, for example, have become significantly less depressed when treated with aerobic exercise (Penninx et al., 2002). Because of the ways in which exercise is related to increased self-esteem and empowerment, exercise appears to be a useful treatment option for depressed women. Vasquez (2002) found support for this relationship in work with Latinas.

Comparisons of therapies

Because a number of treatment options exist, research has been conducted comparing different forms or methods of treatment. Medications have been compared with each other; different methods of psychotherapy, likewise, have been compared with each other; and comparisons have been made between types of treatments.

Within a medical model, psychotherapy is typically relegated to the treatment of milder depression or, for more severe depression, as an adjunct to antidepressant medication (Ebmeier et al., 2006). Other models point to the usefulness of, for example, MBCT compared with anti-depressant medication in terms of relapse prevention, even in the face of discontinuation of medication (Kuyken et al., 2008).

As Cuijpers, van Straten, Andersson, and van Oppen (2008) noted, "[M]ost effects of psychological treatments are caused by common, nonspecific factors and not by particular techniques. These common factors include: the therapeutic alliance between therapist and client, belief in the treatment, and a clear rationale explaining why the client has developed the problem" (p. 909).

Various studies of exercise, as compared with psychotherapy, have consistently found exercise to be a robust intervention for the treatment of depression (Hays, 1999; Johnsgard, 2004). Recently, comparisons of exercise with the use of SSRIs in depressed elderly patients has, again, suggested that exercise is an important and legitimate method of treatment for a wide range of depression (Babyak *et al.*, 2000).

A model of evidence-based practice suggests that the best treatment for any one individual will take into account the research that informs practice, the clinician's various sources of knowledge, and the attitudes, beliefs, and culture of the client (Goodheart, Kazdin, & Sternberg, 2006). This third element, often overlooked, is critical to successful treatment, particularly when changes both to that client's thoughts and moods are involved.

Treatment of depression: the case of Matt

> Depression sits on my chest like a sumo wrestler.
> Sandra Scoppettone, *I'll Be Leaving You Always*

In the short vignette about the runner Matt, which opened this chapter, I was his sport psychologist. A tall, lanky man, Matt exuded an air of somber hopelessness. As if an invisible cloak cut him off from human connection, he sat dejected, responsive to questions but initiating little. Dutifully, he completed a screening tool, the BDI. He admitted that at times, thoughts of being dead were appealing; nonetheless, though he felt that he was dragging himself through life, he had not considered suicide.

Matt was the eldest of three children in an intact family. The children were acutely aware that they should not disturb their mother on the days when she sat utterly still in a darkened room. Matt recalled that his mother had undergone three unexplained hospitalizations. Now as an adult, he surmised that those hospitalizations were for depression.

In high school, and then at university, Matt focused heavily on studying, broken only by his intense involvement and success in track and field. Following graduation, he worked successively at two brokerage firms and was considered a reliable and productive employee. Marrying in his late thirties, he had a stable, if unexciting, relationship with his wife. He surprised himself by the level of his involvement in his children's lives, especially that of his eldest son. During his university years, Matt had felt overwhelmed at times, but he had never experienced this current level of emptiness and despair.

We reviewed his history of running. Taking up running again shortly after his marriage, he enjoyed long solitary runs that prepared him for three marathons a year. He recognized that in addition to the physical benefits, running was critically important to his self-definition; it also might have been important in staving off depression. During this period of injury and recovery, Matt had not explored any other form of exercise.

I focused on three primary tasks in our initial interview: understanding his current symptoms and obtaining relevant history, to form an initial diagnosis and treatment plan; establishing rapport; and initiating some treatment recommendations and suggestions. During this first interview, I asked specific questions and took notes. I responded to Matt's bewilderment and discomfort with careful reflection and explanation of my understanding of his experience.

I concluded the interview by discussing with Matt my diagnostic impression. Based on his symptoms, history, self-presentation, and the BDI results, he appeared to be clinically depressed. I outlined for him what I saw as a likely course of treatment and anticipated outcomes.

Pointing out that the root of his depression might include some genetic factors, I noted that he had a choice of two biochemical-altering treatment options: medication or exercise. Matt was adamant that he did not want to take psychotropic medication. He had been cleared to begin running again, although initially at many fewer miles per week than prior to his injury. He said that he hadn't started running. The task felt too effortful, and he felt too tired. Looking back at other times when he had sustained minor injuries and returned to running, he recalled that once he got started, the process wasn't as arduous as it now felt. He committed to two runs, at the recommended distance, over the next week. I also suggested that he notice his mood both before and after the run (Hays, 1999). Using a 10-point scale, he recorded those two numbers in his BlackBerry. Although Matt was not enthusiastic about swimming, he agreed to check out his local pool and swim once, at least, and use the mood-rating scale for the swim as well.

Matt's problem with sleep was also pivotal in relation to his recovery. We reviewed some elements of sleep hygiene. Additionally, he was intrigued by an initial explanation and demonstration of diaphragmatic breathing for deep relaxation as well as methods for mind-clearing.

Matt was not hopeful at this point, but he left the session with a clearer understanding, less distrust about the process, some specific plans, and a sense of direction. We scheduled a follow-up session for a week later.

At that session, Matt reported two nights of improved sleep: even when awake during the night, diaphragmatic breathing allowed him to drift peacefully. He had complied with the exercise plan. He was surprised that the run was less painful than he had anticipated. He had known intellectually that running improved his mood, but was startled to note that even with a short run, his sense of well-being had shifted 3 points each time. In contrast, even though swimming was of cardiovascular use, it had less effect on his mood.

During this session, we began working much more directly on some of Matt's thoughts and beliefs about himself – his self-statements, capacity to catastrophize and to anticipate dire consequences. We framed out a simple thought record that he could use to record his cognitions. He also was willing to begin making use of "worry time" (30 minutes per day designated specifically for worrying) to contain negative thoughts and anticipations. With plans for a business trip the following week, we scheduled the next appointment for two weeks thence.

Over the next three months, Matt returned for five subsequent appointments. He saw our work together as a collaborative project. His negative bias about psychotherapy decreased; he even encouraged a friend to seek help. He returned to running on the schedule suggested by the physical therapist and supplemented the running with swimming and light weights. Although never enthusiastic about these latter forms of exercise, he recognized that they were helpful physiological adjuncts to his training. Additionally, he appreciated their psychophysiological benefit. Both improved his mood and served as place-markers that kept him from overtraining with running.

Sleep returned fairly rapidly, aided no doubt by the increase in energy expenditure through exercise. Matt developed an ongoing plan for worry time – and built it into his daily schedule of activities. Through the regular use of the thought record, he came to recognize his tendency to anticipate the most dire of consequences. Over time, he learned a number of methods to deal with his thoughts. He could dismiss irrelevant thoughts, challenge and counter them, or use his worry time to explore and resolve troubling issues.

Re-engaging with his family, Matt again took interest in his son's soccer prowess. His daughter and he developed a special weekly time during which he would run while she biked beside him. He incorporated these sessions into his schedule to return to racing. His score on the BDI at this time indicated minimal levels of depression.

Matt recognized the probable genetic component to his depression and the need to actively monitor his tendency toward depression. He contacted me about 18 months later, at a point when his sleep was again becoming disrupted due to new pressures at work. Within a few sessions, Matt was able to re-stabilize his thoughts and emotions and remind himself of the methods that had previously served him well. For future reference, he wrote out a letter to himself of lessons he had learned and made a list of the mental tools he could use, on a continual basis through his life, to retain his equilibrium.

Conclusion

Depression is a complex interaction of thoughts, feelings, and behavior, one of the most frequently diagnosed disorders of mental health. Although all of us feel depressed at times, MDD is characterized by specific symptoms occurring over a period of time and with a certain depth. MDD is diagnosed through a combination of self-report and observation. Because of their general health, physical activity, and sense of purpose, athletes may be somewhat less vulnerable to depression but are by no means immune. Ironically, a number of the symptoms of athletic overtraining are also those characteristic of depression. Various treatment options for MDD include: psychotropic medication, psychotherapy, and physical activity, alone or in combination. In general, people experiencing MDD can be treated effectively; as well, treatment often decreases the likelihood of relapse. See Box 27.1 for take-home messages from this chapter.

Box 27.1

Take-home messages on depression

- Major depressive disorder (MDD) may be caused by any one or a combination of genetic, biochemical, intrapsychic, or situational factors.
- Depression can be differentiated from loss or grief by characteristic symptoms and the number, extent, or duration of these symptoms.
- Depression affects approximately 1/6 of the population at some time in their lives; during any one year, 7% of the population may experience depression.
- A person may experience a number of mental health issues at any one time; depression may also be a symptom of other problems.
- Although exercise is an important component in the prevention of depression as well as its treatment, overtraining can produce symptoms of depression.
- Athletes may be less likely to become depressed, but they are not immune to depression. Various stressors, including performance expectations, the management of weight or injury, and intense interpersonal relationships may increase the risk.

> ▪ A number of treatments for depression exist, including psychotropic medication, psychotherapy, and exercise. The best treatment for a particular person should be based on a combination of relevant research, clinical knowledge, and the client's attitudes, beliefs, and culture.

References

Andersen, M. B. (2002). Helping college student-athletes in and out of sport. In J. L. Van Raalte & B. W. Brewer (Eds.), *Exploring sport and exercise psychology* (2nd ed., pp. 373–394). Washington, DC: American Psychological Association.

Babyak, M., Blumenthal, J. A., Herman, S., Khatri, P., Doraiswamy, M., Moore, K., Craighead, E., Baldewicz, T. T., & Krishman, K. R. (2000). Exercise treatment for major depression: Maintenance of therapeutic benefit at 10 months. *Psychosomatic Medicine, 62*, 633–638.

Beck, A. T., Rush, J., Shaw, B. F., & Emery, G. (1987). *Cognitive therapy of depression.* New York: Guilford Press.

Brewer, B. W., & Petitpas, A. J. (2005). Returning to self: The anxieties of coming back after injury. In M. B. Andersen (Ed.). *Sport psychology in practice* (pp. 93–108). Champaign, IL: Human Kinetics.

Cogan, K. D. (2000). The sadness in sport: Working with a depressed and suicidal athlete. In M. B. Andersen (Ed.), *Doing sport psychology* (pp. 107–119). Champaign, IL: Human Kinetics.

Compton, W. M., Conway, K. P., Stinson, F. S., & d Grant, B. F. (2006). Changes in the prevalence of major depression and comorbid substance use disorders in the United States between 1991–1992 and 2001–2002. *American Journal of Psychiatry, 163*, 2141–2147.

Cuijpers, P., van Straten, A., Andersson, G., & van Oppen, P. (2008). Psychotherapy for depression in adults: A meta-analysis of comparative outcome studies. *Journal of Consulting and Clinical Psychology, 76*, 909–972.

Dunn, A. L., Trivedi, M. H., Kampert, J. B., Clark, C. G., Chambliss, H. O. (2005). Exercise treatment for depression: Efficacy and dose response. *American Journal of Preventive Medicine, 28*, 1–8.

Ebmeier, K. P., Donaghey, C., & Steele, J. D. (2006). Recent developments and current controversies in depression. *Lancet, 367*, 153–167.

Gartlehner, G., Hansen, R. A., Thieda, P., DeVeaugh-Geiss, A. M., Gaynes, B. N., Krebs, E. E., Lux, L. J., Morgan, L. C., Shumate, J. A., Monroe, L. G. & Lohr, K. N. (2007). *Comparative effectiveness of second-generation antidepressants in the pharmacologic treatment of adult depression.* Rockville, MD: Agency for Healthcare Research and Quality. AHRQ Publication No. 07-EHC007-EF

Goodheart, C. D., Kazdin, A. E., & Sternberg, R. J. (Eds.). (2006). *Evidence-based psychotherapy: Where practice and research meet.* Washington, DC: American Psychological Association.

Hays, K. F. (1999). *Working it out: Using exercise in psychotherapy.* Washington, DC: American Psychological Association.

Johnsgard, K. (2004). *Conquering depression & anxiety through exercise.* Amherst, NY: Prometheus.

Kessler, R. C., Berglund, P. A., Demler, O., Jin, R., & Walters, E. E. (2005). Lifetime prevalence and age-of-onset distributions of DSM-IV disorders in the National Comorbidity Survey Replication (NCS-R). *Archives of General Psychiatry, 62*, 593–602.

Kuyken, W., Byford, S., Taylor, R. S., Watkins, E., Holden, E., White, K., Barrett, B. M., Byng, R., Evans, A., Mullan, E. & Teasdale, J. D. (2008). Mindfulness-based cognitive therapy to prevent relapse in recurrent depression. *Journal of Consulting & Clinical Psychology, 76*, 966–78.

Landers, D. M., & Arent, S. M. (2001). Physical activity and mental health. In R. N. Singer, H. A. Hausenblas, & C. M. Janelle (Eds.) *Handbook of sport psychology* (2nd ed., pp. 740–765). New York: Wiley.

McGrath, E., Keita, G. P., Strickland, B. R., & Russo, N. F. (1990). *Women and depression.* Washington, DC: American Psychological Association.

Penninx, B. W., Rejeski, W. J., Pandya, J., Miller, M. E., Di Bari, M., Applegate, W. B., & Pahor, M. (2002). Exercise and depressive symptoms: A comparison of aerobic and resistance exercise effects on emotional and physical function in older persons with high and low depressive symptomatology. *The Journals of Gerontology Series B: Psychological Sciences and Social Sciences, 57,* 124–132.

Thayer, R. E. (2001). *Calm energy: How people regulate mood with food and exercise.* New York: Oxford University Press.

Vasquez, M. J. T. (2002). Latinas: Exercise and empowerment from a feminist psychodynamic perspective. In R. L. Hall & C. A. Oglesby (Eds.), *Exercise and sport in feminist therapy: Constructing modalities and assessing outcomes* (pp. 23–38). Binghamton, NY: Haworth.

Weissman, M. M., Bland, R. C., Canino, G. J., Greenwald, S., Hwu, H.-G., Joyce, P. R., Karam, G., Lee, C. K., Lellouch, J., Lepine, J. P., Newman, S. C., Rubio-Stepic, M., Wells, J. E., Wickramaratne, P. J., Wittchen, H.-U., & Yeh, E. K. (1999). Prevalence of suicide ideation and suicide attempts in nine countries. *Psychological Medicine, 29,* 9–17.

Williams, M., Teasdale, J., Segal, Z. & Kabat-Zinn, J. (2007). *The mindful way through depression.* New York: Guilford Press.

World Health Organization. (2004). *The World Health Report 2004: Changing history, Annex Table 3: Burden of disease in DALYs by cause, sex, and mortality stratum in WHO regions, estimates for 2002.* Geneva, Switzerland: World Health Organization.

28

Anxiety

Daryl B. Marchant

> *Daryl, I want you to walk down the end of the street and meet Julie [older sister] on her way home from school. There is a dog, and she's a bit scared of it; she'll feel much better if you're there to walk her past that part.*
>
> Merle Marchant, circa 1964

The above quote might not be word perfect. My prevailing recollection of the underlying meaning was, "You're a big brave boy, and your five-year-old sister, who is scared of being bitten by the nasty local dog, needs your help." Never mind that I was only four years old, without dog experience, and apparently on the verge of transforming from the unconditioned response of "no fear of dogs" to the conditioned response of a lifelong trepidation and avoidance of anything remotely canine. Amazing, what was my Mum thinking!? Clearly, she had not been subjected to the usual undergraduate psychology learning theory. A bell isn't needed to make a dog salivate; a small child on a fool's errand will do equally well. Nowadays, I don't necessarily walk to the other side of the street when I see a large dog coming my way; I run (only joking). Seriously though, I have never since felt comfortable around dogs and generally avoid them. I mention the story because it is the first I can remember of experiencing anxiety, and because, even some 45 years later, it is vividly etched in my memory. The adage that psychologists enter psychology in an attempt to better understand themselves certainly resonates for me in that I was a relatively anxious child.

Although I will focus largely on sport and competition anxiety in this chapter, the dog story is a reminder that we are all faced with anxiety-evoking situations from an early age. This chapter is largely concerned with working through the process of counseling, including the initial referral or discussion of anxiety with an athlete and the many issues and questions that will inform the work. The questions, issues, and challenges that practitioners and clients negotiate are the main focus here.

Introduction

In reflecting on approximately 50 years of continuous sport anxiety investigations, there was a naïve quality to the early research with uni-dimensional models developed, reworked, and then eventually superseded by more complex, yet similarly inadequate models. A sign of the growing maturity of the field of sport psychology was when researchers took the lead from mainstream psychology and started examining sport anxiety as a multi-dimensional phenomenon. Currently, there is a diverse range of published literature compared to the early research that was largely experimental and quasi-experimental conducted from a narrow quantitative paradigm. I have written this chapter from a practitioner's perspective, and the focus is largely on working through how we might frame our collaborations with anxious athletes. Rather than explaining the fundamentals of anxiety theories, I only touch on the models used in the research in the context of theory informing practice. Undoubtedly, a sport psychology practitioner must have at least a passing understanding of the vast sport anxiety literature. For early career sport psychologists, in particular, there is considerable value in reviewing the key or hallmark sport anxiety papers (e.g., Martens, 1971). Experienced practitioners also sometimes need reminding that new approaches and critical knowledge are regularly being developed and published, and staying abreast of such developments is professionally enriching.

Framing anxiety: complexities in working with anxious athletes

In sport psychology, we are often working in the context of athletes or organizations wanting quick-fix solutions. Sometimes, there is a simple solution; a reliance on quick or generic approaches, however, can trivialize the work. Our training and experience should enable us to provide individualized anxiety interventions that represent state-of-the-art in relation to the currently available evidence in our field.

By the time an athlete seeks or requests help for an anxiety-related issue, there is usually a rich history of unsuccessful (or partially successful) attempts to cope with anxiety. This history needs to be respected and used where applicable. Often, in trainee sport psychologists, I see an overeagerness to move to solutions, treatments, and interventions without fully understanding the personal history and appreciating the unique perspectives and experiences that each client brings to therapy. Perhaps this tendency is borne from practitioners' anxieties around their own skills or insecurities about working in an open framework. Irrespective of the reasons, to provide meaningful solutions for athletes and coaches, superficial or abbreviated processes are generally suboptimal and may have quick, but not long-lasting effects.

Applied sport psychologists can enhance the likelihood of positive outcomes by intentionally managing the working relationship (see Chapter 1) from the outset. Each time we commit to working with a client we embark on a journey together. This journey might be over almost before it begins, unless we attend to some basic, yet essential steps. Many years ago an academic sport psychologist talking about his applied work said to me, "I don't know what it is with clients, but many of them only show up for the first couple of consultations." Although clients can be unreliable, there was clearly an unrecognized problem with how the sport psychologist was framing his work at the outset. Setting-up includes: the initial contact or referral process, managing the working space, introductions, first impressions, sharing expectations, and developing a working alliance. Each step deserves careful consideration, and, when done well will lead to a positive climate for working together, but when done poorly will result in obstruction, confusion, or sabotage of the working relationship.

Logistics and practicalities almost always influence the approaches we take and how we deliver our services. How has the client been referred? Who is funding the services? Is the athlete in season or in a pre-season phase? In what type of environment will the consultations take place (e.g., office, coffee shop/café, sporting venue)? There is little sense planning a lengthy series of psycho-educational sessions when time, resources, or other issues preclude the likelihood of the full intervention being delivered. Poor attention or awareness of practicalities can hijack the working alliance and undermine the practitioners' confidence and clients' motivation to commit to working through the issues.

Because anxiety in sport is multifaceted, exploration or data-gathering is foundational. Most sport psychologists, because of their research and applied training, will feel relatively comfortable in this exploration phase. The initial intake will generally start with demographic, personal, and sport background and at some point move to the presenting anxiety-related issue. Exploration will not only entail polished counseling skills (e.g., attending, active listening, empathic reflection), but also working with anxiety through linking related themes such as stress, arousal, coping, and past history of anxiety experiences. Fortunately, there is an enormous amount of published literature available on sport anxiety, but the sheer volume of literature can be intimidating. Sport psychology researchers have constantly proposed and tested relevant models ranging from arousal-performance explanations to multidimensional anxiety theory. Without a reasonable understanding of the many conceptual advances that have occurred in sport anxiety research, the practitioner's efforts will most likely lead to limited positive (or even negative) outcomes. Leonardo da Vinci's (n.d.) observation that "he who loves practice without theory is like the sailor who boards a ship without a rudder and compass and never knows where he may cast" is relevant here. For busy consulting psychologists engrossed in applied work, it can be a challenge to stay abreast of the published literature.

Getting a handle on the causes and effects of sport anxiety

A central purpose of the exploration process is to jointly discuss, sometimes in considerable detail, anxiety experiences and anxiety-related issues. I liken sport anxiety work to solving a jigsaw puzzle. Rarely are we are faced with a simple 200-piece puzzle, often the puzzle is, metaphorically, 1,000 pieces or more of a relatively unexplored landscape. The simple puzzle might suit neophyte sport psychologists who, being somewhat anxious themselves, are looking to apply basic theory and interventions in a relatively straightforward manner. More experienced and skilled practitioners might be drawn to 1,000-piece anxiety puzzles with unfamiliar terrain, complications, contradictions, and entrenched resistances. Undue haste in moving toward possible solutions without thorough exploration can be counterproductive. In looking for guidance in the types of issues worthy of deeper exploration, the published literature is particularly helpful. Quality research is available in peer reviewed journals relating to virtually all the exploration issues that, for brevity, are simply listed below:

■ Susceptibility, underling causes, triggers, and context (sporting task, level of competition, or environment) – possible parallels in general and other performance domains, state-trait anxiety indicators, defining events, external factors, assessing associated anxiety clusters (e.g., arousal, stress, fear, pressure, self-consciousness, choking, yips);

- Effects – the range of cognitive, somatic, and behavioral manifestations, acute/chronic anxiety, performance facilitation and debilitation, directional interpretations, emotional and motivational consequences;
- Maintenance factors – conscious and unconscious motivation to not resolve anxiety-related issues, role of significant others, environments;
- Coping resources – social and environmental support, coping style, resilience;
- Other factors – personal insight, attempts to self-manage anxiety, personality (e.g., neuroticism), knowledge, evidence of overlapping sport psychology themes (e.g., concentration, self-talk, self-confidence, attributions), understanding and expectations of applied sport psychology assistance.

Sport psychologists borrow the term *treatment* from mainstream psychology, but the term sometimes carries unhelpful connotations, and the word *assistance* might be preferable. There are no definitive lines around where treatment begins. For example, we need to acknowledge that the process of talking about anxiety-related issues, and being heard by an understanding professional, are beneficial for many clients, albeit anxiety-inducing in the short term only. Depending on the approach taken, the talking might even constitute the central feature of the therapy (e.g., narrative therapy). With sport anxiety work there is quite a range of available treatments, programs, techniques, and interventions. The sport psychology literature is replete with research and evidence about the efficacy of treatments. Most practitioners are aware of frequently used approaches such as progressive muscle relaxation, meditation, breathing exercises, autogenic training, and the suite of cognitive-behavioral methods (e.g., rational–emotive behavior therapy, stress inoculation training). A common theme for the neophyte practitioner is the sometimes unrealistic expectations, and occasionally blind faith, accorded to what amounts to packaged treatment programs without due care in individualizing the treatment in the context of the client's particular needs.

Depending on our psychological orientations, the approaches and interventions can differ substantially. Much of the published sport anxiety literature is essentially cognitive-behavioral with infrequent smatterings of alternative approaches. Our frame of reference might be limited because of the paucity of published sport psychology intervention literature reflecting broader perspectives (e.g., humanistic, existential, psychodynamic, narrative).

Hearing the client's story

A number of practical issues warrant further consideration including: psychological orientation or paradigm, practitioners' professional range and skills, integration of client skills, practical considerations, supervision, mentoring, and professional support. Often our approach to therapy is not only guided by our own preferences and expertise but also the working time frame. Athletes who have the time, resources, and patience to commit to long-term therapy are rare.

An initial challenge for the practitioner is in fostering a working alliance whereby negative emotions, such as anxiety, can be discussed openly, authentically, and non-judgmentally. There are some athletes who are especially candid about the effects that their anxieties are having on their sports performances, enjoyment, and their sense of satisfaction. My overriding experience is that athletes, for a range of reasons, tend to minimize the effects of their anxieties. Anxiety, for many athletes, is linked with negative memories, associations, and experiences that can be mentally difficult to share and reconstruct openly. Furthermore, associated emotions of shame, guilt, and embarrassment are often close at hand. Barriers to open disclosure may impede our progress or frustrate our attempts to help athletes. These barriers might represent a lack of trust or confidence in the sport psychologist or in sport psychology. Barriers might also stem from inner struggles to fully acknowledge anxiety, fears of admitting what might be perceived as a weakness, or poor timing with athletes (for myriad reasons) not wanting to work through the issue at present. Also, sometimes athletes unrealistically desire an abbreviated consulting exchange with the hope of a quick outcome in keeping with pressing competition commitments.

A competing athlete is often attempting, simultaneously, to manage the impinging anxiety and trying to foster a positive mindset, whereby negative thoughts and emotions are downplayed. In working with anxiety, we frequently rely on the retrospective recall of clients that, although not deliberately distorted, often entails elements of impression management that diminish the conscious acceptance and verbalization of anxiety. Unless the anxiety is severe and essentially crippling in terms of performance, the reality is that many athletes do not seek professional support.

At some point, usually in the intake session, the client will start to raise anxiety-related themes. Although it may be tempting to dive right into a detailed account of anxiety issues, generally I continue the intake consult taking note of other topics of therapeutic interest. Once I have established the athlete is being affected by anxiety or related issues (e.g., stress, arousal, poor coping), I will start to devise a plan within a particular framework. Another series of self-questions are salient at this point. What approach should I take to fully understand the etiology of the anxiety? For example, will a case history focused on anxiety-inducing events be useful? To what extent are others (e.g., coaches, parents, partners) involved in terms of instigating, reinforcing, understanding, or managing the anxiety? How does the pattern of anxiety being presented fit with examples from previous consultations? What level of self-insight is the client displaying? How do the issues being raised fit with the vast body of available anxiety research including performance-arousal theories, underlying causes and effects of anxiety, multidimensional anxiety theory, and treatment choices? What broad theoretical approach (e.g., cognitive-behavioral, psychodynamic) will frame the treatment? Will observation of the athlete training or competing be useful in understanding how this athlete experiences anxiety? Would administering any of the available anxiety-related tests add to the assessment? These questions and others might best fit under the general aim of what to me is "dwelling in the problem." That is, gathering information, reflecting, observing, developing, and testing tentative hypotheses.

The Edmonton fog: the palpitating effects of anxiety with rifle shooters

When completing my master's research at the University of Alberta in the early 1990s, I was working with a small group of rifle shooters. I had the good fortune to be collecting heart-rate data during the Canadian National Championships when, prior to the first round, a dense fog descended on the shooting range. The ensuing 30 minutes of observation taught me plenty about the realities of anxiety and the range of individual responses. The targets became almost impossible to distinguish at 50 meters; the shooters became anxious, and heart rates escalated. Not surprisingly, shooting performances were relatively poor, but some of the shooters adapted quickly and effectively whereas others appeared to be ill equipped mentally to deal with this unexpected event. The Edmonton fog reinforced how useful first-hand observation can be. In later years when working with anxiety-related issues, I have drawn on lessons learned in the circumstances that morning in Edmonton. I expect other practitioners will have similar experiences where they have witnessed events first hand and gained new insights into how anxiety can manifest in high-level competition. Such learning is not necessarily restricted to situations where we are insiders working directly with athletes. For example, attending high-level sports events as a spectator or observer, although not affording direct interaction with athletes, still represents excellent opportunities to observe athletes coping with pressure and self-managing arousal, stress, and anxiety.

Choking and anxiety

The term choking is closely associated with anxiety and inevitably, for some clients, an assessment of anxiety symptoms will lead to the question: Is this athlete experiencing general anxiety or the more extreme anxiety response of choking? Although there has been a good deal of research on choking in recent years, a differentiation between anxiety and choking is not clear cut. Mesagno, Marchant, and Morris (2008) defined choking as "a critical deterioration in the execution of habitual processes as a result of an elevation in anxiety levels under perceived pressure, leading to a substandard performance" (p. 131) Moreover, the majority of published choking research emphasizes the dual presence of elevated anxiety and ineffective attentional processes in producing choking. Choking is not restricted to sport, and the colloquial understanding of choking is similar to the above definition. For example, popular rapper Eminem recorded the song *Lose Yourself* (2002). The song includes insightful lyrics into a choking experience from the point of view of a musician-performer (the reader can go to any number of websites to read the lyrics, such as http://www.azlyrics.com/lyrics/eminem/loseyourself.html)

Lose Yourself can be a really powerful medium when working with athletes who present with choking. The lyrics encapsulate the choking experience and can really resonate with athletes. In a consultation, choosing to use stimulus material, such as the lyrics of a song, or a powerful image, can circumvent extended descriptive dialogue and help the athlete feel understood. In working with a choking-susceptible athlete, many of the same techniques and topics normally used with anxiety and attention regulation are still relevant (imagery, coping skills, building confidence, working on self-talk, moderating expectations, improving mental toughness). Hill, Hanton, Fleming, and Mathews (2009) recommended multi-modal treatments that might combine elements of the above. In terms of specific choking reduction techniques, two studies have successfully used routines (Mesagno *et al.*, 2008; see also Chapter 56) and music (Mesagno, Marchant, & Morris, 2009) to counter choking susceptibility.

Facilitating change: managing sport anxiety

There is no shortage of applied research and dedicated text chapters specifically about anxiety in sport to inform practitioners; the challenge is in making the right choices about how best to assist an anxious athlete. Some practitioners may choose to use sport anxiety assessment tools (e.g., Sport Anxiety Scale-2; Smith, Smoll, Cumming, & Grossbard, 2006; Competitive State Anxiety Inventory-2; Martens, Vealey, & Burton, 1990). As with all assessment measures, these tools are helpful if they provide additional information, facilitate client-consultant dialogue, or assist in planning individualized treatments.

In working with sport anxiety, we need to draw on what effective coping skills the athlete has already developed. Athletes, often through trial and error, are quite innovative in developing strategies that work for them. Drawing out stories of when the athlete has successfully managed anxiety and performed well can positively change the tone of a consultation. A balanced approach whereby we are focusing on both facilitative and debilitative aspects of anxiety will generally be more engaging to athletes than focusing on debilitative anxiety and failures to cope. A useful initial perspective is thinking in terms of assessing athletes' existing coping resources as balanced against the strength of their anxiety responses. What mental skills (or physical behaviors) do athletes already employ to cope with anxiety? How adaptive or maladaptive are these coping strategies? By staying attuned to clients, we can gain valuable information about their current cognitive and behavioral patterns and other relevant information (e.g., level of insight, willingness to talk openly, level of distress, motivation to develop coping skills). Encouraging client narratives or stories of particular circumstances where anxiety was prevalent is helpful in contextualizing issues and breaking down barriers to open and honest communication. Being patient in these early stages will often not suit the client who may generally want to move quickly into solutions, but a planned approach should set the conditions for a meaningful and ultimately successful working relationship.

I have largely discussed practical considerations and process matters in working with sport anxiety. Planned approaches will normally involve a practitioner taking a theoretical perspective and consequently drawing on treatment objectives and techniques consistent with the chosen model. The practitioner who chooses to use rational–emotive behavior therapy (REBT: see Ellis & Dryden, 2007) will first need to be well versed in the micro-psychology skills of REBT. Second, to draw maximum therapeutic potential, the therapist imbued with a particular psychological framework should ideally also appreciate the philosophical underpinnings, rather than solely concentrating on treatment modalities. That is, the treatment chosen will be more powerful and authentic when the broader background of the underlying psychological framework is well understood. From an REBT perspective, being familiar with Ellis' classic contributions, other leading REBT practitioners (e.g., Dryden, 2009) and sport anxiety adaptations of REBT (see Ellis, 1994; Taylor, 1994) would represent a holistic philosophical-practical approach. I suspect that I am not alone in having occasionally taken the time-poor approach of lifting interventions without due consideration of broader philosophical considerations.

Without digressing into the relative merits of different approaches, the treatment of choice will depend on the athlete, the practitioner's knowledge and skills, and the circumstances. Whatever the treatment used, the likely outcome hinges on a range of factors, such as the micro-skills of the practitioner. I use the term micro-skills in this context to include the breadth and depth of specific knowledge, understanding, and experience in delivering planned anxiety management treatments. Breadth would likely include the range of approaches a practitioner can confidently use. Depth in this context relates to the proficiency of the practitioner in using the full range of tools generally associated with a particular approach. I mention micro-skills because sometimes there seems to be an assumption, especially with sport psychologist trainees, that employing a particular technique will somehow produce predictable results (rarely the case).

If working on a contractual basis with a sports team, psycho-educational approaches to anxiety management can supplement individual work. Applied strategies, such as conducting interactive workshops or focus groups on anxiety will quickly demonstrate how the array of athlete-driven anxiety management strategies is virtually limitless. When one is contracted to provide services to teams, opportunities are usually available to deliver targeted workshops to younger athletes or athletes particularly needing assistance managing anxiety. Embedding a guided interview with an experienced athlete into a workshop is usually well received by younger athletes, assists in terms of providing sport-specific anxiety management strategies, and helps to normalize anxiety. One of the advantages of being a contracted sport psychologist is the opportunity to work closely with athletes in an ongoing manner and seeing athletes in pre-competition and competition modes where behavior can be readily observed. On the subject of pre-competition preparation, I highly recommend non-obtrusive regular observations of individual preparation routines. Attentively observing the symptoms of anxiety and associated behaviors helps in understanding athlete idiosyncrasies and establishing behavioral patterns and benchmarks. This approach fits well with optimal arousal theories such as individual zones of optimal functioning (Hanin, 2000). Once typical anxiety patterns are established, behavioral departures from this normal pattern can be easily identified. Moreover, when substantial increases or decreases in anxiety are observed they can be placed in the context of the many factors that underpin such changes (e.g., specific opponents, game importance, quality of preparation, dispositional factors). Athletes are usually impressed when sport psychologists can later recall specific details of individual athlete competition preparations and signs of anxiety, especially when referenced with performance levels or other relevant factors. Practitioner–athlete conversations are thus likely to reflect the reality for the athletes, and planned management can be tailored to their specific needs and tendencies.

Conclusion

Anxiety remains one of the most intensely researched areas in sport psychology. Sport psychology as a field has moved well beyond the era of simple anxiety-performance theories and generic multi-modal therapies. The practitioner must do more than become familiar with the landmark research and have an appreciation for the many evidence-based treatment approaches and interventions. Flexibility in adapting to the specific circumstances of each athlete who presents with anxiety-related stories, observing and reflecting on each case, and readiness to work through the many challenges that sport anxiety work entails are also essential. See Box 28.1 for key points from this chapter.

Box 28.1

Key points about anxiety

- Anxiety in sport is ubiquitous. Most athletes have personal experiences that will normally enable them to connect their anxieties with triggers, cues, and their past histories.
- Generic treatments (e.g., relaxation) often do not work because sport anxiety is multi-dimensional and dependent on intra-individual circumstances.
- We are entering an era of increased accountability, and practitioners need to consider evidence-based treatments and respond to expectations from organizations about the efficacy of treatments for sport anxiety.
- Case history and in-depth individual work with athletes in the field can provide a useful "hands on" contextual perspective of anxiety-related issues.
- Choking represents the "extreme edge" of anxiety and the current trends toward developing choking-specific interventions should also inform our general understanding of anxiety in sport.
- Athletes may respond well to practitioners who take the time to understand their sports and particularly individual behavioral patterns gleaned from attending and closely observing athletes in competitive situations.
- Anxiety is sometimes best managed by taking a positive perspective and focusing on lessons already learned, assessing coping skills, and attempting to locate zones of optimal performance.

References

da Vinci, L. (n.d.). Online. Retrieved from http://www.brainyquote.com/quotes/authors/l/leonardo_da_vinci.html (accessed 18 June 2010).

Dryden, W. (2009). *Skills in rational emotive behaviour counselling and psychotherapy*. Thousand Oaks, CA: Sage.

Ellis, A. (1994). The sport of avoiding sports and exercise: A rational emotive behavior therapy perspective. *The Sport Psychologist*, 8, 248–261.

Ellis, A., & Dryden, W. (2007). *The practice of rational emotive behavior therapy* (2nd ed.). New York: Springer.

Eminem (2002). Lose yourself. On *music from and inspired by the motion picture 8 Mile* [CD]. Los Angeles, CA: Shady/Interscope Records.

Hanin, Y. L. (Ed.). (2000). *Emotions in sport*. Champaign, IL: Human Kinetics.

Hill, D. M., Hanton, S., Fleming, S., & Mathews, N. (2009). A re-examination of choking in sport. *European Journal of Sport Science*, 9, 203–212.

Martens, R. (1971). Anxiety and motor behavior: A review. *Journal of Motor Behavior*, 3, 151–179.

Martens, R., Vealey, R. S., & Burton, D. (1990). *Competitive anxiety in sport*. Champaign, IL: Human Kinetics.

Mesagno, C., Marchant, D., & Morris, T. (2008). A pre-performance routine to alleviate choking in "choking-susceptible" athletes. *The Sport Psychologist*, 22, 439–457.

Mesagno, C., Marchant, D., & Morris, T. (2009). Alleviating choking: The sounds of distraction. *Journal of Applied Sport Psychology, 21*, 131–147.

Smith, R. E., Smoll, F. L., Cumming, S. P., & Grossbard, J. R. (2006). Measurement of multidimensional sport performance anxiety in children and adults: The Sport Anxiety Scale-2. *Journal of Sport & Exercise Psychology, 28*, 479–501.

Taylor, J. (1994). On exercise and sport avoidance: A reply to Dr. Albert Ellis. *The Sport Psychologist, 8*, 262–270.

29

Sleep

Glenn S. Brassington and Chris Goode

The effect of sleep on athletic performance, and ways to improve the quantity and quality of sleep of athletes, has received little attention in the sport psychology literature. Nevertheless, most athletes and coaches will attest to the importance of feeling fresh and rested for both training and performing. Recent research points to the profound effect that sleep has, not only on athletic training and performance, but also on almost every aspect of athletes' lives (e.g., interpersonal, academic, financial). Unfortunately, people have reported feeling much less satisfied with their sleep and in 2001 were sleeping one hour less per night than people in 1981 (Hicks, Fernandez, & Pellegrini, 2001; Hicks & Pellegrini, 1991).

The goal of this chapter is to provide sport psychology consultants with information and tools to increase the quantity and quality of athletes' sleep. We will provide the rationale and content for sleep improvement education based on current sleep research as well as the first author's experience working with thousands of individual athletes and teams in university and professional settings. We hope that after studying this chapter, the reader will have the resources to provide educational programs for athletes and a basis for further sleep research.

What is sleep and how is it measured?

Sleep has been defined in behavioral terms as a reversible behavioral state of perceptual disengagement from, and unresponsiveness to, the environment. During sleep we are to a great degree cut off from sensory information from the environment, but we can easily be awakened. At the same time we are cut off from the environment, our bodies are undergoing a great deal of activity and change compared to that observed in waking hours (Carskadon & Dement, 2005). Quality sleep refers to an athlete being able to fall asleep within 15–30 minutes of turning out the lights, experiencing few nighttime awakenings (less than 3), waking feeling refreshed, and functioning well throughout the day. A variety of assessments have been created to describe the changes that occur during sleep and form the basis for our definition of sleep. The most commonly used measures of sleep include: polysomnography, actigraphy, questionnaires, Multiple Sleep Onset Latency Test, and sleep logs. Each of these methods of quantifying sleep is described below.

Polysomnography

Polysomnography is a set of physiological recordings taken during sleep. The primary parameters assessed include: electroencephalography (EEG), which records electrical activity on the scalp associated with neural activity in the brain; electro-oculography (EOG), which records eye movement; electromyography (EMG), which records skeletal muscle activity; oximetry, which indirectly measures the oxygen saturation of a person's blood; and respiratory airflow. EEG, EOG, and EMG are used to quantify the types of sleep experienced and oximetry and respiratory airflow are used to diagnose disordered breathing.

Based on polysomnography, normal sleep has been described as consisting of four non-rapid eye movement (NREM) stages and one rapid eye movement stage (REM). NREM sleep generally accounts for 75% of nighttime sleep and REM the remaining 25%. Sleep begins in the NREM stage and passes through four progressively deeper stages until the beginning of REM sleep. This cycle occurs approximately every 90 minutes throughout the night with the percentage of time spent in REM sleep becoming greater in comparison to NREM sleep toward the last third of the night.

Actigraphy

Although polysomnography is considered the gold standard in assessing sleep, newer technologies are being developed that are less expensive, do not tend to disrupt sleep, and capture daytime functioning. One such device is often referred to as an actigraph or actimeter. The actigraph typically is placed on the wrist and records movement with an accelerometer that is then analyzed by a microprocessor to determine how much time the user was awake or asleep (Ancoli-Israel, 2005). Some of the more sophisticated products also capture ambient light. Actigraphy has been shown to be a reliable and valid measure of normal sleep (Littner et al., 2003). Many practitioners use actigraphy in conjunction with polysomnography and sleep logs to inform their overall assessment of a person's sleep.

Multiple sleep onset latency test

To assess how much physiological drive a person has to sleep, Carskadon and Dement (2005) designed a protocol containing a series of four to six opportunities to nap and measurement of how long it takes participants to fall asleep during each attempt throughout the day. Sleep latency in normal adults is from 10–20 minutes with pathological sleepiness as a mean sleep latency of 5–6 minutes. This shorter latency to sleep onset suggests that the individual is experiencing a strong drive to sleep during the day, which is likely the result of insufficient quality nighttime sleep.

Questionnaires

Standardized questionnaires are used to gather self-report data on a person's nighttime sleep and daytime functioning. One of the most widely used self-report measures of sleep quality is the Pittsburgh Sleep Quality Index (PSQI; Buysse, Reynolds, Monk, Berman, & Kupfer, 1989). In this measure, clients answer a series of questions about their sleep over the previous month. One of the benefits of this type of measure is that it captures individuals' subjective experiences of the quantity and quality of their sleep and provides normative data to

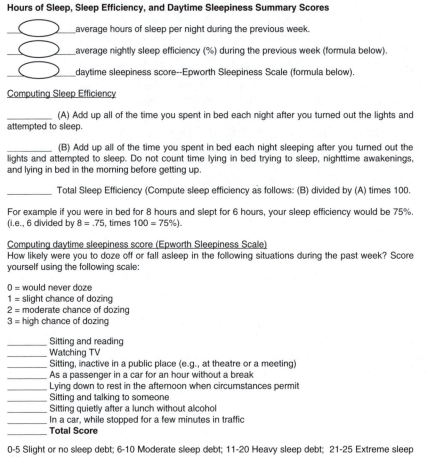

Please compute the following <u>three</u> summary scores: Hours of Sleep, Sleep Efficiency, and Daytime Sleepiness (in the ovals below) for each night of sleep and then average them for the week. These three scores will serve as a summary of important characteristics of your sleep.

Hours of Sleep, Sleep Efficiency, and Daytime Sleepiness Summary Scores

____⬯____average hours of sleep per night during the previous week.

____⬯____average nightly sleep efficiency (%) during the previous week (formula below).

____⬯____daytime sleepiness score--Epworth Sleepiness Scale (formula below).

<u>Computing Sleep Efficiency</u>

_____ (A) Add up all of the time you spent in bed each night after you turned out the lights and attempted to sleep.

_____ (B) Add up all of the time you spent in bed each night sleeping after you turned out the lights and attempted to sleep. Do not count time lying in bed trying to sleep, nighttime awakenings, and lying in bed in the morning before getting up.

_____ Total Sleep Efficiency (Compute sleep efficiency as follows: (B) divided by (A) times 100.

For example if you were in bed for 8 hours and slept for 6 hours, your sleep efficiency would be 75%. (i.e., 6 divided by 8 = .75, times 100 = 75%).

<u>Computing daytime sleepiness score (Epworth Sleepiness Scale)</u>
How likely were you to doze off or fall asleep in the following situations during the past week? Score yourself using the following scale:

0 = would never doze
1 = slight chance of dozing
2 = moderate chance of dozing
3 = high chance of dozing

_____ Sitting and reading
_____ Watching TV
_____ Sitting, inactive in a public place (e.g., at theatre or a meeting)
_____ As a passenger in a car for an hour without a break
_____ Lying down to rest in the afternoon when circumstances permit
_____ Sitting and talking to someone
_____ Sitting quietly after a lunch without alcohol
_____ In a car, while stopped for a few minutes in traffic
_____ **Total Score**

0-5 Slight or no sleep debt; 6-10 Moderate sleep debt; 11-20 Heavy sleep debt; 21-25 Extreme sleep debt

Figure 29.1 Sleep summary worksheet.

which each person can be compared. The PSQI measure provides a global score of sleep quality and seven subscales: sleep quality, sleep latency, sleep duration, sleep efficiency, sleep disturbances, use of medication, and daytime dysfunction.

A commonly used self-report measure of daytime sleepiness is the Epworth Sleepiness Scale (Johns, 1991). On this scale, clients rate from 0 (*slight*) to 3 (*high*), the likelihood that they would doze in a variety of situations such as "sitting and reading," "sitting and talking to someone," and "in a car, while stopped for a few minutes in traffic." This measure asks clients to report their behavior rather than their internal sense of tiredness. The Sleep Summary Worksheet (see Figure 29.1) contains the Epworth Sleepiness Scale, which is an indicator of whether a person's sleep is of sufficient quality to sustain alertness during the day.

Sleep logs

Although the retrospective measures described above provide important information about clients' recollections of their nighttime sleep and daytime sleepiness, prospective sleep logs help overcome some of the biases caused by memories being incomplete and selective. Sleep logs frequently are completed for two weeks and involve clients providing information on their sleep (e.g., how long it took to fall asleep, nighttime awakenings) and on factors that might impair sleep (e.g., caffeine consumption, anxiety, stressful activities engaged in before bed). Sleep log data are used both to inform recommendations for improving sleep as well as to help people understand how particular behaviors affect their sleep (see Figure 29.2).

Negative effects of poor sleep on performance

The duration and quality of an athlete's sleep affects key psycho-physiological factors related to performance including: hypo- or hyper-arousal, inappropriate attention (e.g., too narrow, too broad, not sustained), decreased ability to process information, poor decision making, poor eating (e.g., overeating, eating high fat and sugary foods), poor emotional control, less endurance, inability to regulate energy levels (e.g., get up for an event), immune suppression, and poor memory (e.g., unable to remember coaches' instructions: Reilly, 2009; Samuels, 2008). Even small decrements in functioning in these areas can have significant negative consequences for competitive athletes. It is all too common to see small lapses in judgment and less than optimal execution of a motor skill costing individuals and teams important championships.

Although sleep duration and quality appear to have direct effects on athletic performance, there are likely indirect effects as well. Sleep may increase or decrease athletes' abilities to manage other important areas of their lives such as social relationships, academic tasks in the case of student athletes, or financial/business tasks in the case of professional or Olympic athletes. Figure 29.3 contains a theoretical model of how sleep may directly and indirectly affect competitive performance.

Although, in general, getting sufficient quality sleep contributes to effective training and performance, there may be individuals who experience a performance-enhancing effect of one night of poor sleep. For some athletes, the initial or next-day effect of getting several hours less sleep or having a more fitful sleep is to feel aroused and alert due to increased circulating stress hormones that are secreted into the blood to promote alertness. It is possible that the night-before nerves, which athletes often report before a big event, may in some cases increase the athletes' arousal to a performance enhancing level and give them increased energy and the focus to succeed. One can think of the effects of several hours of sleep deprivation as similar to that of stress in that some stress can be motivating and performance-enhancing but over time can lead to burnout and increased errors. It is important to mention this caveat to athletes so that individuals who are having trouble sleeping before a big event do not worry so much about getting to sleep that they are not able to sleep at all.

Common sleep disorders

Although the primary focus of this chapter is on improving sleep among athletes who have poor quantity and quality of sleep because of modifiable lifestyle factors, it is important to

Day of the Week	Mon	Tue	Wed	Thur	Fri	Sat	Sun
Complete in evening before bed (for that day)							
# of alcoholic beverages							
Time of last alcoholic beverage							
# of caffeinated beverages							
Time of last caffeinated beverage							
Minutes of moderate exercise							
Time of last exercise							
Minutes of meditation/breathing exercises							
Time of last meditation/breathing exercises							
Did you do any other activities in bed except sleep and sex (yes or no)							
Name of stimulating medication (e.g., diet pills)							
Dose of stimulating medication							
Number of cigarettes smoked							
Time of last cigarette smoked							
Number of daytime naps							
Total minutes of time spent napping							
Name of sleep medication							
Dose of sleep medication							
Time you turned off lights and attempted to sleep							
Complete during the night							
Nighttime awaken #1 (time you woke up)							
Nighttime awaken #1 (minutes awake)							
Reason you awakened							
Nighttime awaken #2 (time you woke up)							
Nighttime awaken #2 (minutes awake)							
Reason you awakened							
Nighttime awaken #3 (time you woke up)							
Nighttime awaken #3 (minutes awake)							
Reason you awakened							
Complete upon awakening in the morning							
Time you woke up in the morning							
Time you got out of bed							
# of minutes it took you to fall asleep last night							
How rested do you feel on a scale from (1=not at all rested to 10=very rested)							
Was the room you slept in comfortable (yes or no)							

Figure 29.2 Sleep log.

have at least a basic understanding of the possible psychiatric and medical conditions that may be the cause of an athlete's sleep problems and require medical treatment. Vaughn and D'Cruz (2005) should be referred to for examples of these types of conditions (e.g., insomnia that does not improve with lifestyle changes, pain, anxiety, depression, sleepiness, snoring, apneas [episodes of 10 seconds or more of not breathing]).

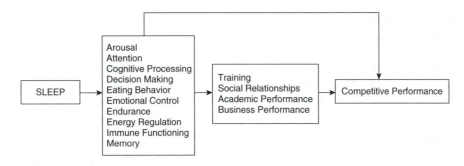

Figure 29.3 Variables theoretically mediating the relationship between sleep and performance.

Necessary conditions for sleep

Sleep and wakefulness are under homeostatic and circadian alerting control. Homeostatic control refers to the phenomenon that the longer we are awake or not experiencing specific sleep stages, the greater the need to make up for the lost sleep or sleep stage. This need is also referred to as sleep drive. Circadian control of the sleep-wake rhythm refers to bio-chemical, physiological, and behavioral processes that encourage wakefulness. When these two regulatory mechanisms are working in synchrony, athletes are able to enter into sleep at regular times each evening, experience deeper stages of sleep (i.e., stages 3 and 4), and remain asleep until it is time to awake, and arise from bed feeling rested. Unfortunately, these two main regulators of sleep can be disrupted by physiological arousal, cognitions, and the environment. It is helpful for athletes to be aware that their cognitions, behaviors, and the environment can work with or against the homeostatic drive and circadian control. Table 29.1 shows theoretically how these factors can inhibit or facilitate sleep. A thorough understanding of how these factors function to promote sleep is central in providing effective educational programs for improving sleep. Each of these factors will be explained in more detail below and together form the theoretical model upon which lifestyle recommendations can be made to athletes.

Sleep drive

The drive to sleep is often referred to as a person's sleep debt. This debt is built up by being awake and is paid back by sleeping. It is not possible to have zero sleep drive because as soon as one did, one would wake up and begin accruing sleep debt. The key understanding here is that it is not "intention to sleep" that promotes sleep, but, rather, the body's drive to sleep that has been built up during wakefulness. Trying to sleep can actually be counter-productive because it generally increases arousal and inhibits sleep.

Table 29.1 Pattern of variables influencing sleep quality.

Sleep drive	Circadian alerting	Somatic arousal	Cognitive arousal	Sleep environment	Sleep quality
High	Low	Low	Low	Dark, Quiet, Safe	High
Low	High	High	High	Light, Loud, Unsafe	Low

Further, falling asleep is not the major problem most people report. Many people routinely experience sleep debt due to curtailing sleep to engage in other priorities. The more common problem is nighttime awakenings and not entering into the deeper stages of restful sleep. Nighttime awakenings often occur as the sleep debt is paid back during the night and the sleep drive is diminished. A limited sleep drive may make it possible for internal (e.g., worries) or external factors (noises) to wake the athlete.

Circadian rhythm

The circadian rhythm, or body clock, coordinates the timing of most physiologic and behavioral processes. Some physiological processes need to be turned on at certain times of the day and night and others need to be turned off. For example, the digestive system needs to be less active in the night so that one can sleep (heavy meals before going to bed will disrupt sleep), and body temperature needs to be lowered during the night to help enter into deeper stages of sleep. Many sleep researchers have posited that circadian alerting works in opposition to the sleep drive to help one stay awake during the day and to consolidate sleep at night. Circadian alerting exerts its effect by creating biological changes that keep organisms alert and then withdrawing these changes to let the sleep drive take its effect.

It is now believed that our sleep–wake circadian rhythm is 10–15 minutes longer than 24 hours requiring us to reset our internal clock each day. The daily pattern of action of circadian alerting is to begin to alert the organism at about 9 a.m. and increasing alertness slowly until 9 p.m. with the greatest alerting effect occurring between 6 p.m. and 9 p.m. Circadian alerting decreases its action slowly, being almost completely withdrawn between 3 a.m. and 6 a.m. Figure 29.4 shows the general pattern of alerting that occurs during a 24-hour period and how this pattern compares with sleep drive (i.e., the opponent process model). One can see from the figure that the afternoon dip in energy (i.e., between 1 p.m. and 3 p.m.) is associated with the withdrawal of circadian alerting and increased sleep drive. Although most people experience changes in circadian alerting in the pattern described, it is important for athletes to understand their own particular cycles through observation and awareness.

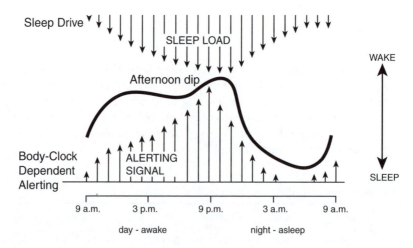

Figure 29.4 Opponent process model of sleep. Reprinted with permission of Tracy Kuo (unpublished figure)

Physiological arousal

Sleep requires quiescence of the sympathetic component of the autonomic nervous system and activities and substances that affect this system. Muscle tension needs to be reduced to a minimum, respiration needs to slow, and one needs to feel comfortable and safe enough in one's environment to encourage sleep. Conversely, sympathetic nervous system activity (e.g., increased muscle tension and stress hormones) inhibits sleep. Commonly referred to as the fight-or-flight response, physiological arousal is associated with alertness and a physiological state of preparing for and taking action. The flight-or-flight response works in opposition to sleep.

Cognitive arousal

Attention to, and processing of, the external and internal world needs to diminish for sleep to occur. One of the biggest barriers to this process of withdrawing from oneself and the world is excessive thoughts about problems in one's life. Thinking about losses, fears, or injustices interferes with sleep by increasing cognitive activity, effort, vigilance, or arousal. Problem solving and preparation for future action are incompatible with the type of diffuse attention required to enter into sleep. For many busy people, as soon as their bodies begin to relax, their minds begin to ruminate about a flood of problems to be solved, which only serves to heighten their alertness. For other people, being in bed is one of the only times in the day that they feel is "their own" time and they resist the urge to sleep so they can enjoy some time of solitude. Another type of cognition that can interfere with sleep arises when athletes worry that they will not be able to fall asleep and get the rest they need to perform well the next day.

Environment

The sleep environment can have a positive or negative effect on sleep. If the environment within and around athletes is relaxed, dark, quiet, and comfortable (neither too hot nor too cold), they will have a better chance of experiencing restful and restorative sleep. The key principle operating here is that the environment needs to be safe and not draw attention away from sleeping.

Sleep management guidelines

Recommendations for lifestyle behaviors relate to the necessary conditions for sleep described above. It is important to emphasize that not every recommendation will apply to every person and that it is up to each athlete to apply the sleep management guidelines and evaluate how each one serves to promote sleep for them.

Sleep drive

Recommendation: Do not go to bed until you feel sleepy.
Rationale: If athletes have not accrued sufficient sleep drive, they will not be able to fall asleep even if they are relaxed, comfortable, and in a safe sleep environment. A common problem is for athletes to go to bed several hours earlier than usual the

night before a big event to try to get extra rest. This tactic often leads to athletes lying in bed and worrying about not being able to sleep and the negative effects this will have on their performance.

Recommendation: Do not take any daytime or evening naps.

Rationale: Daytime naps reduce sleep drive leading to delays in sleep onset and nighttime awakenings. The exception to this recommendation is if daytime naps of less than 1 hour improve recovery after training, are an established sleep pattern, and do not impair nighttime sleep.

Circadian alerting

Recommendation: Expose the body to as much light as is practical during the day.

Rationale: Exposure to light (especially sunlight) signals circadian alerting to maintain its alerting effects. Conversely, withdrawal of light in the evening helps the circadian alerting to withdraw and permit sleep.

Recommendation: Get up and go to bed at approximately the same time (within 1 hour) every day.

Rationale: Maintaining a consistent schedule will help the circadian alerting facilitate alertness during the day and withdraw its effects in the evening. It is not uncommon for athletes to go to sleep after 2 a.m. in the later days of the week only to find that they are not able to fall asleep when they try to sleep before midnight in the earlier days of the week. Moving the sleep-and-wake schedule is equivalent to creating the problems of jet lag every week.

Recommendation: Avoid consuming excess fluids prior to sleeping and avoid eating in the middle of the night.

Rationale: Digestion and elimination are shut down by the circadian clock to promote sleep. Eating late at night or during the night can lead to increased digestion and the alerting activity of the circadian clock.

Recommendation: Do not drink alcohol 2 hours before bedtime.

Rationale: Alcohol may make athletes fall asleep quickly but it reduces the quality (especially REM) sleep they get during the night.

Recommendation: Eat on a consistent schedule during the day and early evening. Do not skip meals. Include healthy food in your diet such as fruits, vegetables, legumes, and grains, and limit refined and sugary foods.

Rationale: Circadian alerting is associated with eating. Healthy eating is associated with overall better physiological functioning responsible for circadian alerting activities.

Recommendation: Do not exercise within 4 hours of bedtime.

Rationale: Exercise raises core body temperature leading to alertness. Core body temperature does, however, tend to decrease within 4 hours of exercise.

Somatic arousal

Recommendation: Do not eat or drink anything containing caffeine or other stimulants after 4 p.m., or within six hours of bedtime. Caffeine increases arousal. Learn all of the foods (e.g., chocolate), drinks (e.g., coffee, tea, soda), and medications (e.g., some over-the-counter cold, headache, and pain relief medications) that contain caffeine and other sympathomimetic substances (e.g., pseudoephedrine, phenylpropanolamine). Some athletes are sensitive to caffeine and other stimulants and need to eliminate consumption to facilitate sleep. Avoid tobacco in the evening.

Rationale: Caffeine, tobacco, and several over-the-counter medications are substances that increase sympathetic nervous system activation and inhibit sleep.

Recommendation: Engage in pleasant, stress-reducing activities, and nurturing relationships.

Rationale: These activities help buffer the effects of stress that can lead to sleep-inhibiting hyper-arousal.

Recommendation: Engage in relaxation training (e.g., progressive muscle relaxation, autogenic training) during the day and before bed.

Rationale: Many athletes have learned techniques for reducing arousal that can be used to facilitate sleep. Athletes need to be careful, however, that the relaxation strategies they have learned to reduce arousal before or during competition do not become associated with sleep. It is often beneficial for athletes to use different relaxation training techniques and strategies to reduce arousal before going to bed than they use in relation to their sports performance. If a clear distinction between relaxing for sleep and relaxing for performance is not made, an athlete may become relaxed and alert while trying to sleep or relaxed and drowsy when trying to perform. It can take some practice to learn to create and distinguish between these different states.

Cognitive arousal

Recommendation: Do not try to make yourself sleep.

Rationale: Trying to sleep is incompatible with the withdrawal of attention and effort required to enter into sleep. Athletes should tell themselves to just let sleep happen and console themselves with the notion that they will eventually sleep, especially as their sleep drive increases. This letting go of effort often leads to sleep.

Recommendation: Avoid working on unpleasant or frustrating tasks just prior to bedtime.

Rationale: It is helpful to reduce cognitive activity that can interfere with sleep prior to going to bed.

Recommendation: Use the last hour prior to bedtime to engage in activities that are enjoyable and relaxing (e.g., taking a warm shower). Take time to wind down from the activities of the day.

Rationale: A pre-bed routine functions to prepare the body and mind for sleep. Similar to pre-performance routines athletes use to increase arousal and narrow focus before a competition, pre-bed routines can help athletes decrease arousal and draw attention away from the concerns of the day.

Recommendation: If worries are making it difficult to fall asleep or stay asleep, consider scheduling a structured time to write about worries and concerns a few hours before going to bed. The act of writing down worries helps some people put them out of their minds and stops them from intruding on their sleep.

Rationale: Writing down worries may reduce the likelihood that an athlete will wake up during the night because of an intrusive worry.

279

Sleep environment

Recommendation: If you go to bed and remain awake for longer than 20 minutes, get out of bed and do something boring (e.g., sit in a chair). Do not return to bed until you feel sleepy. If you return to bed, but again find after 20 minutes that you cannot fall asleep, repeat the instructions.

Rationale: Athletes need to associate the bed with sleeping so that as soon as they enter the bed, body and mind prepare to sleep.

Recommendation: The bed should serve as a cue for sleep. Do not engage in any activity (e.g., watching TV, reading, listening to a radio) other than sleep (and sex) in bed.

Rationale: Athletes need to associate the bed with sleeping as much as possible.

Recommendation: Make the sleep environment conducive to sleep. Arrange for a comfortable temperature and minimal levels of sound. Avoid the use of the radio, stereo, or television to promote sleep. Darken the room as much as possible at night. Make the bedroom feel as safe as possible (e.g., lock windows and doors).

Rationale: Reducing environmental factors that may arouse the athlete from sleep promotes sleep.

Conclusions

Improving the sleep of athletes is a low-cost intervention that sport psychology consultants can use to support the mental and physical training of the athletes with whom they work. Nevertheless, educational programs like the one described in this chapter should not be promoted as a treatment for sleep disorders. Such treatment requires a thorough medical and psychological evaluation and treatment plan. The effects of sleep on athletic performance and the life of the athlete are significant. The challenge for sport psychology consultants is to educate the sports community about the available strategies for improving the sleep of athletes, and, one hopes, the success of both athletes and coaches. We hope that all sport psychology consultants will consider improving sleep as an important part of their intervention repertoires. See Box 29.1 for the main take-home messages of this chapter.

Box 29.1

Take-home messages about sleep

- Sleep influences key biopsychosocial factors related to sports performance.
- Quality and quantity of sleep are determined by the interaction of sleep drive, circadian alerting rhythm, cognitive and somatic arousal, and the sleep environment.
- Implementing behavioral sleep management guidelines can improve the quantity and quality of sleep.

- Athletes should leverage their sleep drive to improve sleep by only going to bed when they feel sleepy and not taking daytime or evening naps that interfere with falling asleep or staying asleep.
- Athletes should entrain their circadian alerting rhythm to withdraw and allow them to sleep by exposing themselves to light as much as possible in the day, maintaining a consistent sleep–wake schedule every day of the week, avoiding excessive fluids before bedtime, refraining from drinking alcohol 2 hours before bedtime, eating consistently throughout the day and avoiding exercise 4 hours before bedtime.
- Athletes should reduce their somatic arousal by reducing caffeine, tobacco, and other sympathomimetics consumption, engaging in pleasant activities, and practising relaxation training techniques.
- Athletes should reduce their cognitive arousal by not trying to make themselves sleep, avoiding frustrating tasks just prior to bedtime, engaging in relaxing and pleasurable activities prior to bed, and managing worry.
- Athletes should make the sleep environment safe, comfortable, and quiet.

References

Ancoli-Israel, S. (2005). Actigraphy. In M. H. Kryger, T. Roth, & W. C. Dement (Eds.), *Principles and practice of sleep medicine* (4th ed., pp. 1459–1467). Philadelphia: Elsevier Saunders.

Buysse, D. J., Reynolds, C. F., Monk, T. H., Berman, S. R., & Kupfer, D. J. (1989). The Pittsburgh Sleep Quality Index: A new instrument for psychiatric practice and research. *Psychiatry Research, 28,* 193–213.

Carskadon, M. A., & Dement, W. C. (2005). Normal human sleep: An overview. In M. H. Kryger, T. Roth, & W. C. Dement (Eds.), *Principles and practice of sleep medicine* (4th ed., pp. 13–23). Philadelphia: Elsevier Saunders.

Hicks, R. A., & Pellegrini, R. J. (1991). The changing sleep habits of college students. *Perceptual & Motor Skills, 72,* 1106.

Hicks, R. A., Fernandez, C., & Pellegrini, R. J. (2001). Striking changes in the sleep satisfaction of university students over the last two decades. *Perceptual & Motor Skills, 93,* 660.

Johns, M. W. (1991). A new method for measuring daytime sleepiness: The Epworth Sleepiness Scale. *Sleep, 14,* 540–545.

Littner, M., Kushida, C. A., Anderson, W. M., Bailey, D., Berry, R. B., Davila, D. G., Hirshkowitz, M., Kapen, S., Kramer, M., Loube, D., Wise, M., & Johnson, S. F. (2003). Practice parameters for the role of actigraphy in the study of sleep and circadian rhythms: An update for 2002. *Sleep, 26,* 337–341.

Reilly, T. (2009). The body clock and athletic performance. *Biological Rhythm Research, 40,* 37–44.

Samuels, C. (2008). Sleep, recovery, and performance: The new frontier in high-performance athletics. *Neurologic Clinics, 26,* 169–180.

Vaughn, B. V., & D'Cruz, O. F. (2005). Cardinal manifestations of sleep disorders. In M. H. Kryger, T. Roth & W. C. Dement (Eds.), *Principles and practice of sleep medicine* (pp. 594–601). Philadelphia, PA: Elsevier Saunders.

30

Identity foreclosure in sport

Albert J. Petitpas and Thaddeus France

From a psychosocial perspective, the primary task of late adolescence is to establish a sense of personal identity. Individuals who explore a variety of activities and interact with people from different backgrounds are in the best position to learn about themselves and to make informed decisions about various life options. Exploratory behavior not only provides the experiences and information that people need to solidify their values, interests, and skills, but also enables them to develop coping strategies and confidence in their abilities to be successful in adult life. Unfortunately, athletes may be prone to putting too much of their time and energy into sport participation and may not engage in the exploratory behavior that is critical to establishing a sense of self-identity (Brown, Glastetter-Fender, & Shelton, 2000). Athletes who do not engage in exploratory behaviors, but make firm commitments to sport as their primary source of identity, have been described as being in a state of identity foreclosure. The purpose of this chapter is to examine the construct of identity foreclosure in athletes and explore related implications for practitioners.

Understanding identity foreclosure

Identity foreclosure is listed as a core knowledge area in the sport psychology proficiencies of the American Psychological Association (2010); however, little has been written about the theoretical development of the construct. The groundwork for the concept of identity foreclosure can be found in the work of ego psychology theorists. Moving beyond the Freudian construct of instinctual id drives, White (1963) proposed that all individuals are motivated by an innate need to master their environments and to move freely in the world. He called this need "effectance" and argued that personal development demanded that individuals not only maintain themselves by satisfying basic instinctual needs, but also grow and gain feelings of efficacy by engaging in activities that influence their environments.

White (1963) believed that infants begin the process of cognitive and motor learning by engaging in simple behaviors such as holding crib toys. By the time infants start to crawl they have had numerous interactions with their environments that begin to shape their beliefs about what they can and cannot do. These beliefs form the basis for self-efficacy.

As children continue to grow, they construct views of their worlds based on what they have learned about their abilities and begin to develop primitive estimates of their levels of personal competence. Without some level of self-efficacy, it is doubtful that young children would have the desire or readiness necessary to imitate the complex behaviors exhibited by older role models.

At school age, children have increased opportunities to interact with their peers and to engage in social comparisons, particularly around physical abilities. Through these interactions, they gain concrete feedback about their competencies and begin to make judgments about the types of activities that are most likely to fulfill their need for effectance (White, 1963). According to Erikson (1959), children who experience success and achieve adequate levels of self-efficacy during latency develop a sense of industry. Children who are not able to meet their effectance needs develop feelings of inferiority and are less likely to take risks or explore new opportunities.

As individuals move into late adolescence, their developmental tasks shift to establishing a sense of personal identity (Erikson, 1959). In traditional psychodynamic views of human development, both separation/individuation and the internalization of self-regulatory functions are critical tasks for optimal identity formation in late adolescence (Kohut, 1971). The process of separation/individuation in adolescence enables individuals to shed family dependencies and loosen infantile object attachments at two levels (Blos, 1967). First, at the object-relations level, adolescents transfer their primary emotional attachments away from parents and on to peer group members. The capacity to attain sufficient freedom from primitive parental identifications allows individuals to benefit from exposure to new role models and experiences without the influence of an overly critical superego (Bourne, 1978). Without this freedom, adolescents would experience significant internal conflict in situations where their needs and goals deviate from the dictates of early parental identifications.

At the second level, the intrapsychic, individuals free themselves of primitive parental identifications internalized during childhood and develop an increasingly stabilized and internalized capacity for self-regulation (Kohut, 1971). As individuals gain separation from parental influences, they often develop new coping resources to manage the demands that come with new experiences and challenges. The internalization of new regulatory functions moves individuals from reliance on external supports to reliance upon themselves as a source of evaluation and self-esteem (Blos, 1967).

Erikson (1959) moved beyond the traditional psychoanalytic views of self and identity to the currently accepted construct of ego identity development. He believed that individuals progress beyond a simple reintegration of early parental identifications to develop consistent and unique personal identities. This process focuses on relationships, knowledge gained from managing the demands presented by new experiences, and the notion of psychosocial reciprocity. Erikson suggested that ego-identity development necessitates that the experiences of childhood and adolescence be formulated into core beliefs about oneself. Individuals look at alternatives and make freely chosen commitments to those choices that seem most consistent with personal values, needs, interests, and skills. Exposure to new people, ideas, and experiences enables individuals to move beyond parental identifications to a position of personal choice and self-identification. Not exploring alternatives or not becoming independent of parental imperatives results in identity foreclosure.

Marcia (1966) extended and operationalized Erikson's concept of identity and presented evidence that identity development was not simply a matter of identity resolution or identity confusion, but rather a factor of exploratory behavior and commitment to personally relevant options across life domains such as career, ideology, and religion. Marcia believed

283

that individuals need to experience crisis in the form of being forced to choose among a series of meaningful alternatives to achieve their unique identities. He postulated that a person's identity status could be determined by examining for the presence or absence of crises. The four original categories were:

1. *Identity achievement*: Individuals have gone through a period of actively exploring meaningful career and ideological alternatives (crisis) and have made firm commitments to those options that provide feelings of continuity within themselves.
2. *Identity moratorium*: Individuals are actively engaged in exploratory behavior, but have not made any firm career or ideological commitments.
3. *Identity foreclosure*: Individuals have not engaged in exploratory behavior, but have made firm career and ideological commitments, typically in directions that would gain parental and societal approval.
4. *Identity diffusion*: Individuals have not engaged in exploratory behavior and have not made any firm career or ideological commitments.

In general, individuals in a state of identity foreclosure have been found to exhibit high levels of authoritarian and stereotyped thinking, an external locus of control, and low levels of autonomy, self-directedness, and moral development (Marcia, Waterman, Matteson, Archer, & Orlofsky, 1993).

Sport participation and identity development

If one accepts the premise that individuals are born with an innate need for effectance (White, 1963), it follows that sport provides a setting where many young people can satisfy this need and develop initial feelings of self-efficacy (Petitpas & Champagne, 2000). Sport participation is highly valued in many cultures and being a successful athlete is usually the most coveted status among junior and senior high school students in the United States (Weiss, 1995). When children participate in sports, they receive concrete feedback about how they compare to their peers. Whether through the informal team selection process that occurs in choosing sides in pick-up games or performance during school or community organized competitions, the feedback children receive about their sport competencies becomes magnified as they move through their school years. Individuals' performances are reported in the media and the intrinsic rewards inherent in mastering one's environment can become superseded by numerous external rewards and recognitions.

As adolescents advance through the various levels of competition, participation in organized sports becomes a process of survival of the fittest, with winning increasing in importance and playing time and opportunities to prove oneself becoming reserved for the more skillful performers. To remain successful, young athletes need to devote more time and energy to sport in efforts to maintain their levels of achievement, and they receive increased pressure from coaches to specialize in one sport (Côté, 2009). During high school, the external rewards associated with athletic success often take on increased importance and skilled performers become identified by their sports accomplishments. Although the literature suggests that there are many benefits to sports participation including better academic performance, increased self-esteem, and better interpersonal skills, there is the danger that too much emphasis on sport may be detrimental, particularly for athletes entering early adulthood (Petitpas & Champagne, 2000).

Elite athletes are frequently engulfed in sport systems that provide them with notoriety, financial support, and other privileges, but also demand large amounts of time, and enormous physical and psychological energy. High-level athletes typically devote at least 20 to 30 hours per week throughout the entire year preparing for and participating in their sports (Brown et al., 2000), making it is easy to imagine that many of them have little desire or time to engage in exploratory behavior.

Developmental theorists contend that exploratory behavior helps individuals acquire and internalize coping skills that enable them to become self-sufficient and prepared to manage various life challenges (Jordaan, 1963). Unfortunately, the structure of most high school and university sport systems promotes conformity and compliance rather than autonomy and independent thinking (Finch, 2009). Many athletes in pursuit of Olympic medals or professional sports careers often comply with team rules and coaches' expectations, rather than engage in exploratory behavior (LeUnes & Nation, 1983).

Studies investigating the link between participation in intercollegiate athletics and identity foreclosure have yielded mixed results. For example, male intercollegiate athletes in revenue-producing sports have been shown to display lower levels of career maturity (Murphy, Petitpas, & Brewer, 1996), career decision-making self-efficacy (Brown et al., 2000), and career planning (Kennedy & Dimick, 1987) than students in the general university population. Identity foreclosure, however, was not related to lower levels of career maturity in samples of community college (Kornspan & Etzel, 2001) or general intercollegiate athletes (Perna, Zaichkowsky, & Bochnek, 1996). The inconsistencies across studies may be a result of the variety of instruments and constructs that have been used to measure identity foreclosure.

Terms such as athletic identity, (Brewer, Van Raalte, & Linder, 1993), role experimentation (Miller & Kerr, 2003), and selective optimization (Danish, 1983) have all been used to describe athletes who have overidentified with the athlete role and have not balanced or invested energy in other academic or career pursuits. Although these terms are related to identity foreclosure, they are each separate constructs. For example, the Athletic Identity Measurement Scale (AIMS; Brewer, 1993) assesses the strength and exclusivity of individuals' identification with sport roles. Although the AIMS is positively correlated with identity foreclosure (Murphy et al., 1996), it does not measure the level of exploration and commitment that individuals report across the domains of career, religion, and politics that are the focus of the Objective Measure of Ego-Identity Status (OM-EIS; Adams, Shea, & Fitch, 1979). Studies using the OM-EIS have found that athletes display high levels of foreclosure when compared to nonathletes (Good, Brewer, Petitpas, Van Raalte, & Mahar, 1993). Intercollegiate athletes were not higher in foreclosure in studies where other instruments (i.e., Modified Erikson Psychosocial Stage Inventory, Commitment to Career Choices Scale) were employed (Perna et al., 1996).

Another feasible explanation for the inconsistent findings on the relationship between identity foreclosure and sport participation can be found in studies of role conflict in student-athletes. Students participating in intercollegiate sports in North America may overidentify with the role of athlete during their first years at university and then begin to place more emphasis on academic and career concerns during their third and fourth years (Miller & Kerr, 2003). The notion that many student-athletes defer role experimentation until they reach the latter stages of their university careers has led some writers to believe that the link between foreclosure and sport participation may have been overgeneralized (Perna et al., 1996), and only those intercollegiate athletes who have a legitimate chance to play professionally would continue to focus exclusively on the athlete role.

Another consideration is the belief that there may be two types of foreclosure. Henry and Renaud (1972) suggested that some individuals who were unable to complete separation/individuation and internalize self-regulatory functions during adolescence could be classified as psychologically foreclosed. These individuals make unwavering commitments to parental- or societal-approved careers and ideological options to avoid identity crises, and this idealized sense of self becomes the central component of their intrapsychic defensive systems. Athletes who are psychologically foreclosed view their sport successes as the only means of maintaining parental acceptance and defend against threats to their ego-identities by avoiding people or situations that might challenge the salience of those identities. In contrast, some individuals make exclusive commitments to the athletic role because sport participation is providing a sense of identity and takes up the majority of their time and energy. These individuals satisfy their needs to establish an identity and sense of belonging through participation in sports resulting in no urgency to explore various life options. Henry and Renaud labeled the identity status of this latter group as situational foreclosure. Student-athletes in situational foreclosure would be more likely to transfer their emphasis away from sport if there were considerable evidence that they would no longer be able to maintain their athletic identities by competing or coaching.

Obstacles in working with an athlete who is foreclosed

Individuals who make premature commitments to sport roles may not initially experience any negative consequences from these decisions. Many of the most sought after careers require an early and exclusive commitment of time and energy. Problems arise for foreclosed individuals only when there are threats to their role identities. For example, a surgeon who has failed to engage in exploratory behavior may be highly confident in the operating room, but may lack the self-awareness and coping skills required to manage family issues at home. The surgeon's confidence and competence is bracketed to the work role and the surgeon can avoid any feelings of self-doubt by simply doing more surgery. Athletes, however, almost always have briefer careers than people in most other occupations (golf being a possible exception), and they are also under constant threat of career-ending injuries or deselection. When most individuals are just establishing themselves in their careers, athletes are faced with the issue of sport career termination.

Coaches and the media reinforce athletes for their work ethic and commitments to improving their sports skills. Success in sports is often predicated on the belief that more is better, and slogans such as "no pain, no gain" adorn locker rooms and are programmed into the mindsets of many elite athletes. Therefore, athletes are not likely to self-refer for personal or career counseling, and many coaches are hesitant to encourage their athletes to engage in any outside activities that could take their focus away from sport.

Issues facing practitioners who work with foreclosed student–athletes include assisting them in managing role conflict and eligibility regulations. Student–athletes who do not engage in exploratory behavior frequently select career tracks that are not compatible with their interests, needs, or skills (Hansen & Sackett, 1993). They often seek out majors and courses that will not conflict with their athletic practice and game schedules, particularly during their first years in university when athletic concerns often supersede academic priorities. Boredom and a lack of interest are just two of the problems associated with the selection of non-personally relevant academic paths (Petitpas & O'Brien, 2008).

Assisting the foreclosed athlete

Many foreclosed athletes have little need or desire to seek out support services. Their strong and exclusive sport identities provide them with the work ethic and focus that enable them to excel in sports and avoid much of the anxiety and uncertainty that accompany establishing a personal identity. Consequently, programs or interventions to assist athletes who have foreclosed on their identities typically result from crises or are built into mandated programs.

A crisis can occur in foreclosed athletes when a severe injury or forced retirement poses a threat to the individual's sport identity. When planning intervention strategies for athletes in crisis, it is helpful to assess their levels of commitment to sport roles and the meanings that they place on their current situations. Typically, this information can be gathered during the rapport-building phase of the counseling relationship and be used to determine if the person is in psychological or situational foreclosure (Petitpas, 2002). In cases where psychological foreclosure is evident, practitioners need to exercise caution and not challenge the efficacy of the strong and exclusive sport identity directly. The therapeutic relationship provides the emotional support that is frequently needed as the person goes through the ups and downs associated with disengagement from sport and establishing a new identity. The process of counseling can take on many of the same characteristics found when working through personality disorders and involves a long process of self-discovery, awareness, and feedback.

Coach-, athletic department-, or club-mandated workshops on career development and life skills provide another avenue to working with foreclosed athletes, who otherwise would have little motivation to participate in any type of self-awareness or life-planning activity. Programs such as the Athlete Career and Education program in Australia offer workshops to elite athletes on a variety of life skills including time management, job hunting strategies, résumé construction, and interviewing skills (Anderson & Morris, 2000). All of these experiences have merit, but the emphasis is often placed on decontextualized skills that have little immediate relevance for the athletes. Even though career development workshops can have positive effects on athletes' career decision-making self-efficacy (Shiina, Brewer, Petitpas, & Cornelius, 2003), it is questionable whether these efforts will result in any concrete actions on the part of unmotivated attendees, particularly, if the underlying issues of motivation, identity, and transferability of skills are not the primary focus.

Kelman's (1958) framework for examining how motivation influences the acquisition of skills can be a helpful tool for planning strategies to reach athletes. In this framework, athletes who participate in mandatory career development workshops to avoid sanctions or to gain coaches' approval would be displaying a *compliance* level of motivation. Those individuals who attend to gain peer approval or social acceptance would be exhibiting an *identification* level of motivation. Both compliance and identification are external motives that rarely lead to lasting change. If athletes are to master skills or form new habits, they must have opportunities to explore and experience the benefits of new behaviors in meaningful contexts. Through these experiences, individuals begin to internalize the new behaviors and the motivation shifts from extrinsic to intrinsic.

When planning career development programs for athletes it is important to remain focused on what motivates them. Practitioners may use compliance- or identification-based strategies to gain athletes' initial participation, but should structure the learning environment to facilitate a progression that allows athletes to create personal relevance through follow-up over an extended period of time. For example, a mandated workshop on identifying transferable skills may initially focus on how specific skills are developed and used in sport contexts. Thus, the career development skills and knowledge to be learned by the athletes are situated in a meaningful context for the participants, sport. Because the context has personal relevance for the participants, they are likely to be interested and to reflect on and internalize potentially beneficial changes.

Athletes can also be motivated to participate in the career development process through identification strategies. Evaluation data from the United States Olympic Committee's Career Assistance Program for Athletes revealed that using well-known former Olympians as part of the training corps brought credibility to the program content and attracted participants (Petitpas, Danish, McKelvain, & Murphy, 1992). Similarly, having recently graduated student-athletes participate in career workshops for intercollegiate athletes is likely to have a greater effect in comparison to career nights where local professionals recount their job achievements. Current student-athletes are more likely to identify with former athletic alumni, who have shared similar concerns, struggles, and transition experiences. Information-sharing networks of former athletes and ongoing support groups are two other methods for keeping the athletes thinking about their career development.

The main challenge for practitioners is to create opportunities that foster learning processes that help foreclosed athletes move from extrinsic motivation to the intrinsic motivation necessary to engage in exploratory behavior. The key to reaching this goal is the quality of the relationship that is established between the practitioner and the foreclosed athlete. Once a relationship has been established, the practitioner can begin to create and provide opportunities that are personally meaningful to the individual athlete. For example, the process of examining skills such as planning and goal setting in sport are transferable to the career development and decision-making process. The practitioner, in this instance, may capitalize on the strong relationship that has been established and work with the athlete to examine the transferability of these skills to other contexts.

Volunteering or taking service learning courses can provide new experiences that challenge athletes to examine career development. Athletes, however, have highly structured lives, and these experiences can be difficult to arrange. So what is the answer? It may simply come down to the quality of the practitioner/athlete relationship. Effective mentoring relationships (i.e., those that are based on empathy, high and positive expectations, and advocacy) can be instrumental in promoting self-awareness and future planning (Cornelius, 2006). Practitioners who are able to create solid mentoring relationships are most likely to facilitate the personal and career development of the student-athletes under their charge.

Conclusions

Although the term *identity foreclosure* was first connected to athletic participation in the 1970s (Petitpas, 1978) and is listed as one of 23 practice areas in the current proficiencies in sport psychology (American Psychological Association, 2010), little has been written about its development or assessment, particularly as it relates to athletes. The purposes of this chapter were: (a) to provide information about identity foreclosure in athletes, (b) to differentiate it from other similar constructs, and (c) to offer suggestions for planning and implementing intervention strategies with athletes who exhibit foreclosure. In general, the ability to differentiate between psychological and situational foreclosure will allow practitioners to plan and deliver interventions that are most appropriate for each group. The defensive structure of the psychologically foreclosed individual presents numerous challenges for practitioners and typically requires them to devote considerable time, to display a lot of patience, and to be able to build strong working relationships before they are likely to see any progress on the part of the athlete. Situationally foreclosed athletes tend to be less defensive and rigid, and are likely to be open to exploring new options, if the information is presented in a personally relevant manner. See Box 30.1 for practical suggestions related to working with athletes in identity foreclosure.

Box 30.1

Suggestions for practitioners working with athletes in identity foreclosure

- Understand the role that sports participation plays in the identity of the athlete.
- Do not directly challenge the efficacy of an exclusive commitment to sport roles.
- Assess for situational versus psychological foreclosure.
- Understand the challenges that can be present when working with athletes who are foreclosed (e.g., bracketed self-confidence, external locus of control).
- Work with coaches and administrators to understand and plan appropriate educational strategies for athletes who display situational foreclosure.
- Establish strong counseling relationships with athletes in psychological foreclosure and assist them through a process of self-discovery, feedback, and awareness.

References

Adams, G., Shea, J., & Fitch, S. (1979). Toward the development of an objective assessment of ego-identity status. *Journal of Youth and Adolescence, 8,* 223–237.

American Psychological Association. (2010). *Public description of sport psychology.* Retrieved from http://www.apa.org/ed/graduate/specialize/sports.aspx

Anderson, D., & Morris, T. (2000). Athlete lifestyle programs. In D. Lavallee & P. Wylleman (Eds.), *Career transitions in sport: International perspectives* (pp. 59–80). Morgantown, WV: Fitness Information Technology.

Blos, P. (1967). The second individuation process of adolescence. *Psychoanalytic Studies of the Child, 22,* 162–186.

Bourne, E. (1978). The state of research on ego-identity: A review and appraisal. *Journal of Youth and Adolescence, 7,* 223–250.

Brewer, B. W. (1993). Self-identity and specific vulnerability to depressed mood. *Journal of Personality, 61,* 343–364.

Brewer, B. W., Van Raalte, J. L., & Linder, D. E. (1993). Athletic identity: Hercules' muscles or Achilles heel? *International Journal of Sport Psychology, 24,* 237–254.

Brown, C., Glastetter-Fender, C., & Shelton, M. (2000). Psychosocial identity and career control in college student-athletes. *Journal of Vocational Behavior, 1,* 53–64.

Cornelius, A. (2006). *Evaluating the mentor-protégé relationship.* Paper presented at Leadership through Academics, Community Engagement, and Service Conference, Springfield, MA.

Côté, J. (2009). The road to continued sport participation and sport excellence. In E. Hung, R. Lidor, & D. Hackfort (Eds.), *Psychology of sport excellence* (pp. 45–52). Morgantown, WV: Fitness Information Technology.

Danish, S. J. (1983). Musings about personal competence: The contributions of sport, health, and fitness. *American Journal of Community Psychology, 11*, 221–240.

Erikson, E. H. (1959). Identity and the life cycle: Selected papers. *Psychological Issues, 1*, 1–171.

Finch, L. (2009). Understanding and assisting the student-athlete-to-be and the new student-athlete. In E. F. Etzel (Ed.), *Counseling and psychological services for the college student-athlete* (pp. 349–378). Morgantown, WV: Fitness Information Technology.

Good, A. J., Brewer, B. W., Petitpas, A. J., Van Raalte, J. L., & Mahar, M. T. (1993). Identity foreclosure, athletic identity, and college sport participation. *Academic Athletic Journal, 7*(1), 1–12.

Hansen, I., & Sackett, S. A. (1993) Agreement between college major and vocational interests for female athlete and non-athlete college students. *Journal of Vocational Behavior, 43*, 298–309.

Henry, M., & Renaud, H. (1972). Examined and unexamined lives. *Research Reporter, 7*(1), 5.

Jordaan, J. P. (1963). Exploratory behavior: The foundation of self and occupational concepts. In D. E. Super, R. Starishevsky, N. Matlin, & J. P. Jordaan (Eds.), *Career development: Self-concept theory* (pp. 46–57). New York: CEEB Research Monographs.

Kelman, H. C. (1958). Compliance, identification, and internalization: Three processes of opinion change. *Journal of Conflict Resolution, 2*, 51–60.

Kennedy, S. R., & Dimick, K. M. (1987). Career maturity and professional expectations of college football and basketball players. *Journal of College Student Personnel, 28*, 293–297.

Kohut, H. (1971). *The analysis of the self: A systematic approach to the treatment of narcissistic personality disorders*. New York: International University Press.

Kornspan, A. S., & Etzel, E. F. (2001). The relationship of demographic and psychological variables to career maturity of junior college student-athletes. *Journal of College Student Development, 42*, 122–132.

LeUnes, A., & Nation, J. R. (1983). Saturday's heroes: A psychological portrait of college football players. *Journal of Sport Behavior, 5*, 139–149.

Marcia, J. (1966). Development and validation of ego-identity status. *Journal of Personality and Social Psychology, 3*, 551–558.

Marcia, J., Waterman, A., Matteson, D., Archer, S., & Orlofsky, J. (1993). *Ego identity: A handbook for psychosocial research*. New York: Springer-Verlag.

Miller, P. S., & Kerr, G. A. (2003). The role experimentation of intercollegiate student athletes. *The Sport Psychologist, 17*, 196–219.

Murphy, G. M., Petitpas, A. J., & Brewer, B. W. (1996). Identity foreclosure, athletic identity, and career maturity in intercollegiate athletes. *The Sport Psychologist, 10*, 239–246.

Perna, F., Zaichkowsky, L., & Bochnek, G. (1996). The association of mentoring with psychosocial development among male athletes at termination of college career. *Journal of Applied Sport Psychology, 8*, 76–88.

Petitpas, A. (1978). Identity foreclosure: A unique challenge. *Personnel and Guidance Journal, 56*, 558–561.

Petitpas, A., & O'Brien, K. (2008). A focus on career considerations. In A. Leslie-Toogood and E. Gill (Eds.), *Advising Student-Athletes: A collaborative approach to success* (Monograph Series Number 18, pp. 133–138). Manhattan, KS: National Academic Advising Association.

Petitpas, A., Danish, S., McKelvain, R., & Murphy, S. (1992). A career assistance program for elite athletes. *Journal of Counseling and Development, 70*, 383–386.

Petitpas, A. J. (2002). Counseling interventions in applied sport psychology. In J. L. Van Raalte & B. W. Brewer (Eds.), *Exploring sport and exercise psychology: A practitioners guide* (2nd ed., pp. 253–268). Washington, DC: American Psychological Association.

Petitpas, A. J., & Champagne, D. E. (2000). Sport and social competence. In S. J. Danish & T. P. Gullotta (Eds.), *Developing competent youth and strong communities through after-school programming* (pp. 115–137). Washington, DC: CWLA Press.

Shiina, S., Brewer, B. W., Petitpas, A. J., & Cornelius, A. E. (2003). Effects of transferable skills workshops on the career self-efficacy of college student-athletes. *Academic Athletic Journal, 17*(1), 54–64.

Weiss, M. R. (1995). Children in sport: An educational model. In S. M. Murphy (Ed.), *Sport psychology interventions* (pp. 39–69). Champaign, IL: Human Kinetics.

White, R. W. (1963). Ego and reality in psychoanalytic theory: A proposal regarding independent ego energies. *Psychological Issues, 3*, Monograph 11. New York: International University Press.

31

Overtraining and recovery

Michael Kellmann

Overtraining develops because the indicators have not been detected over a long period of time and because athletes and coaches have not been aware of the symptoms, have not paid attention, and/or have not linked single indicators to the overall situation the athlete is experiencing. It is easy to overlook indicators considering the time schedule of athletes in the treadmill of sport. For example, Helge Meeuw, five-times German swimming champion, in 2006 described his daily routine before the German Championships:

> I get up at 6:30 a.m. From 7 a.m. until 8:45 a.m. I have water training at the sport school. After that I have a quick breakfast to be at the hospital at 10 a.m. where I am doing my internship. At 3:30 p.m. I head off to the sport school for strength training or physiotherapy, followed by additional water training from 6 p.m. until 8 p.m. At 9 p.m. I am finally at home. In the beginning of this program I felt like I was in a coma. However, I took the day off before the German Championships. The recovery during this period gave me the kick to perform well.
>
> (Körber, 2006, p. 22)

Three elements of this example stand out: (a) the challenge of balancing different tasks and responsibilities (e.g., training, work duties), (b) self-awareness, and (c) well-structured planning. The quote reads as if the recovery day was planned in his schedule and he made a conscious decision that he needed it, because he had some sort of monitoring system that allowed him to judge how he was physically experiencing the effects of his hectic life.

In another example, Whitney Myers, an American swimmer, was probably not aware of the toll overtraining had on her life, as it was described on the website of the New York Times (Reynolds, 2008):

> In 2006, Myers won the women's NCAA title in the 200- and 400-yard individual medleys and, to the surprise of almost everyone, won gold in the 200-meter individual medley at the Pan Pacific Championships. The accolades kept coming: Myers was named an all-American in several events and an NCAA Breakout Performer of the

Year and swam for the United States national team. But barely a year later, she floundered badly at the 2007 long-course championships, making the finals in only one event. For weeks before that, her performance in practices had been miserable: slow times, inert form. "I remember standing behind the starting blocks at the pool and thinking, 'I don't want to be here,'" she says. "I felt terrible, mentally and physically." While trying to build on her breakthrough season, she had pushed too hard. She had overtrained. She was, for a while at least, finished as a swimmer.

Based on this description, it sounds like Whitney had trained too much without taking a break, resulting in a self-generated state of overtraining pushed by a high level of achievement motivation.

A last example comes from the coach of the French national soccer team before the quarter finals in the 2006 World Cup. The press asked him how he trained his athletes so that his team improved their physical condition from game to game. "We have done almost nothing," answered Domenech, "only recovery. You know: old people need care" (Itzel, 2006). Although this quote may sound funny at first, physical and mental rest are important components of fitness and preparation for competition as Richardson, Andersen, and Morris (2008) have recently discussed.

Definition and description of overtraining and recovery

In the conclusion of my chapter "Underrecovery and overtraining: Different concepts – similar impact?" I (Kellmann, 2002a) answered the question in the title clearly with a "yes" and a "no". Yes, underrecovery and overtraining have the same impact – performance declines; no, they are not similar – research has clearly shown that underrecovery is the precursor/cause of overtraining. The key to prevent overtraining is an active and proactive enhancement of recovery. Coaches and athletes need to be educated about the importance of optimal recovery and its effect on performance. Kellmann and Kallus (2001, p.22) defined recovery as

> an inter- and intra-individual multilevel (e.g., psychological, physiological, social) process in time for the re-establishment of performance abilities. Recovery includes an action-oriented component, and those self-initiated activities (proactive recovery) can be systematically used to optimize situational conditions to build up and to refill personal resources and buffers. This definition also illuminates the complexity of recovery as I discussed (Kellmann, 2002a) and highlights the need to identify ideal recovery strategies on an individual basis.

Balancing training stress and recovery are essential to the achievement of optimal performance, and the avoidance of overtraining. Underrecovery can often lead to poor psychological and physical outcomes, including overtraining and burnout. Specifically, a prolonged imbalance of stress (including competition, training, and stress associated with events outside of sport) and recovery, in addition to an increase in the intensity and volume during training, can result in overtraining (Budgett, 1998). Therefore, stress and recovery should be continuously monitored during the training process (e.g., Kellmann, Altenburg, Lormes, & Steinacker, 2001). Overtraining can also result from training factors such as (a) monotonous training programs, (b) more than 3 hours of training per day, (c) failure to alternate hard and easy training days or alternate two hard days followed by an easy training day, (d) no training periodization and respective regeneration micro-cycles after two or three weeks of training, or (e) no rest days (Smith & Norris, 2002). To avoid underrecovery, the precursor of overtraining, physiological and psychological recovery should be an integral part of the training plan (Hooper & Mackinnon, 1995).

Overtraining is characterized by an ongoing performance plateau that does not improve with short amounts of rest and recovery. Common symptoms associated with over-training include depressed mood, general apathy, decreased self-esteem and performance, emotional instability, restlessness, irritability, poor sleep, weight loss, loss of appetite, increased resting heart rate and vulnerability to injuries, hormonal changes, and the absence of supercompensation. Another significant clinical feature of overtraining is an increased risk of infection and other corresponding symptoms, which suggests the presence of an impaired immune response (see Kellmann, 2002a). Alternatively, if the rest interval between consecutive training workouts is of an optimal duration, supercompensation or a training effect is likely to follow a workout that results in a degree of fatigue or depletion. Moreover, supercompensation will be accompanied by an increase in performance ability (Zatsiorsky, 1995).

One objective of studying the effects of overtraining is to establish which signs (symp-toms, markers) predict negative processes. Physiological indicators, such as creatine kinase, represent shifts in training loads, but are an undependable gauge for detecting early overtraining symptoms (Raglin, 1993). Findings from studies of physiological markers of overtraining have been reviewed, but are often inconclusive and even contradictory (Kuipers & Keizer, 1988). Distinguishing normal from abnormal modifications in responses to training is complex because various physiological characteristics alter when one shifts from standard to intense training. Physicians and physiologists stress that no firm physiological marker exists. Studies to establish decisive factors of overtraining have demonstrated, however, that psychological indicators are sensitive and consistent (Kenttä & Hassmén, 1998). The advantage of psychometric instruments is the quick availability of information. Although common blood analyses and/or specific medical/physiological diagnostics may take hours or days (and sometimes even weeks), psychological data become available within minutes.

The phenomenon of overtraining, as described in the literature, is confusing, due, in part, to a lack of international standardized terminology and the absence of clear diagnostic criteria (see Kellmann, 2002a; Richardson et al., 2008). The terms overwork, overreaching, overstraining, staleness, burnout, overfatigue, and short- and long-time overtraining have all been used to describe overtraining. Some authors differentiate between overtraining, staleness, and burnout and describe the different physiological and psychological effects, whereas others do not. Adding to the confusion, terminology differs by geographical location (e.g., Europe, North America) and professional background (e.g., medical staff, sport psychologists).

Interrelations of stress-states and recovery demands

I (Kellmann, 2002a) proposed a general model describing the interrelations of stress-states and recovery demands. The basic assumption of this model (Figure 31.1) is that with increas-ing stress, increased recovery is necessary to stay in the original stress state. Limited resources (e.g., time), however, initiate a vicious cycle: under increased stress and the inability to

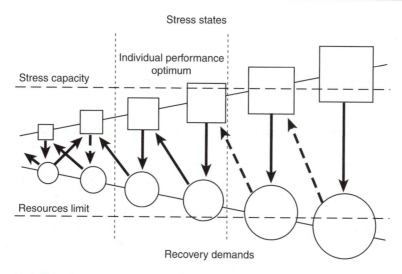

Figure 31.1 The "scissors model" of the interrelation of stress states and recovery demands. Reprinted, with permission, from Kallus, K.W., & Kellmann, M. (2000). Burnout in athletes and coaches. In Y.L. Hanin (Ed.), *Emotions in sport* (p. 212). Champaign, IL: Human Kinetics.

meet increased recovery demands, a person experiences more stress. Recovery demands are defined as the quality and/or quantity of necessary recovery activities to level out the current recovery–stress state. People may be stressed to the point that they fail to find or make time to recover adequately, or to consider better ways of coping with their situations.

With intermediate levels of stress, one can find an area of optimal performance, and thus, an area of adequate recovery. Beyond this point, one cannot meet recovery demands without additional recovery activities. Stress will accumulate, and without intervention, overtraining symptoms are likely to develop. The state of balanced stress and recovery is related to optimal performance. In a state of adequate recovery, the individual can react appropriately and cope successfully with stress without additional recovery activities. A lack of recovery, or underrecovery, can trigger a process that leads to a state of elevated stress. Because increasing stress limits the possibility of recovery, the athlete must be given special opportunities to recover to re-establish an optimal level of performance.

Applying this model to sport may explain how overtraining develops. The axis of the stress-states can be seen as a continuum of an increasing training load, which can be labeled at the extreme end points: *no training* and *overtraining* (see Figure 31.1). With additional training load the organismic recovery demands increase proportionally along the recovery axis. A short-term planned sacrifice of recovery, however, enhances long-term performance effects (e.g., supercompensation). If training load and intensity increase over a longer time with inadequate or inappropriate recovery, the individual experiences long-term under-recovery that may result in overtraining. To reach an optimal recovery–stress state, athletes need to increase their self-initiated activities to fulfil their recovery demands. At each stage of the model, recovery can work as a regulation mechanism, which is caused by an increasing distance between the two axes into a higher recovery debt (days to weeks). The higher a person is on the stress-states or the more extensive the overtraining is, the more recovery efforts are needed to reach the individual optimal recovery–stress state. The model of the interrelation of stress-states and recovery demands implies that it is not negative to be highly stressed as long as a person engages in enough recovery.

Psychometric approaches to monitor training

Athletes do not love paperwork. Many sport psychologists learn this lesson when they try to administer questionnaires to an athlete or sport team during an initial meeting. Due to such experiences, some sport psychologists refrain from using questionnaires as diagnostic tools or they desist from using diagnostics other than observation and more or less systematic interviews. Complete diagnostics, however, are central for a solid data foundation on which to base subsequent interventions for overtraining (Beckmann & Kellmann, 2003). The use of observations, interview techniques, and standardized instruments such as questionnaires is common. Ideally a combination of these approaches should be used (see Chapters 9–12).

In many sports medical doctors are around athletes on a more regular basis than sport psychologists. Verbal interactions between doctors and athletes during sport medical treatments and consultations are often aimed, in part, at detecting signs of overtraining/underrecovery. Intensive consultations depend on the time available. The use of psychometric instruments can be economical and may limit *a priori* biases that can affect the perspectives and perceptions of consultants. The information gained from psychometrically validated questionnaires can be used as a screening method for individual problems in large groups.

To compare athletes with normative data of physiological tests from the general population may be misleading. Inter-individual differences in recovery potential, exercise capacity, non-training stressors, and stress tolerance will affect the degree of vulnerability experienced by athletes under identical training conditions (Lehmann, Foster, & Keul, 1993). Physiological and psychological stress and recovery can be monitored during the training process to prevent overtraining; however, feedback loops of coaches and athletes need to be established on a regular basis to evaluate the scores. The key is to evaluate athletes individually, monitor them regularly, and compare the obtained data longitudinally (Froehlich, 1993).

Monitoring instruments are important for assessing an individual's need for recovery. Research in sport psychology on monitoring training/overtraining/underrecovery has mainly involved the Profile of Mood States (POMS; McNair, Lorr, & Droppleman, 1971/1992) and Borg's Rating of Perceived Exertion (RPE; Borg, 1998). Kenttä and Hassmén (1998, 2002) recently introduced the concept of total quality recovery, which they closely structured around the concept of RPE to emphasize the interrelationship between training and recovery. This new approach is an effective way of addressing the problem of assessing recovery and underrecovery. The POMS and the RPE were not designed for the assessment of recovery in sport, but until recently there had been no instruments available to specifically assess the complexity of recovery and stress.

Hanin (2000, 2002) introduced an alternative individualized approach suggesting that each individual has a zone of optimal functioning. Performance efficiency is maximized when the level of one's subjective emotional experience falls within this zone. The individual zones of optimal functioning (IZOF) model provides an individualized framework and tools to describe, predict, and explain why and how individually optimal and dysfunctional states can affect athletic performance. An important extension of the IZOF model is that idiosyncratic emotion markers of these optimal and dysfunctional performance states are proposed as specific criteria of an optimal (sufficient) recovery process. In each case individually optimal recovery strategies need to be identified.

The Recovery–Stress Questionnaire for Athletes (RESTQ-Sport; Kellmann & Kallus, 2001; Kellmann, Kallus, Samulski, Costa, & Simola, 2009) is an instrument that systematically assesses the recovery–stress state of an athlete. The recovery–stress state indicates the extent to which an individual is physically and/or mentally stressed, and whether or not the person is capable of using individual strategies for recovery, and also assesses which strategies are used. Scales 1 to 7 measure temporary or stable life stresses in general, performance related stress, and physical aspects of stress, and scales 8 to 12 measure temporary or stable non-specific recovery activities (general recovery). Seven sport-specific areas assess additional aspects of stress (scales 13–15, sport-specific stress) and recovery (scales 16–19, sport-specific recovery). All items on the RESTQ-Sport are scored from 0 (*never*) to 6 (*always*). An example of an item would be: "In the past (3) days/nights ... my muscles felt stiff or tense during performance".

The RESTQ-Sport has been used to monitor athletes during the preparation camps for the Rowing World Championships and Olympic Games (e.g., Kellmann *et al.*, 2001; Mäestu, Jürimäe, Kreegipou, & Jürimäe, 2006) and observe the influence of training on stress and recovery (e.g., Coutts, Wallace, & Slattery, 2007). These studies found that increases in training volume were reflected by elevated stress scores and reduced recovery scores measured by the RESTQ-Sport.

During training camps it may be beneficial to provide feedback to coaches and athletes about athletes' current recovery–stress states to initiate interventions aimed at optimal stress–recovery balance. Figure 31.2 provides an example of how the information of the RESTQ-Sport profile has been used. A track and field athlete completed the RESTQ-Sport after arriving at a training camp preparing with the relay team for the next World Championships. Her initial RESTQ-Sport profile is represented by the bold line in Figure 31.2. The profile revealed elevated levels of emotional stress and social stress (scales related to general stress) as well as for all scales of general recovery. In the sport-specific areas, elevated scores of emotional exhaustion and injury could be observed as well as medium levels of recovery. This pattern clearly indicated that something in the life of the athlete was negatively affecting the balance of her recovery–stress state. Knowing that the heavy training was yet to come, and it would even more negatively affect her recovery–stress state, the relay coach approached her and provided feedback on her RESTQ-Sport profile. In this feedback and communication, the athlete shared with the coach a problematic personal situation. Talking to the coach helped her to address the problem and deal with her personal issues. Subsequently, even after the heavy physical training started, her recovery–stress state improved (thin line, Figure 31.2) by the end of the camp.

This example highlights one major component that may help coaches and athletes avoid overtraining: communication. When coaches can acknowledge that athletes have non-sport lives, can create an environment where athletes can express themselves, and do not punish them for being tired, the first step toward a balance between stress and recovery is made. Regular short chats with athletes are important to create that kind of environment, but the process becomes time intensive when a large number of athletes are being coached.

Strategies to prevent overtraining

The most frequent causes of overtraining cited by athletes are (a) too much stress and pressure, (b) too much practice and physical training, (c) physical exhaustion and all-over soreness, (d) boredom because of too much repetition, and (e) poor rest or lack of proper sleep.

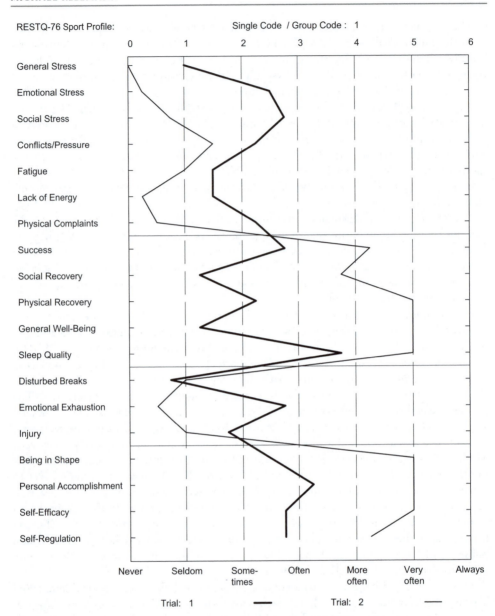

Figure 31.2 Recovery–stress state at the beginning of a training camp (bold line) and at the end of the training camp (thin line).

Holistic training encompasses two ideas: (a) training must be balanced and varied, and (b) non-training time has a major influence on training. All factors outside the realm of training sessions, therefore, need to be evaluated as to their possible negative influences on total fatigue. Insufficient recovery time between practices is the main cause of overtraining. Factors such as nutrition, sleep deficit, sickness, travel, and competitions increase the negative effects of insufficient recovery.

298

Recovery is more than doing nothing and/or resting: it is an active process. Because recovery is specific to each individual, it is important for coaches to plan rest days during regular training, in training camps, and during competition. I (Kellmann, 2002b) suggested some activities such as dancing, meeting friends, stretching, indoor games (e.g., board games, word games, playing cards), reading books, going for walks, sightseeing, trips to a lake including picnics and swimming, or easy runs. These ideas may help coaches and support staff (e.g., sport psychologists) to individualize recovery activities, however not every activity has the same effect of recuperation for all athletes. Recovery activities for athletes can be performed individually or within a group. Sometimes athletes should be left by themselves to do whatever they want to do, and at other times it could be helpful to give some directions. Probably the most important aspect about recovery is that it is a proactive, self-initiated process to re-establish psychological and physiological resources. From this perspective people are responsible for their recovery activities, and can actively initiate them. For example, going to a movie, visiting close friends, or going for a light run can be self-initiated and, therefore, proactively put a person in charge. In regular life there are numerous possibilities for recovery, but during training camps options are limited.

Peterson (2003) identified four steps for coaches and support teams (e.g., sport psychologists) to recognize the symptoms of overtraining and to develop preventive strategies:

Step 1: Know the symptoms of overtraining

- Impaired performance
- No supercompensation in response to taper or rest
- Increased resting heart rate
- Weight loss
- Loss of appetite
- Increased vulnerability to injuries
- Hormonal changes
- Depressed mood
- General apathy
- Decreased self-esteem, emotional instability
- Restlessness, irritability
- Disturbed sleep.

Step 2: Increase level of athletes' self-awareness

- Make it a habit to ask your athletes how they are feeling and listen to their answers.
- Encourage your athletes to keep a regular training log.
- Systematically evaluate athlete performances.

Step 3: Model and teach the value of recovery

- Model good recovery strategies in the context of your own life and work.

Step 4: Keep training fun and sport in perspective

- Coaches should make work fun and incorporate innovations to training programs to reduce stress and make sport enjoyable for their athletes.

- Athletes should maintain balance in their own lives and develop their identities in other realms of interest (e.g., family, school, non-sport careers, outside interests).
- Coaches need to accept the concept of athletes having lives outside of sport.

Conclusions and summary

I (Kellmann, 2002b) have pointed out that it requires a close cooperation between coaches, athletes, sport physicians, and sport psychologists to use the available medical, psychological, and performance data on an interdisciplinary basis. This process starts with open communication, adherence to agreements, quick reactions to feedback, and an openness to learn from others. The athletes are the centre of interest. Ideally the coach receives information dealing with different areas provided by the staff, and makes decisions based on this broad data base. Daily team meetings can ensure that all staff members have the same level of information. Athletes can regularly complete the RESTQ-Sport. Parallel to the questionnaire measurements, a sport medical assessment (e.g., lactate, creatine kinase) can take place. One goal is to identify those athletes whose recovery–stress states deviate from those expected based on individual or group profiles. As athletes complete questionnaires, the coaches and physicians involved receive fast feedback, and therefore, immediate interventions can be provided.

Of course, athletes can intentionally fake good answers on questionnaires, but emphasizing that the key to monitoring training is the principle "honesty first" can limit this behaviour. If the role of questionnaires is accepted, and scoring of the instruments reflects athletes' current conditions, then awareness of the processes affecting their lives increases. A relevant monitoring tool can assess areas not covered in regular coach–athlete talks. For many coaches, life events outside of sport are not relevant to sport performance, or they may think it is too intrusive to ask about private lives. Monitoring, however, can start an educational process for athletes and coaches when the results are shared. This process only works if explanations are provided as to why underrecovery is to be avoided and how questionnaires can be used to optimize training and performance. In my applied work with the German Junior National Rowing Team on recovery monitoring (see Kellmann et al., 2001), up to 80% of the rowers asked for feedback from their questionnaire data and how it related to physiological and medical data. Recognizing they would get feedback and were not just being used as "data gathering subjects" enhanced their commitment to the program (Beckmann & Kellmann, 2003). An open communication process is important to get athletes voluntarily involved in the assessment of recovery.

In addition to the integration of recovery within the training and competition schedule, interdisciplinary cooperation is a key for better diagnosis of the recovery–stress states of individuals. To optimize this process, the consultation with athletes should be done in close cooperation between coaches, sport physicians, and sport psychologists. Therefore, all physiological and psychological data, as well as training and performance data, should be used by the interdisciplinary team (Froehlich, 1993; Kenttä & Hassmén, 1998). This process begins with a complete training documentation, the assessment of subjective and objective physiological and psychological data, and the integration of athletes' perspectives. Clearance from the athlete needs to be obtained to adequately deal with confidentiality issues. See Box 31.1 for a summary of practical take-home messages about recovery.

Box 31.1

Summary of take-home messages regarding recovery

- It is not necessarily bad to have high levels of stress as long as the person knows how to recover.
- Recovery periods must be part of the training plan.
- Recovery is individually specific.
- Monitor the impact of training.
- Recovery involves self-responsibility.
- Regular communication is important to avoid overtraining.
- Sport psychologists can help to facilitate the communication processes and educate coaches and athletes about indicators of overtraining.

References

Beckmann, J., & Kellmann, M. (2003). Procedures and principles of sport psychological assessment. *The Sport Psychologist, 17*, 338–350.

Borg, G. (1998). *Borg's perceived exertion and pain rating scales.* Champaign, IL: Human Kinetics.

Budgett, R. (1998). Fatigue and underperformance in athletes: The overtraining syndrome. *British Journal of Sport and Medicine, 32*, 107–110.

Coutts, A., Wallace, L. K., & Slattery, K. M. (2007). Monitoring changes in performance, physiology, biochemistry, and psychology during overreaching and recovery in triathletes. *International Journal of Sports Medicine, 28*, 125–134.

Froehlich, J. (1993). Overtraining syndrome. In J. Heil (Ed.), *Psychology of sport injury* (pp. 59–70). Champaign, IL: Human Kinetics.

Hanin, Y. L. (2000). Individual zones of optimal functioning (IZOF) model: Emotion-performance relationships in sport. In Y. L. Hanin (Ed.), *Emotions in sport* (pp. 65–89). Champaign, IL: Human Kinetics.

Hanin, Y. L. (2002). Individually optimal recovery in sports: An application of the IZOF model. In M. Kellmann (Ed.), *Enhancing recovery: Preventing underperformance in athletes* (pp. 199–217). Champaign, IL: Human Kinetics.

Hooper, S. L., & Mackinnon, L. T. (1995). Monitoring overtraining in athletes. *Sports Medicine, 20*, 321–327.

Itzel, R. (2006). *Triumph der Edelmänner.* Retrieved April 2, 2009, from http://www.berlinonline.de/berliner-zeitung/archiv/.bin/dump.fcgi/2006/0629/fuballwm2006/0004/index.html

Kellmann, M. (2002a). Underrecovery and overtraining: Different concepts - similar impact? In M. Kellmann (Ed.), *Enhancing recovery: Preventing underperformance in athletes* (pp. 3–24). Champaign, IL: Human Kinetics.

Kellmann, M. (2002b). Current status and directions of recovery research. In M. Kellmann (Ed.), *Enhancing recovery: Preventing underperformance in athletes* (pp. 219–229). Champaign, IL: Human Kinetics.

Kellmann, M., & Kallus, K. W. (2001). *The Recovery–Stress questionnaire for athletes; User manual.* Champaign, IL: Human Kinetics.

Kellmann, M., Altenburg, D., Lormes, W., & Steinacker, J. M. (2001). Assessing stress and recovery during preparation for the World Championships in rowing. *The Sport Psychologist, 15*, 151–167.

Kellmann, M., Kallus, K. W., Samulski, D., Costa, L., & Simola, R. (2009). *Questionário de Estress e Recuperação para Atletas* [The Recovery–Stress Questionnaire for Athletes]. Belo Horizonte, Brazil: Imprensa Universitaria.

Kenttä, G., & Hassmén, P. (1998). Overtraining and recovery. *Sports Medicine, 26*, 1–16.

Kenttä, G., & Hassmén, P. (2002). Underrecovery and overtraining: A conceptual model. In M. Kellmann (Ed.), *Enhancing recovery: Preventing underperformance in athletes* (pp. 57–79). Champaign, IL: Human Kinetics.

Körber, P. (2006). Ich werde nie Profischwimmer. *Wiesbadener Kurier*, p. 22, 28 June.

Kuipers, H., & Keizer, H. A. (1988). Overtraining in elite athletes: Review and directions for the future. *Sports Medicine, 6*, 79–92.

Lehmann, M., Foster, C., & Keul, J. (1993). Overtraining in endurance athletes: A brief review. *Medicine and Science in Sports and Exercise, 25*, 854–861.

Mäestu, J., Jürimäe, J., Kreegipou, K., & Jürimäe, T. (2006). Changes in perceived stress and recovery during heavy training in highly trained rowers. *The Sport Psychologist, 20*, 24–39.

McNair, D., Lorr, M., & Droppleman, L. F. (1971/1992). *Profile of mood states manual*. San Diego, CA: Educational and Industrial Testing Service.

Peterson, K. (2003). Athlete overtraining and underrecovery: Recognizing the symptoms and strategies for coaches. *Olympic Coach, 18* (3), 16–17.

Raglin, J. S. (1993). Overtraining and staleness: Psychometric monitoring of endurance athletes. In R. B. Singer, M. Murphey, & L. K. Tennant (Eds.), *Handbook of research on sport psychology* (pp. 840–850). New York: Macmillan.

Reynolds, G. (2008). *Crash and burnout*. Retrieved April 2, 2009, from http://query.nytimes.com/gst/fullpage.html?res=9A0CE6D81F30F931A35750C0A96E9C8B63

Richardson, S. O., Andersen, M. B., & Morris, T. (2008). *Overtraining athletes: Personal journeys in sport*. Champaign, IL: Human Kinetics.

Smith, D. J., & Norris, S. R. (2002). Training load and monitoring an athlete's tolerance for endurance training. In M. Kellmann (Ed.), *Enhancing recovery: Preventing underperformance in athletes* (pp. 81–101). Champaign, IL: Human Kinetics.

Zatsiorsky, V. M. (1995). *Science and practice of strength training*. Champaign, IL: Human Kinetics.

32

Working with adult athlete survivors of sexual abuse

Trisha Leahy

The systematic documentation of sexual abuse of athletes within sport systems has begun to challenge the commonly accepted view of sport as an unproblematic site of youth empowerment and positive development (Leahy, 2010). Sport psychologists need to be equipped to be able to effectively help athletes through the recovery process without sacrificing their high-performance dreams and goals. Negotiating the complex dynamics of recovery work with profoundly traumatized athlete survivors of chronic sexual abuse poses a significant challenge to even the most skilled sport psychologist. Collaborative decisions about which path to take and which direction to turn, although crucial to an athlete's recovery, may not always be easy to assess from the rapidly evolving knowledge base (Leahy, Pretty, & Tenenbaum, 2003). In this chapter I will focus on the current standard of care guidelines regarding the treatment of survivors of chronic sexual abuse struggling with complex, dissociative posttraumatic conditions, with a particular emphasis on the social context of high-performance athletes.

Sexual abuse and trauma

Researchers and clinicians have for some time been applying a trauma framework to understand the effects of chronic and repeated sexual abuse. Central to this theoretical framework are the concepts of posttraumatic stress disorder (PTSD) and dissociation as key responses to traumatizing events. Core posttraumatic symptoms include re-experiencing, avoidance, and hyperarousal (American Psychiatric Association [APA], 2000). Symptoms related to re-experiencing and hyperarousal can include intrusive thoughts, physiological arousal, reactivity to trauma cues, and hypervigilance. Avoidant symptoms can include avoidance of thoughts, feelings, places, or people associated with the trauma (APA).

Dissociation is "a disruption in the usually integrated functions of consciousness" (APA, 2000, p. 477). Dissociative symptomatology (e.g., amnesia, derealisation, depersonalisation) involves a splitting between the "observing self" and the "experiencing self." During a traumatic experience, dissociation provides protective detachment from overwhelming affect and pain, but it can result in severe disruption within the usually integrated functions of consciousness, memory, identity, or perception of the environment.

Seven areas of functioning are affected through prolonged and repeated abuse, particularly that perpetrated by those in positions of trust, guardianship, or authority (Courtois, 2004). These areas include affect dysregulation (inability to regulate the intensity of affective responses); alterations in attention and consciousness leading to dissociative symptoms; self-perception embedded in a sense of guilt, shame, and responsibility for the abuse; traumatized attachment to the perpetrator, incorporating his (or her) belief system; relational difficulties with trust and intimacy; somatization and medical conditions; and attributions centering on hopelessness and despair (Briere, 2004). Recently, the concept of "complex trauma" has been developed in an attempt to explain these convoluted and intertwined posttraumatic, dissociative, and related symptom clusters (Courtois, 2004). To date, only one group of researchers has investigated the long-term effects on athlete survivors of child abuse using a trauma framework, and their research provided evidence supporting the applicability of the concept of complex trauma to understanding athletes' needs for recovery (Leahy et al., 2003; Leahy, Pretty, & Tenenbaum, 2008).

Sport environment issues

Effective abuse-related therapy must address the sociocultural context of the survivor's distress (Briere, 2004). Particularly evident from research reports across a number of countries is the manner in which certain aspects of the culture of competitive sport provide an environment that facilitates, rather than inhibits, the occurrence of sexual abuse in sport (Brackenridge, 2001). Two sport environment issues, perpetrator methodology and the bystander effect, require our understanding and attention if, as sport psychologists, we are to effectively engage in healing, therapeutic relationships with sexually abused athletes.

Perpetrator methodology

Leahy, Pretty, and Tenenbaum (2004) published qualitative data describing specific perpetrator methodologies sexually abused athletes have experienced within sport. Two key dimensions of perpetrator methodology included strategies designed to simultaneously engender feelings of complete powerlessness in the athlete, and conversely, to present the perpetrator as omnipotent. What seemed to characterize the perpetrator's methodology, and was particularly obvious in cases where the abuse was prolonged and repeated, was the need to impose his version of reality on the athlete and to isolate the athlete within that reality. The perpetrator successfully maintained that reality by controlling the psychological environment, silencing, and isolating the athlete from potential sources of support. In addition to controlling the athlete's outer life, her/his inner life was controlled through direct emotional manipulation, psychological abuse, and the creation of a highly volatile, psychologically abusive training environment. The perpetrator's ability to successfully create and maintain such an environment may be related to the unique sociocultural context of competitive sport in some first-world countries. This context is one that has been criticized as being imbued with an intensely volatile ethos, and within which psychologically abusive coaching behaviors may be normalized as part of the winning strategy (Brackenridge, 2001; Leahy, 2010). This point brings us to the issue of the bystander effect.

The bystander effect

The bystander effect refers to the situation where the victim perceived that others, who knew about (or suspected) the sexual abuse, did not do anything about it (Leahy et al., 2003). For example:

> He was in such a powerful position that no one interfered; I think no one questioned what he was doing. But now when I speak to people, they do say he stepped over the line with us, but ... they didn't say anything, they didn't want to interfere with him, Yeah, I'm a bit angry about that.
>
> (Leahy, 2010, p. 316)

Athletes' experiences of the bystander effect point to the apparent lack of systemically sanctioned accountability in relation to the power of the coach-perpetrator that allowed the abuse to continue for many years unchallenged by other adults in the system. These bystanders included coaching, sport psychology, and other support staff or volunteers who were not as senior in the competitive sport hierarchy as the perpetrator. The bystander effect was especially notable in the elite sport context: "No one ever interfered with us because we were so elite, and no one ever questioned what we were doing." (Leahy, 2010, p. 327).

For children, disclosure may be preempted if the child believes, or is aware that other adults know about the abuse (Palmer, Brown, Rae-Grant, and Loughlin, 1999). If observing adults take no action, the child may assume that the behavior is socially acceptable, or in the case of older children, as mentioned above, that the perpetrator's message that he is omnipotent is really true and that they really are trapped: "it never entered my mind that others could possibly be experiencing the same thing [pause]. ... This was something that was happening to me and it was between me and him and nobody else knew" (Leahy et al., 2003, p. 532).

Disruptions in attachment

Therapy is a trust-based relationship that requires not only authentic engagement but also vigilance in maintaining a healing dynamic within the therapeutic environment. One of the key difficulties in engaging in an effective therapeutic alliance with a chronically abused individual stems from alterations in the individual's capacity to develop and maintain healthy relationships, including the relationship with the therapist (Pearlman & Courtois, 2005). To understand this complex posttraumatic adaptation to prolonged and repeated abuse, particularly that which started from early childhood, we need to draw on attachment theory, and two related coping mechanisms: the locus of control shift, and traumatic attachment to the perpetrator.

Locus of control shift

Attachment theory proposes a biological drive in humans to attach. If attachment does not occur, a child will fail to thrive. Prolonged and repeated abuse by a trusted caregiver presents the child with an overwhelming challenge to the biological need to attach. The child cannot physically escape the abusive situation (e.g., if it is within the family) and cannot choose not to attach. The only developmentally available way of coping is an internal process of dissociating. Amnesia, however, is rarely total, even though specific abusive episodes may be dissociated, so the child has to try to understand why caregivers are hurting him/her.

The meaning likely to be constructed at an early developmental stage, and arguably the only meaning capable of resolving the potential disruption of the attachment systems, is that it is the child who is causing the abuse (e.g., by being bad and, therefore, deserving of such treatment). This locus-of-control shift transfers responsibility for the abuse, or for inability to prevent it, onto the victim (Ross, 1997). This logic simultaneously preserves the idealized trusted caregiver (actively reinforced by the perpetrator methodology and the bystander effect) and allows the victim hope through the illusion of control. It also allows attachment systems to remain intact (Briere, 2004).

Traumatic attachment to the perpetrator

The outcome of the perpetrator methodology, described earlier, and the locus-of-control shift, is the development of a traumatized attachment to the perpetrator. This process has been repeatedly observed in not only chronically abused children but also in adolescents and adults in situations of prolonged traumatization (e.g., domestic violence, captivity; Herman, 1997; Ross, 1997). In these situations in which the victim is repeatedly rendered helpless and powerless, and the perpetrator is presented as omnipotent, with no alternative reference points, the victim becomes entrapped within the perpetrator's viewpoint (Herman, 1997).

In Leahy et al.'s (2004) study, the athletes' reports describe the perpetrator's unpredictable and volatile emotional reward–punishment cycle that pervaded the sports environment. Within such an environment, the isolated victim is likely to become increasingly dependent on the perpetrator both for information and emotional support (Herman, 1997). The unpredictable cycling of fear and reprieve, punishment and reward, in the relatively closed context of an elite competitive sports team can result in a feeling of extreme, almost "worshipful," dependence on the perceived omnipotent perpetrator (Herman, 1997). The more confused and frightened the victim becomes, the more need to cling to the one relationship that is permitted – the one with the perpetrator. A female athlete in the study said of the coach who sexually abused her over a number of years, "To us at that time, his word was like gospel" (Leahy et al., 2004, p. 536).

Traumatized attachment to the perpetrator can continue long after the abuse has stopped, as illustrated in the following comment from an athlete also abused by her coach for many years (Leahy et al., 2004, p. 536):

> I still remember I used to brag to my friends and my parents how great this guy was, how lucky I was, and how he was the best coach in the whole world, you know. I remember I used to say that to people, and he just made us believe that he was just absolutely brilliant and I did believe that. *Yeah, and I still think he's awesome … and I still feel guilty that I did blow the whistle, and I made him lose his job.*

Where the locus-of-control shift and traumatized attachment are key coping strategies, disclosure simply does not happen, and common expectations of visible distress indicators may not be apparent. As the young person attempts to survive the toxic psychological environment, he or she may appear loving, needy, willing to please, and protective of the perpetrator. Silencing is an integral, not separate, part of the experience and is achieved through aspects of the perpetrator's methodology, which keeps the athlete in the state of traumatized entrapment, as a female athlete sexually abused by her coach described: "I didn't realize there was another way out [pause] or there was another option for me like [telling someone]." (Leahy et al., 2003, p. 661).

Some clinicians view the dissociation-facilitated locus-of-control shift and traumatic attachment to the perpetrator as the core therapeutic considerations in working with survivors of chronic childhood sexual abuse (Herman, 1997; Ross, 1997). Failure to recognize these complex dynamics is a potentially therapy-ending error:

> I can't say that I had any thoughts of saying, "No" [to the perpetrator], which is hard to justify to someone who says you're old enough to say no … . and like the [sport psychologist] couldn't understand that, uhm at 17, or 16, I couldn't say no … At the time it was crazy for me to try to explain how I felt, uhm, and so I actually said, "I can't do it" … *I just didn't go back.*
>
> (Leahy *et al.*, 2003, p. 662)

Treatment principles

Research on the efficacy of treatment for complex trauma is just emerging, much of it based on cognitive therapy approaches directed at stabilization of core PTSD and other symptoms (e.g., Reisick, Nishith, & Griffin, 2003). In general, however, there is insufficient evidence to categorically define the nature, longitudinal course, and relationship to PTSD treatment outcomes (Ford, Courtois, Steele, van der Hart, & Nijenhuis, 2005). Nevertheless, there is an evolving standard of care, and the current consensus model of treatment for chronic, complex traumatization is that a phase-oriented approach is necessary, in which treatment is clearly sequenced, tempered and task- and skill-focused (Courtois, 1999). Therapy must be empowering and collaborative and should normalize reactions to trauma. It is multimodal and transtheoretical, employing a variety of therapeutic techniques tailored to the individual needs and requiring a range of linked biopsychosocial treatment approaches (Courtois, 2004).

Within this model, the basic principles of good therapeutic practice remain valid, and it is important that from the outset these are communicated and monitored. These principles include issues of informed consent, confidentiality, clarity of professional role and boundaries, client empowerment and responsibility, issues of safety, emergency procedures, and adjunctive treatment options such as medication and hospitalization, as necessary. Throughout the process of the treatment, care should be taken to ensure that clients are developing the necessary self- and symptom-management competencies to maintain a level of functioning consistent with their lifestyles. For high-performance athletes, this approach will include maximizing the ability to maintain training and performance levels. Finally, vigilance must be maintained to ensure effective management of transferential and countertransferential issues (see Chapter 17). The therapist will need to consciously model self-regulatory skills to manage vicarious trauma reactions while maintaining a therapeutic focus on providing a safe, authentic emotional presence with clear therapeutic boundaries (Pearlman & Courtois, 2005).

The pathway to recovery for complex posttraumatic conditions is likely to require a relatively long time-frame, be intensive in terms of frequency of sessions, and vary in length of each session. Dissociation, avoidance, and motivated forgetting are likely to be extensively used as defense and coping mechanisms to keep painful material, or even the therapist, at a distance. It is important that the psychotherapeutic process proceed slowly and cautiously to avoid prematurely dealing with material that may retraumatize, and overwhelm the individual's ability to cope and maintain daily functioning.

Phases of treatment

The prevailing consensus model of treatment follows a three-phased macro-cycle, within a treatment framework cued to the symptom clusters of complex trauma described earlier. Treatment usually proceeds in a back-and-forth manner, more often taking the form of a recursive spiral, rather than a linear path (Courtois, 1999). The issues addressed in each phase will reemerge repeatedly as treatment progresses, and as the key survival coping mechanisms (dissociation, locus-of-control shift, and traumatic attachment) drive trauma-centric meaning attributions.

The first phase

The first phase focuses on stabilization, the establishment of safety, the development of the therapeutic alliance, symptom management self-care, and skill building. Key tasks that have to be achieved include the development of personal safety strategies; education to demystify the psychotherapy process; education about the nature of trauma and its effects to normalize the often overwhelming trauma symptoms experienced by the client; self-management, and life stabilization skills; and building of social relationships and support systems. Affect regulation and modulation are key targets of skill building interventions, as are body awareness and self-care.

Sport psychology cognitive-behavioral mental skills interventions are applicable in this phase of building healthy coping strategies. For high-performance athletes, self-care will also include attending to the maintenance of proper nutrition, training recovery, and injury prevention. There can be severe physiological sequelae for athletes and their abilities to train and maintain the level of confidence necessary for elite performance. For example, an athlete violently sexually assaulted within her sport environment described how her attempts to cope with the overwhelming trauma psychologically and physically consumed all the energy she had previously directed towards training and competing:

> I was tired, sick. ... I had to really cut down my training because I'd break down [physically]. ... I used to really enjoy training and loved competing [long pause] ... like you know my sport has been the defining thing for me as a person [long pause, weeping].
> (Leahy et al., 2003, p. 662)

The first phase also involves the establishment of the therapeutic alliance. Traumatic attachment processes may present significant challenges to this task. There may be recurrent testing of boundaries and the therapist's trustworthiness, along with fears of future betrayal and violation. If not properly managed by the therapist, these relational dynamics can compound harm by replicating the perpetrator dynamics within the therapeutic relationship. It is crucial that the therapist projects and models and makes available to the client, a stable, secure, reliable, well-bounded treatment relationship framework. This secure environment is the foundation upon which therapeutic work will proceed.

With the focus of the first phase work on skill building and self-management, significant improvements in clients' quality of life are likely to be experienced. For some clients at this juncture, termination or a break in therapy may be requested. Always ensure that an option to return to therapy at a later date remains open. For high-performance athletes, I have found it useful to try to use therapy "micro-cycles" to facilitate the athlete's competition goals, with priority tasks in each micro-cycle geared towards ensuring sufficient self-regulatory skills are in place to allow the athlete to continue to compete at key events. This strategy is important because it is not uncommon that survivors struggle with feelings of being "contaminated" by their traumatic experiences, with a sense of hopelessness about themselves and their lives. Being able to access the parts of their identities (e.g., elite sport performers) that are experienced as being free from this contamination provide an important reparative experience and counter the internalized negative perpetrator messages.

The second phase

In this phase, the therapist and client undertake a gradual, sequenced exposure to traumatic material. The trauma experience or experiences are directly processed to resolve posttraumatic symptoms and to integrate the trauma experiences into the survivor's life in such a way as to allow a forward self-development that is not solely defined by past trauma. This process includes coming to terms with overwhelming affect, gaining control of symptoms, and reducing the need for dissociative defenses to allow a coherent meaning to be constructed that can be lived with. Detailed exploration of traumatic material is not for the purposes of abreaction (release of emotional tension achieved through recalling a traumatic experience), which is not healing, and may simply retraumatize. It is to promote posttraumatic growth (Courtois, 2004).

Before entering this phase, the basic issues of informed consent, clarification of expectations, and demystification of the process must be again revisited. Stabilization skills must be in place, and pacing and intensity has to be planned so that the client leaves therapy sessions in control. I have found that it is during this phase that sessions may require a longer time than the usual therapy hour: up to ninety minutes to ensure this stabilization happens. If pacing and intensity are not managed well, there is a risk of decompensation and the resurgence of maladaptive trauma-based coping behaviors (e.g., self-injury, suicidality).

During this phase, when working with high-performance athletes, I have found guided imagery a useful technique, because athletes are often already familiar with it. Narrative recording, through written or oral presentation, or art and other expressive media, have also worked well. It is important that the therapist is able to be authentically present to acknowledge and normalize responses, and to provide a containing environment for this work. The therapist must also be ready to assist the processing of extremely intense emotions, such as rage, shame, grief, and mourning. Therapist dissociation or withdrawal from the traumatized person's sometimes overwhelming anger and grief are potentially harmful countertransferential responses. If a therapist is uncomfortable with anger or views anger or other negative affects as undesirable, then the practitioner may consciously or unconsciously encourage continued avoidance. Therapists also need to be knowledgeable about methods of safe expression and management of intense affect, to effectively facilitate the recovery of healthy affect regulation.

Common themes reoccurring during this phase will often center on the locus-of-control shift (i.e., the victim is responsible for the abuse) and traumatic attachment to the perpetrator, which can impede the expression and resolution of anger and grief and the development of empowered meaning attributions regarding the abuse. Acknowledging anger and grief is a major step to recovery, but it may be an intolerable step for the survivor unless traumatic attachment to the perpetrator is open for safe therapeutic exploration. Meaning attributions can reveal important underlying information about the locus of control shift and how traumatic attachment bonds are being maintained. The client, however, may perceive this information as unsafe to express if the superficial presentation (e.g., self-blaming attributions) appears to be unacceptable to the therapist who too quickly jumps in with, "It's not your fault" (Leahy *et al.*, 2003). As one athlete succinctly expressed, "Sometimes that makes me angry (pause) because it sounds like it's just a psychologist's spiel rather than sincere, uhm, helping me to understand my confusion." (p. 662). Rather than immediately challenging self-blaming attributions, and insisting that it is not the victim's fault, it may be more productive to respectfully explore the multi-layered construction of the attribution.

The second phase proceeds until PTSD symptoms become manageable. When processing is complete and memory is deconditioned, symptoms often cease and anguish recedes as trauma is integrated with other aspects of life, and clients develop more complete narratives of their lives than they had before (Ford *et al.*, 2005).

The third phase

The third phase involves reconnection with self and reintegration with social relationships and community networks. Therapeutic attention should still be maintained on issues of safety, self-care, and so forth. During this phase, issues related to the development of trusting relationships, intimacy, sexual functioning, vocational and career plans, and other life decisions are often the focus of ongoing work. This phase can also include the challenge of grieving for lost childhood. It may also involve decisions about ongoing relationships with abusive family members and perpetrators still within the client's social environment.

During this phase it is important to continue to facilitate the development of relational skills by modeling healthy negotiation of boundaries and dealing effectively with relational errors or misunderstandings. No therapist is perfect, and inevitably will fail to live up to idealistic projections, miss salient client cues, or fail to perceive accurately the survivors' needs. Modeling how healthy relationships can be preserved and repaired by good communication and emotional processing skills is an important therapist task through this phase to facilitate the development of present-day relationships that are not embedded in traumatized responses (Ford *et al.*, 2005).

Effectively managing the termination process is a challenge when working with traumatized survivors because feelings of abandonment, loss, and grief may re-emerge. Sport psychologists working on an ongoing basis with residential teams may be at an advantage at this point, because both the athlete and the sport psychologist remain in the same environment, allowing a gradual and closely monitored transition. It is helpful to allow for the possibility of return to therapy because future challenges my trigger distress or crises. Therapists should, therefore, be particularly vigilant with this vulnerable group of athletes to not have dual relationships, or post-termination relationships outside the therapy structure, because such involvements would prevent the possibility of a return to a therapy (Pearlman & Courtois, 2005).

Conclusions

> I spoke to the sport psychologist a couple of times but not once did [the sport psychologist] get it.
>
> (female athlete sexually abused by her coach for
> many years; Leahy, 2010, p. 316)

Research and clinical evidence indicates that athlete survivors of sexual abuse, whether perpetrated within sport or outside of sport, form a significant percentage of the athlete population with which sport psychologists will come into contact. Therefore, sport psychologists need to have the skills to be able to integrate effective treatment into the social context of the athlete's life. In this chapter I have described an introductory overview to the key treatment issues. This chapter is not enough to provide anyone with the competencies necessary to start engaging in an effective treatment relationship with traumatized athlete survivors of sexual abuse. Ongoing professional development training in this area should be undertaken before taking on the responsibility of facilitating recovery in this highly vulnerable group of athletes. Personal therapy may be useful to reveal therapist blind spots, and to protect from, or deal with, secondary traumatization. Finally, peer supervision is necessary to ensure the therapeutic process remains free of countertransferential errors that may be experienced by a traumatized athlete as harmful replications of perpetrator dynamics. See Box 32.1 for a summary of key points from this chapter.

Box 32.1

Key points on working with adult athlete survivors of sexual abuse

- Effective therapy must address the client's sociocultural context. Sport psychologists are well-positioned to be able to facilitate recovery, without sacrificing athletes' sporting goals, by integrating treatment into the social context of the athlete's life.
- Therapy is a trust-based relationship that requires authentic engagement, but also vigilance in maintaining a well-bounded, healing dynamic within the therapeutic environment.
- Establishing an effective therapeutic alliance with athlete survivors of long-term sexual abuse is only possible if the therapist is sensitive to the possible alterations in the athlete's capacity to develop and maintain healthy, trusting relationships in light of the confounding influence of ongoing traumatic attachment to the perpetrator.
- Current standard of care guidelines follow a three-phased macro-cycle within a treatment framework cued to the symptoms of complex trauma.
- Collaborative decisions about therapeutic micro-cycles can help ensure the athlete's performance at key competition events is maintained.
- Treatment may take longer than usual therapy, individual sessions may require longer duration, and treatment is unlikely to be linear. Issues may repeatedly re-emerge in different forms as treatment progresses.
- Therapists should be vigilant about having access to ongoing peer-supervision and personal therapy as necessary to ensure the treatment process remains free from harmful transferential and countertransferential contamination.

References

American Psychiatric Association (2000). *Diagnostic and statistical manual of mental disorders* (4th ed., text Rev.). Washington, DC: American Psychiatric Association.

Brackenridge, C. H. (2001). *Spoilsports: Understanding and preventing sexual exploitation in sport.* London: Routledge.

Briere, J. (2004). *Psychological assessment of adult posttraumatic states: Phenomenology, diagnosis, and measurement* (2nd ed.). Washington, DC: American Psychological Association.

Courtois, C. A. (1999). *Recollections of sexual abuse: Treatment principles and guidelines*. New York: Norton.

Courtois, C. A. (2004). Complex trauma, complex reactions: Assessment and treatment. *Psychotherapy: Theory Research, Practice, Training, 41*, 412–425.

Ford, J. D., Courtois, C. A., Steele, K., van der Hart, O., & Nijenhuis, E. R. S. (2005). Treatment of complex posttraumatic self-dysregulation. *Journal of Traumatic Stress, 18*, 437–447.

Herman, J. L. (1997). *Trauma and recovery. From domestic abuse to political terror* (2nd ed.). New York: Basic Books.

Leahy, T. (2010). Sexual abuse in sport: Implications for the sport psychology profession. In T. V. Ryba, R. J. Schinke, & G. Tenenbaum (Eds.), *The cultural turn in sport psychology* (pp. 315–334). Morgantown. WV: Fitness Information Technology.

Leahy, T., Pretty, G., & Tenenbaum, G. (2003). Childhood sexual abuse narratives in clinically and non-clinically distressed adult survivors. *Professional Psychology: Research and Practice, 34*, 657–665.

Leahy, T., Pretty, G., & Tenenbaum, G. (2004). Perpetrator methodology as a predictor of traumatic symptomatology in adult survivors of childhood sexual abuse. *Journal of Interpersonal Violence, 19*, 521–540.

Leahy, T., Pretty, G., & Tenenbaum, G. (2008). A contextualised investigation of traumatic correlates of childhood sexual abuse in Australian athletes. *International Journal of Sport and Exercise Psychology, 4*, 366–384.

Palmer, S. E., Brown, R. A., Rae-Grant, N. I., & Loughlin, M. J. (1999). Responding to children's disclosure of familial abuse: What survivors tell us. *Child Welfare, 78*, 259–283.

Pearlman, L. A., & Courtois, C. A. (2005). Clinical applications of the attachment framework: Relational treatment of complex trauma. *Journal of Traumatic Stress, 18*, 449–459.

Reisick, P., Nishith, P., & Griffin, M. (2003). How well does cognitive-behavioral therapy treat symptoms of PTSD? An examination of child sexual abuse survivors within a clinical trial. *CNS Spectrums, 8*, 340–342, 351–355.

Ross. C. (1997). *Dissociative identity disorder: Diagnosis, clinical features, and treatment of multiple personality*. New York: Guilford Press.

Section V

Team-related issues

33

Constructive communication

Kevin L. Burke

We cannot not communicate. Whether or not we speak, gesture, acknowledge others, or return emails and text messages, we are communicating. Good communication is a central skill sport psychologists and others in sports organizations should possess. Several authors have written regarding communicology, body language, linguistics, proxemics, encoding, decoding, sending, receiving, and other related topics (Burke, 1997). Many universities offer courses and even majors in communication. A book is available entitled *Case Studies in Sport Communication* (Brown & O'Rourke, 2003), and a measure of communication in team sports has been developed (Sullivan & Feltz, 2006). In the business world, studies have shown having good interpersonal relations is a key forecaster of profitability and "bottom-line" advantages (Peters, 1988). Studies comparing communication among sport and business leaders emphasize similar attributes (Weinberg & McDermott, 2002). Whetten and Cameron (1991) suggested supportive communication is a competitive advantage for managers and organizations. Regardless of the setting, effective communication is central to success. Knowing how to be effective communicators may be considered one of the most important skills sport psychologists should strive to hone. Interactions with others will significantly influence our success as practitioners. Understanding the basics of communication provides a foundation for maximizing the components of this talent and potential for continual improvement.

Communication theory and research

There are interpersonal and group communication theories in other areas of study that may be relevant to sport circumstances. One interpersonal communication model, the predicted outcome value theory (Sunnafrank, 1986), concerns anticipated costs and rewards in relationships. Sunnafrank postulated relationships are advanced by the expectation of more positive than negative outcomes. In other words, the rewards and costs expected in a relationship will influence the choice to avoid, constrain, or pursue further involvement with another person. If athletes expect to benefit from consulting with sport psychologists, they are more likely to seek and facilitate these consultations. If athletes expect negative outcomes from sport psychologists, they will communicate in ways that hinder the relationship – even possibly avoiding communication.

The belief that eventual maturity of interpersonal relationships is affected by perceptions of being understood or misunderstood is known as the theory of perceived understanding (Cahn, 1990). For example, if athletes perceive that sport psychologists understand or empathize with them, the athletes will develop feelings of emotional intimacy, which will probably lead to more interactions with sport psychologists. If athletes feel misunderstood by sport psychologists, they will most likely limit further communication.

The previous theories were developed with one-on-one communication issues at the core. There are also models of group communication processes. Two group communication theories/models are: the symbolic convergence theory (Bormann, 1986) and the interaction system model (Fisher & Hawes, 1971). Symbolic convergence (SC) theory emphasizes choices and personal translation, and that the stories and anecdotes members of a group tell disclose important group norms and rules. In a sport setting for example, the anecdotes basketball players share with teammates about each other, or their opponents, augment team norms and help to develop and reinforce team identity. Team members learn about members of the group, and who the group represents, through these symbolic converging behaviors (story telling). SC theory places importance on the meanings stories have for a team or group because these stories help the members form a rhetorical vision (Bormann, 1986). Rhetorical vision is the view of the team identity among group members and in relation to persons outside the group. The strength of the SC theory is the potential to explain group processes such as the development of norms, rules, and cohesiveness (Infante, Rancer, & Womack, 1997).

The interaction systems (IS) model places emphasis on interactions among group members rather than individual actions (Fisher & Hawes, 1971) to explain group behavior. The IS model focuses on group members' behavior patterns, responses, and the interaction of message patterns (Infante et al., 1997). In other words, the IS model explains that to understand team behavior, the interactions among team members should be analyzed, rather than just the behaviors of members within a team. According to Fisher and Hawes, verbal statements may be categorized as to the function performed in the group (e.g., clarification, substantiation, interpretation, decision making). Applied to a sport team, the IS model could be used to attempt to identify how a team interacts (e.g., message patterns among teammates) and the processes transpiring in making team decisions.

In addition to the theories and models above, Byrne's (1971) reinforcement theory proposes that principles of reinforcement explain most interpersonal attraction occurrences. Simply explained, we like and are attracted to people who reward us, and we dislike and are repelled by people who punish us. Byrne also predicted persons with similar attitudes will find their relationship rewarding, and hence, will like each other.

Research related to improving communication in sport teams has been limited in the field of sport psychology (Hanrahan & Gallois, 1993). One 12-week investigation of enhancing interpersonal relations in team sports (DiBerardinis, Barwind, Flaningam, & Jenkins, 1983) showed improvement in communication skills, and those gains were positive predictors of athletic performance. Other related studies investigating team cohesion have found, in interactive team sports, success and performance are dependent upon effective communication (e.g., Nixon, 1976). Studies investigating sport psychologist–athlete relations (e.g., Smith, Smoll, & Curtis, 1979) and co-acting sports (Williams & Widmeyer, 1991) have suggested communication may be integral to success or performance in sport.

316

Types of communication

Communication types may be viewed as intrapersonal and interpersonal. Intrapersonal communication is usually better known as "self-talk" or our inner monologue – the conversations we have with ourselves (see Chapter 53). One could argue that intrapersonal communication is the most important type of communication because it affects one's views on life, confidence, daily actions, and reactions.

Interpersonal communication has usually been defined as meaningful exchanges between two or more persons and refers to a person sending or receiving a message(s) from another individual or group. Interpersonal communication includes not only verbal content, but also nonverbal cues sometimes known as body language (e.g., micro-expressions, posture, facial expressions, voice intonations). Burke (1997) estimated that 50% to 70% of all information exchanged in-person is nonverbal. If this estimate is accurate, then forms of communication not exchanged in-person (e.g., e-mail, text messages, instant messaging, blogging) may be severely limited, or at least much less effective than face-to-face encounters. When communication is disembodied, then the potential for miscommunication and misinterpretation rises substantially.

Communication techniques

Although there is limited empirical research and theory on communication processes in sport, many methods and techniques have been suggested to improve communication processes on sport teams (e.g., Burke, 2005, 2006). Anshel (2003) developed a "ten commandments" of effective communication in sport (See Table 33.1). Although suggested for coaches, sport psychologists may apply these propositions to their interactions with others.

Yukelson (2010) provided several suggestions for how to become an effective communicator. He stated: one must be honest, have good listening skills, be good at asking questions, be able to develop rapport, promote various views of the same situation, use the proper terminology, and establish a trusting relationship. Yukelson also emphasized to become an effective communicator one must take the time to practise these important attributes.

Table 33.1 The ten commandments of communication.

1) Thou shalt be honest.
2) Thou shalt not be defensive.
3) Thou shalt be consistent.
4) Thou shalt be empathetic.
5) Thou shalt not be sarcastic.
6) Thou shalt praise and criticize behavior, not personality.
7) Thou shalt respect the integrity of others.
8) Thou shalt use positive nonverbal cues.
9) Thou shalt teach skills.
10) Thou shalt interact consistently with all team members.

From: Anshel, M. H. (2003). *Sport psychology: From theory to practice* (2nd ed.). Scottsdale, AZ: Gorsuch Scarisbrick.

Communication malfunctions

Although technology has assisted in the rapid exchange of certain types of communications, errors or misperceptions in communications are still frequent, and when communication failures or breakdowns occur, most persons blame the other parties. This bias may keep sport psychologists from thoroughly examining and attempting to improve their interpersonal skills. For accurate communications to occur, all participants must make a substantial effort, which sometimes is challenging. When persons are not "on the same page," communication breakdowns or barriers occur. One of the more common blocks to communication is inattentive listening, which usually occurs because the listener is not interested, is thinking of another topic, or is planning the next response. Another possible communication barrier between individuals is trust. When persons do not share a trust of each other, confidence in the information exchanged is severely affected. Another common cause of communication malfunctions is sending unclear or inconsistent messages. Ambiguous and vague statements are often difficult to comprehend and lead to unintended (mis)interpretations.

Levels of listening

One aspect of improving communication and reducing communication malfunctions is the skill of becoming a better listener (Flynn, Valikoski, & Grau, 2008). Martens (1997) claimed listening effectively is difficult and most untrained listeners hear less that 20% of what is said to them! Martens (1997) suggested one may improve listening skills by recognizing the need to listen, focusing intently on hearing what is said, trying to understand the meaning of the message as well as the facts of the message, avoiding the temptation to interrupt or complete others' statements for them, respecting others' rights to give their viewpoints, and trying not to give an emotional response unless it is suitable. Rosenfeld and Wilder (1990) discussed three levels of listening. Level one represents active listening. In active listening, the receiver is trying to understand the content of the message, the intention of the message, and the feelings accompanying the message. Martens (1997) stated that active listening involves letting the message sender know the message is being understood. Sometimes called reflective listening (Yukelson, 2010), this skill can be accomplished by paraphrasing (restating) what the person said, asking questions, and using body language that communicates attention and engagement. Using these techniques makes the sender aware the receiver is paying close attention and is interested in the message. After the message is received, the listener should honestly and immediately inform the sender how the message is understood in a brief, but clear, manner (Martens, 1987). Another aspect of reflective or active listening is the ability to show empathy (Yukelson, 2010). Being empathetic means the listener is able to view the situation from the sender's perspective. A good listener is able to show the sender caring and concern.

Level two listening refers to hearing only the content of the message. This type of listening may cause the communicator to feel the listener is uninterested or preoccupied. Level three listening occurs when the person receiving the message only hears portions of what is being stated. Attention to the message fades in and out. Receivers may also be so concerned in developing responses that they neglect to hear all of what the sender is attempting to share. Beginning sport psychology graduate students in their first consultation role plays may be an example of this phenomenon.

Weinberg and Gould (2003) discussed using supportive behaviors to indicate one is listening to the message being sent. Some of these actions are: staying open to new ideas, keeping direct eye contact, nodding the head, using receptive facial gestures, acknowledging receipt of the message verbally, and paraphrasing what has been said. Finally, the foundation for improving communication, and lessening the risk of communication malfunctions, is to be motivated to improve. It is likely that the amount of communication enhancement occurring will directly depend on the level of motivation to seek improvement.

Sending effective messages

Being a good communicator involves the ability to communicate in a manner that is clear and concise. Hardy, Burke, and Crace (2005) provided several guidelines for sending effective messages. An initial aspect of what is to be communicated is the development of the message, determining what is to be communicated and attempting to stay within the confines of that message. Avoid adding peripheral statements or information unnecessary to the baseline message. Also, conveying too much information may overload the receiver, particularly when the athlete or coach is under elevated stress. Development of the message can be challenging for sport psychologists in the midst of counseling sessions, due to the small amount of preparation time available in those immediate situations.

Another central element to effective communication is to seek first to understand the person, then seek to be understood (Covey, 1990). This suggestion places importance on showing empathy by understanding the client's goals, interests, values, and frame of reference. By getting to know the coach or athlete first, you will be more likely to communicate with them in a meaningful manner. Another way to be sure communications are being understood is to observe the actions and reactions of the listeners (e.g., body language, micro-expressions). Look for signs the athletes or coaches comprehend what is being said. Finally, one way to help assure your message is received is repetition. Repeat the message as many times as is necessary to be sure it is understood. Although at times it may be necessary to repeat the message in the same manner it was first delivered, find ways of sending the same message in different forms.

In communication, finding a positive manner of stating what needs to be said – even if strong criticism is necessary – can be extremely effective. The "sandwich approach" (Smith & Smoll, 1996) has been a popular method for providing corrective information in a manner in which the person receiving the criticism does not feel attacked, and is instead encouraged by the interaction. Briefly stated, the sandwich approach begins with a positive opening statement, followed by a future-oriented corrective statement, and ends with an encouraging, positive closing remark. In daily interactions with others, finding a positive way to speak with others is almost always more engaging than sarcastic or biting exchanges – no matter what the topic of conversation may be.

The use of humor in communication has been shown to have mental and physical benefits (Burke, 2006). Humor is a basic way of communicating (Lynch, 2002) and can be effective in therapy (Keller, 1984). A good sense of humor can also be an effective coping mechanism (Brooks, Guthrie, & Gaylord, 1999), a relationship builder, and a meaningful communication avenue (Rogers, 1984). Also, studies have indicated humorous individuals have higher popularity (Wanzer, Booth-Butterfield, & Booth-Butterfield, 1996). Currently, it seems there are potentially many benefits to humor, when used appropriately, in communicating with clients.

Nonverbal communication

As mentioned earlier, micro expressions, body language, and facial expressions may be responsible for conveying more information than verbal communication. Body language may be a more salient indicator of what another is thinking and feeling than verbal content, because these subtle (and sometimes not-so-subtle) cues are more difficult to control consciously than spoken language (Burke, 1997). Many individuals are so focused on the verbal aspects of their messages they often give little attention as to whether or not their facial expressions and body postures support what is being said. It behooves sport psychology professionals to learn to pay attention to these potentially valuable clues. Yet, even the most experienced body language experts realize interpreting body language accurately on a consistent basis is challenging.

Although sport psychologists may attend to bodily cues from their clients to better comprehend the overall communication sequence, clients may be engaged in the same analysis. Sport psychology professionals should strive to provide nonverbal communication that supports the messages being sent. For example, using a confident body posture (e.g., shoulders back, chin forward) can help the client have confidence in what is being said.

Electronic communication

One decision sport psychology consultants must consider is how much, if any, electronic communication they wish to use with their clients. With the many communication avenues available (e.g., cell telephone, e-mail, instant and text messaging, Facebook, Twitter, blogs), it is possible to provide an almost unlimited amount of "in touch" services with a client (see also Chapter 44 in this book). Today's "echo boomers" generation (or Generation Y – names given to children of "baby boomers") is the first generation to grow up with computer technology (such as e-mail and text messaging), cell phones, and satellite dishes for television (Leung, 2005). Echo boomers' (EBs) familiarity with these electronic devices, in many cases, means some EBs are much more comfortable communicating in this fashion than many sport psychologists usually are. Therefore, sport psychologists should familiarize themselves with these communication possibilities and at least consider using some of these avenues as a supplement to face-to-face meetings, particularly with EBs. One major drawback of this communication boom, however, is some clients may expect practitioners to be available almost 24/7, which may create dependency issues that must be dealt with by sport psychologists.

"Bull in the ring": a team exercise

When a team experiences communication difficulties, the bull in the ring (BITR) technique (Burke, 2005) may be used to assist with alleviating team disruption and tension. When handled properly, this intervention usually gets the teammates involved and can be an effective eye-opening, group, and self-awareness session. The BITR session may be held in two stages. First, the players are asked to sit in a circle (the ring), and a chair is placed in the center of that circle. For the first part of the session, a team item is placed in the center chair. The item could be a media guide, team jersey (without a player's name or number showing), sport object (e.g., bat, ball), or even a card that has the team's name, mascot, or logo on it. The players are instructed to follow four basic rules:

1. Speak freely, honestly, and forthrightly.
2. Do not explain the brief statements (discussion may occur later).
3. Do not openly react to the statements.
4. Keep an open mind.

Proceeding clockwise around the circle, each teammate is asked to make a constructive, negative statement about their team while looking at the team symbol in the center chair. (For each "round," it is usually a good idea to grant the first person a thirty-second pause to give an adequate amount of time for a thoughtful response.) For this part of the BITR session, players are not allowed to make statements about any individual, but are to only make relevant statements about the team. After hearing all of the constructive negative statements and following the same guidelines, each player is then asked to make a positive statement about the team. After hearing all of the positive statements, each player is then allowed to make *one* comment or ask *one* question of any teammate related to the positive *or* negative comments made in this part of the session.

The second component of the BITR session follows the same format as the first part, but each player sits in the center chair to hear comments directed at him/her. Thus, all players will hear one positive and one negative statement about themselves from each of their teammates. Each center-chair team member (the bull) is given the opportunity to select whether to hear the round of positive or negative statements first. Teammates making the comments may pass (only once) if not ready to respond, and, must look the bull directly in the eyes while making all comments. Each time a new round of comments begins, the teammate next in the circle after the person who last began the previous round, begins the next round of comments.

Obviously this activity can be a sensitive encounter for any team. The sport psychologist's role is to enforce the rules, keep the teammates on task, and help the process flow as smoothly as possible. After all of the players complete their turns in the center chair, then each team member is given a chance to ask *one* question to any *one* of the teammates about the positive or negative comments made. Most bulls tend to ask a question regarding a negative statement from one of their teammates. The sport psychologist should keep these mini-discussions brief. These questions may bring about short discussions and interactions from teammates who sometimes may not interact often. Issues not normally talked about among the teammates who do interact often may be discussed. Then, if the climate is facilitative after the second part of this exercise, allow any teammate *who volunteers*, to make one comment, or ask one question of any other teammate, as long as the comment/ question *does not relate* to the statements made during the BITR session. After the conclusion of the BITR session, the sport psychologist may wish to have the group discuss the process just encountered. Whether or not to have a "debriefing" session after the BITR depends on how the encounters were responded to by the participants. If the sport psychologist believes there may be more issues to discuss or the group would benefit from further discussion of the BITR processes, then further discussion is encouraged.

The BITR exercise can be an excellent method for reducing uncertainty within a team situation. Through these sessions teammates learn what each other is thinking about the team, and how they are perceived by teammates. In circumstances in which there is excellent rapport and trust, coaches and sport psychologists may choose to participate in the BITR.

Another way to incorporate sport psychologists or coaches in the BITR (without players being concerned about retaliation by persons in "positions of power,") is to allow anonymous positive and negative statements to be presented. By learning how one is perceived by others, the BITR session helps promote self-awareness through seeing oneself through others' eyes. Another purpose of BITR is to "clear the air" about issues hurting the team chemistry, and to help promote better communication. Many times the BITR session will promote a bonding experience for the team members. The three Cs or major goals of the BITR intervention are to promote *cohesion*, to improve *communication*, and to *clear* the air.

Closing comments

Even under the best circumstances, maintaining clear and consistent communication is challenging. Many people have a tendency to blame communication mishaps on others, which makes oneself unlikely to seek to improve in this area. Understanding and practising our skills of communication, along with the accompanying engaged, open, and attentive body language, is a major key to being successful as a sport psychology consultant. See Box 33.1 for some take-home messages from this chapter.

Box 33.1

Take-home messages regarding communication

- Communication may be viewed as constantly occurring.
- Communication may be intrapersonal and interpersonal.
- Use the "ten commandments" of communication.
- Make the effort to be an active listener.
- Communicate with others in a manner that is clear and concise, using a positive approach and a sense of humor.
- Be aware of nonverbal communication elements to send effective messages and to understand clients.
- Consider using electronic communication methods – at least as an adjunct to face-to-face encounters.
- Use the "bull in the ring" technique to delve into group or team issues.

References

Anshel, M. H. (2003). *Sport psychology: From theory to practice* (2nd ed.). Scottsdale, AZ: Gorsuch Scarisbrick.

Bormann, E. G. (1986). Symbolic convergence theory and group decision making. In R. Y. Hirokawa & M. S. Poole (Eds.), *Communication and group decision making* (pp. 219–236). Beverly Hills, CA: Sage.

Brooks, N. A., Guthrie, D. W., & Gaylord, C. G. (1999). Therapeutic humor in the family: An exploratory study. *Humor, 12*, 151–160.

Brown, R. S., & O'Rourke, D. J. (2003). *Case studies in sport communication*. Westport, CT: Praeger.

Burke, K. L. (1997). Communication in sports: Research and practice. *Journal of Interdisciplinary Research in Physical Education, 2*, 39–52.

Burke, K. L. (2005). But coach doesn't understand: Dealing with team communication quagmires. In M. B. Andersen (Ed.), *Sport psychology in practice* (pp. 45–59). Champaign, IL: Human Kinetics.

Burke, K. L. (2006). Using sport psychology to improve basketball performance. In J. Dosil (Ed.), *The sport psychologist's handbook: A guide for sport-specific performance enhancement* (pp. 121–137). West Sussex, England: Wiley.

Byrne, D. (1971). *The attraction paradigm.* New York: Academic Press.

Cahn, D. D. (1990). Perceived understanding and interpersonal relationships. *Journal of Social and Personal Relationships, 7,* 231–244.

Covey, S. R. (1990). *The 7 habits of highly effective people.* New York: Simon & Schuster.

DiBerardinis, J., Barwind, J., Flaningam, R. R., & Jenkins, V. (1983). Enhanced interpersonal relation as predictor of athletic performance. *International Journal of Sport Psychology, 14,* 243–251.

Fisher, S. A., & Hawes, L. C. (1971). An interact system model: Generating a grounded theory of small groups. *Quarterly Journal of Speech, 57,* 444–453.

Flynn, J., Valikoski, T., & Grau, J. (2008). Listening in the business context: Reviewing the state of research. *International Journal of Listening, 22,* 141–151.

Hanrahan, S., & Gallois, S. (1993). Social interactions. In R. N. Singer, M. Murphey, & L. K. Tennant (Eds.), *Handbook of Research on Sport Psychology* (pp. 623–646). New York: Macmillan.

Hardy, C. J., Burke, K. L., & Crace, R. K. (2005). Coaching: An effective communication system. In S. Murphy (Ed.) *The sport psych handbook* (pp. 191–212). Champaign, IL: Human Kinetics.

Infante, D. A., Rancer, A. S., & Womack, D. F. (1997). Intercultural contexts. In *Building communication theory* (3rd ed., pp. 371–395). Prospect Heights, IL: Waveland Press.

Keller, D. (1984). *Humor as therapy.* Wauwatosa, WI: Med-Psych.

Leung, R. (2005, September 4). The echo boomers. *CBS News.* Retrieved June 10, 2009, from: http://www.cbsnews.com/stories/2004/10/01/60minutes/main646890.shtml

Lynch, O. H. (2002). Humorous communication: Finding a place for humor in communication research. *Communication Theory, 12,* 423–445.

Martens, R. (1987). *Coaches guide to sport psychology.* Champaign, IL: Human Kinetics.

Martens, R. (1997). *Successful coaching.* Champaign, IL: Human Kinetics.

Nixon, H. L. (1976). Team orientations, interpersonal relations, and team success. *Research Quarterly, 47,* 429–435.

Peters, T. (1988). *Thriving on chaos.* New York: Knopf.

Rogers, V. R. (1984). Laughing with children. *Educational Leadership, 41,* 46–50.

Rosenfeld, L., & Wilder, L. (1990). Communication fundamentals: Active listening. *Sport Psychology Training Bulletin, 1*(5), 1–8.

Smith, R. E., & Smoll, F. L. (1996). *Way to go, coach!: A scientifically-proven approach to coaching effectiveness.* Portola Valley, CA: Warde.

Smith, R. E., Smoll, F., & Curtis, B. (1979). Coach effectiveness training: A cognitive-behavioral approach to enhancing relationship skills in youth sport coaches. *Journal of Sport Psychology,* 59–75.

Sullivan, P. M., & Feltz, D. L. (2006). The preliminary development of the Scale for Effective Communication in Team Sports (SECTS). *Journal of Applied Social Psychology, 33,* 1693–1715.

Sunnafrank, M. (1986). Predicted outcome value during initial interactions: A reformulation of uncertainty reduction theory. *Human Communication Research, 13,* 3–33.

Wanzer, M. B., Booth-Butterfield, S., & Booth-Butterfield, M. (1996). Are funny people popular? An examination of humor orientation, loneliness, and social attraction. *Communication Quarterly, 44,* 42–52.

Weinberg. R., & McDermott, M. (2002). A comparative analysis of sport and business organizations: Factors perceived critical for organizational success. *Journal of Applied Sport Psychology, 14,* 282–298.

Weinberg, R. S., & Gould, D. (2003). *Foundations of sport and exercise psychology* (3rd ed.). Champaign, IL: Human Kinetics.

Whetten, D. W., & Cameron, K. S. (1991). *Developing management skills* (2nd ed.). New York: HarperCollins.

Williams, J. M., & Widmeyer, W. N. (1991). The cohesion-performance outcome relationship in a coacting sport. *Journal of Sport & Exercise Psychology, 13,* 364–371.

Yukelson, D. (2010). Communicating effectively. In J. M. Williams (Ed.), *Applied sport psychology: Personal growth to peak performance* (6th ed., pp. 149–165). New York: McGraw-Hill.

34

Developing a shared identity/vision

Benefits and pitfalls

Traci A. Statler

Good teams become great ones when the members trust each other enough to surrender the Me for the We.

Phil Jackson, Head Coach of the L.A. Lakers

What makes some teams better than others? How do certain teams, with equivalent or even reduced levels of talent, experience, or ability, consistently outperform their opponents? Clearly, the effectiveness of a team is the result of more than the collective combination of the skill levels of its individual performers. As has been established in the sport psychology literature, the characteristics of groups include the constructs of collective identity, a sense of shared purpose, structured patterns of communication and interaction, personal and task interdependence, interpersonal attraction, and a perception of the team as a collective unit (Eys, Burke, Carron, & Dennis, 2010). This chapter focuses on how the elements of collective identity and shared purpose can be developed in a team environment to enhance overall performance and improve the quality of the experience and level of satisfaction for all involved, as well as to overcome some of the more common barriers faced in this process.

When asked to reflect upon their successes, one of the more frequently cited explanations performers give for effectiveness in a team environment is the presence of team unity, harmony, or cohesion. Cohesion has been defined as "a dynamic process that is reflected in the tendency for a group to stick together and remain united in pursuit of its goals and objectives" (Carron, 1982, p.124). Cohesion in sport teams has repeatedly been positively associated with performance success and overall satisfaction in the experience, both in and outside of the sporting environment. Team cohesion is associated with decreased role ambiguity, decreased cognitive anxiety, increased positive affect, decreased social loafing, and increased effort (Carron, Eyes, & Burke, 2007; for an in-depth review of team cohesion, see Carron, Brawley, & Widmeyer, 1998). Developing this sense of team harmony has become a priority for practitioners in team sport settings. The development of team cohesion, harmony, or unity is a dynamic process, occurring in a variety of ways, through numerous planned and unplanned activities over the span of the group's existence. The term *team-building* has become synonymous with activities and initiative games intended to build aspects of team harmony such as trust, communication, leadership, and familiarity. Along with other team-related issues presented in this section, the creation of a shared team identity or group vision can effectively contribute to this sense of overall group cohesion.

Shared identity: establishing who we are as a team

As described earlier, a critical element of any effective group is the perception of that group as a collective unit by its members. This perception necessitates the establishment of a shared identity – one to which each member of the group contributes and supports. In a sport team environment, a portion of this shared identity may already exist prior to the start of pre-season or the formation of that year's team. Returning players, coaches and staff, team traditions, and existing fan-base perceptions may all contribute to the group's existing identity. Although this existing identity is a relevant component of the current team's identity, the addition of new players, the subtraction of players lost, or any other changes to the make-up of the group alter the current environment. Therefore, there is a need to continually reevaluate and reconstruct this shared identity any time these components change.

The simple activity of holding a team brainstorming session or group conversation centered on the idea of answering the questions, "Who are we?" and "Who do we want to be?" can serve to develop a team's identity. Though time consuming, this activity is valuable, both to returning members of the group as well as those joining the group for the first time. For returning members, this activity serves to reinforce similarities to prior groups and clarify modifications for this new group. For newer members, this activity can help them crystallize a rich understanding of the group of which they are now a part, as well as provide an opportunity for them to contribute to the process. This understanding and individual investment additionally contributes to the new members' investment and interpersonal attraction to the team.

Establishing who I am as a team member, and where I fit

In addition to establishing a team identity, it is also important to clarify where each individual player or group member fits into that collective identity. What role do they play in contributing to and enhancing the group identity? If all members actively participated in and supported the outcomes of the group brainstorming activity described above, there will likely be a sense of ownership of that identity. This sense of ownership can enhance motivation and willingness to individually contribute to reinforcing the group identity.

Before team members can contribute to the collective, they first need to determine their personal identities. An effective means of uncovering identities is through an activity similar to the group brainstorming exercise, but on an individual level. Asking the questions, "Who am I?" and "Who do I want to be?" may be too general or philosophical for many to effectively address, so Ravizza and Hanson (1994) have suggested an alternative. In their book *Heads-Up Baseball: Playing the Game One Pitch at a Time*, the authors presented some exercises and a worksheet that prompt players to answer the questions "Why do you play?" to assess personal motivations, "What type of player would you like to be?" to create tangible characteristics that players would like to emulate, and "What would you like to accomplish in your sport?" to identify specific and measurable outcomes that the players can evaluate. The results of this activity can be evaluated in concert with the results of the group identity activity to determine a level of agreement between the group and the self. This comparison may help individuals assess where they "fit" in this group environment.

With a higher perceived level of fit between self- and group identity, there is greater attachment to the group.

An understanding of who one is as an individual team member and where one fits in with the collective identity of the group is essential for the development of a team identity. Members of a team have a choice – they can choose to focus on their own personal goals and identities regardless of fit, risking disharmony between self and the group, or they can choose to emphasize the elements of their individual identities that will enhance the group, making the collective more robust and solidifying this fit for the individual. In ideal circumstances, there is a strong connection between these two elements.

Shared vision: going on a mission

In concert with creating self- and team identities, an effective method of establishing a sense of team vision occurs early in a team's formation, again preferably before the competitive season begins. "A vision not only unites team members around the task of the group but may also enhance emotional commitment" (Stevens, 2002, p. 316). This vision is often referred to as establishing the team's mission. The existence of a cohesive team mission or plan helps give the team direction, provides a sense of collective purpose, and fosters commitment to the group's goal. A team or group "that lacks a sense of mission often fails to perform up to its capabilities" (Ravizza & Hanson, 1994, p.13). When a team has a collective purpose in mind, its members enhance the quality of their performance.

Although some authors have argued that the team vision should come from the coaches or leaders of the team, another approach is to develop this team vision collaboratively, with all members of the group providing their input. Ravizza and Hanson (1994) suggested using an activity to help identify the group's mission. Similar to the group identity exercise described earlier, this activity is most effective when conducted prior to the competitive season and with all members of the group present. This group brainstorming session, however, centers around questions related to what individuals, as a group, would like to accomplish during the season. Some effective guiding questions to use in this brainstorming discussion include:

- What is/are the dream goal(s) for the season?
- What is/are the realistic goal(s) for the season?
- What is it going to take for these goals to be reached:
  - over the season?
  - over the next month?
  - over the next week?
  - in today's practice?
- What are the needed individual contributions?
- What are the barriers that may get in the way of the group's mission?
  - How will we address these obstacles?

Creating the common purpose

This activity, essentially a goal-setting session modified to incorporate the collective input of each member of the group, will help to identify and create the group's common purpose. Starting with a discussion of the ideal long-term goal begins the conversation on a positive note, establishing a dream vision. From this ideal, a discussion of where that dream fits with reality often sets up a prime opportunity for the group to establish clear paths of shorter-term goals that contribute to the overall mission. It is important here not to diminish the dream goal completely in favor of the realistic goal, because the dream holds powerful motivational properties. Employing the philosophy that attaining the realistic goals improves the likelihood of the dream coming to fruition is often positive and confirming.

Next, identification of what individual contributions need to occur for the attainment of those team goals helps members to begin realizing how they each can personally contribute to the team's overall mission. During this part of the activity, it is often useful to have team members clarify what these contributions will look like. For example, if a group member identifies "going all out in practice" as a necessary behavioral component, ask the group to clarify what going all out would entail. An effective probe to elicit this response is to say, "If I were to watch tomorrow's practice, and people were going all out, what kinds of things would I see?" Getting the group to identify tangible behaviors is also an effective tool for reinforcing and rewarding the steps toward these group goals later on because it provides a list of agreed-upon, observable behaviors against which one can compare current actions.

An open discussion of the perceived barriers to accomplishing the mission allows for collective problem-solving, which enhances a sense of team cohesion. Finally, identifying tangible plans for addressing these potential barriers generates a sense of personal responsibility and can help create collective accountability and commitment.

The effectiveness of the activity and the individual commitment to the results are reliant on each member feeling personally included and valued in the discussion. If the group members contributing are only the returning players, or the only ideas supported are those of the starters, the remaining members of the group will not have the same investment and connection to the process. "One important characteristic of team goal setting is member participation. It should be emphasized that group goal setting is more advantageous than individual goal setting, and the more people that participate, the greater the sense of ownership" (Estabrooks & Dennis, 2003, p. 105). Every effort should be made by those leading this discussion to encourage the contributions and ideas of all participants if they wish to develop a shared vision. Because there is a greater sense of ownership among the team members as a result of this mission-building activity, it is anticipated that effort and persistence to the group goals will be intensified.

Developing the group vocabulary

Another important element that develops out of the group identity and group mission discussions is the group vocabulary. In holding these discussions, certain words, terms, phrases, and even images will emerge directly from the members. For example, the group might indicate that one element of their mission is to put aside past performances and focus instead on the task directly ahead of them. They may refer to this focus as "playing forward." In another part of the discussion, the idea of always "giving 100% of what you've got" may emerge as an important cue to reinforce effort. These words, phrases, and concepts are powerful. Time should be taken during these discussions to arrive at operational definitions of these common terms and establish agreement as to what these ideas mean to the group. Using these terms throughout the season – on goal worksheets, in imagery scripts, on motivational messages, in team meetings – will remind members of the team vision and reinforce the collective commitment to it.

Shared vision: sustaining the mission

As with any goal-setting program, simply establishing a mission is not enough to ensure success. One must also implement it, provide support and reinforcement for it, and continually evaluate its effectiveness. The ability to sustain this group mission rests not only in the hands of the coaches or team leaders, but in the hands of each and every member of the group. If team members view their team as united concerning this collective mission, it stands to reason that they would agree with and conform to standards of behavior that are deemed acceptable to the group (Carron *et al.*, 2007). Members of the group are responsible not only for their individual contributions to the group mission, but also for reinforcing this mission with other members of the team. If only a few players are committed to the vision, the likelihood of attaining that goal is diminished. If players only focus on their own responsibilities, the cohesion of the group decreases. Every member must feel invested and reinforced in this process.

Empowering team "buy-in"

Getting all group members on the same page with regard to the team mission and their individual roles within it can be referred to as generating team "buy-in" – getting everyone to buy into the direction and ideas that emerge from the team mission exercise. There are two main factors that must be accounted for to enhance the likelihood of this team buy-in: (a) a belief that the group can attain the goals they have set for themselves, and (b) commitment and acceptance from each member that they understand and will embrace their individual roles in attaining the mission. When either of these factors is missing, solidifying group buy-in becomes challenging.

The collective belief that the group are capable of reaching the goals they have set for themselves is related to the construct of collective efficacy, a widely recognized correlate of cohesion. Collective efficacy represents a "sense of collective competence shared among individuals when allocating, coordinating, and integrating their resources in a successful concerted response to specific situational demands" (Zaccaro, Blair, Peterson, & Zazanis, 1995, p. 309). Because the group's mission, direction, goals, and actions flow directly from their own contributions, conducting the team identity and team mission activities and using the outcomes as the foundation for the rest of the season can increase the likelihood of generating collective efficacy.

The second required factor for buy-in is the recognition and acceptance of one's individual role within the group. "To make a successful team, each athlete must believe he or she makes a difference. The role that each team member plays in goal attainment, and how his or her role fits into the overall vision must be clarified" (Stevens, 2002, p. 318). Team leaders should be reminded to include a broad discussion of the requirements for successful attainment of the mission, not just the requirements for the starters or key personnel. If the importance of even small contributions is emphasized from the start, new players, bench players, or others in supporting roles will be likely to feel their inputs are valued as critical components of overall success. When this reinforcement is included from the start, it may become easier for players in supporting positions to accept their roles, regardless of the size, because their contributions are relevant and valued.

An added benefit of identifying and reinforcing the use of the established team vocabulary can also contribute to this sense of buy-in. The team vocabulary reflects the wording used to identify the collective team needs, desired actions, and repercussions for failing to uphold these ideals. When teammates, coaches, and staff regularly refer back to the words, phrases, and ideas that were generated by the team members themselves, those in the positions of power (e.g., coaches, team captains, team leaders) cannot be viewed as the bad guys. They are the needs *the team* identified. They are the actions *the team* expects. They are repercussions *the team* established. And because each member was present and actively involved in the discussion, *each member is the team!*

Green lights and red flags

It is relatively easy to maintain team buy-in, to embrace this sense of collective efficacy, to continue working away at the short-term, medium-range, and long-term goals when everything is going well – when the "green lights" are indicating everything is right. Nevertheless, not every day in practice or competition is going to be perfect. Not every day is going to give a green light. The less-than-perfect days will likely far outnumber the great ones. It is on these days when things aren't going well and frustration seems more common than patience, when "red flags" seem to be popping up, that commitment to the responsibilities established at the start of the season need to be reinforced. When these less-than-perfect days occur, that is the time when reminders about the solutions generated during the team mission discussion addressing the plans-of-action for anticipated barriers come into play.

When everything is working according to plan, it is fairly easy to identify the steps an individual can take each day to contribute to the group's mission. A simple tool for accomplishing this task is to have each player, at the beginning of the day's practice or competition, ask, "What is today's mission? What do I want to get out of today?" This daily goal should be thought of in terms of its contribution to the collective group goal. "What do I want to contribute to the group goal in today's practice/game?" This series of questions can be used in small groups as well, with players sharing their plans for the day with other teammates. The challenge then becomes keeping this goal at the forefront throughout the day's practice or competition. Sharing each plan with others can help, because when other people know what one is striving for, they can help keep the individual focused. Finally, at the end of practice, or after the competition has ended, time should be taken to evaluate how well athletes were able to stay true to the mission – both individual missions for the day, as well as how those missions fit in with the team mission. When a player or team is experiencing green lights, this process is fairly straight forward and relatively easy. It is when problems start occurring that the team may have to revisit the discussions borne out of the team-mission activity.

Responsibility and accountability

When team members seem to be losing sight of the elements for success required for the team mission, or seem to be straying from agreements made regarding team identity, it can be helpful to revisit the results of these earlier team discussions. An effective way of reiterating these discussions is to remind the group that they are a group, not simply a collection of individuals. Each member of the group is responsible for and to every other member of the group.

All members of any team have (at least) three levels of accountability or responsibility within the group. The first level of accountability or responsibility is to themselves as individuals. This level of accountability is about integrity, about desire and passion for the sport, and about discipline and commitment. If athletes, coaches, and support staff cannot be responsible for and to themselves, how can they expect others to be responsible for themselves? How can they hope to help others if they cannot do the same for themselves? "Discipline and commitment are defined as putting your mission first. You do what your mission 'says' you should do rather than what you feel like doing. Committed athletes are driven by their purpose and not by how they happen to feel on a given day" (Ravizza & Hanson, 1994, p. 15).

Once team members commit to self-accountability, the next level becomes one of accountability to teammates. This level is about holding teammates responsible for themselves. People lose focus at times. Athletes and coaches may find themselves in situations where it is sometimes difficult to hold themselves to the levels they would hope. This is when their teammates are there to support them. The second level of responsibility or accountability is the group process of reinforcing and assisting each other in the personal and group commitments each has made to the team.

The final level of responsibility or accountability is to the coaching staff. This level should be the level of last resort. The coaching staff cannot be responsible for ensuring that all members of the team commit to their goals or that teammates are effectively supporting one another. They have far too many other issues to handle. Nevertheless, when an individual team member is struggling with this first level of self-commitment and teammates are not effectively assisting in this process, or if the coaches see a break in the group's interpersonal support, they can provide the cues and reminders needed to get the team back on track.

Cautionary tales: pitfalls and barriers

The benefits of generating a collaborative team identity and team mission have been discussed throughout this chapter, but a full discussion of this phenomenon would be incomplete without addressing some of the potentially negative outcomes of a group vision or some of the obstacles a group may face in attempting to create them.

Not encouraging every voice

In deciding to hold these group discussions, leaders should be prepared that not everyone will feel comfortable sharing their thoughts in front of the group. Conversely, there may be some who try to monopolize the discussion by contributing more than necessary. The reality of any group discussion is that although everyone potentially has a voice, only certain members use it.

When facilitating these brainstorming discussions, it behooves those leading the discussion to solicit input from all members – seek out the players hiding in corners nodding their heads at others' input, ask other silent players if they agree with what the last contributor said, make an effort to validate the contribution of an overly talkative member while tactfully redirecting the conversation to others. Often group members who volunteer little on their own may voice valid and insightful contributions when specifically given invitations to contribute their thoughts or when an overly vociferous member is temporarily silenced.

One activity for encouraging reserved group members to "use their voices" is through post-it note voting (S. J. Hanrahan, personal communication, October 15, 2009). Once the team has brainstormed a list of values, goals, possible strategies, or repercussions, each athlete is then given a specified number of post-it notes (e.g., three) that they then use to vote by sticking them next to the item or items they support. If they feel strongly about any one particular item, they have the option to put all three votes toward that one item (or two for one item, with their last post-it for another item, or one post-it per item – whatever combination the athlete chooses). This activity is a quick way to get a visual representation of how the group feels about the elements of this list, without individuals having to speak in front of others. A possible variation on this activity could include allowing each person one "veto vote" (perhaps using a different color of post-it) that, although not required, would allow them the choice to indicate items with which they strongly feel they would struggle to comply or elements of the team mission with which they disagree, etc.

Seeking honesty versus speaking the party line

Encouraging the contributions of those members of the group who have previous experience with team missions can be beneficial because they bring a wealth of knowledge and insight into what has worked in the past and what has not. They can provide a solid base of suggestions from which to build upon or modify to reflect the current group. It is important though to strongly encourage honesty in these discussions, from all members, regardless of the popularity of responses. Saying what one knows the coach wants to hear or making suggestions that will be popular with the group, but not actually addressing the reality of the situation at hand, is "speaking the party line." This type of false agreement, or superficial consensus, may make the brainstorming session short and amicable, but will do nothing to significantly address the needs of the team or provide suggestions for dealing with barriers and red flags that will surely confront the group at some point. Encouraging and reinforcing honesty in the discussion from the start will lead to a far better outcome overall.

Unshared identity: when the "I" and the "We" are in conflict

It is important to recognize that getting agreement from *everyone* is highly unlikely, because a team is a collection of individuals with individual motivations, goals, abilities, and commitment levels. A group or team may be able to reach a general consensus on team identity and their group's vision or mission for the season, but there will likely be one or more members whose personal goals or identities are in conflict at some level with the group.

If this conflict is extreme, the athlete, the coach, or both may consider an alternative to this individual's participation in the group. If the conflict is low to moderate, however, the individual may choose to remain a member of the group, despite this lack of total fit or agreement. In this situation, it is useful to have a clear and truthful discussion with the individual about expectations (both the group's expectations of the individual and the individual's expectations of the group), roles, and commitment to the team's mission. "Without commitment, athletes may deliberately pull against the vision because team goals may be incompatible with individual goals" (Stevens, 2002, p. 317). It is acceptable for a player to have a personal mission or identity, as long as it does not actively detract from the group. The acceptance and support for members working toward both personal and team visions concurrently may even serve to solidify their commitments to the team, because they feel personally valued and reinforced without the threat of being pressured to subvert their own needs for the good of the group.

Investment of time, effort, and evaluation

Developing a group identity and vision is a time-intensive process. It takes time to conduct the initial discussions, monitor progress toward the identity mission, and evaluate and modify beliefs and behaviors that result from this process. The suggestions described in this chapter are more than simply activities: they are season-long processes that need to be introduced, integrated, and evaluated throughout the season or lifespan of the group. Were initial goals unrealistic? Was the vision too simplistic? Is the group truly working toward the mission, or are members simply speaking the party line?

For the shared identity to take hold and become a valued characteristic of each member, it needs to be continually recognized and reinforced by the team leaders, coaches, and administrators of the group. It will not flourish if little effort is expended after the brainstorming activity that created it.

As with any effective goal setting program, the value of a defined team vision or mission is only as great as the commitment to working on it. The team vision must be continually re-evaluated and comparisons regularly made between where the team is now and where the team said it wanted to be. Time should be designated within practice schedules to discuss the team mission with an effort toward collective reinforcement of that mission. Without doubt, this process takes commitment, but when effectively integrated into existing team-development practices, it can be rewarding for all members involved. See Box 34.1 for some take-home messages from this chapter.

Box 34.1

Take-home messages about creating a shared identity

- Team unity, harmony, and cohesion will generally improve team effectiveness and member satisfaction.
- Creating a shared team identity and/or group vision can contribute to overall group cohesion.
- Team brainstorming sessions at the start of a season, answering questions such as "Who are we?" and "Who do we want to be?" can be effective activities for establishing a group's identity.
- Establishing an individual's level of fit within the collective team identity is important for ensuring attachment to the group.
- Establishing a collective team mission and purpose, and each individual's responsibility within that mission and purpose, creates commitment and personal connection to the group goal.
- Inclusion of the perspectives of every member of the group is important for ensuring all members buy in to the team vision.
- Reinforcing and reiterating terms and phrases (the team vocabulary) generated when developing the team mission and vision is a useful tool for reminding group members of their commitment to the team.
- All members of a group have three levels of accountability – first to themselves, next to the other members of the group, and lastly to the coaches or supervisors.
- The value of a defined team mission and team identity is only as great as the commitment the group makes to develop, reinforce, and reevaluate it. This process is time-intensive, but it can reap great rewards in terms of team cohesion when effectively implemented.

References

Carron, A. V. (1982). Cohesiveness in sport groups: Interpretations and considerations. *Journal of Sport Psychology, 4*, 123–138.

Carron, A. V., Brawley, L. R., & Widmeyer, W. N. (1998). The measurement of cohesiveness in sport groups. In J. L. Duda (Ed.) *Advances in sport and exercise psychology measurement* (pp. 213–226). Morgantown, WV: Fitness Information Technology.

Carron, A. V., Eys, M. A., & Burke, S. M. (2007). Team cohesion: Nature, correlates and development. In S. Jowett, & D. Lavallee (Eds.). *Social psychology in sport* (pp. 91–101). Champaign, IL: Human Kinetics.

Estabrooks, P, & Dennis, P. W. (2003). The principles of team building and their application to sport teams. In R. Lidor & K. P. Henschen (Eds.), *The psychology of team sports* (pp. 99–113). Morgantown, WV: Fitness Information Technology.

Eys, M. A., Burke, S. M., Carron, A. V., & Dennis, P. W. (2010). The sport team as an effective group. In J. M. Williams (Ed.), *Applied sport psychology: Personal growth to peak performance* (6th ed., pp. 132–148). New York: McGraw-Hill.

Ravizza, K., & Hanson, T. (1994). *Heads-up baseball: Playing the game one pitch at a time.* Chicago: McGraw-Hill.

Stevens, D. (2002). Building the effective team. In J. M. Silva & D. E. Stevens (Eds.). *Psychological foundations of sport* (pp. 306–327). Boston: Allyn & Bacon.

Zaccaro, S.J., Blair, V., Peterson, C., & Zazanis, M. (1995). Collective efficacy. In J. E. Maddux (Ed.). *Self-efficacy, adaptation, and adjustment,* (pp. 305–328). New York: Plenum.

35

Conflict management

Clifford J. Mallett

Conflict is inevitable in most domains of life, including sport, and throughout the lifespan. It is not surprising that issues of power and conflict are commonplace within sporting organizations and teams at all performance levels. Like most work environments, sporting organizations (e.g., teams, clubs) are complex, interpersonal, political, and hierarchical spaces in which there are status differences despite the need for cooperation and teamwork (Boud & Garrick, 1999; Mallett, 2010).

Conflict can be internal (e.g., intrapersonal tension between competing needs) but generally implies a disagreement between people. Conflict can occur between two people (interpersonal conflict), between members of a team (intra-team or intra-group), between groups (inter-group) and between a person and situational factors (Jowett & Lavallee, 2007). There are numerous examples of interpersonal conflict in sport – disagreement between coach and athlete in how the athlete should train leading into an important competition causing coach–athlete tension and conflict. Intra-group conflict in sport is also commonplace, for example, power struggles between two players seeking selection to the same playing position or reserves/substitutes criticizing current team members or the coach of a team. In applied practice, athletes may report the tension between living up to family values associated with drinking and cultural team practices (intra-personal conflict). Conflict can also involve people in specific situations (e.g., a player attending a function and a disgruntled fan verbally abuses the player for below-par performance in a recent match).

Conflict comes in different forms and pervades the sporting community at all performance levels and to varying degrees. Understanding and, when appropriate, managing conflict are important skills for practitioners. The consequences of conflict can be emotionally demanding, especially over an extended period. Often people procrastinate in dealing with conflict, which underscores the key role of a sport psychologist in helping coaches, athletes, and managers to reduce the conflict and its effects. This chapter will provide an understanding of: (a) conflict within the sporting context, (b) individual styles of conflict, and (c) a problem-solving approach to conflict management.

Understanding conflict

Conflict is universal and often occurs because people are competing for similar goals or resources. Competition can be a major catalyst for conflict because in competition there is usually a winner and a loser. Conflict can lead to performance decrements, dissatisfaction, breakdown in communication, and negative emotions (Eunson, 2005).

The term conflict seems to be associated with battles (i.e., winners, losers) and usually has negative connotations, but can conflict be a good thing? A problem-solving approach to conflict may yield positive outcomes such as: better decision-making, behavioral and structural change, alternative perspectives, catharsis, and resolution of inter- and intra-personal strife (Eunson, 2005). Furthermore, understanding and managing conflict can be central to developing team cohesion and its subsequent influence upon player satisfaction with the team and perceived performance (Tekleab, Quigley, & Tesluk, 2009) as well as promoting a strong team identity (Gersick, 1989).

For the purpose of conceptual clarity, it is important to distinguish between conflict resolution and conflict management. *Conflict resolution* is an approach to conflict that usually involves the reduction or elimination of conflict. Conflict resolution is aimed at achieving a positive outcome for both parties; this outcome, however, is rare. Quite often the resolution is temporary because only the symptoms (rather than the causes) are reduced or removed. Resolving conflict may not be the most effective approach in some conflict situations. For example, bringing to the surface players' thoughts and feelings about an issue of infidelity concerning two players on the same team might escalate the conflict. *Conflict management* is an approach to conflict that may involve the elimination, reduction, or increase of, conflict. Some conflicts cannot be resolved, and perhaps monitoring conflict and reducing its adverse effects (conflict management) is a desired outcome. Strategically attempting to manage conflict can be dangerous because the key issues can be much deeper than initially thought and thinking we can always manage conflict is sometimes ambitious and foolhardy. The focus of this chapter is conflict management, but conflict resolution is also a possible outcome.

Causes of conflict

There are many causes of conflict that may work in isolation but often function in combination with each other. Conflicts are variable, and accurately identifying the cause(s) of a conflict is key to managing or resolving it. Some major causes of conflict (Eunson, 2005) are outlined below.

Scarce resources

Often two people want the same thing: for example, competition between two players for the same playing position within a team. Likewise, two assistant coaches wanting responsibility for the more important coaching tasks, and consequently greater recognition of their coaching abilities, might cause conflict between them. Conflict can often result when two or more people want something that cannot be shared.

Adversity

Poor athlete and team performances might increase stress and become a catalyst for conflict between coaches and athletes/teams. It is not uncommon for people to blame others for poor performances. In team sports, one coach might blame another coach for the team's poor performance, creating tension between them. In individual sports, such as swimming, it is not unusual for athletes to blame the coach for their poor performances. Of course, if people view cooperation as the key to resolving the poor performances there is less likelihood of ensuing conflict.

Faulty communication

Ineffective communication (e.g., miscommunication, lack of communication) is a major cause of conflict (Athanasios, 2005). Team sports are fertile contexts for conflict, partly due to the competition for places, but also because coaches are required to communicate with many people in the team (including ancillary staff), a time-consuming task. A football head coach, who has a squad of 40 or more players, faces considerable communication challenges. If he were to spend 15 minutes with each player each week, that would equate to almost 1.5 days of work each week. Limited time and the need to be succinct can promote misinterpretation. The development of effective communication skills is central to reducing spiraling conflict.

Perceived differences

Sporting groups are increasingly populated by people from different cultural backgrounds, which may splinter and alienate people. Limited understanding and acceptance of people from different cultural backgrounds can be sources of tension between individuals and subgroups within teams (see Chapter 48). For example, differing religious beliefs might cause team members to view player alcohol consumption differently.

Biology

Some physiological psychologists (e.g., Burgess & McDonald, 2004) have suggested that people have a predisposition to be in conflict, and to resolve it through verbal or physical aggression. In contrast, other psychologists (e.g., Ury, 2000) have viewed such behaviors as learned. The opposing views should be considered in understanding and managing conflict, especially violent behaviors.

Health

Sub-optimal physical health may also be a cause of conflict. When the body's immune system is under threat, people tend to become less tolerant of others' behaviors. For example, a player who is normally tolerant of another player's arrogant behavior might under less than optimal health verbally berate the person (aggressive reaction) for being arrogant.

The conflict process

The *conflict spiral* is a general model of conflict development that suggests a fairly predictable developmental sequence of conflict events and perceptions (Eunson, 2005). Initially, conflict might start out of the public gaze. For example, one player's seemingly innocuous comment to another player may be interpreted by the receiver as deliberately aggressive, but other players in the team may not interpret the comment as a sign of any tension between the two players. Over time, as the conflict escalates and the comments become more critical and emotionally charged; the tension becomes more public than before. Critical incidents can fuel the conflict, causing people to view only the negative aspects of someone's behavior and ignore any positive aspects. As the conflict escalates, emotions can override rational thinking and cause heated arguments, provocation, possibly retaliation, and perhaps physically aggressive behaviors. When attempting to reduce the conflict, emotions must be brought under control. The sport psychologist, who (one hopes) is perceived as neutral, can play a key role in reducing the emotions of those people involved in the conflict. A useful starting point in mediating the discussions might be acknowledging the perspectives of all people, which can contribute initially to some reduction in emotions. Once emotions are under control, open communication, including disclosure of thoughts and feelings, is possible.

Challenging the spiral early in the process reduces the potential of the conflict spiraling out of control. In the conflict situation, it is one's choice to attempt to resolve or, at least, manage the conflict. Central to any challenging of the conflict spiral is the need to understand and appreciate the emotions of the parties involved before attempting to reduce those emotions.

There are several ways to challenge the conflict spiral at different stages of its development. In the covert stage, challenging negative comments, gossip, and a lack of cooperation can be effective in reducing the potential for conflict to escalate. In the overt stage of conflict the sport psychologist should identify, and subsequently challenge, any distorted perceptions, intimidations, and pressures (Eunson, 2005). Successfully challenging distorted perceptions of an issue, through gentle questioning, paraphrasing, and reframing, might be helpful in reducing emotions, and provide the platform for managing the conflict. Moreover, the sport psychologist should resist recruitment to one side (Eunson, 2005).

Conflict in the coach–athlete relationship

Although there is considerable anecdotal evidence reporting conflicts between coaches and athletes, there has been little research examining that specific topic (Jowett & Lavallee, 2007). This limited examination of conflict within the coach–athlete relationship is surprising considering the problematic nature of coaching. Sports coaching has been described as a complex, social, and dynamic endeavor that can be viewed within a broader set of relations including the interdependency between coaches' interactions with other people (e.g., athletes, other coaches, parents) and the coaching situation and context (Mallett, 2008). This problematized view of coaching mirrors the turbulence in which coaches operate where their emotional connections with athletes are central to coach–athlete–performance relationships. When performance expectations are not met, one party may blame another for the cause, which can be the catalyst for tension between coaches and athletes and between players on a team. For example, when a team is performing poorly, players look for reasons and often lay blame on less skilled performers, which can be the cause of conflict in sporting teams. Common reasons cited for underachievement in sport include poor communication, lack of warmth in relationships, mutual dissatisfaction, limited interaction, mistrust, varying need–satisfaction, insufficient support, incompatibility, and power struggles (Jowett, 2003; Poczwardowski, Barott, & Henschen, 2002); all of which can independently and collectively lead to dissatisfaction, distress, frustration, and anger (Jowett, 2003), and have the potential to increase the probability of conflict occurring between coaches and athletes.

Interpersonal conflict has, at least, two dimensions: content and emotion (LaVoi, 2007). Moderate levels of content conflict (e.g., disagreement between coach and athlete about a training method or how to solve a problem), if expressed unemotionally and with the intention of a positive outcome for both parties, can lead to healthy debate between the two individuals and have the potential to facilitate optimal solutions and perhaps enhance performance. In contrast, emotional (relational) conflict can be debilitative to performance, among other things, producing distrust and suspicion. LaVoi suggested that the inability of people to differentiate between content and relational forms of communication causes most interpersonal conflict.

Although conflict between coach–athlete and athlete–athlete dyads is relatively common, less so is the conflict between a sport psychologist and a client. Nevertheless, tension between the practitioner and the client has the potential to nurture or thwart the relationship and subsequent outcomes. Another common source of conflict is between sport psychologists and coaches, which is a concern for the profession. Coaches' support for sport psychologists assisting the coach–athlete–performance relationship is paramount to future work for practitioners. Athletes often have conflict with their coaches, and in dealing with athlete–coach relationship issues (e.g., athlete dissatisfaction with coach), sometimes sport psychologists marginalize coaches. This sidelining of coaches is not usually perceived well by them and can lead to an escalation of the tension between coach and athlete. Coaches and athletes should be supported and engaged in attempts by the sport psychologist to manage coach–athlete conflicts.

Individual styles of conflict

Typically, people find conflict unpleasant and anxiety provoking. How we respond to conflict is arguably a learned (and consistent) behavior (Ury, 2000), which means we can re-learn how we deal with conflict. The Thomas-Kilmann model of conflict-handling styles (Shell, 2001; Thomas, 2003) is based on the premise that people tend to have dominant reactions (styles) to handling conflict. In the Thomas-Kilmann model, handling conflict occurs along two basic dimensions or continua of behaviors: (a) assertive to unassertive (i.e., high to low concern for self), and (b) cooperative to uncooperative (i.e., high to low concern for others). The five styles of conflict handling include competing, collaborating, compromising, accommodating, and avoiding.

Competing (dominating) involves assertive but uncooperative behaviors between two parties (i.e., high concern for self and low concern for others). It is associated with the pursuit of one's own goals at the expense of positive relationships with others. For example, in a relay team one athlete chooses to produce high quality work when training individually, but not when with other members of the team in specific group training sessions. This style has the potential to be used aggressively. For example, people can use this style to coerce (e.g., bully) others into their way of thinking or viewing the world. In the case of the relay team, a personal coach might coerce another sprinter in the relay team to undertake the same training as his own sprinter so as to advantage the preparation of his own sprinter. Unfortunately, coercion can lead to further conflict.

Collaborating (integrating) involves assertive and co-operative behaviors between parties (i.e., high concern for self and others). Engagement in a truly collaborative approach to conflict can be highly productive, resulting in improved communication and problem-solving. The successful use of collaboration will promote further use of this style, increase communication, and develop healthy relationships. Viewing conflict as potential for personal growth is likely to reduce the negative effects of conflict. Perceptions of conflict can change from negative to positive and lead to productive outcomes for the parties involved. The collaborative style of dealing with conflict is a key strategy to use on a regular basis. Research has shown that teams with higher levels (compared with lower levels) of emotional intelligence preferred to use collaboration in preference to other conflict styles (Jordan & Troth, 2004).

Compromising involves a balance between unassertive–assertive and cooperative–uncooperative behaviors (i.e., moderate concern for self and others). Addressing conflict in most situations is helpful, but compromising one's views might lead to partial satisfaction of the issue. For example, coaches might benefit from exploring players' views on curfews the night before matches and subsequently negotiating with the players about an appropriate decision on team curfews.

Accommodating (obliging) involves co-operative but unassertive behaviors (i.e., low concern for self and high concern for others). This approach to conflict involves people viewing relationships with others as more important than satisfying their own needs. This style results in submissiveness to the demands of others. For example, coaches might accommodate the views of the players because they do not want to upset the players too much. The accommodating style of dealing with conflict can be effective in some situations, for example, when appreciating the importance of building harmony within the team, and when an issue may be of greater importance to another person.

Avoiding involves uncooperative and unassertive behaviors (i.e., low concern for self and others). Avoidance can be used to either ignore the conflict (and hope it goes away) or as a deliberate strategy to control the situation. For example, anecdotal evidence suggests that often people ignore a conflict situation and hope it fades away and sorts itself out, but resolution rarely happens. Some people do not like to confront conflict and therefore tend to ignore it rather than deal with it and seek solutions. In some cases, avoidance can be an effective strategy, for example, a coach may deliberately avoid a player's issue to let an athlete calm down before addressing an important issue, or when the potential negative consequences are not worth the time and effort of dealing assertively with an issue.

Athanasios and Tzetzis (2005) examined the ways in which Greek professional coaches (football, basketball, and volleyball) handled conflict in professional sporting teams. The coaches reported using all five styles in managing conflict, although unsurprisingly, the authors found collaboration and compromising to be the most effective and commonly used styles.

Managing conflict

Managing conflict within teams and training squads can be a major task for practitioners. The various conflict styles and the situations in which they can be effective are presented below.

Competing can be best used when decisive action is necessary, or on important issues upon which the best outcome is sought for the person making the decision. Often coaches are required to make tough and quick decisions about playing personnel. In the selection of team members (e.g., the final team composition for a grand final) the coach does not select a player who has a poor attitude but is considered one of the better performers (competing style).

Collaborating is effective when both parties have positive contributions to make to solving a problem. For example, in sporting teams collaboration between coaches and the players' leadership group to formulate guidelines for agreed-upon behaviors for coaches and players within the organization can be effective in creating a consensus of opinion. This collaboration allows for the perspectives of all parties to be considered before making decisions on potentially contentious issues.

Compromising works well when time is short. and one needs a quick solution. or as an interim step toward resolving a more complex issue. For example, coaches might allow players to attend training late on particular occasions because they know they are having personal problems with their partners, or they are preparing for major university exams.

Accommodating is a style that can work well for coaches when others' views on an issue seem germane, or when coaches believe the approach might facilitate team harmony. For example, a coach might believe that a team curfew when playing interstate should be enforced. The sport psychologist, however, may favor the involvement of the player's leadership group in providing another perspective. In this case, accommodating the views of the players may yield several benefits to the coach–team relationship such as building team harmony through promotion of some player autonomy.

Avoidance is probably the style to use most sparingly. When the issue is minor or when the emotions are high and people need to have time to cool down, the avoidance style can be effective. An example is avoiding a discussion with players about their poor performances in favor of more pressing concerns such as poor attitudes to training. The style may also work well when another person (e.g., another player) can resolve the issue more effectively.

Each conflict style has the potential to contribute to reducing conflict, and knowledge of all five styles is useful. The key is knowing when to use the most suitable style for the specific conflict situation. Using a golf analogy (Goleman, 2000), a player should strategically use the most appropriate club (with or without the aid of a caddy) for the particular shot to be played. Sports psychologists (i.e., the caddy) can guide the coach (golfer) to use the most suitable conflict style (club) for the particular issue (golf shot) in seeking to manage the conflict. You can select the style for the particular situation, but may use some approaches more often than others (e.g., collaboration, compromising). From a practitioner perspective, encouraging coaches and athletes to be adaptable, tolerant, and skilled in the various forms of conflict style can reduce, and in some cases perhaps resolve, conflict. Nevertheless, people need to be realistic in what they can achieve in conflict management. There will be occasions when, regardless of the sport psychologist's actions or interventions, conflict cannot be reduced or even managed.

In many situations, a problem-solving approach to conflict management is recommended, and the following quote serves to support the practice of using conflict styles that address the needs of both parties (e.g., collaborating, compromising):

> The Navajo definition of conflict resolution is to restore harmony. Their experience has convinced them that if one ends a dispute by having a winner and a loser, one dispute may have ended but another dispute will have started because harmony will not have been restored. Behind this is the Navajo recognition that coercion is not an effective way to bring about genuine change in any individual's long term behavior or attitude. Coercion works only as long as one is willing and able to continue the coercion. When the coercion stops, people generally revert to their prior ways, the only

341

real difference being that by then they will have become angry and resentful. Coercion is a short-term, not a long-term, answer.

(Anne Kaas' book, *The Better Way: Navajo Peacemaking*, cited in Adler & Rodman, 1997, p. 240)

The above quote highlights the concomitant issues of coercion and submission in dealing with conflict in selfish (competing) and submissive (accommodating) ways.

Minimizing the potential for conflict

Preventing conflict is impossible, but steps can be taken to minimize the potential harm of its development. The key roles of the sport psychologist in terms of team conflict are two-fold: (a) mediating between parties (e.g., coach and athlete), and (b) providing coaches and athletes with psycho-educational programs aimed at improving communication (e.g., assertiveness training). Practitioners in these roles of mediator and educator can assist coaches and athletes in reducing the potential for conflict in a number of ways.

A focus on effective communication is central to reducing the potential for conflict. Communication should be clear and nonjudgmental, with the focus on behaviors rather than the people. Remaining as calm as possible reduces emotional communication, which is often regretted after the fact.

Approaches to coaching that promote good communication in the coach–athlete relationship, and that are aimed to satisfy the needs of both parties, should be encouraged (e.g., promoting coaches' autonomy-supportive behaviors rather than controlling and autocratic ones). Sport psychologists can encourage coaches to provide athletes with choices, rationales for tasks, non-controlling competence feedback, opportunities for initiative taking, and acknowledgment of feelings and perspectives while avoiding controlling behaviors (Mageau & Vallerand, 2003).

The development of emotional intelligence competencies of coaches and athletes may also be useful. Emotional intelligence (EQ) is concerned with the ability to manage oneself and one's relationships effectively. EQ consists of four major capabilities: self-awareness, self-management, social awareness, and social skill (Goleman, 2000). Key emotional intelligence competencies underpin those four capabilities, which are fundamental to preventing and managing conflict. They include:

- emotional self-awareness;
- self-control, trustworthiness, adaptability;
- empathy, service orientation;
- developing others' communication, conflict management, and teamwork and collaboration.

Summary

Sporting environments are complex, interpersonal spaces in which there are status differences along with the need for solidarity (Mallett, 2010): therefore, conflict is inevitable. The role of the sport psychologist in assisting coaches, players, managers, and parents in managing conflict is pivotal. Specifically, sport psychologists can work effectively with coaches to enhance their interpersonal skills in dealing with conflict (see Box 35.1). There is a range of conflict styles that can be used effectively to deal with situational conflict, and the skill is matching the most appropriate style to suit the particular situation. Assisting others (e.g., coaches, athletes) in developing suitable interpersonal qualities (e.g., emotional self-awareness) can be a key challenge for sport psychologists.

Box 35.1

Practical suggestions for sport psychologists regarding conflict

- There are different forms of conflict – intrapersonal, interpersonal, intra-team, inter-team, and person–situation.
- Conflict is inevitable in the sporting domain; so understand the different forms of conflict and the conflict process.
- Assisting coaches, players, and parents to deal with conflict is a common work task for sport psychologists.
- There are many causes of conflict – identify the cause/s before attempting to manage the conflict. Deal with conflict as soon as you have sufficient information on how to best mediate discussions between people.
- The conflict spiral is a general model of conflict development.
- There are several conflict styles – competing, collaborating, compromising, accommodating, and avoiding.
- Appreciate that some people have a dominant conflict style, but many people can learn other styles.
- Adopt a problem-solving approach to conflict management: be strategic in dealing with conflict. Understand the situation, and select a suitable style.
- A problem-solving approach to conflict can lead to growth in individuals and teams/groups.
- The development of emotional intelligence competencies (e.g., emotional self-awareness, self-control, empathy) can improve communication and the ability to circumvent conflict and manage it.

References

Adler, R. B., & Rodman, G. (1997). *Understanding human communication* (6th ed.). New York: Harcourt Brace.

Athanasios, L. (2005). Communication problems in professional sports: The case of Greece. *Corporate Communication, 10*, 252–256.

Athanasios, L., & Tzetzis, G. (2005). Styles of managing team conflict in professional sports: The case of Greece. *Management Research News, 28*(6), 36–54.

Boud, D., & Garrick, J. (1999). Understandings of workplace learning. In D. Boud & J. Garrick (Eds.), *Understanding learning at work*. London: Routledge.

Burgess, R. L., & McDonald, K. (Eds.). (2004). *Evolutionary perspectives on human development*. Thousand Oaks, CA: Sage.

Eunson, B. (2005). *Communicating in the 21st century*. Milton, QLD, Australia: Wiley.

Gersick, C. J. G. (1989). Making time: Predictable transitions in task groups. *Academy of Management Journal, 32*, 274–309.

Goleman, D. (2000). Leadership that gets results. *Harvard Business Review*, 78(2), 78–90.

Jordan, P., & Troth, A. (2004). Managing emotions during team problem solving: Emotional intelligence and conflict resolution. *Human Performance*, 17, 195–218.

Jowett, S. (2003). When the honeymoon is over: A case study of a coach–athlete dyad in crisis. *The Sport Psychologist*, 17, 446–462.

Jowett, S., & Lavallee, D. (2007). *Social psychology in sport*. Champaign, IL: Human Kinetics.

LaVoi, N. M. (2007). Interpersonal communication and conflict in the coach-athlete relationship. In S. Jowett & D. Lavallee (Eds.), *Social psychology in sport* (pp. 29–40). Champaign, IL: Human Kinetics.

Mageau, G. A., & Vallerand, R. J. (2003). The coach–athlete relationship: A motivational model. *Journal of Sports Sciences*, 21, 883–904.

Mallett, C. (2008). Modelling the complexity of the coaching process: A commentary. *International Journal of Sport Science and Coaching*, 2, 419–421.

Mallett, C. J. (2010). High performance coaches' careers and communities. In J. Lyle & C. Cushion (Eds.), *Sports coaching: Professionalism and practice* (pp. 119–133). London: Elsevier.

Poczwardowski, A., Barott, J. E., & Henschen, K. P. (2002). The athlete and coach: Their relationship and its meaning. *International Journal of Sport Psychology*, 33, 116–140.

Shell, G. R. (2001). Bargaining styles and negotiation: The Thomas-Kilmann Conflict Mode Instrument in negotiation training. *Negotiation Journal*, 17, 155–174.

Tekleab, A. G., Quigley, N. R., & Tesluk, P. E. (2009). A longitudinal study of team conflict, conflict management, cohesion, and team effectiveness. *Group and Organization Management*, 34, 170–205.

Thomas, K. W. (2003). *Intrinsic motivation at work: Building energy and commitment*. San Francisco: Berrett-Kohler.

Ury, W. (2000). *The third side: Why we fight and how we can stop*. New York: Penguin.

36

It's nice to go traveling, BUT ...

Peter C. Terry

Extensive domestic and international travel is a necessity of life for many athletes, particularly those at elite or professional levels. On the one hand, travel opens up exciting opportunities to experience new places, cultures, and people, often providing wonderful memories that will last a lifetime. On the other hand, arduous journeys across multiple time zones are not uncommon and bring with them the challenges of travel fatigue, jet lag, sleep deprivation, and other threats to athletic performance and athlete well-being. Having traveled more than one million miles during the past 25 years in my role as an applied sport psychologist, I have experienced effective and ineffective team travel first hand.

Psychological and physical effects of travel

Travel, whether by air, sea, or land, involves a complex interaction of many disparate influences. Activities such as watching beautiful scenery or interacting with friends are perceived by most people as pleasant things to do, whereas sitting for hours in an airplane or waiting to retrieve luggage at an airport are generally seen as less pleasant, sometimes stressful activities. In this section, I will address the influence on athletic performance of jet lag, sleep deprivation, mood responses, and effects of travel.

Effects of jet lag

One of the most fundamental effects of travel involves interference with the human body clock. If you travel rapidly across multiple time zones, your natural cycle for sleeping and waking becomes out of synchrony with the cycle of natural daylight and darkness at your place of arrival. The site of the human body clock is at the base of the hypothalamus, a region of the brain that is ultimately responsible for many of our daily fluctuations in appetite for food and sleep, which cycle over a period of about 24 hours. These fluctuations are known as *circadian* rhythms, from the Latin word meaning "about a day" (see Waterhouse, Reilly, & Edwards, 2004 for a review).

Jet lag is, in essence, a mismatch between your body clock and the actual time of day. The severity of jet lag symptoms depends upon several factors, including the number of time zones crossed, the duration of the flight, the time of departure and arrival, and the direction of travel, with travel from east to west generally producing less acute effects than travel from west to east. Common symptoms of jet lag include fatigue, insomnia, dizziness, irritability, gastrointestinal problems, general feelings of weakness, and minor cognitive impairments. Additional possible symptoms include attitude and motivation problems, mood swings, decreased general well-being, and increased perceptions of stress. The effects are usually temporary but can persist for over a week in some cases. The usual rule of thumb that is applied to adjustment to jet lag is one day for every hour of time change, although individual differences are substantial and more (or less) time may be required.

Travel-related sleep deprivation

During lengthy periods of travel, it is almost inevitable that some sleep deprivation will occur, either in the duration or quality of sleep, or both. Reilly and Edwards (2007) suggested that some aspects of physical performance, such as muscle strength, swim times, and treadmill running, can be maintained in the face of partial sleep deprivation. Importantly, however, they noted that "while athletes may be able to overcome the adverse effects of sleep loss in single all-out efforts, they may be unable to or unwilling to maintain a high level of performance in sustained exercise and in repeated exercise bouts" (p. 278). Also, Spiegel, Leproult, and Van Cauter (1999) demonstrated that sleep debt has a harmful effect on carbohydrate metabolism and endocrine function. After a relatively short period of sleep restriction (6 days of 4 hours per night), physiological functioning that is critical for athletic performance – glucose metabolism and cortisol secretion – was shown to be depressed by 30–40% compared to a subsequent sleep recovery period (6 days of 12 hours per night) among young, healthy males.

Furthermore, there is evidence that intermittent moderate exercise exacerbates rather than ameliorates the negative effects of sleep deprivation on performance-related indices such as reaction time, depressed mood, fatigue, and vigor (Scott, McNaughton, & Polman, 2006). Strategies to minimize the effects of travel-related sleep deprivation, such as using relaxation strategies to induce sleep while traveling, are probably helpful for athletes who regularly travel long distances to competitions.

Mood responses to travel

Given that mood fluctuations are a common symptom of jet lag and other travel-related matters, there is a strong case for monitoring athletes' mood responses during and after travel, especially across time zones. Such monitoring provides a mechanism for assessing psychological adjustment to the demands of the travel and for providing some forewarning of specific performance-threatening affective responses, such as fatigue, confusion, or depressed mood (Beedie, Terry, & Lane, 2000). Mood monitoring may be especially relevant when travel takes athletes to more extreme environments than they have previously experienced. For example, travel by athletes to extremely hot or cold environments is likely to result in significant mood disturbance, possibly reduced cognitive performance, and associated threats to competition performance (see Lane, Terry, Stevens, Barney, & Dinsdale, 2004).

Figure 36.1 shows mood scores for tension, depression, anger, vigor, fatigue, and confusion reported by a medal-winning bobsled athlete from one day after arrival (Arr +1) in Nagano,

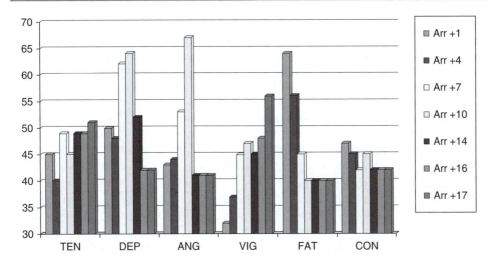

Figure 36.1 Mood profiles of an international bobsled athlete during the 1998 Olympic Winter Games in Nagano, Japan.

Japan for the 1998 Olympic Winter Games through to the two competition days (Arr +16 and Arr +17). Mood responses showed a pattern of rapid fluctuation over the 16-day period, starting with low vigor and high fatigue typically associated with jet lag, and passing through a period of high anger and depressed mood about a week later, before stabilizing into an "iceberg profile" typically associated with superior performance (Morgan, 1980) on the second day of competition when the medals were being decided.

Prior to departing London for Japan at the beginning of February, the bobsled team and its coaching and support team, of which I was a part, had completed a return trans-Atlantic crossing between London and Florida for a training camp in mid-January. Given that Florida is 5 hours behind London and Nagano is 9 hours ahead, this schedule represented a 14-hour time change in the space of less than 3 weeks. The athlete in question experienced acute symptoms of jet lag. The significant mood disturbance he reported could be explained partly by time zone adjustments and sleep disruptions, especially the fatigue and vigor scores. The elevated scores for anger and depressed mood, however, were reflective of his overreaction to relatively minor issues from home that he felt powerless to address while in Japan. These sorts of magnified emotional responses to what would be seen, at other times, as simple daily hassles are part of the emotional intensification brought about by the Olympic experience, but made worse by the underlying irritation that is a common symptom of travel fatigue and jet lag.

Effects of travel on athletic performance

A central question to be addressed is whether long-distance travel has a demonstrably negative effect on athletic performance. A review of the research literature, published in 1990, concluded that "no compelling evidence exists demonstrating that air travel adversely influences athletic performance" (O'Connor & Morgan, 1990, p. 20). Since that review was published, however, further evidence has been produced that suggests that some of the issues commonly associated with travel across multiple time zones, notably jet lag, sleep deprivation, and travel fatigue, may indeed bring about significant performance decrements. Reilly and colleagues, for example, have described a range of associated performance decrements, including reduced muscle strength, slower sprint times, and impaired choice reaction times (see Reilly, Atkinson, & Waterhouse, 1997).

Common difficulties experienced during travel

Although travel is an exciting prospect for many athletes, it can be sufficiently fraught with difficulties to lose its appeal for regular travelers. Air travel can involve the physical stressors of sitting still for long periods of time in a noisy, cramped environment while breathing poor quality air, eating unappealing food, and losing sleep. On top of these conditions, there are the psychological stressors of potential delays and missed flights, forgetting important items, time away from family and friends, guilt about shirking responsibilities back home, and concerns about terrorism. Although there is limited scientific evidence that these stressors, individually or collectively, represent significant threats to sport performance, they appear unlikely to enhance athlete well-being.

A significant travel challenge in some sports involves the safe transport of essential equipment. In tennis or badminton this challenge may involve little more than remembering to pack racquets and clothing, but in other sports, such as kayaking, rowing, shooting, and equestrian, the logistical complications of international travel with boats, guns, or horses are considerable. I have witnessed many occasions where a key piece of equipment was lost, broken, or impounded by overzealous customs officials, and the prospects of competition success disappeared with the equipment. At the 2003 World Shooting Championships, for example, an Olympic medalist's shotgun remained impounded at London's Heathrow airport as he boarded a plane for Cyprus, despite his paperwork being in order. Having to compete with a borrowed gun effectively shattered his chances of a medal, and he finished well down the field. Thorough advance planning and taking all necessary precautions are central to overcoming these types of travel challenges but, in addition, many athletes take crucial items of equipment in their hand luggage where air transport regulations allow.

There are several other seemingly minor but potentially significant challenges associated with successful domestic and international travel, in particular to high security competitions such as the Olympic Games. These challenges include accommodation, nutrition and hydration, local transport, difficulties regarding accreditation and overbearing security arrangements, and acute homesickness as a result of being separated from family and friends for extended periods. Regarding accommodation, it is common for teams with tall athletes, such as basketball, volleyball, or rowing, to find that hotel beds are too small to allow for a good night's rest and, as a result, sleep deprivation becomes a significant issue.

While accompanying teams, I have several times heard defeats on the road attributed to the poor quality of the available food. In one instance, during an overseas trip to Thailand with the Brunei national sepak takraw[1] team, the athletes took several rice cookers and a supply of uncooked rice with them because they did not like the taste of the rice served in Thailand. It is common among athletes traveling overseas to address the problem of unfamiliar and/or unpalatable food by taking their own supplies where customs restrictions allow. Some teams even go to the trouble of taking their own chefs with them to major championships.

Hydration strategies are also of prime importance during travel, given that air-conditioned surroundings and/or humid climates can severely dehydrate athletes. In my experience, many athletes need frequent reminders to carry and consume sufficient quantities of water to prevent the negative effects of dehydration. Avoiding consuming local water is an absolute necessity when traveling to developing countries, especially those where water-borne diseases are prevalent. Although most athletes are sensible enough to drink only bottled water in such destinations, some are caught out by fruit or vegetables washed under restaurant taps or ice cubes made from local water. I have many times counseled athletes who have missed world championship events in places such as Egypt, India, and China because of severe gastrointestinal complaints.

The vagaries of local transport in unfamiliar locations can also produce significant stress. Timely arrival at competition venues, even at events that are otherwise impeccably organized, can prove challenging. For example, arrangements to transfer athletes and officials between the athletes' village and competition venues at the 1996 Olympic Games in Atlanta were, at times, so chaotic and unreliable that some teams relocated, at considerable expense, to rental accommodation nearer their competition venues, and at least one team resorted to hijacking an official bus to drive themselves to their competition, such was their fear of arriving late.

On the issue of security, at many international events, athletes and officials are required to wear accreditation around their necks to identify their status and the areas to which they are allowed access. In the past, some athletes have missed their events at the Olympic Games because they forgot to carry their accreditation, and I personally witnessed tennis champion Steffi Graf being temporarily denied access to the stadium during the Wimbledon Championships for the same reason, until common sense eventually prevailed.

It might be assumed incorrectly that homesickness is primarily restricted to children or inexperienced travelers. On tour with teams, I have often been faced with experienced professional athletes in tears because they were missing their loved ones. Indeed, time spent away from family while traveling with teams is frequently cited by prominent athletes as a reason why they have decided to retire from international competition. To counteract this issue, some international teams have allowed partners and occasionally children to travel with the team for all or part of a lengthy overseas tour. This strategy may help to solve the homesickness issue but may simultaneously create a problem of divided focus among the athletes, and such a strategy requires careful management.

When athletes are on the road, most will naturally want to stay in touch with friends and loved ones via their mobile phones. Not only can this practice prove expensive in many overseas destinations, it also may raise potential problems during competitions. I have known instances where, for example, a partner back home has ended a relationship by text on the morning of an Olympic race, or where a dozen friends have called with good luck messages just prior to competition. Most teams have strict rules about when athletes can and cannot use mobile phones, with many management teams restricting use to post-training or post-competition periods. Having clear rules about phone use becomes paramount when teams are traveling and especially during overseas competitions.

It is not uncommon for traveling athletes to adopt strategies that may inadvertently exacerbate the effects of travel fatigue and jet lag. For example, constantly calculating the time back home when in a new time zone is generally to be avoided. Knowing that it is 2 a.m. the next morning in Sydney while you are in Europe, where it is 4 p.m. the previous afternoon, may help you to avoid waking up a family member or friend in the middle of the night with an ill-timed phone call, but it is also likely to make you feel tired and to slow your adjustment to the new time zone. The usual recommendation is to switch your watch

Table 36.1 Travel recommendations from the Fédération Internationale de Médecine du Sport (based on O'Connor, Youngstedt, Buxton, & Breus, 2004).

1. Before the flight, athletes should:
   - be provided with educational information about jet lag and circadian rhythms;
   - carefully plan for the trip to make it less stressful and more enjoyable;
   - avoid sleep deprivation;
   - consider shifting the sleep schedule (30–60 minutes per day) toward that of the destination for a few days prior to departure;
   - consider using appropriately-timed bright light and darkness, melatonin, or exercise to shift circadian rhythms[1].
2. During the flight, athletes should:
   - drink plenty of water or fruit juices and limit alcohol and caffeine intake to combat dehydration due to the dry air;
   - stretch, perform mild isometric exercises, and walk, at least every hour to minimize muscle stiffness and the risk for thrombosis associated with prolonged inactivity;
   - consider using earplugs or noise-canceling headphones to minimize stressful noise exposure;
   - avoid taking sleeping pills in the absence of a consultation with a physician.
3. After arriving, athletes should:
   - avoid heavy or unfamiliar meals;
   - consider engaging in a low intensity exercise session, which might need to be performed indoors because light exposure at the destination might counter the desired circadian phase shift;
   - consider avoiding heavy training for the first few days after a long flight;
   - consider using appropriately-timed bright light and darkness, melatonin or exercise to shift circadian rhythms.

[1] For a detailed description of how to use appropriately-timed bright light to shift circadian rhythms, the reader is referred to O'Connor *et al.* (2004, pp. 7–9).

to the time zone at your destination as soon as you board the plane and then try, as far as possible, to eat and sleep in accordance with the destination time zone. In-flight meal times, however, often make the latter part of this suggested strategy impractical.

Recommended strategies for effective traveling

There is a wide range of strategies that can minimize the potential negative effects of travel. The Fédération Internationale de Médecine du Sport (FIMS) has produced a position paper that includes a range of recommendations for effective travel (see Table 36.1). Although these recommendations represent sound evidence-based advice, they may not suit everyone or every situation. From my own experiences, I find that a glass of wine with my airline meal (not recommended by FIMS) plus plenty of water to limit dehydration, greatly benefits the quality of my in-flight sleep. Furthermore, having taken an aspirin to guard against risk of deep vein thrombosis, I find an extended sleep to be a better option than a series of catnaps punctuated by on-board exercise breaks, as recommended by FIMS. There are additional specific recommendations for female athletes. Gunning (1999) pointed out the need for women who take oral contraceptives to ensure they continue to take them at the appropriate time of day corresponding to their normal routine at home; otherwise the contraceptives may become less effective.

To augment these recommendations, other strategies can be put in place before, during, and after travel to good effect. Before travel, having all the basics in place related to tickets, passports, visas, vaccinations, currency, insurance, clothing, and equipment helps to minimize stress. Many athletes who travel regularly keep a list of essential items to reduce the risk of forgetting a vital piece of equipment. Also, it is a good idea to use online check-in to pre-book an aisle or exit seat, both of which allow easier movement around the aircraft, and exit seats also have more leg room.

During travel, there are obvious strategies, such as wearing comfortable clothing, trying to secure the best seats possible on a plane, and taking water and snacks with you. More important though is trying to adopt the attitude that you are going to relax and enjoy the experience. I regard this attitude as one of the key aspects of successful travel. On frequent trips between Australia and Europe, the mindset I adopt is that for the next 24 hours (or in some cases 36 hours or even 48 hours) I have no responsibilities other than to turn up for my flight on time, I have no decisions to make other than choice of food, drinks, and movies, and if I want anything I press an overhead button and someone arrives to help me. Adopting a passive approach to travel can make it a much more relaxing experience.

After arrival, certain key strategies will help minimize the negative effects of travel. About two-thirds of those who travel across time zones will experience the effects of jet lag (Rajaratnam & Arendt, 2001). To counteract jet lag, it is important to stay awake during the day and to avoid the temptation to take extended naps, although a short 20-minute nap after you have eaten lunch may prove beneficial (Reilly & Edwards, 2007). Legal stimulants such as caffeine, which is found in a wide range of beverages, may also improve alertness and cognitive performance after a long journey. If possible, try to complete your training in the morning and plan social activities for the afternoon. Another good strategy is to eat a high-protein breakfast, because protein increases adrenaline secretion, which promotes alertness, whereas it is recommended to increase carbohydrate intake during the evening meal, to promote serotonin synthesis, which causes drowsiness.

A somewhat contentious approach to counteracting jet lag symptoms is to use pharmaceutical strategies, such as taking sedatives or melatonin. Sedatives, including low-dose benzodiazepines, will help most individuals sleep better on flights, but they are not effective in helping athletes accelerate their body clock adjustments, and they can even slow this process (Reilly, Atkinson, & Budgett, 2001). Also, given the potential side effects of sedatives for some individuals, such as prolonged drowsiness and disorientation, they are generally not recommended for traveling athletes unless prescribed by a physician.

On the other hand, the sleep hormone melatonin appears to have significant benefits for the traveling athlete, although evidence of its efficacy is somewhat equivocal. Melatonin helps to move the body clock in the opposite direction to bright light. It delays the body clock at times in which bright light advances the body clock, and advances the body clock at times in which bright light delays the body clock (O'Connor, Youngstedt, Buxton, & Breus, 2004). Therefore, if used appropriately in the correct dosage,[2] melatonin can counteract symptoms of jet lag. Lewy, Saeeduddin, and Sack (1995) have clearly demonstrated its effectiveness in phase-shifting the human body clock. Moreover, Petrie, Conaglen, Thompson, and Chamberlain (1989) supported its efficacy for reducing jet lag symptoms more than 2 decades ago using a double-blind, placebo-controlled, crossover design.

Nevertheless, an often-cited study of 257 Norwegian physicians who visited New York for 5 days and were monitored for 1 week after returning to Oslo (Spitzer et al., 1999) showed melatonin to be no more effective at counteracting jet lag than a placebo. Also, a recent meta-analysis concluded that melatonin was not efficacious (Buscemi et al., 2006), although

Arendt (2006) judged this conclusion to be controversial and suggested that it might be explained by variations in quality and content of individual melatonin preparations and the absence of large randomized controlled trials. Other summaries of the literature have strongly supported the efficacy of melatonin in the treatment of jet lag, including a review by Herxheimer and Petrie (2002), which found that of 10 randomized controlled trials that had evaluated melatonin, eight had supported its efficacy in counteracting jet lag.

Although melatonin is a popular and seemingly effective treatment for jet lag, some concerns remain. First, the potency and purity of melatonin products available over the counter in the United States, for example, is not regulated by federal food and drug administration agencies (Naylor & Gleich, 1999). Second, although melatonin is generally regarded as safe with very low incidence of side effects from short-term use (Buscemi *et al.*, 2006), it is not recommended for people with epilepsy or for those taking the anti-coagulant drug, warfarin.

When on tour, especially on rest days, it is important to keep a balance between free time and organized activities. The maxim that idle hands make mischief can apply in several different ways, from athletes staying out too late, overindulging in food and drink, picking up an injury from an impromptu game of soccer, or turning up late or not at all for important team activities. Australian newspapers all too often include reports of rugby league players getting into bar room brawls while on the road, and sports journalists had a field day with the 2008 incident involving cricketer Andrew Symonds, who was omitted from the national team's tour of India for missing a compulsory team meeting because he chose to go fishing instead.

During down time, quite a few athletes like to rest or watch DVDs in their hotel rooms or lounge around the hotel pool, whereas others prefer to go shopping, and some seek out the cultural experience of the local environment. At the 2008 Beijing Olympic Games, the Australian team organized a well-received trip to the Great Wall of China for athletes who had completed their events. Most athletes were delighted by this experience, but not everyone is so enthusiastic about historic visits. One athlete, who finds cultural activities tedious, told me in Beijing that "we have our own walls back home and anyway I've already seen a picture of it."

Although often arduous, well-managed travel can carry significant benefits for sport teams. Road trips are stereotypically seen as positive bonding experiences for the individuals involved. The shared experiences, both positive and negative, can create bonds among players, coaches, and support staff that endure for a long time afterwards. Other obvious benefits of travel lie in the cultural and social experiences that come with it. I always advise athletes to include some sightseeing or visits to local cultural attractions if their training and competition schedules permit. I say this after consulting with many experienced athletes who came to the end of their sporting careers and regretted that they spent so much of their time in airports, hotels, and competition venues, and so little time seeing the wonders of the places they had visited.

Summary

There are many ways in which a sport psychologist can help to promote effective team travel. Analysis of the role of traveling practitioners has shown it to involve about 50% organizational issues (Terry, Hardy, Jones, & Rodgers, 1997). Part of this organizational role is educational, providing athletes, coaches, and other support staff with information to better prepare them for successful travel outcomes. Sport psychologists can also support team management in the planning and implementation of schedules for travel, rest and social activities, monitor the psychological responses of all involved during travel, help to resolve interpersonal issues that might arise on the road, and facilitate subsequent post-event evaluation processes.

At an individual level, travel provides many opportunities to discuss performance-related issues with athletes and coaches. Also, as an experienced traveler, I often keep a close eye on the well-being of the less experienced athletes, including helping to translate in countries where I have more language skills than they do or negotiating on an athlete's behalf if disputes arise. Box 36.1 summarizes some of the principles of successful team travel.

Box 36.1

Principles of successful team travel

- Planning is the key to successful travel for athletes and attention to detail is critical.
- Acknowledge the possible physical and psychological responses to travel.
- Systematically monitor these responses when traveling to increase awareness of the early warning signs of threats to performance and well-being.
- Minimize these potential threats by following recommendations to reduce effects of travel fatigue, jet lag, sleep deprivation, and mood disturbances.
- Pre-plan mood management strategies to counteract performance-threatening emotional responses (see Terry et al., 2006).
- Control what is controllable and accept what is not (hopefully you will have been granted the wisdom to know the difference).
- Enjoy all the positives that travel has to offer.

Notes

1 Sepak takraw is a sport played in Southeast Asia, similar to volleyball, except that players can only use their feet, knees, chest, and head to touch the ball.
2 Doses of melatonin between 0.5 mg and 5 mg have been shown to be effective, although 5 mg doses facilitate faster and better sleep. Melatonin is normally taken close to the target bedtime for the first 2–3 nights after arrival, having crossed five or more time zones (see Herxheimer & Petrie, 2002).

References

Arendt, J. (2006). Does melatonin improve sleep? Efficacy of melatonin. *British Medical Journal, 332*, 550.

Beedie, C. J., Terry, P. C., & Lane, A. M. (2000). The Profile of Mood States and athletic performance: Two meta-analyses. *Journal of Applied Sport Psychology, 12*, 49–68.

Buscemi, N., Vandermeer, B., Hooton, N., Pandya, R., Tjosvold, L., Hartling, L., Vohra, S., Klasses, T. P., & Baker, G. (2006). Efficacy and safety of exogenous melatonin for secondary sleep disorders and sleep disorders accompanying sleep restriction: Meta-analysis. *British Medical Journal, 332*, 385–93.

Gunning, L. (1999). *Travel recommendations for female athletes: Impact of travel fatigue on performance and recovery in elite female athletes*. Concord West, NSW, Australia: New South Wales Department of Sport and Recreation.

Herxheimer, A., & Petrie, K. J. (2002). Melatonin for the prevention and treatment of jet lag. *Cochrane Database of Systematic Reviews, 2*, CD001520.

Lane, A. M., Terry, P. C., Stevens, M., Barney, S., & Dinsdale, S. L. (2004). Mood responses to athletic performance in extreme conditions. *Journal of Sports Sciences, 22*, 886–897.

Lewy, A. J., Saeeduddin, A., & Sack, R. L. (1995). Phase shifting the human circadian clock using melatonin. *Behavioural Brain Research, 73*, 131–134.

Morgan, W. P. (1980). Test of champions: The iceberg profile. *Psychology Today, 14*, 92–108.

Naylor, S., & Gleich, G. J. (1999). Over-the-counter melatonin products and contamination. *American Family Physician, 284*, 287–288.

O'Connor, P., & Morgan, W. P. (1990). Athletic performance following rapid traversal of multiple time zones: A review. *Sports Medicine, 10*, 20–30.

O'Connor, P., Youngstedt, S. D., Buxton, O. M., & Breus, M. D. (2004). *Air travel and performance in sports*. International Federation of Sports Medicine (FIMS) position statement. Retrieved from: http://www.fims.org/files/311417173/PS16%20Air%20travel%20March%202004.pdf

Petrie, K., Conaglen, J. V., Thompson, L., & Chamberlain, K. (1989). Effect of melatonin on jet lag after long haul flights. *British Medical Journal, 298*, 705–707.

Rajaratnam, S. M. W., & Arendt, J. (2001). Health in a 24-h society. *The Lancet, 358*, 999–1005.

Reilly, T., Atkinson, G., & Waterhouse, J. (1997). Travel fatigue and jet lag. *Journal of Sports Sciences, 15*, 365–369.

Reilly, T., Atkinson, G., & Budgett, R. (2001). Effects of low-dose temazepam on physiological variables and performance tests following a westerly flight across five time zones. *International Journal of Sports Medicine, 22*, 166–174.

Reilly, T., & Edwards, B. (2007). Altered sleep-wake cycles and physical performance in athletes. *Physiology and Behavior, 90*, 274–284.

Scott, J. P. R., McNaughton, L. R., & Polman, R. C. J. (2006). Effects of sleep deprivation and exercise on cognitive and motor performance and mood. *Physiology and Behavior, 87*, 396–408.

Spiegel, K., Leproult, R., & Van Cauter, E. (1999). Impact of sleep debt on metabolic and endocrine function. *The Lancet, 354*, 1435–1439.

Spitzer, R. L., Terman, M., Williams, J. B., Terman, J. S., Malt, U. F., Singer, F., & Lewy, A. J. (1999). Clinical features, validation of a new syndrome-specific scale, and lack of response to melatonin in a randomized double-blind trial. *American Journal of Psychiatry, 156*, 1392–1396.

Terry, P. C., Hardy, L., Jones, J. G., & Rodgers, S. (1997). Psychological support at the 1996 Olympic Games. *British Journal of Sports Medicine, 31*, 79.

Terry, P. C., Dinsdale, S. L., Karageorghis, C. I., & Lane, A. M. (2006). Use and perceived effectiveness of pre-competition mood regulation strategies among athletes. In M. Katsikitis (Ed.), *Psychology bridging the Tasman: Science, culture and practice* (pp. 420–424). Melbourne, VIC: Australian Psychological Society.

Waterhouse, J., Reilly, T., & Edwards, B. (2004). The stress of travel. *Journal of Sports Sciences, 22*, 946–966.

37

Bullying and hazing in sport teams

Leslee A. Fisher and Lars Dzikus

What are bullying and hazing in sport? Should sport psychology consultants be concerned with these behaviors? If so, what role should sport psychology consultants play in dealing with abusive relationships in sport? These questions are the major issues we explore in this chapter. We understand bullying and hazing as abusive behaviors related to group dynamics that occur within teams and also when team members harass, bully, or haze non-team members.

The role that power and power dynamics play in sport

As Fisher, Butryn, and Roper (2003) observed, power is a concept not frequently discussed in the field of sport psychology nor in sport psychology consultation. Although sport studies scholars frequently examine power and the power dynamics inherent in sport, only a few sport psychology researchers and practitioners have done so (e.g., Schinke & Hanrahan, 2009). Recently, Fisher, Roper, and Butryn (2009) suggested that such an analysis could provide a meaningful understanding of athlete's experience and welfare. This type of under-standing seems critical for sport psychology consultants, coaches, parents, and administra-tors who work with athletes and care about their overall well-being.

Brackenridge (2008) summarized over 600 cases of sexual abuse and exploitation in sport. Most relevant for this discussion, Brackenridge proposed that there are several aspects of sport that may allow for the exploitation of athletes to occur: we believe these aspects include not only harassment but bullying and hazing as well. In particular, Brackenridge (2001) posited that

> the male-dominated nature of sport, prevalence of high-ranking sport positions popu-lated by men, adherence to hegemonic masculinity, and emphasis on the physical body are each significant contributors to the development and maintenance of a cul-ture of violence and objectification of sport women and men.
>
> (p. 44)

Further, although most sport participants see exploitation and abuse as personally perpetrated and personally experienced, Brackenridge revealed a complex network of stakeholders in abusive and exploitive situations that included coaches, teachers, team managers, trainers, sport organizations, the media, and even peer athletes, parents, and sport scientists. Sport psychology consultants could play an important role in educating such stakeholders about sexually transgressive and other abusive behaviors. At the minimum, consultants could engage stakeholders in discussions about how bullying and hazing are defined. At most, consultants might find themselves in the position of being the first person an athlete tells about being a victim of these behaviors.

In 2003, Fisher *et al.* described how the power dynamics in sport contexts can encourage homophobic, heteronormative, racialized, and classist "accepted" behaviors. To combat such practices, consultants should be aware of how sexuality, race, gender, and class may be "viewed not as simple categories, but as relations of power, as spaces where individuals negotiate for greater agency within the existing power structure" (p. 396). Further, consultants should

> acknowledge gender-biased and homophobic behaviors within the hyper-masculine structure of many sports, as well as to confront ways that consultants, whether male or female, have the potential to be both perpetrators and victims of discriminatory practices themselves.
>
> (p. 393)

Power dynamics are at the heart of many sport behaviors that occur in locker rooms, sport club settings, coaches' houses, and on the field. In these spaces, more experienced athletes and coaches often work hard to maintain their control and power over less experienced participants (Curry, 1991). Actions that are accepted in these contexts may be considered deviant in other spheres of society. For example, it is not unusual for "coaches to scream at athletes, belittle them, or challenge the masculinity of male athletes. At times, it appears only the most outrageous coaching behaviors lie outside the accepted norms" (Coakley, 2007, p. 152). Similarly, in many sports athletes use power via violence, aggression, and intimidation in ways that potentially would be considered criminal behaviors outside the boundaries of sport. Also, the dynamics of bullying and hazing in sport are often not the same as in schools or the workplace (Institute for Global Ethics, 2007).

Some bullying and hazing behaviors in sport may also be rooted in overconformity to what Coakley (2007) referred to as the *sport ethic*. The norms in the sport ethic include athletes' unwavering dedication to their sports, striving for distinction, accepting risks and pain, and overcoming many obstacles in the pursuit of their goals. Bullies often attack those whom they define as outside the range of what they consider acceptable or "normal" in terms of appearance, behavior, musical preference, interests, friends, and so forth (Kimmel & Mahler, 2003). Because athletes often learn to use power strategically in sport via aggression and intimidation and may receive positive feedback for their aggressive behaviors (Coakley, 2007), athletes who bully and haze non-athletes may overconform to notions such as striving for distinction and accepting risks and pains. Similarly, some coach bullying and hazing behaviors could be brought into the locker room because coaches are overconforming to the accepted norm of using intimidation in their sports.

Sport psychology consultants are in a critical position in their work with athletes. Many espouse an athlete-centered approach where athlete welfare is first and foremost (Fisher *et al.*, 2009). As Brackenridge (2008) pointed out, however, practitioners need to also be concerned with sport environments and whether they are safe for those who participate in them. Because of the close relationships developed between consultants and athletes, athletes might reveal incidents of bullying and hazing to consultants before telling others. Therefore, consultants need to develop the necessary skills to educate themselves, athletes, and teams about appropriate and inappropriate sport behaviors including hazing and bullying. They can also develop skills to help athletes once they have been bullied or hazed.

What are bullying and hazing in sport?

Bullying

Bullying in sport is a historical and international problem that affects a broad range of individuals. For example, bullying was a daily occurrence in English public schools from the eighteenth century through to the present. Early forms of student-organized rugby football games became a means for older, stronger boys to exercise control over younger boys (Dunning & Sheard, 2005).

Bullying has been defined as "a conscious, willful, deliberate and repeated hostile activity marked by an imbalance of power, intent to harm, and/or a threat of aggression" (Government of Alberta, 2005, p. 1). Many theorists regard the continued, systematic abuse of power as a defining aspect of bullying; bullying often includes the systematic harassment of weaker individuals via humiliation and torment (Lines, 2008). Specific forms of bulling can occur before, during, and after sport-related events in the form of verbal taunts, social exclusion, physical attacks, and cyber harassment. More specifically, sport bullying could include:

> (a) unwarranted yelling and screaming directed at the [athlete]; (b) continually criticizing the [athlete's] abilities; (c) blaming the [athlete] for mistakes; (d) making unreasonable demands related to performance; (e) repeated insults or put downs of the [athlete]; (f) repeated threats to remove or restrict opportunities or privileges; (g) denying or discounting the [athlete's] accomplishments; (h) threats of, and actual, physical violence; and (i) emails or instant messages containing insults or threats.
>
> (Government of Alberta, 2005, p. 1)

Many insults or put downs of athletes are homophobic, focusing on personal attacks related to athletes' sexual orientation, femininity, or masculinity.

Hazing

Historically, hazing has occurred in universities since medieval times, in the American fraternity and sorority systems, in high school and university athletic settings, and in modern sports (Trota & Johnson, 2004). In recent times, research has been conducted related to hazing in professional hockey (Robidoux, 2001), military combat units (Malszecki, 2004), and even in sport reporting (Nuwer, 2004). Hazing has been defined as "a rite of passage wherein youths, neophytes, or rookies are taken through traditional practices by more senior members in order to initiate them into the next stage of their cultural, religious, academic, or athletic lives" (Trota & Johnson, p. x). Allan and DeAngelis (2004) suggested that based

357

on a United States National Collegiate Athletic Association (NCAA) survey (see Hoover, 1999), hazing can be further delineated into three major categories:

> (a) *questionable behaviors*: Humiliating or degrading activities, but not dangerous or potentially illegal activities; (b) *alcohol-related [behaviors]*: Drinking contests, exclusive of other dangerous or potentially illegal activities; or (c) *unacceptable and potentially illegal behaviors*: Activities carrying a high probability of danger or injury, or which could result in criminal charges.
>
> (p. 63)[1]

Both bullying and hazing can refer to either the actions of an individual or a group or team. Although definitions vary in the degree of specificity regarding individual versus group acts, the systematic and deliberate abuse of power is a main theme in each. Nevertheless, the inclusion of intent in both definitions can often be confusing for those in sport to interpret (Lines, 2008). For example, sport participants may believe that belligerent coaches do not intentionally hurt their athletes; they might believe that coaches intend to bring out "better" performances. In addition, cultural values specific to sports in certain countries may promote an "ends justify the means" approach to sport bullying and hazing. American basketball coach Bob Knight is often discussed in the context of the "potential positive effects of strategic bullying behavior on unit or team performance [including a] ... short-term increase in productivity [and] underperform-ing employees [voluntarily deciding to leave an organization]" (Ferris, Zinko, Brouer, Buckley, & Harvey, 2007, pp. 202–203). Although Knight's treatment of players has long been controversial and has often been used as an example of bullying in sports (Myers, 2000), because Knight was one of the most successful coaches in American men's collegiate basketball, many appear to have championed his style of strategic assertive bullying. Such a positive view of bullying (and by extension, hazing) is obviously problem-atic because it may justify and encourage the use of coach bullying and hazing within sport teams.

Therefore, it is crucial to educate coaches, athletes, consultants, and other stakeholders about how bullying and hazing in sport may make teams appear to perform better in the short term but can have long-term damaging consequences. In addition, given sport psy-chology consultants' ethical codes and laws related to reporting abuse, once consultants are educated about sport bullying and hazing definitions, they may be in a position to report incidents of bullying and hazing before others can (Brackenridge, 2001, 2008; Fisher *et al.*, 2009). Although ethical codes apply to all sport psychology consultants, legal ramifications pertain especially to registered/licensed psychologists. What complicates matters further is that psychologists are bound to confidentiality if a client reveals information in confidence and in the privacy of a one-on-one consultation.

Ethical codes related to sport psychology and athlete welfare

Several national and international professional organizations in sport psychology have ethical codes concerned with the welfare of athletes. Two are reviewed here: the International Society of Sport Psychology (ISSP, n.d.) and the Association of Applied Sport Psychology (AASP, 2005). The ISSP code states that among sport psychology consultants' tasks is the protection of athletes' welfare and the guarding of sport in general "against any dangerous threats to morality" (para. 1). The challenges for consultants are not only to enhance the performance of athletes but also to help "formulate ethical guidelines for conduct of athletic programs" and to "develop means by which athletes are protected against psychological and moral damage" (para. 3). Consultants could contribute their professional expertise to these efforts, focusing on a wide range of stakeholders including athletes, administrators, coaches, parents, physicians, and trainers.

The primary goal of AASP's (2005) code of ethics is "the welfare and protection of the individuals and groups with whom AASP members work" (para. 6). Thus, members of organizations such as ISSP and AASP are called upon to encourage ethical conduct among their members, colleagues, students, and those constituencies with whom they work. Members of these professional bodies can help sports organizations develop and implement their own codes of ethics and policies regarding bullying and hazing. Consultants can partner with athletes, coaches, parents, and administrators to prevent harmful bullying and hazing behaviors as well as help those who have already been hurt.

Specific suggestions for change

As a starting point, we believe that sports teams and clubs at all levels of competition should adopt anti-bullying and hazing policies if they have not done so already. There are several components that should be built into an anti-bullying and hazing policy, including definitions of bullying and hazing, what the punishments for both are, how to report offenders, how to respond to these behaviors when they occur, and, in the case of hazing, how to develop alternative ways to initiate or bond with other athletes (see Crow & Phillips, 2004). Regardless of whether an organization has a policy in place or not, consultants should have an understanding about how to work with athletes who have been bullied, those who bully others, how to work with teams/coaches/parents on these issues, and also how to refer out to a qualified specialist if the situation is beyond their expertise.

Working with athletes who have been bullied

There may be times when athletes come to sport psychology consultants first before telling anyone else that they have been bullied. According to the website for the U.S. Department of Health and Human Services' Health Resources and Services Administration Department (2009), those who are qualified mental health professionals (such as consultants who hold licensure as clinical or counseling psychologists) should help give those who have been bullied:

> (a) permission and support to tell what has happened to them and to talk about their feelings; (b) protection from continued bullying through adult supervision, consequences for those who bully, and adults taking reports of bullying seriously; (c) strong, positive relationships with adults and peers; (d) assistance from peers in feeling that they belong; (e) assistance in not blaming themselves for the bullying; and (f) support with post-traumatic stress symptoms, in some cases, even after the bullying has been stopped.
>
> (HRSA, 2009)

Working with athletes who have bullied others

There may also be times when those same consultants are working with athletes who are bullying others. According to HRSA (2009), qualified mental health professionals should:

(a) help them see the consequences or the cost of bullying behavior and consider alternatives; (b) hold them fully accountable for their actions by confronting excuses that minimize the behavior or externalize the cause of the behavior; (c) help them fully acknowledge their behavior; (d) support authority figures in holding them accountable for their actions and not suggesting or allowing rationalizations; (e) once they are able to recognize problems with their behavior, help them set and work toward goals for change (e.g., channeling aggression into leadership), help them track their progress toward new behaviors, and feel pride about those changes; and (f) help them build genuine empathy and conscience; after learning that their own actions can cause them to get in trouble, they can begin to appreciate the impact of their actions on others.

Working with teams

A recent report in *Sports Illustrated* highlighted the involvement of high school athletes in anti-bullying workshops in California (Roberts, 2008). By sharing their knowledge of sport cultures and moral behaviors, both athletes and consultants could support and facilitate such groups. Consultants could begin by holding workshops to educate athletes about how to critically examine otherwise "accepted" sport behaviors and norms such as overconformity and the concept of the "sport ethic" (Coakley, 2007). They could also help athletes learn to *not* praise overconforming teammates and elevate them to the status of role models for others. Such an approach would not just target bullying and hazing behaviors but could also help teams question behaviors such as athletes playing hurt or practising excessively, above and beyond expectations.

Consultants can also work to educate athletes about what they can do to prevent bullying and hazing on their teams. The Government of Alberta's (2005, p. 2) bullying prevention program tells athletes:

- Trust your instincts. If someone's behavior is making you feel uncomfortable or threatened, don't ignore it. You have the right to be treated respectfully.
- Talk to someone you trust – a parent, friend, coach, manager or another player. Remember to keep speaking up until someone helps you.
- Stay calm. Bullies love a reaction, so don't give them one.
- Project confidence. Hold your head up and stand up straight. Bullies pick on people who they think are afraid. Show them you're not.
- Don't reply to messages from cyberbullies. If you're receiving threatening text messages or emails don't reply, but keep the messages as evidence. The police and your internet service provider and/or telephone company can use these messages to help you.

Consultants can also encourage athletes to interfere when they witness bullying. Instead of fighting the bully physically, speaking up, getting help, and helping the target are appropriate reactions. Quiet bystanders give bullies the audience they want. Once athletes understand bullying and its negative effects, they are more likely to speak up against it. Athletes also need to learn about alcohol responsibility, because many hazing events are fueled by the overconsumption of alcohol. Consultants could then help athletes construct alternative initiations, team-building, or bonding rituals that are not humiliating, degrading, or toxic (Johnson & Donnelly, 2004).

Working with coaches

Once policies have been established related to sport bullying and hazing, coaches should have thorough knowledge about and understanding of those policies, and then provide strong leadership for the athletes with whom they come into contact (Johnson & Donnelly, 2004). These steps require first noticing sport bullying and hazing, then interpreting these behaviors as problems. Next, coaches must recognize their own and others' responsibilities to change a bullying/hazing culture and acquire the skills necessary to make such a change. Finally, they must take action to eliminate bullying/hazing on their teams (see Allan & DeAngelis, 2004, as related to Berkowitz's [1994] five-step model for educating males about sexual violence).

To facilitate these steps, consultants could hold workshops to educate coaches about bullying and hazing and help them learn how to model and reinforce positive behaviors. Coaches' responsibilities include creating "a safe and respectful sport environment by not engaging in, allowing, condoning, or ignoring behavior that constitutes, or could be perceived as, bullying" (Government of Alberta, 2005, p. 2). Consultants can teach coaches how to establish positive communication patterns between all parties involved and how to provide and receive constructive criticism. Most important, such workshops can help coaches become critically reflective practitioners who examine their own behaviors.

Consultants could also help established coaching certification programs to empower coaches to think critically about the structure of their sport programs and encourage them to make changes to the same (Coakley, 2007). Because most coaching certification programs tend to be geared toward helping coaches become "sport efficiency experts rather than teachers who help young people become responsible and informed [about] ... who controls their sport lives and the contexts in which they play sports" (Coakley, p. 148), such workshops could provide a space for coaches to talk openly about pressures related to a focus on winning.

Working with parents

At times, parents become bullies targeting their own children, players on opposing teams, referees, and coaches. Consultants could hold seminar workshops for parents addressing many of the aforementioned issues and strategies. In addition, interested consultants could work with parent sport education programs because parents have become increasingly involved and controlling when it comes to channeling their children into organized, competitive youth sports (Coakley, 2007).

The consultant as part of the problem

Many of the suggestions listed above may appear easy to understand and, by extension, easy to implement. Nothing could be further from the truth for ending sport bullying and hazing.

Consultants can be part of the "bystander effect" or "turning a blind eye" to what is occurring on the teams with whom they work. As Finley and Finley (2006) suggested, hazing is really about *groupthink* or when people act differently in groups versus when they are alone.

The hard reality is that groupthink includes sport psychology consultants who might, for example, quickly report incidents of sexual abuse in children with whom they are working but who are afraid to report incidents of bullying or hazing on sport teams. Consultants may choose not to report bullying or hazing for myriad reasons, including beliefs that: (a) they hold little power in the sport organizations or with the athletes they serve; (b) if they do challenge those in power about the "way things are done," they may find themselves quickly out of a job; (c) they will certainly lose money if the consulting job is lost; (d) they might feel more comfortable trying to effect change by working within the immediate system (e.g., with an individual athlete or team) versus challenging those higher up in the sport structure; and/or (e) they see change in sport organizations as slow and frustrating.

Deciding to report bullying and hazing for whatever reason is certainly difficult and complex. Similar to Brackenridge's (2001, p. 96) assertion about those who experience sexual exploitation in sport, those who know about bullying and hazing also face what seems like impossible choices:

> if [one] speaks out [one's] integrity remains intact but [one's] survival in elite competitive sport is hazarded. If [one] allows the abuse to continue without reporting it, [one's] personal ... integrity [is] violated but [one's] performance in the sport might be salvaged.

Non-reporting has a domino effect. If athletes see consultants and other stakeholders ignoring bullying and hazing, they may conclude that they will not be supported in reporting these behaviors themselves. We strongly suggest that consultants educate themselves about definitions of bullying and hazing and how to work with (or refer out) those who have been a part of these behaviors.

Conclusions

In this chapter, we have suggested that bullying and hazing in sport are serious, problematic behaviors that occur because of power dynamics in sport, sport cultural traditions, and overconformity to the sport ethic (Fisher et al., 2009). We believe that although it will not be easy and will take time, sport psychology consultants can help create sport cultures where bullying and hazing no longer exist. If interested, consultants could play an integral role in changing coach education programs to include bullying and hazing definitions, creating policies related to athlete welfare and behavior, and also helping teams develop healthy and appropriate initiation or bonding alternatives (see Box 37.1). National and international psychology and sport psychology association codes related to the protection of athletes can serve as some guidance in these areas. Further, we believe that consultants could help coaches, athletes, and parents use the process of critical reflection to examine where they get their values about appropriate boundaries in relationships and how athletes should treat each other on teams (Brackenridge, 2008). Finally, as Brackenridge (2001) suggested, sport psychology consultants have specialized training and responsibilities to see that athletes get their psychological needs addressed and psychological injuries prevented.

Box 37.1

What sport psychology consultants can do to help prevent bullying and hazing

- Obtain and share information about the psycho-social conditions that contribute to abuse and exploitation in sport as well as the psychological effects of bullying and hazing.
- Support the adoption of anti-bullying and hazing policies.
- Facilitate workshops to educate coaches, athletes, and parents about bullying and hazing.
- Contribute to the development of coaching certification programs.
- Help teams develop healthy and appropriate initiation or bonding alternatives.
- Intervene by treating or referring out when observing abusive behavior.

Note

1 Although Hoover (1999) examined NCAA athlete hazing behaviors, the NCAA itself has discussed hazing issues but has yet to put any policies in place that we know about as of 2009.

References

Allan, E. J., & DeAngelis, G. (2004). Hazing, masculinity, and collision sports: (Un) becoming heroes. In J. Johnson & M. Holman (Eds.), *Making the team: Inside the world of sport initiations and hazing* (pp. 61–82). Toronto, ON, Canada: Canadian Scholars' Press.

Association for Applied Sport Psychology (2005). *Ethics code: AASP ethical principles and standards.* Retrieved from http://appliedsportpsych.org/about/ethics/code

Berkowitz, A. D. (Ed.). (1994). *Men and rape: Theory, research, and prevention programs in higher education.* San Francisco: Jossey-Bass.

Brackenridge, C. (2001). *Spoilsports: Understanding and preventing sexual exploitation in sport.* London: Routledge.

Brackenridge, C. (2008). Sex, lies, shock, and role: Sport psychologists as agents of athlete welfare. Presentation at the annual conference of the *Association for Applied Sport Psychology*, St. Louis.

Coakley, J. (2007). *Sports in society: Issues and controversies* (9th ed.). Boston: McGraw-Hill.

Crow, R. B., & Phillips, D. R. (2004). Hazing: What the law says. In J. Johnson & M. Holman (Eds.), *Making the team: Inside the world of sport initiations and hazing* (pp. 19–31). Toronto, ON, Canada: Canadian Scholars' Press.

Curry, T. (1991). Fraternal bonding in the locker room: A pro-feminist analysis of talk about competition and women. *Sociology of Sport Journal, 8,* 119–135.

Dunning, E., & Sheard, K. (2005). *Barbarians, gentlemen and players: A sociological study of the development of rugby football* (2nd ed.). London: Routledge.

Ferris, G. R., Zinko, R., Brouer, R. L., Buckley, R. M., & Harvey, M. G. (2007). Strategic bullying as a supplementary, balance perspective on destructive leadership. *Leadership Quarterly, 18,* 195–206.

Finley, P., & Finley, L. (2006). *The sports industry's war on athletes.* Westport, CT: Praeger.

Fisher, L. A., Butryn, T. M., & Roper, E. A. (2003). Diversifying (and politicizing) sport psychology through cultural studies: A promising perspective. *The Sport Psychologist, 17,* 391–405.

Fisher, L. A., Roper, E. A., & Butryn, T. M. (2009). Engaging cultural studies and traditional sport psychology. In R. J. Schinke & S. J. Hanrahan (Eds.), *Cultural sport psychology* (pp. 23–34). Champaign, IL: Human Kinetics.

Government of Alberta. (2005). *Bullying prevention in sports.* Retrieved from http://www.bully freealberta.ca/pdf/Sports_FS.pdf

Hoover, N. (1999). *Initiation rites and athletics for NCAA sports teams: A national survey.* Retrieved on June 4, 2009 from http://www.alfred.edu/sports_hazing/

Institute for Global Ethics (2007). When the coach gets graphic, how important is winning? Retrieved from http://www.globalethics.org/newsline/2007/02/12/when-the-coach-gets-graphic-how-important-is-winning/

International Society of Sport Psychology (n.d.). *Statutes.* Retrieved from http://www.issponline.org/ab_statues.asp?ms=2&sms=2

Johnson, J., & Donnelly, P. (2004). In their own words: Athletic administrators, coaches, and athletes at two universities discuss hazing policy initiatives. In J. Johnson & M. Holman (Eds.), *Making the team: Inside the world of sport initiations and hazing* (pp. 132–154). Toronto, ON, Canada: Canadian Scholars' Press.

Kimmel, M. S., & Mahler, M. (2003). Adolescent masculinity, homophobia, and violence. *American Behavioral Scientist, 46,* 1439–1458.

Lines, D. (2008). *The bullies: Understanding bullies and bullying.* London: Kingsley.

Malszecki, G. (2004). "No mercy shown nor asked" – Toughness test or torture?: Hazing in military combat units and its "collateral damage." In J. Johnson & M. Holman (Eds.), *Making the team: Inside the world of sport initiations and hazing* (pp. 32–49). Toronto, ON, Canada: Canadian Scholars' Press.

Myers, B. (2000, March 26). Knight as a bully. *New York Times,* p. SP12.

Nuwer, H. (2004). How sportswriters contribute to a hazing culture in athletics. In J. Johnson & M. Holman (Eds.), *Making the team: Inside the world of sport initiations and hazing* (pp. 118–131). Toronto, ON, Canada: Canadian Scholars' Press.

Roberts, S. (2008, July 7). Jocks against bullies. *Sports Illustrated, 109,* 90.

Robidoux, M. (2001). *Men at play: A working understanding of professional hockey.* Montreal, QC, Canada: McGill-Queen's University Press.

Schinke, R. J., & Hanrahan, S. J. (2009). *Cultural sport psychology.* Champaign, IL: Human Kinetics.

Trota, B., & Johnson, J. (2004). Introduction: A brief history of hazing. In J. Johnson & M. Holman (Eds.), *Making the team: Inside the world of sport initiations and hazing* (pp. x–xvi). Toronto, ON, Canada: Canadian Scholars' Press.

U.S. Department of Health and Human Services, Health Resources and Services Administration Department (2009). *Stop bullying now.* Retrieved from http://www.education.com/partner/articles/stopbullying/

38

Death of a teammate

Ruth Anderson

It is inevitable that the tragic circumstances that occur in life will also occur in sport, and sport psychologists may play pivotal roles when working with teams to ensure athletes' psychological needs are addressed on and off the sporting field. The death of a teammate is not a situation commonly discussed within sport or in the sport psychology literature. Perhaps to some it seems an unlikely scenario; however, as with all tragic situations, it often happens when it is least expected, and the effects can be far reaching. Death is a reality of life, and the death of an athlete will have a profound and lasting influence on any sporting team. Deaths in sport will occur, and it is important to be adequately prepared to support a team in managing the diverse and complex issues that will arise when a teammate dies (Buchko, 2005; Vernacchia, Reardon, & Templin, 1997).

There are many examples from around the world of athletes dying suddenly and tragically from illness, accidents, and suicide (among other causes: Buchko, 2005). Training accidents across many sports have claimed the lives of athletes. Teams have been involved in accidents, and athletes have witnessed the deaths of teammates. In Australia recently, the nation was shocked at the news of a road accident involving a team of six Australian elite cyclists. The team was on a training ride in a small European town preparing for an upcoming race when a car veered across to the wrong side of the road and crashed straight into the group. It took the life of one cyclist, leaving the five other athletes critically injured. As with many heartbreaking circumstances, this accident happened without warning, and the Australian sport community was faced with a tragedy on a scale that it had not dealt with previously. A rapid and comprehensive response was coordinated, and a team of staff immediately traveled to Europe to facilitate recovery and to assist athletes in coping with the death of their friend. This example is just one of many tragedies that can occur in sport. An unthinkable and unexpected situation occurred outside of anyone's control that required a rapid response. In these types of situations, the sport team and organization tend to immediately look to the sport psychologist for direction on the appropriate strategies and services to best manage the critical incident. Athletes, coaches, and staff are confronted with emotions not usually encountered, when faced with the death of a teammate, and the loss will have an intense effect on the team (Buchko, 2005). Understanding the complexities of grief, designing a

365

helpful intervention plan for the team, and providing grief counseling support will be critical in facilitating recovery.

Understanding grief and loss

Loss is an inescapable part of life, and people experience considerable distress when confronted by the reality of death. Grief is defined as "the pain and suffering experienced after loss" (Humphrey & Zimpfer, 1996, p. 1). Grief is a normal emotional reaction to death, and has significant psychological and physical effects on individual functioning (Raphael, 1994). Although grief is a universal response to loss, there will be individual differences in how each athlete and coach cope with and resolve the loss (Humphrey & Zimpfer, 1996). Grief is an intensely personal experience, and how an individual works through the grieving process will be influenced by a multitude of factors including the relationship to the person who has died, the way it happened, individual personality dispositions, and cultural beliefs about death. There is no correct way to grieve or specific time frames in which grief is resolved (Kübler-Ross & Kessler, 2005). A range of physical, cognitive, emotional, and behavioral symptoms are commonly present in an uncomplicated grief reaction (Worden, 2002), including any of the following:

- *Emotions:* sadness, anger, guilt, anxiety, loneliness, fatigue, shock, numbness;
- *Physical sensations:* tightness in the chest, breathlessness, lack of energy, agitation, dryness in the mouth, fatigue, sense of depersonalization;
- *Cognitions:* disbelief, confusion, helplessness, hopelessness, preoccupation with thoughts of the deceased, poor memory, loss of control;
- *Behaviors:* sleep disturbance, appetite disturbance, absentminded behavior, social withdrawal, avoidance of reminders of the deceased, crying, bad dreams.

Stages of grief

A variety of models have been used to explain the complex reactions following loss (Humphrey & Zimpfer, 1996). Observations that symptoms of grief were often characteristic throughout specific time periods related to the loss, resulted in the development of theories about the experience of grief at certain stages following the loss (Stroebe & Stroebe, 1987). The Kübler-Ross (1993) stage theory is perhaps the most widely recognized. This theory originally focused on the grief process for those who were dying, but in later work was developed to explain the grief process following loss (Humphrey & Zimpfer, 1996; Kübler-Ross & Kessler, 2005). The five stages of grief give insight into the emotional experience of grieving, thereby providing a guide for support throughout the counseling process (Kübler-Ross & Kessler, 2005).

Denial

The first stage helps individuals to unconsciously manage feelings, therefore assisting to initially survive the loss. Denial arises because it is difficult to believe the individual is gone and won't be seen again. The response may be feelings of shock and numbness, and the questioning process begins on how and why it would happen. As individuals ask these questions, denial begins to fade and the reality of the loss begins to be accepted. The movement away from denial begins the healing process, and the feelings previously denied will start to be experienced (Kübler-Ross & Kessler, 2005).

Anger

There are diverse ways individuals may experience the second stage. Anger appears when individuals are feeling safe and able to survive the emotion. Anger will not be logical and can be directed at the one lost, at others for allowing it to happen, or toward themselves for the inability to be able to do something to have prevented the death. Anger presents at the front of many other feelings such as sadness, panic, hurt, loneliness, or guilt. Behind anger is the pain of the reality of being abandoned and of dealing with the loss. Individuals may experience anger throughout the different stages of the grieving process (Kübler-Ross & Kessler, 2005).

Bargaining

It is a natural instinct to want to return to life as it was, and remaining in the past becomes a way of avoiding the hurt. The *if only* or *what if* questions arise as bargaining is used as a means of escape from the pain of the reality. The experience of guilt may arise when questioning what could have been done differently. Although individuals may not always believe the bargaining, it provides temporary relief from the pain and keeps other strong emotions at a distance (Kübler-Ross & Kessler, 2005).

Depression/sadness

As the reality that the loved one is gone is accepted, feelings of sadness may become overwhelming. Life may feel pointless, and the individual may withdraw and struggle with the daily activities of life. The feeling of sadness is not a sign of mental illness at this point, but a natural response to a tragic reality. This feeling is a necessary step of the recovery process, and needs to be experienced to work through the meaning of the loss. It enables individuals to slow down and confront the reality of the loss, allowing for the exploration of thoughts and feelings (Kübler-Ross & Kessler, 2005).

Acceptance

The final stage is when individuals accept that the individual has gone permanently. Learning to live with the new reality and adjusting to living life in a world without the individual become key issues. Ways to remember and commemorate the loss are explored, as individuals reinvest in life (Kübler-Ross & Kessler, 2005).

The stages of grief are intended to be a conceptualization of the process of grieving, not set rules or strict guidelines on where an individual is placed along a prescribed course (Stroebe, Hansson, Stroebe, & Schut, 2001). Kübler-Ross and Kessler (2005) argued that the stage model has often been misunderstood. It was never intended to be a model that compartmentalizes grief, where emotions were neatly packaged into specific stages. The model provides a framework of understanding a complex process experienced while learning how to cope and then live with the loss. There is no typical grief response. Not everyone will go through all of the stages, and there is no simple timeline or structured progression through them (Kübler-Ross & Kessler, 2005). Grieving is a fluid process and individuals may pass both backward and forward among the stages of grief (Raphael, 1994).

Dealing with grief and loss in sport: coordinating a response

On receiving the news of the death of an athlete, the sport organization often will look to the sport psychologist for guidance in managing the aftermath. There are practical considerations when establishing the plan for intervention to make certain the range of issues that may arise will be efficiently and effectively handled.

Practical considerations

Establish who the clients are

It is important to clarify who the primary clients are, and how best to provide services to other parties involved. It is not only athletes and coaches who may need assistance. Consideration needs to be given to what level of intervention is required by family members and staff from the sport organization. Decide with whom you will be working, and how the other parties can receive support if needs are beyond the scope of your practice.

Define the services provided

Be clear in what services you can provide for the team and what your limitations are. If you are working only with athletes, establish referral options for those with whom you will not be directly working, such as family members and staff. Ensure processes put in place and the services provided are culturally specific. If you cannot cater for cultural needs, then use outside resources (Stroebe et al., 2001).

Education of the team/organization on service provision

Inform staff and management within the organization on the types of services that facilitate the process of dealing effectively with the loss. Don't assume people will understand the effect of the death on an athlete or the potential implications for the team. Provide education on the grieving process to highlight the complexity of the nature of grief, thereby assisting in gaining support for the services available over time.

Designing your intervention

Provide a comprehensive assessment

Any plans for intervention should be based on a comprehensive assessment of the effect of the loss on athletes and the current needs of the team. The assessment should include the circumstances of the death, the nature of the relationship with the deceased, and the potential effects of the loss on both individual and team functioning. Because grief will affect individuals and groups in different ways, tailor the interventions to fit the unique requirements of the team. Provide the opportunity to have individual athletes assessed to ensure there are no significant mental health risks present.

Design the intervention plan

Using the assessment as the foundation, design the intervention plan to meet the identified needs of the team. Although there is not a set of prescribed interventions for managing the effects of the death of a teammate, there are key elements of psychological service provision that will facilitate the recovery process. Educate the team on the nature and effects of grief and the support available to them. Develop strategies for working with all involved including athletes, coaches, the team, staff, and family members, by either the direct provision of counseling services or establishing referral options to external psychological services. In collaboration with coaching staff develop strategies for the management of the team dynamics and critical issues. The ongoing monitoring of athletes should ensure any complicated grief reactions are identified and managed. Make provision for longer term counseling support options. As with all interventions, monitor the outcomes and re-evaluate the intervention plan as required.

Call in for assistance

If you are not experienced in delivering grief counseling services, or it is beyond the scope of your role within the team, call in a specialist to assist with service provision. Alternatively, establish a referral system for athletes to access grief counseling.

Counseling principles when working with grief and loss

The aim of grief counseling is to facilitate the process of uncomplicated grieving, supporting the individual to adjust to the loss (Stroebe *et al.*, 2001). Worden (2002) has applied grief and loss theory into a counseling framework, providing counselors with guidelines on the practical application of theory to practice when working with grief.

Goals of grief counseling

Worden (2002) suggested the primary goal of grief counseling is to assist the client to identify, and work through, the four key tasks of mourning. The first task is the cognitive acceptance that the individual has died and will not return. The second task is to experience the affect, pain, and behavioral responses that are an inescapable part of the grieving process. The third task is to learn to adapt to the environment without the deceased. And finally, find a way to remember the deceased while becoming comfortable in reinvesting in life by engaging in other relationships and activities.

General counseling strategies

The counseling process encourages the client to experience the pain of grief, rather than avoid or deny it (Humphrey & Zimpfer, 1996). There are no timeframes for the course of a grief reaction, and issues that may need resolution will vary with the individual (Stroebe & Stroebe, 1987). No prescribed number of sessions for grief is recommended, because it will vary according to a range of influencing factors including the individual's personality and coping skills, the nature of the loss, and the social support available. General counseling principles developed by Worden (2002) provide the practitioner with guidelines to help the client work through the experience of grief (See Table 38.1).

Uncomplicated and complicated grief reactions

Successful adaption to grief results from the interaction of environments, personal resources, the circumstances of the death, and how an individual appraises and copes with the event.

Table 38.1 Grief counseling guidelines (Based on Worden, 2002).

- Help to actualize the loss to assist clients in gaining awareness of the reality of the death.
- Support clients to identify the feelings that may not be recognized, and encourage clients to experience the emotions.
- Assist clients to adapt to living without the deceased.
- Find ways to help clients find meaning in the loss.
- Facilitate the process whereby clients are able to emotionally accept the loss and find a place for the memory of the deceased in their lives to allow the clients to move forward and form new relationships.
- Provide time for clients to grieve.
- Interpret normal behavior to clients so they do not fear there is something wrong.
- Allow for individual differences in the behavioral responses to grief.
- Examine coping styles to help clients develop adaptive coping responses to effectively manage their distress.
- Identify pathology or abnormal reactions that are triggered by the loss and refer on to specialist services. Further assessment from specialist services would be required when the time course and intensity of symptoms differ from what is considered to be a typical grief reaction.

Factors found to facilitate an uncomplicated grief reaction include personality and coping variables, circumstances of the death, relationship to the deceased, social support, and positive family functioning (Schaefer & Moos, 2001). Burnell and Burnell (1989) recognized that unresolved grief can lead to pathological symptoms. Unresolved grief may develop if individuals do not recognize the significance of the loss, display an extreme reaction that is beyond what is considered culturally normal, or have a lack of movement through the grief process and recovery fails to take place (Stephenson, 1985).

It is difficult to make the distinction between what is considered to be a normal grief reaction, and when the reaction becomes pathological, or a complicated grief reaction, because grief reactions do not fit into simple diagnostic criteria. A complicated grief reaction is defined as occurring when the reactions differ from what is considered to be the cultural norm in both the intensity of symptoms or time course of symptoms (Stroebe *et al.*, 2001). The *Diagnostic and Statistical Manual of Mental Disorders-IV-TR* (American Psychiatric Association, 2000) defines unresolved grief as occurring when symptoms are not characteristic of a normal grief response and can be differentiated from the symptoms of a major depression (Humphrey & Zimpfer, 1996).

Identification of individuals at risk of a complicated grief reaction

Preventative intervention will reduce the likelihood of a complex bereavement outcome (Raphael, 1994). Practitioners should identify individuals with unresolved grief issues and those people who may be vulnerable to complicated grief reactions, to ensure they are directed to the appropriate support services (Burnell & Burnell, 1989; Stroebe & Schut, 2001). Factors identified as influencing the likelihood of the development of a poor bereavement outcome include an ambivalent attachment or dependent relationship with the deceased, a sudden, unexpected and untimely death, concurrent stress or crisis, and previous losses, particularly if they have been poorly resolved in the past (Burnell & Burnell, 1989). The therapeutic goal is to help the client proceed through the grieving process, and counseling intervention will assist in shifting the complicated grief reactions to normal responses to grief (Raphael, 1994).

Dealing with traumatic deaths

Loss through violent deaths such as a traumatic accident or suicide may lead to the development of trauma reactions, intensifying the grieving processes for athletes and teams (Bonanno & Kaltman, 1999). Grief over suicide is a unique type of grief. The complex emotions of anger, guilt, fear, and shame are present alongside the stigma that surrounds suicide, and people may be reluctant to discuss suicide. These issues need to be acknowledged in the team, and athletes encouraged to discuss them openly and honestly. The key role of the practitioner is to assist athletes to understand the complexity of emotions that suicide presents, and provide an intervention model that supports athletes to work through their grief (Buchko, 2005, Humphrey & Zimpfer, 1996).

Unexpected loss when associated with the witnessing of traumatic events has been found to be a predictor of a complex grief response (Parkes, 2001). Athletes involved in an accident that results in the death of a teammate will not only be dealing with the loss, but also the trauma of the event. Although relieved to have survived the accident, athletes may feel guilt at surviving the event in which a teammate died. Commonly referred to as survivor's guilt, this emotion can be intense, where individuals feel that their survival was at the cost of another's life (Raphael, 1994). A common reaction is suppressing or denying what happened, which serves as an adaptive function to protect individuals from both confronting the reality of the threat of death to themselves, and identifying with the victim (Raphael, 1994). Intervention in these cases requires careful consideration because trauma is not just loss. The initial focus of the athletes tends to be on their survival of the event, and the athletes will then confront the loss of those who did not survive (Humphrey & Zimpfer, 1996). Individuals will potentially be dealing with both trauma reactions and bereavement (Green, 2000). The role of the counselor is to assess which processes are primary and need attention first. The effects of the trauma will need to be acknowledged before athletes can process the meaning of the loss (Humphrey & Zimpfer, 1996). Exposure to trauma can have significant psychological and physical effects (Vernacchia *et al.*, 1997). Athletes will be dealing with a complex range of emotions in response to many varied issues including a sense of powerlessness, identifying with the victim, and the implications of witnessing the event or being involved in the process of trying to save the individual. A fear of returning to training or participating in similar activities to the accident may become overwhelming. If the issues associated with the trauma are overlooked, it could leave individuals at risk of developing complicated or pathological grief reactions, or other psychiatric problems such as post-traumatic stress disorder (Humphrey & Zimpfer, 1996). Due to the complexity of trauma and grief reactions, long-term psychological support options need to be available to facilitate recovery from the event over the timeframe needed by the athletes.

Memorials

The funeral is a public and a final statement that commemorates death and provides an opportunity to acknowledge the life, express grief, and share thoughts and feelings about the deceased with the support of others (Raphael, 1994). Memorials are often used to perpetuate the memory of the deceased for the team. Annual trophies, sporting scholarships, and game day rituals have all been used to mark the memory of the achievements of the athlete. There are always significant anniversaries following a loss such as the athlete's birthday, last game played, anniversary of the death. People often don't know how to respond and may say nothing in fear of hurting, or bringing up unwanted feelings (Kübler-Ross & Kessler, 2005). It is important to mark the significance of the death by establishing ways for the team to acknowledge the loss at poignant times, particularly at the first year anniversary of the death. Be mindful that there will be individual differences with athletes within the team in how to publicly acknowledge the loss, and for how long the loss should be commemorated.

Managing team dynamics following the death of a teammate

Athletes may be reluctant to acknowledge the effects of the death of a teammate, adopting the notion of "soldiering on" while grieving privately. Sustaining effective team functioning begins with well-functioning individuals within the team. Encouraging the use of grief counseling services will assist in athletes developing adaptive coping skills, which will contribute back to a healthy team environment. Limited information has been written on the management of grief in sporting teams (Vernacchia et al., 1997). Looking to the literature on coping with grief in family units and groups provides insight to the issues that will arise in teams, and the suggested intervention strategies to manage the impact of the loss within a group (Gilbert, 1996). As with all groups, distress of one member will directly influence team functioning (Buchko, 2005). Encouraging the team to assertively and salubriously manage the grief process will assist in recovery and strengthen the team dynamic.

When dealing with the death of a teammate practitioners should consider ways for the team to:

- recognize the death of the athlete and accept the reality of the loss;
- acknowledge the effects of the loss on each individual and the team as a whole;
- reorganize the team following the loss because roles may need to be reassigned and strategies put in place for the team to continue to function without the athlete's contribution;
- recognize the memory of the teammate to assist the team to move forward without feeling the guilt of moving on without that person;
- establish common goals or tasks for the team to work on to assist in rebuilding the team dynamic following the loss (Gilbert, 1996).

Conclusion

Allow for individual differences in the way athletes will cope with and respond to intervention strategies. Emphasizing the importance of open and honest communication, and respect for each other's individual reactions to grief, will contribute to the successful management of the team's response to the death. It is critical that coaches receive support during this time, in both coping with the loss and working with the team. Grief has no timeframe for resolution, so ensure that strategies can be implemented across time and until the team feels it can move forward. See Box 38.1 for key points from this chapter.

Box 38.1

Key points for helping a team deal with the death of a teammate

- The sport psychologist will play a pivotal role in the coordination of the response to a traumatic event, so be prepared to manage the wide range of situations and dynamics that will confront a team following the death of a teammate.
- Understand the complex nature of grief and loss to ensure useful services are provided to facilitate the recovery of individuals and the team.
- Coordinate a comprehensive response that addresses the practical aspects of service delivery within the sport organization, and develop an intervention plan detailing the services to meet the needs of individual athletes and the team as a whole.
- Ensure grief counseling is accessible to assist athletes in working through the grieving process.
- Be mindful of the need to identify athletes who may be at risk of a complicated grief reaction, or who have been through a traumatic event, and refer to specialist services.
- Manage the team dynamics by establishing strategies that address the key aspects of the grief process, allowing the team to grieve, adjust to the loss, commemorate the memory of the athlete, and then unify to move forward.
- Every individual and team will respond differently to loss. Understanding how grief will affect the team enables the sport psychologist to develop targeted interventions to provide comprehensive support and facilitate the recovery of the team following the death of a teammate.

References

American Psychiatric Association (2000). *Diagnostic and statistical manual of mental disorders* (4th ed., text rev.). Washington, DC: American Psychiatric Association.

Bonanno, G. A., & Kaltman, S. (1999). Towards an integrative perspective on bereavement. *Psychological Bulletin, 125*, 760–776.

Buchko, K. J. (2005). Team consultation following an athlete's suicide. *The Sport Psychologist, 19*, 288–302.

Burnell, G. M., & Burnell, A. L. (1989). *Clinical management of bereavement: A handbook for health professionals*. New York: Human Science Press.

Gilbert, K. R. (1996). We've had the same loss, why don't we have the same grief? Loss differential grief in families. *Death Studies, 20*, 269–283.

Green, B. L. (2000). Traumatic loss: Conceptual and empirical links between trauma and bereavement. *Journal of Loss and Trauma, 5*, 1–17.

Humphrey, G. M., & Zimpfer, D. G. (1996). *Counselling for grief and bereavement*. London: Sage.

Kübler-Ross, E. (1993). *On death and dying*. New York: Collier.

Kübler-Ross, E., & Kessler, D. (2005). *On grief and grieving*. New York: Scribner.

Parkes, C. M. (2001). A historical overview of the scientific study of bereavement. In M. S. Stroebe, R. O. Hansson, W. Stroebe, & H. Schut (Eds.), *Handbook of bereavement research: Consequences, coping, and care* (pp. 25–46). Washington, DC: American Psychological Association.

Raphael, B. (1994). *The anatomy of bereavement*. New York: Rowman & Littlefield.

Schaefer, J. A., & Moos, R. H. (2001). Bereavement experiences and personal growth. In M. S. Stroebe, R. O. Hansson, W. Stroebe, & H. Schut (Eds.), *Handbook of bereavement research: Consequences, coping, and care* (pp. 145–168). Washington, DC: American Psychological Association.

Stephenson, J. S. (1985). *Death, grief, and mourning*. New York: Free Press.

Stroebe, W., & Schut, H. (2001). Risk factors in bereavement outcome: A methodological and empirical review. In M. S. Stroebe, R. O. Hansson, W. Stroebe, & H. Schut (Eds.), *Handbook of bereavement research: Consequences, coping, and care* (pp. 349–371). Washington, DC: American Psychological Association.

Stroebe, W., & Stroebe, M. S. (1987). *Bereavement and health*. New York: Cambridge University Press.

Stroebe, M. S., Hansson, R. O., Stroebe, W., & Schut, H. (2001). Introduction: Concepts and issues in contemporary research on bereavement. In M. S. Stroebe, R. O. Hansson, W. Stroebe, & H. Schut (Eds.), *Handbook of bereavement research: Consequences, coping, and care* (pp. 3–22). Washington, DC: American Psychological Association.

Vernacchia, R. A., Reardon, J. P., & Templin, D. P. (1997). Sudden death in sport: Managing the aftermath. *The Sport Psychologist, 11*, 223–235.

Worden, J. W. (2002). *Grief counseling and grief therapy: A handbook for the mental health practitioner* (3rd ed.). New York: Springer.

Section VI

Working with specific populations

39

Children

Melissa A. Chase

Parents and coaches often believe that participation in sport provides children with opportunities for improvement in physical, social, and self-development skills. Nevertheless, involvement in sport, in and of itself, does not necessarily lead to positive outcomes for children (Smith & Smoll, 2002). A positive sport experience that is focused on enjoyment, age-suitable needs of the participants, and intentional practice of mental skills training can make a difference in the overall sport experience for children. The literature has typically defined children as individuals 6–12 years of age and adolescents as 13–18 years of age (Weiss, 1991). In this chapter, the focus will be on the practice of applied sport psychology with children aged 6–12 years.

Mental skills training research with children

Research supporting the effectiveness of applied sport psychology with children has been sparse (Tremayne & Newbery, 2005). As prominent sport psychology consultants have noted, most psychological skills training (PST) programs are geared toward elite athletes, and much of the research has been conducted with young adults, non-elite athletes, and recreational sport participants. Since the early 1980s, practitioners in the field have strongly advocated for PST with children given the millions of children who regularly participate in sport and the ease with which they can learn mental skills (Gould, 1983). Nevertheless, there is limited experimental evidence directly examining the effectiveness of PST with children. Haddad and Tremayne (2009) found that the use of a centering breath by children aged 10–11 years did improve free-throw shooting percentage. In 1998, Atienza, Balaguer, and Garcia-Merita found that imagery training and video modeling improved the tennis serving performance of girls aged 9–12 years. Zhang, Ma, Orlick, and Zitzelberger (1992) found that table tennis players aged 7–10 years who received training in relaxation, video observation, and mental imagery significantly improved their performances. Wrisberg and Anshel (1989) found that boys 10–12 years old improved their free-throw shooting percentages when they practised an imagery and arousal regulation strategy.

In addition to these research studies, support for PST with children is evident from reports of practical and personal experiences, well grounded in psychological theory, from experienced sport psychology professionals. Orlick (1993) has proposed that seven conditions should be in place when conducting PST with children: (a) a fun environment, (b) concrete PST techniques (e.g., place your worries in a bag), (c) individualized instruction, (d) multi-modal instructional approaches, (e) an optimistic outlook, and (f) the use of role models. Gould (1983) and Weiss (1991) have also written extensively on the potential for PST with children and have advocated for a developmental perspective that includes developmentally targeted content and practices. The following sections address their recommendations.

Developmental factors to consider

Special considerations are needed when working with children as compared to working with adults. The popular saying "children are not miniature adults" suggests that techniques that work with adults may not necessarily work with children. Most experienced consultants have recommended using a developmental perspective that encompasses the influences of psychological, biological, social, and physical factors within the social context of youth sports (Weiss, 1991). Gould (1983) wrote:

> to be effective, the objectives and strategies identified for developing psychological skills must be appropriate for the developmental level of the athlete. It is essential that the developmental level of the athlete be considered since children of varying ages have been found to vastly differ in the ability to attend, comprehend, and retain information.
>
> (p. 9)

Several developmental factors affect children's abilities to use and benefit from PST. Weiss and Williams (2004) cautioned that one has to be sensitive to age-related attentional and motivational capabilities of children. Lessons need to be short and interesting to hold their focus. This caution is especially relevant for younger children because attentional processes start to improve from 7–8 years old and mature by about 12 years old (Sherman & Poczwardowski, 2005). Nevertheless, as early as five years old, children may have good memories and self-monitoring skills. Orlick and McCaffrey (1991) have employed some of the same PST approaches used with adults, but modified the approaches so children can understand. Specifically, they adapted the strategies to be simple, concrete, individualized, and fun for children.

Tremayne and Newbery (2005) pointed out in their discussion of developmental issues when conducting PST with children that the field is somewhat limited in understanding at what age (or age range) specific mental skills are most effective. These authors cited the work of Piaget's (1950) cognitive development theory as one way to determine when children are developmentally ready for PST. For example, six-year-old children in the pre-operational stage (think egocentrically and have difficulties taking the viewpoints of others) are different to 7–11-year old children in the concrete operational stage (think and solve problems that apply to actual concrete objects or events, capable of taking the viewpoints of the others), who are different from 12-year-old children in the formal operational stage (have the ability to think abstractly, reason logically, and draw conclusions from the information available). For example, a child 6–7 years old who may still be in the pre-operational stage will have difficulty following PST that uses primarily verbal instructions about actions the child has never seen or done (Tremayne & Newbery, 2005). Children 7–11 years old who may still be in the concrete operational stage may have difficulty thinking abstractly about what they can achieve (e.g., goal mapping). Despite the limited experimental results that pinpoint age-specific PST methods, effective interventions with children do exist and should be implemented with developmental factors in mind.

Suitable PST content for children

Vealey's (1988) view of PST has been well-supported in the literature. She suggested that sport psychologists should focus on skills that individual athletes need to develop and then choose the best methods to deliver the skills. Keeping in mind Vealey's recommendation, there are numerous mental skills that children may use to improve their sport experiences. The following section focuses on an example of one method (goal mapping) and two skills that are developmentally designed for children.

Goal mapping

"Goal mapping is a systematic approach to acting and thinking in purposeful ways to achieve specific accomplishments and personal fulfillment" (Vealey, 2005, p. 149). Goal mapping can be implemented with children by taking them through four simple steps: planning, setting, evaluating, and resetting.

Step 1: Planning

Invite the children to identify their sense of purpose for playing the sport. At this time children can dream big and express their passion for playing. Try to get to the "why" children want to play sport and their answers may reveal something about their motivation. For example, if an athlete's purpose for playing sport is to "win a big trophy," then there may be some reflecting and refocusing needed before the child moves on to setting goals. Help children tell their stories of what makes them happy about playing sport, what makes them feel energized, or what makes them excited about going to practice. Understanding and stating their sense of purpose will allow children to develop and set meaningful goals.

Step 2: Setting

Setting goals can get complicated for children if the different types of goals are described, such as, short-term, long-term, outcome, performance, and process goals or in the language of goal mapping: milestone, challenge, or focus goals. Are all of these types of goals really needed for children 6–12 years old? They are probably not all needed at once but can be added over time as goal-setting techniques improve. Children will likely set outcome goals (short- and long-term) because we live in a goal-oriented society and children can easily identify specific outcomes they want to achieve. One or two outcome goals are fine as long as the goals flow into specific performance or process goals (see Chapter 51).

Step 3: Evaluating

Adults can help children map their goal achievement strategies and think of daily behaviors in which they can engage to evaluate their goals. For example, a few goal achievement strategies for a ten-year-old soccer player aiming to improve her kicking and dribbling skills might be: (a) take 20 shots on goals, (b) practise five penalty shots without a goalie, and (c) do two-minute dribbling drills with a friend before practice. Some children enjoy writing down their goal achievement strategies on a chart and checking off their progress (a goal map). Other children who are not developmentally ready for this task may require a coach or parent to keep track and share their progress periodically. The key is for children to think about and engage in daily activities that will help them meet their goals.

Step 4: Resetting

The last step is resetting or revisiting step 1 so children remember "why" they are playing the sport. By revisiting their passions for playing, children can keep in touch with their internal motivation. Consultants can ask children to reflect upon why they play, what makes them happy about playing, and then discuss how the goals they have mapped are helping them stay passionate about their sports.

Relaxation

There is a common misperception among parents, coaches, and some practitioners that children do not get stressed during sports. The belief that children are not stressed is generally not true and many experts suggest that different forms of arousal control for children are beneficial during sport and everyday life. For example, progressive muscle relaxation techniques have been linked to a reduction in arousal and muscle tension; meditation and distraction control help to quiet counterproductive thoughts and refocus; and guided visual imagery and verbal prompts reduce worry (Vealey, 2005). A simple technique that can be quite beneficial for children is relaxed breathing, combined with self-talk. Relaxed breathing helps children to physically relax by controlling their breathing and reversing the effects of anxiety. Self-talk allows the children to talk themselves into calming down and relaxing with "trigger" relaxation words, such as "breathe easy," "I'm OK," or "take it slow." Children need to recognize that they are experiencing stress before they implement relaxation skills. For example, one way for children to recognize that they are experiencing stress is to recognize that their muscles feel tight and even sore in their necks and shoulders. Suggest that they push two fingers into their shoulder muscles to see whether the muscle feels hard like a chair or soft like a couch. Hard muscles can be one way of their body saying they are experiencing stress and need progressive muscle relaxation. Another symptom of stress in children is an upset stomach. Suggest that children monitor how their stomachs feel. When their stomachs feel like they have been doing flips and are hurting, they may be experiencing too much stress.

Imagery

Imagery is defined as using all the senses to recreate or create an experience in the mind as an internal representation (Vealey & Greenleaf, 2006). Children, more so than adults, seem to have a keen ability to use their senses and imagine real-life and pretend situations.

Weiss (1991) described children's use of imagery as "a natural strategy that is used to rehearse skill sequences." Consultants can ask children to imagine something and discuss: what the image looks like and how to add different senses to enhance their imagery. Imagery with a kinesthetic sense, the feel of their bodies as they move, may be difficult for some young children because they have not yet learned the correct movement pattern so each skill attempt feels different. Children should still try to recognize how their bodies feel during movement. Awareness of their kinesthetic sense may help to provide internal feedback that leads to better technique when learning new skills. Refer to Chapter 50 for a thorough description and implementation ideas of imagery.

In addition to defining and describing imagery techniques to children, it is important to let them know the best times to practise their imagery. For imagery to be effective, children need to systematically practise it just like they practise their physical skills. The best times for imagery practise may be during a cool-down after practice, where they can reflect on the skills they practised that day, or at night as they are getting ready to fall asleep.

These three examples can be effective with children, in addition many other methods and skills should be considered when consulting with young athletes. Orlick's (1993) work has shown that children can use relaxation, imagery, and refocusing through play and fun-oriented games. Gould (1983) has suggested that positive thinking, stress management, focusing, and confidence building are important. Weiss (1991) has advocated problem-solving, self-talk, goal-setting, relaxation, and mental imagery when working with children. Important to keep in mind is that one purpose of interventions with children is to assist them in fulfilling their reasons for participating in sport. Some of the top reasons children participate in sport include: (a) to learn and improve their skills, (b) to have fun, (c) to be with friends, (d) to experience the excitement of competition, (e) to enhance their physical fitness, and (f) to demonstrate competence. For example, goal mapping may assist children in fulfilling their desire to learn and improve their skills or enhance physical fitness. Providing fun-oriented games that teach various PST skills to a team may fulfil their desire to have fun with their friends.

Consulting with children

In addition to considering developmental factors when working with children, there are several issues consultants face that are unique to children. Orlick and McCaffrey (1991) stated:

> To be effective with children we must draw from their qualities and strengths, listen to their perspectives, use their input and, perhaps most important, care about them; otherwise we will never give them the special treatment they need and deserve. More than any other group, children want to know that you care before they care what you know.
>
> (p. 324)

To gain rapport, build trust, and communicate effectively with children, consultants need to be honest and demonstrate they care about the needs of their athletes. Communication with children includes verbal and nonverbal. For example, speaking on the same level as children involves constructing language in terms that they can understand, and physically lowering oneself to a level that is "eye to eye."

Table 39.1 Steps representing the sequence of a PST intervention with children.

1. Have a discussion with parents or coaches about their expectations for what PST can accomplish.
2. Provide a clear explanation about what you can provide in a PST session and privacy policies with athletes, coaches, and parents.
3. Observe the sport environment, and athletes' interactions with coaches, teammates, and parents to gain an understanding of the social context.
4. Meet with children to answer questions and learn about their goals, strengths, and weaknesses; begin to demonstrate a caring attitude, and discuss privacy issues.
5. Develop an individualized plan to meet the specific needs of children which is age-targeted and enjoyable.
6. Meet weekly with children to discuss progress, make refinements, and add new skills while encouraging the daily practice of mental skills when practising physical skills.
7. Share with parents or coaches the daily mental skills so that they can help reinforce, model, and integrate these skills into their normal daily routines.
8. Regularly evaluate whether the PST session is fun for children and meeting their needs.
9. Revisit numbers 1 and 2 with parents or coaches so expectations and implementation are congruent.

Suggestions for how an intervention can be structured and implemented

There are many ways to structure and implement PST with children. Some of the nuances have to do with the personality and strengths (or weaknesses) of the consultant. Table 39.1 illustrates one example of a consulting sequence for PST with children. These general guidelines are suggested as a possible structure for implementing PST with children.

It is probably best to keep strategies simple with a lot of hands-on, real life, tangible examples. For example, if the strategy is for children to stop worrying or change their behaviors, ask them to physically go through the motions of taking the worry or behaviors and putting the worry or behavior somewhere. A bag, backpack, or box can work well as a place to "hold" whatever they are moving. Have the children design a paper "worry bag" – personally decorated – to function as their place to deposit their worries. Another example is asking children to relax their muscles. A simple, real-life example would be the use of objects that children know are relaxed. Orlick (1993) used the example of uncooked and cooked spaghetti to illustrate being tense and being relaxed, respectively. Other examples of relaxed objects would be earthworms or jump ropes. Presenting objects as examples that they can see and touch will help children transfer the concept to how their bodies should look and feel when relaxed.

To promote children's attention and participation, practitioners should construct PST in a way that is viewed as fun by children. Making PST fun may be one of the most difficult aspects of working with children. How can PST be fun and still educational? One suggestion is to use activities that children consider fun, such as pretending, using their imaginations, physically moving (not sitting still), or playing games. Another recommendation by Orlick and McCaffrey (1991) is to use multiple approaches until the one that works is found: so persistence and creativity are also important.

Another guideline found in the PST literature is the use of positive role models. Positive role models include the consultant, significant others, or highly respected athletes. Children respond to seeing and hearing about role models who have overcome obstacles and experienced self-development. The next section focuses on the role of parents during PST with children.

Role of the parents

The role of parents in children's sport experiences is important because children usually view their parents as their most significant adults. Consultants sometimes have a difficult balancing act between dealing with parents and their goals for their children, and the children's goals. A good place to start with parents is to discuss their expectations for their children's sport experiences. One goal for practitioners is to work with parents so that they try to base the success of their children's sport experiences on their children's happiness and not their children's performance successes or failures.

How much should parents be involved in consulting work?

Parents should be involved in their children's PST. There should be a clear understanding from the start about what parts of the conversations between consultants and children are confidential and what parts will be shared with parents. Privacy policies need to be established for all parties to understand what is private, why it is private, and when privacy policies might be renegotiated. Without a clear understanding and agreed upon policy, children may feel they cannot confide in a consultant without everyone hearing their thoughts and parents may worry that they are being left out of the conversation. Children also need to understand that they can talk to their parents or everyone they want about what goes on in a PST session. Parents can also serve as good role models to practise and reinforce the messages the consultant provides and can help reduce unnecessary stress in the environment (Orlick & McCaffrey, 1991).

What happens when the parents are the problem?

For problematic, controlling parents, consultants should provide clear expectations of the parents' roles in the consultation process and try to engage them in interactive communication, while encouraging realistic goal setting with their children. Parents need honest feedback from consultants so they feel informed and educated. It is a good idea to have an established procedure for dealing with individual problems that might arise with parents who do not understand their roles or violate the outlined expectations. For example, some parents might expect the consultant to be available to conduct a PST session immediately after their child's poor performance in a competition. To avoid the parent's emergency phone call, define the word emergency and establish business hours when parents can call with questions or concerns. Stainback and La Marche (1998) have several suggestions for positive, productive parent involvement:

- Encourage parents to understand that fun and family should be emphasized in youth sports.
- Talk with the parents to identify problems, dilemmas, or areas needing improvement.
- Focus on the child's needs and concerns.
- Help develop family communication patterns that facilitate enjoyment and mastery experiences (e.g., the first comment after competition is always about enjoyment of competition and not who won or lost).
- Keep open lines of communication between children, family, and coaches.

Children's situations are difficult to evaluate and understand without understanding the roles of their parents and the communication patterns in the family. Before intervening, have a clear understanding of the family structure and roles of the parents (see Chapter 19).

Role of the coach

Youth sport coaches, even more than parents, need to judge the success of their players' sport experiences on the players' happiness and not competition outcomes. Research has shown that coaches for whom athletes enjoyed playing the most, and who were most successful in promoting children's self-esteem, actually had win–loss records that were about the same as coaches who were less liked and less effective in fostering feelings of self-worth (Smith & Smoll, 2002). Another finding suggested that winning made little difference to children, but they knew that it was important to the adults in their lives.

How much should coaches be involved in consulting work?

The objective of PST is to empower athletes and coaches to reach their goals and enhance their sport experiences. The best relationships between consultants and coaches involve a shared purpose to help children. PST is not intended to undermine the authority of the coach. A coach can and should be involved in consulting work to help reinforce and model the suggestions put forth and provide practice opportunities. Gould (1983) suggested some strategies that coaches can use to assist in the development of mental skills in young athletes:

- Define the objectives of PST.
- Convey the objectives of PST to athletes via individual and/or team discussions.
- Implement systematic goal-setting procedures.
- Use effective role models.
- Employ a positive and sincere approach to communication.
- Develop educational programs for parents of young athletes.

What happens when the coach is the problem?

Similar to the recommendations made for dealing with problematic parents, consultants should provide clear expectations of coaches' roles in the process. Engage coaches in interactive communication so they feel informed and educated. Dissimilar to parents, coaches do not have the right to make decisions about what constitutes a positive sport experience for each child. Coaches should have clear boundaries endorsed by parents as to what coaching behaviors are helpful and beneficial for their children (e.g., not approving the use of physical conditioning drills as a form of punishment for mental mistakes).

Conclusion

In the United States, an estimated 40 million children participate in organized youth sports (Smith & Smoll, 2002). When adult organizers focus on children's personal development in physical, social, and psychological skills, children can benefit greatly from involvement

Table 39.2 Pledge for psychological skills training with children.

As a sport psychology consultant, who values positive sport experiences for all children, I pledge to:

- maintain a positive approach with the goal of improving the sport experience, not just performance;
- modify my approach and PST to be appropriate for each child's developmental needs;
- construct my interventions to meet the reasons why children participate in sport (e.g., to learn and improve skills, to have fun, to be with friends);
- provide PST for all children – recreational to elite;
- work with parents so that they understand their roles and provide positive support systems for their children;
- work with coaches so that they understand their roles and provide positive sport experiences for all children they coach;
- bring positive change to youth sports that encourages the use of PST by athletes, coaches, and parents;
- judge the success of a child's sport experience and PST on the child's happiness and reasons for playing sport and not on the child's performance success or failure.

in sport. PST with children provides unique responsibilities and challenges, and some sport psychology consultants may not be up to the task. For those who wish to work with children, Table 39.2 outlines several key principles for conducting PST with children in the form of a pledge for how to work with children. The pledge for psychological skills training with children concurs with Orlick and McCaffrey's (1991) belief that "every child will experience growth, and some degree of success, if someone who cares devotes time to nurturing important mental skills related to human development" (p. 334). See Box 39.1 for take-home messages from this chapter.

Box 39.1

Take-home messages about psychology with children

- A positive sport experience that is focused on enjoyment, age-targeted needs of the participants, and intended practice of psychological skills training can make a difference for children.
- Most experienced consultants suggest using a developmental perspective that takes into account the influences of psychological, biological, social and physical factors within the social context of youth sports (e.g., Weiss, 1991).
- The sport psychology research is somewhat limited in conveying at what age (or age range) specific mental skills are most effective.
- Sport psychologists should focus on skills that athletes need to develop and then choose the best method to deliver those skills (Vealey, 2005).
- One purpose of interventions with children is to assist them in fulfilling their reasons for participating in sport.
- Each child is unique and so an individual approach is important.
- Parents, coaches, and consultants should base the success of children's sport experiences on children's happiness and not competition outcomes.

References

Atienza, F. L., Balaguer, I., & Garcia-Merita, M. L. (1998). Video modeling and imaging training on performance of tennis service of 9- to 12-year-old children. *Perceptual and Motor Skills, 87*, 519–529.

Gould, D. (1983). Developing psychological skills in young athletes. In N. Wood (Ed.). *Coaching science update* (pp. 4–13). Ottawa, ON: Coaching Association of Canada.

Haddad, K., & Tremayne, P. (2009). The effects of centering on the free-throw shooting performance of young athletes. *The Sport Psychologist, 23*, 118–136.

Orlick, T. (1993). *Free to feel great: Teaching children to excel at living.* Carp, ON, Canada: Creative Bound.

Orlick, T., & McCaffrey, N. (1991). Mental training with children for sport and life. *The Sport Psychologist, 5*, 322–334.

Piaget, J. (1950). *The psychology of intelligence.* London: Routledge.

Sherman, C. P., & Poczwardowski, A. (2005). Integrating mind and body: Presenting mental skills to young teams. In M. B. Andersen. (Ed.), *Sport psychology in practice* (pp. 17–43). Champaign, IL: Human Kinetics.

Smith, R. E., & Smoll, F. L. (2002). Youth sports as a behavior setting for psychosocial interventions. In J. L. Van Raalte & B. W. Brewer (Eds.), *Exploring sport and exercise psychology* (2nd ed., pp. 341–371). Washington, DC: American Psychological Association.

Stainback, R. D., & La Marche, J. A. (1998). Theoretical frameworks: Family systems issues affecting athletic performance in youth. In K. F. Hays (Ed.), *Integrating exercise, sports, movement and mind: Therapeutic unity* (pp. 5–20). New York: Routledge.

Tremayne, P., & Newbery, G. (2005). Mental skills training program for children. In D. Hackfort, J. L. Duda, & R. Lidor (Eds.), *Handbook of research in applied sport psychology* (pp. 93–106). Morgantown, WV: Fitness Information Technology.

Vealey, R. S. (1988). Future directions in psychological skills training. *The Sport Psychologist, 2*, 318–336.

Vealey, R. S. (2005). *Coaching for the inner edge.* Morgantown, WV: Fitness Information Technology.

Vealey, R. S., & Greenleaf, C. A. (2006). Seeing is believing: Understanding and using imagery in sport. In J. M. Williams (Ed.), *Applied sport psychology: Personal growth to peak performance* (5th ed., pp. 306–348). New York: McGraw-Hill.

Weiss, M. R. (1991). Psychological skill development in children and adolescents. *The Sport Psychologist, 5*, 335–354.

Weiss, M. R., & Williams, L. (2004). The why of youth sports involvement: A developmental perspective on motivational processes. In M. R. Weiss (Ed.), *Developmental sport and exercise psychology: A lifespan perspective.* Morgantown, WV: Fitness Information Technology, pp. 223–268.

Wrisberg, C. A., & Anshel, M. H. (1989). The effect of cognitive strategies on the free throw shooting performance of young athletes. *The Sport Psychologist, 3*, 95–104.

Zhang, L., Ma, Q., Orlick, T., & Zitzelsberger, L. (1992). The effect of mental-imagery training on performance enhancement with 7–10-year-old children. *The Sport Psychologist, 6*, 230–241.

40

Masters athletes

Nikola Medic

The objective of this chapter is to provide sport psychology professionals with information and ideas on how to facilitate and optimize sport performance and satisfaction of middle-to older-aged athletes. Information pertaining to the topic is derived from my past and current research work with over 600 athletes aged from 35 to 90+ years in a variety of masters sports including track and field, bowling, golf, marathon, and swimming; my sport psychology consulting experience; and from other existing research conducted with masters athletes.

Opportunities for sport involvement for middle- to older-aged individuals

Masters athletes are individuals who continue or, at some later time in their lives, begin or resume training and competing at events available to middle- to older-aged adults (e.g., masters tournaments, Senior Olympics, Veterans Championships). Each sport governing body determines the status of a masters' athlete based on the age at which peak performance (i.e., the open world record) occurs in a respective sport. For example, the masters' designation begins at 25 years of age for swimming, at 35 years of age for track and field, and at 50 years of age for golf.

The establishment and the expansion of masters sports

Masters sport was established in the 1970s as an alternative to mainstream sport; that is, sports for youth and elite-level athletes. Prior to the 1970s, the exclusion of older people from organized competitions had been attributed to two social norms that were prevalent during that time (Coakley, 2008). First, organized competitive sport was believed to "build character" and should be promoted to young people and males especially. Second, strenuous physical activity was believed to be dangerous to elderly individuals. In the 1970s and 1980s, local masters clubs began to question these biases, and events such as World Veterans Athletic Championships, World Masters Swimming Championships, World Masters Games, and

Senior Olympics emerged as potential opportunities for sport participation and competition for older individuals. Recent trends indicate that the popularity of masters' sports is on the rise as evidenced by increases in participation numbers and in athletes' attendance rates at the major masters' competitions throughout the world. For example, the first two World Masters Games, in 1985 and 1988, each had below 10,000 competitors (i.e., 8,305 and 5,500, respectively). In comparison about 20 years later, World Masters Games in 2002 and 2005 each had over 20,000 competitors (24,886 and 21,600, respectively).

How masters athletes become involved and why they continue participating

The purpose of this section is to provide practitioners with an understanding of the multidimensional nature of motivation and to recommend strategies that can be used to favorably support masters athletes' mental processes and actions such as starting and maintaining sport involvement throughout life. In one of our studies (Medic, Starkes, Young, Weir, & Giajnorio, 2005), we surveyed over 450 masters athletes from track and field and swimming and found that that the three most common ways through which athletes entered into masters sports were: (a) continued involvement in competitive sport; (b) social networks; and (c) community recreational involvement. We found that most masters' athletes had been involved in competitive sport throughout their lives; specifically, 49% of them were continuously involved in their sports since they were young, and 22% switched to their current sports from a different sport. Another common means for entrance into masters' sports was through social networks, which included recommendations from doctors (18%), friends (15%), family (10%), and coaches (8%). The final means of entering masters sport was through community recreational involvement as fans/coaches/officials (9%), after becoming members of community sport programs or local masters clubs (21%), and by learning of opportunities from the local media (9%).

A number of studies conducted to date have shown that masters athletes, regardless of the sport, have a variety of motives for continuing to participate in sport including: enjoyment of the sport, opportunities to test skills, health and fitness concerns, social reasons, and extrinsic rewards (e.g., Medic, Starkes, Young, & Weir, 2006; Tantrum & Hodge, 1993). In addition, a number of studies have shown that masters' athletes tend to be self-determined and goal oriented. Most participants do not intend to stop participating in sport, and the most important motives for continuing to train and compete are intrinsic in nature. Studies also have suggested that masters' athletes' motives for sport differ across age and gender. Specifically, Dodd and Spinks (1995) found that older masters athletes (generally, over 65 years) place greater importance on extrinsic rewards, implying they have a tendency to be attracted by external reinforcers such as athletic awards, medals, and trophies. The results of the studies that have examined masters' athletes' motives for sport as a function of gender suggest that female masters' athletes are likely to give higher importance to intrinsic rewards, enjoyment, and health and fitness and lower importance to extrinsic rewards, competition, and achievement goals (Medic, 2009). In sum, research on masters athletes' motives for sport suggests that to gain the most psychological benefits (e.g., well-being, flow, creativity, self-esteem) from their participation in masters sports, motivational strategies for masters athletes need to be individualized, and personal reasons for participation need consideration.

Masters athletes' passion for sport

Passion is a strong inclination toward an activity individuals like (or even love), find important, invest time and energy in, and is part of their identities (Vallerand et al., 2003). Individuals can have, at least, two types of passion toward an activity. Obsessive passion refers to the motivational force that pushes people toward activities and produces compulsions due to internal forces that seem to control them. For example, an athlete with an obsessive passion for running would report having no choice but to attend a scheduled running workout. Harmonious passion, on the other hand, refers to the motivational force that leads a person to engage in an activity willingly and produces a sense of volition and personal endorsement about pursuing the activity. For example, an athlete with harmonious passion would be able to put aside a running workout if the need arose. Preliminary research has shown that obsessive passion is associated with negative affective and behavioral consequences and that harmonious passion is related to positive outcomes.

In our recent study (Medic et al., 2007b), we surveyed 138 (95 male, 43 female) masters athletes from track and field and found that their scores were very high on harmonious and moderate to low on obsessive passion. We also found that masters athletes whose sport motives were autonomous (intrinsically motivated) and highly internalized (integrated within the individual's self) were the ones who had a high sense of personal endorsement and volition about engaging in their sports, that is high levels of harmonious passion. For these masters athletes, sport involvement is likely to be in harmony with other aspects of their lives, but at the same time not overpower their identities and take over their personal lives.

Our results further suggested that masters athletes whose sport motives were internalized into their identities by external agents are the ones who had high levels of obsessive passion. These internal compulsions (e.g., feelings that they absolutely have to engage in their sports) are likely to lead to feelings of guilt and/or anxiety if one cannot engage in the activity or are likely to lead masters athletes engaging in their sports even when they should not (e.g., due to injury). With this internal pressure to engage in their passionate activities, masters athletes who have high levels of obsessive passion may find it difficult to disengage from thinking about, and participating in, their sports. Masters athletes who have high levels of obsessive passion, when faced with needing to cut back on or cease training and competition, will likely do one of two things: (a) continue engaging in their sports despite unfavorable circumstances (e.g., overtraining syndrome, sport-related injuries) or (b) reflect on their sport involvement and consequently experience negative feelings similar to psychological withdrawal when they are prevented from participating in their sports. From the practical standpoint of the sport psychologist, these situations may call for strategies such as reassessment of short- and long-term goals; cross-training and/or resting; spending more time working on mental skills; and/or starting, maintaining, and reflecting on a training log. Furthermore, depending on the severity of symptoms when obsessively passionate athletes have their sports taken away, the above mentioned strategies may be supplemented with psychotherapy and anxiolytic or antidepressant medication, especially during initial stages.

Dealing with motivational lapses to train

When unmotivated, masters athletes, regardless of their levels of harmonious and obsessive passion, experience feelings of incompetence, lack of control, and/or no purpose with respect to their sports. One approach that sport psychologists can take in working with

Table 40.1 Motivational strategies used by masters athletes to overcome lapses in motivation to train.

Major themes	Minor themes	Gender	
		Male	Female
Self-regulatory strategies	Goal setting	77.1%	54.2%
	Doing imagery to model competition	39.3%	27.1%
	Cross-training	13.6%	13.5%
	Keeping a training log	18.6%	18.3%
	Entering competitions regardless of fitness	5.7%	7.3%
Group-approach strategies	Training in groups	32.1%	45.8%
	Training with younger athletes	9.3%	4.2%
	Commitment to coach	8.6%	16.7%
Timing strategies	Reaching a new age group	11.4%	11.5%
	Taking time off	5.7%	4.2%

masters athletes is to explore why unmotivated feelings are occurring. For some athletes, leaving the sport may be the best alternative. For example, athletes may come to realize that they are in sport only because of habit, and they may want to consider trying new activities. Another approach could involve educating masters athletes about the strategies that can decrease the likelihood of motivational lapses. For example, research (Medic et al., 2005) has found that even though masters athletes report low levels of being unmotivated, about two-thirds of them have at one time or another experienced lapses in motivation to train. Motivational lapses in masters athletes most often occur as a result of injury, burn-out, and family and work responsibilities. The most successful strategies masters athletes report using to overcome motivational lapses are summarized in Table 40.1 and include goal setting, doing imagery to model competition, training with a group or a coach, and keeping a training log. In addition, focusing on performance rather than outcome (e.g., winning medals) may be beneficial for masters athletes' motivation. Research indicated that masters athletes rate their performances (e.g., times) as more successful, and due to more internal and intentional causes, than their outcomes (e.g., placings: Hanrahan & Gross, 2005).

The dark side of masters sport

Despite many positive experiences that can be gained from participating in masters sports, sport psychology practitioners should be aware that there are potentially many dark sides to continuing to train and perform including: experiencing feelings of desperation, trying to fix regrets and past failures, and bringing disruptions to families and professional lives. For example, research has shown that masters athletes are more likely to experience acute and chronic injuries, to have more fears of injury, and to take longer to rehabilitate than younger athletes (Spirduso, Francis, & MacRea, 2005). Furthermore, about 80% of masters athletes report having athletic goals that have remained unaccomplished and that still exert considerable influence on their present motives to continue training and competing in their sports (Medic et al., 2005). Finally, one of my studies has shown that most masters athletes, even though reporting low to moderate levels of obsessive passion for their sport, also reported that they would cease their sport involvement under extreme circumstances related to their health and well-being. The majority of participants (81%) reported that an injury would make them stop; 33% said that very old age and illness would prevent them from participating in sport, and 10% went as far as saying that they will never stop regardless of any condition. The following were some of the unique responses:

I would not stop unless I was injured in such a way that I could not run upright.

(masters runner)

Death or severe ailment close to death would stop me … this is my lifestyle … to stop training is like to stop breathing … I live for training … competitions are just the product of such a lifestyle.

(masters swimmer)

Altogether, these results suggest that sport psychologists need to be aware of these potential problem areas and be ready to deal with them if necessary. For example, consultants and coaches could work with masters athletes on monitoring their levels of sport involvement. Masters athletes might also explore alternative perspectives on what their sport involvement could be about. An example would be to analyze (by identifying strengths and weaknesses) scenarios in which athletes would leave their sports for short periods.

Optimizing sport performance of aging athletes

The purpose of this section is to review evidence on how age-associated decline in athletic performance can be tempered through continued physical training. To effectively assist masters athletes with their training, sport psychology practitioners and coaches need to understand factors that moderate sport performance decline. Some individuals who are having trouble accepting decline in athletic performance as a result of age may ask sport psychologists for assistance.

Various approaches (e.g., analyses of cross-sectional, longitudinal, and world record athletic performance data) have been used with an aim to understand the age-related sport performance declines in masters athletes. Generally, studies have suggested that, after the age of peak involvement (generally about 35 years), performance gradually declines at a rate of 0.5 to 1% per year until approximately the age of 70 years, after which the decline accelerates. Studies have also suggested that the rate of decline is generally greater for long-distance than for middle-distance events (Young, Weir, Starkes, & Medic, 2008), and for swimming and track and field than for golf, and for women more than men (Starkes Weir, & Young, 2003).

Training is, to a certain degree, under the control of individuals if they are motivated; have access to adequate resources such as equipment, coaching, and facilities; are able to remain free of injury; and are not compromised by the effects of secondary processes of aging (Salthouse, 1991). For example, one secondary aging effect is the damage that arises from prolonged training over many years (e.g., arthritis) that in turn may hinder one's ability to train. In an attempt to examine how the typical decline in 10 km running performance of middle-aged masters (40–59 years) can be slowed, we (Young et al., 2008) collected longitudinal performance and training data from 30 masters runners. Our results showed that masters runners who retain high levels of performance do so because they have maintained years of uninterrupted practice (the next section "Choosing when to compete" provides more detail on the importance of continuous involvement), consistently have shorter off-season periods, exhibit higher weekly amounts of sport-specific practice (rather than cross-training), and avoid injury.

Sport psychologists working with masters athletes should be aware that with increasing age, declines in sport performance are inevitable. An exception would be masters athletes who are novices to the sport or those who have switched to different events, for whom performances will likely improve for the first few years, after which their absolute performance will probably start decreasing. There are at least two successful strategies that can be used to assist masters athletes in accepting that decline in athletic performance is inevitable as one ages. One is to help masters athletes reassess their long-term goals and discuss which is more important: continuing to participate in sport for many years in the future (promoting health and well-being) or being able to keep increasing or maintaining their performances, and/or winning medals. The second strategy is to use the age-grading tables that employ mathematical formulae (based on archival performance data) to derive age-corrected times from absolute performance times (age-grading tables are currently available for track and field and swimming). One value of age-grading tables is that a performance-level percentage (higher percentage indicates better performance) can be calculated and used to compare performances across a wide range of events, independent of one's age. The second value of age-grading tables is that one's current performance can be compared to previous performances regardless of age, because all performances are mathematically converted to 35 years of age. For example, an athlete's current running time may be slower when absolutely compared to the performance time achieved five years ago, but the mathematically adjusted time could show that the running performance has actually improved, once age has been considered.

Choosing when to compete

A motivational strategy aimed at establishing a fair playing field in masters sports involves the use of age categories that generally progress in five-year intervals (e.g., 35–39, 40–44, 45–49, and so forth). Nevertheless, anecdotal evidence from masters athletes suggests that as they start approaching the upper ends of their age categories, they feel less motivated to train and compete because of their relative age disadvantage.

To systematically examine the influence of masters athletes' relative age advantages/disadvantages within five-year age categories, our research team (Medic, Starkes, & Young 2007a) analyzed archival data on participation entries and national records set at USA masters championships in track and field and swimming. Based on the five-year age categories in which masters athletes compete, participation entry and record setting ages were each scored separately as frequencies in five separate categories (i.e., years 1, 2, 3, 4, and 5) and were collapsed across all five-year age categories. Year 1 included masters athletes who were in their first year of any five-year age category when they participated or set a record (i.e., those who were age 35, 40, 45, and so forth). Likewise, Years 2, 3, 4, and 5 contained frequencies for participation entries and records set by masters athletes who were in the second, third, fourth, and fifth years, respectively, in any five-year age category. Our results provided strong evidence that the odds of participating in the U.S. national championships were significantly higher for masters athletes who were in their first or second year, and were lower if they were in their fourth or fifth year of any age category. We also found that the odds of setting a U.S. masters record were significantly higher if athletes were in the first year of any five-year age category, and were lower if they were in the third, fourth, or fifth year of an age category. The results for track and field and swimming have been replicated (Medic, Starkes, Weir,

Young, & Grove, 2009). In contrast, for two sports with both age and weight classes (i.e., rowing, weightlifting), we found that the odds of participating in the competition were equally distributed among individuals across all five constituent years of an age category. Altogether, these findings suggest that the perceived age disadvantage that may discourage participation in competition might be less evident for masters athletes competing in sports with both age and weight classes as is the case for weightlifting and rowing, than for masters competitors arranged by chronological age only (e.g., track and field, swimming).

When sport psychologists are notably younger than clients

Finally, when working with this population (especially older masters athletes), practitioners need to be aware of the possibility that they will be substantially younger than the clients. Consultants working with older clients should be aware of the generation gap that may exist between themselves and the clients. Practitioners should find ways to relate to the clients to minimize situations in which misunderstanding can occur due to differences in experiences, opinions, habits, or behaviors. For example, by developing mutual trust and understanding, developing empathy, actively listening, being honest and consistent, occurrences of misunderstanding will be minimized. Finally, practitioners should be aware of their own attitudes, stereotypes, and predetermined beliefs about older people, especially given that many people in Western societies generally hold negative views about the aging process. See Box 40.1 for a summary of suggestions for sport psychologists who are working with masters athletes.

Conclusion

The main objective of this chapter was to provide insights and ideas to sport psychology practitioners on how they can effectively work with middle- to older-aged individuals to enrich and enhance their lives through masters sports involvement. Given that aging individuals are confronted with a number of life issues such as decreased social networks (deaths of loved ones and fellow competitors) and changing relationships with their aging bodies, it is important for practitioners to recognize that in their work with masters athletes the focus should not be exclusively based on them as athletes, but rather on the person as a whole. Based on materials reviewed in this chapter, I suggest that to assist masters athletes in gaining potential psychological and physical benefits from sport involvement, and to enhance their welfare, consultants need to be aware of how they can foster long-term motivation and commitment to sport. For example, practitioners could work with masters athletes on developing sporting environments that: (a) promote training and competitive activities and events that are intrinsically motivating and enjoyable, (b) emphasize the development of new skills and techniques, (c) involve high levels of internalization of the sport activity, and (d) provide high support and low pressure from significant others. Also, practitioners should be aware that extrinsic reasons for masters sport participation at most are moderately important – at most – for the majority of masters athletes. Exceptions may be masters athletes who are 65 years or older, males, and those in the first year of a five-year age category. Thus, to be effective, strategies that can be used to keep masters athletes optimally motivated (providing that athletes want to continue with their sport involvement) need to be individualized so that they complement personal reasons and the specific needs for continuing to train and compete in sport (see Box 40.1).

Box 40.1

Key points when working with masters athletes

- To enhance long-term motivation and maximize benefits that can be gained from sport participation, practitioners could work with masters athletes on developing sporting environments that place emphasis on intrinsically motivating activities, involve high levels of internalization of the sport activity, and have the potential to provide high levels of social support.
- Most masters athletes experience periods when their motivation to train is low. Successful strategies that can be used to overcome motivational lapses are exploration of why feelings of being unmotivated are occurring, goal setting, imagery, group training, and keeping a training log.
- Reassessment of goals and use of age-graded tables can be used to assist masters athletes who have difficulty accepting that decline in athletic performance is inevitable.
- Five-year age categories, an inherent feature of masters sports, can have some negative motivational consequences, especially for those masters athletes who are older relative to their peers in the same age group. To maximize chances of normative or outcome success, practitioners could work with masters athletes on developing strategies that involve entering competitions when they are in the early years of a five-year age category and structuring their training schedules accordingly, and placing an emphasis on performance (e.g., time) rather than outcome (e.g., placing).
- Consultants working with masters athletes who are older than themselves need to be aware that: their clients may have great depth of experience and knowledge in their sports; a generation gap may exist between themselves and their clients; misunderstandings can occur due to differences in experiences, opinions, habits, and/or behaviors; and their own attitudes, stereotypes, and predetermined beliefs about older people may be different from those of their clients.

References

Coakley, J. (2008). *Sports in society: Issues and controversies* (10th ed.). Boston: McGraw-Hill.

Dodd, J. R., & Spinks, W. L. (1995). Motivations to engage in masters sport. *ANZALS Leisure Research Series, 2,* 61–75.

Hanrahan, S. J., & Gross, J. B. (2005). Attributions and goal orientations in masters athletes: Performance versus outcome. *Revista de Psicologia del Deporte, 14,* 43–56.

Medic, N. (2009). Understanding masters athletes' motivation for sport. In J. Baker, S. Horton, & P. Weir (Eds.). *The Masters Athlete: Understanding the role of sport and exercise in optimizing aging* (pp. 105–121). London: Routledge.

Medic, N., Starkes, J. L., Young, B. W., Weir, P. L., & Giajnorio, A. (2005). *Multifaceted analyses of masters athletes' motives to continue training and competing.* Paper presented at the ISSP 11th World Congress of Sports Psychology, Sydney, Australia.

Medic, N., Starkes, J. L., Young, B. W., & Weir, P. L. (2006). Motivation for sport and goal orientations in masters athletes: Do masters swimmers differ from masters runners? *Journal of Sport & Exercise Psychology, 28* (Suppl.), p. S132.

Medic, N., Starkes, J. L., & Young, B. W. (2007a). Examining relative age effects on performance achievement and participation rates of masters athletes. *Journal of Sports Sciences, 25,* 1377–1384.

Medic, N., Starkes, J. L., Weir, P. L., Young, B. W., Wilson, P., Mack, D. E., & Elferink-Gemser, M. (2007b, May). *Do motives for sport predict sport commitment and passion for sport in a sample of highly skilled masters athletes?* Paper presented at the Third International Conference on Self-Determination Theory, Toronto, ON, Canada.

Medic, N., Starkes, J. L., Weir, P. L., Young, B. W., & Grove, J. R. (2009). Relative age effect in masters sports: Replication and extension. *Research Quarterly for Exercise and Sport, 80,* 669–675.

Salthouse, T. A. (1991). *Theoretical perspectives on cognitive aging.* Hillsdale, NJ: LEA.

Spirduso, W. W., Francis, K. L., & MacRae, P. G. (2005). *Physical dimensions of aging* (2nd ed). Champaign, IL: Human Kinetics.

Starkes, J. L., Weir, P. L., & Young, B. W. (2003). What does it take for older athletes to continue to excel? In J. L. Starkes & K. A. Ericsson (Eds.), *Expert performance in sports: Advances in research on sport expertise* (pp. 251–272). Champaign, IL: Human Kinetics.

Tantrum, M., & Hodge, K. (1993). Motives for participating in masters swimming. *New Zealand Journal of Health Physical Education and Recreation, 26,* 3–7.

Vallerand, R. J., Blanchard, C. M., Mageau, G. A., Koestner, R., Ratelle, C., & Leonard, M., (2003). Les passions de l'âme: On obsessive and harmonious passion. *Journal of Personality and Social Psychology, 85,* 756–767.

Young, B. W., Weir, P. L., Starkes, J. L., & Medic, N. (2008). Does lifelong training temper age-related decline in sport performance? Interpreting differences between cross-sectional and longitudinal data. *Experimental Aging Research, 34,* 27–48.

41

Professional athletes

Pippa Grange

Many professional athletes are used to being told how they ought to handle challenges, and their adaptive (and maladaptive) responses to adversity have been reinforced by authority figures (parents, coaches, physicians, trainers) for a considerable time. In a professional environment, where non-sport-related behaviors and activities receive increasing scrutiny, athletes can find themselves needing to operate within a fairly rigid set of behavioral guidelines that do not necessarily leave room for the expression of individuality. An outcome of these restrictions can be that professional athletes enter the therapeutic encounter expecting a similar dynamic. The job of facilitating athletes' choices about what outcomes they would like from the work undertaken together can take substantial time and effort on the psychologist's part. Collaborative effort may be a novelty. It may help to start by asking athletes how they feel about being there and explaining the rules in terms of confidentiality, reporting, and client notes, as well as something about the role of a psychologist. An introduction may go something like, "I'd encourage you to think of this as your space and your time, and what I'm interested in is helping you work through what is going on for you. Over time what I've found is that what seems to work best is when we approach this work together as a team." (see Andersen, 2000).

Professional athletes get lauded for "tough behavior" and "gusting it out" and so help-seeking can seem like a weakness, particularly if the stigma is reinforced by coaches, many of whom came through an era where prowess and heroics would never have been accompanied by the expression of emotional vulnerability. It may feel uncomfortable for professional athletes to acknowledge that they are struggling on any front. One of the things I find useful in opening the door to talking about feelings is to focus on bringing palatable emotions to the fore. These feelings might include passion, anger, or the shattered feeling one experiences after a loss. Making common-sense comparisons and drawing parallels to similar emotions in other aspects of the athletes' lives can help.

On occasion, a medical analogy can help an athlete understand the significance of emotional health and wellbeing. For example, to say "if you were suffering from mononucleosis, would you see it as necessary to deal with it in isolation and not seek help?" Or "playing with depression and ignoring it is possible, like playing with a small broken bone in your foot maybe. But it's uncomfortable and perhaps unnecessary if treatment is available." I also refer to statistics and research because quantification can be useful in the early stages of engagement and rapport building, and athletes are used to quantitative comparisons.

Although professional athletes may not be especially familiar or comfortable with showing vulnerability, they are often used to receiving feedback that most other people would find deflating and demoralizing. Feedback may be given without permission or invitation from the athlete and may be in front of their peers and presented without a right to reply. As a consequence, it seems that some athletes are desensitized and blunt about what is wrong with them (e.g., "I have an addictive personality," "lying is part of my personality"). It might be worth raising a red flag for such comments because they sound suspiciously like other people's diagnoses of the athletes, and those who diagnosed may carry a great deal of weight with the athletes (e.g., coaches, team physicians). These self-views need to be examined carefully because it may be unhelpful to therapeutic relationships in their infancies to place oneself in opposition to important people in the athletes' lives.

Considering things in the third person can assist athletes to access topics until they find a degree of comfort in speaking on a personal level. For example, to ask "what would you think if it were your best mate feeling this way or in this predicament?" It can also help normalize the athletes' experiences (if this approach is suitable) to present de-identified or amalgamated case examples and share them with the clients.

Language

I have heard people say that one needs to dumb down one's language for athletes. I wholeheartedly disagree with the comment. As with any other group, overuse of jargon or psychological terms can be alienating and plain language is best. I have found it useful, however, to use terms that seem familiar to the athletes such as mental practice or mental preparation rather than, say, cognitive restructuring or reframing. I might also reference things physically and start by asking questions such as "what do you feel in your body when that's going on for you, what do you notice?"

It is also worth talking about the technical sport language used when speaking with athletes. As a sport psychologist, you should be at least familiar with the technical terms used within the sports with which you are working, so that your clients can feel confident you are relating to what they say. If your spin bowler (cricket pitcher) is talking about unhelpful cognitive intrusions on the run-up to bowling a "leggy," or feeling consumed with anger if he is accused of "chucking," you need a grasp of the context and an understanding of the terms. Inevitably, however, there will be occasions when you do not understand a technical term or jargon, and these occasions present a great opportunity to learn and to empower the client by asking what that term means. Doing so adds to your competence and provides some balance in the relationship (e.g., client as knowledgeable teacher). On the flip side, the psychologist's overuse of sport-technical terms, and particularly sport jargon, can seem too informal, flippant, and even sycophantic. For example, in Australian rules football sometimes sports commentators will refer to the ball as the pill, the field of play as the paddock, or a pair of football boots as a set of wheels, but using such language with an athlete can make you look like you are trying too hard. I suspect that athletes appreciate that you get it, but also that you are not part of their world, and you represent a space slightly separate from their sports. Perhaps it is best to meet the athletes where they are in terms of language.

Boundaries

Working with athletes can present interesting challenges in regard to one's professional boundaries. In my role as a psychologist working within a player development program for an Australian sports organization, I see athletes one-on-one for therapy, and I see groups for psycho-educational sessions on such topics as depression and anxiety, problem gambling, responsible use of alcohol, and drug education. All of these interactions require trust and rapport, but it is sometimes a fine balance between interacting with the group and keeping the therapeutic relationship with the individual "special." I explain to one-on-one clients that I will not overtly single them out and acknowledge them in group settings because it may be construed as identifying them as clients of mine. It is not uncommon for me to have several clients within the group I am addressing, but they do not know each other as Pippa's clients.

I tend to adopt an open but not "matey" style, which is common in football clubs, and I deliberately approach the captains or club delegates as a point of introduction. Collaboration and relationships with club stakeholders and power brokers is a must in professional environments, and an insider recommendation (from a coach or a club doctor) is potent and credible. Again, the balance is fine because relationships with club doctors or coaches that are too neutral and do not add any value to them in their roles are as damaging as relationships that are too close and breeding grounds for breaches of client confidentiality. For this reason, one needs to be clear and consistent about the professional ethics and boundaries of a psychologist with all parties from day one (Gardner, 1995). A luxury in my current role is that I work across clubs rather than with one club, and so I am seen as neutral and as representing or advocating for the players, not the clubs, which is helpful when the desired outcomes of each are not aligned, and I am clearly signposted as being on the players' side. It is, however, important to remain respectful of the coaches, administrators, and other staff members in each club because there can be strong paternalistic dynamics, and the coach, in particular, is sometimes seen as a singular and omnipotent decision-maker against whom the athletes feel uncomfortable to pit themselves. Part of the privilege of my role is that I can pit my opinion against a coach, respectfully, and voice disagreement, or concern that an athlete may not wish to do something: in effect, giving him a vicarious outlet for the frustration he feels.

Professional club or team-based social occasions can challenge the sport psychologist's professional boundaries. What to do if after a big event or perhaps at the end of the season when the rest of the team, including coaches, physiotherapists, doctors, and administrators, are ready to let their hair down, and invite you to come along? To decline would seem isolating or maybe stand-offish, but to go along and get into the swing of things might put you in a position where your boundaries are stretched: perhaps an athlete may have a few too many drinks and start to probe into your life, or the coach might share way more information than he intended about your clients. Your clients, although seeming comfortable on the surface, might become uneasy about you being so friendly with the people about whom they talk to you week-in-week-out, or alternatively, they may feel restricted in the way they behave because they don't feel comfortable with you in the room. You're supposed to be separate, remember? However close your connection with the team or the athlete, there are few occasions when there is more to be gained from staying for the duration of a social event than attending for a while and making your apologies early and leaving.

Confidentiality

Psychologists operating in any professional domain are ethically bound by and accountable to rules of confidentiality set by their accrediting bodies. This accountability is, in part, designed to engender trust and instill confidence in clients. Psychologists working in sport settings sometimes have these ethics tested because they may have more than one client: the athlete and the person paying the bills (club / coach / parent). Sport psychologists work in myriad settings but are most often associated with teams, clubs, or organizations who refer clients to them. If it is a third-party referral situation, whereby the coach, for example, calls the psychologist to make the referral, sends the athlete along to offices outside of the regular sport setting, and understands that the psychologist is a neutral service provider, the issue of confidentiality may never come up. Likewise, if athletes refer themselves to the psychologist without anyone else being involved, there is no issue. Nevertheless, when the psychologist is contracted or employed by the club or similar body, the reporting lines and responsibilities may become blurred, and the psychologist not only needs to be hyper-vigilant about walking the ethical line, but also needs to be a strong and credible communicator.

Most coaches and administrators have the interests of the athletes at heart and are genuinely looking for positive improvements in their health, performance, and wellbeing (Gardner, 1995). To this end, they seek information about how athletes are progressing, whether they are emotionally fit or ready to perform this week (and if not this week, when?), how they might react to decisions pending (such as being dropped or selected), and what are their abilities to contribute to the team. The coach has to make decisions about fielding the best team and competing optimally week to week, and sees this information as "need-to-know." At other times, the coach may be making decisions about the tenure of the athlete on the team, and the information you hold can significantly influence those decisions. As discussed earlier, the relationship with the professional coach or administrator is a pivotal one for the psychologist, but the presumption needs to be that the information given to you from the athlete is in confidence and is not to be shared with the coach or other stakeholder. In an ideal scenario, you would either have the client present or have been given consent to share specific information on behalf of the client. It doesn't, however, always run so smoothly, and oftentimes psychologists are checking and monitoring themselves along the way. Some psychologists manage to stay flexible by clearly indicating to the group of athletes that particular types of information will be shared with the coach, and letting the athletes know what information has been requested and subsequently shared. Other psychologists carefully pick through their available data and choose what they can talk about, and keep it specific.

Some challenges that I have observed include a situation where a psychologist was involved in the case management of several athletes, one of whom, he was aware, had a pervasive gambling problem that had consumed his attention for many months. Although the athlete had made excellent progress and had finally started putting the problem behind him, legacies of the gambling problem, however, were a serious amount of debt, a broken relationship, and also a lack of focus on planning for life after sport. Two of the members (not psychologists) of the case management team believed that this athlete did not care about his performance, nor did they believe he was invested in the team. He was seen as stand-offish and aloof. Their inclination was to deselect him and elevate someone else to the team. The senior coach asked the psychologist directly whether he knew of any reason why the athlete would have been underperforming that they could take into consideration; if there was no such information, he would not be renewing the athlete's contract. The athlete had not wanted the coach to know about his problem in case he did not get a new contract, which he desperately wanted. The psychologist believed that the deselection of the athlete would be devastating to him, put him under immense pressure, and risk his progress and rehabilitation. But he was also unsure of the amount of empathy the case management team overall would have for the athlete, whom they believed to be difficult at the best of times. In this case, the psychologist asked both the athlete and the senior coach to consider coming together in private to discuss the athlete's position before the case went back to the management team for a decision. The psychologist told the athlete the position he was in and his concerns that he would not be able to represent his situation well and also maintain confidentiality, and explained that he thought that the senior coach might be open to hearing the athlete's story. In this case, the coach and athlete were able to discuss the scenario and reach a resolution whereby the athlete continued his tenure with the team under strict performance improvement criteria.

Another situation involved a sport psychiatrist (with whom I work regularly) who had accepted a referral from a club doctor to work with an athlete on a generalized anxiety issue. The doctor told the psychiatrist that information should be presented back to a particular staff member who was "appropriately trained in psychology." The psychiatrist checked with the client, who concurred that this person was the right person in the club, and all information on players had to go back to him. After giving this person feedback on the athlete's concerns and offering an outline of the deeper psychological processes and long-term issues, it came to the psychiatrist's attention that this man was not a psychologist, but an influential sports scientist and high-performance manager whose priority was the decisions on the playing status of athletes week to week. On further probing, it became clear that the client was under the firm impression that he did not have a choice about information going back to the club. This scenario highlights the importance of explaining confidentiality to each party even when a referral is from a trusted source such as a doctor.

Work environments

The environmental trappings of psychologists working with professional athletes are often unusual. In an ideal consulting situation, a client would see a psychologist in private, comfortable rooms, most commonly set up with two chairs, a table with a box of tissues, access to drinking water, and so forth. The rooms would be reasonably soundproofed, for example, with a door that fully closed and walls that enclosed the rooms, as opposed to partitions. The appointments would be pre-arranged with an acknowledgment that they would go for a set period of time, and the psychologists would have the opportunity to ask a few introductory questions and explain how they work. Sport psychologists sometimes find themselves responding to the question "do you have a couple of minutes to talk?" from an athlete while they are poolside, trackside, courtside, pitchside, or otherwise. There is an emphasis on being accessible, particularly in circumstances where the discipline of psychology is new to a group of athletes, and asking for guidance is openly encouraged by the coach or other staff. There are some advantages to this loose consulting environment that include the normalization of help-seeking behaviors, the integration of sport psychology services into the overall preparation for sport, and the familiarity, rapport, and relationships built between athletes and psychologists (Petitpas, Giges, & Danish, 1999). The priority is to accept the client's invitation to talk, but there is also an onus to protect, as much as possible, the client's privacy and not open up potentially sensitive topics in earshot of other athletes or coaches. Privacy can be achieved by moving away – up to the stands if possible or to the edge of the playing field, but there is still the likelihood of being visible to other people. A good alternative is an administration office or private space that you are able to access, and where you are likely to be undisturbed. Alternatively, if there is some suggestion that the issue up for discussion may leave the athlete feeling vulnerable, it may be prudent to welcome the opportunity to talk and make a time in the near future, outside the setting, where you can meet privately. Many hours of good work have been done by adaptable sport psychologists in local cafés.

Office set-up and location

Even when discrete office space is available there are special considerations with professional athlete populations. For example, it is important to ensure that clients will not be compromised by meeting teammates or players from other teams in your waiting room or at the door as appointments cross over. If clients are well-known public figures, they may request that they have separate entry and/or exit from sessions. On occasion a client will present around an issue that has been in the media, and journalists may turn up at your premises to attempt to photograph or interview the athlete. This situation can present difficulties if you do not have the luxury of a receptionist.

Sometimes, however, the athlete is much more comfortable in a less formal setting. I have noticed that younger male clients and also many Indigenous Australian athletes prefer casual settings. We might go for a walk or meet over a coffee. At my home office, some of my Indigenous clients choose to take their shoes off and sit on the rug leaning against the armchair, rather than sitting in the arm chair. Some of my professional athlete-clients ask me to allow my dogs into the room, who sit close to the clients and become the focus of attention, visually and physically, particularly when the clients venture into emotionally sensitive territory.

A consideration for all psychologists working in private settings, or more casual, informal settings, is personal security. Many sport psychologists work alone and although you may endeavor to "meet the clients where they are" and be flexible, it should never be at the risk of your personal security. If you are one-on-one with a client in private, someone should know where you are working or what time you are scheduled to check in again.

Population

Professional athletes are not a homogenous group. There are, however, some consistent themes or aspects to the athlete population. For example, in professional sport:

- Professional athletes are constantly judged and critiqued by other people.
- Athletes are often displaced geographically, and from family and friends, to train or compete.
- Male team athletes spend an enormous amount of time with other men in large groups, which can create strong cultural norms and dynamics that may seem unusual or extreme to others.
- The conduct of modern professional athletes inside and outside of their sports is regulated tightly (particularly in popular high-revenue sports that attract media coverage).
- Unlike other young men and women, many professional athletes throughout their careers have access to a great deal of support/intervention/assistance/help such as regular access to specialist medical personnel and psychologists (Ray & Wiese-Bjornstal, 1999).
- Professional athletes may have unusually high disposable incomes, significant down time, and access to the means to get into trouble (alcohol, drugs, gambling).

- High-ranking professional athletes lead public (sometimes celebrity) lives and they are often held accountable to the public and the media as role models.
- Athletes cannot have ultimate control over their careers in terms of longevity, injury, or success, and unlike other professionals, who generally progress and grow as they age and become more experienced, professional athletes usually peak at a young age and then find themselves on the brink of deterioration, with their careers at the cusp of being over.
- A professional athlete's life is often in flux and rarely certain or stable. Perhaps because of this instability, in combination with relative financial freedom, it seems that male team sport athletes tend to make commitments in relationships and to family at an earlier age than the general population (Australian Football League Players' Association, 2009).

Professional terms and conditions

Few sport psychologists are employed full-time by professional teams or clubs. Those who do work exclusively with such organizations are usually contracted for a number of hours on a fee-for-service basis, or have restricted terms such as a financial retainer to cover all services provided. Consequently, the amount of time the psychologist is able to dedicate to a client may be necessarily limited. It may be useful to work out with the team or athletes what would happen should athletes require further support. Consideration should be given to whether the athletes pay for extra services themselves or whether the team could extend existing resources. Psychologists should decide whether they are in a position to offer pro-bono services to their clients, but many professional athletes have substantial incomes and could pay for continuing service. It may be possible for clients to claim medical rebates for services that continue beyond the agreement. If there are no options available, psychologists must consider how they will dispense with their duty of care for athletes if they believe they would benefit from further support. It may be necessary to involve another party to assure the safety of the client, for example, a team doctor. In any case, psychologists must clearly communicate to clients the length of time they have available and plan to effectively summarize and terminate the sessions.

For some sport psychologists, getting professional athletes to turn up regularly can be challenging. This limited commitment may be more pronounced when the psychologist is employed or contracted by a third party (team, club, sports governing body) who pays the bills for the athletes rather than athletes paying for services themselves, and so there are no financial consequences for the athlete for not showing up. Cancellations may lessen significantly once a relationship develops between client and psychologist, but in the early engagement phase the commitment may be tenuous. When a client fails to show or cancels without good reason or for a second or third time, it is worth questioning whether the client is making an appointment voluntarily or under the persuasion of the coach or significant other. Athletes may report that training session times are constantly shifting, thus making it difficult to meet external commitments. Professional athletes may be under unrealistic time pressures, or they may not feel ready to meet with a psychologist. I have found it unhelpful to chase up clients beyond the first missed session. Instead, I encourage and welcome them to get in touch if and when they are free and ready. I explain that it might feel a bit awkward at first to talk, but it will be on their terms and at their pace if they choose to come to an appointment. Despite the need for flexibility when working in sport, it is not fair on other athletes (who may need your services) or on you to allow clients to make a habit of canceling without recourse. Possible ways to address this issue may include a three-strikes policy whereby you let the client know that a third cancellation will mean that you do not accept further appointment bookings without a discussion, or clearly explaining that cancellation fees will apply for a second no-show or late cancellation.

Conclusions

Working with professional athletes as a psychologist presents plenty of challenges, including working with dual clients, traveling and unusual hours, managing boundaries in flexible work settings, maintaining confidentiality (when other people may be openly talking about issues in the athletes' lives), and navigating through myriad ethical dilemmas. One dilemma involves the contrasting philosophies within sport about the *raison d'être* of the professional athlete: one side is that the purpose of being is to win at all costs and anything less than winning is failure. On the other side is that the endeavor of elite sport is purpose in itself. In typically short competitive careers, the majority of professional athletes will fail by the criteria of the win-at-all-costs, and the dilemma as a sport psychologist is to assist athletes to strive toward narrowly defined, singular, and extreme goals involving a great deal of compromise and pain, while finding meaning, and staying well. In the big picture of sport psychologists working with professional athletes, performance enhancement is only a small part of the work (cf., Murphy, 2000).

In conclusion, I think that the work of the sport psychologist is far from over when the professional athlete retires from sport. There is a great need for services to assist with transition out of professional sport and adjustment to life thereafter (see Glanville, 2009; Chapter 26). See Box 41.1 for take-home messages from this chapter.

Box 41.1

Take-home messages about working with professional athletes

- Athletes may initially have difficulty in expressing vulnerability, and it can be useful to start with a practical, performance orientation.
- Complex relationships with professional athletes, coaches, and administrators mean that it is especially important to communicate your boundaries to all stakeholders.
- Sport psychologists need to find a balance between being part of the team and being someone neutral and separate in the athletes' world.
- The settings for doing sport psychology with professional athletes are sometimes unusual and practitioners need to be flexible yet discrete.
- Working on performance is only a part of what a sport psychologist does; seeing and valuing the person behind the performer is critical.
- The characteristics and competencies of a good psychologist are the same in sport as in any other environment.
- Sport psychology can offer services to professional athletes beyond their retirement dates.

References

Australian Football League Players' Association (2009). *AFLPA Player Development Program statistics 2005–2009* [Internal business document]. Melbourne, VIC, Australia: Australian Football League Players' Association.

Andersen, M. B. (2000). Beginnings: Intakes and the initiation of relationships. In M. B. Andersen (Ed.), *Doing sport psychology* (pp. 3–16). Champaign, IL: Human Kinetics.

Gardner, F. (1995). The coach and the team psychologist: An integrated organizational model. In S. M. Murphy (Ed.), *Sport psychology interventions* (pp. 147–169). Champaign, IL: Human Kinetics.

Glanville, D. (2009, August 12). The forgotten. *The New York Times*. Retrieved from http://www.nytimes.com/2009/08/13/opinion/13glanville.html

Murphy, S. M. (2000). Afterword. In M. B. Andersen (Ed.), *Doing sport psychology* (pp. 275–279). Champaign, IL: Human Kinetics.

Petitpas, A. J., Giges, B., & Danish, S. J. (1999). The sport psychologist–athlete relationship: Implications for training. *The Sport Psychologist, 13*, 344–357.

Ray, R., & Wiese-Bjornstal, D. M. (1999). *Counseling in sports medicine*. Champaign, IL: Human Kinetics.

42

Working at the Olympics

Ken Hodge

I've always been an advocate of personal best times and to come here [the Olympics] and get two of them, I'm really pleased about that. Only about 30% of swimmers come here and do personal best times; so l made it my personal mission to get inside that 30% ... I set myself a goal and I was pleased with my performance. It won't be my last goal.

Danyon Loader (New Zealand swimmer,
Olympic medalist [Loader, 1996])

As the quote above from double Olympic gold medalist Danyon Loader indicates, the Olympics are challenging (e.g., only 30% of swimmers post a personal best time); a special type of mental toughness is required to succeed at the Olympics. For most athletes, the four-year Olympic cycle generates a level of importance that defines this sporting festival as their career-culminating event (McCann, 2008). As Haberl and Peterson (2006) concluded, the Olympic "crucible creates unique pressures for everyone involved: athletes, coaches, and support staff." (p. 29)

The Olympic context is different

The Olympic context is different and unique, but the basic models of sport psychology consulting, your consulting philosophy, and your ethics remain constant (Andersen, Van Raalte, & Brewer, 2001; Bond, 2001). The Olympic Games are an atypical and unusual sporting experience for most athletes and an alien competition context for some (Greenleaf, Gould, & Dieffenbach, 2001; Pensgaard, 2008). Most elite athletes quickly become familiar with the annual schedule of international events in their own sports (e.g., FINA swimming world cup series; skiing FIS World Cup race circuit) and adjust to the mental demands of such regular elite competitions within their sporting disciplines. The Olympics, on the other hand, only occur every four years, and the Games are a multisport event as opposed to a single sport event.

The quadrennial Olympic cycle offers few opportunities for most athletes to gain experience in the Olympic environment because most athletes only compete at one Games in their careers (Gould, 2001; McCann, 2000). Moreover, as Hodge and Hermansson (2007) contended, the key mental challenge at an Olympics is the multisport aspect of the Games, which can be a distraction as well as obscure the normal exclusive focus on the athletes' own sports.

The prestige and global profile of the Olympics generates huge media coverage and sponsor and public expectations. Consequently, for many sports the Olympics creates a substantially higher public profile and media scrutiny than these athletes typically experience (Haberl & Peterson, 2006; Pensgaard, 2008). The pressures associated with performing under such intense scrutiny can become a burden for many competitors (Blumenstein & Lidor, 2008). The Olympic performance context is often uncomfortable for athletes. They are required to operate outside their normal performance comfort zones. To be successful, Olympic athletes need to learn to be comfortable being uncomfortable (Ravizza, 2005), and to embrace the added pressure as another performance challenge to relish. Clearly, it is not easy being an Olympian, and that is the key point for athletes (and psychologists) to keep in mind when they consider the stress and pressure generated in the Olympic context.

Common psychological issues and challenges at the Olympics

Elite athletes typically work on core mental skills such as motivation, concentration, confidence, controlling arousal/activation, and coping with adversity. Excellent descriptions of Olympic mental skills training programs that focus on these core skills can be found in book chapters by Gould (2001) and McCann (2000). Nevertheless, a number of mental issues and challenges common to the Olympic environment still need to be addressed.

Stress management

Perhaps the most common mental challenge at the Games is stress management and coping (Gould, Eklund, & Jackson, 1993). Competing at the Olympics can be more stressful than competing at annual international competitions, for a number of reasons: (a) the atmosphere of the Games – representing one's country, competing against the world's best with the spotlight on one's performance (McCann, 2008); (b) the global media coverage at the Games (Greenleaf et al., 2001; Pensgaard, 2008); (c) living in the village and dealing with the artificial and sometimes quite foreign surroundings (Blumenstein & Lidor, 2008); (d) transport, security, and organizational hassles (Haberl & Peterson, 2006); (e) interpersonal conflict with teammates, coaches, or managers; (f) dealing with fitness, injury, or health problems; (g) the effort, time, and money required to gain Olympic selection can become a source of stress when the athlete begins to wonder if it is all going to pay off; (h) dealing with the disappointment of a poor performance in the first race/heat/event (Gould, Eklund, & Jackson, 1992); and (i) concerns about life after sport (e.g., "Win or lose at these Games, what will I do next?"). Any one, or a combination, of these sources of stress can cause anxiety, interfere with athletes' mental and physical preparation, and undermine their confidence (Pensgaard & Duda, 2003). It is important to help Olympic athletes identify the issues they can control and then to focus on controlling the controllables (Hodge, 2004).

One particular issue of stress relates to living circumstances (Blumenstein & Lidor, 2008; Hodge & Hermansson, 2007). Village accommodation invariably involves several athletes in the same room in relatively cramped conditions. These living circumstances often cause problems (e.g., noise control, sleeping difficulties, lack of privacy), especially as the Games progress and some athletes finish their competitions. Another potentially powerful stressor for some athletes is that their funding may be strictly tied to their Games performances. If athletes succeed at the Games they will secure funding for the next 1–2 years; if not, their funding is often withdrawn (Haberl & Peterson, 2006). The same is true for coaches' jobs and team funding. If you succeed, you continue; if you don't then you're out as a coach or the funds for the team are cut (Haberl & Peterson, 2006). It is difficult for athletes to remain positive and confident in the Olympic context/situation. For example, Jackie Joyner-Kersee (1992), the U.S. heptathlete and Olympic medalist, said:

> You have to be mentally strong enough to go through pressure [at the Olympics]. It must be practised as much as running or jumping. You have to concentrate on positiveness, feed yourself positive energy. If you tell yourself you can't do something, nine times out of ten you won't be able to do it.
>
> (p. 13)

Pre-event mental preparation

Olympic athletes need to fine-tune their mental preparation to suit the special demands of the Games environment to minimize the stressors identified above (Gould *et al.*, 1992; McCann, 2000). This work typically involves helping athletes modify existing pre-race routines/plans to provide a perception of control over the situation, help deal with stress, and give them confidence that they can perform up to their personal bests (Hodge, 2004). This perception of control is often challenged at the Olympics by the almost inevitable shift toward focusing intently on hoped-for outcomes (Gould, 2001; Hodge & Hermansson, 2007). Given that an athlete's Olympic selection is typically the culmination of years of training, and because there is intense interest in results, athletes struggle more than usual to stay focused on performance objectives. As Barbara Kendall (1992), the New Zealand boardsailor and Olympic medalist, observed, the challenge at the Olympics is to remain performance-focused rather than results/medal-focused:

> Winning a gold medal is an amazing feeling. [But] ... winning a gold medal is not the ultimate now. I went to Barcelona and tried my hardest. I knew I had given my best and that is more satisfying than a gold medal ... If I win the gold medal again [at the 1996 Olympics] that will be fine, but if I finish 10th that will be fine too ... Someone might be better than me. As long as I do my best. That is all I can ask of myself.
>
> (p. 34)

Games wobbles

I created this euphemistic phrase to describe a phenomenon where, despite the added focus on mental preparation mentioned above, some athletes decide to radically change their routines and mental preparation because they are at the Games. Somehow the usual becomes doubted, and athletes sometimes lose trust in their familiar routines (Greenleaf *et al.*, 2001; McCann, 2000). These athletes need to trust themselves and their routines, and with the assistance of their coaches stick to their normal training and competition procedures (Clarke, 2004; Miller, 1997). The sport psychologist can play a key role in reassuring these athletes that their trusted training and mental preparation routines will remain effective if they have the confidence to adhere to them. In addition, these athletes may well benefit from stress management techniques (e.g., cognitive restructuring, relaxation/centering) and coping strategies such as seeking social support (e.g., coaches, teammates) and using imagery of successful coping.

Interpersonal conflict

When competitive people are living closely together in a stressful environment (see issues listed above), there will inevitably be conflict between athletes and their teammates, coaches, or managers (Gould, 2001; Hodge & Hermansson, 2007). Typically, such conflicts develop from, or are exacerbated by, poor communication, limited tolerance, and lack of empathy by both parties (Bond, 2001; Clarke, 2004). A sport psychology consultant often needs to act as a neutral third party who helps negotiate a resolution to such conflicts (see Chapter 35 in this book). Hodge and Hermansson (2007) argued that coaches and managers need to be appointed early in the Olympic cycle by each sport so that the individuals concerned have time before the Games to get to know their athletes (and the athletes get to know the coaches/managers) and develop working relationships.

Psychological aspects of injury and illness

The fear of injury and illness (e.g., flu, respiratory infections), and injury/illness itself, have clear psychological consequences (Williams & Scherzer, 2010), especially in the Olympic context when the four-year cycle offers a small window for participation opportunities. Injured/ill athletes will have to cope with the emotions and stress that accompany the worry that an injury/illness may hinder a top performance or, worse still, prevent them from competing at the biggest event of their sporting careers – one for which they have trained and made sacrifices over a number of years (Greenleaf et al., 2001; McCann, 2008). One feature of sport psychology work with injured/ill athletes is the opportunity for consultants to collaborate with a multi-disciplinary team involving sports medicine personnel such as physiotherapists, massage therapists, and chiropractors (Reid, Stewart, & Thorne, 2004; Vernacchia & Henschen, 2008).

Second-week blues

In my experience (two Olympic Games and three Commonwealth Games), many members of a Games team, not just athletes but coaches, managers, and medical staff, will experience, to some extent, a phenomenon I have labeled "second-week blues". It is normal at the Olympics for athletes and others to get somewhat homesick and irritable after the first week living in the claustrophobic Games environment (Miller, 1997; Vernacchia & Henschen, 2008). Living inside the Games bubble can start to irritate athletes for a number of reasons: the cramped Village, bland bedrooms, lack of privacy, limited spare/private time, monotonous food, travel distances between Village and venues, and the tedious and intrusive security checkpoints. Although such issues, individually, may be minor, collectively they tend to become amplified as the lead-up time to competition shortens and the tension associated with competition expectations builds. Not surprisingly these issues can be especially frustrating for athletes who do not compete until the second week of the Games.

Similar to athletes who may experience Games wobbles, as outlined above, athletes experiencing "second-week blues" may also benefit from stress management techniques and coping strategies. The key issue is that these athletes need to mentally prepare beforehand for the challenge of an extended stay inside the claustrophobic Games environment and the frustrations of waiting to compete until the second week. As with race/game plans, athletes need to plan ahead as to how they will fill in the time productively (a pre-emptive coping plan designed with the help of the sport psychologist), while also adhering to the physical training/tapering program designed by their coaches. Some athletes with second-week blues may benefit from increased communication with family and friends at home (e.g., e-mail, texting, social networking websites), whereas for others such increased communication may exacerbate feelings of homesickness. The sport psychologist can be of assistance to athletes, coaches, and managers by acting as a neutral third party in any discussions about the level of communication with family and friends (see below as well).

Family and friends distractions

Given that Olympic selection is the pinnacle of achievement for most Olympic athletes, many athletes' families and friends make the effort to attend the Games and support their athletes (Haberl & Peterson, 2006). Typically, these supporters will not have been present at the athletes' other international competitions, so their presence can create an unusual environment for the athletes, posing uncommon distractions that they are not used to handling. Many more family members and friends show up at the Olympics than at other events, and they want to connect with their athletes once they arrive. The expectation to interact with family and friends at the Games can put pressure on athletes who don't want to hurt the feelings of Aunty Mary and Uncle Bill who came all the way from Dunedin/Narrogin/Missoula/St. Keverne.

Athletes have told me that new people in a competitive situation can create additional stress, even if they are loving and supportive. For example, an alpine skier commented to me at the 2006 Winter Olympics that he/she was frustrated with her/his parents' well-meaning comments that they "would be happy if she/he just finished the giant slalom/Super-G course," but, as the athlete observed, he/she had not qualified for the Olympics to simply finish the course, she/he wanted to go "fast"! Going fast and potentially crashing or missing a gate is the standard risk that all giant slalom/Super-G skiers negotiate in every international race. This skier's attitude was that anyone could finish the course (if they took a slow, conservative approach to the run), whereas real ski racers focus on going fast and pushing the boundaries to give themselves a chance of posting a competitive time for the run. This skier was dumbfounded and frustrated that after all the years of support, his/her parents still did not fully understand the mindset needed to compete at the international/Olympic level.

Finally, family and friends need to avoid asking their athletes if they think they are going to be selected for the Olympic team. Although this question is sincere, elite athletes know that focusing too much on a potential outcome can interfere with achieving that outcome. Even strong favorites to qualify for the Olympic team hate this question. It makes them nervous. We encourage family and friends to make decisions about going to the Games that are not based upon whether the athletes they know qualify for the team. Athletes often won't know until the last minute whether they have qualified, and knowing that people are waiting for them to qualify before they book air travel and tickets is tremendous additional pressure that is not helpful.

The challenges mentioned above tend to make up the majority of work at the Games for sport psychologists. Much of this work is performance-focused, but a lot of it can be regarded as performance-related (Bond, 2002). As McCann (2008) observed "every issue ... at the

Olympics is a performance issue" (p. 269). Another key issue to be aware of is that the consultant should expect to spend some time helping coaches, not just athletes (Bond, 2002; McCann, 2008; Vernacchia & Henschen, 2008). Compounding the challenges for an Olympic coach may be the presence of an athlete's personal coach who may travel to the Games but live outside the Olympic Village. The presence of personal coaches can be both a help and a hindrance (Vernacchia & Henschen, 2008), and the consultant needs to be alert to the potential influence on the athlete.

Consulting style at the Olympics: "be available, but don't get in the way!"

If I were asked to offer only one key piece of advice regarding consulting in the Olympic environment it would be that sport psychologists at the Games need to master the art of being available and accessible, but not getting in the way (Gould, 2001; McCann, 2000). It is important to avoid unnecessary disruptions to athletes' normal daily training and competition routines and to minimize any potential stigma for athletes who appear to seek help from the "shrink" (Hermansson, 2004). Often sport psychologists who have been officially appointed to Olympic teams for the first time may be too eager to contribute, and to justify their roles by actively seeking clients. Such enthusiasm can be a stressor for some athletes and their coaches. Hermansson likened his approach of developing consulting relationships with Olympic athletes to that of a fly-fisherman:

> I have a line out on the water all the time. Sometimes the fish will disappear on you, other times they might come and take a look and if the timing is right, I might get a bite. The work starts then, when you reel them in, if the line is too tight the fish take off, you have to do it slowly. Establishing credibility and having ongoing exposure to athletes within the Games team selection pool in the lead-up to the Games is central to building a consulting relationship with each athlete (Blumenstein & Lidor, 2008; McCann, 2008).
>
> (p. 12)

As a team sport psychologist you should plan to be readily available for informal chats with athletes in neutral venues such as the dining hall, Games transport/bus, team/TV room, training venues, and physical therapists' rooms. In my experience these informal chats (teachable moments or brief interventions) are often just as effective as a formal mental skills training session (see Giges & Petitpas, 2000; Gould, 2001; McCann, 2000 for detailed examples), and frequently they lead to structured sessions in more controlled settings. Although effective, however, these informal chats in public or semi-public places clearly compromise privacy for the athlete and challenge the need for confidentiality (see Chapter 7).

A number of logistical issues common to the Olympics also need to be taken into account by team consultants: (a) time management – working with multiple athletes and teams across multiple venues and satellite villages using unreliable Games transport; (b) working simultaneously with multiple teams – equity of access and consulting time (Haberl & Peterson, 2006); (c) multiple relationships, and the question of who is the client? – athlete, coach, team manager, parents? (Bond, 2001; Haberl & Peterson, 2006); (d) avoiding overidentification with athletes and their results (Haberl & Peterson); (e) confidentiality and ethics (Andersen, 2001); and (f) self-preservation and "Olympic-size stress" (Haberl & Peterson, p. 38), managing self as the sport psychology provider – time management, sleep, nutrition, exercise, time-out, and seeking peer-supervision (Haberl & Peterson, 2006).

Multidisciplinary support teams

As previously mentioned, one feature of sport psychology at an Olympics is the opportunity to work collaboratively within a multi-disciplinary athlete support team (Reid et al., 2004). Such opportunities may not always be possible when working one-on-one with athletes in the build-up to the Games. When these multi-disciplinary teams work well, the opportunity is there for athletes to benefit from a holistic and unified orientation. The experience of working within a team of providers can be a valuable addition to the effectiveness of sport psychology work. Often the sport psychologist's association with the multi-disciplinary support team can help mitigate the potential stigma of being viewed as the shrink. Such support teams, however, need to be alert to potential problems of task – role overlap, professional territoriality, and role ambiguity across the various support team members.

Team culture

Hodge and Hermansson (2007, 2009) contended that developing a strong overall team culture (as seen in the New Zealand or Australian Olympic teams), along with regular efforts to create unity and strength within sub-units (e.g., hockey, sailing teams/groups), can be a powerful method to counter the pressures that are unique to the Olympics. In my experience, many of the common mental challenges identified above for Olympic athletes can be prevented, or at least managed better, if the overall Games team has a strong team culture (e.g., teamwork, team spirit).

Cohesiveness is an important dynamic for any sporting team (Carron, Coleman, Wheeler, & Stevens, 2002). The same aspiration for cohesion may be as much a need in the overall team as it is for each of its separate units (e.g., different sporting teams and support groups). The development of overall national team cohesion could be seen as a valuable objective for any country participating in the Olympic Games, with the purpose of enhancing team members' satisfaction and performances (see Hodge & Hermansson, 2009, for detailed examples of team-building activities for a national Olympic team). Such team-building, however, is tremendously challenging for large countries such as the USA, China, and Russia, who qualify large teams of athletes (200–300+) for the Olympics.

From a psychological perspective, this team-building philosophy has been helpful in creating a valuable support network as well as an environment where the challenge to perform remains strong. It also provides a settled atmosphere within which individual and team psychological work can take place. These enhanced social-psychological conditions have been important in themselves, but they have also helped underpin the work of the sport psychologist in relation to the kinds of psycho-social challenges previously identified.

Summary

The Olympic context is different and unique, but the basic models of sport psychology consulting, your consulting philosophy, and your ethics remain constant. Olympic athletes need to fine-tune their mental preparation to suit the special demands of the Games environment to minimize the stressors. Sport psychologists at the Olympics need to master the

411

art of being available and accessible, but not getting in the way. It is important to avoid unnecessary disruptions to athletes' normal daily training and competition routines and to minimize any potential stigma for athletes appearing to seek help from the "shrink" (see Box 42.1 for practical take-home messages from this chapter).

Box 42.1

Take-home messages about working at the Olympics

- The quadrennial Olympic cycle offers few opportunities for most athletes to gain experience in the Olympic environment – the key difference about an Olympics is the multisport aspect of the Games, which can be a distraction as well as obscure the normally exclusive focus on the athletes' own sports.
- The most common psychological challenges at the Games are stress management and coping. Competing at the Olympics can be more stressful than competing at annual international competitions.
- Olympic athletes need to fine tune their mental preparation to suit the special demands of the Games environment to minimize the stressors.
- Sport psychologists should expect to spend some time helping coaches, not just athletes.
- Sport psychologists at the Olympics need to master the art of being available and accessible, but not getting in the way. It is important to avoid unnecessary disruptions to athletes' normal daily training and competition routines and to minimize any potential stigma for athletes appearing to seek help from the "shrink."

References

Andersen, M. B., Van Raalte, J. L., & Brewer, B. W. (2001). Sport psychology service delivery: Staying ethical while keeping loose. *Professional Psychology: Research & Practice, 32*, 12–18.

Blumenstein, B., & Lidor, R. (2008). Psychological preparation in the Olympic Village: A four-phase approach. *International Journal of Sport and Exercise Psychology, 6*, 287–300.

Bond, J. W. (2001). The provision of sport psychology services during competition tours. In G. Tenenbaum (Ed.), *The practice of sport psychology* (pp. 217–229). Morgantown, WV: Fitness Information Technology.

Bond, J. W. (2002). Applied sport psychology: Philosophy, reflections, and experience. *International Journal of Sport Psychology, 33*, 19–37.

Carron, A. V., Coleman, M. C., Wheeler, J., & Stevens, D. (2002). Cohesion and performance in sport: A meta-analysis. *Journal of Sport & Exercise Psychology, 24*, 168–188.

Clarke, P. (2004). Coping with the emotions of Olympic performance: A case study of winning the Olympic gold. In D. Lavallee, J. Thatcher, & M. V. Jones (Eds.), *Coping and emotion in sport* (pp. 237–251). New York: Nova Science.

Giges, B., & Petitpas, A. J. (2000). Brief contact interventions in sport psychology. *The Sport Psychologist, 14*, 176–187.

Gould, D., Eklund, R. C., & Jackson, S. A. (1992). 1988 U.S. Olympic wrestling excellence: II. Thoughts and affect occurring during competition. *The Sport Psychologist, 6*, 383–402.

Gould, D., Eklund, R. C., & Jackson, S. A. (1993). Coping strategies used by US Olympic wrestlers. *Research Quarterly for Exercise and Sport, 64*, 83–93.

Gould, D., (2001). Sport psychology and the Nagano Olympic Games: The case of the U.S. freestyle ski team. In G. Tenenbaum (Ed.), *The practice of sport psychology* (pp. 49–76). Morgantown, WV: Fitness Information Technology.

Greenleaf, C., Gould, D., & Dieffenbach, K. (2001). Factors influencing Olympic performance: Interviews with Atlanta and Nagano U. S. Olympians. *Journal of Applied Sport Psychology, 13*, 154–184.

Haberl, P., & Peterson, K. (2006). Olympic-size ethical dilemmas: Issues and challenges for sport psychology consultants on the road and at the Olympic Games. *Ethics & Behavior, 16*, 25–40.

Hermansson, G. (2004). Hermansson hopes the Athens fish are biting. *NZ Coach, 12*, 11–12.

Hodge, K. P. (2004). *Sport motivation: Training your mind for peak performance* (2nd ed.). Auckland, New Zealand: Reed Books.

Hodge, K., & Hermansson, G. (2007). Psychological preparation of athletes for the Olympic context: The New Zealand Summer and Winter Olympic Teams. *Athletic Insight: The Online Journal of Sport Psychology, 9*(4). Retrieved from http://www.athleticinsight.com/Vol9Iss4/NewZealand.htm

Hodge, K., & Hermansson, G. (2009). Psychological preparation of athletes for the Olympic context: Team culture and team-building. In R. Schinke (Ed.), *Contemporary sport psychology* (pp. 55–70). New York: Nova Science.

Joyner-Kersee, J. (1992, March). *NZ Sportswoman*, p. 13.

Kendall, B. (1992, November 12). *Otago Daily Times*, p. 34.

Loader, D. (1996, July 25). *Otago Daily Times*, p. 27.

McCann, S. C. (2000). Doing sport psychology at the really big show. In M. B. Andersen, (Ed.), *Doing sport psychology* (pp. 209–222), Champaign, IL: Human Kinetics.

McCann, S. C. (2008). At the Olympics, everything is a performance issue. *International Journal of Sport & Exercise Psychology, 6*, 267–276.

Miller, B. (1997). *Gold minds: The psychology of winning in sport*. London: Crowood Press.

Pensgaard, A.-M. (2008). Consulting under pressure: How to help an athlete deal with unexpected distracters during Olympic Games 2006. *International Journal of Sport and Exercise Psychology, 6*, 301–307.

Pensgaard, A.-M., & Duda, J. L. (2003). Sydney 2000: The interplay between emotions, coping, and the performance of Olympic-level athletes. *The Sport Psychologist, 17*, 253–267.

Ravizza, K. (2005). *Lessons learned from sport psychology consulting*. Keynote presentation at the 11th World Congress of Sport Psychology. Sydney, August 2005.

Reid, C., Stewart, E., & Thorne, G. (2004). Multidisciplinary sport science teams in elite sport: Comprehensive servicing or conflict and confusion? *The Sport Psychologist, 18*, 204–217.

Vernacchia, R., & Henschen, K. (2008). The challenge of consulting with track and field athletes at the Olympic Games. *International Journal of Sport & Exercise Psychology, 6*, 254–266.

Williams, J. M., & Scherzer, C. B. (2010). Injury risk and rehabilitation: Psychological considerations. In J. M. Williams (Ed.). *Applied sport psychology: Personal growth to peak performance* (6th ed., pp. 512–541). New York: McGraw-Hill.

43

Diverse sexual and gender identities in sport

Kerrie Kauer and Vikki Krane

Sport has long been described as having a homonegative climate: one that is disinviting and often hostile toward lesbian, gay, bisexual, and transgender (LGBT) athletes and coaches (Griffin, 1998; Messner, 2002). Although there are signs that some sport environments are becoming open and comfortable (e.g., Kauer & Krane, 2006), it is probably safe to assume that many, if not most, sport environments are grounded in heteronormativity. That is, acknowledgment of sexual or gender identities other than heterosexual typically does not occur. Heteronormativity is the privileging of "normal" heterosexual identities and behaviors, with the concomitant assumption that everyone on the team must be heterosexual, and marginalization of other sexual and gender identities (Hall, 2003). When such assumptions permeate sport environments, intentionally or not, they send messages that lesbian, gay, bisexual, and transgender athletes are not welcome.

In this chapter, we emphasize *inclusive excellence* for sport participants of all sexual and gender identities. Inclusive excellence is a concept introduced by the Association of American Colleges and Universities that re-envisions diversity and inclusion to reflect new forms of excellence in learning in all aspects of higher education. Diversity is a systematic process that engages differences and transforms learning environments with a primary aim toward reflecting, supporting, and sustaining goals of inclusion and excellence (Williams, Berger, & McClendon, 2005). In other words, excellence is achieved by embracing multicultural and diverse individuals. We believe this concept is particularly appropriate for challenging the heteronormative environments of sport. Excellence already is a common goal in sport, and inclusiveness reflects the group dynamics within a team vying for excellence (Krane, 2008).

Embracing inclusive excellence includes challenging normative assumptions about gender and sexual orientation as well as recognizing the vast diversity of gender and sexual identities. Sexual orientation is one's emotional and affectional attraction to another person, whereas sexual identity refers to individuals' personal definitions of their sexual desires and expressions (Cho, Laub, Wall, & Daley, 2004). Gender identity is self-expression of gender, which may or may not be consistent with biological sex or social expectations related to biological sex (Cho et al., 2004). We believe it is essential to include gender identity when addressing homonegativism because often homonegative discrimination and bullying is based on lack of adherence to "appropriate" gender presentation (Brackenridge, Rivers, Gough, & Llewellyn, 2006). Males and females not fitting traditional masculine and feminine characteristics, respectively, often are labeled as gay or lesbian (Krane, 2008). It is gender expression, not sexual orientation per se, that leads to biased, discriminatory, and possibly violent interactions (i.e., differently masculine males may be heterosexual, yet still be taunted with homonegative epithets). Individuals in an inclusive climate recognize and value the diversity of self-expression relative to gender and sexual identities For example, Carl Joseph Walker-Hoover, an 11-year-old football player from Springfield, Massachusetts who did not identify as gay, was the target of severe homonegative taunting. Because of his choice in clothing and commitment to schoolwork, he repeatedly was called "gay" by his classmates. The tragic outcome was that he hung himself in March 2009.

Consistent with our previous work (e.g., Krane, 2008; Krane & Kauer, 2007), social identity perspective grounds our approach for creating inclusive excellence. Our primary focus is the development of team social norms that encourage productive assimilation of all team members en route to team goals. Such a focus can benefit team dynamics as well as lead to improved team productivity and performance. A major premise of the social identity perspective is that when individuals adopt new social identities, such as becoming members of a new team, they will learn the expected values and behaviors of the group, and their behaviors will become consistent with these team norms (Turner, Hogg, Oakes, Reichter, & Wetherell, 1987). Such actions will increase the likelihood of gaining acceptance and approval from established team members and will lead to collective esteem or team pride.

Fitting in is a strong motivator for athletes, which will often lead to the adoption of team norms to gain acceptance (Waldron & Krane, 2005). Ideally, athletes embrace healthy and productive team norms. Creating inclusive excellence depends on athletes accepting norms supporting inclusion. The team is the superordinate identity for athletes; it is the overarching identity that joins together all team members. Embracing individual differences among team members can be a strong foundation for maintaining a sense of belonging to the team (Rink & Ellemers, 2007). This sense of belonging, then, will enhance motivation and commitment (Krane, 2008). Inclusive teams appreciate sexual and gender diversity, as well as, for example, multiplicity in race and religion, and consider them as team strengths. The rest of this chapter will focus on how to develop inclusive excellence, especially as it relates to creating inclusive team norms regarding diverse sexual and gender identities on sport teams.

Developing inclusive norms and positive team climates

In this section we provide a variety of suggestions that sport psychology practitioners can use with coaches and athletes. Our approach is both proactive (developing and maintaining inclusive climates) as well as reactive (what to do in response to a negative action or climate).

Being proactive: creating inclusive excellence

Josh, a sport psychology practitioner, is approached by a new coach. First, Coach Tuttle asks Josh to work with her soccer team. Then, she also confesses that on her previous team, serious cohesion problems arose due to homophobic taunting and "accusations" that some players were lesbian. She wants to avoid such problems with her current team, but she does not know how to go about telling athletes that she thinks it's okay if they are lesbian and that it is not okay to be prejudiced about any

415

personal characteristic. Coach Tuttle asks Josh what he can do to help and what advice he may have for her.

A practitioner initiating work with a team can establish the goal of developing inclusive excellence. Inclusion can be explained as acceptance of any differences among players: religion, race and ethnicity, body size/shape, skill level, age, and sexual and gender identities. The concerns voiced by the coach can be framed within the context of inclusive excellence. Making it clear that discrimination based on any social identity will impede achievement of team goals lays a foundation for guiding productive team behavior. For example, practitioners can begin a discussion about what makes a team successful (Barber & Krane, 2005). Athletes most likely will mention characteristics such as being cohesive, having good communication, trusting players, and being supportive. These concepts easily can be extended and applied to the development of inclusive excellence.

Typically, silence is the foundation for heterosexism and expectations of homonegative reactions from coaches and teammates, whereas creating safe spaces for dialogue about individual differences is a key aspect of inclusive excellence. As long as issues about sexual and gender identities remain unspoken, some LGBT athletes will assume the worst. Often silence is the outcome of not knowing how to address LGBT issues or being fearful of offending a player or teammate. Therefore, signs of acceptance are needed to create LGBT inclusive climates.

> This involves publicly declaring, through visible signs, that physical premises such as your offices, team rooms, locker rooms, classrooms, or the entire facility, are 'positive spaces.' Respect is mandatory in such a space and lesbian and gay persons and other minorities can expect to feel welcome and secure in a safe space. The simple act of putting up posters or stickers can be extremely empowering for the minorities who participate in your programs and facilities, and sends an important message that the area is a welcoming space to lesbian and gay people.
>
> (Corbett, 2006, p. 9)

Another component of inclusive excellence is providing overt support for diverse individuals. Many schools have "safe zone" programs that provide resources and training for faculty and staff. Coaches who have participated in this or similar programs can display a sign or sticker indicating their commitment to inclusiveness. Having books about diverse topics in sport on their bookshelves also sends a subtle yet important message (Barber & Krane, 2005). Examples include *Strong Women, Deep Closets: Lesbians and Homophobia in Sport* (Griffin, 1998), *In the Game: Gay Athletes and the Cult of Masculinity* (Anderson, 2005), *Jocks 2: True Stories of America's Gay Male Athletes* (Woog, 2002), or any of a number of recent biographies of gay male athletes (e.g., Amaechi, 2007; Tewksbury, 2006; Tuaolo, 2006).

As Hornsey and colleagues (Hornsey & Hogg, 2000; Hornsey & Jetten, 2004) suggested, embracing individual differences and establishing individual distinctions as part of the foundation supporting team success creates a strong framework for cohesion and productive team norms. One step toward such inclusion is showing interest in the activities of diverse team members. For example, during ordinary conversations coaches can mention the Gay Games, if they are in the news, or talk about openly LGBT athletes, such as mentioning out athletes competing in the Olympics (e.g., Australian diver Matthew Mitcham, U.S. soccer player Natasha Kai). Awareness of pronoun use and unintended heterosexist inferences is another strategy for normalizing diverse gender and sexual identities. For example, using the term partner instead of boyfriend allows lesbian athletes to become part of a conversation. Always saying he or she when talking about dating or about who's going with whom to special events includes all team members in the conversation, regardless of sexual orientation. Such language may open athletes' minds to the possibility that a teammate may have a same-sex partner or date. Importantly, such language also sets a tone of inclusion. Applying an inclusive excellence model begins to change the atmosphere of the team. As Rink and Ellemers (2007) found, as athletes recognize individual characteristics and identities, they acknowledge that they are meaningful contributions to team success.

Teachable moments

Avery was "out" to many friends in his high school, but the team climate on his club soccer team made him fearful to tell anyone connected to the team. Almost daily, in practices and in the locker room, Avery heard his teammates and coaches use words such as faggot, sissy, and homo as well as make other derogatory comments about gay males. Although he hated hiding his partner from his teammates, whom he considered close friends, he did not feel it would be safe to come out to them.

Often coaches and athletes do not recognize the power of their words or the implicit messages they send. Given the strong heteronormative climate of sport, it is likely many athletes assume that everyone on the team is heterosexual, and they do not consider how hurtful some words could be to someone. Unfortunately, in many sport environments, using homonegative language is standard (Curry, 1991). Having a commitment from coaches, as well as sport psychology practitioners, is integral to changing homophobic and heterosexist environments. Having the coach's 100% active backing of anti-homophobic language and environment would be ideal: however, this support might not always be the case. Practitioners may want to consult with coaches regarding their roles in creating environments that work toward inclusion with the intent on creating excellence. Within the framework of inclusive excellence, not only are athletes challenged to confront unproductive team norms, a structure and support for doing so are created.

For this example, we offer two suggestions for practitioners: (a) challenging the athletes to consider that not all male athletes are straight, and (b) changing the team norms surrounding their language. An important first step in making these changes is talking about the issue. Initiating such a conversation for the first time may feel uncomfortable or intimidating. Nevertheless, there are a number of ways to introduce the topic. If the practitioner is just beginning to work with a team, a statement noting her or his discomfort with the commonly used homonegative language could provide an opening. Alternatively, if the practitioner hears a comment directed at a particular player, that may provide an opportunity for dialogue. For example, during conditioning Pete starts complaining. John replies, "Quit being such a fag, suck it up and keep going." The coach or practitioner could say "That kind of commentary is not appropriate here." The comment is likely to get some laughter or strange looks, but the conversation can continue, "Maybe someone else here *is* gay or maybe someone has a gay brother, cousin, or friend … " In this instance, the dialogue may lead athletes to consider that they may actually know someone who is a gay male and that their language is insulting and hurtful toward that person. Obviously, a single brief exchange is not going to change common attitudes and language, but the door has been opened for further discussion and for reproaching subsequent use of homonegative language.

It is critical that team leaders model and encourage acceptable language as well as constructively point out when teammates use insensitive words (Krane, 2008). Practitioners and coaches can, and should, teach positive leadership. Such lessons can be imparted to select individuals (e.g., captains, oldest members of a team, individuals teammates already look up to). Athlete leaders should be taught to consider it their responsibility to encourage respect of all players. Providing athlete leaders with pre-determined statements in response to homonegative language will be especially helpful. Sport psychology practitioners often teach athletes to use thought stoppage to change unproductive thoughts, and an initial step is to determine acceptable replacement thoughts. In this situation, athlete leaders can brainstorm acceptable responses to teammates' cavalier homonegative commentary. To carry the thought stoppage analogy further, all team members can be instructed to say STOP anytime they say or hear a homonegative comment. In this way, teammates encourage each other to change unacceptable language. Concurrently, alternative phrases need to be introduced. Replacement terms such as doofus or dingbat may get a laugh, but at the same time, athletes will begin to recognize that homonegative language is as unacceptable as racist and other derogatory language. Although not easy, changing team norms is possible; challenging athletes to take responsibility for redirecting team norms is an important step in creating inclusive excellence.

> Lindsey is a member of a high profile university field hockey team. She has been in a relationship with another female athlete on campus for several years, but has never mentioned it to her teammates. One day in the locker room after practice, one of the captains comes up to Lindsey taunting her about her disgusting relationship with Carmen. Several other players join the banter, which turns ugly. The coach overhears just enough of the discussion to understand what is going on and decides that she needs to intervene and discuss the situation with the team. The coach spends the whole evening and next day agonizing about how to go about addressing this issue.

It seems that too often coaches are not willing to take a strong stand upon hearing about intra-team conflict regarding sexual orientation. Often coaches believe that it is not their place to discuss athletes' personal lives or that other professionals should address these issues (Krane & Barber, 2005). Nevertheless, coaches using an inclusive excellence framework accept responsibility for making sport a safe place for all athletes. Gaining coach "buy-in" may be challenging, yet sport psychology practitioners who explain the potential benefits of supporting inclusion and diversity may gain the support of coaches. For example, embracing the individuality and skills of all team members can lead to improved team communication, motivation, and performance (Krane, 2008).

Within an inclusive excellence approach, the sport psychology practitioner can assist the coach in addressing the team climate. In this example, the coach and sport psychology practitioner decide that the coach will meet with Lindsey before talking with the whole team. She will state her support for Lindsey, give her a "heads-up" that the issue will be talked about with the team that afternoon, and give her a choice of whether or not she wants to be at the meeting. Next, the coach and practitioner develop a plan for approaching the team as a whole.

The coach can express her disappointment with the discriminatory nature of the comments while at the same time taking an educational approach to explain why it is not productive among teammates striving toward the same goals. The discussion can be framed within the context of team goals. Players can be asked to reiterate their aspirations and to highlight how each athlete contributes to team excellence. Then, if not mentioned by the athletes, the sport psychology practitioner can explain how homonegativism among teammates will interfere with team goals – that is, impede inclusive excellence. Further, if needed, the coach or sport psychology practitioner can talk about how sport is changing; that although at one time it was acceptable to exclude players because of skin color or use racially derogatory language, no longer do we support such practices in sport. Today, there is recognition that some athletes are LGBT. Just as racially charged language is insensitive, so too is negative commentary referring to sexual orientation or gender identity. Throughout the conversation, the focus on inclusive excellence will point athletes toward productive behaviors and may initiate attitude changes among team members.

Dialogue about gender identity

Tracy is a member of a high-level track club. Consistently, she is one of the top sprinters on the team, and her current goal is to compete at national level. For years, Tracy has grappled with her gender identity. She has never felt comfortable "being female." Although she has never self-identified as lesbian, she often has been the target of homonegative actions by her peers. After talking with her parents, who were exceptionally understanding and supportive, she has begun identifying as male. At this time, Tracy has not taken any hormones, but has changed her appearance (e.g., shorter hair, baggier clothes) and has asked that male pronouns be used.

An aspect of inclusive excellence is appreciation for diversity within gender identity. The team sport psychology practitioner can work with Tracy to help him feel comfortable discussing these issues with teammates. Alternatively, the sport psychology consultant can act as a resource and assist team members in understanding Tracy's gender identity. Very likely, a combination of these approaches will be helpful. Perhaps framing the issue as relating to team dynamics and inclusive excellence will help team members understand the significance of supporting their teammates. Helping teammates focus on inclusive excellence can reinforce a climate in which Tracy can focus on performance, rather than manage criticism and bigotry.

The sport psychologist working with the team can gather resources, such as information from the Women's Sport Foundation (2008a) – in particular the *It Takes a Team* educational materials (e.g., Women's Sport Foundation, 2008b). If the sport psychology practitioner is comfortable with the content, she or he can lead a discussion about transathletes and assist in dispelling myths or misinformation. The term "transgender" encompasses an array of different forms of gender identity. In general, transgender refers to gender identities that do not coincide with the gender assigned at birth (Plante, 2006). Some transgender people, such as Tracy, are not comfortable with the gender assigned to them, yet also do not desire to undergo physical changes to their bodies. Transsexuals are people who use hormone therapy and who have had sex reassignment surgery (Cho *et al.*, 2004). In Tracy's situation, he is not undergoing any hormonal or anatomical changes to his physiology or anatomy, but he is making changes in gender expression. Because he has not undergone hormone therapy, Tracy is only changing his outward appearance. His body is no different than it was previously and there are no performance advantages. At the present time, Tracy has no desire to compete on a male team and wishes to remain a part of the female team with which he has established cohesion, and dedicated many hours. Through team discussions, the practitioner can reinforce team commitment to inclusive excellence. By supporting Tracy, the team will be reinforcing norms of inclusion as well as continuing progress toward team performance goals. If the sport psychology practitioner does not feel comfortable leading this discussion, she or he can bring in individuals from a university LGBT resource center, women's center, or multicultural center to help.

Summary

In this chapter, we challenge sport psychologists to embrace inclusive excellence and work toward eliminating heterosexism and homonegativism in sport. Because language creates a structure for understanding the norms in sport (Sykes, 1998), a prominent focus in this chapter has been to challenge and change heteronormative language on sport teams. Employing the strategies and proactive measures provided in this chapter can work toward this end. Heterosexism and homonegativism adversely affect all participants in sport, regardless of sexual orientation or gender identity. These institutionalized and systematic behaviors and norms create unproductive (and often hostile) team climates and further embed heteronormativity in sport. Applying an inclusive excellence model to sport provides concrete examples for how to approach these issues.

Inclusive excellence provides a framework for sport psychology consultants to address issues of diversity within sport teams. Combined with our social identity perspective, developing productive team norms while viewing individual difference as a team strength can create a sense of belonging for all team members. Thus, all members, regardless of gender and sexual expression, can feel part of a larger structure that values and supports them. Within this context, sport then provides social and psychological benefits to all of its participants, even if they do not fit into dominant gender or sexual ideologies.

Sport psychology practitioners who embrace inclusive excellence will help change the existing culture of sport where heterosexism is the norm. Although changing established team climates will be challenging, we believe that sport psychology practitioners can and should be at the forefront of such a movement. It is our hope that this chapter will allow existing and future professionals to rise to that challenge and work toward a type of excellence that values each team member and embraces everyone who shares a common love – sport! See Box 43.1 for a summary of strategies for developing inclusive excellence.

Box 43.1

Strategies for developing inclusive excellence

- Establish a superordinate identity as "team member" that embraces all athletes.
- Recognize diversity in gender identity, sexual orientation, race, religion, and other social identities as a team strength.
- Use inclusive language and avoid assumptions that everyone on the team is heterosexual or gender normative.
- Encourage open conversation about individual differences.
- Openly display signs of support for diverse sexual and gender identities (e.g., with "safe zone" stickers, LGBT-focused books).

■ Educate team members about the diversity among gender and sexual identities.
■ Refer to available resources (e.g., campus organizations, websites such as www. ittakesateam.org) as necessary.
■ Encourage athletes, especially team leaders, to model productive inclusive behaviors and challenge unproductive team norms.

References

Amaechi, J. (2007). *Man in the middle*. New York: ESPN.

Anderson, E. (2005). *In the game: Gay athletes and the cult of masculinity*. Albany, NY: State University of New York Press.

Barber, H., & Krane, V. (2005). The elephant in the locker room: Opening the dialogue about sexual orientation on women's sport teams. In M. B. Andersen (Ed.), *Sport psychology in practice* (pp. 259–279). Champaign, IL: Human Kinetics.

Brackenridge, C. H., Rivers, I., Gough, B., & Llewellyn, K. (2006) Driving down participation: Homophobic bullying as a deterrent to doing sport. In C. Aitchison (Ed.), *Sport and gender identities: Masculinities, femininities and sexualities* (pp. 122–139). London: Routledge.

Cho, S., Laub, C., Wall, S. S. M., & Daley, C. (2004). *Beyond the binary: A tool kit for gender identity activism in schools*. Retrieved from http://www.transgenderlawcenter.org/pdf/beyond_the_binary.pdf

Corbett, R. (2006). *A position paper on homophobia in sport: Seeing the invisible, speaking about the unspoken*. Retrieved from http://www.caaws.ca/pdfs/CAAWS_Homophobia_Discussion_Paper_E.pdf.

Curry, T. J. (1991). Fraternal bonding in the locker room: A profeminist analysis of talk about competition and women. *Sociology of Sport Journal, 16*, 119–135.

Griffin, P. (1998). *Strong women, deep closets: Lesbians and homophobia in women's sport*. Champaign, IL: Human Kinetics.

Hall, D. E. (2003). *Queer theories*. New York: Palgrave.

Hornsey, M. J., & Hogg, M. A. (2000). Assimilation and diversity: An integrative model of subgroup relations. *Personality and Social Psychology Review, 4*, 143–156.

Hornsey, M. J., & Jetten, J. (2004). The individual within the group: Balancing the need to belong with the need to be different. *Personality and Social Psychology Review, 8*, 248–264.

Kauer, K., & Krane, V. (2006). "Scary dykes and feminine queens": Stereotypes and female athletes. *Women in Sport and Physical Activity Journal, 15*(1), 43–56.

Krane, V. (2008). Gendered social dynamics in sport. In M. Beauchamp & M. Eys (Eds.), *Group dynamics advances in sport and exercise psychology: Contemporary themes* (pp. 159–176). New York: Routledge.

Krane, V., & Barber, H. (2005). Identity tensions in lesbian college coaches. *Research Quarterly for Exercise and Sport, 76*, 67–81.

Krane, V., & Kauer, K.J. (2007). Out on the ball fields: Lesbians in sport. In E. Peele & V. Clark (Eds.), *Out in psychology: Lesbian, gay, bisexual and transgender perspectives* (pp. 273–290). West Sussex, England: Wiley.

Messner, M. A. (2002). *Taking the field: Women, men, and sports*. Minneapolis: University of Minnesota Press.

Plante, R. F. (2006). *Sexualities in context: A social perspective*. Boulder, CO: Westview.

Rink, F., & Ellemers, N. (2007). Diversity as a basis for shared organizational identity: The norm congruity principle. *British Journal of Management, 18* (Suppl.), S17–S27.

Sykes, H. (1998). Turning the closets inside/out: Towards a queer-feminist theory in women's physical education. *Sociology of Sport Journal, 15*, 154–173.

Tewksbury, M. (2006). *Inside out: Straight talk from a gay jock.* Hoboken, NJ: Wiley.

Tuaolo, E. (2006). *Alone in the trenches: My life as a gay man in the NFL.* Naperville, IL: Source books.

Turner, J. C., Hogg, M. A., Oakes, P. J., Reichter, S. D., & Wetherell, M. S. (1987). *Rediscovering the social group: A self-categorization theory.* Oxford, England: Basil Blackwell.

Waldron, J. J., & Krane, V. (2005). Whatever it takes: Health compromising behaviors in female athletes. *Quest, 57,* 315–329.

Williams, D. A., Berger, J. B., & McClendon, S. A. (2005). *Toward a model of inclusive excellence and change in postsecondary institutions.* Retrieved on the Association of American Colleges and Universities Web site: http://www.aacu.org/inclusive_excellence/documents/Williams_et_al.pdf

Women's Sport Foundation (2008a). East Meadow, NY. Retrieved from http://www.womenssports-foundation.org

Women's Sport Foundation (2008b). *It takes a team! Video evaluation executive summary 2005–2006.* East Meadow, NY: Women's Sport Foundation. Retrieved from http://www.womenssportsfounda-tion.org/Content/Articles/Issues/Homophobia/I/It-Takes-A-Team-Video-Evaluation-Executive-Summary-2005-2006.aspx

Woog, D. (2002). *Jocks 2: True stories of America's gay male athletes.* New York: Alyson.

44

Psychological services for rural athletes

Jack C. Watson II and Damien Clement

Professionals in the field of psychology have been cognizant of the needs of psychologists with regard to their work with rural populations since the 1980s (Murray & Keller, 1991), as evidenced by increased writing and the existence of journals dedicated to this topic (e.g., the *Australian Journal of Rural Health*, and the *Journal of Rural Community Psychology*). Sport and exercise psychologists, however, have been slow to address this area of concern. The only references we could identify in current sport and exercise psychology literature that pertained to working with rural populations were specific to populations in Australia. Because of the paucity of research and writing in this area, we aim in this chapter to present sport psychology consultants with useful information related to working in rural settings and with rural athletes, using material gathered primarily from the parent field of psychology.

For the purposes of this chapter, we define the term "rural" using a multidimensional perspective, as an area that satisfies the rural triad (i.e., ecological, occupational, and socio-cultural components). That is, a rural area is one in which the population is relatively sparse and isolated from metropolitan areas, where occupations within the area are primarily based around agriculture or extracting industries, and values and ideals such as self-reliance and ethnocentricity form the basis of community interactions. Furthermore, because of financial factors associated with the industries that support these populations, individuals who reside in these areas have an increased likelihood of being economically disadvantaged (Murray & Keller, 1991).

Cultural considerations for working with rural athletes

Even though residents of rural communities tend to be more heterogeneous than homogeneous, many common traits tend to exist within these groups. Rural residents often attempt to take care of their own problems or rely on family and close friends, only seeking help when the aforementioned options have been exhausted. This self-reliance may lead rural residents to believe that their problems should stay "in-house" and not be discussed with strangers or outsiders. Moreover, for many rural individuals, seeking help can be analogous to showing personal weakness, a trait that is not consistent with many rural cultures. Thus, sport psychology professionals may only be approached by rural athletes when a problem has become detrimental to self-esteem, functioning, or athletic performance.

Rural residents tend to be distrusting of outsiders, and may be resistant to setting up appointments with healthcare providers, especially those who are from outside their local areas. When rural athletes first meet with sport psychology professionals, they may not be forthcoming about the gravity of the current situation and their reasons for scheduling the appointment. Furthermore, the "goldfish bowl phenomenon when everyone expects to know everyone else's business" (Slama, 2004, p. 10) also plays a role in perpetuating distrust of outsiders because there is a common perception among rural residents that the details of such sessions will become shared knowledge within the community. These issues can contribute to a pervasive stigma with regard to seeking help within rural communities. The belief that privacy and confidentiality will be lacking, coupled with the associated stigma toward seeking help, often leads to rural individuals being less likely to request services.

Another characteristic to consider when working with rural populations is the possibility that they may possess stigmatic negative attitudes toward mental health professions. Residents in rural areas have been known to avoid seeking mental health services because they perceive these services to be unsuitable avenues for assistance. When rural residents seek help for mental health issues, they often request such assistance from general practitioners (Judd et al., 2006) or clergy, stemming from their established relationships with these practitioners. Consultants should not only be aware of the prevailing help-seeking stigma present in rural communities, but also the associated beliefs and behavioral tendencies (e.g., resistance against seeking help, limited beliefs in the efficacy of services, inclinations to seek out general practitioners).

Psychology professionals who practise in rural areas should also be aware of the time and work demands often present in these communities. Rural residents can sometimes ill afford to miss time away from work to bring their children to regularly scheduled sessions or attend sessions themselves (Bischoff, Hollist, Smith, & Flack, 2004). For this reason, rural residents may be less consistent than other clients in attending appointments, and may be late or leave sessions early. Additionally, the financial burden associated with sport psychology sessions may sometimes necessitate clients being creative with regard to payment (e.g., installment plans, bartering).

Rural athletes may have limited knowledge and exposure to psychology and psychologists, and may tend to first seek the services of professionals in other fields. Therefore, a central task for the rural practitioner is to explain what sport psychology is to individuals and influential community members (e.g., coaches, pastors, physicians), and to address any associated myths, stereotypes, and stigmas. Some of the most popular myths and misconceptions that should be addressed from the onset are: only problem athletes seek help, the consultations are not confidential, only crazy people see psychologists, and, only weak people ask for help. If sport psychology consultants are proactive in addressing these concerns early, the likelihood of receiving referrals, and of individuals entering into and continuing with sessions, will be increased. Research has shown that the traditional urban model of delivery is not often a good fit in rural communities (Helbok, 2003), and it would be wise for psychologists to tailor their approaches to meet the needs of rural athletes.

Practising sport psychology in rural settings

Although the overall process for sport psychology consultations with rural athletes may not vary considerably from the processes used with urban athletes, there are issues that should be considered throughout traditional face-to-face and teletherapy sessions with rural athletes. These issues generally result from the social, economic, and cultural experiences of rural athletes. Although many of the qualities of rural individuals discussed in the previous section are not consistent across rural athletes, consultants should be aware of this information and know some basic strategies to help promote successful consultations. Practitioners should use this information as a starting point to improve communication. This section focuses on suggestions for consultants to consider when working with rural athletes either face-to-face or via some form of teletherapy.

Suggestions for in-person services with rural athletes

Face-to-face encounters with rural clients often closely resemble traditional service delivery. Consultants should be aware of, and take steps to use, information about common issues with rural clients. These concerns include: acknowledging unique qualities, addressing confidentiality and trust concerns, exploring knowledge/expectations about sport psychology, taking a culturally sensitive approach, and developing working alliances within the community.

It is important that the individual's decision to seek help be recognized and validated prior to beginning the consultation. Such recognition can be accomplished by thanking the client for coming in and acknowledging any difficulty/apprehension associated with beginning the consultation. Rural psychologists may then encourage conversations about issues such as weather, local news, and school events prior to commencing the session as a way to help put the client at ease, but also create a sense of shared experiences between the consultant and client that can be used as a base upon which a relationship can be built. Once some rapport has been established, we recommend that consultants discuss confidentiality. Affirming confidentiality and discussing issues such as how to greet/acknowledge each other in public if paths should cross in the community can help the therapist avoid potential problems (e.g., client public discomfort) in the future.

Another way to help alleviate some client concerns is by asking clients questions that they will likely feel comfortable answering, such as "How did you get involved in sport?" The initial session is a great time to help clients feel knowledgeable about the discussion topics, and can also provide an opportunity for clients to speak about concerns they may have about talking to a sport psychologist. Many rural clients may have little understanding of sport psychology and may only expect what they have seen on television. Such conversations often produce a laugh and help with the rapport-building process.

Sport psychology consultants need to establish working alliances with their clients from the outset. Rural consultants need to let clients know that they empathize with their situations, in addition to having their best interests at heart. Furthermore, this alliance is presented as a collaborative endeavor whereby both the psychologist and client establish goals that they will work toward achieving. Moreover, establishing a working alliance early in the consultation process has been shown to be a critical variable in predicting treatment outcomes (Hovarth & Greenberg, 1994; see also Chapter 1). This working alliance may be even more important when working within rural populations, because rural residents are often distrusting of outsiders and helping professionals.

425

Practitioners need to make every effort to incorporate aspects of multicultural counseling into their consultations with rural athletes. They should actively strive to become aware of the biases (e.g., by identifying personal experiences with this population and identifying how these experiences have influenced perceptions), values, and assumptions they may have with regard to rural populations because the possibility exists that the aforementioned experiences may interfere with their abilities to work effectively with rural clients. Sport psychology practitioners should strive to be nonjudgmental about the views expressed by rural clients because any inadvertently insensitive remarks could negatively affect the therapeutic relationship. Furthermore, practitioners should acknowledge if they were not raised in a rural area, and more important, should attempt to acquire as much practical information as they can about their rural clients (e.g., background, daily living experiences).

Sport psychologists should be cautious about routinely applying standard psychological interventions with rural populations. Rural areas are often inhabited by economically disadvantaged individuals who do not take well to "talk therapy," because self-disclosure is typically contrary to traditional values. Finally, sport psychology professionals who intend to work with rural populations should make every effort to obtain coursework and training to help prepare themselves to work effectively with this population. Beneficial courses and experiences include multicultural counseling, cultural diversity, issues in rural mental health, and other internship or practical placements with rural populations (for more information please see Table 44.1).

Suggestions for teletherapy with rural athletes

Sport psychology is a relatively new and specialized field, but the demand for practitioners is growing. At present, there is not a large enough market in most rural communities to financially support a sport psychology practitioner. Therefore, if consultants want to make a living working with athletes in rural settings, they should also be trained as general counselors or psychologists, and be willing to work with non-athletes. Furthermore, there are not enough competently trained sport psychology professionals to directly serve many rural communities. If rural athletes want to have access to a sport therapist, they usually either drive to an urban area or consult via teletherapy (e.g., telephone, email, internet messaging, web camera).

Table 44.1 Additional training resources for working with rural athletes.

Australian Psychological Society: http://www.psychology.org.au/publications/inpsych/rural_remote/

American Psychological Association (2002). *Guidelines on multicultural education, training, research, practice, and organizational change for psychologists.* Available from http://www.apa.org/practice/guidelines/multicultural.pdf

Hargrove, D. S. (1991). Training PhD psychologists for rural service: A report from Nebraska. *Community Mental Health Journal 2*, 293–298.

Sears, S., Jr., Evans, G., & Perry, N. (1998). Innovations in training: The University of Florida rural psychology training program. *Professional Psychology: Research and Practice, 29*, 504–507.

Stamm, B. H. (Ed.). (2003). *Rural behavioral health care: An interdisciplinary guide.* Washington, DC: American Psychological Association.

Stuart, R. (2004). Twelve practical suggestions for achieving multicultural competence. *Professional Psychology: Research and Practice, 35*, 3–9.

Sue, D. W., & Sue, D. (2003). *Counseling the culturally diverse: Theory and practice.* New York: Wiley.

The process of working with clients from a distance is one that needs to be considered closely before initiating consultations. Beyond the many ethical and legal issues affecting such services, there are several other factors that rural psychologists should take into consideration to enhance teletherapy interactions. These factors include suggestions for initial meetings, assessing cultural issues, acquiring local knowledge, discussing possible communication problems and solutions, disclosure of common identifying information, and confidentiality concerns. It is also important to note that rural athletes may not have access to computers given the possible economic hardships associated with living in a rural area.

Strategies for successful internet consulting

When starting professional relationships with rural athletes, we encourage practitioners to schedule the first one or two sessions in person or over a web camera. Such meetings will facilitate the intake process by allowing the consultant to use both verbal and nonverbal information. Because of the importance of nonverbal communication in client conceptualization, it is important for the consultant to have as much visual information available as possible. During these initial sessions, the client and therapist should work on developing rapport, learn about communication styles, and discuss future communication patterns and techniques for dealing with potential communication problems. These initial sessions provide an opportunity to ask important cultural questions and to formulate a basic treatment plan. Future sessions in some situations can be carried out using a web camera or telephone with periodic in-person meetings, but may also take place over protected e-mail or the internet (live "messenger" services).

Because clients living in a different area may be affected by community issues that may not be affecting the practitioner, it is important for the consultant to stay current on the community issues occurring in the client's town. For example, drought, flood, fire, pest infestation, or other regional issues may be affecting the client. To stay on top of such local developments, professionals may try to periodically read the client's hometown paper on the internet. When possible, consultants may also try to visit the client's town to learn more about the culture and other background issues.

Beyond learning about a client's culture and hometown, when therapists work via the internet or e-mail, we also encourage them to discuss with clients possible strategies for clarifying communication. For example, the use of emoticons (i.e., text-based characters inserted into communications to help describe the emotion that one is currently feeling) can help both parties express emotion in text. Further, because of the lack of nonverbal communication and higher likelihood of communication mistakes caused by typing, grammar, or reading errors, both parties must understand how to clarify discrepancies. Such strategies include follow-up phone calls or web camera sessions, and encouraging and empowering clients to ask questions.

On a similar note, communication mistakes via internet consultations are common for individuals who do not type well, have writing difficulties, or dislike typing. Consultants will note that such clients are brief with their responses and often do not do a good job of expressing themselves. These situations can lead to multiple communication problems. To avoid such difficulties, therapists should assess potential problems before entering into an internet consultation, and consider not using these modalities when working with such people.

In a traditional session, when clients come in to meet with a sport psychologist, they learn information about the practitioner that they might not necessarily learn during internet consulting. This information includes approximate age, appearance, race/ethnicity, office memorabilia, and speech patterns. Although many of these issues are not absolutely pertinent to the sessions, this information affects rapport building. Sport psychology consultants should provide similar information to clients either through a brief description on a webpage, or keeping an up-to-date picture of oneself on the webpage.

Ethics and the rural community

Consultants should be aware of the potential ethical dilemmas they may face when working in rural settings. Some of these ethical dilemmas and potential solutions are directed at consultants who live and work in rural communities, whereas others are for practitioners who may live in an urban setting, but see clients from rural communities. The primary issues to consider include multiple role relationships, confidentiality, competency/scope of practice, limited supervision and consultation, visibility in the community, and other issues related to the use of the internet in consultations (see Helbok, 2003, for an overview).

Ethical issues for those living and working in a rural community

One of the benefits of living in a small town is the depth of the relationships that an individual can develop with friends and neighbors. Because of the often limited resources available in rural areas, individuals living in the region often take on multiple roles for the benefit of the community (e.g., youth coach, Sunday school teacher, postmaster). Such roles are also likely to occur for sport psychology professionals living in rural communities. Although this immersion in a small community may be appealing to many, it can cause problems for consultants who are concerned about developing multiple-role relationships with clients or potential clients. Taking on such roles, however, may help sport psychology consultants extend their client base and referral networks, as well as develop trust, respect, and credibility in the community. Although the ethical concern related to multiple-role relationships is important to consider, this is not to say that consultants should not take on other roles within a small community, but more that they should be careful about the relationships that they develop. Multiple-role relationships, especially in rural communities are not usually unethical. Such relationships become unethical when there is a conflict of interest between the two roles or when a power differential exists between practitioner and client that increases the likelihood for harm or exploitation of the client, affects the client's ability to make decisions, or impairs the practitioner's objectivity, competence, or effectiveness.

As mentioned previously, confidentiality is a big concern in rural communities. In a small community everyone tends to know everyone else, and news travels quickly. When clients come in to see a sport psychologist, they may be identified by support staff, clients' cars may be identified outside the office, or others may spot awkward interactions between consultants and clients in the supermarket. Any of these seemingly innocuous issues can affect the client, the practitioner, and the working relationship.

Working within one's area of competency is an expectation of all practitioners, but this principle may be challenged when working in rural regions. In small communities, it is unlikely that there will be many options for receiving psychological services. Therefore, consultants may be approached for any number of sport- and non-sport related issues. Some of these issues may fit neatly within one's competency areas, but other issues may not.

With few (or no) other practitioners around for referrals, difficult decisions about service provision need to be made. In an urban setting, sport psychologists are much more likely to have colleagues to whom they refer clients when presenting concerns are outside of their competencies. In rural communities, practitioners may be faced with difficult decisions about providing services outside of their competency areas or leaving potential clients with no options for services. Further confusing the situation is that there are not likely to be (m)any professionals around from whom to receive supervision or to consult to help consultants develop new areas of competence. Although telesupervision may be an option to help one remain ethical in such situations, finding a supervisor who is willing to work with you from a distance can be challenging. Rural practitioners often find themselves in positions without much support. Not only is practising near or outside of one's competency dangerous, but it is also taxing, and can lead to burnout.

Ethical issues for teletherapy with rural athletes

Although practitioners who live and work in a rural setting should strongly consider the ethical issues mentioned above, it is unlikely that many professionals will actually set up shop in a rural community with a limited client base. Sport psychology consultants are more likely to live and work in larger cities and either travel to rural communities to see clients, or consult with rural athletes via teletherapy (i.e., phone, email, internet messaging, web camera). The ethical issues related to teletherapy are important to consider, but due to space considerations in this chapter, only a few of these issues will be discussed: confidentiality, credentialing, competency, relationship development, and treatment efficacy. Other issues such as scheduling, response time, and rates of payment will not be discussed (see Watson, Tenenbaum, Lidor, & Alfermann, 2001, for a more complete description of these and other issues).

It is not earth-shattering news that e-mail is not confidential. Computer servers are frequently hacked, and anyone who has been to internet cafés to send e-mails may have had their information hacked by someone who has gained access via that public server. Therefore, conducting therapy via the internet should not be a decision made lightly. It would be a good idea to use encryption software, and to have a visible notice on all e-mails and even a waiver for clients to sign indicating that internet communications are not confidential but that reasonable efforts will be made to maintain confidentiality. Such reasonable efforts probably entail having developed a competency for understanding internet-related technologies and how to consult effectively via this medium. Because rural clients often have strong concerns about confidentiality, professionals may want to make sure that clients clearly understand the confidentiality issues related to this medium of consultation. Such discussions may take place effectively in person, over the phone, or using a web camera.

Credentialing is another issue to consider when working with clients from a distance. It is important to realize that if consultants are communicating with clients over state, provincial, or country lines, they may not be credentialed to provide services in this new jurisdiction. In such cases, professionals may be doing something that is unethical and illegal. We encourage practitioners to check the laws that govern the areas where clients are located. In many cases, licensed practitioners may apply for short-term privileges to work in different jurisdictions.

Sport psychology consultants should develop competencies for working with all mediums they choose for consultations. Some of the major issues associated with teletherapy modalities of service delivery involve the ability to develop effective rapport and to have a treatment approach that is based upon evidence of success. Consultants should be extra conscious about developing rapport through honest and accurate communications, given that the majority of all face-to-face communication is nonverbal (Poyatos, 1992). Therefore, when using non-face-to-face modalities such as the internet for consulting, practitioners will have significantly less information available to them. Limited information has the potential to affect information gathering, diagnosis, and treatment. Even when using web cameras for consulting, a camera provides a two-dimensional image of a limited area. Extra time must be taken to get to know the client, ask specific questions about feelings and behaviors, and develop honest and open two-way communication.

Because of these above-mentioned communication concerns, and limitations with regard to building rapport, it is important that professionals think carefully about clients' presenting issues before consulting with them via teletherapy. For example, adopting an educational approach to help a client learn how to concentrate may be an appropriate intervention to deliver over the internet, but it is probably not a good idea to deal with complex eating or mood disorder issues via the internet. Sport psychology consultants must choose wisely the issues with which they are willing to work from a distance, because some issues are more easily dealt with in situations with restricted communication and less access to nonverbal communication. Practitioners should also make sure that they are aware of efficacious techniques for dealing with communication concerns using their chosen medium of consultation.

Conclusion

Although rural athletes are probably more similar to urban athletes than they are different, it would be a mistake for sport psychologists to treat them the same. Rural athletes are exposed to cultural, economic, and social systems within their communities that are often different from those to which urban athletes are exposed. Therefore, it is important for consultants to be knowledgeable about these potential differences and have strategies for dealing with them if they are to work successfully with rural athletes. In this chapter, we have outlined many potential differences for practitioners to consider in their work with rural athletes. Knowledge of these potential differences should be used as a basis for inquiry to help sport psychology consultants understand their clients, their presenting concerns, and their potential treatment options. One should not assume that treatment approaches that have been validated with urban athletes will necessarily be effective with rural athletes. Although these approaches may be effective with rural athletes, there is the possibility that the cultural, economic, and social differences in their communities call for different tactics (see Box 44.1).

We have identified several ethical issues of which practitioners should be aware when working with rural athletes either in person or via teletherapy. Even though the same ethical principles and standards apply for working with rural and urban clients, sport psychology professionals who work with rural athletes are more likely to be faced with certain ethical dilemmas. These dilemmas include, but are not limited to, problems with multiple roles, confidentiality, client concerns about confidentiality and privacy of internet communications, competency, credentialing, and appropriateness of working with some issues. Although there are many other ethical issues of which therapists should be aware, those mentioned here tend to be the major concerns faced when consulting with rural athletes.

Box 44.1

Take home messages about working with rural athletes

- Be aware of common rural characteristics such as self-reliance, distrust of outsiders, and stigmatic attitudes toward seeking help when working with rural clients.
- Be conscious of biases and assumptions toward rural clients. These biases could affect the therapeutic relationship.
- Be mindful of the unique social, economic, and cultural experiences of rural athletes.
- If planning to work with rural clients, attempt to obtain as much training (coursework, practical, or internship experiences) in preparation for working with this population.
- Teletherapy may be one option that enables work with rural clients when face-to-face sessions are not feasible.
- When using teletherapy communication, ground rules must be established to avoid miscommunications and to deal effectively with communication mishaps.
- Be especially cautious to adhere to appropriate ethical codes when working with rural clients, especially when using teletherapy.

References

Bischoff, R., Hollist, C. S., Smith, C. W., & Flack, P. (2004). Addressing the mental health needs of the rural underserved: Findings from a multiple case study of behavioral telehealth project. *Contemporary Family Therapy*, 26, 179–198.

Helbok, C. M. (2003). The practice of psychology in rural communities: Potential ethical dilemmas. *Ethics & Behavior*, 13, 367–384.

Hovarth, A. O., & Greenberg, L. S. (1994). *The working alliance: Theory, research, and practice*. New York: Wiley.

Judd, F., Jackson, H., Komiti, A., Murray, G., Fraser, C., Grieve, A., & Gomez, R. (2006). Help-seeking by rural residents for mental health problems: The importance of agrarian values. *Australian and New Zealand Journal of Psychiatry*, 40, 769–776.

Murray, J. D., & Keller, P. A. (1991). Psychology and rural America. *American Psychologist*, 46, 220–231.

Poyatos, F. (1992). *Advances in non-verbal communication: Sociocultural, clinical, esthetic, and literacy perspectives*. Philadelphia: Benjamins.

Slama, K. M. (2004). Toward rural competence. *Minnesota Psychologist*, 53, 6–13.

Watson, J., Tenenbaum, G., Lidor, R., & Alfermann, D. (2001). Ethical uses of the internet in sport psychology: A position stand. *International Journal of Sport Psychology*, 32, 207–222.

45

Athletes with physical disabilities

Jeffrey J. Martin

Disability sport, particularly at the highest levels (e.g., Paralympics), is becoming increasingly competitive. Athletes with disabilities, like able-bodied athletes, may benefit from working with sport psychologists by learning mental and life skills applicable to sport and everyday life. Researchers have determined that many athletes with disabilities already use psychological skills (Perreault & Vallerand, 2007), desire to learn more about psychological skills (Kirkby, 1995), and have positive attitudes toward sport psychologists (Page, Martin, & Wayda, 2001). Reviewing the role of psychological skills for performance-enhancement purposes, however, is just one goal of the current chapter. Consistent with the major focus of this text, the athlete's quality of life, health, and happiness are also central considerations that should also be a focus of a sport psychologist's work. Numerous researchers examining the sport experiences of youth and adults have indicated that sport can provide multiple benefits to individuals with disabilities (Hutzler & Bar-Eli, 1993). The ability to reduce loneliness by developing friendships with other athletes with disabilities is a particularly important quality of life benefit of sport participation.

Building on the personal development model advocated by Danish and Hale (1981) and elaborated on by Vealey (1988), Martin (1999; 2005) adapted it to disability sport. Martin urged sport psychologists to employ it with their clients to enhance their quality of life and to help them achieve in their sports. Specifically, Martin indicated that sport psychologists should help athletes with disabilities develop the three foundation skills of self-esteem, self-determination, and self-awareness. Given that many individuals with disabilities report feelings of powerlessness, exploring issues related to self-determination may be particularly relevant.

The purpose of this chapter is to explore significant issues for practitioners who choose to work with athletes with physical disabilities. In particular, my goal is to help sport psychologists understand both the disability world and the world of disability sport, and the challenges athletes face in these overlapping worlds. Although practitioners are sure to learn much from reflective hands-on experiences, my hope is that I can provide a modest head-start to their efforts by concisely illustrating some unique considerations present when working with athletes with physical disabilities.

The athlete, the person

It is important to view athletes with disabilities as people first and to focus on their lives and athletic pursuits in a realistic manner. One of the difficulties individuals with disabilities often face from others in society is being equated with their disabilities, stigmatized, and having other qualities (e.g., athletic skill, intelligence, social competence, sense of humor) minimized, or go unacknowledged. In contrast to the above negative view is the "supercrip" perspective that is often framed as a positive portrayal of athletes with disabilities. The supercrip image suggests that people with disabilities are heroes by engaging in regular activities such as going to school and participating in sport. The supercrip image also implies that accomplishing significant goals (e.g., wheeling a marathon) is a sign of overcoming the disability.

Disability scholars tend to see the supercrip image as a patronizing consumer-driven media image. Furthermore, the problem with the supercrip stereotype is that most people with disabilities do not view themselves as heroes or their achievements as overcoming their disabilities. Although some athletes with disabilities view the supercrip model as inspiring, others see the heroic label as inaccurate because they view their sport successes as normal athletic achievements (Hardin & Hardin, 2004). Elite wheelchair athletes routinely became frustrated when labeled as courageous and strong for successfully managing simple activities of daily living. For example, one athlete in a recent study (Hardin & Hardin, 2004) reported that he had been praised countless times for doing various things that he considered mundane (i.e., going to a nightclub). From the athlete's perspective, there was nothing heroic about accomplishing such tasks. A clear source of the athlete's frustration was the perception that being viewed as brave for being disabled *and* an athlete was patronizing.

Berger (2008) suggested that the supercrip stereotype can simultaneously be both a disempowering and empowering model for individuals with disabilities. Hardin and Hardin (2004) offered a similar perspective when they noted that one athlete in their study felt that people viewed him as both helpless and a hero. Most elite-level athletes with disabilities do not want to be reduced to a "supercrip" stereotype and would rather be recognized for their legitimate athletic accomplishments (Berger). Sport psychologists working with athletes with disabilities should avoid inadvertently replicating common societal perspectives that serve to unrealistically minimize or glorify athletes with disabilities. In other words, sport psychologists should treat athletes with disabilities as people who play sport and happen to have disabilities, and focus on their abilities, not their disabilities.

The disability

Approximately 15% of athletes have lived with their disabilities since birth (i.e., they have congenital disabilities) and have not experienced life without a disability. Most athletes with disabilities (i.e., 85%), however, have acquired disabilities, which means they have endured a progressive disease over time or had a serious traumatic injury. One major ramification of experiencing a sudden and permanent injury is a serious disruption of psychological equilibrium.

Tremendous, and usually psychologically and physically painful, adjustment demands land on individuals when they go from running and playing catch one day to, in cases of people with quadriplegia, being unable to move their arms or legs the very next day. Indicating the severity of how some athletes feel, one athlete stated, "Now I am nothing. Life moves on, without me. That is how it is. How it will always be. I just survive. No ambitions. Nothing … Sometimes I don't think I can go on." (Smith & Sparkes, 2005, p. 1101).

Although many people eventually adjust to an acquired disability, this quote illustrates how devastating a disability can be. Not only is a loss of function an obvious and far-reaching ramification of acquiring a disability, but it often becomes the most dominating feature of the disability experience. In brief, a primary characteristic of experiencing a significant and permanent injury is a loss of function, and people often become defined as their disabilities in their own eyes and in the eyes of others.

A second major area of disruption is relational. For example, Lyons, Ritvo, and Sullivan (1995) interviewed a 43-year-old woman with a spinal cord injury (SCI) who stated, "Your friendships are greatly affected by your disability. I don't have any friends except maybe two from the pre-disability days" (p. 38). Lyons *et al.* found that people with disabilities see their friends less, have more difficulty relating to old friends, and often experience rejection by old friends. For married individuals, the marital union is often disrupted and disability is a risk factor for divorce. For adult athletes with disabilities who are parents, parent–child relationships are also affected.

One of Kleiber, Brock, Lee, Dattilo, and Caldwell's (1995) participants, Donald, stated "another thing that makes it hard is the fact that I can't run with them [his children]" (p. 293). Young children's inability to understand exacerbates the difficulty parents have in managing the change in the parent–child relationship. For example, Donald reflected on his daughter and reported that, "She's not accepting the fact, I don't think, that I can't walk, she'll tell me to put on my shoes, and I can walk. So, see that makes it hard on me." (p. 293).

Sparkes and Smith (2002) and Smith and Sparkes (2005) described men's SCI-related experiences. For able-bodied male athletes who had strong masculine athletic identities and who derived substantial self-worth from sport, both of these critical aspects of their self-concepts were severely damaged when they became disabled. One participant indicated, "Your masculinity is gone, broken, you just struggle to live up to it [being a man]" (Sparkes & Smith, 2002, p. 269). Some athletes may completely disregard disability sport as an option. One man, for example, stated, "How can you play sports like that? I mean I can understand people using sport for rehabilitation and everything. For me though, they aren't real sports, not really" (Sparkes & Smith, 2002, p. 270). A related sentiment was expressed by a former able-bodied basketball player who noted, "No way would I settle for less with a sport I had excelled in on my feet. So in the hospital I set my mind on the triathlon" (Hutchinson & Kleiber, 2000, p. 50).

In sum, experiencing an acquired disability has far-reaching ramifications. Athletes heavily invested in sports and struggling with disruptions to their athletic identities may face particularly difficult times. What makes the preceding information particularly relevant is that some elite athletes start sport shortly after their acquired injuries and then have short careers (e.g., lasting less than two years). Furthermore, adjusting to a major trauma may take as long as two years, and adjusting one's self-concept may take as long as four years (Trieschmann, 1988). Sport psychologists may find themselves working with athletes adjusting to significant trauma, getting ready for a major competition, managing a secondary disability such as a chronic injury, and possibly leaving high-level disability sport in the near future.

The disability world

The picture I paint in this section is one of generalizations. My suggestion is to use the following information as a general guide to understanding athletes' lives early in the consulting relationship given that there is no substitution for first-hand knowledge obtained directly from athletes. My premise for this section is that athletes with disabilities live in a world that is quite different from the able-bodied world, and their life experiences will indirectly, and directly, influence their sporting aspirations.

The effect of a disability is felt across virtually all life dimensions such as employment, education, friendships, and health. Children without disabilities, for example, may view children with disabilities as less attractive compared to children without disabilities. Adolescents and young adults with disabilities in sport settings have reported that they commonly were recipients of pitying "poor you" looks (Goodwin, Thurmeier, & Gustafson, 2004). Individuals with disabilities often receive negative evaluative judgments about their appearances from others, making it difficult to construct positive body images.

People with disabilities tend to have lower levels of income and live in homes with less income compared to people with no disabilities. Similarly, based on data from the USA, a greater percentage of individuals with disabilities live in poverty and live alone, compared to people with no disabilities. A far greater percentage of people without disabilities also graduate from high school and college compared to individuals with disabilities. Individuals with disabilities are also more likely to be the victims of crime. Women with disabilities, for example, have a 40% greater chance of being physically or sexually assaulted compared to women without disabilities. Even simple tasks such as hailing a taxi can be problematic because some taxi drivers do not want to deal with storing a wheelchair in the trunk. In brief, an athlete with a disability, with whom a sport psychologist might work, lives in a world that can be profoundly different from the one in which an able-bodied person lives.

Coaching issues

Many athletes with disabilities lack coaches, or have coaches who lack a sport science foundation and are volunteers. Even elite athletes (e.g., Kenyans competing in the Paralympic Games) may have no coaches (Crawford & Stodolska, 2008). Although athletes from countries with strong support systems (e.g., Canada) may have access to the same high level coaches as non-disabled athletes (Cregan, Bloom, & Reid, 2007), there may still be a shortage of coaches in some wealthy countries (e.g., USA). For example, in 1996 only 58% of 319 elite adult athletes from the USA (Ferrara & Buckley, 1996) and 33% of a diverse group of international athletes (e.g., Australian, Dutch, Japanese; Liow & Hopkins, 1996) reported having coaches who directed their training sessions. Even wheel-chair racers from Britain, a country with a strong history in disability sport, have limited access to coaches.

Because of limited coaching, athletes often end up training inconsistently, in non-sport-specific ways, do not taper for major competitions (Liow & Hopkins, 1996), and overtrain when they should be resting. When attempting to self-coach, athletes have difficulty locating reputable material. In brief, sport psychologists may have to consider helping their clients find a coach. Ignoring counterproductive physical training is tantamount to sport psychologists sabotaging their own efforts at helping athletes develop their mental and life skills. Assuming a non-traditional sport psychology role, in addition to mental and life skill development, is not without precedent. For example, at the Paralympics Brooks (2007) explained his role as a "gofer" (e.g., shopping, doing odd jobs) and Jackson (2007) was the video analyst. Furthermore, Jackson incorporated knowledge from the video analysis in his sport psychology services (e.g., feedback, team role clarification) and in the process gained credibility with his athletes. Ethical issues (e.g., conflicts of interest) related to dual relationships, however, contraindicate sport psychologists acting as coaches. To summarize, sport psychologists working with athletes with disabilities should be cognizant of the potential to at least consider broadening the range of services they provide.

Injury/illness and pain/fatigue

Compared to able-bodied performers, athletes with disabilities lose more training time due to injury. The disability condition, sport-specific stressors, and the use of any adaptive, assistive, or guidance aids (e.g., prosthetic devices) often interact, leading to increased likelihood of injury. Athletes with unilateral leg amputations (i.e., one leg) experience a high incidence of injury in the joints of the contralateral whole limb. Shoulder injuries are quite common among wheelchair athletes and often occur from wheeling for both training and everyday activities of living in combination with inadequate rest and recovery time. Because athletes with SCIs have difficulty regulating body temperature, especially in hot weather, there is also an increased risk of heat exhaustion and heat stroke.

For athletes with disabilities, fatigue, discomfort, and pain are a significant aspect of the sport experience. Pain may be particularly relevant for athletes with SCIs because up to 94% of people with SCIs indicate that they experience daily chronic pain. Although limited research on pain has been conducted with athletes with disabilities, it is clear that pain and fatigue are common barriers limiting physical activity in children and adults with disabilities (Martin Ginis et al., 2003). Pain and fatigue related to both disability and sport can affect training (e.g., missing practice) and performance. Simply put, managing pain, fatigue, and training; avoiding injury, illness, and overtraining; and effectively tapering for major competitions may be difficult for athletes with disabilities.

In summary, practitioners should remind athletes and coaches to be aware of their training loads in order to avoid overtraining, injury, and illness. The additional consideration of pain in the equation may make sport psychologists' and athletes' tasks particularly challenging. For example, discerning between pain that is temporary and fatigue-related versus pain that is serious and indicative of further injury is often difficult.

Classification

Although able-bodied athletes are classified by gender and sometimes by weight (e.g., wrestling, rowing), most athletes know their classifications or can reasonably predict or control them. Athletes with disabilities are also classified based on their functional abilities. In the functional classification system, athletes are graded based on their abilities to perform physical tests. Athletes with different disabilities may compete against each other if they have the same functional classification. For example, swimmers with SCIs, cerebral palsy, or amputations may all compete in one race.

The classification process can be stressful. First, the process itself might be stressful, irrespective of the outcome, if athletes fear being reclassified at a different level than they have historically been rated at. Second, if athletes are reclassified at a more functional level they will compete against athletes who can, presumably, perform better (e.g., faster times) than their previous competitors. The idea of facing more accomplished athletes can impair confidence and promote anxiety at the most inopportune time possible (e.g., 24–48 hours prior to competition). The classification procedure is unique to disability sport and is clearly a potential stressor. Sport psychologists should help their athletes prepare for the classification process (e.g., by practising anxiety management) and a potentially negative classification outcome (i.e., being reclassified). A variety of psychological methods (e.g., self-talk, relaxation, goal setting) will be of use in coping with classification.

Mental skill development adjustments

In this section I provide information related to mental skill development methods and specific mental skills, as well as practical suggestions.

Communication

Individuals with cerebral palsy (CP) often take longer to articulate a sentence if their speech is impaired. Page and Wayda (2001) suggested that sport psychologists working with athletes with CP use multiple forms of communication in case athletes also have auditory impairments. Simple adjustments such as sitting or kneeling may also be necessary for adequate eye contact with an athlete in a wheelchair.

Imagery

One use of imagery is for mental practice, making it particularly helpful for athletes with physical disabilities when they cannot, as is often the case, physically practise skills (e.g., because of limited transportation, no teammates, or inferior equipment). Practitioners should be aware that a source of frustration for amputee athletes, while imaging, may be imaging missing limbs. Visuomotor behavior rehearsal (VMBR) might be useful for athletes with cerebral palsy because the relaxation element of VMBR may reduce spasticity.

Imagery can also be considered an internal form of modeling. Recognizing that model similarity is important for building self-efficacy, sport psychologists have recently started to employ self-modeling strategies. For example, sport psychologists might work with athletes and their coaches to splice together footage of successful performances to promote skill development as well as enhance motivation and efficacy. An added advantage of this strategy is that although most athletes are surprised and even shocked at viewing themselves, they are quite enthusiastic about this type of mental skill intervention (Ram & McCullagh, 2003).

Relaxation

Although relaxation may reduce muscle spasticity, muscle spasticity in turn can make some relaxation exercises difficult. Cognitively oriented relaxation techniques, such as autogenic training, might be more effective than muscle-based methods. For example, Page and Wayda (2001) noted that spasticity (i.e., muscle contractures), athetosis (i.e., uncoordinated muscle movement), and ataxia (i.e., low muscle tone) all made it difficult for CP athletes to learn traditional progressive muscle relaxation.

Self-talk

Because athletes may have more control over their thoughts than their physiology, managing self-talk for relaxation purposes might be important. Self-talk, in the form of cue words (e.g., eye on the ball), can also be used to correct technique in sports such as wheelchair basketball and tennis. In a recent study of wheelchair basketball players, researchers examined the influence of self-talk on passing and dribbling performance (Harbalis, Hatzigeorgiadis, & Theodorakis, 2008). The self-talk group improved in both skills relative to the control group, providing support for the value of teaching self-talk skills. Athletes with disabilities may also be overly self-critical, but psychological skills training has helped Paralympic wheelchair basketball players reduce their negative self-talk.

Martin (2008) found that wheelchair basketball players expressing confidence in their abilities to maintain positive thoughts during times of distress also reported more positive affect and less negative affect compared to athletes who reported less confidence in their abilities to maintain positive thoughts during anxious times. Martin's findings suggest that sport psychologists who can help athletes effectively manage their self-talk may also help them enhance their quality of life (e.g., enjoy more positive affect and less negative affect). Finally, verbalizations of self-talk can also provide sport psychologists with potential insights into athletes' self-esteem.

Preparation

Traveling across time zones, trying to understand foreign languages, and enduring different climates all take a toll on athletes' emotional and physical resources. At the Paralympics, athletes often cannot practise at the competition site and sometimes must room with individuals they do not know and who do not compete in their sports (Katz, 2007), adding another layer of stress to their sporting experiences. Visiting the competition site and obtaining video images of the competition site will help athletes use imagery to prepare for competition. Sport psychologists can also help athletes view rooming with strangers as a positive aspect of the Paralympic experience and an event to embrace rather than fear.

Goal setting

Goal setting is a psychological technique often recommended to enhance motivation and efficacy. Athletes with disabilities have expressed limited training efficacy relative to performance efficacy (Martin, 2008). Because these athletes often face many barriers to training (e.g., few training partners) and, as mentioned earlier, have limited coaching, sport psychologists should pay particular attention to helping athletes formulate training goals (see Chapter 51) based on effective goal-setting guidelines.

Summary and conclusion

Current delivery of psychological services to athletes with disabilities is minimal. To the degree that limited information on disability sport psychology is a barrier, I hope that the information contained in the current chapter is helpful. See Box 45.1 for a summary of practical suggestions.

Box 45.1

Practical suggestions for sport psychologists working with athletes with disabilities

- Treat athletes as whole people, not just athletes.
- Do not focus on the disability, unless that is what the athlete wants to explore.
- Understand the potential trauma resulting from the injury.
- Be aware of non-sport challenges (e.g., reduced social contact).
- Consider helping athletes obtain adequate coaching.
- Be cognizant of the influence of disability-related pain and chronic injuries.
- Prepare for the classification procedure.
- Learn disability-specific changes in psychological skill development delivery.

References

Berger, R. J. (2008). Disability and the dedicated wheelchair athlete: Beyond the "Supercrip" critique. *Journal of Contemporary Ethnography, 37*, 647–678.

Brooks, J. (2007). Reflections on the Athens Olympics and Paralympics: My work as a sport psychologist working with Equestrian. *Sport & Exercise Psychology Review, 2*(2), 35–40.

Cregan, K., Bloom, G. A., & Reid, G. (2007). Career evolution and knowledge of elite coaches of swimmers with a physical disability. *Research Quarterly for Exercise and Sport, 78*, 339–350.

Crawford, J. L., & Stodolska, M. (2008). Constraints experienced by elite athletes with disabilities in Kenya, with implications for the developmental of a new hierarchical model of constraints at the societal level. *Journal of Leisure Research, 25*, 128–155.

Danish, S. J., & Hale, B. D. (1981). Toward an understanding of the practice of sport psychology. *Journal of Sport Psychology, 3*, 90–99.

Ferrara, M. S., & Buckley, W. E. (1996). Athletes with disabilities injury registry. *Adapted Physical Activity Quarterly, 13*, 50–60.

Goodwin, D. L., Thurmeier, R., & Gustafson, P. (2004). Reactions to the metaphors of disability: The mediating effects of physical activity. *Adapted Physical Activity Quarterly, 21*, 379–398.

Harbalis, T., Hatzigeorgiadis, A., & Theodorakis, Y. (2008). Self-talk in wheelchair basketball: The effects of an intervention program on dribbling and passing performance. *International Journal of Special Education, 23*, 62–69.

Hardin, M. M., & Hardin, B. (2004). The "Supercrip" in sport media: Wheelchair athletes discuss hegemony's disabled hero. *Sociology of Sport Online*. Retrieved from http://physed.otago.ac.nz/sosol /v7i1/v7i1_1.html

Hutchinson, S. L., & Kleiber, D. A. (2000). Heroic masculinity following spinal cord injury: Implications for therapeutic recreation practice and research. *Therapeutic Recreation Journal, 34*(1), 42–54.

Hutzler, Y. & Bar-Eli, M. (1993). Psychological benefits of sports for disabled people: A review. *Scandinavian Journal of Medical Science and Sports, 3*, 217–228.

Jackson, R. C. (2007). Reflections on the Athens Paralympics: Working with wheel-chair rugby. *Sport & Exercise Psychology Review, 2*(2), 41–45.

Katz, J. (2007). Reflections on the Paralympic HQ psychology service: Athens 2004. *Sport & Exercise Psychology Review, 2*(2), 25–28.

Kirkby, R. J. (1995). Wheelchair netball: Motives and attitudes of competitors with and without disabilities. *Australian Psychologist, 30*, 109–112.

Kleiber, D., Brock, S., Lee, Y., Dattilo, J., & Caldwell, L. (1995). The relevance of leisure in an illness experience: Realities of spinal cord injury. *Journal of Leisure Research, 27*, 283–299.

Liow, D. K., & Hopkins, W. B. (1996). Training practices of athletes with disabilities. *Adapted Physical Activity Quarterly, 13*, 372–381.

Lyons, R. F., Ritvo, P. G., & Sullivan, M. J. L. (1995). *Relationships in chronic illness and disability.* Thousand Oaks, CA: Sage.

Martin, J. J. (1999). A personal development model of sport psychology for athletes with disabilities. *Journal of Applied Sport Psychology, 11*, 181–193.

Martin, J. J. (2005). Sport psychology consulting with athletes with disabilities. *Sport and* Exercise Psychology Review, *1*(2), 33–39.

Martin, J. J. (2008). Multidimensional self-efficacy and affect in wheelchair basketball players. *Adapted Physical Activity Quarterly, 25*, 275–288.

Martin Ginis, K. A., Latimer, A. E., McKechnie, K., Ditor, D. S., McCartney., N., Hicks, A., L., Bugaresti, J., & Craven, B. C. (2003). Using exercise to enhance subjective well-being among people with spinal cord injury: The mediating influences of stress and pain. *Rehabilitation Psychology, 48*, 157–164.

Page, S. J., & Wayda, V. K. (2001). Modifying sport psychology services for athletes with cerebral palsy. *Palaestra, 17*, 10–14.

Page, S. J., Martin, S. B., & Wayda, V. K. (2001). Attitudes toward seeking sport psychology consultation among wheelchair basketball athletes. *Adapted Physical Activity Quarterly, 18*, 183–192.

Perreault, S., & Vallerand, R. J. (2007). A test of self-determination theory with wheelchair basketball players with and without disability. *Adapted Physical Activity Quarterly, 24*, 305–316.

Ram, N., & McCullagh, P. (2003). Self-modeling: Influence on psychological responses and physical performance. *The Sport Psychologist, 17*, 220–241.

Smith, B., & Sparkes, A. C. (2005). Men, sport, spinal cord injury, and narratives of hope. *Social Science and Medicine, 61*, 1095–1105.

Sparkes, A. C., & Smith, B. (2002). Sport, spinal cord injury, embodied masculinities, and the dilemmas of narrative identity. *Men and Masculinities, 4*, 258–285.

Trieschmann, R. B. (1988). *Spinal cord injuries: Psychological, social and vocational rehabilitation* (2nd ed.). New York: Demos.

Vealey, R. S. (1988). Future directions in psychological skills training. *The Sport Psychologist, 2*, 318–336.

46

Working with athletes with intellectual disabilities

Melanie Gregg

Intellectual disabilities are "characterized by significant limitations both in intellectual functioning and adaptive behavior as expressed in conceptual, social, and practical adaptive skills" (American Association on Mental Retardation, 2002, p. 6). Individuals with intellectual disabilities are generally described using ten adaptive skill areas – for example: social, communication, and employment (Conyers, Martin, Martin, & Yu, 2002). For the applied sport psychology practitioner, familiarity with these adaptive skills is more relevant than the classification of the degree of intellectual disability. Understanding the needs and abilities of athletes, both those with and without intellectual disabilities, is necessary for effective service delivery.

When considering organized sport, the most widely available resources for athletes with intellectual disabilities are the Special Olympics programs. Founded in 1968, these programs have grown to include more than 2.5 million athletes, in over 180 countries (Special Olympics, 2009). The mission of the Special Olympics centers on participation with the added intentions of enhancing fitness levels, motor skills, confidence, and self-concept. Sport participation at elite levels takes place through the International Sports Federation for People with an Intellectual Disability (INAS-FID). The INAS-FID fosters competitive sport environments for athletes who choose open competition governed by the rules of the international sport federations (INAS-FID, 2009). Working in a complementary fashion, the Special Olympics and the INAS-FID aim to improve society's perceptions of individuals with intellectual disabilities through sport participation. Athletes may participate in events hosted by either, or both, organizations.

Practical considerations for working with athletes with intellectual disabilities are examined throughout this chapter and include: ethical considerations, communication and feedback, motivation, and group interactions. Finally, I discuss how traditional mental skills for performance enhancement may be effective when suitably adapted for the specific population.

Ethical considerations in service delivery

Athletes with intellectual disabilities commonly have difficulties making autonomous decisions and may be reliant on (and vulnerable to) the influences of others. Ethical principles that guide sport psychology practitioners (e.g., American Psychological Association [APA], 2002) must be upheld at all times. It is essential that sport psychology practitioners treat all athletes with dignity and respect, and allow athletes to make their own decisions. Athletes with intellectual disabilities must be given the opportunities to consent to, or withdraw from, working relationships with sport psychologists, and as sport or research participants. It is best to inform important others such as caregivers, parents, or coaches, of the nature of the working relationship. Involving important others in the process will help ensure the athletes' needs are being met, and will foster understanding. Athlete participants must give their own assent or consent to participate, overriding that of important others (see the APA's ethical principles for further guidelines).

Practitioners' stereotypes about athletes with disabilities should be identified and resolved as much as possible. The APA guidelines recommend that practitioners reduce the effect of their biases based on disability. Rather than focusing on the disabilities of the athletes, effective practitioners will focus on their abilities (Hanrahan, 2004) and construct programs that will encourage the development of these abilities for positive outcomes (Travis & Sachs, 1991). Practitioners need to address their own biases and limited experiences when working with athletes with intellectual disabilities.

Communication and feedback

Sport is often a safe setting where athletes with intellectual disabilities may be challenged and take risks (Travis & Sachs, 1991). It is important to acknowledge the athletes' abilities and help them to cope with challenges rather than taking on a protective role (Gorely, Jobling, Lewis, & Bruce, 2002). A paternalistic approach to communication and the consultation process is not useful (Travis & Sachs, 1991) and will hinder the practitioners' rapport with athletes (Farrell, Crocker, McDonough, & Sedgwick, 2004). Some athletes may be nonverbal, posing particular challenges to communication. Others may have limited verbal and written communication skills. These challenges to communication will require creativity on the part of the sport psychologists to develop novel and effective methods of conveying their messages and to ensure they are clearly receiving the athletes' communications. Athletes indicate they want input into their training and for coaches to be open to their ideas (Farrell et al., 2004); it would not be unreasonable for athletes to have the same expectations for their sport psychology practitioners. Much of the advice in this chapter applies to both coaches teaching physical skills and sport psychologists instructing athletes in cognitive and emotional techniques for their sports.

Sport psychologists may find that athletes with intellectual disabilities have a propensity for acquiescence, or a tendency to answer positively. Though potentially problematic, with careful planning acquiescence can be circumvented (Matikka & Vesala, 1997). A combination of observation and interviews or questioning techniques is more likely to provide a complete picture rather than using only one technique (Mactavish, Lutfiyya, & Mahon, 2000). Questions that require dichotomous (yes/no) responses should be avoided, because these types of questions are most likely to lead to acquiescent responses (Matikka & Vesala, 1997). Questions that require athletes to consider their answers allow practitioners to garner valuable information (e.g., "Can you tell me a time when the cue word 'ice' might be useful?"; Gorely et al., 2002, p. 361). Asking athletes to repeat instructions back to the practitioner is another useful strategy (Travis & Sachs, 1991). Working with athletes' communication strengths will help build rapport and lead to better information. For example, when working with athletes who have limited verbal communication or writing skills, using visual cues such as pictures or having the athletes draw may be more effective methods for the athletes to express themselves than oral interviews or written questionnaires.

As Hanrahan (1998) suggested, *specific* praise and feedback are core practitioner behaviors when working with athletes with intellectual disabilities. Using abstract terms such as "Great!" or "Do your best" are too vague and may be confusing. Instead, tell the athlete precisely what was great (e.g., "Your cue words 'go, go, go!' are really good.") or what is expected of them (e.g., "When you breathe in make your tummy stick out."). Keep concepts simple, particularly when teaching a new skill, and break these skills into parts (Hanrahan, 2007). Repetition of instructions and practising parts of the skill may be necessary. Concepts that are generally assumed to be understood may need to be explained: it is important to adapt coaching and teaching styles to the level of the individual's understanding (Hanrahan, 2004). For example, in the middle of an interval on the track an athlete with an intellectual disability may stop to tie her shoe in the lane rather than moving to the side of the track out of the way of the other runners. Corrective feedback instructing the athlete to move off the track to tie the lace would solve the issue.

Frequent positive feedback and praise lead to feelings of competence and control (Farrell *et al.*, 2004) and are important for developing and maintaining motivation. Caution must be used when providing negative feedback because it could lead to withdrawal from sport (Farrell *et al.*, 2004). As with all athletes, positive feedback and praise should outnumber instances of negative feedback. In particular, athletes with intellectual disabilities often have self-doubts, and benefit from the reassurance and support from important others. This support leads to the sense that their participation in sport is valued (Farrell *et al.*, 2004). Gillespie (2003) indicated that every-trial knowledge of results enhances the acquisition of new sport skills in youth with intellectual disabilities. Compared to every-trial knowledge of results, summary knowledge of results following several practice attempts of the skill has a greater influence on skill retention. When athletes are given visual and verbal cues that serve as reminders, combined with knowledge of results, their performances on closed-skill tasks (e.g., basketball free throws, overhand softball throws, dart throws) can be improved (Yang & Porretta, 1999).

Providing frequent positive feedback during the early stages of sport participation fosters skill acquisition, self-efficacy, motivation, and long-term sport participation. As athletes' commitment to participation increases and self-efficacy for participation improves, a schedule of summary feedback may be introduced leading to long-term participation and skill retention. Regardless of the schedule of feedback, effective communication combined with positive feedback and valuing athlete input will help create a positive sport experience.

Motivation

Athletes with intellectual disabilities participate in sport for similar reasons as athletes without disabilities: fun, fitness, affiliation, competency, and to experience success (Farrell *et al.*, 2004; Shapiro, 2003). Athletes have many motives for participating in sport, but generally they can be grouped into task, ego, or social approval orientations of competence (Shapiro). Athletes with strong task orientations are driven by a desire to develop competence, test themselves, and compare themselves to their own standards or previous levels of performance. Individuals with strong ego orientations compare themselves to others, play to win, and compete against others. Athletes participating for social incentives seek recognition from important others, and feelings of relatedness. Athletes with intellectual disabilities from a variety of sports rate task and social motives as more influential to participation than ego-oriented motives (Shapiro, 2003).

All athletes who participate in Special Olympics events receive a tangible reward (e.g., medal, ribbon) for their participation. Because *all* participants receive an extrinsic reward for participation, the focus is not on being better or worse than others: "coaches and athletes perceive an emphasis on the accomplishment of personally relevant goals, effort, and improvement rather than on winning and success" (Shapiro, 2003, p. 157). Farrell *et al.* (2004) supported this notion, and Požėrienė, Admomaitienė, and Ostasevičienė (2008) suggested that the medals and ribbons for Special Olympians emphasize information about the athletes' competencies.

Travel is rated low in importance as a participation motive for athletes without disabilities. In contrast, athletes with physical and intellectual disabilities indicate travel to competitions and practices as a relatively important motive (Shapiro, 2003). This difference in the motivational role of travel may be because of fewer overall opportunities to travel, reliance on others for travel, and increased opportunities for social interaction (described in the following section) as a result of travel.

Coaches and sport psychologists can reinforce a task orientation and create opportunities for social incentives in the sport environment (Shapiro, 2003). One method of developing and reinforcing social competencies is to involve athletes with intellectual disabilities as assistant coaches. This approach reinforces the sport knowledge and abilities that experienced athletes bring to the training environment, can positively influence newer athletes by providing models to which to aspire, and may keep athletes involved in sport by helping them feel valued and by continuing to challenge them (Farrell *et al.*, 2004).

Athletes with intellectual disabilities indicated that they have higher participation motivation when they are in a self-determined environment. Farrell *et al.*'s (2004) interviews with 38 Special Olympians, training and competing in a variety of sports, revealed that the athletes preferred to train in an autonomous or self-determined environment and to have input in their training programs. Coaches who listen to their athletes, take their suggestions on board, are flexible and knowledgeable about the sport, and value the participants' experiences and ideas, are favored. Assigning roles to athletes to give them opportunities to act as leaders and provide input for their programs will go a long way toward meeting the needs of the athletes and fostering their motivation.

Group interactions

The need for relatedness and social support may be more important for athletes with intellectual disabilities than autonomous experiences and feelings of competence, because these athletes generally have smaller social networks than athletes without intellectual disabilities (Farrell *et al.*, 2004). The sport environment provides opportunities for interaction and striving for achievement as a team (Požėrienė *et al.*, 2008). Part of this motivation results from the positive feeling of belonging associated with involvement in a social group (Požėrienė *et al.*, 2008). Sport participation by athletes with intellectual disabilities facilitates social integration, leading to a greater sense of autonomy when athletes feel as though their input into the program is valued (Farrell *et al.*, 2004). Enhanced social skills that transfer to daily life outside of sport may also result. In particular, sport participation leads to the development of friendships with teammates and competitors. These social relationships are significant because individuals with intellectual disabilities often experience difficulties making friends and tend to have limited social circles (Zoerink & Wilson, 1995). Social approval for participating in sport, coming from friends, family, support workers, and coaches, helps to enhance the athletes' feelings of self-efficacy and leads to positive emotions (Farrell *et al.*, 2004). Opportunities for socializing should be built into sport programs, and team building can be used to help develop relationships.

Mental skills for performance enhancement

Most of the literature in the area of sport psychology and athletes with disabilities has focused on descriptive profiles of these competitors and comparisons to athletes without disabilities (Zoerink & Wilson, 1995). There has only been limited exploration of the effectiveness of psychological skills training for athletes with intellectual disabilities. It is important to modify psychological skills training programs to meet the needs of any individuals, but these modifications may be particularly salient for athletes with intellectual disabilities (Hanrahan, 2004) where a textbook approach may be suboptimal.

In one of the few published reports of psychological skills interventions with athletes with intellectual disabilities, Gregg, Hrycaiko, Mactavish, and Martin (2004) successfully modified existing interventions with three athletes in a Special Olympics track and field program. Several modifications suitable to the functioning levels of the athletes were made (e.g., happy, sad, and neutral faces rather than Likert scales were used to describe goal attainment). The athletes engaged in the psychological skills of goal setting, self-talk, and imagery of goal achievement. Following the intervention, the participants spent more time on-task, had overall increases in work output, and were successful in setting and achieving their practice goals. Gregg *et al.* suggested that although it is possible to use a standard packaged approach when delivering psychological skills to athletes with intellectual disabilities, it may be more pragmatic to use psychological skills one at a time rather than in combination, such as imagery alone. It is most efficacious for the athletes to learn one psychological skill at a time and have the athletes integrate those skills into their regular training program. Similarly, Gorely *et al.* (2002) recommended limiting the use of psychological skills to include only the most pertinent ones, and pointed out that interrelated skills are likely to be most effective and easier for the participants (athletes and coaches) to manage.

Goal setting may help direct athletes' attention, improve effort, encourage athletes to persist for longer, and enhance athletes' sense of independence and self-efficacy, leading to feelings of autonomy (Hanrahan, 1998). The effectiveness of goals is improved by setting cooperative goals and through record keeping. Cooperatively set goals are more effective than assigned or self-selected goals (Hanrahan, 1998); to foster goal effectiveness the coach or sport psychologist should assist the athlete in setting realistic goals. In preparation for the state championships for athletes with intellectual disability, a men's basketball team used team goal-setting to help direct effort and clarify roles (Gorely *et al.*, 2002). Modifying the recording of goals by using audio recordings may avoid issues with literacy and writing ability (Hanrahan, 2004). Gorely *et al.* (2002) also used audio recordings to remind athletes how and when to use their cue words to help them relax, focus, and listen, to use deep centered breathing, and to replace negative thoughts with positive ones.

Athletes with intellectual disabilities, like other athletes, often experience anxiety prior to competition, and this anxiety may adversely affect their performances (Porretta, Moore,

445

& Sappenfield, 1992), and this heightened state anxiety may result in a corresponding performance decrement. Gorely et al. (2002) successfully used cue words and deep centered breathing to teach relaxation to basketball players with intellectual disabilities. The players reported using the techniques in basketball as well as in daily life, including "when frustrated, when trying to sleep, and before free throws" (Gorely et al., 2002, p. 358). The keys to the success of the techniques were the coaches' reinforcement and repetition throughout training sessions and at competitions. Athletes with intellectual disabilities have also successfully engaged in guided progressive muscle relaxation (Hanrahan, 2004). Relaxation and anxiety management techniques provide the athletes with direction rather than simply leaving the athletes on their own to manage their anxieties, but repetition and reminders may be required. Any pre-existing self-management skills may be limited due to "shortened attention spans, indecision about what to do, or inability to remember the process" (Hanrahan, 1998, p. 352). Abstract concepts are challenging for athletes with intellectual disabilities; using concrete instructions and examples will allow the athletes to be more successful in their anxiety management (e.g., "put your hand on your belly and notice as you breathe out your belly slowly goes down", Hanrahan, 2004).

Pre-competition plans help athletes enter competition confidently and minimize stressors. These plans should include elements such as: travel arrangements, food, water, competition schedule, equipment and uniforms, and general and specific on-site physical and mental warm-up activities. Planning may help athletes feel autonomous and reduce reliance on others for assistance prior to competition (Hanrahan, 1998). Given that athletes with intellectual disabilities often have difficulties making decisions, developing alternatives in case things do not go as planned (e.g., competition is behind schedule, resulting in a need for a longer physical warm-up) should help athletes cope with the changes. Familiarity with facilities and routines leads to feelings of comfort (Hanrahan, 1998) resulting in less pre-competition anxiety. Coaches and sport psychologists should assist athletes in developing pre-competition plans and their alternatives, have the athletes practise the plans in training before entering the competition environment, and give feedback and suggest modifications to the plans. Making recordings of the pre-competition plans is helpful because it will prompt athletes to follow their plans, and may help athletes overcome challenges with memory and stay on task (Hanrahan, 1998).

Imagery is the most commonly used mental skill in interventions for individuals with intellectual disabilities (Gorely et al., 2002). Athletes have a clearer image of their physical skills when they combine their physical practice with imagery practice. Imagery combined with physical practice improves performance beyond physical practice alone (Porretta & Surburg, 1995). Porretta and Surburg suggested that imagery helps athletes with intellectual disabilities to anticipate appropriate responses and overcome limitations of attention capacity, with almost an immediate influence on performance. Furthermore, Porretta and Surburg stated that "[i]magery practice in conjunction with physical practice seems to provide subjects with the time needed to attend to the task as long as they are given direction by the teacher or coach" (p. 1180). Providing concrete cues while requesting the athletes engage in imagery practice helps direct the athletes' attention to task-relevant cues. Gregg et al. (2004), for example, provided participants with a picture of the athletic facility to help them to imagine participating in that venue.

Frequently athletes with intellectual disabilities have been encouraged to imagine specific sport skills such as a start in running events (e.g., Gregg et al., 2004). Imagery may also be used for mastery experiences such as imagining oneself in a difficult situation, and then imagining overcoming that difficulty (e.g., seeing oneself behind at the start of a race and then successfully catching the pack.) These types of images can help increase athletes' self-efficacy. Gorely *et al.* (2002) suggested that the use of videos may be helpful to aid athletes in forming images for these additional purposes. Qualities such as being relaxed, focused, and confident may be modeled by others; athletes may learn to image and perform these qualities by observing and imitating the model.

Maintaining focus and managing distractions is necessary when coaching or consulting with athletes with intellectual disabilities. Gregg *et al.*'s (2004) primary intervention outcome was frequency and duration of off-task behavior (e.g., talking to other athletes during intervals other than scheduled rest periods). The psychological skills training program was effective at reducing the duration and frequency of off-task behaviors of the athletes. In an evaluation of a psychological skills intervention in a physical activity program for children with intellectual disabilities, parents reported their children had improved focus during the physical activity sessions as a result of the intervention, which included positive thinking, autonomous behavior, relaxation techniques, imagery, and goal setting (Spassiani & Fraser-Thomas, 2008). Activities aimed at improving concentration should be modified to a suitable level so the athletes do not get frustrated trying to do a task that is overly difficult (Hanrahan, 1998).

Creative approaches may be useful in assessing an individual athlete's understanding of mental skills and how to apply them. Practice situations, such as competition simulations where the athletes try to apply the techniques, can provide information about the consolidation of the skills (Gorely *et al.*, 2002). Gregg *et al.* (2004) used log books and one-on-one interviews to check for understanding. A simpler method, particularly when working with a large group of athletes, is to ask questions to test for understanding. When athletes are taught mental skills that are modified for their needs and abilities, systematically integrated into practice and competition settings, and frequently reinforced, these skills can help the athletes achieve success in their sport performance, and facilitate enjoyment of their sport experiences.

Conclusion

In this chapter I examined practical considerations for working with athletes with intellectual disabilities. Many of the recommendations in the chapter are suitable for athletes with and without intellectual disabilities. Practitioners should not shy away from working with athletes with intellectual disabilities; by making minor modifications and planning in advance, this challenge is rewarding and fosters innovation. To enhance the effectiveness of sport psychology programs practitioners must gain rapport with the athletes by avoiding a paternalistic approach and encouraging the athletes to take active roles in the process. Athletes can, and should, make decisions and provide input into the program. Practitioners must check for their own understanding as well as the athletes', to ensure effective communication in both directions. Using concrete statements and repetition will improve the clarity of instructions and enhance the acquisition of mental skills such as relaxation techniques. Athletes will be motivated to participate in the program if they have opportunities to master tasks and to engage in social interaction. Athletes can benefit from mental skills training, but to be effective the programs need to be modified to suit individual needs. See Box 46.1 for practical suggestions for sport psychologists working with athletes with intellectual disabilities.

Box 46.1

Practical suggestions for practitioners working with athletes with intellectual disabilities

- Provide opportunities to experience and develop autonomy.
- Avoid acquiescence with creative approaches to assessment.
- Focus on and work within athletes' abilities.
- Provide frequent, positive, and specific feedback and praise.
- Speak in simple, concrete terms.
- Provide opportunities for travel and socializing.
- Focus on and reinforce a limited number of psychological skills.
- Assist athletes in setting goals.
- Guide athletes through relaxation exercises.
- Use routines to help alleviate stressors.
- Combine imagery with physical practice.
- Provide instruction to help athletes attend to appropriate cues.

References

American Association on Mental Retardation (2002). *Mental retardation: Definition, classification, and systems of support* (10th ed.). Washington, DC: American Association on Mental Retardation.

American Psychological Association (2002). Ethical principles of psychologists and code of conduct. *American Psychologist, 57,* 1060–1073.

American Association on Mental Retardation (2002). *Mental retardation: Definition, classification, and systems of support* (10th ed.). Washington, DC: American Association on Mental Retardation.

Conyers, C., Martin, T. L., Martin, G. L., & Yu, D. (2002). The 1983 AAMR manual, the 1992 AAMR manual, or the Developmental Disabilities Act: Which do researchers use? *Education and Training in Mental Retardation and Developmental Disabilities, 37,* 310–316.

Farrell, R. J., Crocker, P. R. E., McDonough, M. H., & Sedgwick, W. A. (2004). The driving force: Motivation in Special Olympians. *Adapted Physical Activity Quarterly, 21,* 153–166.

Gillespie, M. (2003). Summary versus every-trial knowledge of results for individuals with intellectual disabilities. *Adapted Physical Activity Quarterly, 20,* 46–56.

Gorely, R., Jobling, A., Lewis, K., & Bruce, D. (2002). An evaluative case study of a psychological skills training program for athletes with intellectual disabilities. *Adapted Physical Activity Quarterly, 19,* 350–363.

Gregg, M. J., Hrycaiko, D., Mactavish, J. B., & Martin, G. L. (2004). A mental skills package for Special Olympics athletes: A preliminary study. *Adapted Physical Activity Quarterly, 21,* 4–18.

Hanrahan, S. J. (1998). Practical considerations for working with athletes with disabilities. *The Sport Psychologist, 12,* 346–357.

Hanrahan, S. (2004). Sport psychology for athletes with disabilities. In T. Morris and J. Summers (Eds.), *Sport psychology: Theory, application and issues* (2nd ed., pp. 572–583). Brisbane, QLD, Australia: Wiley.

Hanrahan, S. J. (2007). Athletes with disabilities. In G. Tenenbaum & R. C. Eklund (Eds.), *Handbook of sport psychology* (3rd ed., pp. 845–858). Hoboken, NJ: Wiley.

International Sports Federation for People with an Intellectual Disability (2009). Retrieved from http://www.inas-fid.org/

Mactavish, J. B., Lutfiyya, Z. M., & Mahon, M. J. (2000). "I can speak for myself": Involving individuals with intellectual disabilities as research participants. *Mental Retardation, 38,* 216–227.

Matikka, L. M., & Vesala, H. T. (1997). Acquiescence in quality-of-life interviews with adults who have mental retardation. *Mental Retardation, 35*, 75–82.

Porretta, D. L., & Surburg, P. R. (1995). Imagery and physical practice in the acquisition of gross motor timing of coincidence by adolescents with mild mental retardation. *Perceptual and Motor Skills, 80*, 1171–1183.

Porretta, D., Moore, W., & Sappenfield, C. (1992). Situational anxiety in Special Olympics athletes. *Palaestra, 8*, 46–50.

Požėrienė, J., Admomaitienė, R., Ostasevičienė, V. , Rėklaitienė, D., & Kragnienė, I. (2008). Sport participation motivation of athletes with intellectual disabilities. *Education. Physical Training. Sport,* 3 (70), 69–75.

Shapiro, D. R. (2003). Participation motives of Special Olympics athletes. *Adapted Physical Activity Quarterly, 20*, 150–165.

Spassiani, N. A., & Fraser-Thomas, J. L. (2008, October). *Evaluating the effectiveness of a mental skills intervention in a routine-based physical activity program with children with disabilities.* Poster session presented at the annual conference of the Canadian Society for Psychomotor Learning and Sport Psychology, Canmore, AB, Canada.

Special Olympics (2009). Retrieved from http://www.specialolympics.org/

Travis, C. A., & Sachs, M. L. (1991). Applied sport psychology and persons with mental retardation. *The Sport Psychologist, 5*, 382–391.

Yang, J. J., & Porretta, D. L. (1999). Sport/leisure skill learning by adolescents with mild mental retardation: A four-step strategy. *Adapted Physical Activity Quarterly, 16*, 300–315.

Zoerink, D. A., & Wilson, J. (1995). The competitive disposition: Views of athletes with mental retardation. *Adapted Physical Activity Quarterly, 12*, 34–42.

47

Athletes who are blind/visually impaired or deaf/hard of hearing

Jennifer E. Vose, Rebecca A. Clark, and Michael L. Sachs

Almost all the material one reads about sport psychology is based on work with able-bodied athletes, including those with no or minimal sensory deficits. And yet there are millions of individuals who have sensory deficits, specifically visual and hearing impairments. Some compensate quite well for these deficits, with glasses/contact lenses or hearing aids/lip reading skills, whereas others have deficits that are not amenable to such corrections. The majority of adult individuals have some visual impairment (people using glasses/contact lenses) or some degree of hearing loss (fewer wear hearing aids, but many do). These losses don't affect the ability of most of these individuals to compete in athletic endeavors.

Although there are exceptionally few elite athletes who are blind/visually impaired or deaf/hard of hearing (hoh), there are many who do participate on a regular basis, some in competition with sighted/hearing athletes, and many others as part of disability-specific groups such as the United States Association of Blind Athletes (USABA), Confederação Brasileira de Desportos dos Surdos (CBDS), Deaf Sports Australia (DSA), Korean Deaf Sports Federation (KDSF), or USA Deaf Sports Federation (USADSF). A few athletes who are deaf/hoh have competed in the Olympic Games. They include: Angel Acuna (Mexico – basketball), Tony Ally (UK – synchronized diving), Frank Bartolillo (Australia – fencing), Tamika Catchings (USA – basketball), Juri Jaansen (Estonia – rowing), and Terrance Parkin (South Africa – swimming). Jeff Float, a deaf swimmer, was the captain of the USA 1984 Olympic swimming team who won a gold medal in the 4 x 200 m relay. He also won ten gold medals in ten events in the 1977 Deaflympics. One elite visually impaired athlete, Marla Runyan (who has Stargardt's disease), has competed as an Olympian and a Paralympian in middle distance running (as the dust jacket of her book [2001] notes, the "first legally blind athlete to compete in the Olympic Games"). This chapter, however, is not oriented toward the professional/elite athlete per se, but toward all athletes with sensory impairments, whether they compete in elite competition or recreational sport events.

Athletes who are blind/visually impaired

Whether practitioners have worked with individuals with visual impairment (VI) in the past, or are simply interested in learning more about working with this population, the tools and tips in this section are designed to provide some food for thought as consultants embark on work with athletes who present a set of strengths and challenges that may be unfamiliar to many practitioners. We hope that readers will emerge from this chapter with some new perspectives and ideas for working with athletes with VI.

Individuals with VI may possess some visual ability, enough to drive a car (with some assistive technology) and read regular-size print, may be totally blind, or may fall somewhere in between. VI may also affect vision in different ways. For example, vision loss may be more pronounced in an individual's peripheral field (in the case of retinitis pigmentosa), or may be more pronounced in an individual's central vision (as in the case of macular degeneration or Stargardt's disease). We encourage readers to consult other resources, such as Lighthouse International (2010), to obtain more in-depth information on specific types of VI. In addition, organizations such as the International Blind Sports Federation (IBSA: 2010a) and the United States Association of Blind Athletes (USABA: 2010), a US Olympic Committee member organization, can be consulted for more information about organizational support for sport opportunities for the visually impaired, ranging from sport skills camps for youth to elite-level, Paralympic competition. In addition, IBSA provides specific medical criteria that athletes must meet with regard to their visual abilities to be eligible to compete in IBSA-affiliated events (IBSA, 2010b).

When consultants first meet athletes with VI, it is likely that questions will arise such as: "What can you see?" and "What does the world around you look like?" Although such questions may seem direct and somewhat brusque, the answers may provide practitioners with valuable information as they begin work with the athletes. The answers to these questions most likely lie in observations of the athletes, as well as in the insights the athletes are able to provide. Understanding athletes' strengths, needs, and challenges is central for establishing positive rapport, providing helpful support, and implementing effective interventions.

So, where to begin? Sport psychologists should not be afraid to be curious about observing athletes in their surroundings, or hesitate to engage in one-on-one conversation with athletes so they can help better understand their needs. When observing and conversing, it may be helpful to learn more about how much vision the athlete possesses, whether one eye is stronger than the other, the degree to which the athlete relies more heavily on central or peripheral vision, whether the athlete is able to drive or read regular size print, which color contrasts work best for the athlete to be able to perceive detail, and whether there was once a time when the athlete possessed better vision.

Conversations about the athlete's VI should be approached with sensitivity, respect, and genuine interest. Some athletes may be more comfortable discussing their VI than others, so proceed with conversations accordingly. Some athletes may be eager to enlighten practitioners as to their needs and circumstances, whereas others may seem distant and reluctant to share details. In the case of the latter, observational skills may be called upon more heavily until the athlete feels comfortable enough to talk more openly.

Consultants should consider how best to communicate with athletes with VI, given the critical role communication plays in the sport psychology consultant-athlete relationship. An emphasis on descriptive, accurate, verbal communication is critical. It is best that any live or video-taped demonstrations, pictures, or other visual media are accompanied by accurate descriptions of what is being depicted. Minimize background noise to enable the athlete to focus on your voice or the voices of others. When engaged in a group discussion in which individuals are taking turns to speak, call upon individuals by name to speak rather than using nonverbal cues such as pointing or head nods. When speaking directionally, use clear terms such as "to the right," "to the left," "forward," or "backward" rather than vague terms such as "over here" or "over there." In addition, any directional gestures such as pointing should be accompanied with clear directional terminology.

When communicating with athletes via emails or blogs, consider that the athletes may require the use of magnification or screen reader software to engage in such communication. Check with the athletes ahead of time to be sure that the means by which you are communicating electronically are compatible with their assistive technology. In addition, if the athletes use screen reader software, avoid the use of bold or colored type face for emphasis. Such software may not distinguish between different font styles and colors, thus your intended emphasis will not be clear to the athlete.

Aside from using more verbal communication, when working with athletes with VI, what practitioners do will not change much, but how they do things may require special consideration. For interventions that are best facilitated through the use of printed material, for example, consultants should learn from the athletes ahead of time how they can best avail themselves of this material. Some options include providing materials in large print; providing materials using different color contrasts (e.g., black paper with white writing); providing materials in electronic form to be viewed on a personal laptop computer by the athletes; having a fellow athlete, with whom the visually impaired athlete is comfortable, read the printed material aloud to the athlete; providing an audio recording of the printed material (and a personal listening device, if needed) for the athlete; and offering any printed material in Braille format (for those athletes who are able to read Braille). Regardless of the format that is most appropriate, make these arrangements ahead of time so that the athletes are able to take part in the sharing of information at the same time as their fellow athletes (rather than the athletes having to wait until a later time to view or hear the material).

Sport psychology practitioners commonly introduce imagery and mental practice activities with both individuals and teams. Given the usually visual nature of imagery, some practitioners may erroneously presume that athletes with VI cannot participate in and benefit from imagery exercises. Many visually impaired individuals, however, either have, or used to have, some visual ability, so they may be able to benefit from and appreciate such sensory information. In addition, imagery is most effective when the most salient sensory information is included. Thus, for a visually impaired athlete (and any other athletes for that matter), the inclusion of auditory, olfactory, and kinesthetic, along with some visual images, might help to create mental representations to which the athlete can relate (the more polysensory the image the better). The athletes can play an active role in creating these images by describing their world as they "see" it, feel it, smell it, and so forth.

With regard to team-building activities, practitioners need to take care ahead of time to be sure that activities are adapted to enable athletes with VI to participate fully and safely. Of particular emphasis might be team-building activities focused on enhancing verbal communication among teammates during practice and competition. Given the possibility that nonverbal on-field communication may not be receivable or useful for an athlete with VI, it would be helpful for the team to develop and practise effective, agreed upon, verbal communication strategies. Consultants may consider helping the athletes develop and practise a system of code or cue words that can be easily communicated to one another in competitive situations, as well as practising speaking loudly enough to one another so that they deliver information accurately. It may also be important to facilitate practice situations that simulate competition, complete with game-day noises in the background, so that all team members can practise communicating with one another in this context.

Athletes with VI, at one time or another, are likely to express a certain degree of anxiety about having to travel to and practise/compete in new and unfamiliar facilities. Navigating in new, unfamiliar environments may be a highly anxiety-provoking experience for individuals with VI, and consultants may be called upon to assist athletes in making this transition smoothly. This assistance is important because athletes' energy is likely to be better used in preparing for the competitions rather than on worrying about finding the bathrooms or not tripping up and down stairs. If possible, travel with the athletes to the new facility to provide them with opportunities to become familiar with the surroundings. It might be helpful to obtain a map of the facility and, using the map, develop a tactile representation of its layout. The athletes can then use their hands to explore the layout of the facility. Consultants may also assist in identifying members of the teams with whom the athletes are comfortable and who can assist the athletes in getting around the facility once they arrive. Consultants may also help the athletes identify and practise the navigational/mobility skills they already possess and use in the community, and discuss how these skills can be used when transitioning to the new sport contexts.

Athletes who are deaf/hard of hearing (deaf/hoh)

There are excellent opportunities for sport psychology practitioners to work with deaf/hard of hearing (hoh) athletes. The world population for people with these hearing impairments was estimated to be 560 million people in 2005 and expected to increase to 900 million in 2025 (Davis, 1995). Chances are high that sport psychologists will encounter athletes with these "hidden" disabilities at some point in their careers. Hearing loss is considered a hidden disability in that without visual external devices such as hearing aids and cochlear implants, it is invisible to others. Furthermore, not all athletes benefit from these listening devices and those who do, often do not wear them while competing, for any number of reasons (e.g., lack of sweat-proof devices, vulnerability of breaking, rules banning them from competition). Athletes who are deaf/hoh may share many characteristics in common with hearing athletes, but may also exhibit some unique characteristics.

Athletes who are deaf/hoh are a diverse population with varying degrees of hearing loss, educational backgrounds, different communication methods, and athletic skills. How athletes feel about their hearing loss plays an important part in their personal identification. Athletes with a hearing loss can identify themselves as deaf, Deaf, or hard of hearing. For example, athletes who were born deaf, communicate in native sign language (e.g., British [BSL], Chinese [ZGS], Israeli [ISL], Kenyan [KSL], Mexican [MSL]), and socialize mainly with the deaf community may identify themselves as Deaf. The uppercase Deaf refers to a cultural and linguistic minority rather than a medical condition to which the lowercase deaf refers (Padden & Humphries, 1988).

The audiological definition of hearing loss ranges from mild to profound, and involves age of onset and the ability of the individual to use any hearing for communication purposes. Hard of hearing individuals tend to have mild to moderate hearing loss and are able to make use of hearing aids and assistive listening devices for communication purposes. Most often these individuals communicate orally (speech) although some learn sign language. Deafness is medically defined as a severe profound hearing loss and the inability to rely on hearing for communication. These individuals may or may not identify themselves with the deaf community. Some learn to speak well; some don't. Some depend on lip reading and others immerse themselves in deaf culture and learn to communicate in their native sign languages (there are 121 sign languages in the world).

Deaf/hoh athletes compete in sports and exercise for the same reasons other people do – for fitness, fun, socialization, and competition. These athletes are "able-bodied" and do not have a physical or mental disability that prevents them from participating in sports and exercise activities with their hearing competitors. There are no changes in rules or special classifications. Visual and/or tactile cues are substituted in place of auditory cues. For example, a flashing light or wave of a flag/hand is used simultaneously with a starter's gun to signal the beginning of a race. Most deaf/hoh athletes have some hearing and may be able to hear some sounds.

Elite deaf/hoh athletes

Just as there are elite hearing athletes who compete in the Olympics, there are some exceptional elite deaf/hoh athletes who have competed in the Olympics as well as the Deaflympics. The governing body of deaf sport, International Committee of Sports for the Deaf (ICSD), formerly Comité International des Sports des Sourds (CISS), identified "the top ten deaf Olympians of the Century," including Ignazio Fabra (four Olympic Games, wrestling, Italy), Terence Parkin (2000 Olympics silver medalist, swimming, Republic of South Africa), and Susan Jane Pedersen (1968, two gold and two silver medals, swimming, USA); Lovett, Eickman, & Giansanti, 2001).

Athletes who compete in competitions sanctioned by ICSD must have a minimum of a 55 decibel per tone average hearing loss in their better ear (Deaflympics, 2010b). Any kind of amplification gives an unfair advantage for those who can use them (e.g., the sound of the bat or hand on the ball provides auditory information on how hard or soft the ball was hit or hearing a teammate shout "pick" on a defensive play); thus, hearing aids and external cochlear implant parts are banned in deaf sport competitions (e.g., Deaflympics, Deaf World Championships, European Deaf Swimming Championships). Athletes do not need to know sign language to participate in Deaf Sport events, although it is encouraged. For more in-depth information about ICSD, its rich history (including co-founder of the International Paralympics), listings of sporting events, national sports governing bodies, and volunteer opportunities, and so forth, please visit the ICSD website (Deaflympics, 2010a).

Communication strategies

Sport psychologists may work with deaf/hoh athletes as part of a team or one-to-one. Frequently, the first encounters with these athletes are when they are part of a hearing team as opposed to a team of all deaf/hoh athletes. Generally, there are no differences in delivery of psychological skills training or counseling services with these athletes as part of an all deaf or mixed team of deaf and hearing athletes. As with all athletes, it is important to establish good rapport and, to do this, one must have good communication skills. In terms of deaf/hoh athletes, sport psychologists need to find out the specific communication methods they use. These methods may range from spoken language to sign language or a combination of both. Do not assume that all deaf/hoh athletes can lip read. Even the best lip readers miss a lot of information due to not all phonemes of spoken language being visible on the lips. Ask the athletes what their desired communication methods are. For those who lip read, do not exaggerate your lip movements. Speak clearly and make sure you are facing the athletes when you are talking. Be mindful of anything obstructing the view of your lips (e.g., facial hair, chewing gum, hands, clipboard).

When working with athletes who communicate in sign language (this does *not* mean gesturing), learn the specific sign language of the athletes or use qualified sign language interpreters. Sign language is learned at the same rate as any other language and one's fluency depends on using the language (signing) regularly. Sport psychologists can learn sign language at local universities and through nonprofit-/profit-making agencies that offer courses. There are private teachers/tutors, as well as various media/internet products/services that offer sign language classes. One can hire sign language interpreters through most university offices of students with disabilities, or via businesses that provide interpreting services. A consultant should talk directly to the deaf/hoh athlete when using an interpreter. Video Remote Interpreting (VRI) is available for free or at a low cost and requires web camera, TV or computer monitor, and telephone access number. There are a variety of different new technologies in which VRI or direct communication (sign to sign) is accessible (most recently, the Ojo Personal Video Phone). Please note that even in English-speaking countries (e.g., UK, USA, Australia), their sign languages are different. Furthermore, in the USA, American sign language has various regional signs. For example, the word "anxiety" is signed away from the body in New York but close to the body in Texas. One needs to be aware of these types of regional "accents" of sign language that are present in many large countries.

When working with two or more athletes who sign, or in situations where sign language may be understood by hearing athletes, coaches, trainers, or spectators, the sport psychologist needs to be sensitive about communicating confidential information. Sign language is visual and anyone who knows it can see what is being discussed. So if the information being shared is confidential, then the practitioner needs to be sure to communicate with the athlete privately.

When preparing for competition in mainstream environments, one should consider ahead of time the challenges the athletes might face (e.g., "hearing" a call to report to a certain place for an event); coaches, psychologists, and support staff can anticipate some of these challenges and make plans ahead of time to insure the athletes are where they need to be. Deaf/hoh athletes will not be able to hear a practitioner when they are actively performing, therefore staff need to give their instructions prior to performance (e.g., warm-up, time-out, half-time). Some athletes may have had some hearing in the past, thus allowing them the advantage of using memory of auditory cues in imagery and relaxation exercises. Hard of hearing athletes have some hearing that they can use when working with consultants. Consider the degree to which the athletes are able to hear the crowd and use this information when helping the athletes develop strategies to either block out the noise or use the crowd noise to "psych up" for performance.

Some hard of hearing athletes are able to hear music and use various auditory relaxation methods. For deaf athletes who are not able to use the regular "sound" modes of relaxation such as music and audiotapes, alternative methods include self-guided progressive muscular relaxation, deep breathing exercises, and massage/tactile relaxation methods.

Sport psychologists can conduct relaxation and imagery exercises with deaf/hoh athletes using either written or signed instructions first, then use light, vibrations, and/or appropriate tactile (touch) methods (with or without eyes opened) in lieu of sound. Boundaries, however, must be established, and discussion should take place regarding the type of touch that is acceptable to use for purposes of communication. Also be cognizant of the "speed" of your signs, which can assist in the relaxation and imagery process. For example,

455

a sport psychologist using his/her calming, soothing voice on a relaxation tape with hearing athletes can also achieve the same in sign language by signing in a soothing, calm manner; not signing LOUDLY, LARGELY and in the athlete's personal space.

Intervention strategies

For all deaf/hoh athletes, make eye contact and otherwise get their attention. A wave of the hand, a touch on the shoulder, flashing lights, or waving flags are some practical ways of gaining athletes' attention. Be mindful of the position of the light or sun when talking/signing. If the sun or light is behind you, it will impair the athlete's view. Facial/body language should be consistent with the practitioner's sign/verbal language. Use visual communication tools such as computers (e.g., Power Point, word processing), dry erase/chalk boards, flip charts, overhead projectors, text messaging, captioned and/or signed videos, web cameras, and written and/or signed instructions in your work with this population. If working with large groups, divide into smaller groups to facilitate ease of communication. You can also demonstrate your instructions and ask the athletes to mirror your movements or ask them to repeat instructions to check for communication understanding.

When working with these athletes on hearing teams, team-building exercises can assist the deaf/hoh athlete(s) to feel included, and aid in overall cohesiveness of the team. These methods may entail instructing hearing teammates about visual cues, signs, and gestures that help facilitate communication. Deaf/hoh athletes should also be encouraged to inform teammates and coaches of their specific needs. These athletes have similar performance issues as hearing athletes, and it should not be assumed that performance problems are related to their deafness. Please note when using sport psychology tests/inventories with Deaf athletes whose native language is not English (or specific spoken language of these tests), videotaped translations in the athletes' native sign language or qualified sign language interpreters should be provided (Clark & Sachs, 1991).

Deaf/hoh athletes are a heterogeneous population who share many of the same characteristics as hearing athletes. The difference in working with this population may be in communication methods and the highly visual nature of deaf/hoh athletes. These athletes seek optimal performance enhancement as much as other athletes. Sport psychologists have many opportunities to provide psychological skills training and other services for this generally underserved group of athletes.

Athletes who are deaf-blind

Sensory impairments may occur in combinations, as seen in athletes who are deaf and blind. Some individuals may be Deaf-blind, some deaf-Blind, some Deaf-Blind, and some legally deaf and legally blind, so there are many different definitions (culturally and linguistically). Similarly, many different communication methods must be used, depending on the deaf-blind person. For example, some deaf-blind have more hearing and poor vision, thus relying on speech and sounds for communication; others are deaf but have some vision, and communicate in sign language. Others have some vision, some hearing; some have neither and communicate via tactile means. The bottom line in working with deaf-blind athletes is to begin with the strategies indicated above for blind/VI and deaf/hoh athletes, but then tailor specific strategies to the needs of the individuals with whom you are working. Establishing and working with their preferred communication methods are essential.

The category of deaf-blind as a disability is officially recognized and included as part of the Paralympics. There are active deaf-blind athletes at different levels in many competitive sports, such as tandem cycling, speed skating, lawn bowling, running, and judo. Rules are altered as needed for deaf-blind participation.

Conclusion

The content of sport psychology sessions with athletes who are blind/visually impaired or deaf/hoh will be similar to sessions held with athletes without sensory impairments. The main differences will be in terms of the methods of communication. Competent professionals providing sport psychology services for athletes with sensory impairments will be aware of these similarities and differences and use them to their advantage in working most effectively with these athletes. See Boxes 47.1 and 47.2 for the main practical suggestions for working with these populations.

Box 47.1

Practical suggestions for working with athletes who are blind/visually impaired (VI)

- Talk with and observe the athletes to better understand the nature of their vision loss, as well as their strengths and challenges.
- Be sure that communications with athletes with VI are highly descriptive, accurate, and verbal.
- In using print or electronic media when working with athletes with VI, be sure to use methods that are compatible with the athletes' capabilities and resources.
- Athletes with VI may be able to appreciate the inclusion of visual information in imagery exercises because many currently have some visual ability, or have had it at some point in time.
- Assist athletes with VI and their fellow athletes in developing clear and effective on-field verbal communication strategies.
- Assist athletes with VI in preparing for travel to new, unfamiliar facilities for practice and/or competition. This preparation may help athletes reduce anxiety associated with the transition, thus allowing for increased attention on their athletic endeavors.
- Planning ahead and consulting with the athletes regarding any adaptations that may be necessary helps to ensure that athletes with VI are able to participate safely and as fully as possible alongside their athlete peers in any interventions that are implemented.

Box 47.2

Practical suggestions for working with athletes who are deaf/hoh

- Find out from the athletes what their preferred communication methods are. If the athletes communicate in sign language, then learn sign language or use a qualified sign language interpreter. Note that different sign languages are used in different countries, even those that speak the same language (e.g., UK, USA, Australia).
- Speak clearly and slowly but DO NOT EXAGGERATE your lip movements.
- For athletes who lip read, be sure to face the athlete when speaking. Also be aware of anything obstructing the view of your face/lips.
- Be aware of the position of the sun or light when communicating with all deaf/hoh athletes. If the sun or light is behind the sport psychologist, it will block the athlete's view. Therefore, the sport psychologist should make sure the light is in front or to the side of him/her.
- Make eye contact with, and otherwise get the attention of, the athlete. A wave of the hand, a touch on the shoulder, flashing lights, and waving flags are some practical ways of gaining the deaf/hoh athlete's attention.
- Use visual communication tools – such as computers (e.g., PowerPoint, word processing), dry erase/chalk boards, flip charts, overhead projectors, text messaging, captioned and/or signed videos, web cameras, and written or signed instructions.
- If working in large practice groups, divide into smaller groups because this tactic will facilitate ease of communication.
- Demonstrate instructions and ask the athletes to mirror your movements.
- Be aware that deaf/hoh athletes will not be able to hear you when they are actively performing. Give your instructions prior to performance (e.g., warm up, time out).

References

Clark, R. A., & Sachs, M. L. (1991). Challenges and opportunities in psychological skills training in deaf athletes. *The Sport Psychologist, 5*, 392–398.

Davis, A. (1995). *Hearing in adults*. London: Whurr.

Deaflympics (2010a). Deaflympics: Frederick, MD. Available from www.deaflympics.com

Deaflympics (2010b). *Eligibility*. Deaflympics: Frederick, MD. Available from www.deaflympics.com/athletes/?ID=239

International Blind Sports Federation (2010a). Vancouver: IBSA. Available from http://www.ibsa.es

International Blind Sports Federation (2010b). *Medical Classification*. Vancouver: IBSA. Retrieved from http://www.ibsa.es/docinteres/HTM/MedicalClassification.htm

Lighthouse International (2010). New York: Lighthouse International. Available from http://www.lighthouse.org

Lovett, J. M., Eickman, J., & Giansanti, T. (2001). *CISS 2001: A review*. Ossett, England: Red Lizard.

Padden, C., & Humphries, T. (1988). *Deaf in America: Voices from a culture*. Cambridge, MA: Harvard University Press.

Runyan, M. (2001). *No finish line: My life as I see it*. New York: Putnam's.

United States Association of Blind Athletes (2010). Colorado Springs, CO: USABA. Available from http://www.usaba.org

48

Culturally competent practitioners

Stephanie J. Hanrahan

In this book there are chapters about counseling skills, various frameworks and theories of therapy, issues experienced by individuals and teams, traditional mental skills, and population considerations. One factor overarching all of these elements is culture, or perhaps more accurately, cultures. The population chapters touch on cultures in terms of age, level of sport (e.g., professional sports, Olympics), sexual orientation, community (i.e., rural communities), and disability. The authors of Chapter 14 (acknowledging that cognitive behavioral therapy may have limited application within certain multicultural contexts) and Chapter 35 (stipulating that limited understanding and acceptance of people from different cultural backgrounds can be sources of tension between individuals and subgroups within teams) specifically mentioned culture, but cultures are a factor in every human interaction (and therefore every sport psychology session).

Norms, beliefs, values, and behaviors

We are all cultural beings. Both we and our clients have norms, beliefs, values, and behaviors that have been molded by cultures. Norms are the patterns, models, or standards regarded as typical within a particular culture. For example, when meeting people the cultural norm may be to shake hands, kiss, or just nod. In terms of psychology, in many mainstream cultures the norm for assessment and diagnosis is to use standardized and validated assessment instruments and a diagnostic manual such as the *Diagnostic and Statistical Manual of Mental Disorders* (American Psychiatric Association, 2000). In other cultures these forms of assessment and diagnosis may be seen as culturally invalid, with practitioners relying on observation and input from the family or community. Beliefs are opinions or convictions, confidence in the truth or existence of something not immediately susceptible to rigorous proof. Cultures differ in beliefs, for example in terms for and representation of God(s). Examples related to psychology and cultures include beliefs in evidence-based treatment, traditional healers, or healing rituals.

Values refer to relative worth, merit, or importance. Higher education, life experience, age, and accumulation of wealth are examples of values that vary by culture. Western psychologists

460

tend to value particular models (e.g., medical or biopsychosocial). In other cultures, where moral and spiritual laws are valued, psychological problems may be perceived to result from transgressing these laws.

Cultural behaviors are relatively objective, observed aspects of life such as language, dress, and what and how one eats. In terms of one-on-one psychological consultations, culture can influence punctuality, preferred distance from the psychologist, and whether or not eye contact is made. Norms, beliefs, values, and behaviors are interrelated. For example, in a team in which the time of each member is valued equally, there may be the belief that everyone (e.g., athletes, managers, coaches) should be treated equally, and team members should behave in accordance by arriving at the time a meeting is scheduled to begin. Another team, where the time of senior group members is valued more than that of junior members, beliefs likely reflect that team members have different levels of status, with senior staff and athletes regarded as having the most to offer to team decisions. In this case, junior team members may arrive to team meetings before senior members, with a meeting only beginning after the senior members have arrived (Schinke, Hanrahan, & Catina, 2009).

Culture: more than just nationality or race

We often tend to think of cultures in terms of people in different countries having different cultures. A Japanese kimono, Italian risotto, or Cuban salsa (the dance, not a sauce) are internationally recognized representations of different cultures. With the globalization of society, chances are slim that everyone on a team will have the same national heritage. Even a team that visually appears to be of similar heritage may be of English, German, and Swedish heritage or Ethiopian, Liberian, and Kenyan heritage (although here I would like to point out that there are Black Germans and White Kenyans). Aside from race and nationality, cultures are also determined by factors such as religion, socio-economic status, gender identity, sexuality, (dis)ability, type of sport, club tradition, neighborhood, and even family. Through socialization, groups of people who live in close proximity and/or under similar living conditions develop shared values, beliefs, and norms, as well as behaviors that are conducive to the particular situation.

We have all been enculturated; we have been socialized. We have learned the customs of the society in which we live and the ways of specific social groups within that society. For example, we have learned roles, norms, values, beliefs, and attitudes from family, peers, school, media, coaches, and society in general. How we act can change depending on the social environment in which we find ourselves. For example, I think most of us would have some variance in our behaviors (e.g., dress, tone of voice, specific actions) depending on whether we were in a cathedral, a pub, a hospital, a plane, or at a rock concert. Similarly, cultural norms vary by sport (e.g., synchronized swimming, boxing, surfing, archery.) We can consider these sports as different microcultures. Most people have experienced multiple microcultures.

When individuals experience a different macroculture, they begin a process of acculturation where they start to adopt a culture other than their original culture. When living in a new culture, some individuals retain the practices of their original culture and live in a community with others who have the same background and traditions; some retain their customs and language, but also integrate some of the customs and language of the new culture; bicultural individuals balance the two cultures; and finally, acculturated individuals fully adopt the ways of the new culture (Thomason, 1991). Because our clients can be in different places along this continuum of acculturation, we cannot assume what their values, norms, and beliefs might be just by being familiar with their culture of origin. It is also possible that clients, in a state of flux and confusion while in the process of acculturation, may benefit from the direct exploration of the differences in values of the culture of origin and the adopted culture. Children of first-generation immigrants may struggle with family friction that can develop because children tend to acculturate at a more rapid rate than their parents do (Roemer & Orsillo, 2009).

Within a single team, not only may people have different national heritages, if they are originally from another country (as an aside, 20% of the Australian population was born in a country other than Australia) they will have different enculturation experiences, different levels of acculturation, and different exposure to a potentially huge variety of different microcultures. Identifying a client's cultural background requires a lot more than simply knowing where they were born. Before worrying about the cultural factors that may influence our clients, however, we should begin with a bit of self-reflection. Particularly true for those of us who are members of the mainstream macroculture (i.e., the majority), we are often unaware of our own cultural identities. Nevertheless, as cultural beings, our values, beliefs, and behaviors are influenced by our cultures.

Collectivistic and individualistic cultures

The dominant cultural groups in Western societies such as Europe and the United States are individualistic. Characteristics of individualistic societies include independence, individual achievement, self-expression, individual thinking, personal choice, flexibility in roles, private property, and individual ownership (Ranzijn, McConnochie, & Nolan, 2009). The dominant cultural groups in many Eastern countries and most Indigenous cultures in the world are classified as collectivistic. Characteristics of collectivistic societies include interdependence, group success, adherence to norms, respect for authority and elders, group consensus, hierarchical roles, shared property, and group ownership (Ranzijn et al., 2009). Conflicts or misunderstandings can occur when people are unaware of, or do not accept, the different ways of thinking and acting that can occur when a team has individuals from both individualistic and collectivistic cultures. Athletes from individualistic cultures may be used to people owning their own gear, striving for personal bests, taking responsibility for their own fitness or strength training, and making decisions regarding strategy. Those from collectivistic societies may be accustomed to equipment being accessible to anyone, focusing only on team performance, waiting for others to guide them in all aspects of fitness training, and relying on the coach or extremely experienced players to determine strategy. An athlete from a collectivistic culture may use someone else's equipment (in a team in an individualistic country) with the belief that it is there for use by everyone, but the owner of the gear may think of the action as disrespectful or even theft. What one person may interpret as being slack and not taking responsibility or ownership may be perceived by another as being respectful to those of higher status. How athletes define success and whether one-on-one or group-based psychological interventions are most effective depend in part on whether they are from an individualistic or collectivistic culture (Schinke et al., 2009).

As practitioners we need to be aware of biases we might have, and be vigilant that we do not try to influence our clients to act in ways that are consistent with our own values. For example, psychologists from individualistic cultures may value personal fulfillment and engagement in personally meaningful activities, whereas athletes from collectivistic cultures may value providing for extended families and contributing to the community. I worked with an athlete from a collectivistic culture who began to miss training sessions and put in less than full effort when at training. Before exploring the situation with the athlete, I was assuming that either he was losing interest in the sport or that he was having issues with motivation. In reality, he was feeling guilty for putting time and effort into his own personal performance when he could be spending time with his family or using the time and energy to do something that might directly benefit his extended family and community.

In addition to collectivism versus individualism, cultures also have been classified in terms of their degrees of power distance, masculinity, and uncertainty avoidance (Hofstede, 2001). Power distance refers to the power differential between the rulers and those being ruled. Generally, democratic societies have a low power distance, and autocratic societies have a high power distance. If individuals from a culture with a low power distance find themselves in a culture with a high power distance, they may be seen as arrogant, aggressive, or rude, when their intentions were only to contribute to the team. Masculinity denotes how much value a culture places on traditionally male attributes (e.g., dominance, competitiveness) or female attributes (e.g., nurturing, fostering relationships). Within many sports masculinity is valued (even in women's teams). Sometimes coaches who have backgrounds in men's sports may find it challenging to coach women when competitiveness is valued, but athletes still may want to foster relationships. Uncertainty avoidance refers to how much cultures rely on well-established rules of behavior to resist change (Hofstede, 2001). Sport psychologists may face uncertainty avoidance when first working with a club or sport with strongly established traditions that do not include the development of psychological skills or communication. As with any aspect of culture, these classifications (i.e., individualistic/collectivistic, power distance, masculinity, uncertainty avoidance) only describe tendencies and do not predict individuals' behaviors and attitudes.

Cultural influences on personal space and time

We tend to feel uncomfortable when people crowd our personal space, yet may feel there is something wrong with us if people stay too far away. Cultural challenges may arise because the interpersonal space at which people feel comfortable can vary by more than four feet. A distance that is too close in one culture may be perceived as too far away in another. Norms for personal space also vary depending on the sport (i.e., the microculture). As consultants, we should take the lead from our clients in terms of personal space, rather than imposing our own norms onto our clients. In addition to the amount of space between client and consultant, we should also be aware of furniture arrangements and the setting. In some cultures it may be preferable to sit at an angle beside the client rather than face-to-face in one-on-one situations (Dudgeon, 2000). Meeting in an office may be uncomfortable for some (and impractical in some sporting situations). In some cultures (e.g., in Buenos Aires), seeing a psychologist is an accepted, common behavior. In other cultures (e.g., in rural areas in the United States and Australia), people may not want to be seen entering a psychologist's office because of a feeling of shame in having to seek help.

Cultures also influence concepts of time. The two main ways to conceptualize time are clock-based and event-based. In clock-based time (adhered to in Western mainstream cultures), people organize their schedules according to the clock with appointments scheduled to begin (and often end) at particular times. Clock-based time has advantages in situations where people are juggling meetings with different people in different places. There are, however, cultural differences in terms of clock-based time. In many Latin American cultures, schedules are made based on clock time, yet it is not unusual for the actual start time to be 30 or 45 minutes after the specified time. Arriving 30 minutes after the scheduled time is not considered as being late. In Ghana, GMT refers to Ghana Maybe Time (instead of Greenwich Mean Time); individuals can turn up an hour after an arranged time and not be late (Diehl, Hegley, & Lane, 2009).

Event-based time involves organizing a schedule using a relational strategy with the order of events established, but with no clear tie to the clock. Event-based time allows individuals to prioritize the process of a meeting and the exchange of ideas without keeping an eye on the clock, resulting in less-hurried exchanges. When we are working with people who have concepts of time that are different from our own, we need to discuss the issue openly and arrive at an agreed understanding, rather than get upset because others are late, assume lack of punctuality means a lack of interest or a lack of respect, or be confused because of others being upset by our behaviors.

Communication

To be useful consultants we need to be able to communicate effectively with the teams and athletes with whom we work (see Chapters 2 and 33). Psychological practice is reliant on communication. Just as with other behaviors and norms, aspects of communication are influenced by culture. Language is the most noticeable culturally affected component of communication. In addition to obviously different languages (e.g., English, Spanish, Mandarin), there also are differences in terminology and pronunciation in different countries or regions that speak the same language (e.g., English in Mississippi, Newfoundland, Dublin, Johannesburg, and Sydney; Spanish in Barcelona, Buenos Aires, Havana, Panama City, and Santo Domingo). Even seemingly simple words can have multiple meanings. In response to a question, "yes" may mean someone wants to be obliging and thought well of, someone has heard the question, or that someone agrees (Hanrahan, 2009).

Cultures can also differ in how information is obtained or conveyed, even if limiting the situation to one-on-one and in person. During intake interviews, psychologists may have a tendency to directly question clients, with the aim of obtaining answers to specific questions. For clients from cultures with strong oral traditions, a narrative approach that invites individuals to use their own words to tell their own stories would probably be more effective than a question-and-answer format. Although relying on hints and indirect questions may seem time consuming, this approach can sometime obtain more information than direct questioning, which can result in clients shutting down because of a feeling of being interrogated.

Many of us probably have worked with teams and have used a variety of methods to reach team consensuses about various issues (e.g., training times, uniforms, team captains, team rules and responsibilities, team cohesion). Athletes from different cultures may vary in their willingness to express firm opinions. Athletes may not respond to a comment or question, not because they don't have an opinion, but because they feel they are not in a position to make a comment (Dudgeon, 2000). For example, athletes may not feel it is warranted to express their opinions in front of the coach, even if the coach is directly asking them a question. Some individuals may be unwilling to state their opinions in a team meeting even if the coach is not present, particularly if they perceive their views to be in conflict with the opinions of others. As consultants, we need to ensure that we do not assume that a lack of response means a lack of interest. One way around this potentially problematic situation is to use post-it note voting (see Chapter 34) or other methods of obtaining viewpoints anonymously.

Eye contact is another component of communication whose meaning varies across cultures. Many of us were probably taught in basic counseling courses to make eye contact with clients because it shows that you are paying attention and are interested in what they have to say. In some cultures eye contact is part of being polite (e.g., the parental demand to "Look at me when I'm talking to you"). In other cultures avoiding eye contact is a sign of respect. In yet other cultures prolonged eye contact may be considered offensive, intrusive, aggressive, or even an attempt at seduction (Dudgeon, Garvey, & Pickett, 2000). The key, as with many other cultural differences, is to take our cues from our clients and/or openly discuss the issue.

A continuum of cultural competence

Wells (2000) developed a series of six stages from cultural incompetence to cultural proficiency. The first three stages, cultural incompetence, knowledge, and awareness, make up the cognitive phase and emphasize acquiring knowledge and understanding. The final three stages, cultural sensitivity, competence, and proficiency, form the affective phase and focus on changes in attitudes and behaviors as a result of applying the knowledge obtained in the cognitive phase. Wells argued that individuals (or institutions) must actually experience working with individuals from other cultures to progress through the affective stages. See Table 48.1 for a description of the six stages.

As an individual it is difficult to develop cultural competence if working within a culturally incompetent organization. Wells (2000) would argue it is not viable for an individual to be culturally proficient within a culturally incompetent organization. It may be almost impossible to engage in culturally appropriate practices if management has rigid structures in place that do not allow for individual variations. The value of a culturally competent practitioner could be undermined by a culturally incompetent receptionist. A challenge for all of us may be to consider how we might increase the cultural competence of the organizations

Table 48.1 A continuum of culture competence based on Wells (2000).

Phase	Stage	Description
Cognitive	Cultural incompetence	No knowledge of the cultural influences or implications of behavior
	Cultural knowledge	Learning the components of culture and their role in determining behavior
	Cultural awareness	Recognizing and understanding the cultural influences and implications of behavior
Affective	Cultural sensitivity	The integration of cultural knowledge and awareness into behavior
	Cultural competence	The routine application of culturally appropriate practices and interventions
	Cultural proficiency	The integration of cultural competence into professional practice, teaching, and research of the individual and the organization

and institutions within which we work. Providing information about culture(s) can help with the cognitive phase of development, but the affective phase requires interactions, discussions, and experience. In some sporting clubs where cultural differences are ignored, or worse, a cause for bullying, we may be in a position to model cultural competence; reinforce instances of cultural awareness, sensitivity, or competence in others; or challenge rules, regulations, or policy that get in the way of the development of a culturally proficient organization.

Worldviews

We all hold worldviews, or mental representations of the world, that are developed by socialization and life experiences. Worldviews help us make sense of what we observe and what we do, providing a feeling of security due to some sense of predictability. We have a tendency to assume, unconsciously, that our worldview, or concept of reality, is the correct one. When we stay predominantly within one culture, we tend not to be aware of our worldviews because the main components are shared by those around us, and are therefore not brought into question. As Ranzijn *et al.* (2009) noted:

> Trying to describe our own worldview is like a fish trying to describe what water is: a fish could not describe water, since it is immersed in water all of the time. However, if you take a fish out of water it knows instantly what water is, since it now experiences what water is not. ... Similarly, we may find it hard to describe our own worldview until it is challenged, perhaps through interacting with or encountering people with very different worldviews.
>
> (p. 14)

Cognitively it is relatively easy to understand that others' worldviews have as much validity and value as our own, but emotionally it may be challenging to accept the values, beliefs, and concepts of worldviews that are dramatically different from our own. Our worldviews filter how we interpret the behaviors of others. When people from different cultures attempt to understand each others' worldviews, they do so through their own filters, making it potentially impossible to truly understand. As consultants, we need to be aware of how our own worldviews may be filtering what our clients say and the behaviors we observe. The good news is that immersing ourselves in other cultures, whether for an hour at a local community center or for months in another country, can open us to the worldviews of others (and perhaps begin to change our own). Getting to know each of our clients as individuals, with regular checks of our own assumptions, can result in a respectful relationship and be a step toward cultural competence.

Conclusion

Almost all of us are working, or will work, with individuals from a variety of macrocultures. All of us do work with individuals from an array of microcultures, and we should strive not only for cultural awareness, but also cultural competence (and ideally working within organizations that are culturally proficient). We need to reflect on how our own cultural backgrounds can influence how we perceive and interact with our clients. By being genuinely interested in and interacting with individuals, we can get an idea of their worldviews and how their cultural backgrounds might influence the client–practitioner relationship. Although I recommend that sport psychologists become familiar with ethical guidelines related to culture provided by their professional organizations (e.g., American Psychological Association, 2003), reading and having a cognitive understanding of culture are only the first steps. For effective multi-cultural practice (i.e., all practice), we need to experience other cultures, reflect on our own, and learn to apply routinely the knowledge we have gained in the form of culturally appropriate practices and interventions. See Box 48.1 for the key points from this chapter.

Box 48.1

Key points about culture

- We and our clients have been molded by cultures.
- Norms, beliefs, values, and behaviors are influenced by cultures. These norms, beliefs, values, and behaviors influence how we practise psychology.
- Cultural identity is difficult to determine because many of us have been exposed to multiple macrocultures, and all of us have experienced numerous microcultures.
- Characteristics that we value may not be valued by some of our clients, because of cultural differences such as individualism/collectivism, power distance, masculinity, and uncertainty avoidance.
- Clients may differ in how they conceptualize time, the interpersonal space they find to be comfortable, and the settings in which they prefer to meet for consultations. The key is to discuss these issues openly and come to a shared understanding.
- Cultural backgrounds influence how people communicate. Language, terminology, pronunciation, questioning, stating opinions, and eye contact are just some of the facets of communication affected by culture.
- The development of cultural competence has cognitive and affective components. Cultural proficiency requires individual as well as organizational cultural competence.
- As consultants we need to be aware of how our own worldviews may filter what our clients say and the behaviors we observe.

References

American Psychiatric Association (2000). *Diagnostic and statistical manual of mental disorders* (4th ed., text Rev.). Washington, DC: American Psychiatric Association.

American Psychological Association (2003). Guidelines on multicultural education, training, research, practice and organizational change for psychologists. *American Psychologist, 58*, 377–402.

Diehl, C., Hegley, A., & Lane, A. M. (2009). Working with Ghanaian athletes. In R. J. Schinke & S. J. Hanrahan (Eds.), *Cultural sport psychology* (pp. 173–183). Champaign, IL: Human Kinetics.

Dudgeon, P. (2000). Counseling with indigenous people. In P. Dudgeon, D. Garvey, & H. Pickett (Eds.), *Working with indigenous Australians: A handbook for psychologists* (pp. 249–271). Perth, WA, Australia: Gunada Press.

Dudgeon, P., Garvey, D., & Pickett, H. (2000). *Working with indigenous Australians: A handbook for psychologists.* Perth, WA, Australia: Gunada Press.

Hanrahan, S. J. (2009). Working with Australian Aboriginal athletes. In R. J. Schinke & S. J. Hanrahan (Eds.), *Cultural sport psychology* (pp. 185–192). Champaign, IL: Human Kinetics.

Hofstede, G. (2001). *Cultural consequences: Comparing values, behaviors, institutions, and organizations across nations* (2nd ed.). Thousand Oaks, CA: Sage.

Ranzijn, R., MacConnochie, K., & Nolan, W. (2009). *Psychology and indigenous Australians: Foundation of cultural competence.* South Yarra, VIC, Australia: Palgrave Macmillan.

Roemer, L., & Orsillo, S. M. (2009). *Mindfulness- & acceptance-based behavioral therapies in practice.* New York: Guilford.

Schinke, R. J., Hanrahan, S. J., & Catina, P. (2009). Introduction to cultural sport psychology. In R. J. Schinke & S. J. Hanrahan (Eds.), *Cultural sport psychology* (pp. 3–11). Champaign, IL: Human Kinetics.

Thomason, T. C. (1991). Counseling Native Americans: An introduction for non-Native American counselors. *Journal of Counseling and Development, 69,* 321–327.

Wells, M. I. (2000). Beyond cultural competence: A model for individual and institutional cultural development. *Journal of Community Health Nursing, 17*(4), 189–199.

Section VII

Mental skills

49

Activation/arousal control

Robert Weinberg

I love the pressure. I just look forward to it.

Daly Thompson, Olympic decathlon gold medalist

The thing that always worked best for me whenever I felt I was getting too tense to play good tennis was to simply remind myself that the worst thing – the very worst thing that could happen to me – was that I'd lose a bloody tennis match. That's all.

Rod Laver, Hall of Fame tennis champion

Most competitive athletes spend a great deal of time physically practising their skills and honing the precise movement patterns necessary to perform at high levels. Sooner or later athletes have to perform their skills in competition where there are usually competitors, spectators, and coaches present. In addition, society places a premium on winning, and there may be high expectations placed on athletes. Expectations usually result in athletes feeling pressure to perform and becoming highly aroused, which often translates into decreases in performance. This scenario, however, does not have to be the case. We all know athletes who seem to thrive under pressure and perform at their best. The two quotes above highlight how athletes may experience and interpret pressure and arousal symptoms differently.

Definitions of arousal and anxiety

The terms arousal and anxiety are often confused and used interchangeably. Although there is some overlap, they are conceptually different. Arousal is defined as a blend of physiological and psychological activity in a person falling along a continuum from deep sleep to extreme excitation. Arousal is not automatically associated with either pleasant or unpleasant events. For example, individuals could become highly aroused winning the lottery or learning about a death in the family. Increases in arousal are intimately associated with sympathetic nervous system activation, whereas it is the parasympathetic nervous system that is engaged when an athlete becomes more relaxed.

Anxiety is defined as a negative emotional state (feeling fearful and uncomfortable, experiencing dread) characterized by nervousness, worry, and apprehension and associated with activation or arousal of the body. Anxiety has a thought component (e.g., worry, apprehension) called cognitive anxiety. It also has a somatic component that is the degree of physical activation (e.g., increased heart rate, generalized muscle tension, galvanic skin response). So, a racing heart and an increased respiration rate could be an increase in arousal or anxiety depending on the context of the situation.

Assessment of arousal

The primary way to determine athletes' arousal levels is to observe or measure their physiological reactions. Athletes can sometimes hide symptoms, making it difficult to determine arousal levels simply by observing athletes' physical reactions. In addition, sport psychology consultants often do not observe athletes extensively when the latter are actively engaging in their sports, so they do not notice these symptoms if they happen to be there. Despite these limitations it is instructive to know typical physiological reactions to increases in arousal that directly involve the cardiovascular system and the classic "flight or fight" response with blood rushing to the large muscle groups as the body prepares for action. Some typical sympathetic physiological reactions include (a) accelerated heart rate, (b) increases in galvanic skin response (sweating), (c) increased blood pressure, (d) nausea or abdominal distress, (e) shortness of breath, (f) increased generalized muscle tension, (g) trembling or shaking, and (h) feeling dizzy, lightheaded. These symptoms should not be confused, however, with the normal physiological reactions to physical activity. Heart rate monitors, for example, cannot differentiate between increased heart rate as a result of running and rapid heart rate due to perceived excitement or fear. Although not as observable, some cognitive and behavioral symptoms of increases in arousal can include (a) excess worry and apprehension, (b) difficulty concentrating, (c) difficulty making decisions, (d) rumination, (e) withdrawal or isolation, and (f) difficulty staying on task.

Arousal–performance relationship

Over the years there have been many theories put forth to explain the relationship between arousal and performance, but one constant has been the idea that there seems to be an optimal level of arousal at which athletes perform their best. Instead of attempting to review all the theories and their different predictions, I will focus on one approach that has practical implications for consulting with athletes.

Zones of optimal functioning

Using his initial consulting practice and then conducting supportive empirical research, Hanin (1997) found that different athletes appear to have different optimal levels of arousal (anxiety levels in particular) for their best performances. In essence, Hanin argued for an individual differences approach to finding athletes' optimal levels of arousal. Instead of athletes comparing themselves to others, they need to become aware of their own individual zones of optimal functioning. We all know some athletes who need to be at high levels of arousal (pumped up), whereas others need to be at low levels (cool and calm). So, how does one go about finding an athlete's optimal level of arousal?

Initially, we have to find what level of arousal is most associated with high levels of performance. Hanin (1997) originally attempted this determination using the State Anxiety Inventory (Spielberger, 1966) before several competitions (or retrospectively after several competitions), to find an athlete's individualized zone of optimal functioning (IZOF). In his more recent work, however, Hanin (2000) has expanded to studying optimal zones for different emotions and feeling states. He has used items from the Positive and Negative Affect Scale (Watson, Clark, & Tellegen, 1988) to measure certain emotional states.

Hanin has argued that there are pleasant states that may have positive influences on performance (e.g., energetic, motivated, charged, confident), pleasant states that may have negative influences on performance (e.g., easygoing, tranquil, relaxed), unpleasant states that may have negative influences on performance (e.g., tired, sluggish, depressed, lazy), and unpleasant states that may have positive influences on performance (e.g., tense, dissatisfied, nervous, angry). Hanin (2000) has focused on the notion of direction (interpretation) of arousal states in addition to the typical focus on intensity (the amount of arousal). Jones and colleagues popularized this concept of direction in the mid-1990s and focused on whether the anxiety felt by a performer was perceived as facilitative or debilitative to performance (Jones & Swain 1995; Jones, Swain, & Hardy, 1993). For example, two athletes listening to the national anthem right before a game might have their hearts start to beat really fast and get queasy feelings in their stomachs. However, one athlete interprets this queasy feeling as facilitative ("I'm ready to go") whereas the other athlete perceives it as debilitative ("I'm so nervous I hope I don't mess up"). Alternatively, one athlete might view the emotion of tranquility either positively or negatively. Therefore, athletes might benefit from being taught to interpret their arousal symptoms in a facilitative manner (to help performance) as well as develop techniques that will help them be optimally ready for competitions. These techniques might involve reducing or increasing arousal levels, and they will be the main focus of the remainder of the chapter.

Matching best performance with arousal levels

Determining arousal levels is only one part of what is needed; over several competitions, performance should also be assessed. Performance can be measured either objectively or subjectively. For example, in assessing basketball performance, one could simply look at a player's objective performance in relation to such things as scoring (shooting percentage), assists, rebounds, steals, and so forth and develop a composite performance assessment. Alternatively, the athlete (or the coach) could rate her performance in relation to how she normally plays from "1" (much worse than usual) to "11" (much better than usual). The first way appears to be the more objective, but it is dependent on the performances of teammates and opponents.

After assessing both arousal and performance for several competitions, one is now ready to create a zone of optimal functioning using the best performances and the arousal states that are associated with these top performances. In Hanin's (1997) original work, he used plus/minus a half of a standard deviation (that was plus or minus 4 on the State Anxiety Inventory). But you can create a zone you want based on scores on a test (e.g., Positive and Negative Affect Scale) or on certain autonomic nervous system reactions such as heart rate or breathing rate. The goal, then, would be to regulate arousal levels so that the desired optimal levels (associated with top performance) would be achieved at least just prior to performance. It then becomes the athlete's responsibility to try to maintain this zone throughout competition. The next section contains some techniques and references for regulating arousal levels.

Relaxation strategies

For most athletes, the problem is usually too much arousal as opposed to too little, particularly during important competitions or games. Therefore, the focus has often been on reducing arousal, because the many potential negative effects, both physical (e.g., tight muscles, racing heart) and mental (e.g., inappropriate attentional focus, poor decision making), can produce decreases in performance. The old adage of "giving 110%" does not really work because athletes tend to tense all their muscles in attempting to give 110% effort (not to mention it being impossible to give more than 100%). Skilled performance usually involves an intricate interplay between having some muscles relaxed while others are contracting. Simply trying to relax usually will not work. The relaxation techniques need to be systematically practised so that athletes learn different techniques to achieve relaxation. Consultants working with athletes should always be cognizant of the matching hypothesis, which basically states that an arousal management technique should be matched to meet the needs of the individual. For example, worry and apprehension should be treated with techniques that focus on calming the negative cognitions, and unwanted physiological activation should be treated with physical relaxation (e.g., progressive muscular relaxation, diaphragmatic breathing).

Breath control

One of the easiest but most effective ways to reduce arousal is through breath control. When under pressure, many athletes do not breathe efficiently. All breaths have inhalation and exhalation phases with inhalation producing tension and exhalation producing relaxation. In many relaxation exercises the inhalation phase is be shorter than the exhalation phase (a 1:2 ratio is often used). That is, if athletes inhale for two seconds they should exhale for approximately four seconds, or if they inhale for three seconds they should exhale for six seconds. A final point is that each breath should come from the diaphragm (belly) because this produces deeper and slower breathing by drawing the breath fully into the lower parts of the lungs.

To practise breath control, athletes should take a deep complete breath and imagine the lungs are divided into three levels. They should focus on filling the lower level of the lungs with air, first by pushing the diaphragm down and forcing the abdomen out. Then they should fill the middle portion of the lungs by expanding the chest cavity and raising the rib cage. Finally, the upper level of the lungs should be filled by raising the chest and shoulders slightly. After briefly inhaling, exhale slowly by pulling the abdomen in and lowering the shoulders and chest. By focusing on the lowering (inhalation) and rising (exhalation) of the diaphragm, they will experience an increased sense of stability, centeredness, and relaxation.

Breath control is particularly useful during a break in the action or before performing a specific skill such as serving in tennis, hitting a golf ball, kicking a field goal, taking a penalty shot in soccer, or before starting a gymnastic routine or figure skating program. Finally, although breathing generally is a somatically-based strategy, if athletes focus on their breathing, breath control has the added benefit of reducing negative thoughts because cognitions such as mentally counting the seconds of inhalation and exhalation keep one focused on numbers and breathing so there is little room for other unwanted thoughts.

474

Progressive muscular relaxation

When it comes to relaxation, the "gold standard" is probably progressive muscular relaxation (PMR) originally developed by Jacobson (1938). PMR rests on several basic assumptions: (a) it is possible to learn the difference between tension and relaxation in the muscles; (b) tension and relaxation are mutually exclusive – it is not possible for a muscle to be tense and relaxed at the same time; and (c) relaxation of the body through decreased muscle tension will lead to fewer anxious thoughts because one cannot be worried and relaxed at the same time.

It is called progressive muscular relaxation because one progressively contracts and relaxes each major muscle group until all targeted muscles are relaxed. The tension–relaxation cycles develop an athlete's awareness of the difference between tension and lack of tension in the muscles. Each cycle involves maximally contracting one specific muscle group and then attempting to relax that same muscle group as much as possible, all the while focusing on the different sensations of tension and relaxation. With practise, athletes can detect tension in a specific muscle or area of the body, and then relax that muscle. Prior to or within competition, if athletes feel that they are tight/tense in certain areas of the body (e.g., many people manifest anxiety in the neck and shoulder areas), then they can scan their bodies for any residual tension and use PMR to relax those specific muscles. The first few sessions of progressive relaxation can take about 30 minutes, although less time is necessary as athletes develop the ability to relax.

Because the original PMR protocol can take some time to learn and implement, Ost (1988) developed a variation of PMR that allows athletes to relax in a shorter time frame. Specifically, the first phase of training involves a 15-minute progressive relaxation session practised twice a day in which targeted muscle groups are tensed. The individual then moves to a relax-only phase that takes 5–7 minutes. The time is next reduced to a 2- to 3-minute version with the use of the self-instructional cue, "relax." This time is finally reduced until only a few seconds are required, making the technique useful in actual sport situations.

Relaxation response

Herbert Benson popularized a clinically validated way of relaxing that he called the relaxation response (Benson & Proctor, 1984). Benson's method applies the basic principles of meditation, but does not contain any spiritual or religious connotations. The state of mind produced by this technique is characterized by keen awareness, effortlessness, relaxation, spontaneity, and focused attention. The four basic steps include the following (20–30 minutes):

1. *Quiet environment:* External distractions are at a minimum.
2. *Comfortable position:* No set position as long as the athletes can hold the position throughout the procedure.
3. *Mental device:* Focusing on a single thought or word and repeating it over and over. For example, words such as ease, calm, or relax would be repeated in conjunction with exhaling.
4. *Passive attitude:* If while repeating the mental devices other thoughts enter their minds, the athletes should not attend to them and instead let them simply go out of their minds. Athletes should then refocus attention on the mental devices.

475

Autogenic training

Schultz developed autogenic training in the 1930s and refined it with the help of Luthe in 1969 (see Schultz & Luthe, 1969). This relaxation process has been used extensively in Europe but less so in North America. Autogenic training consists of a series of exercises designed to produce sensations of warmth and heaviness. Basically it is a technique of self-hypnosis where attention is focused on the sensations one is trying to produce. The autogenic training program is based on six hierarchical stages that usually are learned in the following order: (a) heaviness in the extremities, (b) warmth in the extremities, (c) regulation of cardiac activity, (d) regulation of breathing, (e) abdominal warmth, and (f) cooling of the forehead.

The statements "my right arm is heavy," "my right arm is warm and relaxed, "my heartbeat is regular and calm," and "my forehead is cool" are examples of commonly used verbal cues in autogenic training. It may take several months of regular practice (10 to 40 minutes per day) to become proficient in experiencing warmth and heaviness in the legs along with changes in cardiac and respiratory cycles (that is one reason why it probably did not catch on in time-poor North America).

Pre-competition routines

Two sources that may bring about debilitative arousal in athletes are uncertainty and loss of control. There are many things in athletes' environments that are out of their control, such as the weather, officials, opponents, spectators, and coaches. These situations and people external to athletes can cause arousal levels to rise past optimal levels. One way to take control of the situation is through the use of pre-competition or competition routines. Routines are structured, systematic ways of thinking and behaving when preparing for competition or for events occurring throughout competition. These routines are within the control of athletes and can be followed regardless of the situation or external events. In addition, routines work by helping athletes divert their attention from task-irrelevant (usually negative thoughts such as "what will my teammates think if I miss this field goal") to task-relevant cognitions ("just keep your head down"). Routines may increase the likelihood that athletes will not be distracted internally or externally prior to, or during performance. For example, many athletes have developed specific routines before performance such as serving in tennis, hitting a golf ball, kicking a field goal, shooting a free throw, and taking a penalty shot. See Chapter 56 for more information about pre-performance routines.

Cognitive-affective stress management training (SMT)

SMT is a comprehensive package of techniques designed to produce an integrated coping response (Smith, 1980). SMT offers specific intervention strategies, such as relaxation (PMR), cognitive restructuring (reframing, positive self-talk), and self-instructional training ("keep your head down"). There are four distinct phases: (a) pretreatment assessment – assessing the situations causing stress, the athletes' reactions to stress, and how stress affects the athletes; (b) treatment rationale – understanding their stress reactions and that the treatment is to assist them in gaining control and coping with stress; (c) skill acquisition – learning different skills including relaxation, cognitive restructuring, and self-instructional cues; and (d) skill rehearsal – deliberately introducing stress so athletes can use the skills acquired to practise coping with the stress.

Imagery

One of the easiest ways for athletes to relax is through imagery. By consciously visualizing a relaxing image, athletes allow their bodies to unwind and relax. For example, athletes can imagine the blood flowing into their muscles to increase their warmth and elasticity or imagine drinking a warm liquid and feeling it seep through their bodies, relaxing their arms, legs, shoulders, necks, backs, and trunk. Furthermore, athletes can imagine a situation that has caused them to become overaroused in the past (e.g., shooting critical free throws at the end of a game) and see themselves coping with this overarousal (by using one of the aforementioned techniques). Imagined events stimulate us, much like real events, so athletes can practise their relaxation through imagining themselves, for example, staying calm in a tense competitive situation. See Chapter 50 for additional information about imagery.

Self-talk

Self-talk is basically a verbal monologue athletes have with themselves that can either be out loud or just inside their heads (auditory imagery). Although self-talk can take many forms, it is usually categorized into three types: positive (motivational) self-talk (e.g., "I can do it") that focuses on increasing energy and effort and staying positive; instructional self-talk (e.g., "bend your knees") that helps athletes stay focused on task-relevant cues; and negative self-talk (e.g., "that was a stupid shot") that usually creates unease and fosters self-doubt. The basic idea of using some sort of positive/instructional self-talk is that athletes gain the ability to talk themselves into calming down, putting forth effort, or staying focused. Words and phrases such as "slow down," breathe and relax," and "calm" are self-suggestions that can remind athletes to stay calm and relaxed during critical and stressful points during competition or regularly throughout competition. For example, runners could remind themselves to "keep their shoulders relaxed" or golfers could remind themselves to "relax and take a deep breath" before important shots.

It is often assumed that negative events cause stress. Psychologists, however, have come to understand that it is often the self-talk that comes after the negative event that produces athletes' stress reactions. For example, after a poor performance, a baseball player might say "I just can't play in the major leagues," which could result in the player feeling stressed, anxious, frustrated, and hopeless. Given the same situation, however, another player might say "I just need to work more on being more patient at the plate," which could result in increased effort, motivation, and optimism. Research (see Weinberg & Gould, 2007 for a review) across a wide variety of sports has consistently revealed that performance is increased after positive and instructional self-talk but decreased after negative self-talk. Changing negative to positive self-talk may not only reduce stress but may also increase performance. See Chapter 53 for additional information on self-talk.

Arousal-inducing techniques

As noted earlier, a major problem for athletes is being over-aroused or being too "pumped up." There are, however, times when intensity levels need to be increased, such as when athletes are feeling lackadaisical, tired, or possibly overconfident. Under-arousal is usually more of an issue during training than during competition. Whenever it occurs, coaches need to be careful not to overly psych athletes up with pre-game pep talks and motivational speeches because these talks can be debilitative for some athletes. So if arousal is going to be raised, it should be done in a deliberate fashion with awareness of optimal arousal states. Some signs of being underactivated or underaroused might include (a) constantly wandering thoughts, (b) feeling bored or uninterested, (c) heavy feeling in the legs, (d) moving slowly, and (e) lack of anticipation/enthusiasm. There are a number of techniques that athletes can use to become more energized including the following:

Increase breathing rate

Short, quick breaths can help energize athletes. When increasing activation the focus is on inhalation instead of exhalation. To increase the effect, athletes say "energy in" with each inhalation and "fatigue out" with each exhalation.

Physical activity

Jumping up and down, slapping thighs, and pumping fists can all stimulate blood flow and increase activation. For example, tennis players often bounce on the balls of their feet before serving or receiving serve. In addition, before competition, some athletes like to work out and get a sweat going to get themselves activated for competition.

Mood words/positive statements

Thinking can certainly affect physiology. For example, saying or thinking mood words (e.g., hustle, strong, move, tough, quick) can get the athlete activated. In addition positive self-statements such as "hang in there," "get tough," "get going," and "I can do it" can also raise arousal levels.

Act energized

Sometimes athletes might not feel energetic and motivated, but if they act pumped up they can often recapture their high energy levels. Head up, shoulders back, and walking quickly are some actions that can increase arousal.

Upbeat music

Listening to fast, upbeat music or a favorite tune can sometimes help athletes become activated, enthusiastic, and ready for competition. Many athletes now use headphones and iPods to listen to energetic music before competition to help increase arousal and create positive feelings.

Energizing imagery

As noted earlier, imagery can be used for relaxation. Imagery can also be used to generate positive feelings and energy. Energizing imagery involves visualizing something that is exciting to the individual. For example, a sprinter might imagine a cheetah running swiftly over the plains or a swimmer might imagine moving through the water like a shark.

Summary

In this chapter I have discussed the arousal–performance relationship, with a special focus on ways in which to regulate arousal levels. Box 49.1 summarizes some of the main points from this chapter.

Box 49.1

Main points about arousal control

- Arousal and affect can be measured through the use of questionnaires (e.g., Positive and Negative Affect Scale) or through physiological reactions (e.g., heart rate, breathing rate).
- Compared to the traditional intensity of anxiety/arousal symptoms, the direction of anxiety/arousal (interpretation as facilitative or debilitative) seems to be more critical to performance.
- All athletes have an optimal level or zone of arousal where they experience their top performances.
- These zones of optimal functioning are different for different athletes.
- Creating an optimal zone requires a number of arousal assessments (either before competition or retrospectively) correlated with performances (subjective or objective).
- Arousal reducing techniques are usually focused on physical relaxation (e.g., progressive muscular relaxation, breath control) or mental relaxation (relaxation response, self-talk).
- Typical arousal-inducing strategies include energizing imagery, mood words/positive statements, physical activity, upbeat music, and increased breathing rate.

References

Benson, H., & Proctor, W. (1984). *Beyond the relaxation response*. New York: Berkeley.

Hanin, Y. (1997). Emotions and athletic performance: Individual zones of optimal functioning. *European Yearbook of Sport Psychology 1*, 29–72.

Hanin, Y. (2000). *Emotions in sport*. Champaign, IL: Human Kinetics.

Jacobson, E. (1938). *Progressive relaxation*. Chicago: University of Chicago Press.

Jones, G., & Swain, A. (1995). Predisposition to experience debilitative and facilitative anxiety in elite and non-elite performers. *The Sport Psychologist, 9*, 201–211.

Jones, G., Swain, A., & Hardy, L. (1993). Intensity and direction dimensions of competitive state anxiety and relationships with performance. *Journal of Sport Sciences, 11*, 525–532.

Ost, L. (1988). Applied relaxation: Description of an effective coping technique. *Scandinavian Journal of Behavior Therapy, 17*, 83–96.

Schultz, J., & Luthe, W. (1969). *Autogenic methods* (Vol. 1). New York: Grune and Stratton.

Smith, R. (1980) A cognitive-affective approach for stress management training for athletes. In C. Nadeau, W. Halliwell, K. Newell, & G. Roberts (Eds.), *Psychology of motor behavior and sport -1979* (pp. 54–72), Champaign, IL: Human Kinetics.

Spielberger, C. D. (1966). Theory and research on anxiety. In C. D. Spielberger (Ed.), *Anxiety and behavior* (pp. 3–20). New York: Academic Press.

Watson, D., Clark, L., & Tellegen, A. (1988). Development and validation of brief measures of positive and negative affect: The PANAS scales. *Journal of Personality and Social Psychology, 54,* 1063–1070.

Weinberg, R., & Gould, D. (2007). *Foundations of sport and exercise psychology* (4th ed.). Champaign, IL: Human Kinetics.

50

Imagery

Tony Morris

Imagery is a mental process that is almost always with us. When we feel hungry and think about a bacon sandwich, we see the cooked bacon curling out of the sides of the bread, smell the unique aroma, and taste the salty smoked meat. When we must give somebody bad news, knowing they will be upset, we rehearse the words we will use to deliver the news and the soft, somber tone of voice, then we perceive their distraught reaction. All these sights, sounds, tastes, smells, and emotions are aspects of imagery, a rich multi-sensory experience that we create intentionally, but which sometimes seems to arise automatically.

Athletes often generate imagery about their sports. They imagine themselves performing the technical skills; they picture themselves playing well or badly; they go over mistakes in their minds; they experience anxiety about upcoming competition; they think about winning or losing and their reactions to each (e.g., Morris, Spittle, & Perry, 2004). Imagery is a ubiquitous process, and researchers have found that it is the most widely-used psychological skills training (PST) technique among athletes, coaches, and sport psychologists (e.g., DeFrancesco & Burke, 1997). Nevertheless, the automatic imagery experiences athletes have about their sports are often negative (Morris, Spittle, & Watt, 2005). Because imagery can have a powerful influence on thoughts, feelings, and behaviors, all of which affect how athletes play their sports, imagery has been applied extensively for performance enhancement in sport (Morris *et al.*, 2005).

Given that imagery appears in infinite forms in all aspects of our lives, psychologists have, for a long time, applied imagery in a great diversity of contexts (e.g., Stewart, 1996) that go well beyond the confines of PST and even the variety of approaches grouped under the rubric of cognitive-behavioral therapies (CBT), which form the majority of PST techniques. Thus, in this chapter I also describe and exemplify use of imagery in a psychotherapeutic context, involving mindfulness meditation and acceptance and commitment therapy (ACT; Harris, 2008).

What imagery is

Imagery is an ephemeral process. We can't see it, hear it, or touch it, so defining imagery has proved challenging. In sport, the definition Richardson (1969) proposed is widely accepted. Morris et al. (2005) expanded on it a little to suggest:

> Imagery, in the context of sport, may be considered as the creation or re-creation of an experience generated from memorial information, involving quasi-sensorial, quasi-perceptual, and quasi-affective characteristics, that is under the volitional control of the imager and which may occur in the absence of the real stimulus antecedents normally associated with the actual experience.
>
> (p. 19)

This definition emphasizes that, although the generation of imagery is based on past experience, it is possible, and often desirable, to imagine something one has never actually experienced, such as performing a triple back somersault, running a marathon, or winning an Olympic final. The definition also makes it clear that people can control what they imagine, but when it is not consciously controlled our imagery is often unhelpful or even mischievous.

How imagery works

Many theories have been proposed to explain how imagery affects thoughts, feelings, and behavior. In sport, the focus has been on explaining how imagery can enhance learning and performance. An enduring explanation is the psychoneuromuscular theory (Jacobson, 1930). Jacobson argued that imagery triggers low-level innervation of the muscles involved in performance, strengthening those specific brain-to-muscle connections through feedback similar to that experienced when the task is performed physically. Symbolic learning theory (Sackett, 1934) focuses on cognition. Sackett specifically claimed that imagery involves rehearsal of the symbolic aspects of tasks, such as sequences of actions. Lang (1977) proposed a bioinformational theory, arguing that imagery involves representations of aspects of experiences, which he called propositions. Stimulus propositions represent the stimuli that signal action, whereas response propositions represent characteristics of the action taken. According to Lang, imagery that involves response propositions is particularly powerful. Lang's interest was in the emotions that accompany behaviors, so bioinformational theory emphasizes affective response propositions. Although research has provided some support for each of these theories, no theory is without noteworthy limitations. Low-level innervations have been recorded in the muscles involved in specific movements, but critics argue that these are only by-products of the imagery process. Tasks involving larger cognitive components have shown greater performance effects during imagery than tasks with substantial motor components, but there is no direct evidence that imagery primarily has a cognitive focus. Studies have shown greater performance effects when response propositions are employed than for stimulus propositions alone. Other theories propose cognitive-, arousal-, attention-, or motivation-based explanations. Proponents of these explanations of imagery argue that imagery works by creating the appropriate arousal level for effective performance, by focusing attention on task-relevant cues, or by increasing motivation, so greater effort is applied to performance. Theories of imagery are addressed in detail elsewhere (Morris et al., 2005).

What is known about imagery

Imagery is one of the most frequently-researched concepts in sport psychology. A question commonly studied is whether imagery leads to enhanced performance (Morris *et al.*, 2005). Studies have employed a range of different research designs to examine this issue. Often this research has taken the form of laboratory or field studies, where real-world complexities are reduced to increase control. Other studies have employed single-case designs, developed to examine the efficacy of psychological interventions in authentic circumstances. Here, sample size and strict control are sacrificed for greater ecological validity. Meta-analyses of studies have consistently concluded that imagery does enhance performance. Various factors affect the strength of the effect, including age and skill level of participants; type of task; imagery delivery variables, including length of imagery sessions, and frequency and duration of the imagery program; and method used to measure performance. There is also research evidence supporting the use of imagery to influence psychological variables (see Morris *et al.*, 2005). Most frequently studied in this respect are arousal level and motivation. Studies have indicated that imagery can increase or decrease arousal level, whereas enhancing motivation is common, especially for strength and endurance tasks. Related to motivation is the demonstration of increases in self-efficacy, which can be interpreted as task-specific self-confidence. Several researchers have also reported increases in self-confidence more broadly related to sport performance. Another key variable associated with performance is attention. Research evidence also supports the application of imagery to enhance attention in sports tasks (Farrow & Kemp, 2003).

Sport psychology researchers have tested predictions from the major theories and models of imagery with varying success, as reported earlier in this chapter. The findings from this research have not ruled out any major theory, but they have shown limitations of each approach. A substantial amount of research has also been focused on the development of measures of imagery.

How imagery is measured

In early research in sport psychology, researchers employed imagery assessment techniques that had been developed in other areas of psychology. Following the principle that sport-specific measures are usually more sensitive, researchers developed instruments in the contexts of sport and movement. The assessment devices developed in this way measure two aspects of imagery, namely imagery use and imagery ability.

Measures of imagery use assess the extent to which athletes' imagery is directed to each of several uses. The best-established measure of imagery use is the Sport Imagery Questionnaire (SIQ: Hall, Mack, Paivio, & Hausenblas, 1998). Hall *et al.* developed the 30-item SIQ from an earlier measure, the Imagery Use Questionnaire (IUQ), based on Paivio's (1985) two-dimensional classification of cognitive/motivational and specific/general imagery functions. In exploratory factor analysis, however, items generated to assess the four categories of imagery use derived from Paivio's classification produced five factors. In the main, the expected categories emerged: namely cognitive specific imagery (e.g., imagining specific skills), cognitive general imagery (e.g., imagining broad strategies), and motivational specific imagery (e.g., imagining striving for and attaining specific goals). In addition, however, motivational general imagery split into two factors, one concerned with imagery being used for the management of arousal and the other focused on imagery use associated with the experience of mastery. The five-factor SIQ has been widely examined in relation to key issues, such as type of sport, skill level, performance, and psychological variables. The SIQ is useful in the development of imagery programs, where it has been applied to identify the imagery use categories most frequently or effectively employed in a specific context. Then the content of imagery scripts can be written to concentrate on those types of imagery use.

Two measures of imagery related to movement have been widely used in sport, and they are the Movement Imagery Questionnaire (MIQ; Hall & Pongrac, 1983) and the Vividness of Movement Imagery Questionnaire (VMIQ; Isaac, Marks, & Russell, 1986). These measure imagery of simple movements only and focus on the visual and kinesthetic senses. This limitation raises concerns about their ecological validity for use in sport. They are described in detail elsewhere (Morris *et al.*, 2005).

Watt *et al.* (2004) developed the Sport Imagery Ability Measure (SIAM), in which several common scenes from sport are described and each is imagined and then rated. The SIAM presents four scenes and respondents rate them on five dimensions (vividness, controllability, speed, ease, and duration of imagery), six sense modalities (visual, kinesthetic, auditory, tactile, gustatory, and olfactory), and emotion. Ratings are performed on 100 mm analogue scales to add sensitivity. The SIAM has been used in a wide range of sports and has produced equivalent factor structures among large samples in several countries, each using different languages (i.e., Finland, Israel, Sweden, Thailand). Strengths of the SIAM include its ecological validity for use in sport, the breadth of dimensions and senses assessed, and the sensitivity of the analogue scales. Given its greater breadth in terms of sense modalities and dimensions compared to other measures of imagery ability in movement and sport, the factor structure of the SIAM is more complex than the MIQ and the VMIQ.

Applying imagery

As previously remarked, we can imagine anything that we can think of. Which 15-year-old developing 1,500 meter athlete has not imagined sitting on the shoulder of the Ethiopian reigning champion and sprinting past her in the final straight to take Olympic gold to the roar of the crowd? For most 15-year-olds this event is not possible, but it can be imagined. The key question for sport psychologists is not *whether* it is possible to imagine, but *how* should *this athlete* in *this sport context* use imagery most effectively?

Using imagery in psychological skills training

Imagery has long been a major aspect of psychological skills training (PST) in sport, which is the application of psychological techniques for the purpose of optimizing athletes' sport experiences. Most sport psychologists agree about a number of ways in which imagery can be used effectively in PST. These uses include imagery for learning/practising skills, learning/practising strategies/moves, previewing performance, reviewing performance, enhancing motivation, building confidence, reducing anxiety, increasing concentration, and recovering from injury or heavy training (Morris *et al.*, 2004). A number of sources provide detailed descriptions of the use of imagery in these contexts (see Morris *et al.*, 2005).

An aspect of the use of imagery that cannot be stressed too strongly is that it is important to enlist the commitment of the athletes for whom the imagery training is devised. Without a high level of motivation toward achieving, and some would even say belief in the potential for imagery to influence performance directly (or enhance psychological variables that influence performance), the effectiveness of imagery will be limited. Reading a chapter like this one will not greatly influence most athletes. Hearing positive statements from a credible source, such as their coach, might have some influence, but, for most athletes, physically experiencing imagery is most effective. A simple example could be to ask athletes to imagine smelling and biting into a lemon and note the response of real salivation. A more substantial example is the string-and-bolt activity (see Morris et al., 2004).

A more systematic approach to assessing athletes' current capacities for imagery, however, is to employ psychometrically-validated self-report measures of imagery ability, such as the SIAM. Using such measures in preparation for the application of imagery is important to the effectiveness of the training program. It can even help practitioners shape the content of the program. First, if athletes score low on most aspects of imagery, it is unwise to go straight into sport performance imagery. Imagery can be trained. Technically the term "imagery ability" is a misnomer, because abilities, as defined in psychology, are fixed capacities, whereas imagery *skill* can be increased by specific practice. Such practice often starts by imagining simple, static targets with the greatest meaning for the individual, such as visual images of faces of close family, the ball from the athlete's sport, or auditory images of a favorite piece of music or the crowd cheering. Practice then moves to more complex imagery, perhaps involving more than one sense modality or multiple targets. Next, movement is added to the imagery. Once complex, dynamic imagery has been mastered, athletes can move to sport performance imagery. Second, where the measure of imagery ability indicates some imagery strengths, but other areas of weakness, and the strengths match the imagery skills needed in that sport, imagery programs might focus on those skills, especially if there is some urgency. For example, although visual imagery dominates in many sports, in sports such as diving kinesthetic imagery is usually much more important. Sport performance imagery should be acceptable (using kinesthetic imagery) provided the divers score high on kinesthetic imagery on the imagery ability questionnaire. If divers report high visual imagery, but low kinesthetic imagery, then training to enhance kinesthetic imagery is needed prior to sport performance imagery, otherwise a lot of effort could be wasted by the athletes trying to use an imagery training program for which they lack the imagery skill. Monitoring imagery ability plays an important role in matching imagery training to the imagery skills of each athlete, taking into account the profile of the sport in terms of factors such as sensory involvement and duration.

Just as measures of imagery ability should be used to guide the use of imagery with athletes and the design of imagery training, athletes' current imagery use can be informative to practitioners. Measures such as the SIQ can be used to identify current use. Research and expert knowledge can inform practitioners about the most important categories of imagery use for effective imagery related to a specific sport context. Then the athletes and the context can be matched in a manner similar to that proposed for imagery ability.

So much research has been conducted on aspects of imagery and their relationships to various personal and contextual variables that it is difficult to bring it all together in a meaningful way. The PETTLEP (physical, environmental, task, timing, learning, emotion, perspective) model (Holmes & Collins, 2001) provides useful guidance, but even with its seven elements, it does not cover all considerations.

Morris et al. (2005) proposed an Imagery Training Program (ITP) model, which does not attempt to address all the specific variables that can influence how we design an imagery program in a specific context, but focuses attention on the generic components to be considered. *Prerequisites* for imagery training are those personal factors that affect the design of an ITP, including age and gender, skill level, imagery use preferences, imagery ability, and internal and external imagery perspectives. *Environment* for imagery training refers to those situational factors that affect the design of the ITP, including the training or competition setting, noise level, physical location, whether imagery is dynamic or static, and whether the skills are open or closed. Pre-requisites and environmental components are *pre-existing* factors that should be considered first. They influence the three factors that follow, which are components related to structure and content. *Content* for imagery training is the central component, what we actually put in the ITP. This component includes use of sense modalities, perspective selection, choice of real time versus slow motion or fast forward imagery, skills (cognitive) focus, and motivational content. *Rehearsal routines* for imagery training are characteristics associated with the delivery of the ITP; that is, when and how it is rehearsed. They include duration of ITP sessions (how long they last), scheduling of sessions (how often they occur, what time of day, what relationship they have to training and competition), and patterning of sessions (e.g., from static to dynamic, from simple to complex). *Enhancements* for imagery training are ways in which ITPs can be improved, for example, by use of technology. Enhancements include use of cues and triggers, audio scripts, modeling, using video or portable devices, biofeedback, and flotation. Once the ITP has been operational for a short time, it is important to regularly assess how well it is working. Such evaluation should first be done soon after the ITP starts, so athletes do not continue to use ineffective or counterproductive imagery, and any misuse of techniques is quickly resolved. *Evaluation* of the imagery training program is the use of systematic techniques to judge what is (and is not) working. These assessments include formative and summative testing, verbal discussions with athletes, written reports by athletes, athlete self-evaluation ratings, and sport psychologist and coach observations of the athlete.

An advantage of such a generic model (see Figure 50.1) is that it does not lose currency when research identifies new key pre-requisites or aspects of content. In applying the ITP model, practitioners should always consider the most current evidence related to each component. Morris *et al.* (2005) did not claim to have identified every component, so other researchers and practitioners are free to propose additional components and relationships for the ITP model.

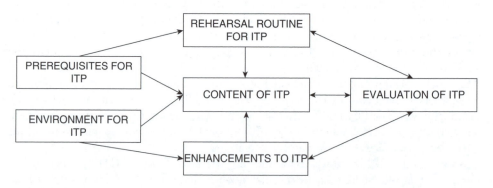

Figure 50.1 The Imagery Training Program (ITP) model. Adapted from *Imagery in Sport* by T. Morris, M. Spittle, and A. P. Watt, 2005. Copyright 2005 by Human Kinetics.

Using imagery in athletes' lives

Published descriptions of imagery in sport usually focus on the use of imagery in PST either to enhance performance directly or to manage psychological variables that affect performance. Imagery can be applied to any aspect of athletes' lives that affects their well-being. Imagery can also be employed within any psychological perspective.

Case study: Kathy's depressed mood

Kathy was a 15-year-old member of an age-group elite swimming squad. Recently, her development had stalled, and her performances seemed to be going backwards. She decided to see a psychologist to sort out her performance issues. For several sessions, discussion was superficial, but the psychologist noted that Kathy's mood was flat. As trust developed, Kathy talked about her hopes and dreams and then burst into tears. She then revealed that she was a fraud. She believed she shouldn't be in the squad because she wasn't good enough and would never "make it." As the psychologist asked why Kathy had these beliefs, it became clear that Kathy's coach was giving her a hard time. Kathy's negative perceptions of herself turned out to be based on statements made by the coach. Kathy's depressed mood was based on the thought that she was worthless, emanating from her ruminations about the negative comments made by the coach, who was the most important voice in Kathy's head at this point in her life.

Circumstances dictated that Kathy could not follow her swimming dream unless she stayed in the squad, so avoidance was a last resort. The psychologist decided to adopt an acceptance and commitment therapy (ACT; Harris, 2008) approach to help Kathy to manage her negative thoughts and feelings, so she could function effectively in the present environment. ACT is a mindfulness therapy, based on the importance of being in the present moment (see Chapter 21). Training in mindfulness allowed Kathy to observe her own thoughts and feelings. Acceptance is a key aspect of ACT, in which Kathy accepted her negative thoughts and feelings, especially about worthlessness, as something that everybody experiences, but that simply having them does not make them real; they are only some of the thousands of thoughts she has had that never amount to anything. What is important is action, particularly action based on core values. Kathy identified swimming to the best of her ability as a core value for her. This value was the basis for an imagery script that Kathy and the psychologist developed together.

In the imagery script, Kathy imagined herself at swimming training. Just as she was about to slip into the pool, the coach came up and made a typical negative comment to her. Kathy imagined feeling deflated and not up to pushing herself at training. At this point, Kathy imagined using her mindfulness skills to explore her thoughts and feelings. She accepted the negative thoughts and feelings she was experiencing, and then recognized that they were just her mind messing with her again. Kathy focused on her core value and determined to act to achieve the goals associated with that value. Kathy imagined jumping into the pool and training as hard as she was able. In her imagery, she was in the moment, acting in accordance with her goals and values. Kathy imagined ending the session tired, but very satisfied. In some imagery sessions, Kathy imagined her performance being timed and the times showing stabilization and then improvement. She and the psychologist then devised a modified script in which training was replaced by competition. Kathy imagined a typical comment from the coach ("don't let yourself down again!"), accepted her thoughts and feelings about it, focused on her core value, and produced a personal best in her race.

487

In discussion with the psychologist after working with these imagery scripts for several weeks, Kathy observed two things: first, the coach seemed to talk to all the swimmers this way – it was just the coach's misguided idea of motivating them; second, the coach didn't seem to say negative things to Kathy as often as before. The psychologist also noted a marked improvement in Kathy's mood and a reinvigoration of her commitment to her swimming dream.

Conclusions

Despite the extensive publication of theory, research, and practice related to imagery in sport, there still seems to be more that is not known about imagery than is unequivocally determined. Clearer direction for future research based on well-founded theory is required to direct effective application of imagery in sport. Nonetheless, practitioners continue to recommend imagery, and athletes and coaches use it and report positive effects. See Box 50.1 for a summary of key points from this chapter.

Box 50.1

Summary of key points about imagery

- Imagery is the psychological skills training technique most widely used by athletes, but it is not well understood how best to use imagery to enhance performance and well-being in sport. Athletes often have negative sport-related imagery experiences, so it is preferable to manage athletes' imagery, based on the best evidence available.
- Theories and research have not produced definitive principles of imagery use, but can be used to guide practice with caution. Practitioners should reflect on the information that is available in a systematic way to help them devise the most efficacious imagery training programs. The Imagery Training Program model can guide this systematic process of imagery program development.
- Practitioners should also use a range of assessment methods, including observations, interviews, and psychometric measures. Assessing athletes' imagery abilities can help to determine how to frame an imagery script, for example, in terms of use of sense modalities. Examining imagery use can help to focus imagery on the most effective categories of use for the specific situation.
- Imagery can be used in almost all therapeutic contexts. Devising an imagery program for therapeutic purposes should be based on a thorough understanding of the individual, the issues to be addressed, the therapeutic framework, and the best evidence available regarding the effective use of imagery.

References

DeFrancesco, C., & Burke, K. L. (1997). Performance enhancement strategies used in a professional tennis tournament. *International Journal of Sport Psychology, 28*, 183–193.

Farrow, D., & Kemp, J. (2003). *Run like you stole something (the science behind the score line)*. Sydney, NSW, Australia: Allen & Unwin.

Hall, C. R., Mack, D. E., Paivio, A., & Hausenblas, H. A. (1998). Imagery use by athletes: Development of the Sport Imagery Questionnaire. *International Journal of Sport Psychology, 29,* 73–89.

Hall, C., & Pongrac, J. (1983). *Movement imagery questionnaire*. London, ON, Canada: University of Western Ontario.

Harris, R. (2008). *The happiness trap: Stop struggling, start living*. Wollombi, NSW, Australia: Exisle.

Holmes, P. S., & Collins, D. (2001). The PETTLEP approach to motor imagery: A functional equivalence model for sport psychologists. *Journal of Applied Sport Psychology, 13,* 60–83.

Isaac, A. R., Marks, D. F., & Russell, D. G. (1986). An instrument for assessing imagery of movement: The Vividness of Movement Imagery Questionnaire (VMIQ). *Journal of Mental Imagery, 10,* 23–30.

Jacobson, E. (1930). Electrical measurement of neuromuscular states during mental activities: Part 1. Imagination of movement involving skeletal muscle. *American Journal of Physiology, 91,* 567–606.

Lang, P. J. (1977). Imagery in therapy: An informational processing analysis of fear. *Behavior Therapy, 8,* 862–886.

Morris, T., Spittle, M., & Perry, C. (2004). Mental Imagery in sport. In T. Morris & J. Summers (Eds.) *Sport psychology: Theories, applications and issues* (2nd ed., pp. 345–387). Brisbane, QLD, Australia: Wiley.

Morris, T., Spittle, M., & Watt, A. P. (2005). *Imagery in sport*. Champaign, IL: Human Kinetics.

Paivio, A. (1985). Cognitive and motivational functions of imagery in human performance. *Canadian Journal of Applied Sport Science, 10* (Suppl.), 22S–28S.

Richardson, A. (1969). *Mental imagery*. New York: Springer.

Sackett, R. S. (1934). The influence of symbolic rehearsal upon the retention of a maze habit. *Journal of General Psychology, 10,* 376–395.

Stewart, W. (1996). *Imagery and symbolism in counselling*. London: Kingsley.

Watt, A. P., Morris, T., & Andersen, M. B. (2004). Issues in the development of a measure of imagery ability in sport. *Journal of Mental Imagery, 28,* 149–180.

51

Motivation and goal setting

Glyn C. Roberts and Elsa Kristiansen

> *Confusion of goals and perfection of means seem, in my opinion, to characterize our age.*
> Albert Einstein

In sport and physical activity, we can manage our own motivation or motivation can be managed by others – parents, teachers, coaches, peers. One of the most powerful strategies for managing motivation and performance is the use of goal setting. But first, let us look at what is motivation. Motivation has often been confused with other constructs (e.g., arousal, positive thinking). The important assumption with which most contemporary theorists agree is that motivation is a *process*, and not an entity. To understand motivation and be able to enhance it in the context of sport, we must make an attempt to understand the process of motivation and the constructs that drive the process, and how goal setting becomes an integral part of the process.

Motivational processes can be defined by the psychological constructs that energize, direct, and regulate achievement behavior (cf., Roberts, 2001). First, motivation processes are qualities of the person and the person's perception of the context. What are the criteria of success and failure for the person? These criteria are the central issue in understanding motivation in physical activities and other achievement arenas. Although motivation may be partially understood in terms of the context (e.g., the goals coaches or parents may have for athletes), it is the influence of the environment on personal assessments that is important. The environment has no motivational qualities unless it is perceived as such by the participant. Thus, motivation is a process that resides within the person and how the person assesses what is needed to succeed. Second, motivation processes help people anticipate and predict future events and potential consequences that are meaningful to them. These processes form the basis from which decisions are made about how much of personal resources (e.g., talent, money, time, effort) one is prepared to invest in the activity to reach the valued goal. Motivation prepares the individual to move forward to reach desired goals or to produce desired outcomes. Third, motivation processes are evaluative in character. These evaluations may be self-referenced or may involve pertinent others as criteria of reference. Motivation involves the person assessing whether to increase or decrease behavioral striving to affect the desired outcome or goal. The outcome or goal, however, is subjectively defined and varies from person to person. What is success for one may not be success for another. Thus, one is seen to be motivated, or demotivated, through assessments of one's competencies within the achievement context, by using self or other referenced criteria, and the meaning or value of the context to the person.

To be effective applied consultants we need to understand what goals individuals want to achieve, and their criteria for success in achieving those goals. Locke and colleagues (Locke, Shaw, Saari, & Latham, 1981) in their seminal work on goal setting defined a goal as "attaining a specific standard of proficiency on a task" (p. 145). Goal attainment is the demonstration of competence within a specified task. Locke and Latham (1990) viewed goals as direct motivational strategies because they direct action by focusing attention, increasing effort and intensity, encouraging persistence in the face of failure or adversity, and promoting the development of new task or problem-solving strategies. Embedded in the practice of goal setting are two specific characteristics of the goal, its content and its intensity. The content refers to the exact nature of the goal and what is to be accomplished, and goal intensity reflects the degree of difficulty and effort needed to reach the goal (Hall & Kerr, 2001).

Researchers (e.g., Roberts, Treasure, & Conroy, 2007) have argued for two types of goals because the demonstration of competence takes two forms: self-referenced competence, where one attempts to better one's own previous performance; or other-referenced competence, where one tries to outperform relevant others. In motivation terms, these types are termed mastery (or task involved) goals and performance (or ego involved) goals (see Roberts *et al.*, 2001). When athletes have mastery goals, they are concerned with demonstrating effort, learning, and getting better. When athletes have performance goals, they focus on being superior, winning, and beating others.

Some researchers describe outcome, performance, and process goals (e.g., Hardy, Jones, & Gould, 1996; Kingston & Wilson, 2009). What these researchers term performance goals are *mastery goals* as we define them in this chapter, and what are termed outcome goals are *performance goals*. We use the terms mastery and performance goals to be consistent with the vast literature on motivational goals, both within sport and other contexts. Process goals are defined (e.g., Gould, 2006) as procedures in which the performer engages during performance (e.g., a skier focusing on keeping his/her hands in front of him/her). Process goals, however, are inherent in both performance and mastery goals (e.g., an athlete with a performance goal who tries to win without apparently trying hard, because that demonstrates even greater competence; or an athlete with a mastery goal who concentrates on the dynamics of the skill because this tactic will assist learning). To be consistent with motivation theory, we make the distinction between mastery and performance goals and recognize that process goals are embedded within both mastery and performance goals. Motivation theory, then, has the potential to inform goal setting in sport.

The setting of goals

Initiated by Locke and colleagues (Locke *et al.*, 1981), goal setting has been applied to various laboratory, field, and real-world settings, using myriad tasks. Individuals who set specific and challenging goals perform better than people who set no goals or who are simply told to do their best. Goal setting is a popular basic sport psychology technique, and it is often the one first introduced when implementing mental training because, some authors claim, it is fundamental for maximizing athletic potential (Hardy *et al.*, 1996). Goal setting consistently facilitates performance and led Locke *et al.* to state that it was one of the most robust and replicable findings in psychology.

Goal setting is now so universally known that athletes often understand that goal setting is useful, but they may struggle on how best to set goals that will optimize their performances. Despite the general knowledge and understanding of how goals should be implemented and what type of goals to use, coaches and athletes frequently forget that many factors may affect the goal-setting process. Although practitioners use and recommend goal setting, researchers continue to investigate why, and how well, it works. What has troubled many are the inconsistencies in the findings within sport psychology (e.g., Hall & Kerr, 2001; Kingston & Wilson, 2009). The research in sport simply does not replicate the work of Locke and colleagues (1981) within the organizational psychology literature. Hall and Kerr argued that goal setting is a "double edged sword" and that it is "not so much a flawed methodology that renders goal-setting research in sport problematic but rather a conceptual narrowness that encourages a preoccupation with performance effects while largely ignoring how athletes who are striving for goals process performance information" (p. 185).

A search for theory

In one of the first studies in sport on goal setting, Burton (1984) applied motivation theory to goal setting. Burton looked at the effect of a goal-setting program on performance and certain cognitions of intercollegiate swimmers. Burton applied mastery goals (he called them performance goals) rather than performance goals (he labeled them outcome goals, and it is to this study that we can lay the blame for the subsequent mislabeling of the goals!) and found that those swimmers who focused on mastery goals had better performances and more positive cognitions (lower in anxiety, higher in self-confidence). Most of the subsequent research in sport has been atheoretical in that the studies applied specific goal-setting techniques (e.g., setting short-term, specific, discrete, and/or challenging goals) to sport tasks (see Burton, Naylor, & Holliday, 2001). The studies have shown that goal setting generally has positive performance outcomes (e.g., Kyllo & Landers, 1995), despite not replicating all the findings of the goal-setting literature in organizational psychology.

Most practitioners are interested simply in *whether* goal setting works, but some researchers also are interested in *why* it works. Burton and Naylor (2002) again used achievement goal theory to suggest that the type of goal affects the goal setting-performance relationship. Burton and Naylor argued that athletes holding mastery goals are best served by goal-setting programs. Consistent with the arguments of achievement goal theory (e.g., Roberts *et al.*, 2007), athletes with performance goals may be affected by their perceptions of their own abilities. If athletes have performance goals and high perceptions of ability, then they believe they can achieve (i.e., they are success-oriented) and goal setting is effective, but not as effective as it is for athletes with mastery goals. If individuals have performance goals and low perceptions of ability, then they believe they have little likelihood of achieving (i.e., they are failure oriented) and therefore goal setting is less likely to work with these athletes.

Drawing on contemporary motivation theory, Hall and Kerr (2001) argued that there are beneficial aspects to understanding goal setting within an achievement goal theory perspective. First, researchers and practitioners would be able to understand better why athletes make the motivational choices that they do. As Hall and Kerr stated, understanding achievement goal theory will "enable us to go beyond noting that an athlete is energized to achieve discrete goals, to explain why the athlete is energized and what the accompanying cognitions might be" (p. 231). Second, motivation theory can help researchers understand some of the idiosyncratic findings within the sport context. Athletes asked to "do their best" often do as well as athletes given discrete goals, which is contrary to Locke et al.'s (1981) findings. This finding makes sense if the athletes asked to do their best are mastery oriented and already have the goal of doing their best. In other words, the meaning of achievement within the context needs to be taken into account to understand goal setting. Finally, the traditional goal-setting literature shows that researchers are preoccupied with performance effects and have not appreciated that athletes' achievement goals give meaning to the context so that any feedback may have adaptive and maladaptive motivational effects. As an example, the literature suggests that performance goals and public goals are more effective for performance (e.g., Kyllo & Landers, 1995) than mastery goals. This finding is part of the "double edged sword" syndrome in that it is known that performance goals are "fragile" over the long term (e.g., Roberts et al., 2007). When the meaning and value of the context are taken into consideration, then the ultimate effect of performance goals can be demotivational, especially if the perceived competence of the athlete is low. Therefore, only when we consider goal-setting strategies with an understanding of what success and failure mean to the athlete within a specific context will we be able to fully understand goal-setting strategies, and practitioners be able to optimize the goal-setting strategies for that athlete.

Applying achievement goal theory

As we stated at the outset, when considering goal setting for motivation, we have two facets of the equation. First, how can sport psychologists help coaches, teachers, and even parents give motivational succor to athletes in their endeavors? We call this managing the motivation of others, versus aiding athletes to manage their own motivation. It is the latter to which the vast majority of the goal-setting literature addresses itself.

Managing the motivation of others

One of the most fundamental aspects of achievement goals is the central role the situation plays in the motivation process. The perceived criteria of success and failure coaches (parents, teachers, sport psychologists) hold within an environment can make it more or less likely that achievement behaviors, thoughts, and feelings associated with being mastery- or performance-involved are adopted. The perceived criteria of success and failure affect the achievement behaviors, cognitions, and affective responses through the perceptions of the participants of the behaviors necessary to achieve success. In other words, athletes recognize what the coach believes is important to achieve success within that context. This area of research recently has become popular in the sporting world with the growing recognition that the way coaches coach affects not only the beliefs and perceptions of athletes, but also the cognitive, behavioral, and affective outcomes of the competitive experience (see Roberts et al., 2007).

The two dimensions, mastery and performance, are central to understanding achievement cognitions and behaviors in achievement contexts (i.e., *motivational climate*). Coaches foster a mastery climate when they focus on learning and self-referenced improvement, emphasize effort in the learning of new skills, and regard mistakes as an aspect of learning. In such a climate, athletes are likely to perceive that success is achieved when effort is displayed and mastery is demonstrated. Coaches promote a performance climate when they focus on interpersonal competition, publicly evaluate performance, provide normative feedback, punish mistakes, and temper reinforcement by the demonstration of normative competence. Here athletes perceive that success is achieved when superiority is displayed and normative competence demonstrated.

The focus on mastery as success is likely to result in athletes' perceptions that effort and self-referenced accomplishment are valued and important. A focus on mastery also is likely to lead to positive outcomes such as intrinsically regulated motivation and autonomy in that the intrinsic value of the task is highlighted. In addition, athletes are likely to experience positive affect and positive consequences of participating in sport. The focus on performance as success is likely to deny players making the connection between effort and success, and may lead to the perception that to be worthy is to beat others. Also, a focus on performance is likely to lead to negative outcomes such as extrinsically regulated motivation, in that the extrinsic nature of evaluation is highlighted. In addition, players are likely to experience negative affect and negative consequences of participating in sport (Roberts et al., 2007).

Goal-setting procedures can be introduced to child and adolescent athletes as well as elite adult athletes. The important issue is how the sport psychologist or coach adapts the procedure to make sport training effective without taking out the fun element. Coaches can create stimulating environments that interest young athletes in what they do at training, and guide them to structure and take charge of their own training. Some intuitively use this means to enhance performance. Peter Shilton (1992; retired English goalkeeper) provided a good example of effective concrete mastery goals:

> When I was 11, I would come home and do drawings of practice and training routines. I would also draw diagrams to work out the sort of angles I should be taking to stop shots and cut crosses. Then I'd take my studies down to the park and get my friends to help me put them into practice. Instead of just kicking the ball around and shooting, I would work on certain disciplines to attempt to improve my skills. You should not think that because you are still young you cannot work constructively on your game.
>
> (p. 17)

Shilton found training meaningful when clear goals were set before practice, and this procedure gave him a head start in his professional career. But generally, young athletes are not so astute. Coaches need to help children and young adolescents develop their talents.

The superstars of child and adolescent sport programs are usually the physiologically mature. Yet it is the physiologically immature child athletes who may become the superstars of the adult athletic world. But coaches often make selections for advanced training regimens from the physiologically mature athletes, ignoring the rest. With young athletes, sport psychologists and coaches should take the long view and introduce goal-setting programs to keep all athletes interested and developing. Practitioners should take a developmental stance with children and young adolescents, adopt a mastery climate, and set mastery goals.

Mastery goals are not only to be set at the beginning of a season; they need to be sustained throughout the season. We all have anecdotal experience with coaches "losing it" during important competitions. What coaches may not realize is how athletes perceive their actions.

An interview with a young athlete demonstrates the effect of a coach who apparently changed his goal focus at a major youth competition (Kristiansen & Roberts, 2010):

> My coach totally changed focus as soon as we arrived in Belgrade. He told me that I had to reach the finals, "*I had to prove that I deserved to be in* [the event]," and he told me "*you must win.*" That totally blew it for me; usually he is such a good coach always focusing on the task ahead. But in major competitions he becomes another person, he takes off. His comments affected my results, everything went wrong, and it was hard to concentrate. It took me a few days to get the right task focus back.
>
> (p. 692)

Normally, the coach was mastery goal oriented, but at the competitive venue, the coach suddenly became performance oriented. The National Governing Body (NGB) of his event had told the coach that future funding was dependent on the results of the competition. What the coach had done is transfer the performance goals of the NGB onto the athlete. The coach shifted the perceived motivational climate from mastery-based criteria of success to performance-based criteria of success. With young and inexperienced athletes, this shift may create serious problems of focus. With more mature athletes, it is less of a problem.

The "bottom line" of managing the motivation of others is to do one's best to create a mastery motivational climate for the athletes in both practice sessions and competitive events. Even elite athletes prefer their coaches to have a mastery approach to performance because it helps to alleviate stress (Pensgaard & Roberts, 2002). But, for some elite athletes who are secure in their perceptions of competence, being performance oriented is acceptable, and even preferred.

Managing one's own motivation

Individual goal setting became popular in sport because of the mounting evidence, and coaching folklore, that it facilitates performance. It is also a way to structure and organize daily training and frame the entire competitive season, and one characteristic of a highly successful athlete is the practice of setting clear daily practice goals. There are several goal-setting guidelines for effective goal setting. One of the best is Gould's (2006) goal staircase model. The starting point is the present ability of the athlete. The staircase has a long-term mastery goal, and to get to that goal, the athlete follows several short-term mastery goals that increase in competence demands. This staircase is a coherent way of approaching goal setting for performance and for motivation. The short-term goals are for immediate improvement and motivation to work harder for the long-term goals. The long-term goals give achievement meaning for the athlete.

Short-term goals need to be specific and measurable. Researchers, over the last 40 years, have advocated these types of goals rather than "do-your-best" goals (see Locke *et al.*, 1981) that are almost impossible to measure and are not in accord with the theoretical claim of relevance to progress. The short-term goals should be moderately difficult and realistic (Kyllo & Landers, 1995). A goal should require some effort to be achieved, but be in accordance with the athlete's view of his/her own capacity to achieve the goal. Having demands that consistently exceed competence may lead to anxiety, stress, and in the worst cases, burnout.

Goal setting can become complicated because it is pertinent to have performance goals as part of a goal-setting staircase. For example, the long-term goal may be to become an Olympic athlete: The short-term goals become steps in that process of becoming an

Olympic athlete. The important point is that the performance goals are not to be considered ends in themselves, but are a means by which the athlete can observe progress relative to others. It is at this point that a coach or sport psychologist should help the athlete interpret the performance goals as steps in the process. Target days for reaching the different short- and long-term goals may be advantageous. Intense training periods, the timing of different events, and the end of a season are dates that help structure training and motivation enhancement. In a goal staircase, goals for training and competition should be set and implemented by the sport psychologist, the coach, and athlete together.

Make goal setting a coach–athlete project

Efficient goal setting is mostly a result of identifying the needs of the athlete, planning the goals, and then splitting them into short-term goals that prepare the athlete for the long-term goals with the present capacity of the athlete in mind. Both coaches and teams/ athletes have to be committed to the goals and work hard to reach them. Hall and Kerr (2001) have identified two moderators of goal-setting performance in sport: commitment and feedback. No matter how well-structured the planning process, if the coaches and athletes are not committed to the goals and do not evaluate progress, or lack of progress, then the likelihood of success is reduced. Feedback should be given in ways that will assist athletes to continue with their mastery goals, and should be provided to show performance in relation to these goals (Locke et al., 1981). The feedback system is one way of trying to avoid problems in goal setting. Experienced coaches, and coaches being advised by sport psychologists, may easily detect problems such as setting too many goals too soon, and revise general and unrealistic goals. When first introducing this mental skill, some neophyte practitioners think they can change every bad habit simultaneously. Prioritization and moving on as one progresses is the best advice (Gould, 2006). Nevertheless, an experienced athlete may handle a larger number of goals.

How coaches and sport psychologists choose to use goal setting with their teams or individual athletes will depend on personal preferences, but we recommend introducing routines within a *mastery climate*. The recording of daily training results and goals before sharing them with the coach (and/or sport psychologist) seems to be common practice in many sports, and it is a great measure of personal progress and a tool to help keep athletes focused on their own progress.

Practical advice

Choosing a mastery approach is not about not wanting to win, but it is the most efficacious way of taking a long-term dream goal and focusing on the steps (short-term mastery goals) toward achieving that goal. As the first author likes to say to his clients when they are faced with impending competitive contests, "all you can do is to simply focus on your role and strategies in the contest and take care of business." To illustrate how elite athletes "take care of business," we conclude with two pieces of advice.

The first piece of advice is to stick to your goals. For example, in one of the premier elite divisions of European professional football during 2008, one of the teams had agreed among themselves to focus on mastery goals and to take one game at a time. They concentrated on the tasks within their specific roles on the team for each match. And they did well, much better than they or the media expected. Halfway through the season, they were ranked sixth in the division. Through mutual agreement their goal changed: they decided to try to win the league championship. One of the players commented in an interview (Kristiansen & Roberts, 2010):

> We did so well before the summer, and we started to aim for the top ... which was possible as we were number 6 [in the league standings] for a while. But I think we started to aim high too early, and the upcoming losses became much harder than they should have been for the team's self-confidence ... we did not make it, and the guys started to "hang their heads." There was less laughter in the locker room, and in the end all we could think of was "we have to stay in the Elite Division."

The change from a mastery to a performance goal led to a catastrophe for the team. Instead of taking each game at a time and focusing on the short-term goals, they were motivated to win the championship. This shift of focus caused a disruption in their rhythm and each loss meant that they were failing, and that caused them to become despondent. They had to fight to prevent being relegated from the Elite Division by the end of the season. It was not what the coach said that changed the goal; the players spontaneously changed their group goal. If the team had had a sport psychologist working with them (they did not), or a more knowledgeable coach, then it might have been possible to intervene and ask the players to continue to stay focused on one game at a time.

Finally, our second piece of advice is that athletes should be careful about stating their performance goals in public to opponents or the media. They can divulge this information to the sport psychologist, who is bound by the ethics of confidentiality, but keep dream (performance and long-term) goals private! Previous research has suggested that perform-ance improvements will be greater with public goals than with private ones (Kyllo & Landers, 1995), but such a suggestion is inconsistent with what we know about achievement goals. When performance goals become public, then the media and the sporting public are able to evaluate progress (or lack of progress), creating a performance-oriented motivational climate. Having publicly stated performance goals puts performance pressure on the athlete. Instead, athletes should talk about the short-term mastery goals if asked to comment upon their hopes for the upcoming event or when goals are to be stated in a public forum.

Conclusions

In this chapter, we advocate that sport psychologists and coaches use goal-setting procedures within the framework of contemporary motivation theory. Our goal-setting strategies are con-ceptually coherent and consistent because the theory provides a base from which our strategies emanate. By using motivation concepts, we give meaning to the short-term goals, and more importantly, reflect the long-term achievement goals of the athletes. The theory gives a framework within which practitioners can work. The evidence in favor of goal-setting strategies based on achievement goal theory is overwhelming, in both sport and academic contexts. And the evidence is clear: Motivation is better served with mastery-based short- and long-term goals. As professionals, it is incumbent on us to use the extant evidence in our field to inform our applied practice. As responsible professionals, we must use evidence-based mental skill strategies. When motivation is the issue, use motivation theory and evidence to inform your mental skills strategies. See Box 51.1 for some practical suggestions from this chapter.

Box 51.1

Practical goal-setting suggestions

- Mastery goals are preferable to performance goals, especially for younger athletes.
- Long-term goals should be achieved through a series of short-term mastery goals in a staircase model.
- Short-term goals should be broken down into daily practice goals.
- With children and young adolescents, use mastery goals in a developmental model. Teach children mastery goal setting as soon as possible.
- Especially during the adolescent growth spurt, give young athletes mastery and persistence goal-setting feedback.
- The most crucial people in the goal-setting paradigm are the coaches. Their role is not simply to coach the sport and advocate winning, but to maintain and enhance the motivation of athletes to persist and develop competence. To do this, the setting of goals should be done in a mastery framework.

References

Burton, D. (1984, February). Goal setting: A secret to success. *Swimming World*, 25–29.

Burton, D., and Naylor, S. (2002). The Jekyll/Hyde nature of goals: Revisiting and updating goal-setting in sport. In T. S. Horn (Ed.), *Advances in Sport Psychology* . Champaign, IL: Human Kinetics, pp. 459–499.

Burton, D., Naylor, S., & Holliday, B. (2001). Goal setting in sport: Investigating the goal effectiveness paradox. In: R. N. Singer, H. A. Hausenblas, & C. M. Janelle (Eds.), *Handbook of research on sport psychology* (2nd ed., pp. 497–528). New York: Wiley.

Gould, D. (2006). Goal setting for peak performance. In J. M. Williams (Ed.), *Applied sport psychology: Personal growth to peak performance* (5th ed., pp. 240–259). New York: McGraw-Hill.

Hall, H. K., & Kerr, A. W. (2001). Goal setting in sport and physical activity: Tracing empirical developments and establishing conceptual direction. In G. C. Roberts (Ed.), *Advances in motivation in sport and exercise* (pp. 183–233). Champaign, IL: Human Kinetics.

Hardy, L., Jones, G., & Gould, D. (1996). *Understanding psychological preparation in sport: Theory and research*. Chichester, England: Wiley.

Kingston, M., & Wilson, K. M. (2009). The application of goal setting in sport. In S. Mellalieu & S. Hanton (Eds.), *Advances in sport psychology: A review* (pp. 75–123). New York: Routledge.

Kristiansen, E., & Roberts, G. C. (2010). Young elite athletes and social support: Coping with competitive and organizational stress in "Olympic" competition. *Scandinavian Journal of Medicine and Science in Sport*, 20, 686–695.

Kristiansen, E., & Roberts, G. C. (2010). *Coping with organizational stress in elite football*. (Manuscript submitted for publication).

Kyllo, L. B., & Landers, D. M. (1995). Goal setting in sport and exercise: A research synthesis to resolve the controversy. *Journal of Sport & Exercise Psychology*, 17, 117–137.

Locke, E. A., & Latham, G. P. (1990). *A theory of goal setting and task performance*. Englewood Cliffs, NJ: Prentice Hall.

Locke, E. A., Shaw, K. N., Saari, L. M., & Latham, G. P. (1981). Goal setting and task performance: 1969–1980. *Psychological Bulletin, 90*, 125–152.

Pensgaard, A. M., & Roberts, G. C. (2002). Elite athletes' perception of the motivational climate: The coach matters. *Scandinavian Journal of Medicine and Science in Sports, 12*, 54–59.

Roberts, G. C. (2001). Understanding the dynamics of motivation in physical activity: The influence of achievement goals on motivational processes. In G. C. Roberts (Ed.), *Advances in motivation in sport and exercise* (pp. 1–50). Champaign, IL: Human Kinetics.

Roberts, G. C., Treasure, D. C., & Conroy, D. E. (2007). Understanding the dynamics of motivation in sport and physical activity: An achievement goal interpretation. In G. Tenenbaum & R. E. Eklund (Eds.), *Handbook of sport psychology* (3rd ed., pp. 3–30). Hoboken, NJ: Wiley.

Shilton, P. (1992). *On goalkeeping*. London: Headline.

52

Concentration/attention

Aidan Moran

Without question, at the top level, concentration is a big part of a player's game – whether they're a keeper or outfield.

Sir Alex Ferguson, manager of Manchester United, 2009
Premier League champions, on a new record set by
Edwin van der Sar for the longest time spent
by a goalkeeper without conceding a goal;
cited in Northcroft, 2009, p. 12

As top coaches, like Sir Alex Ferguson, have discovered from experience, the ability to concentrate, or focus on the task at hand while ignoring distractions (Moran, 2004), is central to successful performance in sport. This claim is supported by a combination of anecdotal, descriptive, and experimental evidence. First, anecdotally, many sports performers have emphasized the great importance that they attach to concentration skills. For example, Paul McGinley, the Irish golfer, reported what he focused on when he faced a tricky putt to win the 2002 Ryder Cup match for Europe against the USA:

> At no time did I even consider the mechanics of the stroke … I became absorbed in the line of the putt. I could see it exactly from beginning to end. My only job at that moment in time was to set the ball off on the line that I had chosen. That was the only thing I could control.

> (cited in Clarke, 2005, p. 63)

McGinley's insights are interesting because they highlight the importance of concentrating on a specific external target (the line of the putt) and because they indicate the practical value of dwelling only on actions that are under one's control. Second, at the descriptive level, the capacity to become absorbed in the present moment is a key component of peak performance experiences in athletes (Jackson & Kimiecik, 2008). Finally, many laboratory experiments show that there is a relationship between focus of attention and skilled performance. More precisely, Wulf's (2007) review of relevant evidence concluded that an external focus of attention (where performers direct their attention at the effects that their movements have on the environment) is usually more effective than an internal one (where performers focus on their own body movements) in the learning and performance of motor skills.

Despite agreement among coaches, athletes, and psychologists about the importance of concentration in sport, at least four theoretical and practical questions remain unresolved in research in this field. First, what exactly is "concentration" and how is it related to the broader psychological construct of attention? Second, why do athletes appear to "lose" their focus so easily in competitive situations? Third, what psychological principles govern effective concentration in athletes? And finally, what practical techniques can athletes use to improve their concentration skills in competitive situations? The purpose of this chapter is to make a start in attempting to answer these and other relevant questions.

Attention and concentration

Concentration is part of the multi-dimensional construct of attention that Goldstein (2008) defined as "the process of concentrating on specific features of the environment, or on certain thoughts or activities" (p. 100). The main dimensions of attention are selectivity of perception, the ability to coordinate two or more actions at the same time, and concentration (Moran, 2004). These dimensions can be explained as follows.

Selective attention

Selective attention is the perceptual skill of zooming in on relevant information while ignoring potential distractions. For example, goalkeepers in soccer must be able to focus on the flight of an incoming ball while disregarding the distracting movement of players in their penalty area.

Divided attention

Divided attention is the mental time-sharing ability that enables skilled athletes to coordinate several simultaneous actions. For example, an expert basketball player can dribble the ball while simultaneously scanning the court for a teammate who is in a favorable position to receive a pass.

Concentration

Concentration involves the deliberate decision to invest mental effort in information that seems most important at any given time. For example, during a team talk before a crucial match, players will usually make an effort to focus carefully on their coach's instructions.

For many psychologists, concentration is best understood as a mental spotlight that illuminates what we pay attention to either in the world around us or in the private theatre of our own thoughts and feelings (Kremer & Moran, 2008). In some ways, it resembles the head-mounted torches that miners, divers, and spelunkers wear in dark environments. No matter where these explorers look, their targets are illuminated. This spotlight metaphor of concentration has two important practical implications. First, it shows us that although athletes' concentration can never be really lost (one's mental spotlight has to be shining *somewhere*), it can be directed at the wrong target – one that is irrelevant to the task at hand. This attentional misdirection happens regularly in everyday life. For example, have you ever had the experience of suddenly discovering that you've been reading the same sentence in a book or newspaper over and over again without comprehension because your mind was miles away? If so, then what has happened is that you have distracted yourself by allowing a thought, daydream, or feeling to become the target of your own mental spotlight. The second practical implication of the spotlight metaphor is that it suggests that athletes are in control of where they choose to "shine" their concentration beam at any given moment. For example, a midfield player in soccer who has gained possession of the ball must quickly scan the field before attempting a pass to a teammate. Here, he uses a broad external focus of attention. By contrast, a gymnast rehearsing a complex movement in her mind before a competition is using an internal focus of attention. Unfortunately, even the best athletes in the world sometimes allow their mental spotlights to wander. Let us now consider why this problem occurs.

Why do athletes lose their concentration?

Athletes frequently complain of being distracted or losing their focus during competitive action. But, as I have just explained, attention is never lost – just misplaced. So, what factors distract an athlete's spotlight from its intended target?

In general, distractions fall into two main categories – external and internal (Moran, 1996; 2004). External distractions are objective events and situations (such as crowd noise) that divert an athlete's attentional spotlight away from its intended target, whereas internal distractions include thoughts, feelings, and bodily sensations (e.g., pain, fatigue) that impede a performer's efforts to concentrate on the job at hand. Regardless of where they come from, distractions are particularly damaging for elite athletes because of the automaticity of their skills. Because such athletes have largely automated their technical skills as a result of extensive practice (typically amounting to 6–8 hours a day over many years), they tend to have extra mental capacity available to devote to other concurrent tasks – thereby increasing their distractibility.

Typical external distractions include such factors as spectator movements, sudden changes in ambient noise levels (e.g., the click of a camera), gamesmanship (e.g., "sledging" or verbal taunting of opponents) and unpredictable weather conditions (e.g., tennis players can get distracted if gusty conditions affect ball tosses). Usually, these distractions impair athletic performance. For example, Roger Federer's victory over Robin Söderling at the 2009 French Open tennis championship was jeopardized by the sudden appearance of a spectator who jumped onto the court and approached him. Clearly rattled by this distraction, Federer lost the next three points and admitted afterwards, "it definitely threw me out of my rhythm" (cited in Sarkar, 2009). Fortunately, he regained his composure and won the match. In soccer, noisy supporters can distract players. For example, fans of the Turkish football club, Galatasaray, are infamous for using flares, drums, smoke, and incessant shouting to intimidate visiting teams at their home ground, which is known to visitors as "Hell" (Ronay, 2008)! Not surprisingly, some of the world's leading soccer teams (e.g., AC Milan, Barcelona, Manchester United, Real Madrid) have been defeated in this hostile cauldron. Another example of the deliberate, tactical use of distractions comes from the verbal taunting of opponents – a practice that Steve Waugh, the former Australian cricket captain, justified as a means to achieve the "mental disintegration" of opponents (McIlvanney, 2008).

As the term suggests, internal distractions come from inside performers themselves. They include disruptive, self-defeating thoughts such as wondering what might happen in the future, regretting what may have happened in the past, and worrying about what other people might think or say. They also include feelings of being tired or emotionally upset. A classic example of a costly internal distraction occurred in the case of the American golfer Doug Sanders who missed a putt of less than three feet that would have earned him victory at the 1970 British Open championship. This error not only prevented him from winning his first major tournament but also deprived him of millions of pounds in prize-money, appearance fees from subsequent tournament invitations, and advertising endorsements. Remarkably, Sanders' attentional lapse was precipitated by an internal distraction – thinking too far ahead. "I made the mistake about thinking which section of the crowd I was going to bow to!" he confessed (cited in Gilleece, 1999, p. 23). By his own admission, Sanders had distracted himself by allowing his mental spotlight to shine into the future instead of on the task in hand. As he acknowledged:

> I had the victory speech prepared before the battle was over ... I would give up every victory I had to have won that title. It's amazing how many different things to my normal routine I did on the 18th hole.
>
> (cited in Moran, 2005, p. 21)

Sanders' sudden anticipation of future success led to a costly lapse in attention. But dwelling on a previous success (or failure) can be equally damaging to an athlete's focus. For example, Stephen Hendry, the 7-times world champion snooker player, slipped up mentally after he had achieved a rare feat – scoring a maximum "break" in his match against Shaun Murphy in the 2009 World Snooker Championship. Having won £157,000 for this achievement, he said, "After I made the maximum, my concentration was nowhere ... I was so elated ... in the next break, I missed a red" (in Skilbeck, 2009, p. 16). Fatigue can also serve as an internal distraction. For example, Paula Radcliffe, the British runner who has won the New York marathon three times, admitted that, "When you're tired, it's easy to drift off and suddenly have run 20 seconds slower for that mile, so you need to stay focused. I count to myself to break down the miles, and stay in the moment" (cited in *The Guardian*, 2009, p. 35)

Unfortunately, few studies have been conducted on internal distractions in elite athletes, and we know relatively little about how and when they arise. Let us now consider the building blocks of effective concentration in sport.

Principles of effective concentration

Figure 52.1 summarizes five key principles of effective concentration in sport (derived from Kremer & Moran, 2008).

Athletes have to decide to concentrate – it will not happen by chance

To concentrate properly, athletes have to prepare to focus by making a deliberate decision to invest mental effort in their sporting performances. Many expert sport performers understand this link between deciding to concentrate and subsequently performing to their full potential. For example, Ronan O'Gara, the British and Irish Lions' rugby outside-half

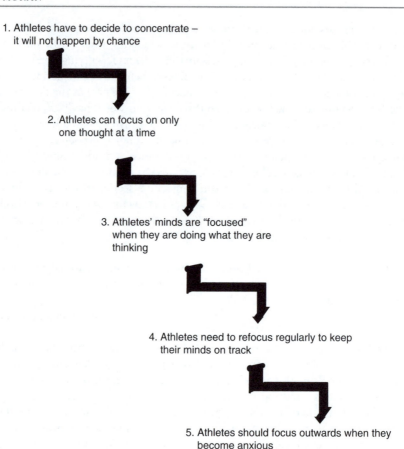

1. Athletes have to decide to concentrate –
   it will not happen by chance

2. Athletes can focus on only
   one thought at a time

3. Athletes' minds are "focused"
   when they are doing what they are
   thinking

4. Athletes need to refocus regularly to keep
   their minds on track

5. Athletes should focus outwards when they
   become anxious

Figure 52.1 Concentration principles (based on Kremer & Moran, 2008; Moran, 1996).

stated, "I have to be focused. I have to do my mental preparation. I have to feel that I'm ready" (cited in English, 2006, p. 70).

Many athletes use mental imagery to distinguish between "switch on" (focused) and "switch off" (relaxed) zones in their sports. For example, when tennis players want to switch off for a few seconds during a match, they may look for towels from ball-persons behind the baseline of the court between points to dry themselves. But when they want to switch on their minds again, they step forward to begin their pre-service or pre-return routine.

Athletes can focus on only one thought at a time

A second building block of effective concentration is the "one-thought principle" – the idea that athletes can focus consciously on only one thought or action at a time. Given this limited attention span, the ideal thought for a performer should be a single word or phrase designed to trigger the appropriate feeling or tempo of the action to be executed (e.g., "slow and smooth" for a golf drive) rather than a complex technical instruction (e.g., "transfer your weight and turn your shoulders"). This one-thought principle is epitomized by the

U.S. swimmer Michael Phelps, who revealed that, "You have to go one day at a time, one meet at a time, and one practice at a time. Everything is about steps and constantly improving on your own times and achievements" (cited in Walsh, 2008, p. 13).

Athletes' minds are "focused" when they are doing what they are thinking

A third principle of effective concentration is that when athletes' minds are truly focused there is no difference between what they are thinking about and what they are doing at that moment. This harmony between thought and action is characteristically evident in peak performance experiences in sport. For example, Roger Bannister (2004) experienced a unity of thought and action when he became the first athlete to run a sub 4-minute mile in May, 1954, "There was no pain, only a great unity of movement and aim" (p. 12). Based on these insights, it seems plausible that peak performance stems from a fusion of thinking and action. Such fusion is facilitated by concentrating on tasks that are specific, relevant, and under one's own control.

Athletes need to refocus regularly to keep their minds on track

Because our concentration system is rather fragile, skilled performers have to learn to refocus regularly by switching their attention back to the present moment as often as possible. An example of such refocusing comes from Paula Radcliffe, the world-class British marathon runner, who uses a counting strategy to keep her mind on track during a race, "At marathon pace, if I count to 100 three times it's about a mile" (cited in *The Guardian*, 2009, p. 35)

Athletes should focus outwards when they become anxious

The final building block of effective concentration is the idea that when athletes become anxious, they should focus outwards on what they have to do – not inwards on self-doubts. This outward focus is necessary because nervousness tends to make people self-conscious or self-critical. The adoption of an external focus of attention is consistent with recommendations arising from Wulf's (2007) review of the research literature.

Practical concentration techniques

Sport psychology researchers have developed a variety of practical strategies that seem to improve concentration skills in athletes (see Greenlees & Moran, 2003; Kremer & Moran, 2008).

Specifying action goals

Psychologists (e.g., Hardy & Jones, 1994) commonly distinguish between outcome goals (e.g., the result of a match), performance goals (i.e., the specific end-products of performance that lie within the athlete's control such as attempting to achieve 90% serving accuracy in tennis), and process goals (i.e., specific behavioral actions that need to be undertaken to achieve a specific goal such as deliberately swinging slowly in golf). Using this distinction, sport psychologists suggest that focusing on actions (i.e., performance and process goals) can help to improve athletes' concentration skills. See also Chapter 51 in this book.

505

Using pre-performance routines

Most top-class athletes display characteristic and consistent sequences of preparatory actions before they perform key skills. For example, golfers tend to adopt the same set-up for every shot and waggle their clubs and take the same number of practice swings before striking the ball. These preferred action sequences or repetitive behaviors are called *pre-performance routines* and they are designed to take the performer from thinking to action – one step at a time. They are typically performed prior to the execution of self-paced skills (i.e., actions that are carried out largely at one's own speed and without interference from other people).

Top athletes attach great importance to pre-performance routines in their quests to achieve optimal concentration before competition. For example, Martin Corry (2007), the former England rugby player, stated:

> I believe that the only way to cope is to establish a routine, almost to go on automatic pilot. That way you are free to think about the game, rather than constantly fret about where you're supposed to be … I used to like switching the dressing room light off, to signify the end of our preparations and the start of something new.
>
> (p. 3)

Singer (1988) described a useful five-step pre-performance routine for self-paced skills. Applied to golf, this routine involves *readying* (preparing to perform by adopting a comfortable stance and taking a few practice swings), *imaging* (visualizing a target at which to aim), *focusing* (directing one's mental spotlight at a specific part of the golf ball such as its number), *executing* (swinging the club as smoothly as possible) and, if feasible, *evaluating* (or checking whether or not one is happy with the shot played). See also Cotterill (2008) and Chapter 56 in this book.

In competitive situations, routines are often combined with other concentration techniques. For example, the Irish rugby player Ronan O'Gara incorporated the use of mental imagery and trigger words into his routine before kicking the winning penalty for Munster in the 2006 final of the Heineken Cup against Biarritz:

> It was obvious how important it was, but I just had to get into my routine and block everything else out. Usually, there's a mark in the centre of the crossbar and I focus on that. Thomond Park has a black dot, at Lansdowne Road it's green. I imagine a little hoop between the sticks, like a gymnasium hoop, and I picture the ball going through that. I stepped back and the buzz words in my mind were, "Stay tall and follow through."
>
> (cited in English, 2006, p. 233)

Using "trigger words" as cues to concentrate

Many athletes talk to themselves covertly when they compete, in an effort to motivate themselves or to keep their minds on track. Such silent cognitive activity has attracted research interest from psychologists in recent years (e.g., Zourbanos, Hatzigeorgiadis, Chroni, Theodorakis, & Papaioannou, 2009). Usually, what athletes say to themselves silently takes the form of praise (e.g., "Well done! That's good"), criticism ("You idiot – that's a stupid mistake"), or instruction ("Swing slowly"). It is this third application of self-talk that interests us here in our discussion of athletes' use of trigger words. For example, the U.S. tennis champion Serena Williams used trigger words during the 2002 Wimbledon ladies' singles tennis final against her sister, Venus. In this match, Serena (who defeated Venus 7–6, 6–3) was observed by millions of viewers reading something as she sat down during the changeovers between games. Afterwards, she explained that she had been consulting notes that she had written to herself as trigger words or instructional cues to remind her to "hit in front" or "stay low" (Williams, 2002, p. 6). Serena Williams also used trigger phrases such as "get low," "add spin," or "move up" during her defeat of Daniela Hantchukova in Wimbledon 2007 (Martin, 2007). Hatzigeorgiadis, Theodorakis, and Zourbanos (2004) have reported evidence for the efficacy of trigger words on performance. They encouraged participants to use verbal cues such as "ball" or "target" in an effort to concentrate on the most important elements of the execution of an open skill (e.g., water polo ball throwing). They found that this use of self-talk not only improved skilled performance in water-polo but also decreased the prevalence of intrusive thoughts among the players concerned. See also Chapter 53 in this book.

Imagery

Earlier, I mentioned that some athletes use their imaginations to create switch on and switch off zones. More generally, imaging involves "seeing" and "feeling" a skill in one's mind's eye before actually executing it (Driskell, Copper, & Moran 1994). Although there is considerable empirical evidence that mental practice facilitates skill-learning and performance, its status as a concentration technique remains uncertain. Anecdotally, however, mental imagery is used widely by performers for focusing optimally. For example, the English rugby star, Jonny Wilkinson (2006), revealed that his imagery involves

> a sort of clarified daydream with snippets of the atmosphere from past matches included to enhance the sense of reality. It lasts about twenty minutes and by the end of it I feel I know what is coming. The game will throw up many different scenarios but I am as prepared in my own head for them as I can be. If you have realistically imagined situations, you feel better prepared and less fearful of the unexpected.
>
> (p. 58)

In Wilkinson's quote, we discover that mental imagery may help athletes prepare for various hypothetical scenarios, thereby ensuring that they will not be distracted or upset by unexpected events. This hypothesis, however, has not been tested adequately to date. Additional research is required on athletes' knowledge about, and views on, imagery techniques in sport. See MacIntyre and Moran (in press) and Chapter 50 in this book.

Conclusions

Concentration, or the ability to focus on the task at hand while ignoring distractions, is central to successful performance in sport. It is part of the construct of "attention" that is concerned with focusing mental effort on sensory or cognitive events. Other dimensions of this construct include selective attention (the perceptual skill of zooming in on relevant information while ignoring distractions) and divided attention (the mental time-sharing ability that enables us to perform several simultaneous actions equally well). For cognitive psychologists, concentration resembles a mental spotlight that illuminates what we pay attention to – either in the world around us or in the private theatre of our own thoughts and feelings. An important aspect of this spotlight metaphor is the idea that concentration can never be lost but can be directed at the wrong targets (i.e., things that are irrelevant to the task at hand). Research-based principles of effective concentration include the ideas that one has to *decide* to concentrate in the first place, one can focus on only one thing at a time, one should try to do exactly what one thinks, one needs to refocus regularly, and one should focus outwards when anxious. Practical concentration techniques include setting action goals, establishing pre-performance routines, using trigger words, and visualizing future actions. Overall, this chapter has shown that far from being something fleeting or mysterious, concentration is a mental skill like any other that can be improved with appropriate training and practice. See Box 52.1 for some take-home messages from this chapter.

Box 52.1

Take-home messages about concentration

- Concentration, or the ability to focus on the task at hand while ignoring distractions, can have a significant influence on performance outcomes.
- Concentration is best understood as a mental spotlight that shines at targets either in the external world or in the internal world of thoughts and feelings.
- Whenever the concentration beam shines at a target that is irrelevant to the job at hand, focus can be lost.
- One is truly focused when there is no difference between doing and thinking.
- To concentrate effectively, one needs to prepare properly (by deciding to focus on a job that is under one's control), be single-minded, and remember to re-focus when distracted.
- Popular practical concentration techniques include setting action goals for performances, following pre-performance routines, using trigger words to remind oneself about what to concentrate on, and using imaginations to "see" and "feel" exactly what to do next.

References

Bannister, R. (2004, May 1). Fear of failure haunted me right to the last second. *The Guardian*, pp. 12–13.

Clarke, D. (with K. Morris) (2005). *Golf: The mind factor*. London: Hodder & Stoughton.

Corry, M. (2007, October 13). Broccoli, foul focus drinks and hip-hop: How we will prepare for the big kick-off. *The Guardian*, p. 3.

Cotterill, S. (2008). Developing effective pre-performance routines in golf. *Sport & Exercise Psychology Review*, 4(2), 10–15.

Driskell, J. E., Copper, C., & Moran, A. (1994). Does mental practice enhance performance? *Journal of Applied Psychology*, 79, 481–492.

English, A. (2006). *Munster: Our road to glory*. Dublin, Ireland: Penguin.

Gilleece, D. (1999, July 6). So near and yet so far. *The Irish Times*, p. 23.

Goldstein, E. B. (2008). *Cognitive psychology: Connecting mind, research, and everyday experience* (2nd ed.). Belmont, CA: Thompson/Wadsworth.

Greenlees, I., & Moran, A. (Eds.). (2003). *Concentration skills training in sport.* Leicester, England: British Psychological Society.

Hardy, L., & Jones, J. G. (1994). Current issues and future directions for performance-related research in sport psychology. *Journal of Sports Sciences, 12,* 61–92.

Hatzigeorgiadis, A., Theodorakis, Y., & Zourbanos, N. (2004). Self-talk in the swimming pool: The effects of self-talk on thought content and performance on water-polo tasks. *Journal of Applied Sport Psychology, 16,* 138–150.

Jackson, S. A., & Kimiecik, J. C. (2008). The flow perspective of optimal experience in sport and physical activity. In T. S. Horn (Ed.), *Advances in sport psychology* (3rd ed., pp. 377–399). Champaign, IL: Human Kinetics.

Kremer, J., & Moran, A. (2008). *Pure sport: Practical sport psychology.* London: Routledge.

MacIntyre, T., & Moran, A. (2010). Meta-imagery processes among elite sports performers. In A. Guillot & C. Collet (Eds.), *The neurophysiological foundations of mental and motor imagery* (pp. 227–244). Oxford, England: Oxford University Press.

McIlvanney, H. (2008, January 13). Slippery slope of sledging. *The Sunday Times* (Sport), p. 24.

Martin, A. (2007, July 3). More than words: Book of Serena the answer to Williams' prayers. *The Guardian* (Sport), p. 5.

Moran, A. P. (1996). *The psychology of concentration in sport performers: A cognitive analysis.* Hove, England: Psychology Press.

Moran, A. P. (2004). *Sport and exercise psychology: A critical introduction.* London: Psychology Press/ Routledge.

Moran, G. (2005, July 12). Oh dear, so near but yet so far away. *The Irish Times,* p. 21.

Northcroft, J. (2009, February 8). They shall not pass. *The Sunday Times* (Sport), pp. 12–13.

Ronay, B. (2008, July 2). The peculiar power of the centre court crowd. *The Guardian* (g2), pp. 6–9.

Sarkar, P. (2009, June 7). Open: Federer unnerved by spectator intrusion. Retrieved from http://www. guardian.co.uk/sport/feedarticle/8546123

Singer, R. N. (1988). Strategies and metastrategies in learning and performing self-paced athletic skills. *The Sport Psychologist, 2,* 49–68.

Skilbeck, J. (2009, April 30). Snooker. *Irish Independent* (Sport), p. 16.

The Guardian. (2009). *The Guardian and Observer guides to getting fit with Britain's medal winners.* London: The Guardian.

Walsh, D. (2008, July 6). Is this the world's greatest athlete? *The Sunday Times* (Sport), pp. 12–13.

Wilkinson, J. (2006). *My world.* London: Headline Books.

Williams, R. (2002, July 8). Sublime Serena celebrates the crucial difference. *The Guardian,* p. 6.

Wulf, G. (2007, June 5). Attentional focus and motor learning: A review of 10 years of research. *Bewegung und Training* (e-journal), 1–11. Retrieved from http://web.visu.uni-saarland.de/ejournal /Diskussionsforum//DCForumID2/13.html

Zourbanos, N., Hatzigeorgiadis, A., Chroni, S., Theodorakis, Y., & Papaioannou, A. (2009). Automatic Self-Talk Questionnaire for Sports (ASTQS): Development and preliminary validation of a measure identifying the structure of athletes' self-talk. *The Sport Psychologist, 23,* 233–251.

53

Self-talk

Judy L. Van Raalte

Some athletes maintain an ongoing internal dialogue while competing: "I really need this putt," or "I couldn't hit the side of a barn today," or "I own this court." Other athletes shout aloud in frustration or exhilaration. "You cannot be serious!!" or "Come on!! Get there!" And then there are times when athletes compete in silence, step up, take a deep breath, and execute.

What mindset should athletes have to perform their best? Does thinking or talking to oneself affect sport performance? According to Confucius (n.d.), "the more man meditates upon good thoughts, the better will be his world and the world at large." Many athletes and coaches believe that being positive enhances sport performance. But is being positive always right? James Hagerty (n.d.) once said, "One day I sat thinking, almost in despair; a hand fell on my shoulder and a voice said reassuringly: cheer up, things could get worse. So I cheered up and, sure enough, things got worse." If positive thoughts are not always effective and sometimes things get worse, then perhaps negative self-talk, a mental kick in the butt, could be an alternative performance strategy. And what about the athletes who are "in the zone" or performance flow states and don't seem to be thinking or talking to themselves at all?

These questions pertain to self-talk and the relationships among self-talk, personal factors, environmental factors, and sport performance. In this chapter, I will define self-talk, present research related to self-talk in sport settings, and finally, discuss how to apply research findings to work with teams and athletes. Understanding self-talk can help athletes, coaches, and sport psychology consultants meet their sport, exercise, and other goals.

What is self-talk?

Self-talk is a term used widely in the research literature to describe what athletes say to themselves out loud or internally and privately. A number of terms have been used to describe self-talk, including inner or internal dialogue, monologue, voice or speech, auditory imagery, private speech, self-statements, stream of consciousness, and more (Brinthaupt, Hein, & Kramer, 2009). Given this broad range of descriptive terms, it is not surprising that definitions of self-talk range greatly in breadth and scope. Some definitions of self-talk focus only on self-directed verbalizations; other definitions include imagery, inner or internal speech, hand and body gestures, and even some verbalizations that appear to be directed at others (Van Raalte, Brewer, Cornelius, & Petitpas, 2006). The inclusion of gestures in definitions of self-talk seems to be warranted, based on recent cross-cultural research indicating that gestures are intimately tied to language acquisition and use (Guidetti & Nicoladis, 2008).

Consideration of self-talk definitions may seem to be solely an academic exercise but there are applied benefits. Defining self-talk facilitates clarification and a shared understanding of the construct. Broad definitions of self-talk suggest that a range of strategies might be used in self-talk interventions.

Types of self-talk

To help understand self-talk more clearly, researchers have classified self-talk according to a number of coding schemes. For example, self-talk has been categorized according to the manner in which it occurs. Some self-talk is self-determined, occurring spontaneously such as when an athlete shouts out a frustrated "I stink!" after a missed shot or an enthusiastic "awesome!!" after a great one. Other self-talk is purposefully used to change mood or behavior and may be chosen by an athlete or assigned by a coach or researchers as part of an experiment (Zinsser, Bunker, & Williams, 2010).

Spontaneously occurring self-talk has been categorized as positive, negative, and instructional (Van Raalte, Brewer, Rivera, & Petitpas, 1994). Positive self-talk includes statements that people say to themselves that are encouraging or reflect favorable emotions. In a sport setting, positive self-talk might include statements such as "I can do it," or "Yes!" Negative self-talk involves statements that are negative and /or reflect anger or discouragement such as "you are slow!" or "that's horrible." Instructional self-talk involves providing self-direction about the performance of a particular skill or strategy such as "nice loose swing" or "move your feet." More recently, motivational self-talk such as "hang in there" or "come on!" has also been studied in sport settings (Zervas, Stavrou, & Psychountaki, 2007). Research on spontaneous self-talk has shown that discouraging events such as losing points in tennis can lead to negative self-talk (Van Raalte, Cornelius, Hatten, & Brewer, 2000). Further, spontaneous negative self-talk can lead to poor performance (Van Raalte et al., 1994). These results suggest that spontaneous negative self-talk is problematic for competitors.

If spontaneously occurring negative self-talk hurts performance, it might make sense that reducing negative self-talk and/or using positive self-talk would be helpful for performance. Research has been conducted to examine the effects of self-talk that athletes and coaches intentionally choose to use. Laboratory studies exploring the relationship between self-talk and performance usually involve participants coming into a laboratory setting and performing sport-like tasks such as throwing darts at a target (Van Raalte et al., 1995). Much of this research involves college undergraduates who are not competitive athletes and are not performing in real sport settings. In these studies, the preponderance of research data suggests that positive self-talk is associated with better performances than use of negative self-talk and that motivational self-talk is particularly effective for tasks requiring power (Edwards, Tod, & McGuigan, 2008). For tasks requiring precision, instructional self-talk is superior to motivational or no self-talk (Hatzigeorgiadis, Theodorakis, & Zourbanos, 2004).

From this laboratory research, it appears that intentional use of positive, instructional, and motivational self-talk may be helpful in sport settings. Field studies involving athletes performing sport tasks in non-competitive and actual competition settings confirm that negative self-talk can disrupt performance and that instructional self-talk is a preferred approach. For example, Harvey, Van Raalte, and Brewer (2002) found that golfers who were told to use instructional self-talk while putting showed benefits in terms of consistency. In contrast, the more positive and negative self-talk that golfers used, the less accurate were their putting performances.

Similar research conducted with endurance athletes has typically involved assessment of the effects of athletes' associative and dissociative self-talk. Associative self-talk, a form of instructional self-talk, involves a focus on body sensations and noticing how performance is proceeding with self-statements such as "my legs are OK" or "keep shoulders down." Dissociative self-talk involves self-distraction, thinking about tasks to be completed or other people or even listening to music. Skilled performers, especially those working at high levels of effort, perform best when using associative/instructional self-talk (St Clair Gibson & Foster, 2007). When considering laboratory and field studies together, it appears that negative self-talk can be harmful to sport performance and that instructional self-talk can be helpful.

How does self-talk affect sport performance?

A number of mechanisms by which self-talk affects sport outcomes have been proposed. Specifically, it has been proposed that self-talk affects sport performance by causing emotional (e.g., mood, motivation, anxiety) and/or cognitive (e.g., self-instruction, distraction reduction) changes (Zinsser et al., 2010). Emotional changes may help athletes maintain appropriate levels of motivation, reduce negative emotions and perhaps negative self-talk, and increase self-confidence. Cognitive changes can direct attention to the appropriate movement and help athletes correct errors and focus effectively on the task at hand.

If so much is understood about self-talk and the mechanisms by which self-talk affects performance in sport, then why isn't self-talk used by athletes most of the time? The challenge related to self-talk is knowing exactly what type and how much self-talk is most effectively used for which athletes under which circumstances. Research on choking in sport has demonstrated that instructional self-talk can be performance enhancing for novices. The same type of instructional self-talk can induce choking in skilled performers. For example, Ford, Hodges, and Williams (2005) had skilled soccer players use instructional self-talk, directing attention to their feet during a soccer dribbling task. Those using instructional self-talk dribbled the ball more poorly than did those who did not use self-talk. Beilock, Carr, MacMahon, and Starkes (2002) demonstrated similar results in their study on soccer players and golfers. Overall, it seems that for highly skilled athletes, use of instructional self-talk can lead to increased attentional monitoring and worse performances, or to put it another way, under certain circumstances, skilled athletes using instructional self-talk may experience paralysis by analysis.

If too much instructional self-talk is problematic for skilled performers, then perhaps turning off self-talk is ideal for optimal performance. Leary and Tate (2007) discussed the mental states associated with peak performance, flow states, and mindfulness and noted that reduced self-talk is a defining characteristic of optimal performance mental states. It is not clear, however, if the beneficial effects of mindfulness are due to reduced self-talk or to the effectiveness of the other components of mindfulness. It may be possible for athletes to use self-talk to achieve peak performance and flow states but then experience reduced self-talk during the actual experience of peak performances. This interpretation is supported by qualitative research with high performers and athletes describing flow and peak experiences. Athletes and coaches consistently indicate that self-talk is one of the key components that has contributed to their optimal peak performances (Krane & Williams, 2010).

Personal factors related to self-talk use

Another reason that it may be difficult to determine exactly what self-talk is ideal for performance enhancement is that a "one size fits all" approach may not work well for self-talk. Personal and environmental factors can come into play such that certain types and amounts of self-talk are effective for some people and not as effective for others. Van Raalte *et al.* (2000) studied competitive adult tennis players and found that nearly 75% of the athletes spontaneously used negative self-talk after losing a point, perhaps to express frustration. Half of the tennis players used positive self-talk after they lost a point, perhaps to get back on track and to perform better. When it came to the next point, almost all the tennis players performed worse after using negative self-talk, but one player tended to perform better. With regard to positive self-talk, only one player performed better after using positive self-talk, two players performed worse, and the rest were unaffected. These data suggest that there are trends in the ways that people use self-talk but also that there are important individual difference in self-talk uses and effects. What works for some may not work for others.

Wood, Perunovic, and Lee (2009) looked at another individual characteristic, self-esteem, to examine the effects of self-talk. High and low self-esteem participants in their study were asked to repeat positive self-talk statements or were assigned to a no-statement control condition. It might be expected that positive self-talk would be particularly helpful for the low self-esteem participants who might especially need encouragement. Instead, results showed that low self-esteem participants who used positive self-talk such as, "I'm a lovable person" or focused on how that statement was true actually felt worse than those low self-esteem participants who focused on how the statement "I'm a lovable person" could be true or not true. Further, low self-esteem participants who used positive self-talk also reported feeling worse than those who did not use positive self-talk at all. For high self-esteem participants, a limited benefit of positive self-talk use was found. Thus, use of positive self-talk may benefit certain people, but may be least effective for those with low self-esteem who *appear* to need positive self-talk the most. Clearly, further research exploring self-talk and other personal factors is needed. When applying these findings, performers may want to try using positive self-talk to see how it works. If positive self-talk appears to be helpful, then continued use makes sense. If not, then other strategies might be worth considering.

Environmental factors related to self-talk use

Self-talk affects individuals, but it is important to remember that individuals are not alone, but rather, function within an environmental context. When talking about environmental factors that contribute to self-talk, I use the term "environment" in a broad sense. That is, it includes the social team environment created by other athletes and coaches as well as the specific sport environment involving practice and competition settings. Research exploring self-talk across settings indicates that self-talk typically used in practice differs from that used in competition. As might be expected, more self-talk is used during competition when intensity is high (Hardy, Hall, & Hardy, 2005). Self-talk use also differs across cultures. Peters and Williams (2006) compared East Asian and European American students in their use of self-talk and the effects of self-talk on performance. They found that East Asian students used a greater proportion of negative to positive self-talk than did European American students. This greater negative to positive self-talk ratio resulted in better performance for the East Asian students than it did for the European/American students. Thus, the social, sport, and cultural environments may all contribute to how and when self-talk is used and the effects that self-talk has on individuals. For those who find self-talk to be an effective or useful strategy, developing a self-talk plan that includes self-talk use that is matched to the environment and that is flexible might be a valuable tactic for training and competition.

Using self-talk in sport performance

The body of research reviewed above suggests that using self-talk can be a valuable strategy. How then might an effective self-talk program be designed? Based on the research highlighting individual differences in the effects of self-talk (Van Raalte et al., 2000), it is useful to start by understanding how teams or individual performers currently use self-talk. Is self-talk used at all? If so, is it spontaneously generated self-talk, or is it self-talk that has been selected by athletes, coaches, sport psychologists, or important others for a specific purpose? Under what circumstances is self-talk used or does self-talk occur? How does self-talk affect personal factors (e.g., self-esteem, confidence, motivation)? What is the environment like and how does self-talk fit into that particular environment? How are self-talk and performance related? That is, would reducing negative self-talk be helpful or do certain types of negative self-talk provide motivation?

Answering these sorts of questions usually requires athletes to think about themselves, their environments, and sport performances in an unfamiliar manner. Some athletes benefit from self-talk journals, in which they write down their self-talk used and the effects of such self-talk. Some athletes might speak their talk aloud and record it to assess their actual self-talk use. Other athletes might prefer a less academic approach, using imagery to recollect their self-talk or simply choosing to be more aware of their self-talk and then considering how (and if) they might like to use self-talk in a more systematic manner.

Once an understanding of current self-talk use is gained, it is important to consider the individual athlete involved. There are a number of self-talk techniques that may be effective for athletes in general. The challenge is finding the right techniques to consider for each individual athlete in his or her individual situation. Several self-talk techniques are described below.

Self-instruction

For athletes who want to correct or develop specific sport skills, instructional self-talk may be their strategy of choice. For these athletes, simple phrases such as "turn, hit," are reminders that can help athletes reap the benefits of instructional self-talk. The goal is to select instructional self-talk that is at the appropriate level so that the performance decrements due to excessive attentional monitoring are minimized (Beilock et al., 2002). Instructional self-talk can also be used to develop psychological skills. For example, athletes may use self-talk to improve mood by choosing self-talk statements to use at critical times that help them feel better, such as "I love this sport." Self-talk can also be used to increase effort, "I can take more pain. I have trained, and I am ready for anything!" or to control attentional focus, "there is only the ball and me."

Thought replacement

For athletes who find that they are overwhelmed by negative self-talk, thought replacement may be implemented to counteract the problematic effects. Thought replacement is based on the idea that suppressing negative self-talk ("don't think about it any more") works temporarily at best and sometimes cannot be accomplished at all (Zinsser et al., 2010). To use thought replacement, athletes identify their problematic negative self-talk. Next, they come up with and use alternative thoughts to replace the identified self-talk statements. For example, "this is too hard, I will never get it" might be replaced by, "I've learned hard things before. I can learn this, too." In high pressure situations that lead athletes to say to themselves things such as, "I don't belong here, the competition is too good," negative self-talk can be replaced with the statement made famous by tennis star, Billie Jean King (n.d.), "Pressure is a privilege – it only comes to those who earn it." With thought replacement, the intentional use of helpful self-talk is designed to provide direct benefits that replace the harmful effects of negative self-talk.

Mindfulness

Both self-instruction and thought replacement are effortful techniques that require athletes to purposely change their self-talk behaviors and patterns. Inherent in these approaches is a sense that self-talk is insufficient or wrong and should be controlled, eliminated, or improved. Athletes who attempt to suppress problematic self-talk such as "don't think about how much I suck" may experience ironic effects of mental control or action such that the thoughts are suppressed for a time but then rebound more strongly later.

Mindfulness and acceptance approaches are based on the idea that self-talk and related internal cognitive and emotional states do not need to be replaced or eliminated (see Chapters 20 and 21). With regard to self-talk, positive outcomes can be achieved by practising nonjudgmental, present-moment awareness and acceptance of naturally occurring self-talk followed by commitment to action. Mindfulness states have been shown to be similar to flow states suggesting that athletes who use mindfulness may be likely to experience flow states more often (Bernier, Thienot, Codron, & Fournier, 2009).

As with any behavioral intervention, it is useful to get a baseline of the behavior in question, to try an intervention to enhance performance, and then to evaluate the effectiveness of the intervention. Modifications to the self-talk plan can then be made to help reach optimal performance states. This approach can work for athletes, coaches, and sport psychology consultants.

Conclusion

Self-talk, broadly defined, includes what athletes say to themselves via word or gesture, out loud, or internally and privately. Although more narrow definitions of self-talk exist, this one encompasses the full range of self-talk and related phenomena. Research conducted on self-talk in experimental and field settings generally suggests that negative self-talk is associated with poor performance. Instructional self-talk can be useful in certain circumstances. Positive self-talk seems to enhance performance primarily in the laboratory. These generalizations should be carefully considered when applying self-talk interventions to any specific individual. There are large individual and environmental differences in terms of self-talk use and its effects. People who want to try using self-talk in a systematic way can begin by assessing their current self-talk use and its effects. Next, an intervention can be designed to modify self-talk in a particular way. Finally, the intervention can be evaluated and changed to better reach desired results. Athletes and coaches have identified self-talk as a key component in sport success. It seems valuable to consider self-talk as a part of a comprehensive sport or exercise training program. See Box 53.1 for a summary of practical points from this chapter.

Box 53.1

Summary of practical points about self-talk

- Self-talk broadly defined includes gestures and self-directed thoughts and talk.
- Negative self-talk is associated with poor performance.
- Positive self-talk use may result in lower self-esteem for some athletes.
- If choosing among positive, negative, and instructional self-talk, instructional self-talk is associated with the best performances.
- To use self-talk effectively, athletes should identify how and when they use self-talk, determine the effects of self-talk, implement interventions, and evaluate self-talk.
- One should modify self-talk strategies as skill and sport needs evolve.

References

Beilock, S. L., Carr, T. H., MacMahon, C., & Starkes, J. L. (2002). When paying attention becomes counterproductive: Impact of divided versus skill-focused attention on novice and experienced performance of sensorimotor skills. *Journal of Experimental Psychology: Applied, 8*, 6–16.

Bernier, M., Thienot, E., Codron, R., & Fournier, J. F. (2009). Mindfulness and acceptance approaches in sport performance. *Journal of Clinical Sport Psychology, 4*, 320–333.

Brinthaupt, T. M., Hein, M. B., & Kramer, T. E. (2009). The Self-Talk Scale: Development, factor analysis, and validation. *Journal of Personality Assessment, 91*, 82–92.

Confucius. (n.d.). Retrieved from http://www.worldofquotes.com/author/Confucius/1/index.html

Edwards, C., Tod, D., & McGuigan, M. (2008). Self-talk influences vertical jump performance and kinematics in male rugby union players. *Journal of Sports Sciences, 26*, 1459–1465.

Ford, P., Hodges, N. J., & Williams, A. (2005). Online attentional-focus manipulations in a soccer-dribbling task: Implications for the proceduralization of motor skills. *Journal of Motor Behavior, 37*, 386–394.

Guidetti, M., & Nicoladis, E. (2008). Introduction to Special Issue: Gestures and communicative development. *First Language, 28*, 107–115.

Hagerty, J. (n.d.). Retrieved from http://quotationsbook.com/quote/35822/

Hardy, J., Hall, C., & Hardy, L. (2005). Quantifying athlete self-talk. *Journal of Sports Sciences, 23*, 905–917.

Harvey, D., Van Raalte, J. L., & Brewer, B. W. (2002). Relationship between self-talk and golf performance. *International Sports Journal, 6*, 84–91.

Hatzigeorgiadis, A., Theodorakis, Y., & Zourbanos, N. (2004). Self-talk in the swimming pool: The effects of self-talk on thought content and performance on water-polo tasks. *Journal of Applied Sport Psychology, 16*, 138–150.

King, B. J. (n.d.) Retrieved from http://www.tennisontheline.org/quotes.shtml

Krane, V., & Williams, J. M. (2010). Psychological characteristics of peak performance. In J. M. Williams (Ed.), *Applied sport psychology: Personal growth to peak performance* (6th ed., pp. 169–188). New York: McGraw-Hill.

Leary, M. L., & Tate, E. B. (2007). The multi-faceted nature of mindfulness. *Psychological Inquiry, 84*, 251–255.

Peters, H. J., & Williams, J. M. (2006). Moving cultural background to the foreground: An investigation of self-talk, performance, and persistence following feedback. *Journal of Applied Sport Psychology, 18*, 240–253.

St Clair Gibson, A., & Foster, C. (2007). The role of self-talk in the awareness of physiological state and physical performance. *Sports Medicine, 37*, 1029–1044.

Van Raalte, J. L., Brewer, B. W., Cornelius, A. E., & Petitpas, A. J. (2006). Self-presentational effects of self-talk on perceptions of tennis players. *Hellenic Journal of Psychology, 3*, 134–149.

Van Raalte, J. L., Brewer, B. W., Lewis, B. P., Linder, D. E., Wildman, G., & Kozimor, J. M. (1995). Cork: the effects of positive and negative self-talk on dart throwing performance. *Journal of Sport Behavior, 18*, 50–57.

Van Raalte, J. L, Brewer, B. W., Rivera, P. M., & Petitpas, A. J. (1994). The relationship between observable self-talk and competitive junior tennis players' match performances. *Journal of Sport & Exercise Psychology, 16*, 400–415.

Van Raalte, J. L., Cornelius, A. E., Hatten, S. J., & Brewer, B. W. (2000). The antecedents and consequences of self-talk in competitive tennis. *Journal of Sport & Exercise Psychology, 22*, 345–356.

Wood, J. V., Perunovic, W. Q. E., & Lee, J. W. (2009). Positive self-statements: Power for some, peril for others. *Psychological Science, 20*, 860–867.

Zervas, Y., Stavrou, N., & Psychountaki, M. (2007). Development and validation of the Self-Talk Questionnaire (S-TQ) for Sports. *Journal of Applied Sport Psychology, 19*, 142–159.

Zinsser, N., Bunker, L., & Williams, J. M. (2010). Cognitive techniques for building confidence and enhancing performance. In J. M. Williams (Ed.), *Applied sport psychology: Personal growth to peak performance* (6th ed., pp. 305–335). New York: McGraw-Hill.

54

Confidence

Robin S. Vealey and Dan Vernau

Athletes know two things about confidence. One, confidence makes them feel bulletproof. When they believe in themselves – that they have the resources and abilities to perform successfully – their performances flow automatically and easily. Two, athletes also know that confidence is fragile. Certain circumstances, such as failure in a critical competitive moment, can lead to chinks in athletes' bulletproof armors, or even a total collapse of confidence and an inability to successfully perform a skill in competition. Elite athletes have stated that the most important ingredient in mental toughness is a deeply rooted self-confidence that is strong and resilient in the face of setbacks and obstacles (Bull, Shambrook, James, & Brooks, 2005).

Because confidence is foundational, but sometimes fragile, athletes and coaches often identify it as an important mental skill to be nurtured and maintained. Research suggests that confidence may be enhanced through various types of mental training (e.g., Vealey & Chase, 2008). So what strategies can be used to help athletes gain and maintain confidence? How can we individually use and collectively package the tools in the mental training "toolbox" described in this section of the book to build confidence? And how can we, or even can we, help athletes develop the deep, resilient confidence identified as a key to mental toughness or feelings of "bulletproofness?"

How confidence is built

To organize our thinking about how to build confidence in athletes, we've boiled down what research and best practices in sport psychology have taught us to create the illustration shown in Figure 54.1. Here are the key points to be extracted from the illustration:

1. There are four broad categories to draw from in building confidence. The boxes on the left side identify the four main sources of confidence in sport (Bandura, 1997; Hays, Maynard, Thomas, & Bawden, 2007; Vealey, Hayashi, Garner-Holman, & Giacobbi, 1998). How do athletes build confidence? They (a) physically train and prepare exhaustively, (b) engage in self-regulatory strategies (e.g., self-talk, imagery,

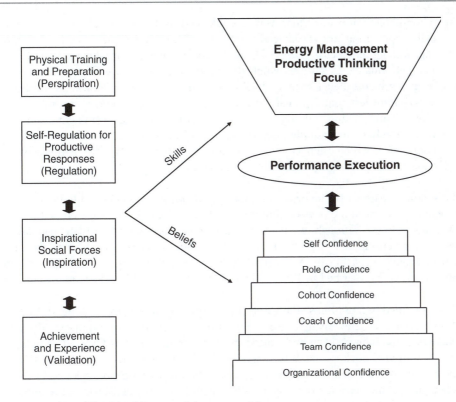

Figure 54.1 A model for building confidence in athletes.

energy management, behavior monitoring) to habituate productive responses in competition, (c) gain inspiration and support from others (e.g., teammates, family, coaches), and (d) progressively achieve success and gain experience in succeeding in diverse situations. Or, a more colorful way to describe it is to say that athletes gain confidence through: perspiration (hard work), regulation (mental training), inspiration (socially from others), and validation (seeing their hard work and preparation pay off in successful performance).

2. Athletes' self-confidence is nested within a complex range of social contexts, so it is important to account for all these types of confidences. This point is illustrated by the "stair steps" on the right side of Figure 54.1. Athletes' self-confidence is embedded within increasingly broader social layers, such as confidence in their abilities to succeed in their roles and within their specific cohorts (e.g., line in hockey, doubles partner in tennis) as well as confidence in their coaches, teams, and organizations. An abusive coach, team conflict that negatively affects performance, and/or a dysfunctional athletic department or organization can all serve to undermine an athlete's confidence or sabotage attempts to build self-confidence.

3. The direct pathway to building confidence is using the four sources of confidence to create and enhance strong, resilient beliefs about one's abilities (lower long arrow). These strong and resilient beliefs about abilities create feelings of confidence, which enable athletes to engage in successful performance execution. This pathway is best thought of as building confidence for performance success.

4. The indirect pathway to increasing confidence is to build one's physical and mental skills (upper long arrow) that lead to effective energy management, productive thinking, and optimal focus. These qualities are controllable mental skills that guide optimal performance execution, which then enhances confidence. The premise is that even if athletes' belief systems (feelings/thoughts about abilities and probability for success) are less than optimal (as when one lacks confidence), they can use their physical and mental training to focus on relevant cues, manage energy, and think productively to successfully perform. Successful performance execution then builds confidence, which then enhances performance, and so on. This pathway is best thought of as building performance success for confidence.

This indirect pathway is important because confidence is a difficult skill to mend once it has been shaken by failure or poor performance, because one main source of confidence is performance success. Through systematic physical and mental training, athletes can develop an automatic performance response that will allow them to succeed, even when their confidence is shaky. This application of mental skills to enhance performance at a time of shaky confidence is aptly described by Peter Vidmar, U.S. Olympic gold medalist in gymnastics:

> I was petrified because I missed my first two routines. I was starting to panic thinking I might not make the Olympic team, even though I was still in third place. All of a sudden, I just calmed down and started thinking straight. Just as I started thinking, things started to click for me. It turned out to be the best routine of my life up to that point. I don't have that type of panic anymore. As the years went on, I got rid of that element of panic because I triggered myself somehow into saying, "Okay, something is wrong now. What can I do about it?" as opposed to saying, "Something's wrong. I can't believe it's happening!"
>
> (Ravizza, 1993, p. 96)

Building confidence through "perspiration"

Confidence is earned through persistent, deliberate practice and training (or "perspiration"). There are no shortcuts or quick fixes when it comes to confidence. Systematic physical preparation allows athletes to trust themselves in executing their skills during the pressure of competition. Here are some specific ways to build confidence through perspiration:

1. Incorporate training strategies that simulate pressure situations and create unexpected scenarios to train adaptability. Practise against a six-player defense in basketball; use multiple balls and rapid-fire sequencing in volleyball defensive drills; turn the heat up (literally!); systematically practise last-minute plays and strategies, and use the scoreboard to create specific situations for athletes (e.g., down by six points with a minute left, up by two points with a minute left). Some coaches are masters at these tactics, with the intent being that competition will rarely be more intense than the training.
2. Set up a team or programmatic mantra or attitude that defines the work ethic of the team and how they can "live" this work ethic. Work with team leaders to create the "how we do it here" norm for training intensity and practice expectations. One example mantra is "I see me." A team with whom we worked bought into the idea that "details make champions," and then they committed to that by emphasizing the

importance of everyone taking personal responsibility for the details of becoming champions. "I see me" meant that no one had to be watching or evaluating for each player to take care of the smallest details in training and preparation. The phrase was extended as players would say "I see you, Robin" to acknowledge and show appreciation for a teammate's hard work or extra effort.

3. Teach athletes to focus on performing at their best level "that day." Perspiration is particularly needed by athletes on those days when things don't come easy for them. Confidence affects our effort and persistence, without us even realizing it. Athletes must understand how important it is for them to focus and "grind" out their best performances when they aren't "in the zone" or when they are not feeling naturally confident. Challenge them to focus on performing at their best for that day. If they feel like they're not at 100%, focus on the 80% that they have. This situation is an important mental test for athletes. Great athletes don't wait until they feel like performing great; they attempt to perform great even when they don't feel like it. An important part of athletes' confidence is their beliefs in their abilities to perform well on "off" days.

4. Ask athletes to assess their preparation and commitment to training. In a team meeting, ask athletes to grade (from 0 to 100%) their team's commitment to physical conditioning, physical skill execution, and mental skill development. Then post all the team members' scores on a chalkboard for all to see. Lead a discussion about the various grades assigned to each category. Then, in small groups followed by a collective team discussion, have athletes generate ideas about how to raise the team's grade in each category.

Another exercise to assess athletes' effort in training is asking them to consider their training efforts compared to key competitors (Selk, 2009):

1. Who is your toughest competitor, the person you most enjoy outperforming?
2. On a scale of 1 to 10, rate how much effort you think this person puts into training. (1 = *very little effort*, 10 = *as much effort as possible*)
3. On the same scale, rate how much effort you put into training.
4. If your number is less than 10, what changes would need to be made for you to put a 10-level effort into your training? Be specific, and describe what a 10 would look like for you in your training.

Building confidence through regulation

Perspiration is the first step in building confidence, so that athletes have foundations to be confident. Just like the endless physical training repetitions that athletes undergo to hone their physical skill execution, they must also undergo deliberate mental repetitions to systematically train productive responses to competitive demands. This psychological training could include many of the mental strategies presented in this book, including self-talk training, imagery, energy management, and the development and use of focus plans. Below are a few specific tips about how to "package" various self-regulatory skills to enhance confidence.

1. Fake it 'til you make it. Athletes should attempt to exude a physical or behavioral level of confidence as much as they can. Athletes will benefit from controlling their

body language, facial expressions, and posture so that they convey a sense of confidence and personal control. This faking it until you make it should be explained, practised, and monitored in training sessions, because physical poise and behavioral confidence are an essential part of a team culture or program "code." Responding with outer poise or confidence makes it easier to respond with inner confidence, or to believe in self. Although faking it 'til you make it refers to an outward appearance of confidence, it also can apply to internal beliefs. Athletes should adopt a key affirmation that describes their idealized self-image, or what they want to be. Affirmation statements should always be stated in the present tense to project to themselves that they are what they intend to be. Affirmations should also be simple, active, emotive, and positive. Examples are: "I'm a relentless scorer," "I love the pressure because it draws out my best," and "I'm prepared, strong, and focused." Affirmations work if athletes believe in themselves enough to program thoughts toward their desired goals and achievements.

2. Learn to "respond" with confidence. We believe that athletes should focus on responding with confidence and control, as opposed to reacting with emotion or unproductive behaviors. Practice is needed because competitive sport involves failures, mistakes, inequity, criticism, embarrassment, aggression, and opponents whose goal is to block athletes from achieving their goals. Athletes should develop thoughtful, planned responses to situations that jolt their confidence or distract their focus. These situations include such things as receiving criticism from coaches, making performance errors, suffering a heartbreaking defeat, dealing with rough play, and taking bad luck in stride (such as a poor call from an official or a freak, lucky play from an opponent). Effective self-regulation means that athletes are mentally efficient and emotionally adaptive, no matter what occurs in competition.

How can athletes learn to respond with confidence? By practising it – in training and through imagery. We suggest using "I respond with confidence" as a go-to phrase that athletes learn to repeat when training their response-ability. Everyone has the ability to respond more effectively: it just takes a commitment to change and practice in making the new response automatic. Below is an example of a response plan that athletes could develop and practise for those moments when they lose focus, make a critical error, or feel as if they are "choking."

The acronym ACT gives athletes three steps to follow in responding with confidence: Accept, Center, Think. Accept the dreadful feelings, and tell yourself that it's okay; you understand what's happening and expected that you could feel this way. Don't try to suppress or hide the bad feelings – acknowledge them. Own them, or they will own you. Center yourself physically. Create a confident posture; inhale deeply, thinking about infusing your body with feelings that you need (e.g., strength, readiness, relaxation), and then exhale the tension, negative thoughts, and bad feelings. Think intentionally by directing your thoughts to your "go-to" self-talk strategy, such as the, "I respond with confidence" statement to center yourself, followed by a performance-oriented go-to thought that focuses on controllable things and the process of performance. Continuously occupy your mind by thinking on purpose, instead of letting your thoughts wander in unproductive ways.

Athletes should ACT, not just fall victim to random thoughts and feelings that enter their minds. Athletes can successfully ACT if they have planned productive mental responses to specific situations that undermine their confidence and focus, and then mentally practise these responses over time to make them habitual.

3. When responding effectively to adversity, athletes self-regulate their performances to "stay within themselves." An ineffective response to mistakes, poor team performance, or other obstacles is to try too hard or to attempt to make up a mistake with an exceptional play. But by trying to take it up a notch or do something spectacular, athletes forego the disciplined, trained performance responses that lead to success. Tell athletes: what happens to you is not nearly as important as how you respond to what happens to you. After a triple-bogey, golfers should program their focus to respond with a solid tee shot on the next hole (as opposed to ripping a career shot). A struggling volleyball hitter should attack aggressively to attempt to put the ball down, but not spectacularly in attempting an unbelievable shot. Attempting to do something great, in responding to mistakes, often leads to more mistakes. Help athletes understand how to make the solid play as a confident response.

4. Create and re-create personal images of successful experiences. Athletes should "see" what they want to happen (successful performance) and replay past successes. Many athletes today have personal highlight videos of themselves to view, a motivational and confidence-building technique. In addition to using technology in this way, athletes should create their own mental personal highlight videos using creative imagery. Athletes can create whatever highlight video they want, but a good formula to follow is to make about a minute or two highlight of a previous peak performance or combination of highlights from the past (see Selk, 2009). Then immediately follow that up by creating images of how they will feel, think, and perform in an upcoming competition. Athletes should outline on paper the key images that will make up both parts of their imagery highlight videos. This method makes their mental approach systematic as they experiment with images to find the ones that work best for them.

Building confidence through inspiration

Systematic physical and mental training helps athletes gain confidence through perspiration and regulation, and is the most direct method to build confidence. We also know that athletes thrive when they perform within a "culture" of confidence. Such a culture involves supportive and trusted interpersonal relationships between athletes, teammates, and coaches. Team building and communication activities may enhance not only team cohesion, but also team and athlete confidence. Consultants and coaches should choose team-building activities that focus on trust and personal self-disclosure, understanding and embracing diversity, and creating a collective sense of team identity. The leadership and decision-making of coaches has also been shown to be an important source of confidence for athletes (Vealey et al., 1998), and coaches should be sensitive to the needs of the team and individual athletes in terms of confidence. Frequent, yet short and concise team meetings to consistently reinforce productive interpersonal patterns might be helpful. For example, 5 minutes at the end of training sessions could be scheduled for team members to give feedback and evaluate the quality of the workout as well as the team's progress. Questions might include: What went well? What needs work? How can coaches help you? How can teammates help you? Confidence in teams is also enhanced by having strong athlete leaders. Coaches and sport psychology consultants should initiate team discussions around leadership to specifically identify what it means to be a leader for this group and what the team needs in terms of leadership.

Building confidence through validation

The strongest source of confidence is success. The biggest reason that athletes lose and lack confidence is that they allow others to define success for them. Each athlete can develop a personalized goal map that identifies specific and individualized mastery and performance goals (process goals are embedded in both; see Chapter 51), as well as time-bound goal achievement strategies (e.g., Vealey, 2005). Athletes who buy into their personal goal maps gain control over their own success, which is central to building confidence. Coaches should reinforce progress and achievement for each individual athlete based on their personal goal maps. Particularly in relation to self-confidence, athletes need help in identifying and pursuing challenging yet achievable goals. Athletes should be encouraged to push their limits and extend their performance and skills, but not at ridiculously unrealistic levels and definitely not as defined by others. Stable, resilient confidence is based on the pursuit and achievement of goals within personalized goal maps.

A case example: the line is mine

Here we present a case example of a basketball player in a crisis of confidence. Multiple strategies were used to rebuild this athlete's confidence, including physical and mental training to integrate perspiration and regulation within an inspirational climate to achieve personal validation and performance success.

Description

Kyra was the starting point guard for her college team. In a key game in early December against a highly ranked opponent, she missed two free throws in the closing seconds, which could have won the game for her team. Immediately after that game, Kyra's confidence at the free-throw line plummeted and her shooting percentage dropped from a heady 87% to a dismal 50%. Kyra's coach told her to, "Relax and don't worry about it," but Kyra continued to struggle at the line. In a holiday tournament, the coach had to substitute another player for Kyra late in the game to ensure that she had a ball handler on the floor who could make critical free throws down the stretch. Kyra understood the decision, continued to practise more and more free throws, but she still could not regain her confidence and free-throw shooting percentage.

Assessment

Kyra had fixated on the key free throws she had missed at a critical time. Her images and self-talk had become negative and less controllable than before, and her attentional focus at the line turned inward as she was paralyzed into controlled processing (thinking about how to shoot) as opposed to allowing her shot to flow freely through automatic processing. She lost her belief in herself to make free throws, particularly in critical situations.

Intervention

When the team had a week off for final exams, with a 2-week break between games, Kyra met with a sport psychology consultant. She stated that she wanted to "regain her confidence" in her free throw shooting, that she "knew she was still a good shooter," but that "she didn't believe she could transfer being a good shooter into putting the ball in the basket at this point." The consultant clarified that Kyra meant that she knew her solid shooting was still in there, but she had too much mental interference to "let it happen" naturally as it had in the past.

Kyra and the consultant agreed to combine a progressive physical training strategy with a mental training strategy designed to "clear" her mental interference. Basically, the intervention was to "rearrange" Kyra's focus, self-talk, and personal images. Because Kyra lost confidence in her free-throw shot, she agreed to change her pre-shot routine (somewhat radical for a college basketball player in the middle of a season) to wipe away the negative memory and triggers that reminded her of the missed free throws. She described it as wanting to leave the old free-throw "problem" behind by changing her routine, and liked the concept of a fresh start.

To create this new routine, Kyra engaged in a centering exercise where she carefully considered how she wanted to feel physically as well as what she wanted to think about when she got to the free-throw line. She decided to engage the feeling of being strong in her legs and balanced at the line. She would take her stance carefully and flex her knees a few times to cue the strong and balanced feeling. Her attentional focus was a smooth uncoiling of her body and the ball floating softly over the front of the rim. Her self-talk mantra was "strong, smooth, soft," which verbally and visually led her through the steps of her routine.

She noticed that her new routine at the line was working, but she still felt out of control at the initial moment when she was fouled and realized she was going to the line. She said she would have a quick "Oh, no!" moment where she felt fear about going to the line. Through discussion, the first thing Kyra came to realize and accept was that fear is okay and normal in that situation. She learned a response plan for the moment she was fouled, in which she could acknowledge her fear but also her confidence that she "had the shot." She chose to focus her attention immediately on how prepared she was to shoot the free throw by repeating to herself, "The line is mine; the line is mine – strong, smooth, soft." "The line is mine" created a strong overall feeling of confidence, and the words "strong, smooth, soft" locked her mind on her specific pre-shot routine and the needed focus for the shot. She worked on physically portraying confidence in her posture, walking to the line, and visually rehearsing the thoughts, feelings, and posture in which she would engage prior to shooting.

Once her routine was created, she began practising it in sets of 10 repetitions at 5 feet, 10 feet, and then 15 feet (the free-throw line) in front of the basket. This tactic gave her a progression to follow, with the intent of practising the routine enough to make it automatic and useful. And prior to physically practising at each station, she mentally practised her new routine and shooting the 10 reps at each spot. As time progressed in training sessions with the team, the coaches eased Kyra back into pressure situations by having her shoot free throws with consequences (e.g., taking a "time out" and going through mental rehearsal again) if she missed. This tactic allowed her to practise her new routine in simulated competitive situations.

Outcome

Kyra really liked creating a new routine and leaving her problem behind her, and the fresh start and mental plan coupled with systematic physical practice allowed her to overcome her "choking" response at the line. In time, Kyra learned to trust her preparation and follow her mental plan, and was able to do so because she spent extra time physically practising her free throws within the new routine. She described the experience as "breaking through the barrier" that kept her true shot from coming out at the line. Her confidence was mended through mental training to manage her thinking in such a way as to perform better, which then built back her confidence.

Conclusions

The overall goal for athletes is not a quick fix of confidence here and there to keep them going. Strong and resilient confidence is based on a challenging physical training foundation, practiced self-regulatory skills, strong leadership and a supportive team/organizational culture, and success that is personally validating of one's abilities and achievements. But athletes must accept that confidence is not a shatterproof shield or magical state. What is important is that athletes believe that they have multiple ways to gain or restore confidence and their performance abilities. See Box 54.1 for a summary of key points from this chapter.

Box 54.1

Key points about confidence

- Athletes gain confidence through (a) physical training and preparation, (b) self-regulatory strategies to habituate productive responses in competition, (c) inspiration and social support from significant others, and (d) progressive achievement and success.
- Athletes' self-confidence is nested within broader social layers, including confidence in their roles, cohorts, teams, coaches, and organizations.
- Confidence is built directly by creating and enhancing strong resilient beliefs about one's abilities, and is also built indirectly by applying physical and mental training to achieve performance success, which then leads to greater confidence.
- Specific activities and techniques may be used based on the four confidence-building strategies of perspiration, regulation, inspiration, and validation.

References

Bandura, A. (1997). *Self-efficacy: The exercise of control.* New York: Freeman.

Bull, S. J., Shambrook, C. J., James, W., & Brooks, J. E. (2005). Toward an understanding of mental toughness in elite English cricketers. *Journal of Applied Sport Psychology, 17,* 209–227.

Hays, K., Maynard, I., Thomas, O., & Bawden, M. (2007). Sources and types of confidence identified by world class sport performers. *Journal of Applied Sport Psychology, 19,* 434–456.

Ravizza, K. (1993). An interview with Peter Vidmar, member of the 1994 U.S. Olympic gymnastics team. *Contemporary Thought on Performance Enhancement, 2,* 93–100.

Selk, J. (2009). *10-minute toughness*. New York: McGraw-Hill.

Vealey, R. S. (2005). *Coaching for the inner edge*. Morgantown, WV: Fitness Information Technology.

Vealey, R. S., & Chase, M. A. (2008). Self-confidence in sport. In T. S. Horn (Ed.), *Advances in sport psychology* (3rd ed., pp. 65–97). Champaign, IL: Human Kinetics.

Vealey, R. S., Hayashi, S. W., Garner-Holman, M., & Giacobbi, P. (1998). Sources of sport-confidence: Conceptualization and instrument development. *Journal of Sport & Exercise Psychology, 20*, 227–243.

55

Time management

Edward Etzel and Samantha Monda

In his wonderful tale, *The Little Prince* (de Saint-Exupéry, 1943/2000), Saint-Exupéry's central character observed that the most important things in life are those we cannot see. Time is one of those invisible things that is central to our lives Along with our health and the company of others, time is perhaps the most precious commodity we have. Active people and high achievers in sport, exercise, the performing arts, and elsewhere recognize the usefulness of taking advantage of the limited time we have on the planet. They find ways to accomplish the things that are meaningful to them and those that are not so significant. Many, however, do not take advantage of the time they have to live fully. How can we best use our time to make the most of our lives?

We are often asked to do more, often with less – sometimes with little at all. Multi-tasking is the norm for many of us. Multiple responsibilities and distractions challenge the focus that high-achieving people want and need to do their best. Technology has evolved at a dizzying pace with the evolution of the internet, email, personal digital assistants (PDAs), cell phones, and so forth. The conflicting demands of the interests and the work-related tasks of helping professionals, and those they serve, may lead to achievements below personal potential, discouragement, and disengagement from potentially rich life experiences.

A case from the world of work and sport

Geoff, a semi-pro golfer, had been consulting sport psychologist, Dr. Ann, for performance reasons for several months. He had been relatively successful in his sport but struggled with consistency of play in tournaments. His work responsibilities included being an assistant pro at a country club golf course, giving lessons, working in the pro shop, and running tournaments. During one session, Geoff lamented to Dr. Ann that it was "real tough" for him to squeeze in training and competitions with everything else. He felt tired most days and sometimes was unmotivated to "get himself into gear." Members at the club thought he appeared to be insufficiently engaged (feedback provided by the head pro).

Geoff was also recently engaged to be married. In his sessions with Dr. Ann, he revealed some personally dysphoric pressure from his soon-to-be spouse to spend more time with her.

In one session, Geoff revealed that he was thinking about giving up his competitive aspirations in golf and the golf business. He said, "I just don't know where I'm going to find enough time to get everything done that I need to do these days! I'm not really enjoying golf as much as I used to. My lifestyle's made me act kind of moody. I don't have the sense of being able to be successful I used to have – even a year ago, and I'm certainly not getting as much done. I worry about how my relationship will be affected if I continue."

Time management as stress management

Sound familiar? With all of the responsibilities people have, it can be difficult to get so much done – let alone done consistently well. There are costs associated with having a full plate in life, such as this ambitious young man had. What could one to do to help Geoff help himself?

One of Geoff's complaints surrounded the multiple responsibilities in his life as an employee, golfer, and soon-to-be husband. One source of stress shared by high achieving people is taking on too much. Some see being extremely busy as part of the lifestyle of winners, but biting off more than one can chew has consequences. A busy life of work and outside personal activities is usually filled with a mix of both negative (distressful) and positive (eustressful) thoughts, feelings, and experiences. Geoff sensed that aspects of his life were progressively slipping out of his control, increasing his distress. From a positive perspective, however, he was looking forward to his marriage and still enjoyed many aspects of his work.

Dr. Ann suggested that Geoff consider the things in his work, sport, and outside life that were in his control as well as those things that were not so much in his control. After a review of his responsibilities and activities, they determined that much of his day was often controllable (i.e., he mostly had choices in these matters), and that there might be some practical benefits of improved time management in his life. She suggested that more effective time management might take the edge off of some of Geoff's distress so that he could feel more in control of his life, work and train more efficiently, and regain some satisfaction in his work and personal life. Geoff agreed with Dr. Ann's suggestions and expressed interest in further addressing his time management skills.

Self-monitoring

It is often useful for sport psychology professionals to initially inquire about, and assess, how their clients organize their days. Just as we frequently do not have a good sense of how we spend our money, we often do not think about how we spend our time. Our daily experiences can become a blur as we rush from task to task. Self-monitoring can be an enlightening experience that can foster change. Awareness of our priorities, responsibilities, and realities of how we are actually spending our time can help us determine the best use of the time that we have. Writing down what we have to do (i.e., "to-do" lists) or logging what we have done for a training/work day or week in a planner or log can be useful. Geoff sensed that he had lost some control over time, and investing even a week in this tracking activity might well lead to increased awareness, life reorganization, and possibly stress reduction.

Another simple exercise is to have a client create a three-column list of daily experiences on a sheet of paper. Consultants may want to craft such forms to give to clients in advance.

They are asked to assign daily experiences to: (a) distressful (negative), (b) eustressful (positive), or (c) neutral columns. In the following session, consultants can examine and discuss this material with the client. It is often constructive to discuss which activities are "life required" (e.g., Geoff having to show up to the golf course at 6.30 a.m. Tuesday through Sunday) versus those that are "personal choices" (e.g., practice, tournaments, cooking dinner with his fiancée). It may also be useful to discuss the following questions: (a) What was it like to engage in self-monitoring? (e.g., was it boring, easy to do, frustrating?) (b) How meaningful was this activity to the client? (c) How does the client perceive and react to the organization of daily activities as recorded? (d) Are there any patterns, useful or otherwise, that emerge? (e) What are the chances that the client might continue to do this type of practice in the future? and (f) How might this practice be useful for meeting the client's needs?

From the above activity, Geoff and Dr. Ann would likely learn useful things to help him gain an increased sense of control over his moments, days, and weeks. Another important task for Dr. Ann would be to help Geoff invest more of his time in constructive and meaningful activities, and less in unimportant tasks. Designating time for responsibilities that Geoff sees as essential may help him feel more in control. Self-monitoring and determining his priorities may reduce the negatives and likely increase the positives in his busy life.

Time management and goal setting

There are only 24 hours in a day – realistically, only about 10 to 12 hours at most – for the high achiever to be productive. Lakein (1997a) emphasized that every moment during the day is a potentially manageable gift and opportunity to contribute to one's life purposes, goal achievements, and change. Like Geoff, high-achieving people would seem to benefit from deciding what is most personally important and meaningful. Given the time pressures and limitations each day, setting goals – very short, short, medium, and long-term – is instrumental to success and often provides a feeling of accomplishment.

Using goal setting to deal with time pressures should come as no surprise to students and practitioners of sport psychology. The psychology and sport psychology literature contains abundant support for at least the moderate effectiveness of goal setting (Burton, Naylor, & Holliday, 2001). Generally, goal setting has been established as a reliable and effective technique to enhance motivation to achieve (Locke & Latham, 2002). See Chapter 51 for more information about goal setting.

In concert with Dr. Ann, Geoff learned some things from his self-monitoring activities. For example, he learned that he spends time talking with club members and staff at the pro shop and around the course. Although a somewhat constructive part of his job, this chatting cuts into precious time that he could be using to attend to other tasks. Talking with members left him less time to practise his golf game before work. Geoff also observed that his golf practice habits at the club were unfocused and inconsistent.

These revelations led him to set simple goals linked to his time management work with Dr. Ann. For example, Geoff decided that it would be useful to create a training schedule. As part of this task, he would arrive at work 30 minutes earlier each day (6.00 a.m.) and train for an hour uninterrupted. He would stretch for 5 minutes, hit one large bucket of golf balls as he worked on his swing, digitally record his daily range practice with equipment at the course, review his swing tapes at the end of each session (possibly with feedback from the head pro, with whom he did not regularly consult), and play at least one competitive practice round per week with a player of comparable skill.

What can the reader take from the above? As creatures of habit, we frequently engage in activities that are familiar but not necessarily useful to our goals. Perhaps it would be helpful to regularly reassess what our purposes are. What do we really value and need to invest our time and effort in? What have we become accustomed to doing but could change or get rid of with some benefit? We can also glean from Geoff's plan that, even though one may not have a lot of time to devote to important tasks, taking advantage of small segments of quality time can be an efficient approach.

Overall, it appears that high-achievers in sport and other areas of challenging endeavor have to become efficient time managers. They also have to commit to the regular practice of time management skills and habits to work toward realistic goals in meaningful areas of achievement. Regular reassessment and readjustment of daily habits are of considerable value for this purpose.

Time management as a transferable life skill

High achieving individuals often learn that time management can help them achieve their goals and reduce distress in their lives. Time management is not only useful in situations such as the one Geoff was facing, but can also be helpful in future athletic and non-athletic situations. As employees, parents, students, or athletes, our clients will most likely encounter circumstances where their responsibilities outweigh the time they have to dedicate to them. Teaching the fundamentals of time management helps clients develop a life skill that can be transferred to other situations that they may face throughout their lifetimes. Clients can use their time management skills to negotiate new responsibilities and demands. As Geoff's life roles change – perhaps he moves to a higher level of competition or welcomes a new baby into his family – he will need to adapt his schedule to meet his needs and the changing needs of others around him. With the help of time management tools and strategies he developed with Dr. Ann, Geoff can be in greater control of demands and outcomes in his life because he can make adjustments whenever he sees fit.

Some people may not recognize that they have already experienced success with time management that can help them with current challenges. Taking time with a consultant to examine how they have been successful in managing their responsibilities in the past can help clients understand that they have the capability to take charge of their lives in the future. Mapping out situations in which clients have had to manage their time to accomplish their goals can help them to apply this skill in future situations and benefit from this life skill beyond sport.

Many people maintain that sport is a microcosm of the real world, teaching athletes skills that they can use in other areas of life. For example, athletes who are entering the work force or transitioning into different careers can use their time management skills as selling points when interviewing and negotiating for jobs, internships, or positions in graduate school. The ability to manage time demonstrates maturity, is an attractive skill to employers, and may set the individual apart from other candidates. Whether it is in a sport transition, a new career, or a job as a parent, time management can be used to make our lives more enjoyable and less stressful.

Barriers to efficient time management

Even if we are motivated to be better time managers, several practices and personal factors can get in the way of doing so. Impediments to effective time management include: (a) taking on too much, (b) being too accessible to others, (c) perfectionism, (d) fear of failure, (e) distractibility, and (f) procrastination (George Washington University, 2009). Modern technology, although useful, can also be an impediment to effective time management. These issues are often topics of concern to sport psychology consultants and their clients. Given the limitations of this chapter, we have chosen to briefly discuss two common obstacles (technology and procrastination) below.

Technology: making it work for us rather than against us

Our world is swimming with technologies designed to make information sharing more accessible. Email, cell phones with internet access and media libraries, social networking sites such as Facebook and Twitter, and online media sites such as YouTube have become common time-consumers in the lives of today's athletes. The benefit of these technologies is that people have instant access to a vast array of information while not needing to be in a certain place to acquire and use it. These tools permit flexibility while traveling, and many life responsibilities can be addressed through these modalities. For example, PDAs and organizational software can help arrange and simplify schedules, creating a visual represen-tation of the athlete's responsibilities and reminding them when and where they need to be. Athletes who struggle to maintain personal and professional relationships while they are away can update friends and family about their training and competitions through webcams and blogs. Athletes enrolled in universities can take online classes during the course of a competitive season. Because they can access information for courses and submit homework assignments online, athletes who travel can keep up with their studies without having to be present in classrooms.

In many cases, these technologies help save time and energy by allowing athletes to multi-task and keep in touch electronically. Nevertheless, the potential for technology overload is a real threat to time management skills. Here are a few examples of technology overload and suggestions for how to overcome it.

Time wasters

Surfing the internet, visiting social networking sites, repeatedly checking email and sports scores, or playing videogames may turn from recreational activities into time wasters. Sometimes we may use these activities to distract ourselves from our priorities; at other times we may not even realize how much of our day is being taken up with meaningless activities. Although we may perceive that we do not have enough time in our day, activities that we designate as time wasters may be expendable and can lead to the opening of avail-able time that can be used for something more productive. Examining a daily log of activi-ties and how much time is being devoted to each of them can help identify problem activities. Once people recognize their time wasters, they can begin to minimize them. They can set limits on time wasters (e.g., check email only twice a day, surf the internet for 5 minutes as a time-out and then return to work responsibilities.) When people catch themselves in time-wasting activities, it may be helpful to stop what they are doing, return to the moment, encourage themselves to adhere to their established limits, and engage in meaningful activities. The more individuals can catch themselves in a time-wasting activities and return to more productive ones, the easier it will be to minimize technological distractions.

Communication overload

If clients are high achieving individuals, they probably have many people with whom they would like to be in contact and vice versa. Prior to many of the new technologies, individuals were less likely to experience communication overload because they could be unavailable while traveling, training, vacationing, or working. Email, electronic chatting, cell phones, and text messages, however, make us accessible to anyone at any given time. Pressure to maintain communication can become overwhelming for some people and impede their abilities to manage their time. To avoid communication overload, here are a few tips:

1. Stick to your priorities. Ask yourself, what will happen if I don't respond? Is this important? Is this time sensitive? If not, either ignore it or wait until you have finished your most important tasks rather than distracting yourself from your priorities. If it is important and you make the mistake of ignoring it, you will surely hear about it again.
2. Train others to understand your communication style. Instead of trying to be on top of all modalities, let people know what type of communication you prefer. Do you like to answer emails or have people leave messages so that you can call them back at your convenience? If others have a clear understanding of when and how you are likely to communicate with them, they will be prone to adhere to your communication pattern.
3. Choose a time of the day that you check and respond to your email. Instead of replying as soon as you receive a message, which may distract you from your priorities, designate specific times for returning emails. Set limits for the length of time you will dedicate to replying to messages.

Procrastination

Procrastination is an avoidance behavior that involves intentionally delaying responsibilities even when a person is aware of the potential consequences (Klassen, Krawchuk, & Rajani, 2008; Schraw, Wadkins, & Olafson, 2007). Although procrastination can be adaptive in the short term (e.g., delays stress and anxiety, increases motivation and productivity), it may come at a cost in the long run. High levels of procrastination have been linked to distress, anxiety, illness, fear of failure, and under-achievement (Klassen *et al.*, 2008). Research has shown, however, that even as little as a month of time management training can help reduce avoidance behavior and worry (Van Eerde, 2003). To be excellent in work, sport, and elsewhere, individuals such as Geoff must become master time managers and learn to resist the impulse to put things off until later.

So how can athletes learn to become champions of self-regulation? First, they need to become aware of when they are procrastinating and what they are doing in place of their responsibilities. Good time managers are able to identify their priorities and attend to the activities that are most important and time sensitive. Great time managers plan ahead and attend to activities that are important *before* they become time sensitive.

Procrastinators often choose to attend to activities that are neither important nor time sensitive.

Coming up with ways to make avoided tasks less threatening or more enjoyable may help people feel more motivated to address them. With a goal or an attractive outcome in mind, people can focus on what they need to complete to achieve an outcome. In the case of Geoff, training may take the backseat to work or socializing, but reminding himself that attending to his most important tasks will give him an opportunity to return home earlier to his new fiancée, and may help motivate him to stay on track during the day. Another way Geoff could address procrastination is to set a goal for his golf game. If he wanted to reach a certain competition or score by a certain time, he may become more motivated to attend to the tasks that will lead him to success. Breaking the cycle of procrastination and building on time management successes can help develop self-efficacy and reduce procrastination behavior.

Practical time management tips

Pinkney (1991) observed that acquiring and using effective time-management habits involves a commitment to a personal attitude shift about what we choose to do with our days. He noted that many of our responsibilities tend to be less attractive than others. Clearly, most of us are more readily inclined to invest time and energy in activities we find meaningful and enjoy doing, such as being around family and friends, watching a movie versus working on a project, doing an extra workout, or practising mental training. The first, and perhaps most important, step in taking control of time is making a simple yet challenging commitment to deal with the mundane tasks that are not so stimulating versus other more meaningful, higher priority activities. For many people who have not developed useful personal organizational skills, or who have limited experience regularly applying them, this first step is quite difficult to take.

Several simple practices can help people become efficient time managers. For example, many portable scheduling tools are currently available. Perhaps the simplest example is the personal planner. Although there are many sophisticated electronic planners, an inexpensive planner in small book form is a useful start. Not only does a planner help individuals create to-do lists and serve as a physical reminder for them to do things, it also serves as a record of what they have done. Using a simple planner can reinforce useful time choices and behaviors. Like any tool, a planner is helpful only if one regularly uses it and does not lose it! Dr. Ann's client Geoff warmed up to the idea of using a small pocket planner versus a less convenient and more expensive PDA. He began keeping one in his back pocket and believed that it helped remind him of what he needed to do to stay on track during his busy days at the course.

What else could be useful to a person like Geoff? In his practical bestseller, *How to Get Control of Your Time and Your Life*, Lakein (1997b) offered tips consultants can pass on to their clients to assist them in managing their time. They are: (a) recognize the time of day that clients are most productive, and encourage them to work on priority tasks during these prime periods; (b) work on less challenging, simple tasks (e.g., domestic responsibilities) during non-prime time; (c) if possible, reserve some daily free blocks of time to attend to unexpected responsibilities; and (d) invest some time daily to recover and recharge their personal batteries.

Geoff found these suggestions helpful. He reported to Dr. Ann that he was probably "a morning person" who accomplished more from the time he arrived at work until around noontime. As noted earlier, Geoff decided that he would train early in the morning and devote his time in the afternoons to more mundane responsibilities. Geoff further decided that he would take care of personal responsibilities after work or on weekends, versus running off at noon to attend to these things. Although he felt his time was too limited to set aside an entire hour to rest a bit and recover during the day, Geoff did get permission from his boss to take 20 minutes at noon to rest and take a power nap.

Conclusions

Time is one of our most precious commodities, but we do not always know how to manage it. Poor time management skills can lead to distress and can affect a client's work, performance, and personal well-being. Sport psychology consultants can help clients regain satisfaction in their lives through the development of time management skills. Self-monitoring activities can help clients identify priorities and current behavior patterns. Goal-setting can help clients develop new habits that align with their priorities. Planners can help to visually keep track of responsibilities so that they do not become crises. Finally, working during their primetime hours and setting aside recharging time can help clients maximize efficiency so that they can approach or reach peak performance in their most important roles. Nevertheless, clients may encounter barriers to achieving their time management goals. Learning how to identify time-wasting activities, limiting distracting technologies, and committing to completing both exciting and unexciting responsibilities can help clients stay on track with their time management goals. Time management is also a transferable life skill that can help clients achieve short-term success and may also help them succeed throughout their lives. See Box 55.1 for take-home messages from this chapter.

Box 55.1

Take-home messages about time management

- Time is invisible but central to our lives and every momentary experience.
- Individuals can attend to their priorities by addressing the most meaningful activities first and minimizing time wasters.
- Sticking to priorities, helping others understand one's preferred communication formats, and establishing specific email or message time periods can help individuals avoid communication overload.
- Use of a planner can help athletes keep track of short- and long-term responsibilities and events before there is a time crunch.
- Efficient time management is a marketable life skill that can be applicable and useful in future situations.

References

Burton, D., Naylor, S., & Holliday, B. (2001). Goal setting in sport: Investigating the goal effectiveness paradox. In R. N. Singer, H. A. Hausenblas, & C. Janelle (Eds.), *Handbook of sport psychology* (2nd ed., pp. 497–528). New York: Wiley.

de Saint-Exupéry, A. (2000). *The Little Prince* (R. Howard, Trans.). New York: Mariner Books (Original work published 1943).

George Washington University (2009). Identify obstacles to time management. Retrieved from http://ccvillage.buffalo.edu/vpc.html

Klassen, R., Krawchuk, L., & Rajani, S. (2008). Academic procrastination of undergraduates: Low self-efficacy to regulate predicts higher levels of procrastination. *Contemporary Educational Psychology, 33*, 915–931.

Lakein, A. (1997a). *Give me a moment and I'll change your life*. Kansas City, MO: Andrews McMeel.

Lakein, A. (1997b). *How to get control of your time and your life*. New York: Penguin.

Locke, E., & Latham, G. (2002). Building a practically useful theory of goal setting and task motivation. *American Psychologist, 57*, 705–717.

Pinkney, J. W. (1991). Student-athletes and time management for studying. In E. F. Etzel, A. P. Ferrante, & J. W. Pinkney (Eds.), *Counseling college student-athletes: Issues and interventions* (pp. 121–143). Morgantown, WV: Fitness Information Technology.

Schraw, G., Wadkins, T., & Olafson, L. (2007). Doing the things that we do: A grounded theory of academic procrastination. *Journal of Educational Psychology, 99*, 12–25.

Van Eerde, W. (2003). Procrastination at work and time management training. *Journal of Psychology, 137*, 421–434.

56

Pre-performance routines

Ronnie Lidor

Skilled athletes who regularly perform sporting acts such as shooting free throws in basketball, swinging in golf, and serving in tennis or volleyball demonstrate a consistent use of behavioral routines prior to performance. It seems that they attempt to repeat the same patterns of behavior each time they perform; they don't try to vary these routines, but perform them as fixed rituals. For example, when looking at mega-star athletes such as Cristiano Ronaldo, Kobe Bryant, or Serena Williams, one can observe that they all use some kind of well-established preparatory routine before performing their respective sporting acts – the 11-meter penalty kick in soccer, the free throw in basketball, and the serve in tennis. Scientific and anecdotal evidence suggests that preparatory routines can help performers attain better achievements, if they practise the routines consistently.

The purpose of this chapter is threefold: first, to briefly review the experimental, observational, and anecdotal evidence supporting the use of pre-performance routines in self-paced tasks; second, to present the instructional foundations of a three-phase model for teaching pre-performance routines, including two practical examples of how to use this model; and third, to provide practical tips for sport psychology consultants who work with athletes on developing pre-performance routines.

Pre-performance routines: definition and settings

A pre-performance routine has been defined as a set of physical and psychological behaviors that is used prior to the performance of self-paced events (Lidor & Mayan, 2005). This set is typically composed of motor, cognitive, and emotional behaviors that are regularly performed immediately before the execution of self-paced tasks. The resulting routine is part of an athlete's repertoire when preparing to perform.

Self-paced events are those that take place in relatively stable and predictable settings, where adequate time is given to prepare for their execution (Lidor, 2007). Examples of these events are golf strokes, a penalty kick in football, and diving (springboard or platform). Table 56.1 presents a number of self-paced sport tasks in which performers are provided with short-duration time intervals (e.g., 3–20 s, according to the rules of a given sport),

Table 56.1 Self-paced skills and the time periods allowed for preparation.

Self-paced skills	Official preparation time (sec)	Source
Free-throw shot (basketball)	5	International Basketball Federation (2008)
7-meter throw (handball)	3	International Handball Federation (2005)
Serve (volleyball)	8	Fédération Internationale de Volleyball (2004)
Serve (tennis)	20 before the first serve; No preparation time available before the second serve. The server should serve without delay.	International Tennis Federation (2008)

to prepare themselves for these acts. In these events, performers know in advance what they are going to do, how they are going to do it, and how much time they have to prepare. They activate a ritual of physical and psychological behaviors, or what is termed in this chapter a "pre-performance routine."

The use of pre-performance routines in self-paced tasks: scientific and anecdotal support

The usefulness of pre-performance routines in self-paced tasks has been indicated in scientific investigations as well as in anecdotal reports from elite performers, leading coaches, and sport psychology consultants.

Scientific support

Scientific evidence suggests that pre-performance routines are an effective means of promoting physical and psychological readiness prior to the execution of self-paced sport skills (Lidor, 2007; Lidor & Mayan, 2005). Data supporting the use of preparatory routines have emerged from two types of studies: observational and experimental. In observational studies, researchers observe performers' overt patterns of behaviors in natural settings, such as when athletes are preparing themselves for self-paced tasks in actual competitions or games (Thomas & Nelson, 2005). In this type of study, the observer (i.e., the researcher) can accurately and authentically describe behaviors that those skilled athletes exhibit before they perform self-paced tasks. In experimental studies, the researcher can manipulate conditions or treatments that have the potential to enhance behavior (Thomas & Nelson, 2005). In the case of pre-performance routines, one of the objectives of researchers has been to examine the influence of a given physical/psychological routine on sport performance.

Observational studies

In one typical observational study, Crews and Boutcher (1987) looked at pre-shot routines for two shots in golf – the full swing and putting – in 12 tour players of the Ladies Professional Golf Association. They found that all the players were consistent in their pre-shot behaviors and the time they used to prepare themselves for the strokes. Some of the patterns of behaviors observed prior to each stroke included: standing behind the ball, setting the club behind the ball with one glance at the target, and setting the feet. The authors also found that the more successful golfers used longer periods of time in preparing for the strokes. Precise information on athletes' patterns of behaviors before performing other self-paced tasks can be found in studies on free-throw shots in basketball (Wrisberg & Pein, 1992), serving in volleyball (Lidor & Mayan, 2005, Study 1), and kicking in rugby (Jackson, 2003).

Two conclusions can be made based on the observational data collected in the studies on pre-performance routines. First, skilled performers maintain a consistent set of physical (e.g., positioning, setting the body/body parts, holding the ball/club/racquet, dribbling) and psychological (e.g., external attentional focus, imagery, self-talk) routines during the preparation time provided to them for a given self-paced act. Second, although different performers in a given self-paced act use different routines, a number of physical and psychological behaviors are common among performers.

Experimental studies

Experimental studies have examined the effectiveness of pre-performance routines in self-paced events such as free throws in basketball (e.g., Southard & Miracle, 1993), strokes in golf (e.g., Beauchamp, Halliwell, Fournier, & Koestner, R., 1996), and serves in volleyball (Lidor & Mayan, 2005, Study 2). Two manipulations were typically performed in these studies: manipulations of the regular routines used by the performers (mainly physical routines), and manipulations of imposing psychological routines (e.g., focusing attention, imagery, relaxation) on athletes. When examining the results of the experimental studies on preparatory routines, two main observations can be made. First, imposed pre-performance routines such as external focusing-attention, imagery, and relaxation can facilitate accuracy of self-paced tasks. Second, maintaining a consistent sequence of pre-performance routines can result in improved levels of proficiency.

Anecdotal support

Additional support for the use of task-pertinent pre-performance routines can be found in anecdotal evidence. Elite athletes, experienced coaches, and sport psychology consultants have all developed pre-performance routines for self-paced tasks. For example, Larry Bird, the basketball legend and former NBA coach, advised his beginning and advanced basketball players to follow a six-step routine when preparing themselves for a free-throw shot (Bird, 1986). Among the steps in his routine were: getting ready (i.e., feeling relaxed and confident when going to the line), getting set (i.e., being in balance at the line), and aiming (i.e., concentrating on the target). For the same skill, the combined efforts of a sport psychology consultant and another leading college basketball coach resulted in the establishment of a six-step routine composed of both physical and psychological elements (Burke & Brown, 2003). Among the physical routines were getting into position at the line, taking a deep breath while holding the ball, and staring at the rim. Examples of the psychological routines were using quick imagery and counting each dribble performed before the shot.

For the swing in golf, Coop and Fields (1993) developed a pre-shot routine consisting of five steps including signaling entrance to the concentration zone, choosing an intermediate target on the intended line of the shot, and providing a cue or thought that would allow the player to give up voluntary control of the swing and shift to involuntary action.

For another self-paced task, serving in tennis, Yandell (1999) developed a pre-shot visualization technique focusing on four core serving elements: the ready position, the racket drop, the contact point, and the finish position. Servers create images of these elements to build effective physical and mental models of these patterns of movements. Loehr (1990), who observed elite tennis players' patterns of behavior between points, proposed another pre-performance routine for serving in tennis. According to his observations, servers should use visualization and relaxation techniques to ready themselves psychologically for the serve, as well as for maintaining a physical routine such as bouncing the ball a minimum of two or three times prior to the serve, and pausing just after the last bounce.

Based on this anecdotal evidence we can conclude that practitioners recommend using physical and psychological routines prior to the execution of self-paced sport tasks. Their practical recommendations are in line with most of the findings from observational and experimental studies; namely, that performers could benefit from developing a consistent set of behaviors, and that this set should match their needs and preferences.

Benefits of the use of task-pertinent pre-performance routines

There are a number of explanations for the benefits obtained through the use of task-pertinent preparatory routines. First, performers are able to establish plans of action before they perform their self-paced tasks. They can plan in their minds what needs to be done, how it should be done, and how long it will take them to do it. In essence, pre-performance routines serve as a last-minute preparation for the act. Second, performers can stay focused and overcome external distractions (e.g., noise generated by the audience) and negative internal thoughts (e.g., "I am going to miss this shot"; Moran, 1996). In this respect, the process of focusing attention is enhanced. Third, performers feel in control over what they are doing (Lidor, 2007). They feel that by performing their systematic physical and psychological routines they will be ready to perform and can achieve their best.

Three-phase model for teaching pre-performance routines

Based on empirical inquiries and anecdotal evidence, some of which have been reviewed in this chapter, I am proposing a three-phase model for teaching pre-performance routines. The model contains the following phases: preliminary preparatory instructions (Phase 1), task-specific preparatory instructions (Phase 2), and preparatory instructions for the real-life self-paced event (Phase 3). Detailed information on this model can be found in Lidor (2007).

Phase 1: preliminary preparatory instructions

The objective of Phase 1 is to expose learners to basic fundamentals of both physical and psychological preparatory routines associated with self-paced tasks. It should be explained to learners that preparatory routines are integral to self-paced tasks. The verbal instructions given to the learners, combined with a set of actual demonstrations (i.e., modeling) of the task, should convince them that the routines need to be an integral part of the task. In this phase, learners are provided with various opportunities for practising different routines.

They are told what the typical routines are that can be performed before the task, and are provided with the instructional opportunities to practise all of them. They need to experience different physical and psychological routines to be able to select the most appropriate ones for them. Phase 1 of the model reflects a collaborative instructional process. For example, one of the instructional objectives of sport psychology consultants is to determine which routines the athletes prefer to use, and what they actually think about the new routines they are trying to adopt. The perceptions and thoughts of the learners about what might be the most effective routines for them should be considered in the initial phase of the preparatory instructions.

During this phase of learning, emphasis should be made on the psychological routines (e.g., focusing attention, imagery, self-talk) that the learners perform prior to the self-paced event. The physical preparatory routines can be naturally integrated into the specific learned task, for example dribbling before serving in volleyball (Lidor & Mayan, 2005), or dribbling before shooting free throws in basketball (Lidor, 2009). Nevertheless, this "natural fit" may not be the case with psychological routines: learners may have difficulty integrating psychological skills into the learning process if they are not explicitly taught how to do so (Sinclair & Sinclair, 1994). Therefore, learners should not be only instructed how to apply psychological routines such as imagery and external focusing/attention, but must also be provided with enough time to practise these routines so that they will be able to select the ones most appropriate for their own use.

Phase 2: task-specific preparatory instructions

The objective of this phase is to enable learners to adopt a consistent set of physical and psychological routines that best reflect their individual needs and preferences. After practising and experiencing different physical and psychological routines during Phase 1, in Phase 2 learners should select one set of physical and psychological routines that will be performed each time they ready themselves for a specific self-paced event. Athletes should feel comfortable in performing their selected set of routines; they should feel that this set is an integral part of the learned/performed self-paced task.

Sport psychology consultants can motivate learners to adopt a set of preparatory routines by sharing with them those routines that skilled athletes regularly perform. They can run videos of well-known athletes who are preparing themselves for self-paced acts, and discuss what the most salient physical elements are that these athletes consistently use in their routines. Instructors in this phase can also use findings from observational studies examining the use of physical routines in skilled performers (e.g., Lidor & Mayan, 2005, Study 1). As in Phase 1, emphasis is placed on adopting a consistent set of psychological routines prior to the execution of the self-paced task. These routines should be practised repeatedly until the athletes feel comfortable using them in real self-paced events, namely those that occur in competitions and games.

Phase 3: preparatory instructions for the real-life self-paced event

The objective of this phase is to enable athletes to practise their selected preparatory routines in settings that reflect the actual real-life self-paced events they may potentially face in competitions and games. In this phase, the routines are practised while taking into account two situational conditions: time constraints and external distractions. In most self-paced events, performers face time constraints when preparing themselves for the act.

For example, according to the rules of international basketball, players standing on the free-throw line are allowed 5 seconds to prepare themselves for the free-throw shot after receiving the ball from the official (International Basketball Federation, 2008). While practising preparatory routines before self-paced tasks, learners should ensure that the physical and psychological routines they have selected can be performed within the allowed preparatory time intervals.

In this phase, learners should also practise their routines under distracting conditions, such as loud crowd noises. Whereas in Phases 1 and 2 the athletes practise the routines under relatively relaxed learning conditions, in Phase 3 they are taught to use the routines in more challenging situations. For example, in real-life ball games, players who are preparing themselves for self-paced events are typically faced with external distractions from players on the opposing team (e.g., "trash talk," hostile verbal behavior), as well as noise generated by the crowd. Practising the routines under challenging conditions should help learners effectively transfer them to real-life events, particularly if the training situations are similar to the ones they will face in actual competitions.

Applying the teaching model to sport skills

I have selected two self-paced sport skills, shooting free throws in basketball and performing a golf stroke from a tee, to demonstrate the use of the proposed model in teaching pre-performance routines. The reason these skills were selected is that there is a considerable amount of scientific and anecdotal support for the effectiveness of the physical and psychological routines accompanying these skills.

Shooting free throws in basketball

Pre-performance instructions are given for each phase. In each phase, instructions are given separately for developing the physical and psychological components of the routines.

Phase 1: preliminary preparatory instructions

The objective of this phase is to help learners practise those behaviors that they may use while standing at the free-throw line and preparing themselves for the shooting act. Learners should experience various physical and psychological behaviors before selecting one set of behaviors that they will use consistently prior to each shooting attempt. Nevertheless, for shooters to effectively perform the proposed physical and psychological routines, they can start using them from the moment they know that they are going to make a free-throw shot (e.g., after the player has been fouled). Lidor (2006) found that approximately 19 seconds (unofficial pre-performance time) were available to adult and youth basketball players before the ball was actually handed to them by the referee. During this interval, players went to the free-throw shooting area, and while waiting at the shooting line they bent their knees, wiped their hands with a towel, and adjusted their shorts and tops. When standing at the free-throw line shooters also used this unofficial pre-performance time to imagine themselves performing the shot, focus attention at the rim, and verbalize selected cue words, such as "calm" and "focus." Appropriate use of the unofficial pre-performance interval can create a longer period of time for preparation, and therefore benefit those performers who may need additional time for readying themselves for the free-throw shot.

Physical routines

While at the free-throw line, learners should:

- search for the most comfortable area facing the rim;
- decide on the most comfortable readying position;
- dribble the ball while standing at their preferred position: the number of dribbles should be varied – 2 dribbles, 3 dribbles, 4 dribbles – according to the number that is most comfortable for the player;
- hold the ball while inhaling deeply and exhaling slowly: The time of holding should be varied – 1 s, 2 s;
- spin the ball with the hands; time of spinning should be varied – 1 s, 2 s– shoot the ball at the basket.

Psychological routines

While standing at the free-throw line, learners should:

- search for the most appropriate area at the front of the rim for an external focus of attention;
- image themselves shooting the ball while focusing attention at the front area of the rim;
- decide on verbal cues to be used before each shot; athletes should experience the use of different words, or short sentences, which they would feel comfortable verbalizing while preparing themselves for the shot.

Phase 2: task-specific preparatory instructions

The objective of this phase is to enable learners to establish a consistent set of physical and psychological routines that they will perform before each free-throw attempt. After experiencing different routines in Phase 1, one routine composed of both physical (e.g., dribbling the ball four times consecutively, holding the ball for two seconds) and psychological (e.g., imaging a successful shot for two seconds, verbalizing the word "high") behaviors should be selected. Learners should be aware of the established order of both the physical and psychological components in the routines they use. They should also use structured self-reflection for assessing the contribution of the selected routines to their shooting performance. Emphasis should be made on consistent use of the selected routine, regardless of the outcome of the shot.

Phase 3: preparatory instructions for the real-life self-paced event

The objective of this phase is to enable learners to practise the established routines under challenging conditions. In this phase the periods of time used by shooters prior to each free-throw attempt after they receive the ball from the referee should be measured, to ensure that they do not use more time for preparation than the time intervals allowed according to the rules of the game (i.e., 5 s). In addition, shooting attempts should be made under distracting conditions, such as noise generated by a tape recorder located about 2-3 m from the shooter, or verbal interference made by the sport psychology consultant or teammates (e.g., "you are going to miss the shot," "think what happens if you miss this shot"). As in Phase 2, emphasis should be made on consistent use of the routines before each shooting act.

Performing a golf stroke from the tee

Pre-performance instructions are given for each phase, and for the physical and psychological routines separately in each phase.

Phase 1: preliminary preparatory instructions

The objective of this phase, as in the basketball free-throw example, is to enable golfers to practise those behaviors that they may use while standing behind/beside the tee (ball) and preparing themselves for the stroke act. Learners perform various physical and psychological behaviors before selecting one set of behaviors they will regularly use prior to each tee shot.

Physical routines

While standing behind/beside the tee (ball), learners should:

- search for the most appropriate distance from the ball;
- select the most comfortable readying position behind/beside the ball;
- set the feet;
- set the club;
- set the grip;
- perform a number of continuous practice swings – 1 swing, 2 swings, or 3 swings, according to the number that is most comfortable for the player;
- inhale deeply and exhale slowly (take a deep diaphragmatic breath);
- swing the club to contact the ball.

Psychological routines

While standing behind/beside the ball, learners should:

- look at the target;
- imagine themselves hitting the ball while at the same time glancing at the target;
- decide on verbal cues (e.g., "I am ready," "distance," "go") to be used before each stroke.

Phase 2: task-specific preparatory instructions

The objective of this phase is to enable learners to develop a fixed set of physical and psychological routines they will use prior to each stroke. A developed routine may be composed of physical components such as one comfortable readying position and a fixed number of continuous practice swings, and psychological components such as looking at the target and imagining a successful stroke.

Phase 3: preparatory instructions for the real-life self-paced event

In this phase, learners practise their established golf routines under challenging conditions. For example, routines should be performed while playing on different courses and at different distances from the target. As in Phase 2, emphasis should be made on consistent use of the routines, regardless of the outcome of the stroke.

The routines proposed for free-throw shots in basketball and strokes in golf reflect both scientific and anecdotal evidence. These routines illustrate a few physical and psychological behaviors that can be used effectively by performers readying themselves for self-paced events. Performers can develop other task-pertinent routines according to their needs and preferences. They should spend time not only on developing their routines, but also on practising them repeatedly so that they will become an integral part of the self-paced task. The three-phase model proposed in this chapter can help performers plan effective learning environments for pre-performance routines. A number of practical suggestions for teaching routines are given in Box 56.1.

Box 56.1

Practical suggestions for teaching pre-performance routines

- Effective pre-performance routines should be composed of both physical and psychological components. Practice should be devoted to both components.
- Physical routines (e.g., positioning, dribbling, holding the ball) are perceived as an integral part of the self-paced skill. These routines can be presented to the learner as part of the physical and technical foundations associated with the task.
- Instructional effort should be made to develop task-pertinent psychological routines. Routines such as an external focus of attention, imagery, or self-talk should be presented at early phases of learning, and integrated naturally into the physical routines (e.g., focusing attention at the rim while dribbling the ball before shooting a free-throw shot).
- Athletes should experience various physical and psychological routines at early phases of learning before selecting one fixed routine.
- Instructors should encourage learners to use the physical and psychological routines demonstrated by skilled performers, but these routines should be modified according to the learners' own preferences.
- Athletes should practise their selected routines not only under relaxed learning conditions (Phases 1 and 2 of the proposed model), but also under distracting conditions (Phase 3) that reflect actual competition and game situations.

References

Beauchamp, P. H., Halliwell, W. R., Fournier, J. F., & Koestner, R. (1996). Effects of cognitive-behavioral psychological skills training on the motivation, preparation, and putting performance of novice golfers. *The Sport Psychologist, 10*, 157–170.

Bird, L. (1986). *Bird on basketball*. Reading, MA: Addison-Wesley.

Burke, K., & Brown, D. (2003). *Sport psychology library: Basketball*. Morgantown, WV: Fitness Information Technology.

Coop, R., & Fields, B. (1993). *Mind over golf: How to use your head to lower your score*. New York: Macmillan.

Crews, D. J., & Boutcher, S. H. (1987). An exploratory observational behavior analysis of professional golfers during competition. *Journal of Sport Behavior, 9*, 51–58.

Fédération Internationale de Volleyball (2004). *Official volleyball rules*. Seville, Spain: Fédération Internationale de Volleyball.

International Basketball Federation (2008). *FIBA activities*. Retrieved from http://www.FIBA.com.

International Handball Federation (2005). *Rules of the game*. Basel: Switzerland.

International Tennis Federation (2008). Rules of tennis. Retrieved from www.ITFTENNIS.com

Jackson, R. C. (2003). Pre-performance routine consistency: Temporal analysis of goal kicking in the Rugby Union World Cup. *Journal of Sports Sciences, 21*, 803–814.

Lidor, R. (2006). Pre-performance routines in self-paced tasks: Duration and sequences. In *The Proceedings of the 2006 International Forum of the Psychology of Olympic Excellence* (pp. 62–65). Taiwan.

Lidor, R. (2007). Preparatory routines in self-paced events: Do they benefit the skilled athletes? Can they help the beginners? In G. Tenenbaum & R. C. Eklund (Eds.), *Handbook of sport psychology* (3rd ed., pp. 445–465). New York: Wiley.

Lidor, R. (2009). Free throw shots in basketball: Physical and psychological routines. In E. Tsung-Min Hung, R. Lidor, & D. Hackfort (Eds.), *Psychology of sport excellence* (pp. 53–61). Morgantown, WV: Fitness Information Technology.

Lidor, R., & Mayan, Z. (2005). Can beginning learners benefit from preperformance routines when serving in volleyball? *The Sport Psychologist, 19*, 343–362.

Loehr, J. E. (1990). *The mental game: Winning at pressure tennis*. New York: Stephen Greene Press/ Pelham Books.

Moran, A. P. (1996). *The psychology of concentration in sport performers: A cognitive analysis*. East Sussex, England: Psychology Press.

Sinclair, G. D., & Sinclair, D. A. (1994). Developing reflective performers by integrating mental management skills with the learning process. *The Sport Psychologist, 8*, 13–27.

Southard, D., & Miracle, A. (1993). Rhythmicity, ritual, and motor performance: A study of free throw shooting in basketball. *Research Quarterly for Exercise and Sport, 3*, 284–290.

Thomas, J. R., & Nelson, J. K. (2005). *Research methods in physical activity* (5th ed.). Champaign, IL: Human Kinetics.

Wrisberg, C. A., & Pein, R. L. (1992). The pre-shot interval and free throw shooting accuracy: An exploratory investigation. *The Sport Psychologist, 6*, 14–23.

Yandell, J. (1999). *Visual tennis: Using imagery to perfect your stroke techniques*. Champaign, IL: Human Kinetics.

57

Mental toughness

Daniel F. Gucciardi and Clifford J. Mallett

Researchers and practitioners have long considered psychological factors as essential ingredients for performance excellence and well-being across a number of settings. Athletes and coaches commonly describe an athlete's "mental game" as one of the key distinctions between good and great athletes. Mental toughness is the umbrella term that coaches, athletes, sport psychologists, and the media use when referring to the constellation of psychological factors that appear to discriminate good and great athletes. Although once considered a little-understood construct, the knowledge base contributing to current conceptualizations of mental toughness now has some scientific rigor owing to the efforts of several groups of researchers. Researchers have studied the perceptions of athletes and coaches from a variety of team (e.g., rugby union, netball, football) and individual sports (e.g., swimming, triathlon, boxing) in an attempt to identify the make-up of mentally tough performers. Recent investigations have adopted a context-specific approach in which mental toughness is examined within a single sport (e.g., cricket, soccer) to provide a context-rich understanding of this construct (for a review, see Gucciardi, Gordon, & Dimmock, 2009a).

Core components of mental toughness

Perhaps the most common finding from the available empirical literature is that mental toughness appears to be multifaceted with multiple key components. These key components can be broadly classified as values, attitudes, cognitions, and emotions. Among these broad components, there seem to be several central characteristics (e.g., self-belief/confidence, personal values, attentional control, self-motivation, positive and tough attitudes, enjoyment and thriving through pressure, resilience, sport intelligence) that are common across all the sports sampled thus far, suggesting that this constellation of core psychological characteristics would not vary significantly by sport. The cohorts sampled in the investigations to date, however, are certainly not representative of most sport participants. There are some variances in key characteristics that seem to provide sport-specific information

Deci, E. L., & Ryan, R. M. (1985). *Intrinsic motivation and self-determination in human behavior.* New York: Plenum.

Gucciardi, D. F., & Gordon, S. (2009). Revisiting the performance profile technique: Theoretical underpinnings and application. *The Sport Psychologist, 23,* 93–117.

Gucciardi, D. F., Gordon, S., & Dimmock, J. A. (2008). Towards an understanding of mental toughness in Australian football. *Journal of Applied Sport Psychology, 20,* 261–281.

Gucciardi, D. F., Gordon, S., & Dimmock, J. A. (2009a). Advancing mental toughness research and theory using personal construct psychology. *International Review of Sport and Exercise Psychology, 2,* 54–72.

Gucciardi, D. F., Gordon, S., & Dimmock, J. A. (2009b). Development and preliminary validation of a mental toughness inventory for Australian football. *Psychology of Sport and Exercise, 10,* 201–209.

Gucciardi, D. F., Gordon, S., & Dimmock, J. A. (2009c). Evaluation of a mental toughness training program for youth-aged Australian footballers: I. A quantitative analysis. *Journal of Applied Sport Psychology, 21,* 307–323.

Kobasa, S. C. (1979). Stressful life events, personality, and health: An inquiry into hardiness. *Journal of Personality and Social Psychology, 37,* 1–11.

Loehr, J. E. (1986). *Mental toughness training for sports: Achieving athletic excellence.* Lexington, MA: Stephen Greene Press.

Maddi, S. R., & Khoshaba, D. M. (2001). *Personal Views Survey* (3rd ed., Rev.). Newport Beach, CA: Hardiness Institute.

Mageau, G. A., & Vallerand, R. J. (2003). The coach-athlete relationship: A motivational model. *Journal of Sport Sciences, 21,* 883–904.

Mallett, C. J. (2004). Reflective practices in teaching and coaching: Using reflective journals to enhance performance. In J. Wright, D. Macdonald, & L. Burrows (Eds.), *Critical inquiry and problem-solving in physical education* (pp. 147–158). London: Routledge.

Mallett, C. J. (2005). Evidence-based coaching practice: A case study using SDT. *The Sport Psychologist, 19,* 417–429.

Middleton, S. C., Marsh, H. W., Martin, A. J., Richards, G. E., Savis, J., Perry, C., Jr., & Brown, R. (2004). The Psychological Performance Inventory: Is the mental toughness test enough? *International Journal of Sport Psychology, 35,* 91–108.

Rutter, M. (2006). Implications of resilience concepts for scientific understanding. *Annals of the New York Academy of Sciences, 1094,* 1–12.

Ryan, R. M., & Deci, E. L. (2000). Self-determination theory and the facilitation of intrinsic motivation, social development, and well-being. *American Psychologist, 55,* 68–78.

Schön, D. A. (1983). *The reflective practitioner: How professionals think in action,* New York: Basic Books.

Seligman, M. E. P., & Csikszentmihalyi, M. (2000). Positive psychology: An introduction. *American Psychologist, 55,* 5–14.

Vealey, R. S. (2007). Mental skills training in sport. In G. Tenenbaum & R. C. Eklund (Eds.), *Handbook of sport psychology* (pp. 287–309). Hoboken, NJ: Wiley.

Index

557